The Entrepreneur and Small Business Problem Solver

The Entrepreneur
and Small Business
Problem Solver

An Encyclopedic
Reference
and Guide

William A. Cohen

A Ronald Press Publication

John Wiley & Sons

New York • Chichester • Brisbane • Toronto • Singapore

Published by John Wiley & Sons, Inc.

Library of Congress Cataloging in Publication Data:

Cohen, William A., 1937–
      The entrepreneur and small business problem solver.

   "A Ronald Press publication."
   Includes index.
   1. Small business.   2. Entrepreneur.   I. Title.
HD62.7.C63 1983   658'.022   82–20311

ISBN 0-471-86740-3 (cloth)
ISBN 0-471-80795-8 (paper)

Printed in the United States of America

10 9 8 7 6 5 4 3

This book is dedicated to Barak and Nimrod,
who will take the entrepreneurial spirit
into whatever lifework they choose.

Preface

When I first started my own entrepreneurial activities years ago, there was no such book as this. There were and are many books on marketing, finance, accounting, management, and other functional aspects of business. There were and are numerous books on small business as a distinct and separate area of interest. Yet, I could not go to any one book or any one source for the plain, simple information that I needed in order to start or expand my various prospects and businesses. As a result, in order to get the answers to my questions, I spent many hours over many days at several different libraries. This was not only a waste of my time; it actually cost me money. Countless opportunities were lost because I did not obtain the information until it was too late to be of any use.

In recent years, as a business professor, the director of the Small Business Institute at California State University, Los Angeles, and a management consultant for small business and big business, I have been continually amazed at the variety of information about small business and the starting of small businesses required by investors, entrepreneurs, and even people who have been in business for many years. Most of this information *is* available, but either it must be researched by the individual at the cost of many hours spent on the problem, or a management consultant must be hired for $100 an hour or more to provide the answer. Sometimes a consultant's expertise is needed and well worth the fee. But there are other questions which have simple, easily understood answers—if only you could find them.

The purpose of this book is to place this essential information at your fingertips. In it I have gathered together the answers to the questions most frequently asked of me by business clients and entrepreneurs whom I help. This book is designed to do the following things for you:

1. Save hours, days, and perhaps months of research for any business problem that you want answered
2. Save the cost of hiring consultants when such consultants are not necessary to solve your problem
3. Enable you to know when and how to get help if you do need it, and how to do so at the lowest possible cost.

The purpose of this book, summarized in one sentence, is this: It was written to help you to be successful with your small business or entrepreneurial project. Each chapter was designed to stand by itself and assist you with a certain class of business problems. Chapter 1 covers the legal aspects of going into business. Chapter 2 covers sources of capital and how to get a loan. Chapter 3 covers business insurance; Chapter 4, business planning, including marketing planning, which is crucial for success and yet which may cost $5,000 or more if you must have it done by someone else. Chapter 5 covers recruiting employees for your business as it grows. Chapter 6 covers buying a business that is already in existence. Chapter 7 tells you how to protect your idea, whether your idea is an invention, something written, or something that is not covered by patent, trademark, or copyright law. Chapter 8 covers the important area of buying or leasing equipment, including whether to replace old equipment or whether it is more profitable to retain it. Chapter 9 covers all aspects of record keeping. Chapter 10 is about personnel management, including how to recruit employees as well as how much to pay them and how to keep them happy and doing their best for you. Chapter 11, on financial management, discusses the various tools of financial management and working with an accountant. Chapter 12 covers embezzlement, theft, and bad checks, and how to eliminate or minimize them. Chapter 13 will assist you with credit collection. Chapter 14 concerns advertising and public relations, which are essential if you are going to sell your product or service. Chapter 15 tells you how to do your own marketing research and how to do it at low cost. Chapter 16 covers personal selling, how to do it, and how to manage a force that does it for you. Chapter 17 is all about trade shows; Chapter 18, about pricing the products. What you will learn here about pricing may surprise you—that frequently a higher price will bring you more sales as well as additional contribution to margin. Finally, Chapter 19 will show you how to develop and introduce new products which will make your enterprise profitable.

The appendices cover everything from location of important government offices to government aids to small business, a sample business plan, and other useful information.

Throughout, specific examples have been used to show you step by step what to do, and forms and checklists are contained in every chapter. A glance at the Contents and the chapter titles and subheadings will give you some idea of the concrete assistance this book can give to anyone interested in beginning a small business or anyone who has already established one.

If this book doesn't save you five times its cost the first time you use it, I will be surprised. If the use of the book enables you either to save or to make at least 1,000 times its price during the years you use it, I won't be surprised at all.

WILLIAM A. COHEN

Pasadena, California
February, 1983

Acknowledgment

I wish to thank the Small Business Administration, especially the staff of the Los Angeles Office, through whose courtesy many of the excellent checklists, bibliographies, sources, and other information published by the SBA were obtained.

W.A.C.

Contents

1

The Legal Aspects of Going into Business

In this chapter, we're going to cover the essential legal aspects of going into business, including setting up the legal structure for your firm, obtaining business licenses and paying local taxes, dealing with the state board of equalization and resale permits, registering a fictitious name, setting up the books, and handling federal tax obligations and income taxes, Social Security taxes, excise taxes, unemployment taxes, state taxes, local taxes, and records for income tax reporting.

SELECTING THE LEGAL STRUCTURE FOR YOUR FIRM

There are several different legal structures for your firm from which you can choose. These are: the sole proprietorship, the partnership, and the corporation. Each has its own particular advantages and disadvantages, depending upon your situation. We'll look at each in turn.

THE SOLE PROPRIETORSHIP

The sole or single proprietorship is a business structure for a firm, which is owned and operated by only one person. To establish a sole proprietorship, all you need to do is obtain whatever licenses are needed in your local area to begin operations. This means it is the easiest of the legal structures to set up, and it is also the most used form of small business legal structure.

Advantages of the Sole Proprietorship

Ease and speed of formation. With the sole proprietorship, there are fewer formalities and legal restrictions. A sole proprietorship requires little or no government approval and you usually need to spend only a few minutes with your city or county clerk to obtain a relatively inexpensive business license.

Reduced expense. The sole proprietorship is less expensive to set up than either a partnership or a corporation. This is because of the minimal license fees and legal help needed to set up this type of business organization.

Complete control. Since in a sole proprietorship there are no partners or other owners to consult with, you have total control over the business, and you can run it yourself as you see fit. You make all the decisions. There is no board of directors or any other boss except your customers to direct you, tell you what to do, supervise the decisions you make, or criticize your errors. As a result, you can quickly respond to business needs on a day-to-day basis. Win, lose, or draw, you are the whole show and what you say goes.

Sole recipient of profits.   Since you are the sole proprietor, you are not required to share profits with anyone. The profits are all yours.

Relative freedom from government regulations and taxes.   For taxes, the government treats you and your sole proprietorship as one. If you actually end up losing money over the first year, then having this form of legal structure is an advantage since you may deduct those losses on your tax return against any other income that you may have earned during the year. This can be especially valuable if you run your business part-time while at the same time you have cash flow from a position held within a larger company. Naturally, the same advantage continues if you must run in the red for several years.

Termination.   Termination is also very easy with a sole proprietorship. You can liquidate your assets, pay your debts, turn out the light, and your entire operation is completely shut down. Or you can sell your business if you wish to do so with few restrictions. With a sole proprietorship, it is as easy to get out of business as it is to get into business.

Disadvantages of the Sole Proprietorship

Unlimited liability.   One major disadvantage of the sole proprietorship is that you have unlimited personal liability in your business. This means that you are responsible for the full amount of business debts, which could exceed your total investment in the business. This liability extends to all your assets, such as home and car. If your business fails owing money to various creditors, those monies which you still owe can be collected from your personal assets. Of course, you can lessen the risk of liability in the case of physical loss or personal injury by obtaining proper insurance coverage. This will be discussed later in the book. Also, these liabilities may not be of substantial importance in your situation under certain conditions. If you borrow money for your business, the bank will usually require that you personally guarantee your loan. In this way, even if you are incorporated, you may become personally liable. Also, for many types of businesses, the chance of your being sued because of a failure of your product is very slim. The manufacture and sale of greeting cards, personalized stationery, or costume jewelry are examples. Therefore, even though you are totally responsible, your risks are minimal.

Total responsibility.   Since in a sole proprietorship you are essentially a one-man band, you are limited to and by your own skills and capabilities. This means, for example, that you may not be able to take a long vacation, or that your enterprise could be put in serious jeopardy, or even terminated, by a serious illness or something else which takes you away from your business for some extended period of time. The fact that only your skills and experiences are brought to the business means there are fewer resources available to your firm than to another firm in which more than one are contributing experiences and personal resources.

Difficulties with capital.   Again, since you are but one individual, it may be more difficult to obtain capital for your business than it is for other types of legal business structures with more than one individual involved. Also, it is difficult to get financing, since you alone must make good a debt. As the investor sees it, if you have a partner, this doubles the chances of getting his money back. The bottom line is that the sole proprietorship is the most difficult business structure for which to obtain financing.

THE PARTNERSHIP

The partnership is also fairly easy to get into, although written articles of partnership are customarily executed with the help of an attorney. Many states have adopted a uniform partnership act which defines a partnership as an association of two or more persons to carry on as co-owners of a business for profit. The contract or articles developed for use in your partnership may be very simple or fairly complex. They typically cover the following aspects:

1. Absence and disability
2. Arbitration
3. Authority of individual partners in conduct of business
4. Character of partners including whether general or limited, active or silent
5. Contribution by partners both now and at a later period
6. Dissolution and winding up
7. Division of profits and losses
8. Draws and/or salaries
9. Duration of agreement
10. Employee management
11. Expenses and how to handle them
12. Name, purpose, and domicile of partnership
13. Performance by partners
14. Records and method of accounting
15. Release of debts
16. Required acts and prohibited acts
17. Rights of continuing partner
18. Sale of partnership interest
19. Separate debts
20. Settlement of disputes

Characteristics That Distinguish a Partnership from a Sole Proprietorship

Certain characteristics distinguish a partnership from a sole proprietorship and other business structures. These are as follows: (1) co-ownership of the assets; (2) limited life of the partnership; (3) mutual agency; (4) share in management; (5) share in partnership profits; (6) unlimited liability of at least one partner.

Types of Partners

In a partnership, there can be different types of partners which have different responsibilities to the business. An *active partner* is one who is active in the business. A *dormant partner* is inactive and not known or held out as a partner. A *limited* or *special partner* is a partner who risks only his agreed investment in the business. He or she is usually not subject to the same extent as a general partner to the liabilities of the firm, nor does he or she participate in the management and control of the firm or in the conduct of the firm's business. A *nominal partner* is not a partner in the sense of being a party to the partnership agreement. However, the nominal partner represents him- or herself as a partner or permits others to make representation by the use of his or her name. Therefore, under the law, a nominal partner is as liable as if he or she were a partner to another party who has acted on the reliance on the truth of true partnership. An *ostensible partner* is an individual who is active and is known as a partner. A *secret partner* is a partner who is active but is not known or presented to be a partner. A *silent partner* is inactive, but he or she may be known to be a partner. A *subpartner* is an individual who is not a member of the partnership but contracts with one of the partners and participates in the interest of the partner in the firm's business and profits.

Advantages of a Partnership

Additional capital to start your business.   Your partner or partners are themselves sources of additional capital.

Help in decision making.   Two heads are better than one, and so your partners provide additional resources and help in decision making and the work of the business.

Ease of formation.   The legal formalities and expenses are not great. Although they are greater than those of a sole proprietorship, they are less than those of the development and creation of a corporation. Like a proprietorship, a partnership is easy to set up. Usually, you obtain a business license from your county clerk or city clerk, and the cost for the license is the same as for the proprietorship license.

Relatively stable business life.   In a partnership situation, you have double the resources to apply in solving problems or in handling such mundane decisions as when to go on vacation. There is more stability built into a partnership structure than into that of a sole proprietorship.

Relative freedom from government control and special taxation.   As with the sole proprietorship, there is a minimum amount of paperwork associated with a partnership as opposed to a corporation. There is a form that you must fill out each year for the IRS known as Form 1065, U.S. Partnership Return of Income, but basically the monies you receive from the partnership are treated as ordinary income as are the monies you receive from a sole proprietorship. You can deduct losses in the partnership from other sources of income when you complete your income tax just as you can for a sole proprietorship.

Share in profits.   All partners, to a greater or lesser degree, are motivated to apply their best abilities and put in the time by direct sharing of the profits from the business.

Flexibility.   Like a sole proprietorship, a partnership is reasonably flexible in that it can respond rapidly to changing conditions of business. On the other hand, because more than one individual is involved, the decision-making process is less flexible than that of the sole proprietorship.

Disadvantages of a Partnership

All partners are bound by the actions of one partner. This is perhaps the major disadvantage of a partnership: you are liable for the actions and commitments of your partners. A single partner can expend the company's resources in a business commitment and all partners are liable to that commitment, whether they agree with it or do not agree.

Organizational problems. Organizational responsibilities must be clearly written into the articles of partnership or else you'll run into problems trying to figure out who's in charge of what and who has the final say on various business matters.

Unlimited liability of at least one partner. By law, at least one partner has unlimited liability, just as with a sole proprietorship. Other partners may have similar liabilities, depending upon what's written into the articles of partnership.

Relative difficulty in obtaining capital. For a partnership, you can obtain capital more easily than you can for a sole proprietorship. However, it is much more difficult to obtain capital for a partnership than it is for a corporation.

Disposing of partnership interests. Buying out one partner may be very difficult unless the terms have been stated in the written agreement contained in the articles which formed the partnership.

THE CORPORATION

Unlike the other business structures, the corporation is not a simple structure. Usually you must have the help of an attorney to incorporate, although there are several books which can enable you to set up your corporation by yourself. One book on this subject is *How To Form Your Own Corporation Without A Lawyer For Under $50,* by Ted Nicholas, published by the Enterprise Publishing Co., 1000 Oakfield Lane, Wilmington, Del. 19810. Since state laws differ regarding corporations, many books have been written by experts discussing how to incorporate in their various states. Frequently these books have tear-out forms for you to use. If you're interested, check a local bookstore and find out if such a book is available for your state.

Corporations which do business in more than one state must comply with the federal laws regarding interstate commerce and with the various state laws. These may vary considerably from state to state. In general, to form a corporation, subscriptions to capital stock must be taken and a tentative organization created. Then, approval must be obtained from the secretary of the state in which the corporation is to be formed. The approval is in the form of a charter for the corporation stating the powers and limitations of the particular enterprise.

Advantages of the Corporation

Limited liability. Perhaps the major advantage that exists over the other two forms of business ownership and structure is limited personal liability. With a corporation, your liability is limited to the amount of your investment in the business. Accordingly, your creditors cannot take your personal holdings or assets should the corporation fail or be sued for more funds than are available in the corporation.

Income taxes. Currently a corporation pays taxes to the maximum of 48% of its net profits. Since personal income tax is currently 50%, and in the past this has been 90%, there may be some very real tax advantages for you in a corporation. The money you would normally pay in tax can be used to help your company to grow. At some time in the future you can sell this expanded business and pay capital gains taxes rather than income taxes. Since capital gains taxes are lower, the net result could be big savings.

Ease in securing capital. Various lenders, including banks, venture capitalists, and others, are generally much more willing to make loans to a corporation that has been operating successfully than to a sole proprietorship or a partnership. Also, capital may be obtained through issuance of various stocks and long-term bonds.

Increased resources available. Since a corporation will generally include more than one individual in its organization, the corporation has the ability to make use of multiple skills and resources.

Corporate benefits. As a corporation, you and other members in your business will be able to take advantage of fringe benefits such as pension plans, insurance, company cars, and so forth.

Permanence of existence. A corporation has a life of its own and continues to exist and may do business even after the death or illness of the principal officer in the corporation.

Disadvantages of the Corporation

Paperwork. There is a tremendous amount of paperwork associated with a corporation, for taxes and for other reasons. Getting this paperwork done takes time, effort, and money.

Government regulations. Your activities in the corporation are limited by various laws of the government. In fact, of the three types of business structures, this is the one over which the government has the most control. You must make numerous reports to the federal, state, and local governments.

Inability to take losses as deductions. As noted earlier, in both the partnership and the sole proprietorship, if you lose money in your business, these losses can be taken as deductions from other earned income at income tax time. However, this is not true with losses sustained by a corporation. Your corporation may lose money, but until such time as you sell your stock or the business fails, these losses cannot be taken against other earned income. (There is an exception to this in a Subchapter S corporation which will be discussed later.)

Lessened control. As pointed out earlier, corporations are very closely regulated by the state in which you are registered. This control can restrict your business activities. Furthermore, your corporation is required to have a board of directors and hold stockholders' meetings. Even though you can stack the board of directors in your favor so that you can still run the company, your control over your business and the decision-making process does suffer from this limitation.

Taxes. Depending upon your situation and the profits in your business, the fact that you are incorporated may be a disadvantage because of double taxation. Corporate profits are taxed once through the corporation itself as a taxable legal entity and a second time through your salary or when profits are distributed to you as a stockholder. You then pay tax on this as ordinary income. If profits are sufficiently high, this is of little consequence since you will be building your business and taking your money out later. However, if profits are not that high, you'll be losing money to Uncle Sam through taxation instead of saving it. Again, a Subchapter S corporation can help.

A Guide to Decision Making

In summary, in considering which form of legal structure to adopt, you should weigh the following factors:

1. Cost
2. The value of partners in either a partnership or a corporation in both capital and personal resource contributions
3. Organizational flexibility
4. Stability of business during illness or when you want to take time off
5. Risks associated with each type of organizational structure
6. The taxation situation
7. The influence of laws, federal, local, and state
8. The importance of other factors that are peculiar to your business.

HOW TO INCORPORATE A SMALL BUSINESS

In general, to incorporate a small business you should either see an attorney or refer to one of the books on self-incorporation discussed earlier. However,. this section will provide you with an overall view of the process and what is required.

Generally, the first step in incorporating is preparation of a certificate of incorporation. Many states require that the certificate be prepared by three or more individuals who are legally qualified, but the current trend is to require only one incorporator.

Before a certificate of incorporation is filed, however, you must consider the location of the corporation since it has important bearing on taxation and other aspects of your business.

Most small and medium-size businesses obtain their charters from the state in which the greatest part of their business is conducted. However, sometimes there are advantages or benefits to be gained from incorporation in another state. To the state in which you are located, yours would be known as a "foreign corporation." Advantages may include lower state taxes, fewer restrictions on corporate powers and lines of businesses in which your company may engage, and lower capital requirements for incorporation. On the other hand, foreign incorporation may also have significant disadvantages. For example, under the laws in many states, you may be taxed twice, that is, by the state in which you incorporated and the state in which your business is located. Under the laws of some states, the property of a foreign corporation is subject to less favorable treatment than that of a corporation located in the state. Also, some states require a foreign corporation to obtain certification to do business in their state, and without this certification your corporation may be deprived of the right to sue in those states. Finally, there is no standard fee, and the fee for a corporation and the organizational tax charged for a corporation vary greatly from state to state.

Certificate of Incorporation

Many states have a standard certificate of incorporation form which you can use. You can obtain copies of this form from the designated state official who grants charters or, in some states, local stationery stores. Also, if you intend to incorporate by yourself and you obtain one of the books mentioned earlier, these forms will frequently be found as tearouts. In most cases, the following information is required on these forms:

1. *Corporate name of the company.*   The name chosen cannot be similar to the name of any other corporation authorized to do business in the state so as to lead to confusion. Also, the name that you choose may not be deceptive; it may not mislead the public. To save yourself much time, you can check out the availability of names through an official in your state whose job it is to handle such inquiries. You should do this prior to drawing up a certificate of incorporation. There are companies that will perform this service for you which you can locate either through the state offices or through the telephone book. In many states there are certain procedures that are used to reserve a name for your corporation. Again, the proper state official can supply you with this information.

2. *Purposes for which the corporation is formed.*   Most states require very specific information in this section. You must state in precise language the purposes of your corporation. However, several states will allow you to use very broad language in stating the purpose of your corporation; the purpose can be written in such a way as to allow you to pursue virtually any lawful enterprise. There are advantages for stating the purpose of your corporation specifically and for stating it in general terms. The advantage in stating the purpose in general terms is that if the corporation decides to change its business, reincorporation will not be required. On the other hand, in dealing with financial institutions, a specific purpose will give a very clear picture of what you are doing. Also, a specific purpose will prevent problems in qualifying your corporation to do business in other jurisdictions.

3. *Length of time for which the corporation is being formed.*   Here you may indicate a certain number of years or you may indicate that the length of time is in perpetuity.

4. *Names and addresses of the incorporators.*   This requirement is a simple one, although you should know that in some states one or even more of the incorporators are required to be residents of the state within which the corporation is being organized. You should check and find out what is required in the state in which you intend to incorporate.

5. *Location of the principal office of the corporation in the state of incorporation.*   In those situations in which you decide to obtain your charter from another state, you will be required to have an office in that state. However, there is an alternative: you may have an agent in the state to act for you. The agent is required to represent your corporation, maintain a duplicate list of stockholders, and receive or reply to suits brought against the corporation in the state of incorporation.

6. *The maximum amount and type of capital stock which the corporation is authorizing for issue.*   Under this paragraph, you indicate the capital structure of the corporation, including the number and the classification of shares and the rights, preferences, and limitations of each class of shares and stock.

7. *Capital required at time of incorporation.*   Some states require that a specific percentage of the par value of the capital stock be paid in cash and placed in a bank to the corporation's credit before the certification of incorporation is submitted for approval.

8. *The names of the stockholders and the number of shares to which each stockholder subscribes.*

9. *The names and addresses of persons who will serve as directors until the first meeting of stockholders or until their successors are elected and qualify.* For purposes of expediting the filing of the articles, sometimes dummy incorporators are employed. These dummy incorporators are usually associated with a service company that performs this or with an attorney for the organizers. Typically they elect their successors and resign at the first meeting of the incorporators.

Assuming that the name of the proposed corporation is satisfactory, that the certificate contains the information required and is properly executed, and that there is nothing in the certificate or in the proposed activities of the corporation that violates any law of the state or public policy, the charter is issued. The next step is an officers' and stockholders' meeting.

Officers' and Stockholders' Meeting

The officers' and stockholders' meeting is necessary to complete the incorporation process. This very important meeting is usually conducted by an attorney or someone familiar with corporate organizational procedure. Three basic things are accomplished during this meeting. First, corporate bylaws are adopted. Second, a board of directors is elected. And third, the board of directors elects the officers who will actually run the corporation on a day-to-day basis. It is possible in a small corporation for members of the board of directors to be elected officers of the corporation.

Bylaws of the Corporation

The bylaws of the corporation repeat some of the items already covered in the certificate of incorporation, but they also cover additional points. These include the following: (1) location of the principal offices and other offices of the corporation; (2) the time, place, and required notice of annual and special meetings of stockholders, the quorum necessary at the meetings, and the voting privileges of the various stockholders; (3) the number of directors, their compensation, if any, their term of office, how to elect them, and the methods of creating and filling vacancies on the board of directors; (4) the time and place of regular and special directors' meetings, as well as notification and quorum requirements; (5) the process for selecting officers and their titles, duties, terms of office, and salaries; (6) the issuance and form of stock certificates, how to transfer them, and their control in the company books; (7) dividends, when they are declared, and by whom they may be declared; (8) the fiscal year of the corporation, the corporate seal, the authority to sign checks, and the preparation of an annual statement; (9) the procedure for amending the bylaws which have been established.

SUBCHAPTER S CORPORATIONS

Subchapter S corporations were created by Congress to give tax relief to small companies. Specifically, the purpose of Subchapter S is to permit a small business corporation to have its income taxed to the shareholders as if the corporation were a partnership, if it so desires. The advantages of a Subchapter S corporation are twofold. One, it permits you to avoid the double tax feature of taxation of corporate income. Two, it permits you as a shareholder to have the benefit of offsetting business losses incurred by the corporation against your income. Thus, you have the advantage of the protection of incorporation as well as the tax advantage of a partnership.

You should be aware that it is *not* to your advantage to have a Subchapter S corporation if your corporation enjoys substantial profits. When this happens, your personal income will be taxed at a rate appreciably higher than the maximum corporate rate of 48% because of your much higher tax bracket.

In order to qualify as a Subchapter S corporation, you must meet the following requirements: (1) you must have no more than 10 shareholders, all of whom are individuals or estates; (2) you must have no nonresident alien shareholders; (3) you must have only one class of outstanding stock; (4) all shareholders must consent to the election of a Subchapter S corporation; and (5) a specified portion of the corporation's receipts must be derived from actual business activity rather than passive investments.

In a Subchapter S corporation, no limit is placed on the size of the corporation's income and assets.

1244 CORPORATIONS

IRS Code 1244 grants ordinary rather than capital treatment of losses on certain small business stock. That is, if investment funds are lost in a new, small firm, these losses may be charged against normal income on your federal income tax return. In such a situation, the amount of such losses is limited to $500,000.

To qualify for Section 1244 stock, your stock must meet the following requirements: (1) the stock must be common stock; (2) the stock must be issued by the corporation for money or other property pursuant to a written plan containing several limitations; (3) the amount of contribution received for the stock and equity capital of the corporation must not exceed certain maximum dollar limitations.

OBTAINING BUSINESS LICENSES AND PAYING LOCAL TAXES

Federal, State, and Local Licenses

For most small businesses, you will only need a local business license. This may mean either a municipal or county license, or both. These are payable at your city or county hall. To get the license, you may be required to conform to certain zoning laws and to meet building codes and other regulations set by the local health, fire, or police department. Permits may be required by these agencies for activities which are considered hazardous to the community. If you are required to have special permits, you will be informed at the time of the purchase of your business license.

State Licensing Requirements

Some states require licensing for particular occupations, and licenses are granted according to standards of professionalism and ability. Usually the requirement for state licensing will be indicated at the time of your purchase of your local business license. However, for more specific information, check with your state's department of commerce.

Federal Licensing Requirements

The federal government regulates interstate commerce and also requires federal permits or licenses for any enterprise involving preparation of meat products for transportation or sale, operation of a common carrier, construction of a radio or TV station, production of drugs or biological products, operation of an investment advisory service, and certain other businesses. Again, you usually will be informed of the necessity of an additional license at the time of purchase of a local business license. However, to be certain, you can contact the department of commerce (addresses listed in Appendix I).

Dealing with the State Board of Equalization and Resale Permits

The state board of equalization is the government agency to which you pay state taxes which you collect if your state has a sales tax. Usually the same agency will enable you to secure a seller's permit which allows you to buy tangible personal property which you intend to resell without paying sales or use tax to your vendor. In order to do this, you must give your vendor a signed resale certificate showing your seller's permit number.

To obtain a seller's permit, contact the sales and use tax department of your state (address listed in Figure 1.1). If a fee is required for a seller's permit, the appropriate office listed will inform you. Sometimes this office requires some security from you for the payment of future tax, since this office is the one to which you pay sales tax if applicable. If so, the amount is determined at the time you make your application for the permit required. This security deposit protects the state, because if you fail to pay any sales tax due, the state can deduct the amount that you owe them from the security which you posted with them.

Clearly it is to your advantage not to leave a security deposit for your seller's permit at all. How much security is required, however, or whether any is required, depends on the information that you provide on the application form which they will give you to fill out. The security amount required may be less than $100. However, the requirement for security can vary in any one state from no deposit at all to several thousand dollars. In some cases, where the security deposit required is very high, installment payment arrangements can be made. The minimum is generally required if you own your own home and have substantial equity in it, if the estimated monthly expenses of your business are low, if your estimated monthly sales are low, if you are presently employed and this is a part-time business, if you have no employees, and if you have only one place of business. According to your own situation, additional amounts may or may not be required.

FICTITIOUS NAME REGISTRATION

You may or may not need fictitious name registration. Whether or not you must file a fictitious business name statement and get the publicity as required in your state depends on the law in your area of operations. Usually you must file a fictitious name registration statement if the business name which you select is within the definition of the fictitious business name used in your geographic area. What this generally means is that you are using a name in doing business which is other than your own or those of partners whom you may be associated with, that the name varies from the corporate name, that it does not include the surnames of all owners, or that it implies the existence of additional owners.

ALABAMA
Department of Revenue
Sales and Use Taxes
Montgomery, Alabama 36130

ALASKA
Department of Revenue
Pouch S
Juneau, Alaska 99801

ARIZONA
Sales Tax Division
Phoenix, Arizona 85007

ARKANSAS
Sales and Use Tax Division
Department of Finance and Adminis-
tration
Little Rock, Arkansas 72201

CALIFORNIA
Department of Business Taxes
State Board of Equalization
P.O. Box 1799
Sacramento, California 95808

COLORADO
Department of Revenue
State Capitol Annex
Denver, Colorado 80203

CONNECTICUT
Sales, Use and Excise Tax Division
Hartford, Connecticut 06115

DELAWARE
State Division of Revenue
Wilmington, Delaware 19801

DISTRICT OF COLUMBIA
Department of Finance and Revenue
300 Indiana Avenue, N.W.
Washington, D.C. 20001

FLORIDA
Sales Tax Bureau
Department of Revenue
Tallahassee, Florida 32304

GEORGIA
Sales and Use Tax Unit
Department of Revenue
Atlanta, Georgia 30334

HAWAII
Department of Taxation
State Tax Office Building
425 Queen Street
Honolulu, Hawaii 96813

IDAHO
Sales Tax Division
State Tax Commission
Boise, Idaho 83707

ILLINOIS
Department of Revenue
Springfield, Illinois 62706

INDIANA
Sales Tax Division
Department of Revenue
100 N. Senate Avenue
Indianapolis, Indiana 46204

IOWA
Division of Retail Sales and Use Tax
Department of Revenue
Lucas State Office Building
Des Moines, Iowa 50319

KANSAS
Sales and Compensating Tax Division
State Revenue Building
Department of Revenue
Topeka, Kansas 66612

KENTUCKY
Sales Tax Division
Department of Revenue
Frankfort, Kentucky 40601

LOUISIANA
Collector of Revenue
Baton Rouge, Louisiana 70821

MAINE
Sales Tax Division
Bureau of Taxation
Augusta, Maine 04330

MARYLAND
Retail Sales Tax Division
Treasury Department
301 W. Preston Street
Baltimore, Maryland 21201

MASSACHUSETTS
Sales and Use Taxes
Department of Corporations & Taxation
Boston, Massachusetts 02133

MICHIGAN
Sales and Use Taxes
Department of Treasury
Revenue Division
Treasury Building
Lansing, Michigan 48922

Figure 1.1. Sales and use tax departments.

MINNESOTA
Sales and Use Tax Division
Department of Taxation
Centennial Office Building
St. Paul, Minnesota 55101

MISSISSIPPI
Sales and Use Tax Division
State Tax Commission
Jackson, Mississippi 39205

MISSOURI
Sales and Use Tax Bureau
P.O. Box 840
Jefferson City, Missouri 65102

NEBRASKA
Sales and Use Tax Unit
Department of Revenue
Box 4818, State Capitol
Lincoln, Nebraska 68509

NEVADA
Nevada Tax Commission
Carson City, Nevada 89701

NEW JERSEY
Division of Taxation
Department of the Treasury
Trenton, New Jersey 08625

NEW MEXICO
Revenue, Bureau of Revenue
Santa Fe, New Mexico 87501

NEW YORK
Sales Tax Bureau, State Tax
Commission
Department of Taxation and Finance
Tax and Finance Building 9,
State Campus
Albany, New York 12226

NORTH CAROLINA
Sales and Use Tax Division
Main Office—Revenue Building
Raleigh, North Carolina 27611

NORTH DAKOTA
Enforcement Director (Sales Tax)
State Capitol Building
Bismarck, North Dakota 58501

OHIO
Sales and Excise Division
Department of Taxation
68 East Gay Street
Columbus, Ohio 43151

OKLAHOMA
Sales and Use Taxes
Oklahoma Tax Commission
2101 Lincoln Blvd.
Oklahoma City, Oklahoma 73105

PENNSYLVANIA
Bureau of Taxes for Education
Department of Revenue
Harrisburg, Pennsylvania 17128

RHODE ISLAND
Department of Administration
49 Westminster Street
Providence, Rhode Island 02903

SOUTH CAROLINA
Sales and Use Tax Division
South Carolina Tax Commission
Columbia, South Carolina 29201

SOUTH DAKOTA
Sales and Use Tax Division
Department of Revenue
Pierre, South Dakota 57501

TENNESSEE
Sales and Use Tax Division
Department of Revenue
War Memorial Building
Nashville, Tennessee 37219

TEXAS
Comptroller of Public Accounts
Austin, Texas 78711

UTAH
Auditing Division (Sales Tax)
State Tax Commission
201 State Office Building
Salt Lake City, Utah 84114

VERMONT
Department of Taxes
State of Vermont
P.O. Box 547
Montpelier, Vermont 05602

VIRGINIA
Sales and Use Tax Division
Department of Taxation
P.O. Box 6L
Richmond, Virginia 23215

WASHINGTON
Department of Revenue
Olympia, Washington 98501

Figure 1.1. (Continued)

WEST VIRGINIA
    Sales and Use Taxes
    State Tax Department
    Charleston, West Virginia 25305

    Business and Occupation Tax
    State Tax Department
    Charleston, West Virginia 25305

WISCONSIN
    Income, Sales, and Excise Tax Division
    Department of Revenue
    P.O. Box 39
    Madison, Wisconsin 53702

WYOMING
    Sales and Use Tax Division
    State Tax Commission
    Cheyenne, Wyoming 82002

Figure 1.1. (Continued)

Obtaining fictitious name registration is usually very easy, and the fact that you must register it should not be considered an impediment to selecting a name that people will notice and associate with your business. To find out the law in your state, consult your telephone book and contact the appropriate agency listed under city, county, or state government, and they will give you the information regarding the requirements in your area. Typically, there will be a small registration fee of $10 or so, and within a period of the registration you must publish notice of the fictitious trade name in a general circulation newspaper in the area where the business is located. This may cost you another $30 or so. You then file an affidavit confirming such publication at the county clerk's office. In practice, this is a very easy matter. Frequently the form can be obtained at the office of the newspaper in which you intend to publicize your notice, and they will handle everything for you, including filing the affidavit after publication. The form is usually a simple one, and filling it out will take you less than five minutes. Some states will allow you to obtain more than one fictitious name on one form. For some types of businesses, such as certain types of consultancies or researchers, this is an advantage, since these firms may legally use any of the fictitious names which are listed on the form. Usually the fictitious name is good for five years or so and then must be renewed. You are generally informed well ahead of expiration. If you use your own name as that of your business, fictitious name registration is not required, nor is it required if you use your corporate name in the business.

SETTING UP THE BOOKS

Good records in your business are necessary for several purposes, including taxes, measurement of management effectiveness and efficiency, uncovering employee theft, material waste, and obtaining loans.

Essential records should include the following: (1) a daily summary of cash receipts taken from sales receipts; (2) an expense ledger tallying both cash and checks disbursed for expenses such as rent, payroll, and accounts payable; (3) an inventory purchase journal showing shipments received, accounts payable, and cash available for future purchases; (4) an employee compensation record listing hours, pay, and withheld deductions for both part-time and full-time workers; (5) an accounts receivable record for credit sales. Forms suitable for these purposes are shown in Figures 1.2 through 1.6.

Day/Date

Item Sold or Service Performed	Amount	
Total amount received today		
Total amount received through yesterday		
Total amount received to date		

Figure 1.2. Form for daily summary of cash receipts.

FEDERAL TAX OBLIGATIONS

There are four basic types of federal taxes. These are: income taxes, Social Security taxes, unemployment taxes, and excise taxes. We will discuss each in detail.

Income Taxes

The amount of federal income taxes which you will owe depends on the earnings of your company, as well as the type of business or organizational structure you choose, sole proprietorship, partnership, or corporation. If you choose either the sole proprietorship or the partnership structure, your other income exemptions and nonbusiness deductions and credits will also be important factors. If you are a sole proprietor, your income tax is paid just as if you were working for someone else. The big difference is that your income is derived from the earnings of your business instead of from a salary or wage. You file the identical form that the individual taxpayer working for someone else files. The only difference here is that you file an additional form which in effect identifies items of expense and income

Date	To Whom Paid	Purpose	Check Number	Amount	
		Total expenditures			

Figure 1.3. Form for an expense ledger tallying both cash and checks disbursed.

Expenditure Summary

Purpose	Total This Period		Total up to This Period		Total to Date	
Advertising						
Car and truck expense						
Commissions						
Contributions						
Delivery expense						
Dues and publications						
Employee benefit program						
Freight						
Insurance						
Interest						
Laundry and cleaning						
Legal and professional services						
Licenses						
Miscellaneous expense						
Office supplies						
Pension and profit sharing plan						
Postage						

Figure 1.3. (Continued)

Purpose	Total This Period		Total up to This Period		Total to Date	
Rent						
Repairs						
Selling expense						
Supplies						
Tax						
Telephone						
Traveling and entertainment						
Utilities						
Wages						
Totals						

Figure 1.3. (Continued)

from your business. That form is Schedule C of 1040, Profit or Loss from Business or Profession. If your business is a partnership, the partnership must file a return to reflect the income and expenses of the business, and you will report only your share of the profit on your return.

One important difference as an individual proprietor or a partner in a partnership is that you are required by law to pay federal income tax and self-employment tax as income is received. You do this by filing a Declaration of Estimated Tax (Form 1040ES) on or before April 15 of each year. This declaration is an estimate of the income and self-employment taxes you expect to owe based on expected income and exemptions. You then make payment on this estimate each quarter, on or by April 15, June 15, September 15, and January 15. At the time of each payment, adjustments to the estimates can be made. As the owner of a new

Date	Inventory Ordered	Shipments Received/Date	Accounts Payable	Cash Available for Future Purchases
	Carried Forward			

Totals

Figure 1.4. Form for an inventory purchase journal.

Name _____ Social Security No. _____

Date	Period Worked (hours, days, weeks, or months)	Wage Rate	Total Wages		Deductions					Net Paid	
					Soc. Sec.	Fed. Inc. Tax	State Inc. Tax				

Totals

Figure 1.5. Form for an employee compensation record.

Date	Customer/Client Name	Products/Services	Amount Owed	Payments Made/Date

Figure 1.6.   Form for an accounts receivable record for credit sales.

business, you may be required to file a declaration on a date other than April 15 if your expected income or exemptions change during the year. One example of this might be if you stop working as an employee and your wages were subject to withholding. You would then be required to file a declaration as follows: If the change occurred after April 1 or before June 2, you must file by June 15. If the change occurred after June 1 and before September 2, you must file by September 15. If the change occurred after September 1, then you must file by January 15 of the following year.

If your business is a corporation not filing Subchapter S discussed previously, it pays taxes on its profits. Also, as an owner of the corporation, you pay an additional tax on the salary you receive or dividend which your corporation pays to you.

Income tax rates for a corporation are currently set as follows: All taxable income is taxed at 22%. In addition, a surtax of 26% is imposed on taxable income over $25,000. This increases the effective rate of taxation to 48%.

The income tax return for a corporation is due on the 15th day of the third month following the end of each taxable year. The corporation may select as its taxable year a period which does not coincide with the calendar year.

While income tax returns are typically filed annually, payment of the taxes is made on an "on-account" basis by most firms, quarterly. Every corporation whose estimated tax is expected to be $40 or more is required to make estimated tax payments.

It is extremely important that you have the necessary funds to pay your income taxes on time. To assist you in paying income taxes as well as other taxes, it is recommended that you use Figure 1.7, Worksheet for Meeting Tax Obligations, which was developed by the Small Business Administration.

Withholding Income Taxes

By law, you must withhold the federal income tax payments for your employees. These payments are passed on to the government periodically. This process begins when you hire a new employee. Your new employee must sign Form W-4, Employee's Withholding Allowance Certificate. On it, your employee lists the exemptions and additional withholding allowances which he or she claims. The completed Form W-4 certificate is your authority to withhold income tax in accordance with the withholding tables issued by the Internal Revenue Service. If an employee fails to furnish a certificate, you are required to withhold tax as if he were a single person with no withholding exemptions. Before December 1, you should ask your employees to file new exemption certificates for the following year if there has been a change in their exemption status since they last filed their certificate. At the end of the year, you are required to furnish each employee copies of Form W-2, Wage and Tax Statement, for him- or herself and each taxing jurisdiction, that is, the state and local government. The employee files a copy with his or her income tax return and keeps one. You, the employer, must also furnish a copy of Form W-2 to the Internal Revenue Service on or before February 28. For complete details of how to do this and the necessary forms, contact the local office of the IRS.

Withholding Social Security Taxes

In paying Social Security taxes, you also deduct the necessary tax which each employee owes. However, by law, you are required to match these deductions. If you are using Social Security for your own retirement, you must pay the tax for yourself. If your type of business involves tips, an employee receiving cash tips of $20 or more in a month while working for you must report these tips to you for income tax and Social Security purposes. This must be accomplished on or before the 10th day of the following month. You then deduct the employee's Social Security income tax from wages due the employee. However, you are required to match only deductions you made on the employee's wages. You need not match the Social Security taxes you deduct on the employee's tips.

Remitting Federal Taxes

To remit federal taxes, you take two actions. One, you report the income and Social Security taxes which you withheld from employees' pay, and, two, you deposit the funds which you withheld.

This worksheet is designed to help the owner-manager to manage his firm's tax obligations. You may want your accountant or bookkeeper to prepare the worksheet so you can use it as a reminder in preparing for and paying the various taxes.

Kind of Tax	Due Date	Amount Due	Pay to	Date for Writing The Check
Federal Taxes				
Employee income tax and Social Security tax				
Excise Tax				
Owner-manager's and/or corporation's income tax				
Unemployment tax				
State Taxes				
Unemployment taxes				
Income taxes				
Sales taxes				
Franchise tax				
Other				
Local Taxes				
Sales tax				
Real estate tax				
Personal property tax				
Licenses (retail, vending machine, etc.)				
Other				

Figure 1.7. Worksheet for meeting tax obligations.

To report withholding and Social Security remittances to the federal government, use Form 941. A return for each calendar quarter is due on the last day of the following month, that is, April 30, July 31, October 31, and January 31. In many cases, remittances of taxes are required before the due date of the return. These dates depend on your situation.

To make deposits, you complete Form 501, Federal Tax Deposits, Withheld Income and FICA Taxes. This form, with a check, is sent to the Federal Reserve Bank which serves your district, or to a commercial bank that is authorized to accept tax deposits. Your local bank or a Federal Reserve Bank can give you the names of such commercial banks. In general, the smaller the amount of your tax liability, the less frequently you are required to make a deposit. The basic rules are as follows:

1. If you have less than $200 liability per quarter, no deposit will be required. The total liability for the quarter will be remitted with the return on or before the last day of the month following the close of the quarter.

2. If at the end of the first month in the quarter the cumulative liability is less than $200, but by the end of the second month it is $200 or more, the employer must deposit the cumulative amount by the 15th day of the third month in the quarter. The liability for the third month of the quarter may be remitted with the return that will be due on or before the last day of the month following the close of the quarter. If the cumulative liability does not reach $200 until the third month of the quarter, the total liability must be deposited by the last day of the month following the close of the quarter.

3. For each of the first two calendar months in the quarter, if the cumulative liability for the quarter is $200 or more and less than $2,000, deposits will be required on or before the 15th day of the next month. For the last month in the quarter, employers will not have to deposit until the last day of the month following the close of the quarter.

4. If on the 7th, 15th, 22nd, or last day of the month cumulative liability is $2,000 or more, a deposit will be required within the next three banking days.

Excise Taxes

Federal excise taxes are posed on the sale or use of certain items or certain transactions, and on certain occupations. Examples are occupational tax on retail dealers in beer, retail liquor dealers, and wholesale beer and liquor dealers. Diesel fuel and certain special motor fuels carry a retailer's excise tax. There are manufacturer's excise taxes on trucks and equipment and on petroleum products and firearms. If a business involves liquor, gambling, or firearms, it may be subject to an occupational excise tax. To determine whether or not you are subject to a federal excise tax, contact your local Internal Revenue Service office. Certain excise taxes are due without assessment or notice. With others, you must file a quarterly return on Form 720. When you owe more than $100 a month in excise taxes, you must make monthly deposits of that tax in a Federal Reserve Bank or other authorized depository. Semimonthly rather than monthly deposits of excise taxes are required if you are liable for more than $2,000 in excise taxes reportable on Form 720 for any month during the previous quarter.

Unemployment Taxes

If you paid wages of $1,500 or more in any calendar quarter, or you had one or more employees on at least some portion of one day in each of 20 or more calendar weeks, either consecutive or nonconsecutive, your business is liable for federal unemployment taxes. If your liability from deposits of federal unemployment taxes exceeds $100 for any calendar quarter and any preceding quarter, you must deposit the tax with an authorized commercial bank or a Federal Reserve

Bank within one month following the close of the quarter. Each deposit must be accompanied by a preinscribed Federal Unemployment Tax Deposit Form, Form 508. A supply of these forms will be furnished to you automatically if you have applied for an employer identification number. But in any case, they must be obtained from the IRS where you file returns.

An annual return must be filed on Form 940 on or before January 31 following the close of the calendar year for which the tax is due. Any tax still due is payable with the return. You must file Form 940 on a calendar year basis even if you operate on a fiscal year basis. Form 940 may be filed on or before February 10 following the close of the year if all the required deposits are made on time, in full payment of the tax due, deposited on or before January 31. Usually the Internal Revenue Service will mail copies of Form 940 to you. However, if you fail to receive them, copies may be obtained from your local IRS office.

Obtaining an Employer's Identification Number

An employer's identification number is required on all employment tax returns to the federal government. You obtain this by filing a Form SS-4 with your regional Internal Revenue Service Center. Please note that this identification number is not the same as your Social Security number required on your individual income tax returns. At the time that you apply for an employer's identification number, you can request your business tax kit which is IRS 454. This tax kit has additional information on taxes pertinent to each particular business.

STATE TAXES

State taxes vary from state to state. However, the three major types are unemployment taxes, income taxes, and sales taxes. It is critical for you to know what your state taxes are and what your state requires you to pay as well as what it requires you to collect as an agent of the state. In some states, if you fail to remit withheld state taxes, you can be charged with embezzlement.

Every state has state unemployment taxes. The rules and requirements vary state by state; however, they usually are based on the taxable wage base of a quarter, and the rate of tax charged is determined by your unemployment experience coupled with the unemployment experience of your state.

State income taxes are imposed by many states. If your state does so, you are required to deduct this tax from your employees' wages just as you deduct the federal tax. Sometimes these taxes are assessed in a fashion similar to the assessment of the federal tax, and sometimes not. If the requirements differ, make sure that your records will allow you the necessary information for the state income taxes.

To meet the sales tax obligation, if your state has sales tax, you must act as if you were an agent. You collect the tax and pass it on to the appropriate state agency. This was discussed earlier in the section dealing with the state board of equalization and resale permits.

LOCAL TAXES

Counties, towns, and cities impose various kinds of taxes. These include real estate taxes, personal property taxes, taxes on groceries, receipts of businesses, and unincorporated business taxes. A business license is also a tax, although you may not have thought of it as such. Local taxes may actually include income tax for very large cities. To insure that you are paying the proper taxes, check with your local tax authorities.

TAX CREDITS

Tax credits are credits against the income tax which you pay and, as such, they are not deductions but account for much more. The two basic types of tax credits at the federal level are investment tax and business energy investment.

Investment Tax Credit

The investment tax credit allows for qualified investment in certain types of new and used equipment. This provision of the IRS allows a business owner to take a tax credit of up to 10% of the amount of the qualified investment in new property and up to 10% of the first $100,000 invested in used property. The credit applies only to certain property and the property must have a useful life of at least three years to be eligible for any portion of the credit. Expenditures on the rehabilitation of buildings in use for 20 years that have not been rehabilitated during that period may also qualify for investment tax credit if used for business or commercial activities after rehabilitation.

Business Energy Investment Credit

Business energy investment credit is allowed under the Energy Tax Act of 1978 which permits you to claim a 10% investment credit on energy property installed after September 30, 1978, and before January 1, 1983. Qualifying properties include alternate energy property, solar or wind energy properties, specially defined energy property, and recycling equipment. This tax credit is determined separately from the regular investment tax credit discussed previously. If the energy property is also tangible personal property that qualifies for investment tax credit, both credits may be claimed.

OUTSIDE HELP

For help with the legal aspects of going into business, you may need an attorney and an accountant. Whenever there's a doubt about a legal question, an attorney's help should be sought. An accountant can help you determine what records to keep and advise on techniques so you don't pay unnecessary tax. Both accountants and lawyers can advise on changes in tax laws that may require adjustments in the kind of facts necessary for tax reporting. Although use of attorneys and accountants will cost additional money, they may save you much more than their fees, not only in the long run, but also in the short run.

You will find a complete list of U.S. government tax publications in Figure 1.8. Any of these publications can be obtained free from any Internal Revenue Service office.

Tax Publications

The discussions in *Tax Guide for Small Business,* Publication 334, generally will answer you questions about Federal tax laws that apply to business. However, sometimes other IRS publications on individual topics are suggested for more information. You will find these publications listed below in alphabetical order. All of these publications are available free from any Internal Revenue Service Office.

Title	No.
Accounting Periods and Methods	538
Administrators, Survivors, and Executors, Tax Information for	559
Aliens, U.S. Tax Guide for	519
Annuity and Pension Income	575
Annuity Programs, Tax-Sheltered, for Employees of Public Schools and Certain Tax-Exempt Organizations	571
Appeal Rights, Examination of Returns, and Claims for Refund	556
Assets, Sales and Other Dispositions of	544
Bad Debts, Deduction for	548
Basis of Assets	551
Business Expenses and Operating Losses	535
Business, Small, Recordkeeping for a	583
Business Use of Your Home	587
Buying or Selling Your Home, Tax Information on	523
Canada-United States Income Tax Treaty, Information on the	597
Casualty Losses, Disasters, and Thefts, Tax Information on	547
Child and Disabled Dependent Care	503
Circular E, Employer's Tax Guide	15
Civil Aircraft, Federal Use Tax on	582
Civil Service Retirement and Disability Retirement, Tax Information on U.S.	567
Civil Service Retirement Benefits, Tax Guide for U.S.	721
Claims for Refund, Examination of Returns, and Appeal Rights	556
Clergy and Religious Workers, Social Security for Members of the	517
Collection Process, The	586A
Commerical Fishermen, Tax Guide for	595
Community Property and the Federal Income Tax	555
Condemnations of Private Property for Public Use	549
Condominiums and Cooperative Apartments, Tax Information on	588
Contributions, Charitable	526
Cooperative Apartments and Condominiums, Information on	588
Corporations, Subchapter S, Tax Information on	589
Corporations, Tax Information on	542
Credit, Earned Income	596
Credit for the Elderly	524
Credit Sales by Dealers in Personal Property	512
Deductions, Miscellaneous	529
Dental and Medical Expenses	502
Depreciation	534
Disability Payments	522
Disability Retirement and U.S. Civil Service Retirement, Tax Information on	567
Disabled Dependent and Child Care	503
Disaster, Casualty Losses, and Thefts, Tax Information on	547
Disaster Loss Workbook	584
Divorced or Separated Individuals, Tax Information for	504
Donated Property, Valuation of	561
Earned Income Credit	596

Title	No.
Educational Expenses	508
Elderly, Credit for the	524
Employee Benefit Plans, Filing Requirements for	1048
Employer's Tax Guide, Circular E	15
Energy Credits for Individuals	903
Entertainment, Travel, and Gift Expenses	463
Estate and Gift Taxes, Federal	448
Estimated Tax and Tax Withholding	505
Examination of Returns, Appeal Rights, and Claims for Refund	556
Excise Taxes for 1980	510
Executors, Survivors, and Administrators, Tax Information for	559
Exempt Organizations, Tax on Unrelated Business Income of	598
Exempt Status for Your Organization, How to Apply for and Retain	557
Exemptions	501
Farmer's Tax Guide	225
Federal Income Tax, Your	17
Fishermen, Commercial, Tax Guide for	595
Foreign Scholars and Educational and Cultural Exchange Visitors	518
Foreign Tax Credit for U.S. Citizens and Resident Aliens	514
Fuel Tax Credit or Refund for Nonhighway and Transit Users, Federal	378
Gift and Estate Taxes, Federal	448
Gifts, Computing the Interrelated Charitable, Marital, and Orphans' Deductions and Net	904
Highway Use Tax on Trucks, Truck-Tractors, and Buses, Federal	349
Home, Business Use of Your	587
Home, Tax Information on Buying or Selling Your	523
Homeowners, Tax Information for	530
Income Averaging	506
Income from Tips, Reporting	531
Income, Investment, and Expenses	550
Income, Pension, and Annuity	575
Income, Taxable and Nontaxable	525
Individual Retirement Arrangements, Tax Information on	590
Installment and Deferred-Payment Sales	537
Interest Expense	545
Investment Credit	572
Investment Income and Expenses	550
Jobs, Targeted and WIN Credits	906
Losses, Operating, and Business Expenses	535
Medical and Dental Expenses	502
Miscellaneous Deductions	529
Moving Expenses	521
Mutual Fund Distributions	564
Nontaxable and Taxable Income	525
Older Americans, Tax Benefits for	554
Optional Self-Employment Tax Tables	421
Overseas, Income Tax Benefits for U.S. Citizens Who Go	593
Partnerships, Tax Information on	541
Pension and Annuity Income	575
Political Campaigns, Voluntary Tax Methods to Help Finance	585
Private Foundations and Foundation Managers, Tax Information for	578
Publications, Index to Tax	900
Recordkeeping for a Small Business	583
Recordkeeping Requirements and a List of Tax Publications	552
Rental Property	527
Reporting Requirements and Withholding Taxes	539
Retirement Benefits, U.S. Civil Service, Tax Guide for	721
Retirement Plans, Self-Employed, Tax Information on	560
Retirement, U.S. Civil Service, and Disability Retirement, Tax Information on	567

Title	No.
Sales and Other Dispositions of Assets	544
Scholars, Foreign, and Educational and Cultural Exchange Visitors	518
Scholars, U.S., Tax Information for	520
Self-Employed Retirement Plans, Tax Information on	560
Self-Employment Tax	533
Self-Employment Tax Tables	421
Selling or Buying Your Home, Tax Information on	523
Separated or Divorced Individuals, Tax Information for	504
Social Security Tax Guide for Employers in the Virgin Islands, Guam, and American Samoa, Federal	80
Sponsors of Contests and Sporting Events, Tax Information for	558
Subchapter S Corporations, Tax Information on	589
Survivors, Executors, and Administrators, Tax Information for	559
Targeted Jobs and WIN Credits	906
Tax, Your Federal Income Tax Calendar for 1980	509
Tax Changes, Highlights of 1979	553
Tax-Sheltered Annuity Programs for Employees of Public Schools and Certain Tax-Exempt Organizations	571
Tax Treaties, U.S.	901
Tax Treaty Countries, Certification for Reduced Tax Rates in	686
Taxable and Nontaxable Income	525
Thefts, Disasters, and Casualty Losses, Tax Information on	547
Tips, Reporting Income from	531
Travel, Entertainment, and Gift Expenses	463
Treaty Countries, Certification for Reduced Tax Rates in Tax	686
Unemployment Compensation, Tax Information on	905
U.S. Citizens Abroad, Tax Guide for	54
U.S. Citizens Who Go Overseas, Income Tax Benefits for	593
U.S. Government Civilian Employees Stationed Abroad, Tax Information for	516
U.S. Possessions, Tax Guide for U.S. Citizens Employed in	570
Valuation of Donated Property	561
Visitors to the United States, Tax Information for	513
WIN and Targeted Jobs Credits	906
Withholding of Tax on Nonresident Aliens and Foreign Corporations	515
Withholding Tax and Estimated Tax	505
Withholding Taxes and Reporting Requirements	539
Your Federal Income Tax	17

Spanish Language Publications

Guía para preparar la declaración del impuesto federal sobre ingreso personal	579S
Proceso de Cobro (Deudas del Impuesto Sobre Ingreso)	586S
Revisión de las Declaraciones de Impuesto, Derecho de Apelación y Reclamaciones de Devolución	556S

Other Helpful Publications

The Small Business Administration has available a number of informative publications. SBA 115A contains a list of free publications; and SBA 115B provides a list of the for-sale booklets. Both SBA 115A and SBA 115B are available through SBA's Washington and field offices or write to the Small Business Administration, Washington, D.C. 20416.

Figure 1.8. Complete list of government tax publications.

SOURCES OF ADDITIONAL INFORMATION

The Drafting of Corporate Charters and Bylaws, by Kurt Pantzer and Richard Deer, published by the Joint Committee on Continuing Legal Education of the American Law Institute and the American Bar Association, 4025 Chestnut St., Philadelphia, Pa 19104.

Tax and Business Organization of Small Business, by Jonathan Sobeloff, published by the Joint Committee on Continuing Legal Education of the American Law Institute and the American Bar Association, 4025 Chestnut St., Philadelphia, Pa 19104.

Tax Guide for Small Business, IRS Publication No. 334, published by the Superintendent of Documents, Washington, DC 20402.

2

Sources of Capital
and How to Get a Loan

THE BEST SOURCE OF CAPITAL

The best source of capital for any new business is your own money. The reason it's best is that it's the easiest to make use of and, of course, it's also the quickest to get. In addition, you don't need to worry about paying the money back and you don't have to surrender equity in your business. You should recognize that many outside sources of capital will expect you to put up *some* of your own money before they will agree to invest. This gives these sources greater confidence that you will not easily give up when the going in your business gets rough, and also that you are as convinced that your idea will succeed as you appear to be.

OBTAINING MONEY FROM FRIENDS AND RELATIVES

Friends and relatives are also a good source of money. This is the second fastest, easiest, and cheapest source of cash that you need for your business, with fewer legal problems and with far less paperwork required. If you do raise money from friends and relatives, try not to surrender control of your business. That is, make this money a loan and do not give up stock in your business. If you do become partners with friends or relatives, you may find it difficult to keep them out of day-to-day operations and decision making. Unless they have know-how to contribute as well as money, there is no reason for their participation.

BORROWING FROM THE BANK

There are various types of bank loans, and the difficulty of getting them varies considerably. Basically, the bank is a very conservative lender that will insist upon collateral and will want to be absolutely certain that it will get its money back from you. If you have money in a savings account, you can borrow against this money. The cost of such a loan is usually low, because the savings institution in which you have the money can use your savings as collateral until your loan is repaid. There is an advantage to this type of loan: the money you have in the savings account continues to draw interest while you have the loan, even while it is being held as collateral. Accordingly, if your money is normally earning 9½% interest and if the loan is costing you 15½%, the real cost of the loan is only 6% interest.

It might also be relatively easy for you to get a loan using your life insurance as collateral. This is possible if your life insurance policy has cash value. If so, you can generally obtain a loan up to 95% of the money that has been accumulated. With this type of life insurance loan, you don't actually have to repay the loan; you pay only the interest each year along with your premium. Of course, if you don't replace the money that you borrowed from your life insurance, that amount is deducted from the face value of the policy paid to any beneficiary.

Another type of bank loan which is relatively easy to get, if your credit is good, is a signature or personal loan for several thousand dollars. If you have dealt with the same bank for some time, sometimes you can get an even larger loan if they feel that you are a good risk. These types of loans are short-term and usually must be paid off within from several months to several years. Depending on your negotiations with the bank, these loans may be paid off on an installment plan or in a lump sum at a specified time.

TYPES OF BANK LOANS

The *commercial loan* is a short-term loan from a bank which is usually paid off in a lump sum within a six-month period. Stocks and bonds, the cash value of life insurance, or a personal guarantee may be accepted as collateral for this type of loan. If the loan exceeds a certain amount, some banks will require that the borrower maintain a reserve of cash in a bank account. This reserve is known as a compensating balance. Its size will depend on a number of factors, but usually will not have to be more than 20% of the amount borrowed.

Accounts receivable financing is credit extended from the bank, unsecured, against money owed you by your customers. Usually the bank will advance you up to about 80% of the receivable value. You are required to sign the receivables over to the bank. When you receive payment, you send payments to the bank which credits this amount against your loan along with the interest agreed upon. Your customer is not involved in any way and pays you in the usual manner.

Inventory financing uses raw materials or finished goods in your inventory as collateral. You usually can get this type of loan only up to 50% of the value of the inventory.

Loans against real estate can usually be made for up to 75% of the property value and amortized over a fairly long period, in some cases up to 20 years. A bank will also provide residential mortgages and real estate refinancing.

If you intend to buy major equipment, banks will make *equipment loans* for up to about 80% of the equipment's value. The maximum length of this loan is usually five years or the maximum life of the equipment.

SMALL BUSINESS ADMINISTRATION LOANS

Small Business Administration (SBA) loans have been a good source of capital; however, they are far from automatic and, like any loan, they require a completed loan package developed by the entrepreneur or small businessperson. You should also allow yourself lead time of a year to 18 months from the time you apply for the loan until it will be fully approved and you actually have the money. As this is being written the SBA's loan program is under review. Therefore, check with your local SBA office.

By law, the SBA may not make a loan if you can obtain funds from a bank or other private source. Therefore, you must seek private financing before applying for an SBA loan. This means that you should apply to your bank or other lending

institution for a loan, and if you live in a city with a population of more than 200,-
000, you are required to apply to two banks before applying for a direct SBA loan.

There are various types of SBA loans, and their structures change from time to
time. Therefore, you should check with the local office of your SBA (see Appendix II) to get the latest information. However, basically there are two types of
loans which you may qualify for: business loans and economic opportunity loans.

SBA business loans are for businesses, including farms, that are independently
owned and operated and not dominant in their fields, that are unable to obtain
private financing under reasonable terms, that are qualified as "small" under SBA
size standards based on various factors. These factors are currently under review.
According to an SBA bulletin issued in July 1982:

> The Small Business Act of 1953 broadly defines a small business as independently
> owned and not dominant in its field. The act authorizes the administrator of the U.S.
> Small Business Administration (SBA) to establish more specific, industry-related
> criteria that can be used to identify the small business community in order to deter-
> mine eligibility for SBA program benefits, procurement set-asides, regulatory ex-
> emptions, and other forms of Federal assistance. The size standards developed
> through these criteria are of vital concern to every business that considers itself to be
> small.
>
> Existing size standards were developed through a consensus process with each in-
> dustry. While these standards vary markedly between industries in order to reflect
> the specific characteristics of each industry, they lack an underlying comprehensive
> rationale or a cohesive logic. In some cases these standards reflect the special inter-
> ests of procurement agencies, Congress, or the historical view of specific businesses.
>
> Currently, SBA utilizes a variety of measures for size determinations. The largest
> number of businesses in retail, service, wholesale, construction, and agriculture, for
> example, are measured by annual receipts criteria (averaged over 3 years). Manufac-
> turing, research and development, and mining are measured by employee criteria.
> Criteria used to determine business size in other industries include such measures as
> the number of hospital beds and barrels of oil refined per day.
>
> In 1978, the SBA initiated a comprehensive study of its size standards, and as a result
> has announced that it intends to propose sweeping revisions. While these revisions
> are fundamentally a bureaucratic exercise, they are necessary in order to bring co-
> herence to SBA's policies regarding loans, procurement assistance, and advocacy.
>
> On March 10, 1980, SBA issued its first advance notice of proposed size standard re-
> visions. The SBA held ten regional hearings on the notice and received over 1,500
> comments. Over 80 percent of these comments criticized the new measure. The Sen-
> ate Select Committee on Small Business also held hearings on the notice on May 5,
> 1981, at which the public was once again invited to participate.
>
> On May 3, 1982, the SBA issued its second advance notice of proposed size standard
> revisions which reflected the comments received on the first proposal. The May 3 no-
> tice uses one criteria for measuring business size—number of employees—but re-
> tains the annual receipts criteria for measuring business size in agriculture and con-
> struction. (Measuring employment in the agriculture industry presents problems of
> determining whether family members and relatives are considered employees. In
> construction the question is whether employees of subcontractors, which are used
> widely in this industry category, should be included in the employee count. Both
> problems were resolved by the annual receipts approach.)
>
> The May 3 notice establishes a maximum employee limit above which a business is
> no longer considered by the SBA to be small. In the manufacturing industry, the
> proposed limit has been set at 500 employees. This is a significant reduction from the
> 2,500 employee ceiling proposed in the 1980 notice.

Upper limits were also imposed on the major industry categories in retail, wholesale, service, transportation, and finance. These ceilings, proposed in the May 1982 notice, range from 25 to 500 employees depending on the type of firm. (In the 1980 proposal, some ceilings were as low as 15 employees.)

This adjustment corrects one inequity noted by the Office of Advocacy regarding the first advance notice in 1980. For example, under that proposal, a large manufacturer with just under 2,500 employees would have been eligible for SBA assistance. At the same time, a retailer owning a hardware store with eight employees, and a small grocery store with eight employees, would have been classified as a large business, and no longer eligible for SBA assistance. The adjustment restores some equity among industry categories.

In addition, the May 3 notice clarifies SBA's intent to average full-time and part-time employees so that seasonal fluctuations in employment will not significantly affect a firm's size status. Those industries relying heavily on part-time employees were reviewed carefully, and standards were adjusted accordingly.

In the interest of administrative simplicity and uniformity, SBA has also proposed several procedural changes in its size standard regulations. These include:

Eliminating geographical differentials.

Basing all SBA size standard categories on the Office of Management and Budget's published Standard Industrial Classification codes, in lieu of written descriptions.

Eliminating broad-based non-manufacturing size standards and replacing them with industry-specific size standards.

Eliminating the special size standards for the surety bond guarantee program.

Increasing small business size standards by 25 percent for businesses located in labor surplus or redevelopment areas.

Check with your SBA office for the official definition at the time of your loan application.

You can use the SBA business loan for conversion or expansion, purchase of equipment, facilities, machinery, supplies, materials, and working capital. The maximum amount of this loan at the present time is $500,000. However, this maximum figure can be obtained only in exceptional circumstances under which you pay an interest rate which does not exceed the rate set by a statutory formula relating to the cost of money to the government. Normally you are required to pay this loan off within 10 years, unless it is a working capital loan, in which case you will be required to pay the loan off in 6 years. On the other hand, portions of loans for construction and acquisition of real estate may go as long as 20 years.

As collateral for an SBA loan, you may be required to put up a mortgage on land, buildings and/or equipment, assignment of warehouse receipts for marketable merchandise, a mortgage on chattels or guarantees of personal endorsements, and, in some cases, assignment of current receivables.

Economic opportunity loans are similar to business loans except they are for low-income or disadvantaged persons who lack the opportunity to start or strengthen a small business and cannot obtain the necessary financing from other sources on reasonable terms. Usually these loans are limited to $100,000 to any one borrower. The money can be used for purposes similar to those stated for the business loan, and the interest rate is set by a statutory formula. Major differences here have to do with the maximum period of time for repayment of the loan. There is a maximum of 15 years, with a maximum of 10 years for a working capital loan. Also, the collateral that is required may be any worthwhile collateral which is available or will be acquired with the proceeds of the loan.

How to Apply for an SBA Loan

There are many companies around which will offer to carry out the entire SBA loan application procedure for you, for a fee. In most cases, you will be able to do the same job for yourself at a much lower cost. You should be aware that no preparer can guarantee that you will get your loan approved. Be wary of any company that even implies that your loan approval is assured if they prepare your loan package. The SBA recommends the following sequence to obtain one of their loans:

1. Prepare a current financial statement balance sheet listing all assets and all liabilities of your business.
2. Have a profit and loss statement for the previous full year and for the current period to the date of the balance sheet.
3. Prepare a current personal financial statement of yourself as owner or each partner or stockholder owning 20% or more of the corporate stock in the business.
4. List collateral to be offered as security for the loan with your estimate of the present market value of each item.
5. State amount of loan requested and explain exact purposes for which it will be used.
6. Take this material with you and see your banker. Ask for a direct bank loan and, if declined, ask the bank to make the loan under the SBA's loan guarantee plan or to participate with the SBA in a loan. If the bank is interested in an SBA guarantee or participation loan, ask the banker to contact SBA for discussion of your application. In most cases of guarantee or participation loans, the SBA will deal directly with the bank.
7. If a guarantee or participation loan is not available, write or visit the nearest SBA office and they will give you the additional information required.

For new businesses, follow these procedures:

1. Describe in detail the type of business to be established.
2. Describe experience and management capabilities.
3. Prepare an estimate of how much you or others have to invest in the business and how much you will need to borrow.
4. Prepare a current financial statement balance sheet listing all personal assets and all liabilities.
5. Prepare a detailed projection of earnings for the first year the business will operate.
6. List collateral to be offered as security for the loan, indicating your estimate of the present market value of each item.
7. Take this material and go see your banker. Ask for a direct bank loan and, if declined, ask the bank to make the loan under the SBA's loan guarantee plan or to participate with the SBA in a loan. If the bank is interested in the SBA guarantee or participation loan, ask the banker to contact the SBA for discussion of your application. In most cases of guarantee or participation loans, the SBA will deal directly with the bank.
8. If a guarantee or participation loan is not available, write or visit the nearest SBA office for additional information.

See Chapters 9 and 11 for information on preparation of financial statements.

OBTAINING MONEY FROM FACTORS

Obtaining money from factors involves the outright sale of your accounts receivable to another party. Essentially, you get paid cash on delivery of your product or service while your customers receive credit on terms that they require. This differs from accounts receivable financing in that factoring is not a loan. The factor actually purchases your accounts receivable for their full value, usually for up to 80% of their worth, at the time that you ship the goods. The remainder of their worth is given to you when your customers pay. The factor checks the credit of each of your customers' accounts and purchases these receivables from you without recourse, which means that the factor absorbs any bad debt losses. To compensate for these risks, factors typically charge a 1 to 2% fee for each invoice, plus interest, on the advance that they make to you. The total amount is usually greater than bank and commercial finance company rates for comparable loans. However, factors do not require as extensive a loan package as other lenders. Also, obtaining money from a factor can be fast, and sometimes once your credit references and other financial statements are supplied and the credit of the account has been confirmed, you can obtain money in as little as 24 hours.

FINANCE COMPANIES

Finance companies will assume a greater amount of risk in the loan than will banks. Whereas a bank may deny you the loan if you have a high degree of debt or may be running into financial difficulties, a commercial finance company makes loans on the strength of your collateral rather than your track record or potential. Commercial finance companies will make loans much as banks do to include equipment leasing and factoring. Naturally you will pay more money in interest for a commercial finance company loan than for a bank loan. To obtain the loan usually requires several days up to a few weeks.

USING SUPPLIERS FOR A LOAN

Your suppliers are a frequently overlooked source of a loan. Suppliers may be those selling you stationery and printing supplies, or various components or materials that are used in something that you manufacture. In effect, a loan exists if your supplier will not require a payment until the delivery of supplies. In addition, sometimes suppliers will grant you 30, 60, or 90 days, or even more time to pay for whatever material you have purchased from them. Clearly, the effect is that of a loan, even though a loan as such has not been negotiated. Usually suppliers will give a discount for early payment of purchased supplies; typically, this discount is 2% for payment within 10 days. This 2% savings should be weighed against your need for funds in the business. You should never be afraid of asking for credit to enable you to pay later if you need this money for some important business purpose.

CREDIT CARD LOANS

Credit cards are another frequently overlooked source of "loans." Depending upon the particular credit card and the amount of credit that you are permitted with that card, you may be able to get several thousand dollars, with which you can purchase supplies or materials for your business. This credit is easy to get and requires no special paperwork as long as you do not go above the amount which has been established for you with the particular credit card. Be careful of the interest rate on these, however; it can be extremely high, and you should weigh against the easy acquisition of this money the amount of interest charged.

EQUITY CAPITAL FINANCING

Equity capital financing is selling off a portion of your business to another investor who contributes capital and may or may not participate in the management of your business. Your business has no legal obligation for repayment of the amount invested or for payment of interest for the amount of the funds. The investor shares in the ownership of the business and is entitled to participate in any distribution of earnings through dividends in the case of corporations or any draw in the case of a partnership. How much the investor participates in the distribution of earnings depends upon the number of shares that he or she holds; or in a partnership, the percentage of the business which the partnership owns. Since you do not have to pay a debt, equity financing may appear to be an easy way to obtain capital for your business. However, it has the following disadvantages:

1. The share in the success must be extended to other owners in your business.
2. You lose some control over your business. In some types of equity financing you will have to give up a majority control. You should most definitely consult your attorney before taking on any equity investors.

HOW TO VALUE EQUITY CAPITAL

A primary question once the decision has been made to use equity capital is how to value it. In a start-up situation, for example, it is fairly typical for the individual with the idea or product innovation to get 50% equity and the investors to get the other 50% equity. If the innovator also has capital to contribute, he is given the same proportion of equity for his additional capital as the investors are given for theirs. Although the 50–50 rule is fairly common, another way of doing this is to put some value on the contributions of the individual starting the company. For example, if a price tag can be put on patents that he is contributing, specific knowledge, and so forth, then this would help to place a value on the equity which is given to the investors in exchange for capital. Of course, all terms are negotiable and the valuation of the innovator's contributions versus capital contributions will vary from situation to situation.

VENTURE CAPITAL

Venture capital is generally used for relatively new businesses that are somewhat risky, but that have both a successful track record and a clear potential for high growth and return on investment. Venture capital firms and individuals who venture their own capital are interested in many of the same factors that influence other lending organizations. That is, they want to know the results and ratios of past operations, how much money is wanted, what the money is wanted for, and financial projections. But venture capitalists will look much more closely at the features of the product or service being offered and the potential in the market than do many other lending organizations. As a result, venture capitalists very frequently have definite preferences for certain types of industries, certain types of products, and certain locations.

Before you even consider this source, you should know that venture capitalists are interested in being owners. That is, they will insist on an equity type of financing. Further, in most cases, venture capitalists will insist upon owning more than 50% of the business. However, this may not be as critical a factor as it seems. Although in theory, the venture capitalist will control the company by owning a majority of the stock, these companies are normally not interested in running the business on a day-to-day basis, or in exerting their control so as to interfere in your business management.

Despite the fact that venture capitalists insist on equity financing and owning a controlling interest in the businesses they finance, they are usually in a buyers' market. Typically venture capital firms will receive hundreds, if not thousands, of proposals during the course of the year. They may reject 95%. It is important to remember, therefore, that in order to interest a venture capital firm in your business, you must do the selling. Understand that they are only interested in companies with some sort of track record and will only invest in firms that they believe can rapidly increase in sales and generate substantial profits with the money they provide. Typically, venture capital companies seek a return of three to five times their investment in only five to seven years. And, also typically, venture capital firms are interested in investment projects requiring an investment of from $250,000 up to about $2 million.

Selling the Venture Proposal

Inasmuch as 90% or more proposals to venture capital firms are rejected, you must do your homework and recognize what a venture capital firm is looking for when you prepare your venture proposal. This proposal should emphasize the market potential and competitive position of the company, along with its products, present and potential customers, suppliers, production costs, financial condition, and the character and competence of the management including experience and background.

The proposal should be upbeat without lying. Difficulties should be clearly indicated, but each problem stated should also include a solution. The proposal should be under 50 pages and should cover the following areas in detail: purposes and objectives of the project, the proposed financing including the amount of money that you'll need, how the money will be used and how you plan on structuring the financing, marketing including the marketing segment that you are after, competitors that are in the market and how you will beat them, characteristics of the market, and costs of executing the marketing plan you are proposing. You should also have a history of your firm including the significant milestones since founding, prior financing, your success, company organization, financial relationships with banks and other lending institutions, and a detailed description of your product or service and the costs associated with it. As for financial statements, you should include balance sheets, income statements, and cash flows for the last three years, as well as projections for the next three years which include the effect with the proposed project for which financing is being obtained. You should also include an analysis of key factors which may affect the financial performance, as well as the result if the level of sales projected is not attained. You should have a complete list of shareholders in your company, the amounts invested to date, and the form of capitalization equity per debt. Biographical sketches of résumés and the qualifications and experience of key owners and managers of the company should be included and should emphasize experience and accomplishments which have a bearing on the operation of your firm. You should include a list of your main suppliers and your main customers, and problems that you anticipate or that are possible, as well as actions that you would take in the event that these problems became a reality. Finally, you should have a section detailing the advantages of your firm, its product, service, plans, personnel, and the project for which you need the money. Finally, you should emphasize why and how your unique advantages cannot fail, but will surely result in success for this project.

For a list of venture capital companies, get a copy of *The Guide To Venture Capital Sources,* published by the Capital Publishing Corp., 10 South LaSalle St., Chicago, Ill. 60603.

SMALL BUSINESS INVESTMENT COMPANIES AND MINORITY ENTERPRISE SMALL BUSINESS INVESTMENT COMPANIES

Small business investment companies, or SBICs, and minority enterprise small business investment companies, or MESBICs, are both regulated and sponsored by the Small Business Administration. In fact, the government puts up a great deal of the capital for these firms to invest in young companies. The major difference between the SBIC and the MESBIC is that the MESBIC must invest only in minority-owned and minority-managed firms. The rules and regulations are relaxed significantly for these firms and the money leveraging capabilities are increased significantly.

SBICs and MESBICs make both equity investments and long-term loans. These loans can be as large as their equity investments—30% of the MESBIC's private capitalization or 20% of the SBIC's private funds. Most of these loans are made for from 5 to 7 years, although they can go as high as 20 years, and they are generally made for business expansion purposes. Typical charges for SBIC and MESBIC loans are the going bank rate in your state, and both loans and equity investments from either SBICs or MESBICs will take from several weeks to several months.

You will find a list of SBICs in Appendix V.

SMALL BUSINESS DEVELOPMENT COMPANIES

Small business development companies, or SBDCs, operate in the same fashion as SBICs except that they are capitalized entirely by private sources, including banks, large manufacturing firms, utility companies, transportation firms, and so forth. Like the SBICs and the MESBICs, they make loans on a long-term basis or purchase stock in the venture. Information on small business development companies can be obtained from your local chamber of commerce.

STATE BUSINESS AND INDUSTRIAL DEVELOPMENT CORPORATIONS

Many states have their own development corporations which are capitalized through funds from the state. These SBIDCs make long-term loans rather than equity investments, specializing in from 5- to 20-year loans for the expansion of facilities and the purchase of equipment. SBIDC interests and priorities vary from state to state. Some are particularly interested in making high-risk loans for businesses which cannot otherwise obtain loans from banks. Others will only lend capital when the risk is minimal. To get more information on SBIDCs, check with your state business development office or chamber of commerce or the SBA office in your area.

LOCAL DEVELOPMENT COMPANIES

Local development companies (LDCs) are resident-organized and capitalized. However, they solicit SBA and bank loans to buy or build facilities for local small businesses. Once they have identified small businesses in the local area which are in need, they are eligible for one SBA loan or guarantee up to $1 million annually, and unlimited bank loans for each small business they assist. Typically, an LDC supplies only 10% of a project's cost; the remainder must be obtained through combined SBA and bank loans or one SBA guarantee bank loan. Also, an LDC can finance all of a company's facilities, but it cannot supply working capital or fund the purchase of inventory supplies or freestanding fixtures and equipment.

High-risk ventures are good candidates for an LDC loan because the LDC and not the small business is the actual loan recipient. Some LDCs are nonprofit corporations and therefore will charge minimum interest on their 10% of the funds lent. Others that operate for a profit will charge rates which are comparable with those of banks.

In order to use and get an LDC loan, you must first be approved by the LDC using a standard loan package which is described at the end of the chapter. You are then evaluated by the SBA and then by the participating bank. Lead time for the LDC loan in its entirety is from two to four months.

To find out the LDCs in your area, consult Appendix II and contact the SBA field office in your area.

USE OF FINDERS IN LOCATING LOANS

Finders are individual financial consultants who are paid a percentage of the loan by you to locate a loan for you. These finders may be obtained by word of mouth from other entrepreneurs and small businesspeople or from your attorney, accountant, or banker. Sometimes finders can be found through advertisements in financial papers or the classified section of your local newspaper, or the *Wall Street Journal*. Finders' fees vary greatly. They may be as low as 1% or as high as 15%. Therefore, if you use a finder, make certain that you ask for enough money in the loan to include the fee.

HOW TO DECIDE WHICH TYPE OF FUNDING TO USE

To determine which source of funding is best for you in your situation, you should consider the following factors primary. They are:

1. *Cost.* How much will each type of capital cost and how will each source affect the earnings of the present owners of the business?
2. *Risk.* How does each source of funding affect your business or expose it to risk?

3. *Flexibility.* What conditions imposed by each source of funding affect your flexibility either in seeking additional capital or in using the capital generated the way you wish and according to your best judgment?

4. *Control.* How is your present control of the business affected by the source of funding? Will loss of control prevent you from making operating and daily business decisions that you consider to be in your best interest?

5. *Availability.* Which sources are in fact available for you to use and which are not?

These five factors should be weighed and all tradeoffs considered in order to arrive at the optimal method of funding for your particular situation.

PUBLIC STOCK OFFERINGS, MERGERS, AND CASHING IN

When your business is first organized, equity capital is usually secured from a combination of sources including your own personal savings and money from friends, relatives, and so forth. Then, as you grow, you will need additional capital through professional finders, venture capitalists, SBICs, and other sources. Finally, as very high levels of capital are needed, you will have basically two choices. One option is to merge with a larger company for an infusion of capital, and a second is to sell shares through public offering. The public offering seeks to attract a large number of investors to purchase stock. Both stock offerings and mergers provide a way in which you can cash in on your business. For example, a merger may entitle you to stock from the larger firm which can be held or turned into cash, plus a management position and salary if you desire to continue managing the enterprise which you started, or a fee over a period of years as a consultant or as part of an agreement not to compete with the firm with which you've merged. Selling capital stock of a corporation is closely regulated and can fail. It is done through your local investment banker when your enterprise is a corporation. And through the use of different types of stock, common versus preferred, you may retain your control over the corporation since while preferred stock has a priority of dividends it does not have a voting privilege as does common stock. Therefore, by retaining the majority of common stock in a corporation, you can retain control.

The banker prepares a detailed study of your projections and plans for your firm which he issues in the form of an offering. The investment banker's charges will depend upon whether he guarantees sale of the full amount or whether the stock is sold on a "best efforts" basis. The first type of offering is usually reserved for large enterprises that have a considerable track record. The investment banker, for a fee, can also analyze your business plan and loan package and prepare an offering of your company's stock to its investment contacts. This private placement may be in the form of a stock equity or long-term debt, but it is not intended for public trading and therefore is not registered with the Securities and Exchange Commission (SEC).

THE LOAN PACKAGE

The loan package is extremely important for all types of loans. Figure 2.1 shows a loan package outline from the Small Business Administration itself. Figure 2.2 shows a loan package outline and example.

U.S. Small Business Administration

APPLICATION FOR BUSINESS LOAN

I. Applicant

30

Trade Name of Borrower		Street Address	
32		34	

City	County	State	Zip	Tel. No. (Inc. A/C)
36		37	39	

Employers ID Number	Date of Application	Date Application Received by SBA	Number of Employees (including subsidiaries and affiliates)
33		5	

Type of Business	Date Business Established	☐ Existing Business	At Time of Application _____
		☐ New Business	If Loan is Approved _____
Bank of Business Account		☐ Purchase Existing Business	

II. Management (Proprietor, partners, officers, directors and stockholders owning 20% or more of outstanding stock)

Name	Address	% Owned	Annual Comp.	*Military Service From	To	*Race	*Sex
			$				
			$				
			$				
			$				

*This data is collected for statistical purposes only. It has no bearing on the credit decision to approve or decline this application.

III. Use of Proceeds: (Enter Gross Dollar Amounts Rounded to Nearest Hundreds)	Loan Requested	SBA USE ONLY Approved	2 SBA Office Code	1 ① SBA Loan Number
⑤ Land Acquisition	$			
⑥ New Plant or Building Construction			**IV. Summary of Collateral:**	
⑦ Building Expansion or Repair			If your collateral consists of (A) Land and Building, (D) Accounts Receivable and/or (E) Inventory, fill in the appropriate blanks. If you are pledging (B) Machinery and Equipment, (C) Furniture and Fixtures, and/or (F) Other, please provide an itemized list (labeled Exhibit A) that contains serial and identification numbers for all articles that had an original value greater than $500. Include a legal description of Real Estate offered as collateral.	
⑧ Acquisition and/or Repair of Machinery and Equipment				
⑨ Inventory Purchase				

	Loan Requested	SBA USE ONLY Approved		Present Market Value	Present Mortgage Balance	Cost Less Depreciation
⑩ Working Capital (Including Accounts Payable)						
⑪ Acquisition of all or part of Existing Business			A. Land and Building	$	$	$
⑫a Payoff SBA Loan			B. Machinery & Equipment			
⑫b Payoff Bank Loan (Non SBA Associated)			C. Furniture & Fixtures			
⑫c Other Debt Payment (Non SBA Associated)			D. Accounts Receivable			
⑬ All Other			E. Inventory			
⑭ Total Loan Requested	$		F. Other			
Term of Loan			Total Collateral	$	$	$

V. Previous Government Financing: If you or any principals or affiliates have ever requested Government Financing (including SBA), complete the following:

Name of Agency	Amount	Date of Request	Approved or Declined	Balance	Status
	$			$	
	$			$	
	$			$	

③ Previous SBA Financing (Check One) ☐ (1) No ☐ (2) Repaid/Other ☐ (3) Present Borrower	④ Loan Number of 1st SBA Loan

VI. Indebtedness: Furnish the following information on all installment debts, contracts, notes, and mortgages payable. Indicate by an asterisk (*) items to be paid by loan proceeds and reason for paying same (present balance should agree with latest balance sheet submitted).

To Whom Payable	Original Amount	Original Date	Present Balance	Rate of Interest	Maturity Date	Monthly Payment	Security	Current or Delinquent
	$		$			$		
	$		$			$		
	$		$			$		
	$		$			$		

SBA Form 4 (9-81) REF SOP 50 10 1   PREVIOUS EDITIONS ARE OBSOLETE   (OVER)

Figure 2.1. Loan package outline from the SBA.

All Exhibits must be signed and dated by person signing this form.

1. Submit SBA Form 912 (Personal History Statement) for each person e.g. owners, partners, directors, major stockholders, etc; the instructions are on SBA Form 912.

2. Furnish a signed current personal balance sheet (SBA Form 413 may be used for this purpose) for each stockholder (with 20% or greater ownership), partner, officer, and owner. Social Security number should be included on personal financial statement. Label this Exhibit B.

3. Include the statements listed below: 1, 2, 3 for the last three years; also 1, 2, 3, 4 dated within 90 days of filing the application; and statement 5, if applicable. This is Exhibit C (SBA has Management Aids that help in the preparation of financial statements.)

    1. Balance Sheet   2. Profit and Loss Statement
    3. Reconciliation of Net Worth
    4. Aging of Accounts Receivable and Payable
    5. Earnings projections for at least one year where financial statements for the last three years are unavailable or where requested by District Office.

        (If Profit and Loss Statement is not available, explain why and substitute Federal Income Tax Forms.)

4. Provide a brief history of your company and a paragraph describing the expected benefits it will receive from the loan. Label it Exhibit D.

5. Provide a brief description of the educational, technical and business background for all the people listed in Section II under Management. Please mark it Exhibit E.

6. Do you have any co-signers and/or guarantors for this loan? If so, please submit their names, addresses and personal balance sheet(s) as Exhibit F.

7. Are you buying machinery or equipment with your loan money? If so, you must include a list of the equipment and the cost. This is Exhibit G.

8. Have you or any officers of your company ever been involved in bankruptcy or insolvency proceedings? If so, please provide the details as Exhibit H. If none, check here ☐

9. Are you or your business involved in any pending lawsuits? If yes, provide the details as Exhibit I. If none, check here ☐

10. Do you or your spouse or any member of your household, or anyone who owns, manages, or directs your business or their spouses or members of their households work for the Small Business Administration, Small Business Advisory Council, SCORE or ACE, any Federal Agency, or the participating lender? If so, please provide the name and address of the person and the office where employed. Label this Exhibit J. If none, check here ☐

11. Does your business have any subsidiaries or affiliates? If yes, please provide their names and the relationship with your company along with a current balance sheet and operating statement for each. This should be Exhibit K.

12. Do you buy from, sell to, or use the services of any concern in which someone in your company has a significant financial interest? If yes, provide details on a separate sheet of paper labeled Exhibit L.

13. If your business is a franchise, include a copy of the franchise agreement and a copy of the FTC disclosure statement supplied to you by the Franchisor. Please include it as Exhibit M.

CONSTRUCTION LOANS ONLY

14. Include in a separate exhibit (Exhibit N) the estimated cost of the project and a statement of the source of any additional funds.

15. File all the necessary compliance documents (SBA Form Series 601). The loan officer will advise which forms are necessary.

16. Provide copies of preliminary construction plans and specifications. Include them as Exhibit O. Final plans will be required prior to disbursement.

DIRECT LOANS ONLY

17. Include two bank declination letters with your application. These letters should include the name and telephone number of the persons contacted at the banks, the amount and terms of the loan, the reason for decline and whether or not the bank will participate with SBA. In cities with 200,000 people or less, one letter will be sufficient.

AGREEMENTS AND CERTIFICATIONS

Agreement of Nonemployment of SBA Personnel: I/We agree that if SBA approves this loan application I/We will not, for at least two years, hire as an employee or consultant anyone that was employed by the SBA during the one year period prior to the disbursement of the loan.

Certification: I/We certify: (a) I/We have not paid anyone connected with the Federal Government for help in getting this loan. I/We also agree to report to the SBA Office of Security and Investigations, 1441 L Street N.W., Washington, D.C., 20416 any Federal Government employee who offers, in return for any type of compensation, to help get this loan approved.

(b) All information in this application and the Exhibits is true and complete to the best of my/our knowledge and is submitted to SBA so SBA can decide whether to grant a loan or participate with a lending institution in a loan to me/us. I/We agree to pay for or reimburse SBA for the cost of any surveys, title or mortgage examinations, appraisals etc., performed by non-SBA personnel provided I/We have given my/our consent.

(c) I/We give the assurance that we will comply with sections 112 and 113 of Title 13 of the Code of Federal Regulations. These Code sections prohibit discrimination on the grounds of race, color, sex, religion, marital status, handicap, age, or national origin by recipients of Federal financial assistance and require appropriate reports and access to books and records. These requirements are applicable to anyone who buys or takes control of the business. I/We realize that if I/We do not comply with these non-discrimination requirements SBA can call, terminate, or accelerate repayment of my/our loan. As consideration for any Management and Technical Assistance that may be provided, I/We waive all claims against SBA and its consultants.

I/We understand that I/We need not pay anybody to deal with SBA. I/We have read and understand Form 394 which explains SBA policy on representatives and their fees.

For Guaranty Loans please provide an original and one copy (Photocopy is Acceptable) of the Application Form, and all Exhibits to the participating lender. For Direct Loans submit one original copy of application and Exhibits to SBA.

It is against SBA regulations to charge the applicant a percentage of the loan proceeds as a fee for preparing this application.

If you make a statement that you know to be false or if you over value a security in order to help obtain a loan under the provisions of the Small Business Act, you can be fined up to $5,000 or be put in jail for up to two years, or both.

_____
Signature of Preparer if Other Than Applicant

_____
Print or Type Name of Preparer

_____
Address of Preparer

If Applicant is a proprietor or general partner, sign below:

By:_____
                                                Date

If Applicant is a corporation, sign below:

_____
Corporate Seal   Date

By:_____
                       Signature of President

Attested by: _____
                     Signature of Corporate Secretary

Figure 2.1. (Continued)

A SUGGESTED FORMAT FOR LOAN APPLICATIONS

Any presentation whose objective is to obtain a loan or investment capital should be prepared by the applicant so that any lender or investor has sufficient information from the presentation alone upon which to base a decision as to whether to make a loan or an investment. With this thought in mind, each of the following categories should be carefully considered for the presentation.

THE BUSINESS STRUCTURE

When was the business formed? Is it a sole proprietorship, partnership, or corporation. Who are the owners, and what percentage of the business does each own? Includes personal financial statement(s) of principal owners or partners. A statement as to the type of business the firm is engaged in or proposes. A condensed narrative of history of the firm's operation including copies of last three year-end financial statements of your business (balance sheets and operating statements) or for entire period of operation if less than three (3) years. Copy of most recent financial statement (not older than 90 days).

PERSONNEL

Brief resumes including the background of education and experience of the principals and key employees should be part of the presentation with special emphasis on their experience in the type of work in which the firm is to be engaged.

PHYSICAL FACILITIES

A statement of physical facilities available which should include the location, square footage, and the equipment. One list should show the facilities currently owned or available and the second list the facilities to be acquired. Each item on the list should be followed by the cost of that item.

SPECIAL ASSETS

This should contain a listing of patents, designs, copyrights, prosessing or manufacturing techniques with the estimated value of each.

PRODUCTS & SERVICES

A comprehensive statement of the products and/or services the firm will offer with special emphasis on any unique or advantageous features.

MARKETING INFORMATION

A statement of the total market potential within the area of the operation of the firm. Make a statement as to the present and anticipated competition with the relative advantages and disadvantages of the firm in meeting this competition. A statement to the expected amount of the total potential that the firm expects to obtain over a stated period of time. If possible include letters or other documents from prospective customers that indicated that they are willing to buy from your firm.

PLAN OF ACTION

A statement of the proposed actions for the coming year including expansion of facilities, hiring of personnel, advertising proposed, sales efforts proposed, production efforts proposed, and any direct action that the management plans to take.

USE OF LOAN FUNDS

How the funds applied for are to be used.

FORECASTS - BUDGETS

A projection by month for at least one year but not less than that period of time required to show a positive generation of cash (spendable money). This projection should include: sales, cost of sales, expenses, profits, income, disbursements, cash flow monthly and cash flow cumulative. In addition, if the firm will gross over $250,000 in sales during the next year a pro-forma balance sheet should be made as of the end of the first year forecast.

Figure 2.1. (Continued)

2 SBA Office Code	U.S. SMALL BUSINESS ADMINISTRATION **LENDER'S APPLICATION FOR GUARANTY OR PARTICIPATION** *(Numbers in circles or squares are SBA codes only)*	SBA Loan Number 1 (1)

Name of Applicant:

30

WE PROPOSE TO MAKE A (Check One)

	Lenders Share	SBA Share	Term of Loan	Monthly Payment
Guaranteed Loan	%	%	Years	$
	Lenders Share	SBA Share	Lenders Interest Rate	Payment Beginning
Immediate Participation Loan (Lender to make and service)	%	%	% Per Annum	_____ Months from Date of Note

Amount of Loan $

If Interest Rate is to be Variable

		Rate Adjustment	Base Rate Source
Base Rate:	Spread:	Other ☐ Quarterly ☐ (Specify)	

TERMS AND CONDITIONS OF LENDER: *(Attach additional sheets if more space is needed.)*

I approve this application to SBA subject to the terms and conditions outlined above. Without the participation of SBA to the extent applied for we would not be willing to make this loan, and in our opinion the financial assistance applied for is not otherwise available on reasonable terms. I certify that none of the Lender's employees, officers, directors or substantial stockholders (more than 10%) have a financial interest in the applicant.

Signature:	Title:	Date:

Name of Lender 40	Telephone (Inc A/C)	Financial Institution I.D. Code 41
Street Address 42	City 43	State 44	Zip 45

FOR SBA USE ONLY

Loan Officers Recommendation

☐ Approve   ☐ Decline   State Reason(s)

Signature:	Title:	Date: 3

Other Recommendation, if Required

☐ Approve   ☐ Decline   State Reason(s)

Signature:	Title:	Date:

THIS BLOCK TO BE COMPLETED BY SBA OFFICIAL TAKING FINAL ACTION

☐ Approve   ☐ Decline   State Reason(s)

Signature:	Title:	Date:

BUSINESS LOANS ONLY

4 Program Struct. Code	6 MTY (MOS)	9 SMR	46 No. of Employees	47 Franchise Code	48 New Bus 1-No 2-Yes	49 Women 1-No 2-Yes	50 Viet Vet. 1-No 2-Yes	51 Organ. Code 1-Indiv. 2-Part. 3-Corp.
10 City Code	11 State Code	12 Loan Type (1) Dir. (4) IPSBA (3) IPBK (7) Guar.	52 SIC Code	53 Location 1-Urban 2-Rural	54 EOL Family Income ($ Only) $	55 Poll. Code	56	
13 Sub Program Code	14 County Code	15						

SBA LOAN PAY OFFS: LIST ALL SBA LOANS BEING REFUNDED

Loan Amount Approved	% Participation	Interest Rate	(15a) Loan Number cc 11-20	(15b) Loan Type cc 21	(15c) Loan Status cc 22	(15d) Amount
16 SBA	19 %	21 %	cc 11-20	cc 21 (1) Direct (2) Part. (3) Guar.	cc 22 (1) Curr. (4) C/D (2) P/D (5) Liq. (3) Del.	$
17 Bank	20 %	22 %	cc 29-38	cc 39 (1) Direct (2) Part. (3) Guar.	cc 40 (1) Curr. (4) C/D (2) P/D (5) Liq. (3) Del.	$
18 Total			cc 11-20	cc 21 (1) Direct (2) Part. (3) Guar.	cc 22 (1) Curr. (4) C/D (2) P/D (5) Liq. (3) Del.	$

23 Minority Code	24 O/S SBA Loan 1-No 2-Yes	25 Const. Cont. Amt. $	IF MORE THAN 3 LOANS ARE PAID OFF ENTER TOTAL OF REMAINING LOANS (16) $
26 New Construction 1-No 2-Yes	27 Real Collateral 1-No 2-Yes	28	**PRIOR SBA LOANS:** LIST LOAN NUMBERS OF ALL PRIOR SBA LOANS TO BORROWER
29	31 Soc. Sec. No.		(17a) cc 11-20 (17b) cc 21-30 (17c) cc 31-40
33 Employer ID No.		35 Borrower Alpha Code	

SBA Form 4-I (9-81) REF SOP 50 10 1   PREVIOUS EDITIONS ARE OBSOLETE

Figure 2.1. (Continued)

INSTRUCTIONS: The information requested below must be supplied with the application package.

FINANCIAL SPREAD

BALANCE SHEET	As of	Fiscal Year Ends	AUDITED ☐	UNAUDITED ☐
		DEBIT	CREDIT	PRO FORMA
Assets				
Cash	$	$	$	$
Accounts Rec.				
Inventory				
Other				
Total Current Assets				
Fixed Assets				
Other Assets				
Total Assets	$	$	$	$
Liabilities & Net Worth				
Accounts Payable	$	$	$	$
Notes Payable				
Taxes				
Other				
SBA				
Total Current Liabilities	$	$	$	$
Notes Payable	$	$	$	$
SBA				
Other				
Total Liabilities	$	$	$	$
Net Worth	$	$	$	$
Total Liab. & Net Worth	$	$	$	$
Profit & Loss	YEAR	YEAR	YEAR	YEAR
Sales	$	$	$	$
Depreciation				
Income Taxes				
W/D Officer Comp.				
Net Profit After Tax/Deprec.	$	$	$	$

PRO FORMA SCHEDULE OF FIXED OBLIGATIONS

	YEAR 1	YEAR 2	YEAR 3	YEAR 4
	$	$	$	$

Lender should comment on the following (Continue on separate sheet if needed):

1. Balance sheet and ratio analysis - comment on trends, debt to worth and current ratio.
2. Lenders analysis of repayment ability.
3. Management skill of the applicant.
4. Collateral offered and lien position, and analysis of collateral adequacy.
5. Lenders credit experience with the applicant.
6. Schedule of insurance requirements, standby agreements and other requirements.

Lenders Analysis:

☆ U.S. Government Printing Office: 1981—352/853/5576

Figure 2.1. (Continued)

	Prior to Loan	1st Month	2nd Month	3rd Month	4th Month	5th Month	6th Month	7th Month	8th Month	9th Month	10th Month	11th Month	12th Month	Total for Year
1. Total Sales (Net)														
2. Cost of Sales **														
3. Gross Profit (line 1 minus line 2)														
4. Expenses (operating): *******														
5. Salaries (other than owner)														
6. Payroll Taxes														
7. Rent														
8. Utilities (incl. phone)														
9. Insurance														
10. Professional Services (i.e., acct.)														
11. Taxes & Licenses														
12. Advertising														
13. Supplies (for business)														
14. Office Supplies (forms, postage, etc.)														
15. Interest (on loans, contracts, etc.)														
16. Depreciation														
17. Travel (incl. operating costs of veh.)														
18. Entertainment														
19. Dues & Subscriptions														
20. Other														
21														
22. Total Expenses (add line 5 thru 21)														
23. Profit Before Taxes (line 3 minus 22)														

44

24. Income (cash received)															
25. Cash Sales															
26. Collection of Accounts Receivable															
27. Other															
28. Total Income (add lines 25, 26, & 27)															
29. Disbursements (cash paid out)															
30. Owner's Draw															
31. Loan Repayments (principal only)															
32. Cost of Sales (line 2)															
33. Total Expenses (minus line 16)															
34. Capital Expenditures (equip. bldgs, veh., leasehold impr.)															
35. Reserve for Taxes															
36. Other															
37. Total Disbursements (add line 30 thru 36)															
38. Cash Flow Monthly (line 28 minus 37)															
39. Cash Flow Cumulative (line 38 plus 39 of previous month).															

**Line—Cost of Sales: Retail—beginning inventory-purchase minus ending inventory
Manufacturing —cost of material, labor manufacturing

Figure 2.1. (Continued)

Statements Required by Laws and Executive Orders

Federal executive agencies, including the Small Business Administration are required to withhold or limit financial assistance, to impose special conditions on approved loans, to provide special notices to applicants or borrowers and to require special reports and data from borrowers in order to comply with legislation passed by the Congress and Executive Orders issued by the President and by the provisions of various inter-agency agreements. SBA has issued regulations and procedures that implemented these laws and executive orders and they are contained in Parts 112, 113 and 116, Title 13 Code of Federal Regulations Chapter 1, or SOP's.

This form contains a brief summary of the various laws and executive orders that affect SBA's business and disaster loan programs and gives applicants and borrowers the notices required by law or otherwise. The signatures required on the last page provide evidence that SBA has given the necessary notices, that the signatory understands that special information will be required in some cases and that he or she may be required to complete and submit reports to SBA.

Freedom of Information Act
(5 U.S.C. 552)

This law provides that, with some exceptions, SBA must supply information reflected in Agency files and records to a person requesting it. Information about approved loans that will be automatically released includes, among other things, statistics on our loan programs (individual borrowers are not identified in the statistics) and other information such as the names of the borrowers (and their officers, directors, stockholders or partners), the collateral pledged to secure the loan, the amount of the loan, its purpose in general terms and the maturity. Propriety data on a borrower would not routinely be made available to third parties. All requests undet this Act are to be addressed to the nearest SBA office and be identified as a Freedom of Information request.

Privacy Act
(5 U.S.C. 552a)

Disaster home loan files are covered by this legislation because they are normally maintained in the names of individuals. Business loan files are maintained by business name or in the name of individuals in their entrepreneurial capacity. Thus they are not files on individuals and, therefore, are not subject to this Act. Any person can request to see or get copies of any personal information that SBA has in the requestor's file. Requests for information about another party may be denied unless SBA has the written permission of the individual to release the information to the requestor or unless the information is subject to disclosure under the Freedom of Information Act. (The "Acknowledgement" section of this form contains the written permission of SBA to release information when a disaster victim requests assistance under the family and individual grant program.)

Under the provisions of the Privacy Act, loan applicants are not required to give their social security number. The Small Business Administration, however, uses the social security number to distinguish between people with a similar or the same name. Failure to provide this number may not affect any right, benefit or privilege to which an individual is entitled by law but having the number makes it easier for SBA to more accurately identify to whom adverse credit information applies and to keep accurate loan records.

Figure 2.1. (Continued)

NOTE: Any person concerned with the collection of information, its voluntariness, disclosure or routine use under the Privacy Act or requesting information under the Freedom of Information Act may contact the Director, Freedom of Information/Privacy Acts Division, Small Business Administration, 1441 L Street, N.W. Washington, D.C. 20416, for information about the Agency's procedures on these two subjects.

Right to Financial Privacy Act of 1978
(12 U.S.C. 3401)

This is notice to you, as required by the Right to Financial Privacy Act of 1978, of SBA's access rights to financial records held by financial institutions that are or have been doing business with you or your business, including any financial institution participating in a loan or loan guarantee. The law provides that SBA shall have a right of access to your financial records in connection with its consideration or administration of assistance to you in the form of a Government loan or loan guaranty agreement. SBA is required to provide a certificate of its compliance with the Act to a financial institution in connection with its first request for access to your financial records, after which no further certification is required for subsequent accesses. The law also provides that SBA's access rights continue for the term of any approved loan or loan guaranty agreement. No further notice to you of SBA's access rights is required during the term of any such agreement.

The law also authorizes SBA to transfer to another Government authority, any financial records included in an application for a loan, or concerning an approved loan or loan guarantee, as necessary to process, service or foreclose a loan or loan guarantee or to collect on a defaulted loan or loan guarantee. No other transfer of your financial records to another Government authority will be permitted by SBA except as required or permitted by law.

Flood Disaster Protection Act
(42 U.S.C. 4011)

Regulations issued by the Federal Insurance Administration (FIA) and by SBA implement this Act and its amendments. These regulations prohibit SBA from making certain loans in an FIA designated floodplain unless Federal flood insurance is purchased as a condition of the loan. Failure to maintain the required level of flood insurance makes the applicant ineligible for any future financial assistance from SBA under any program, including disaster assistance.

Executive Orders — Floodplain Management and Wetland Protection
(42 F.R. 26951 and 42 F.R. 2961)

The SBA discourages any settlement in or development of a floodplain or a wetland. This statement is to notify all SBA loan applicants that such actions are hazardous to both life and property and should be avoided. The additional cost of flood preventive construction must be considered in addition to the possible loss of all assets and investments in future floods.

Lead-Based Paint Poisoning Prevention Act
(42 U.S.C. 4821 et seq)

Borrowers using SBA funds for the construction or rehabilitation of a residential structure are prohibited from using lead-based paint (as defined in SBA regulations) on all interior surfaces, whether accessible or not, and exterior surfaces, such as stairs, decks, porches, railings, windows and doors, which are readily accessible to children under 7 years of age. A "residential structure" is any home, apartment, hotel, motel, orphanage, boarding school, dormitory, day care center, extended car facility, college or other school housing, hospital, group practice or community facility and all other residential or institutional structures where persons reside.

Figure 2.1. (Continued)

Equal Credit Opportunity Act

(15 U.S.C. 1691)

The Federal Equal Credit Opportunity Act prohibits creditors from discriminating against credit applicants on the basis of race, color, religion, national origin, sex, marital status, age (provided that the applicant has the capacity to enter into a binding contract); because all or part of the applicant's income derives from any public assistance program; or because the applicant has in good faith exercised any right under the Consumer Credit Protection Act. The Federal agency that administers compliance with this law concerning this creditor is the Federal Trade Commission, Equal Credit Opportunity, Room 500, 633 Indiana Avenue, N.W., Washington, D.C. 20580.

Civil Rights Legislation

All businesses receiving SBA financial assistance must agree not to discriminate in any business practice, including employment practices and services to the public, on the basis of categories cited in 13 C.F.R., Parts 112 and 113 of SBA Regulations. This includes making their goods and services available to handicapped clients or customers. All business borrowers will be required to display the "Equal Employment Opportunity Poster" prescribed by SBA.

Executive Order 11738 — Environmental Protection

(38 F.R. 25161)

The Executive Order charges SBA with administering its loan programs in a manner that will result in effective enforcement of the Clean Air Act, the Federal Water Pollution Act and other environmental protection legislation. SBA must, therefore, impose conditions on some loans. By acknowledging receipt of this form and presenting the application, the principals of all small businesses borrowing $100,000 or more in direct funds stipulate to the following:

1. That any facility used, or to be used, by the subject firm is not listed on the EPA list of Violating Facilities.

2. That subject firm will comply with all the requirements of Section 114 of the Clean Air Act and Section 308 of the Water act relating to inspection, monitoring, entry, reports and information, as well as all other requirements specified in Section 114 and Section 308 of the respective Acts, and all regulations and guidelines issued thereunder.

3. That subject firm will notify SBA of the receipt of any communication from the Director of the Environmental Protection Agency indicating that a facility utilized, or to be utilized, by subject firm is under consideration to be listed on EPA List of Violating Facilities.

Occupational Safety and Health Act

(15 U.S.C. 651 et seq)

This legislation authorizes the Occupational Safety and Health Administration in the Department of Labor to require businesses to modify facilities and procedures to protect employees or pay penalty fees. In some instances the business can be forced to cease operations or be prevented from starting operations in a new facility. Therefore, in some instances SBA may require additional information from an applicant to determine whether the business will be in compliance with OSHA regulations and allowed to operate its facility after the loan is approved and disbursed.

In all instances, signing this form as borrower is a certification that the OSHA requirements that apply to the borrower's business have been determined and the borrower is, to the best of its knowledge, in compliance.

Figure 2.1. (Continued)

48

Consumer Credit Protection Act

(15 U.S.C. 1601 et seq)

This legislation gives an applicant who is refused credit because of adverse information about the applicant's credit, reputation, character or mode of living an opportunity to refute or challenge the accuracy of such reports. Therefore, whenever SBA declines a loan in whole or in part because of adverse information in a credit report, the applicant will be given the name and address of the reporting agency so the applicant can seek to have that agency correct its report, if inaccurate. If SBA declines a loan in whole or in part because of adverse information received from a source other than a credit reporting agency, the applicant will be given information about the nature of the adverse information but not the source of the report.

Within 3 days after the consummation of the transaction, any recipient of an SBA loan which is secured in whole or in part by a lien on the recipient's residence or household contents may rescind such a loan in accordance with the "Regulation Z" of the Federal Reserve Board.

Applicant's Acknowledgement

My (our) signature(s) acknowledges receipt of this form, that I (we) have read it and that I (we) have a copy for my (our) files. My (our) signature(s) represents my (our) agreement to comply with the requirements the Small Business Administration makes in connection with the approval of my (our) loan request and to comply, whenever applicable, with the hazard insurance, lead based paint, civil rights or other limitations contained in this notice.

My (our) signature(s) also represents written permission, as required by the Privacy Act, for the SBA to release any information in my (our) disaster loan application to the Governor of my (our) State or the Governor's designated representative in conjunction with the State's processing of my (our) application for assistance under the Individual and Family Grant Program that is available in certain major disaster areas declared by the President.

Business Name
_____ BY _____
Date   Name and Title

Proprietor, Partners, Principals and Guarantors

_____
Date   Signature
_____
Date   Signature
_____
Date   Signature
_____
Date   Signature

SBA Form 1261 (9-81) SOP 50-10-1

Figure 2.1. (Continued)

United States of America

SMALL BUSINESS ADMINISTRATION

STATEMENT OF PERSONAL HISTORY

Please Read Carefully - Print or Type

Each member of the small business concern requesting assistance or the development company must submit this form in TRIPLICATE for filing with the SBA application. This form must be filled out and submitted:

1. If a sole proprietorship, by the proprietor;
2. If a partnership, by each partner;
3. If a corporation or a development company, by each officer, director, and additionally, by each holder of 20% or more of the voting stock;
4. Any other person, including a hired manager, who has authority to speak for and commit the borrower in the management of the business.

Name and Address of Applicant (Firm Name)(Street, City, State and ZIP Code)

SBA District Office and City

Amount Applied for:

1. Personal Statement of: (State name in full, if no middle name, state (NMN), or if initial only, indicate initial). List all former names used, and dates each name was used. Use separate sheet if necessary.

   First   Middle   Last

2. Date of Birth: (Month, day and year)

3. Place of Birth: (City & State or Foreign Country)

U.S. Citizen? ☐ yes   ☐ no

If no, give alien registration number:
#

4. Give the percentage of ownership or stock owned or to be owned in the small business concern or the Development Company.

Social Security No.

5. Present residence address
   From   To   Address

   City   State

   Home Telephone No. (Include A/C)

   Business Telephone No. (Include A/C)

   Immediate past residence address
   From   To   Address

BE SURE TO ANSWER THE NEXT 3 QUESTIONS CORRECTLY BECAUSE THEY ARE IMPORTANT.

THE FACT THAT YOU HAVE AN ARREST OR CONVICTION RECORD WILL NOT NECESSARILY DISQUALIFY YOU. BUT AN INCORRECT ANSWER WILL PROBABLY CAUSE YOUR APPLICATION TO BE TURNED DOWN.

6. Are you presently under indictment, on parole or probation?

   ☐ Yes   ☐ No   If yes, furnish details in a separate exhibit. List name(s) under which held, if applicable.

7. Have you ever been charged with or arrested for any criminal offense other than a minor motor vehicle violation?

   ☐ Yes   ☐ No   If yes, furnish details in a separate exhibit. List name(s) under which charged, if applicable.

8. Have you ever been convicted of any criminal offense other than a minor motor vehicle violation?

   ☐ Yes   ☐ No   If yes, furnish details in a separate exhibit. List name(s) under which convicted, if applicable.

9. Name and address of participating bank

The information on this form will be used in connection with an investigation of your character. Any information you wish to submit, that you feel will expedite this investigation should be set forth.

Whoever makes any statement knowing it to be false, for the purpose of obtaining for himself or for any applicant, any loan, or loan extension by renewal, deferment or otherwise, or for the purpose of obtaining, or influencing SBA toward, anything of value under the Small Business Act, as amended, shall be punished under Section 16(a) of that Act, by a fine of not more than $5000, or by imprisonment for not more than 2 years, or both.

Signature

Title

Date

It is against SBA's policy to provide assistance to persons not of good character and therefore consideration is given to the qualities and personality traits of a person, favorable and unfavorable, relating thereto, including behavior, integrity, candor and disposition toward criminal actions. It is also against SBA's policy to provide assistance not in the best interests of the United States, for example, if there is reason to believe that the effect of such assistance will be to encourage or support, directly or indirectly, activities inimical to the Security of the United States. Anyone concerned with the collection of this information, as to its voluntariness, disclosure or routine uses may contact the FOIA Office, 1441 "L" Street, N.W., and a copy of §9 "Agency Collection of Information" from SOP 40 04 will be provided.

SBA FORM 912 (3-79) SOP 50 10 1 EDITION OF 5-78 WILL BE USED UNTIL STOCK IS EXHAUSTED

1. SBA FILE COPY

Figure 2.1.   (Continued)

PERSONAL FINANCIAL STATEMENT As of _____ , 19 ___.	**Return to:** Small Business Administration	**For SBA Use Only** **SBA Loan No.**

Complete this form if 1) a sole proprietorship by the proprietor; 2) a partnership by each partner; 3) a corporation by each officer and each stockholder with 20% or more ownership; 4) any other person or entity providing a guaranty on the loan.

Name and Address, Including ZIP Code *(of person and spouse submitting Statement)* **SOCIAL SECURITY NO.** _____ **Business** *(of person submitting Statement)*	This statement is submitted in connection with S.B.A. loan requested or granted to the individual or firm, whose name appears below: **Name and Address of Applicant or Borrower, Including ZIP Code**

Please answer all questions using "No" or "None" where necessary

ASSETS	LIABILITIES
Cash on Hand & In Banks . . . . $ _____	Accounts Payable . . . . $ _____
Savings Account in Banks . . . . _____	Notes Payable to Banks . . . . _____
U. S. Government Bonds . . . . _____	(Describe below - Section 2)
Accounts & Notes Receivable . . . . _____	Notes Payable to Others . . . . _____
Life Insurance-Cash Surrender Value Only . . _____	(Describe below - Section 2)
Other Stocks and Bonds . . . . _____	Installment Account (Auto) . . . . _____
(Describe - reverse side - Section 3)	Monthly Payments $ _____
Real Estate . . . . _____	Installment Accounts (Other) . . . . _____
(Describe - reverse side - Section 4)	Monthly Payments $ _____
Automobile - Present Value . . . . _____	Loans on Life Insurance . . . . _____
Other Personal Property . . . . _____	Mortgages on Real Estate . . . . _____
(Describe - reverse side - Section 5)	(Describe - reverse side - Section 4)
Other Assets . . . . _____	Unpaid Taxes . . . . _____
(Describe - reverse side - Section 6)	(Describe - reverse side - Section 7)
	Other Liabilities . . . . _____
	(Describe - reverse side - Section 8)
	Total Liabilities . . . . _____
	Net Worth . . . . _____
Total . . . . $ _____	Total . . . . $ _____

Section I. Source of Income *(Describe below all items listed in this Section)*	CONTINGENT LIABILITIES
Salary . . . . $ _____	As Endorser or Co-Maker . . . . $ _____
Net Investment Income . . . . _____	Legal Claims and Judgments . . . . _____
Real Estate Income . . . . _____	Provision for Federal Income Tax . . . . _____
Other Income (Describe) * . . . . _____	Other Special Debt . . . . _____

Description of items listed in Section I _____

_____
_____
_____
_____
_____
_____

* Not necessary to disclose alimony or child support payments in "Other Income" unless it is desired to have such payments counted toward total income.

Life Insurance Held (Give face amount of policies - name of company and beneficiaries) _____

_____
_____
_____
_____
_____
_____
_____
_____
_____
_____

SUPPLEMENTARY SCHEDULES

Section 2. Notes Payable to Banks and Others

Name and Address of Holder of Note	Amount of Loan		Terms of Repayments	Maturity of Loan	How Endorsed, Guaranteed, or Secured
	Original Bal.	Present Bal.			
	$	$	$		

Figure 2.1. (Continued)

Section 3. Other Stocks and Bonds: Give listed and unlisted Stocks and Bonds *(Use separate sheet if necessary)*

No. of Shares	Names of Securities	Cost	Market Value Statement Date Quotation	Amount

Section 4. Real Estate Owned. *(List each parcel separately. Use supplemental sheets if necessary. Each sheet must be identified as a supplement to this statement and signed). (Also advises whether property is covered by title insurance, abstract of title, or both).*

Title is in name of	Type of property

Address of property *(City and State)*	Original Cost to (me) (us) $ _____ Date Purchased _____ Present Market Value $ _____ Tax Assessment Value $ _____
Name and Address of Holder of Mortgage *(City and State)*	Date of Mortgage _____ Original Amount $ _____ Balance $ _____ Maturity _____ Terms of Payment _____

Status of Mortgage, i.e., current or delinquent. If delinquent describe delinquencies

Section 5. Other Personal Property. *(Describe and if any is mortgaged, state name and address of mortgage holder and amount of mortgage, terms of payment and if delinquent, describe delinquency.)*

Section 6. Other Assets. *(Describe)*

Section 7. Unpaid Taxes. *(Describe in detail, as to type, to whom payable, when due, amount, and what, if any, property a tax lien, if any, attaches)*

Section 8. Other Liabilities. *(Describe in detail)*

(I) or (We) certify the above and the statements contained in the schedules herein is a true and accurate statement of (my) or (our) financial condition as of the date stated herein. This statement is given for the purpose of: *(Check one of the following)*

☐ Inducing S.B.A. to grant a loan as requested in application, of the individual or firm whose name appears herein, in connection with which this statement is submitted.

☐ Furnishing a statement of (my) or (our) financial condition, pursuant to the terms of the guaranty executed by (me) or (us) at the time S.B.A. granted a loan to the individual or firm, whose name appears herein.

Signature	Signature	Date

SBA FORM 413 (12-78) REF: SOP 50 50 Page 2 GPO : 1979 O - 286-301

Figure 2.1. (Continued)

Summary of Collateral

OFFERED BY APPLICANT AS SECURITY FOR LOAN AND SBA APPRAISER'S VALUATION REPORT

	EMPLOYER ID NO.
Name and Address of Applicant: (Include Zip Code) _____	
	SBA LOAN NO.

IMPORTANT INSTRUCTIONS FOR PREPARING THE LISTING OF
COLLATERAL OFFERED AS SECURITY FOR LOAN

Page 1. Summary Of Collateral Offered By Applicant As Security For The Loan: This is a summarization of the detailed listing on SBA Form 4, Schedule A. If collateral is to be acquired, with proceeds of loan describe the collateral in detail *on an attachment* to Schedule A with the notation "To be acquired".

Show exact cost. If assets were acquired from a predecessor company at a price other than cost less depreciation.

The figures to be entered in the net book value column must agree with the figures shown in the balance sheet, on page 2 of the application, except for the assets, if any, not being offered as collateral and non-business assets, if any, which are being offered to secure guarantees.

If a recent appraisal has been made of the collateral offered, it should be submitted with the application.

Any leases on land and buildings must be described, giving date and term of lease, rental, name and address of owner.

Page 2. Real Estate:

Item 1 - Land And Improvements: (a) legal description from deed on the land - location - city where deed is recorded. Book and page numbers of Official Records. Describe the land improvements such as paving, utilities, fence, etc. (b) cost of land when purchased.

Item 2 - Buildings: (a) general description, describe each building or structure on the land. Include size, type of construction, number of stories, date erected, use and condition. (b) amount of taxes and the assessed value from tax bills. (c) total amount of income received by owner from rental of the described property. (d) cost of building when purchased.

INADEQUATE OR POORLY PREPARED LOAN APPLICATION AND LISTING OF COLLATERAL ON PAGE 3 WILL CAUSE DELAY IN THE PROCESSING OF LOAN APPLICATIONS.

Page 3 - It is most **IMPORTANT** that applicants make an **ACTUAL PHYSICAL INVENTORY OF THE EQUIPMENT** being offered as collateral. **DO NOT TAKE FROM BOOK RECORDS.** Actually list each in accordance with the classification, e.g.: 1. Machinery and Equipment; 2. Automotive Equipment; 3. Office furniture and equipment; 4. Other—jigs, dies, fixtures, airplanes, etc.

Page 4 - Is a continuation of Equipment being offered.
Group items in accordance with the above classifications

Show: manufacturer or make, model and serial numbers, size, year, whether purchased new, used, or rebuilt. BE SURE ITEMS LISTED CAN BE **READILY INSPECTED** BY SBA APPRAISERS.

SUMMARY			Not to be used by applicant
Item	Cost	Net Book Value	
1. Land and land improvements			
2. Buildings			
3. Machinery and Equipment			
4. Automotive Equipment			
5. Office furniture and equipment			
6. Other			
7. Total			
8. Real and chattel mortgages (Not to be paid from SBA loan req.) Attach details	X X X X		
9. Equity	X X X X		
10. To be acquired (Cost)		X X X X	
11. Total			

THE APPRAISER CERTIFIES that he has personally and thoroughly inspected the collateral as listed in this Report. Furthermore, as of _____ the market values shown in the above Summary are fair and reasonable as of that date. Additional comments are attached to this Report.

SBA Appraiser's Signature	Date of Report

SBA Form 4 Schedule A (8-66) REF ND 510–1A previous editions of sheets 1, 2 and 3 are obsolete.

Figure 2.1. (Continued)

Real Estate

OFFERED BY APPLICANT AS SECURITY FOR LOAN AND SBA APPRAISER'S VALUATION REPORT

Name and Address of Applicant (include Zip Code)	Parcel number _____	SBA LOAN No.
	Title data: ☐ Title Insurance ☐ Abstract ☐ Other (indicate)	
Address of Realty Offered _____	Realty in name of _____	
	Recorded Book_____ Page_____ County_____	

1. Land and land improvements (Do not include buildings - see Sec. 2 below)

Cost_____   date acquired_____

Legal description (Attach if too long) *

* If available, attach plat survey.

2. Improvements   Cost (If separate from land) $_____

Building description: List each building separately with brief description and dimensions.

Income if Applicable.

Rent $_____ Month ☐ Annually ☐ Lease ☐ _____ Term.

Assessed Value	
Land	_____
Improvements	_____
Taxes	_____

SBA Form 4 Schedule A (8-66) previous editions are obsolete

Figure 2.1.   (Continued)

54

Personal Property (Chattels)

OFFERED BY APPLICANT AS SECURITY FOR LOAN AND SBA APPRAISER'S VALUATION REPORT

The following described chattels are located or headquartered at (include Zip Code) _____	EMPLOYER ID NO.
	SBA LOAN NO.
Above location is owned ( ) leased ( )	

It is most **IMPORTANT** that applicants make an **ACTUAL PHYSICAL INVENTORY OF THE EQUIPMENT** being offered as collateral. **DO NOT TAKE FROM BOOK RECORDS.** Actually list each item in accordance with the classification, e.g.:* 1. Machinery and Equipment 2. Automotive Equipment 3. Office furniture and equipment 4. Other - jigs, dies, fixtures, airplanes, etc.

Show: manufacturer or make, model and serial numbers, size, year, whether purchased new, used or rebuilt.

List chattels at different locations on separate sheets. ⁂ Description of _____	Model	Serial Number	New Used Rebuilt	NOT TO BE USED BY APPLICANT	
				Cond.	Market Value
Carry Totals of Each Classification to Page 1 (Summary) Lines 3, 4, 5, and 6.				Total	

INADEQUATE OR POORLY PREPARED LOAN APPLICATION AND LISTING OF COLLATERAL WILL CAUSE DELAY IN THE PROCESSING OF LOAN APPLICATIONS. BE SURE ALL ITEMS CAN BE READILY INSPECTED BY SBA APPRAISER.

I, _____ _____ ,
　　(Signature of owner, partner, or corporation officer)　　　　(Title)

of the _____
　　　　　　(Name of Firm)

certify that the above machinery and equipment listing represents an *actual physical inventory* taken on (date) _____ ; Mark items (in column 2) with an asterisk if they are subject to conditional bills of sale or chattel mortgages the balance of which will not be paid off from an SBA loan. Carry total of such balances to line 8, page 1 (Summary).

SBA Form 4 Schedule A (8-66) previous editions are obsolete

Figure 2.1. (Continued)

Continuation of Personal Property (Chattels)

Description of_____

	Model	Serial Number	New Used Rebuilt	NOT TO BE USED BY APPLICANT	
				Cond.	Market Value
Carry Totals of Each Classification to Page 1 (Summary) Lines 3, 4, 5, and 6.			Total		

SBA Form 4 Schedule A (8-66) previous editions are obsolete

Figure 2.1. (Continued)

The Loan Package

The **outline of a complete loan package** below illustrates the type of detailed presentation sometimes required by lenders such as banks and the Small Business Administration. However, this degree of detail is often unnecessary for stable businesses already known to the lender. Many debt sources never require such complete documentation. Instead, they seek the particular information described in their respective sections of this report.

The **sample loan documentation** on the following pages demonstrates an acceptable rendition of **only the major parts** of a loan package. It does not represent the complete loan package outlined below, and it adheres to the business buyout format, rather than the forms for business start-up or expansion.

This particular example involves a hypothetical SBA-guaranteed bank loan.

SAMPLE LOAN PACKAGE OUTLINE

I. Summary

  A. Nature of business
  B. Amount and purpose of loan
  C. Repayment terms
  D. Equity share of borrower (equity/debt ratio after loan)
  E. Security or collateral (listed with market value estimates and quotes on cost of equipment to be purchased with the loan proceeds)

II. Personal information (on persons owning more than 20% of the business)

  A. Educational and work history
  B. Credit references
  C. Income tax statements (last three years)
  D. Financial statement (no older than 60 days)

III. Firm information (whichever is applicable below—A, B or C)

  A. New business
    1. Business plan (see outline of business plan sections page 9)
    2. Life and casualty insurance coverage
    3. Lease agreement

  B. Business acquisition (buyout)
    1. Information on acquisition
      a. Business history (include seller's name, reasons for sale)
      b. Current balance sheet (not over 60 days old)
      c. Current profit and loss statements (less than 60 days old)

      d. Business' federal income tax statements (past three to five years)
      e. Cash flow statements for last year
      f. Copy of sales agreement with breakdown of inventory, fixtures, equipment, licenses, goodwill and other costs
      g. Description and dates of permits already acquired
    2. Business plan
    3. Life and casualty insurance

  C. Existing business expansion
    1. Information on existing business
      a. Business history
      b. Current balance sheet (not more than 60 days old)
      c. Current profit and loss statements (not more than 60 days old)
      d. Cash flow statements for last year
      e. Federal income tax returns for past three to five years
      f. Lease agreement and permit data
    2. Business plan
    3. Life and casualty insurance

IV. Projections

  A. Profit and loss projection (monthly, for one year) and explanation of projections
  B. Cash flow projection (monthly, for one year) and explanation of projections
  C. Projected balance sheet (one year after loan) and explanation of projections

Figure 2.2. Loan package outline from *Financing Small Business.* (Reprinted with permission from Bank of America, NT & SA, "Financing Small Business," *Small Business Reporter,* Vol. 14, No. 10, Copyright 1980.)

1

SUMMARY OF LOAN APPLICATION

Applicant	Mr. Sammy I. Lee phone: 555-3742 3578 35th Avenue Oakland, California 94923
Eligibility	Applicant is of a socially and economically dis- advantaged group and qualifies for a loan under Small Business Administration requirements as to size and type of business.
Amount Requested	$38,000
Term Requested	Five years, with no prepayment penalty.
Interest Rate	Current small business rate
Security	Business assets Personal guarantee SBA's 90% guarantee
Debt/Equity Ratio— after loan	$38,000/$33,075
Purpose of Loan	Loan will enable applicant, Mr. Sammy Lee, to pur- chase Good Times Liquor Store. Sales price of $60,000 includes all furniture, fixtures and equipment; sign (in working condition); inven- tory; liquor license and goodwill. (See Sales Agreement for other details.) Cash payment re- quired is $60,000; no deposit has been paid to date.

2

The table that follows shows how the purchase will be financed and the
distribution of loan proceeds and equity.

USE OF FUNDS   SOURCE OF FUNDS

	Loan	Equity	Total
Purchase of Business			
Inventory	$28,000	$ 2,000	$30,000
Ice Machine		1,170	1,170
Wine Case		578	578
Deli Case		307	307
Appliances and Fixtures		374	374
Liquor License	10,000		10,000
Goodwill		17,571	17,571
Subtotal	$38,000	$22,000	$60,000
Other			
Station Wagon		$ 3,450	$ 3,450
Cash		7,625	7,625
Subtotal		$11,075	$11,075
TOTAL	$38,000	$33,075	$71,075

COLLATERAL AND CONDITIONS

The following are offered as collateral and conditions for the loan

1 Security interest under the uniform commercial code on all fixtures, equipment and inventory

2 Borrower will assign life insurance in the amount of the loan
and keep it in force by punctual payments of required premiums

3 Second deed of trust on borrower's residence

4 Borrower will maintain hazard insurance in the amount and type
required by lender with loss payable endorsement

5 Borrower will deliver to lender quarterly financial statements

6 All loan documents will be signed by spouse (mandatory for SBA
loan only)

3

RESUME

Name	Sammy I. Lee
Address	3578-35th Avenue Oakland, California 94923
Phone	555-3742
Personal	Born: February 23, 1938 Married Two children
Education	Oakland High School Oakland, California
	Merritt College Oakland, California A.A. degree in Accounting
	Hayward State College Hayward, California B.A. degree in Business Administration
Employment and Business Experience	Lee's Grocery Store (family store) 325 9th Street Oakland, California Duties: Served customers, checked groceries, made deliveries, stocked shelves 1951 – 1959
	Standard Forms & Supplies 1717 San Pablo Avenue Oakland, California Duties: Managed office and kept books Supervised staff of three 1959 – 1964

4

RESUME continued

Employment and Business Experience	Bay Area Auto Supply Co. Inc. 2905 Bayshore Avenue South San Francisco, California Duties: Managed warehouse, filled orders, maintained inventory records 1964 – 1970
	Sunshine Liquor Store 7789 MacArthur Boulevard Oakland, California Duties: Managed store 1970 – 1972
	Happy Liquor Store 1535 Scotch Street San Francisco, California Duties: Managed store for brother 1973 – present

PERSONAL CREDIT REFERENCES

Bank of America
Broadway-MacArthur Branch
Oakland, California

Savings Account   4578 – 02039
Checking Account   7641 – 02666

Golden East Savings and Loan
5546 Telegraph Avenue
Oakland, California

Auto Loan No. 05532 – 14684
Home Loan No. 308 – 055921

Figure 2.2. (Continued)

5

PERSONAL FINANCIAL STATEMENT

Assets

Cash on hand and in banks	$ 250
Savings account in banks	29,375
U.S. government bonds	12,000
Accounts and notes receivable	0
Life insurance cash value	0
Other stocks and bonds	540
Real estate	43,600
Automobile	3,450
Other personal property	0
Other assets	0
TOTAL ASSETS	$89,215

Liabilities

Accounts payable	$ 0
Notes payable to banks	0
Notes payable to others	0
Installment account (Auto)	0
Installment account (Other)	0
Loans on life insurance	0
Mortgages on real estate	28,473
Unpaid taxes	0
Other liabilities	0
TOTAL LIABILITIES	$28,473

NET WORTH	$60,742

6

BUSINESS PLAN

Name of Firm	Good Times Liquor Store
Owner-to-Be	Sammy I. Lee Sole proprietor
Method of Acquisition	Buy-out
Type of Business	Retail liquor store with some grocery and delicatessen items
Hours of Operation	9 a.m. to 10 p.m. Will be open seven days a week and on all holidays.
Location	575 Bourbon Avenue San Francisco, California 94112

Above location is in an area suitable for retail trade, a very busy area with numerous other business establishments. Surrounded by home owners, is easily accessible by public transportation and personal conveyance.

Shopping area draws from a vicinity of approximately one square mile with a population of 47,347. (See attached data and map.)

Area includes such ethnic groups as Latinos, Filipinos, Blacks, Asians, Irish and Italians.

The above will be the target area for potential customers.

7

Potential of the Business	As of 1970, San Francisco had 196 liquor stores with yearly income of $53,709,000. (Of the 196 stores, 145 have employees on their payrolls. The yearly income of these 145 stores is $49,775,000. This brings the yearly average per store to $343,275.) With a population in San Francisco of 715,674 the yearly average spent by each person would be about $75. With a population in the sales area of 47,347 the potential income of the area would be $3,551,025. This appears to be an ample reservoir of customers to tap.
	Source: 1970 census, population and housing. Prepared by San Francisco Department of City Planning, March, 1975. (See attached map.)
Competition	There is one other liquor store and one liquor/grocery store within a six-block radius.
History of Firm	Good Times Liquor Store is presently owned by Mrs. William Win who acquired sole proprietorship after the death of her husband about three years ago. The store has been in operation since 1935.
	For the past three years the store has been run by Mr. Win's brother, brother-in-law and Mrs. Win.
	Mrs. Win's physician has advised her to stop working so she has decided to sell the business. Her brother and brother-in-law are also nearing retirement and have no interest in running the business.
Sales Plan	Mr. Lee believes the store has declined in recent years due to lack of interest on the part of current owners. He feels that through new ownership the store could develop into a profitable business.

8

The store now closes at 8 p.m. Mr. Lee plans on extending the business hours from 9 a.m. to 10 p.m., an additional two hours per day. Also, he intends to be open seven days a week and on all holidays.

An innovation by Mr. Lee will be to sell cold sandwiches and magazines. The store has ample room for display of inventory and a back room for storage.

Mr. Lee will also utilize to better advantage the ice machine, wine case, delicatessen case and appliances and fixtures.

The atmosphere in the store could be made pleasant and comfortable with bright, new decoration.

Mr. Lee plans local advertising through the neighborhood newspaper, leafleting and door-to-door personal contact with his neighbors.

Managerial Capability	Mr. Lee has acquired the background to own and operate a liquor store through practical experience. He operated and managed his brother's liquor store on Scotch Street. Thus he is familiar with all aspects of the retail liquor business.
Personnel	The liquor store at present has three employees working as cashiers and clerks. Mr. Lee plans to use only one clerk. He and Mrs. Lee will work the other hours. This will be a savings of approximately $20,000 per year.
Prices and Margins	There are no problems of price cutting competition. Analysis of the historical data, however, shows that gross profit margins have fluctuated widely. Mr. Lee plans to bring this under control by keeping a close watch on inventory.

Figure 2.2.   (Continued)

GOOD TIMES LIQUOR STORE
PREVIOUS YEAR AND PROJECTED PROFIT & LOSS STATEMENT

	1974 $	1974 %	Oct (1975)	Nov (1975)	Dec (1975)	Jan (1976)	Feb (1976)	Mar (1976)	Apr (1976)	May (1976)	June (1976)	July (1976)	Aug (1976)	Sept (1976)	Total	%
Gross Sales	203.491	100	15.000	15.500	15.500	16.000	16.500	16.500	17.000	17.500	17.500	18.000	18.500	19.000	202.500	100
Less Cost of Sales	171.812	84.4	11.250	11.625	11.625	12.000	12.375	12.375	12.750	13.125	13.125	13.500	13.875	14.250	151.875	75
Gross Profit	31.679	15.6	3.750	3.875	3.875	4.000	4.125	4.125	4.250	4.375	4.375	4.500	4.625	4.750	50.625	25
Controllable Expenses																
Salaries	27.184	13.3	600	600	600	600	600	600	600	600	600	600	600	600	7.200	3.6
Payroll Taxes	1.622	.8	57	57	57	57	57	57	57	57	57	57	35	35	640	.3
Alarm Service	318	.2	30	30	30	30	30	30	30	30	31	31	31	31	364	.2
Advertising	68	0	35	35	35	35	35	35	35	35	35	35	35	35	420	.2
Automobile	156	.1	90	93	93	96	99	99	102	105	105	108	111	114	1.215	.6
Bad Debts	315	.2	15	15	15	15	15	15	15	15	15	15	15	15	180	.1
Collection Fees	157	.1	15	15	15	15	15	15	15	15	15	15	15	15	180	.1
Dues & Subscriptions	11	0	5	5	5	5	5	5	5	5	5	5	5	5	60	0
Laundry & Linen	20	0	8	8	8	8	8	8	8	8	8	8	8	8	96	0
Legal & Accounting	855	.4	100	100	100	100	100	100	100	100	100	100	100	100	1.200	.6
Office Expense	134	.1	10	10	10	10	10	10	10	10	10	10	10	10	120	0
Professional Fees	96	0	8	8	8	8	8	8	8	8	8	8	8	8	96	0
Maintenance & Repairs	662	.3	50	50	50	50	50	50	50	50	50	50	50	50	600	.3
Store Supplies	262	.1	25	25	25	25	25	25	25	25	25	25	25	25	300	.2
Telephone	456	.2	46	46	46	46	46	46	46	46	46	46	46	46	552	.3
Utilities	1.336	.7	90	90	90	90	90	90	90	90	90	90	90	90	1.080	.5
Miscellaneous	341	.2	25	25	25	25	25	25	25	25	25	25	25	25	300	.2
Total Controllable Expenses	33.993	16.7	1.209	1.212	1.212	1.215	1.218	1.218	1.221	1.224	1.225	1.228	1.209	1.212	14.603	7.2
Fixed Expenses																
Depreciation	149	.1	85	85	86	86	86	86	87	87	87	87	87	87	1.036	.5
Insurance	1.335	.6	125	125	125	125	125	125	125	125	125	125	125	125	1.500	.7
Rent	2.400	1.2	300	300	300	300	300	300	300	300	300	300	300	300	3.600	1.8
Taxes & Licenses	1.744	.9	150	150	150	150	150	150	150	150	150	150	150	150	1.800	.8
Interest on Loan			325	320	316	312	308	303	299	295	290	286	281	277	3.612	1.9
Total Fixed Expenses	5.428	2.8	985	980	977	973	969	964	961	957	952	948	943	939	11.548	5.7
TOTAL EXPENSES	39.421	19.5	2.194	2.192	2.189	2.188	2.187	2.182	2.182	2.181	2.177	2.176	2.152	2.151	26.151	12.9
Net Profit (Loss)	(7.742)	(3.1)	1.556	1.683	1.686	1.812	1.938	1.943	2.068	2.194	2.198	2.324	2.473	2.599	24.474	12.1

Figure 2.2. (Continued)

10

EXPLANATION OF PROJECTED PROFIT AND LOSS STATEMENT

Gross sales. For each month and the year. Projections are based on analysis of previous monthly sales from sales tax returns. The business averaged $16.957 a month for 1974. Although sales for early 1975 (not shown) averaged just below $15,000, projections for the first year under new management show a return to 1974's level. This is attributed to staying open longer hours and more vigorous management.

Cost of sales. Projected at 75% of sales. This is based on data from the State Board of Equalization. Retail Sales Tax Division: The Robert Morris Associates Annual Statement Studies: Almanac of Business and Industrial Financial Ratios: Bank of America Small Business Reporter for Independent Liquor Stores: and contact with the industry.

Gross profit. This is the difference between sales and cost of sales.

Controllable expenses. Controlled expenses are itemized below.

Salaries. This will be reduced nearly $20,000 by eliminating two clerks. The owner and family will operate the necessary hours with one employee.

Payroll taxes. This includes employer's share of 5.85% on Social Security: 3.6% on up to $4,200 of unemployment tax.

Alarm service. For use of burglar alarm service.

Advertising. For advertising in local newspaper, printing flyers.

For expense of station wagon to be used 75% of the time for deliveries, pickups, etc.

Bad debts. For direct write-offs of uncollectible accounts. Based on historical experience of 0.1%.

Collection fees. Fees paid for collection of delinquent accounts. Based on historical experience of 0.1%.

Dues and subscriptions. For trade journals.

Laundry and linen. Smocks for clerks and restroom towels.

Legal and accounting services. For outside accountant and legal assistance. Based on historical costs plus added service.

Office expense. Includes stationery and miscellaneous office supplies like postage, etc.

Professional services. For outside technical advice and assistance. Based on historical experience.

Repairs and maintenance. Projected on historical experience of 0.3% of sales.

Stores supplies. For storeroom, cartons, etc.

Telephone. Projected on historical experience of 0.4% of sales.

Utilities. Electricity, gas, water, trash, etc. Projected on historical experience of 0.5% of sales.

Miscellaneous. For sundry items.

Total controllable expenses. Total of items from salaries through miscellaneous.

Fixed expenses. The detailed fixed expenses are itemized below.

Depreciation calculated by straight line depreciation method as follows:

Item	Cost	Life	Amount
Ice Machine	$1,170	10 yrs.	$ 117
Wine Case	578	5 yrs.	116
Delicates. Case	307	8 yrs.	38
Appliances & Fixtures	374	5 yrs.	75
1973 Chev. Sta. Wagon (personal)	4,600	5 yrs.	920 x 75% = 690
			$1,036

Insurance on inventory and building for fire and theft; also public liability, life insurance for loan and workers' compensation. Projected on historical experience of 0.7% of sales.

Rent. Based on new lease agreement at $300 per month.

Taxes and licenses. Property tax plus business license.

Interest on loan. Calculated on $38,000 loan requested, over five years at 10.4%.

Total fixed expenses. Sum of items from depreciation through interest on loan.

Total expenses. Sum of controllable expenses and fixed expenses.

Net profit or loss. Difference between gross profits and total expenses. Net earnings are expected to total over $24,000.

Figure 2.2. (Continued)

GOOD TIMES LIQUOR STORE

PROJECTED CASH FLOW

	Oct.	1975 Nov.	Dec.	Jan.	Feb.	March	April	May	June	July	Aug.	Sept.	TOTAL
								1976					
Cash on Hand and in Banks (before purchase of business)	29.625												29.625
Cash Sales	13.500	14.000	14.000	14.500	15.000	15.000	15.500	16.000	16.000	16.500	17.000	17.500	184.500
Sales Tax Collected	878	906	907	936	965	965	994	1.024	1.024	1.053	1.082	1.112	11.846
Payments on Accounts Rec.	0	1.500	1.500	1.500	1.500	1.500	1.500	1.500	1.500	1.500	1.500	1.500	16.500
Loan Injection	38.000												38.000
TOTAL Cash Available	82.003	16.406	16.407	16.936	17.465	17.475	17.994	18.524	18.524	19.053	19.582	20.112	280.471
Cash disbursement													
Owner's Draw	1.000	1.000	1.000	1.000	1.000	1.000	1.000	1.000	1.000	1.000	1.000	1.000	12.000
Payment on Inventory Purchases	0	11.250	11.625	11.625	12.000	12.375	12.375	12.750	13.125	13.125	13.500	13.875	137.625
Payroll & Withholding Taxes Payable (quarterly)				579			579			579			1.737
Sales Tax Payable	0	878	906	907	936	965	965	994	1.024	1.024	1.053	1.082	10.734
Purchase of Business	60.000												60.000
Total Operating Expenses Less: Payroll Taxes. Depreciation and Bad Debt Write-off	1.916	1.914	1.910	1.909	1.908	1.903	1.902	1.901	1.897	1.896	1.894	1.893	22.843
Loan Payment Principal	488	492	496	500	505	509	513	518	522	527	531	536	6.137
TOTAL Disbursements	63.404	15.534	15.937	16.520	16.349	16.752	17.334	17.163	17.568	18.151	17.978	18.386	251.076
Cash Flow Monthly	18.599	872	470	416	1.116	713	660	1.361	956	902	1.604	1.726	29.395
Cash Flow Cumulative	18.599	19.471	19.941	20.357	21.473	22.186	22.846	24.207	25.163	26.065	27.669	29.395	

Figure 2.2. (Continued)

11

EXPLANATION OF CASH FLOW PROJECTION

Cash on hand and in bank. From personal financial statement. $29,625.

Cash sales. Total sales less receivables due.

Sales tax collected. Estimated at 6.5% on 90% of cash sales.

Payments on A/R. Collections from accounts receivable of previous month. Mr. Lee's plan is to limit credit sales to no more than $1,500 a month.

Loan injection. This is the loan of $38,000 being requested.

Total cash available. The sum of items from cash on hand through loan injection.

Cash disbursements, detailed below.

Owner's draw of $1,000 per month is sufficient for owner to cover living expenses, income taxes and residential real estate loan payments. However, this could be adjusted depending on the business.

Cost of sales is taken from the projected profit and loss statement, the second line, allowing 30 days' credit from suppliers.

Payroll and withholding taxes payable projected on the basis of one employee. 11.7% Social Security, state and federal income taxes withheld; 3.6% on up to $4,200 for unemployment tax and disability tax withheld from employee.

Sales tax payable. Payments on sales tax collected for the previous month.

Purchase of business for $60,000. This is the use of the $38,000 loan that is being requested. Owner is providing $22,000 to complete the purchase from accessible cash.

Total operating expenses. Total expenses including loan interest payments.

Loan payment principal. Only the principal portion of the loan repayment is shown because the interest portion has already been included under fixed expenses. Payments are based on a five-year loan.

Total disbursements. The sum of items from owner's draw through loan payment principal.

Cash flow monthly. The difference between total cash available and total disbursements for each month represents a positive flow.

Cash flow cumulative. A $29,395 excess of current receipts over all current disbursements is expected for the 12-month period. This indicates a substantial cushion for repayment of the loan.

Figure 2.2. (Continued)

12

13

GOOD TIMES LIQUOR STORE

Projected Balance Sheet

Current Status (after purchase of business) vs. One Year Later

	I Oct. 1, 1975	II Oct. 1, 1976
ASSETS		
Current Assets		
Cash on Hand and in Bank	7,625	29,395
Accounts Receivable	0	1,500
Inventory	30,000	30,000
Total Current Assets	37,625	60,895
Fixed Assets		
1973 Vega Station Wagon	3,450	3,450
Ice Machine	1,170	1,170
Wine Case	578	578
Delicatessen Case	307	307
Appliances and Fixtures	374	374
Total	5,879	5,879
Less Allowance for Depreciation	0	(1,036)
Net Fixed Assets	5,879	4,843
Other Assets		
License (Market Value)	10,000	10,000
Goodwill	17,571	17,571
Total Other Assets	27,571	27,571
TOTAL ASSETS	71,075	93,309
LIABILITIES		
Current Liabilities		
Accounts Payable	0	14,250
Federal Income Tax Withheld	0	252
State Income Tax Withheld	0	33
Federal S.S. Tax Payable	0	210
State Disability Tax Payable	0	18
Sales Tax Payable	0	1,112
State Unemployment Tax Payable	0	22
Principal Payments Due, Long-Term Loan	6,137	6,794
Total Current Liabilities	6,137	22,691
Long-Term Loan	31,863	25,069
TOTAL LIABILITIES	38,000	47,760
NET WORTH	33,075	45,549
Total Liabilities Plus Net Worth	71,075	93,309

Figure 2.2. (Continued)

14

EXPLANATION OF PROJECTED BALANCE SHEET

<u>ASSETS</u>. Current, fixed and other.

<u>Current</u> <u>assets</u>. Detailed below.

<u>Cash</u> <u>on</u> <u>hand</u> <u>and</u> <u>in</u> <u>bank</u>. 1976 balance is taken from projected cash flow statement.

<u>Accounts</u> <u>receivable</u>. Determined by calculating charge sales ($18,000) and deducting receivables payments ($16,500).

<u>Inventory</u>. Projected on the basis that inventory would remain constant at $30,000.

<u>Total</u> <u>current</u> <u>assets</u>. Sum of 3 items above.

<u>Fixed</u> <u>assets</u>. Detailed below.

1973 Vega station wagon. Based on 75% of cost of $4,600, as it will be used on that percentage.

The values of the following fixed assets were taken from C-3 1974 income tax return (original cost).

   Ice machine. $1,170

   Wine case. $678

   Delicatessen case. $307

   Appliances and fixtures. $374

<u>Total</u> <u>fixed</u> <u>assets</u>. Sum of items from station wagon through appliances and fixtures.

Less <u>allowance</u> <u>for</u> <u>depreciation</u>. Amount taken from projected profit and loss statement.

<u>Net</u> <u>fixed</u> <u>assets</u>. Total fixed assets less allowance for depreciation.

<u>Other</u> <u>assets</u>. Detailed below.

License. Fair market value for license issued in 1935.

Goodwill. Amount of purchase price over assets acquired.

<u>Total</u> <u>other</u> <u>assets</u>. Sum of license and goodwill.

<u>Total</u> <u>assets</u>. Sum of current, fixed and other assets.

<u>LIABILITIES</u>. Current and long-term liabilities detailed below.

<u>Current</u> <u>liabilities</u>. Detailed below.

Accounts payable. Cost of sales less payments to suppliers.

Federal income tax withheld. From employee for the quarter—$252.

State income tax withheld. From employee for the quarter—$33.

Federal Social Security tax payable. 11.7% of wages for the quarter—$210.

State disability tax payable. Amount withheld from employee for the quarter—$18.

Sales tax payable. Sales tax collected for September.

State unemployment tax payable: 3.6% of balance of wages up to $4,200 (3.6% x $600), for July, 1976, only; August and September wages went beyond $4,200 maximum.

Principal payments due on long-term loan—amount payable within one year. Taken from cash flow projection then calculated for year beginning October 1, 1976.

<u>Total</u> <u>current</u> <u>liabilities</u>. Sum of items from accounts payable through long-term loan payments.

<u>Long-term</u> <u>loan</u>. Original $38,000 minus principal already paid as current liability.

<u>Total</u> <u>liabilities</u>. Sum of total current liabilities and balance on long-term loan.

<u>Net</u> <u>worth</u>. Total assets less total liabilities (owner's equity).

$33,075	October, 1975 Net Worth
+24,474	Projected net profit (bottom line, projected profit and
$57,549	loss statement)
-12,000	Owner's draw, cash flow statement
$45,549	October, 1976 Net Worth

Total Liabilities plus Net Worth should balance Total Assets.

Figure 2.2. (Continued)

SOURCES OF ADDITIONAL INFORMATION

Anatomy of a Merger, by Robert Q. Parsons and John Stanley Baumgartner, published by Prentice-Hall, Inc., Englewood Cliffs, NJ 07632.

Business Loans, 2nd edition, by Rick Stephan Hayes, published by CBI Publishing, Inc., 51 Sleeper St., Boston, MA 02210.

Financing For Small And Medium-Sized Businesses, by Harry Gross, published by Prentice-Hall, Inc., Englewood Cliffs, NJ 07632.

Going Public, by Daniel S. Berman, published by Prentice-Hall, Inc., Englewood Cliffs, NJ 07632.

How To Finance a Growing Business, by Royce Diener, published by Frederick Fell Publishers, Inc., 386 Park Ave., New York, NY 10016.

How to Negotiate a Business Loan, by Richard C. Belew, published by Van Nostrand Reinhold Co., 135 Weston St., New York, NY 10020.

Money Raising and Planning for the Small Business, by David L. Markstein, published by Henry Regnery Co., 114 West Illinois St., Chicago, IL 60610.

Small Business Reporter, Vol. 13, No. 10, "Financing Small Business," published by the Bank of America, Department 3120, P.O. Box 37000, San Francisco, CA 94137.

Winning the Money Game, edited by Donald Dible, published by The Entrepreneur Press, Santa Clara, CA 95051.

3

Business Insurance

WHY BUSINESS INSURANCE IS NECESSARY

Business insurance is extremely important for your business because it provides a means of protection against many business risks. You pay a relatively small amount of money to insure your business against the loss of a far greater amount. It is not an understatement that the relatively small insurance fee that you pay may actually save your company from going under.

RISK MANAGEMENT

Use of insurance for a business is really a way of managing risk in your business. This means identifying and controlling the exposure of your business or your personal assets to loss or to injury. Proper risk management is done in a four-step process as follows:

1. Identify the risk to which your business will be subjected.
2. Evaluate the probability of the occurrence of each risk which you have identified, along with the cost to you should it occur and the cost of insurance coverage protecting you against this risk.
3. Decide the best way to allow for each risk: whether to accept all of it, part of it, or to minimize the risk through insurance.
4. Control the risk by implementing what you have decided is the best method.

To identify each risk, you should think of everything which poses a threat to your business. This includes strikes by your employees, death or temporary ill health of key personnel, losses due to fires, through a product causing some injury and your being sued, and so forth. You should list every single threat that you can think of.

Now you must decide whether each risk that you have listed describes an event that is likely or unlikely. Further, if the event is likely, what can it cost you or your firm? For example, if you are sued because of a defect in your product which causes injury, how much are you likely to be sued for? If you have a fire, what is the fire likely to destroy and what is the dollar value of what is destroyed? After doing this, then investigate the insurances involved and how much insurance would cost to protect your business in each case.

After finding the cost of insurance protection, you must decide the best way to handle each of the threats to your business. In other words, you make some decisions about each risk. In some cases you may be able to avoid the risk entirely by having someone else perform the task which leads to the risk. For example, you can avoid certain of the fire risks and risks of injury to your employees by subcontracting the manufacture of your product to someone else. Another alternative is spreading the risk. You can duplicate various valuable documents, keeping them in two different locations, so that if a fire destroys one set the other set is still available. Some risks may be prevented. Safety equipment may prevent injury; sprinkler systems and fire alarms minimize the potential for loss due to fire. Finally, you can transfer the risk. Transferring the risk is done through contracts entered into with insurance companies. The insurance companies assume the risk of losses due to fire and so forth in return for a payment of a fee. This fee is called a "premium." Finally, if the risk is slight, you may simply accept it as a cost of doing business.

After weighing all alternatives, you must take the action to implement the decision which you have made. In many cases some type of insurance will be the best course of action. Now the problem is to develop an overall insurance program to implement this decision.

DEVELOPING AN INSURANCE PROGRAM

Developing an insurance program requires three basic actions: (1) getting exact insurance costs; (2) developing an insurance plan for your business; and (3) getting professional advice. Let's look at each in turn.

Getting Exact Insurance Cost

In order to decide how to handle the risk, it is necessary to obtain a rough idea of insurance costs. However, before you actually purchase any insurance, you should investigate the methods by which you can reduce the cost of your coverage. These methods are listed below.

1. Use as high a deductible as you can afford.
2. Make certain there's no duplication in the various insurance policies that you have.
3. Buy your insurance in as large a unit as possible. Certain package policies are suitable for different types of small businesses.
4. Review your insurance program periodically to insure that your coverage is adequate and that your premiums are as low as possible, consistent with the protection that you seek.

Developing a Business Insurance Plan

You must plan in order to manage your insurance program, receiving the necessary coverage at the lowest possible cost. Some general principles will help here. Write out clear statements of what you expect insurance to do for you and your firm. Try to select only one agent to handle your insurance. This fixes responsibility in one single individual or company. If you personally are not handling the insurance, make certain that whoever is handling it for your company understands the importance of his or her responsibility. Don't try to con your insurance agent.

An insurance agent is like an attorney. In order to give you maximum help, he or she should know everything possible about risks to your business and its exposure to loss. Be careful about underinsuring in areas that can cause major loss even if the probability of the loss's occurrence is small. Premiums vary depending upon probability. So if the probability of occurrence is small, the premium will probably be small as well. Keep accurate and complete records of your insurance policies as well as your premiums, losses, and loss recoveries. You can use this information as your business grows to make better decisions about insurance coverage in the future. Finally, make certain that your property is appraised periodically by independent appraisers. In this way you will know what your exposure to risk actually is.

Getting Professional Advice

Insurance, like any other aspect of your business, can be complex. You cannot expect to master it by yourself unless you have very limited coverages. Therefore, an agent who is professionally qualified, a broker, or some other consultant can be worth the fees that you pay for this service many times over—just as are fees you pay for the services of an attorney or an accountant or any other business professional.

THE THREE BASIC TYPES OF INSURANCE

There are three basic types of insurance. They are: liability insurance, life and health insurance, and property insurance.

Liability Insurance

Any business is subject to laws governing negligence, and this includes negligence to customers, employees, or anyone else with whom you may happen to do business or with whom you have contact in the course of business, or who is on your property. If you are negligent, you fail to do something, and in the case of liability, negligence refers to failing to exercise a degree of care which might be expected or required under your particular situation or circumstances. An example might be failing to clear snow properly from the walkway in the entrance to your premises, or permitting a hazard to exist due to the manufacturing processes that you employ. You may be liable through negligence even if you have signs posted specifically warning of this hazard, or if you have cleaned the snow from the walkway to your own satisfaction. It may be that an accident occurs due to carelessness on the part of the injured. It doesn't seem to make much difference. Many courts judge in favor of the plaintiff anyway; the business is assumed to be responsible for any accidents happening on the premises, even though the injured person's carelessness may contribute to the mishap.

But there are even more important kinds of liabilities to your business than accidents or mishaps which may occur on your premises. One example is product liability. You are liable for the effects of the product that you produce. There is also liability as a result of an automobile accident by one of your employees while on the job. The bottom line is that you may have to purchase separate liability protection against potential liabilities which are not included in a general comprehensive liability policy.

General Liability Coverages

In general, liability insurance policies cover the following types of losses:

1. Payments which are required due to bodily injury or damage to the property of others that you cause accidentally
2. Medical services necessary at the time of the accident
3. Costs of defending lawsuits that allege bodily injury or property damage including expenses in investigation and settlement
4. The cost of any court bonds or other judgments during appeal

There are various exclusions and limitations on most liability policies. Some policies may exclude obligations under workers' compensation laws since this is covered by special workers' compensation insurance, as we will discuss shortly. Also excluded may be damage to property of others which is in your care or control. This exclusion may usually be eliminated by payment of an extra premium. Finally, a major exclusion will include liability resulting from war, mishaps involving nuclear energy, blasting operations, and similar situations. Limits to liability may be on a per-person or on a per-accident basis. For example, automobile liability insurance may limit you to $100,000 per person injured or to a total of $400,000 in any one accident. This means that if two persons are injured in a single automobile accident for which you are covered by liability insurance and the judgments are $200,000 each, the policy will only pay $200,000 because of the limit of $100,000 per person. On the other hand, if four individuals were injured and the judgment is $100,000 each, the policy would cover the total amount. Other limitations may include a single limit applying to bodily injury and property damage, or in property liability insurance or as a limitation on product liability that applies to a certain group or batch of bad products. You should be well aware of all limitations before purchasing the insurance. Now let's look at several types of liability insurance.

Automobile Liability Insuance.   You will generally be required to maintain insurance on all automobiles or other vehicles that you operate as a part of your business. You should also be aware that you can be legally liable for accidents by vehicles owned by others, either employees, vendors, or even customers who are involved in these accidents while they are using their vehicles on behalf of your business.

Typical coverage for automobile liability insurance includes insurance for damages from collision, fire, theft, and other physical perils. Physical damage or perils can be subdivided into several types. These include collision damage which can be insured separately from other types of losses. Collision insurance does not cover glass breakage and damage from falling objects, missiles, windstorms, hail, malicious mischief, and vandalism. With your automobile liability insurance you can insure all types of physical loss except collision by taking out a comprehensive policy. A comprehensive policy generally excludes only the following: losses from wear and tear; losss to tires unless owing to fire, malicious mischief, or vandalism arising from collision; loss from radioactive contamination and loss from freezing or from mechanical or electrical breakdown. However, if any of these losses except for those covered by radioactive contamination result from theft, you are covered. The alternative to buying comprehensive insurance is to insure against each peril separately.

How much you have to pay for automobile insurance or physical damage insurance can vary widely depending upon the vehicle itself, including its age, type, the territory including the location and distance traveled, and the age of the driver or drivers. Sometimes special physical damage rates can be obtained if you own more than one vehicle. These are called "experience rates" and give individual physical damage rates based upon experience over a period of several years. Other special physical damage rates can be given under safe driver plans or merit rates for which you as the individual owner may qualify. In these days of very high insurance rates, obtaining a policy that allows for a deductible amount will permit you to save a significant amount of money on your collision coverage. This means that you yourself assume the obligation for a certain amount of damage in the event of an accident. Let's say you agree to a $500 deductible coverage. If you suffer damage to $500, you receive no reimbursement from the insurance. You are assuming the risk to that amount. Above $500, the policy would cover your losses. Again, you must weigh your loss in the event of damage, the probability of occurrence, and other factors to develop a risk tradeoff which will help you decide how much obligation you should assume in any given situation.

Product Liability Insurance. Product liability insurance is useful to you as a manufacturer or, in some cases, a retailer of products which may cause injury or damage to the user of the product. However, even though this is known as "product" liability insurance, services too can cause damage and may be subject to product liability. Today, judgments against physicians for incorrect or incompetent medical decisions are common. The insurance which physicians carry to protect them against judgments in such suits is a type of product liability insurance. In the same fashion, an automobile mechanic who does a repair job incorrectly could be liable for an injury caused due to the service performed. Product liability insurance can be very expensive depending upon the likelihood of your product's causing injury or damage or even allowing it to happen if your product is protective in nature. However, the awards in the event of an injury or death caused by your product may be so high as to make such insurance imperative.

Workers' Compensation Insurance. Usually workers' compensation insurance is required by law. It protects the employer against liability in the event of an accident to the employee. By law, you are required to provide employees with a safe place to work, hire only competent employees so they will not endanger one another, provide safe tools to work with, and warn employees of any existing dangers which may exist or develop while they are doing their job for you. If you fail to take any of these actions, not only in your eyes but in the eyes of the court you are liable for damage suits brought against you by your employees. The mere fact that you try to do these duties to the best of your ability is not sufficient, and under workers' compensation insurance an employee can collect payment for doctors' bills and medications, as well as hospital expenses and income payments for time lost beyond a specified minimum period. If injuries are received which result in permanent damage, the employee may collect a lump sum payment to compensate for that loss.

These workers' compensation awards are not automatic and are made on the basis of the hearing by a special examiner or board. At this board, you will have the right to be represented either directly or jointly with the insurance company. Awards made to the employee may be smaller in the case of carelessness by the employee or when the loss is the result of an injury caused by a fellow employee.

All-Inclusive Policies. You may also purchase overall insurance which can cover exceptionally large liabilities above and beyond your basic coverage. Such a policy may cover a multimillion-dollar lawsuit for the loss of life in an accident on your premises. Fortunately these general coverages or umbrella policies are not as expensive as one might think because the insurance company which provides them need only fulfill the few claims that exceed the basic insurance coverage. The result is that for a relatively small cost these all-inclusive policies can protect you against extremely severe losses. As to whether you need such policies or not, it is important to read the fine print carefully and take the time to have the insurance agent explain to you exactly what you are covered for and exactly what you are not covered for under the basic insurance policies that you purchase.

Life and Health Insurance

Life and health insurance provides extra compensation to employees, owners, or the business itself for losses that are sustained as a result of illness or death. These are not required by law, but most businesses today do carry them for their employees—in addition to the basic workers' compensation insurance. You will probably have to carry such life and health insurance policies for your employees in order to be competitive with what is offered by other companies in your industry. Typical coverages for this type of policy include basic life insurance, basic health insurance, major medical insurance coverage, dental insurance, and even eyeglass insurance in some cases. Life insurance is used to provide financial protection to the employee's family in the event of the employee's death. Some group life insurance plans are tax deductible for you as the employer. Also, group coverage can frequently be obtained at lower rates even if your firm includes only one or two employees. Generally a life insurance policy is offered in conjunction with some form of basic health or major medical insurance.

Health and medical insurance may include basic hospitalization and medical plans, major medical plans, and disability plans. Basic hospitalization medical plans pay the cost of hospitalization, medical care, and medication during hospitalization, and they also pay for medical care outside of hospitals and diagnostic services such as blood tests, x-rays, urinalyses, and so forth. These policies, in some cases, may be split between medical and surgical on one hand and hospitalization on the other. Usually basic medical insurance is less expensive in group plans, except in the case of small groups. If the group or firm has very few employees, it may be less expensive to cover them with individual policies. Again, here's a tradeoff which you should calculate after apeaking with your insurance agent.

Major medical or catastrophic plans are intended to meet the cost of catastrophic illnesses. They usually contain deductible clauses so that they apply only after the payments covered by basic medical and hospitalization plans. For the same reason that all-inclusive policies are not expensive, major medical plans are not expensive, even for small companies.

In some states, disability plans are required by the law. These plans pay the employees a proportion of their salary during temporary or extended absences due to illness or accidents that are work related.

It is possible to use life insurance annuities to provide pension benefits to your employees. These pension and retirement plans are frequently offered by many large and small companies, but they are complex and they can be very expensive. Therefore, you must be very careful about these plans to make sure that you will not have increasing premium payments and that your business has sufficient income to make pension payments over the long run. Pension plans are also subject to federal laws and IRS regulations. Therefore, they represent a major insurance decision for your firm, and you should be certain that the plan that you intend to adopt meets all federal requirements.

There is an alternative to pension retirement plans. The Individual Retirement Account (IRA) is available for employees, and you may qualify for the Keogh Plan as an owner. Because of tax deferments for various other reasons, these may be more advantageous to you than a very small pension plan. Check into these plans with your bank and insurance agent and again compute the tradeoffs to yourself, your employees, and your firm.

Property Insurance

Property insurance protects against losses which may occur to your business property. This includes real property or buildings, personal property including machines, office supplies, and equipment, finished goods, and so forth. Property coverages that you may want to consider include the following:

1. Automobile damage collision insurance
2. Comprehensive property insurance
3. Crime insurance for theft, burglary, and/or robbery
4. Fire insurance
5. Flood insurance
6. Hail and windstorm insurance
7. Inland marine insurance
8. Vandalism

Automobile Damage Insurance. Automobile damage insurance is usually included as part of the automobile liability insurance policy discussed earlier. Therefore, it is usually excluded from all-purpose property policies.

Comprehensive Property Insurance. This is an all-risk policy which generally covers all perils except those which are specifically excluded and named in the policy. An all-risk policy has certain advantages:

1. You avoid gaps in your coverage since you know that you are covered for all perils not specifically excluded.
2. You are less likely to duplicate your coverage with additional policies than if you tried to get the same insurance by purchasing several different policies.
3. In general, it is easier to obtain settlement for lawsuits with an all-risk policy. This is because owning several policies which cover a single loss may lead to a conflict as to how much each policy is to contribute toward coverage of the loss.
4. The total premium on an all-risk policy is generally less than the same coverage obtained by several different policies.

The areas which all-risk policies do not usually cover include such items as accounting records, automobiles, cash, jewelry, machinery, manuscripts, and like items, which are protected by other types of policies.

Crime Insurance.   Some types of crime insurance can be included in comprehensive all-risk policies. However, other types of crimes such as off-premise robberies, disappearance of money, employee theft, and embezzlement are not included. Typical types of crime insurance include burglary insurance covering your safes and inventory of merchandise; robbery insurance which will protect your from loss of property, money, and securities by robbery either on or off the premises; comprehensive crime policies which can cover other types of theft loss in addition to burglary and robbery including destruction or disappearance of property; and storekeepers' burglary and robbery policies which are designed specifically for small businesspersons and cover up to a certain amount of loss for each occurrence of certain types of crime such as inside robbery, outside robbery, stock burglary, kidnapping of the owner, and so forth.

Crime insurance rates are generally high. They do, of course, depend on many factors, including your type of business, the location, kinds of loss prevention measurements such as safes, burglar alarms, and so forth, and various other factors.

Fidelity bonds are a type of insurance that protects you against a serious potential loss that is caused by a special kind of crime: dishonesty of your own employees. For example, an embezzler may steal small amounts from you over a number of years, but the grant total may be quite high. A fidelity bond can insure you against this type of theft. Furthermore, the act of requiring an employee to be bonded may itself discourage stealing. Also, the character investigation performed by the bonding company may disclose unfavorable facts about an employee, enabling you to take preventive measures before a theft can occur.

Fire Insurance.   Fire insurance is standardized in the United States. A standard policy covers three basic perils: fire, lightning, and losses to goods temporarily removed from their premises because of the fire. For any additional perils you must pay extra. For example, a standard fire policy excludes theft and failure to protect the property after a fire. Also, a special policy which extends the standard fire policy is needed to cover loss by fire of accounts, bills, currency, deeds, evidence of debt, and securities.

Flood, Hail, Windstorm, and Vandalism.   The perils of windstorm, hail, and vandalism are frequently covered under comprehensive all-risk property insurance policies discussed earlier. However, flood damage is not, and such a policy is usually purchased separately.

Inland Marine Insurance.   The inland marine floater policy is designed for specialized types of retailers and wholesalers, including equipment dealers, furriers, jewelers, and launderers, that are not covered by general all-risk commercial property insurance because their property is highly susceptible to loss. The type of insurance available may be all-risk or there may be specifically named peril contracts.

SPECIAL-PURPOSE INSURANCE COVERAGES

Various additional coverages can be obtained to protect you against the potential of large losses. These include the following:

1. Business interruption insurance
2. Credit insurance
3. Glass insurance

4. Key employee insurance
5. Power plant insurance
6. Profits and commission insurance
7. Rent insurance
8. Sprinkler leakage insurance
9. Surety bonds
10. Transportation insurance
11. FAIR plan program

Let's look at each of these in turn.

Business Interruption Insurance

Any business will lose money if you are shut down as a result of a major disaster including fire, earthquake, flood, or storm. Further, even after repairs have been made, you will have to continue paying expenses such as salaries of employees, taxes, and so forth, even though there may be little or no money coming in. Business interruption insurance can help you with this problem.

Credit Insurance

Credit insurance is of several types. Credit life insurance is generally used by retail firms which sell on credit. It insures that the outstanding debt of the customer will be paid off in the event of his death. Commercial credit insurance enables you to have an open account of credit that you can extend to buyers of merchandise for commercial purposes. Installment sales floaters protect you against loss which has a potential for occurring when a purchaser has not insured goods bought on credit. In other words, they assure you for payments for goods that you have already sold.

Glass Insurance

Glass insurance protects you against breakage of large and expensive plate glass windows, signs, and showcases.

Key Employee Insurance

Key employee insurance insures you against losses resulting from the death or total disability of a key employee in your firm, including owners and partners. Thus, if a good deal of business depends on a single individual in your firm, this potential loss can be insured.

Power Plant Insurance

Certain types of machinery which can explode are not covered under all-risk or comprehensive property insurance. Therefore, these require separate policies. This category includes power plants, boilers, and other like machinery or electrical equipment.

Profits and Commission Insurance

This type of insurance enables you to insure profits or commissions you would lose if some named peril destroyed the merchandise involved.

Rent Insurance

Rent insurance is insurance for rent on property that you lease. It will reimburse you if your tenant fails to pay.

Sprinkler Leakage Insurance

This insurance covers losses resulting from leakage from water sprinklers used in fire protection of your building.

Surety Bonds

Surety bonds enable you to compete on an equal footing with larger or better-known firms. Basically, surety bonds are a guarantee that you will carry out work according to contract. Typically, surety bonds are issued for persons or firms doing contract construction, for those connected with court actions, or for those seeking licenses or permits. The bond guarantees that you are honest and have the necessary ability and financial capacity to meet the obligations required. The surety bond will also back your credit and vouch for your ability to perform. As with a fidelity bond, the bonding firm will require extensive information about you. They also require you to put up collateral before the bond will be issued. In the event of loss, sureties have the right to collect from you any amount they are required to pay to the person or company protected. You can see how such bonds put you on an equal footing with much larger firms since your ability to perform is guaranteed even though you may not be known to the individual paying for the job.

Transportation Insurance

Transportation insurance covers you while transporting goods. Many businessmen do not realize that common carriers are not always liable for losses to the goods which they may be carrying for you. For example, common carriers are not liable for loss from floods, storms, earthquakes, or other perils or acts of God which cannot reasonably be guarded against by the carrier. Therefore, transport insurance is of some importance.

Two basic types of transportation insurance are *inland transit policy* and *blanket motor cargo policy*. Inland transit policy is most frequently used for land shipments. It covers those perils which are not the liability of the common carrier. The coverage includes collision, derailment, and acts of God. Pilferage is usually excluded, but theft of an entire shipping package or container can be covered. Typical exclusions for the inland transit policy are those arising from strike, riot, civil commotion, war, delay of shipment or loss of market, and leakage or breakage—unless caused by one of the perils insured against. Certain types of property are also excluded, including accounts, bills, deeds, evidences of debt, money, notes and securities, and exports after arrival at seaport. Certain coverages in these provisions can be negotiated. Rates for an inland transit policy vary widely. You can save insurance costs by using a released bill of lading which makes the common carrier liable for only $50 worth of damage. This can result in a reduction in transit rates which is usually more than enough to pay for the inland policy insurance.

A blanket motor cargo policy is issued to truckers and to those who ship by truck. All states require truckers to have certain minimum coverages, including their legal liability for loss of a shipper's goods. Federal laws also require inter-state truckers to carry certain coverages. As a shipper, you may wish to obtain your own coverage rather than relying solely on the truckers since these mini-mums may not offer you full protection. Also, even if the trucker carries more than the minimum required by law, you have no assurance that the policy cannot be voided by breach of warranty or exclusions of various types. Finally, of course, the trucker's policy will not cover acts of God. Therefore, blanket motor cargo policies can be obtained which cover fire, flood, collisions, explosions, and other perils. Typical exclusions for this type of policy are strikes, war, illegal trade, and civil commotion.

The FAIR Plan Program

The FAIR (Fair Access to Insurance Requirements) plan is a riot insurance pro-gram established by the U.S. Housing and Urban Development Act of 1968. In states accepting the plan, the state, the insurance industry, and the federal gov-ernment cooperate to make property insurance available in certain high-risk areas at moderate rates. If your business is in an area generally known to be sub-ject to riots or serious vandalism, and you are unable to get adequate insurance in the normal manner or cannot get insurance without paying excessively high pre-miums, this plan may help you out. In fact, you may not be turned down because of being located in a riot-prone area subject to vandalism. It is therefore in your interest to find out whether your state has a FAIR plan and where to apply if this situation applies to you. To do so, contact your state insurance commissioner.

HOW TO BUY INSURANCE

Direct Writers and Agents

There are basically two different types of insurance sellers. These are the direct writer and the agent. The direct writer is a commissioned employee of the in-surer. The business he or she writes belongs to the insurance company itself, which may turn it over to someone else who is also an employee of the firm. The agent is an independent businessperson who has negotiated with the insurer to represent him or her in a given territory. The agent is also compensated on a commissioned basis.

There are advantages in dealing with either the agent or the direct writer. An independent agent may represent many different insurers. Therefore, such an agent will be able to offer you a wide choice among a number of different cover-ages. Also, if this independent agent handles many different types of insurance, you need deal with only this one seller to obtain the same coverage that you would otherwise have to obtain from several different insurance sellers. Also, be-cause the insurance agent may deal with a variety of different coverages, he or she may have greater knowledge of the overall field than a direct writer who would be limited to the line of the employer insurance company. Finally, inas-much as the business is all his or hers, the independent agent has a greater finan-cial motivation to give you the best service possible.

Advantages in dealing with direct writers include lower costs, since the com-mission paid the direct writer by his or her own company is less than that paid the independent agent. Also, the direct writer becomes a specialist in whatever area or line of insurance he or she is handling. Thus, whereas the independent agent has general knowledge, the direct writer has in-depth, specialized knowledge in one area. This may be advantageous to you, depending upon the type of insurance that you are interested in and your business situation.

How to Pick an Insurer

The decision to pick one insurer over another generally is based upon four factors. These are cost, type of insurance offered, flexibility in coverage, and financial stability of the firm.

Cost.   To evaluate the cost factor, set up a matrix as shown in Figure 3.1. Using this matrix, you would select the insurer who offers the lower cost for the coverage and deductible that you decide upon. Note that there may be more to it than just the lower premium to consider. Some insurers charge a lower initial premium; however, another insurer, which charges a higher premium, may pay a dividend to its policyholders. Therefore, to make an accurate comparison, you must compare not only the initial premium involved but also the probable size of dividend if one is being paid.

If the premium is extremely low, you should be particularly careful that this low premium is not made possible by extremely strict claim settlement policies, the setting aside of inadequate loss reserves, or such low commissions to their agents that the agents will not be motivated to render quality service.

Type of Insurance Offered.   Some insurers may specialize in certain types of insurance, and even in insurance for a specific industry. If you choose an insurer offering this sort of specialization, you will obtain coverages that are specifically applicable to your business, and the cost of the coverages can be lower than that which other firms offer for a similar type of insurance.

Flexibility in Coverage.   Various insurers are able to tailor their policies specifically to the type of buyers that they envision. Also, some insurers will enable you to insert certain provisions which may affect the final premium you pay or other factors. In some cases and with some insurers, you may negotiate depending on your situation and an insurance rating calculated according to the likelihood of the occurrence of the event for which you are to be insured. All of these factors can affect both the exact type of insurance coverage that you receive and the cost of the premiums.

Financial Stability of the Firm.   In most cases, the agent representing the firm will be your normal source of information about it, and generally you will not be misled. In dealing with an agent with whom you have not dealt before, you must also recognize that the agent may have some motivation for recommending one insurance company over another. For example, one insurance company may pay him more. In this and similar situations, it is important that you know that the insuring company recommended has financial stability. Be especially careful when a policy is issued that has a provision that allows policyholders to be assessed additional premiums if the resources of the insurer are insufficient to pay claims against it. You should check to see whether the proposed policy is assessable or not. In general, you should purchase assessable policies only when nonassessable policies are not available and never if the insurance firm is unstable financially. To check on the financial stability of an insurance firm other than through the

Insurance Company	Coverage	Deductible Amounts $ 500	$1000	$2000	
Insurance Company A	$80,000	$1400	$1200	$ 800	
	85,000	1460	1245	830	Required premiums less dividends
	90,000	1520	1300	860	
Insurance Company B	$80,000	$1525	$1300	$ 835	
	85,000	1580	1335	910	
	70,000	1670	1410	960	

Figure 3.1. Decision Matrix for Insurance Based on Cost and Deductibles.

agent, consult a publication known as *Best's Insurance Reports*. *Best's Insurance Reports* publishes ratings which describe firms' reliability in their dealings with policyholders, their size of net worth and other important factors. Most ratings fall in the three highest classes, A+, A, and B+. If the company that you are investigating does not fall in one of these three classes, you should look at it much more closely.

How Much Deductible?

You can decide on how much deductible or which policy or coverage to purchase with the matrix method also. Let's consider the case of the deductibles in Figure 3.1. Because of basic costs, we have already decided to do business with insurance company A, and now the question is—how much deductible to take? First, we decide on how much insurance is adequate for our purposes. Let us assume that the answer is $80,000. Now we have three options: $500 deductible for a premium of $1,400; $1,000 deductible for a premium of $1,200; and $2,000 deductible for a premium of $800. Let us say that we calculate that on the average we will suffer a $500 loss every two years, a $1,000 loss once every four years, and a $2,000 loss once every six years. We can then make the following calculations. For the $500 deductible policy, we would pay six times $1,400 or $8,400 for their premium plus three times $500 or $1,500 for the three losses during the six years, for a total of $9,900. If we chose $1,000 deductible, we would pay six times $1,200 or $7,200 for the premium and suffer an average of one and one-half losses during the six-year period. That is one and one-half times $1,000 or $1,500, for a total of $8,700. Or, considering our third option, $2,000 deductible, we would pay six times $800 or $4,800 for our premium and during the six-year period suffer one loss of $2,000, for a total of $6,800. Since $6,800 is lower than either $8,700 or $9,900, it would pay us to take the $2,000 deductible policy.

How to Save Money with Your Insurance

To save money in buying your insurance, you should do the following:

1. Get competitive bids on all of your policies, review using the matrix system shown in Figure 3.1, and compare the alternatives.
2. Don't rely totally on your agent. Review your alternatives to be sure that your agent has not neglected to suggest the best possible coverage for your situation.
3. Over a period of time, evaluate how your agent has performed in getting compensation for your losses.

4. Make certain that you evaluate the use of deductibles in your insurance program.

5. Check with your agent where you can reduce premiums through assuming certain obligations, for example, a sprinkler system, a burglar alarm system, and so forth.

SETTLING INSURANCE LOSSES

Notice of Loss

All insurance policies will require you to notify the insurer as soon as the loss occurs. Do not violate this rule as you may endanger your right of recovery. As soon as practicable after the loss occurs, make certain that the insurer is informed.

Proof of Loss

Insurers will require some proof of the loss that has occurred. Generally this will amount to some sort of documentation, accounting records, death certificate in the case of life insurance, a complete inventory of destroyed property in the case of fire insurance, and so forth. To do this, you should keep good records ahead of time and expect to have to prove the loss that occurred. However, do not delay the notice of loss in order to get the full proof. You will have a reasonable period in which to provide the proof required.

Paying for Losses

Your local agent is generally authorized to settle small claims. However, larger claims are usually handled by company representatives. The company representative's job is to evaluate the loss and arrive at the settlement that will compensate you in accordance with your policy.

Basic Insurer Options

Generally, the insurer has three options in order to fulfill the terms of the policy which you have taken. These include: (1) paying a cash settlement for your loss, (2) repairing the property, or (3) replacing the property with goods of like kind and quality. Naturally, a cash settlement is the most frequent means of settling the claim.

Arbitration

A careful reading of your policy will indicate arbitration procedures if you and your insurer do not agree on the amount to be paid in cases of loss. The general procedure is for each party to select an independent and competent appraiser as well as a disinterested party to act as judge. The appraiser assesses the loss separately and submits any differences between your value and the insurance company's to the judge or umpire. Usually no lawsuit can be initiated unless these arbitration procedures have been carried out first. Also, there is a limitation regarding the time when a lawsuit can occur. This information can be found in your insurance policy.

Potential Problems in Settlement

There are certain potential problems in settling your claim, and the time to consider them is when you purchase your insurance and not after the loss occurs. The main problems of this type are overlapping coverage, nonconcurrency, and spread-out coverage.

Overlapping Coverage. This means that two or more policies cover the same risk or property. Intentionally obtaining overlapping coverage is a mistake because it inflates your cost as well as hindering settlement when and if a loss occurs. What happens is this: If a loss occurs, each insurer may try to make its policy that which pays the excess over the other insurance policy. Thus, both end up denying the basic liability and resulting legal litigation may mean that you won't get a settlement for years. Be very careful about overlapping coverage. In some cases, it may be difficult if not impossible to avoid, but in every instance in which it can be avoided, do so.

Nonconcurrency. This refers to a discrepancy among different policies covering identical property. This occurs because of conflicting provisions of different policies or overlapping coverage. Again, a close reading of your policies before the loss occurs can help you avoid lots of difficulty later on.

Spread-Out Coverage. This refers to spreading out your insurance among several different agents. This increases the chances of overlapping coverage and nonconcurrency. It also means that no one agent is completely responsible for your entire insurance program. Spread-out coverage should be minimized or, if possible, eliminated. The only exception is in the case where the advantages of using direct writers described earlier are so significant that they outweigh this major disadvantage.

COMMON INSURANCE TERMS

Beneficiary. This is a person who is designated to receive the face amount of the policy.

Cash value of policy. This is the amount of insurance a company will pay if the policy is canceled, generally in the case of life insurance.

Coverage. This is the type of loss for which a policy will pay you. For example, most liability policies will pay for the amount you become legally obligated to pay because of bodily injury or damage to property that you accidentally caused, and the expense of settling a liability suit.

Deductibles. Deductibles are a specified dollar amount and percentage of loss above which the insurance company will pay.

Face amount of policy. This is a life insurance term which refers to the amount paid by the insurance company in the event of the death of the insured.

Exclusions. These are the types of losses for which a policy will not pay.

Indemnity. This is a principle which permits you to collect only the actual amount of the loss and not an amount named in the policy as the policy limit. This concept prevents excessive insurance coverage.

Limitations. This is the maximum amount of payment which the policy will provide in the event of a loss.

Loan value of policy. This, again, has to do with life insurance and is the amount of insurance that the insurance company will loan if you wish to borrow against the cash value of the policy.

Paid-up policy. This is also a life insurance term. It is a policy in which no further premiums are required. It may also be a new policy for less than the face value of an older policy which is given to the insured in the event the insured desires to cancel the original policy and take a policy of less than the original face, but pay no more premiums.

Premium. This is the amount paid to maintain the policy in force.

Subrogation. This is a principle under which the insured gives to the insurer his right of recovery against liable third parties, to the extent that the insurer indemnifies the insured for loss.

INSURANCE CHECKLIST FOR SMALL BUSINESS

The following insurance checklist for small business was developed by Mark R. Greene, Distinguished Professor of Insurance at the University of Georgia.[1] This checklist will enable you to discover areas in which your insurance program can be improved, costs can be saved, and the effectiveness of your insurance can be increased. It will also serve as a guide on points to talk about with your insurance agent, broker, or other insurance counselor.

THE CHECKLIST

The points covered in the checklist are grouped under three general classes of insurance: (1) coverages that are essential for most businesses, (2) coverages that are desirable for many firms but not absolutely necessary, and (3) coverages for employee benefits. For each of the statements, put a check in the first answer column if you understand the statement and how it affects your insurance program. Otherwise, check the second column. Then study your policies with these points in mind and discuss any questions you still have with your agent.

Essential Coverages

Four kinds of insurance are essential: fire insurance, liability insurance, automobile insurance, and workers' compensation insurance. In some areas and in some kinds of businesses, crime insurance, which is discussed under "Desirable Coverages," is also essential.

Are you certain that all the following points have been given full consideration in your insurance program?

[1] Mark R. Greene, *Insurance Checklist for Small Business*, Small Business Administration (1979).

Fire Insurance

	No action needed	Look into this

1. You can add other perils—such as windstorm, hail, smoke, explosion, vandalism, and malicious mischief—to your basic fire insurance at a relatively small additional cost.   ____ ____

2. If you need comprehensive coverage, your best buy may be one of the all-risk contracts that offer the broadest available protection for the money.   ____ ____

3. The insurance company may indemnify you—that is, compensate you for your losses—in any one of several ways: (1) It may pay actual cash value of the property at the time of loss. (2) It may repair or replace the property with material of like kind and quality. (3) It may take *all* the property at the agreed or appraised value and reimburse you for your loss.   ____ ____

4. You can insure property you don't own. You must have an insurable interest—a financial interest—in the property *when a loss occurs* but not necessarily at the time the insurance contract is made. For instance, a repair shop or drycleaning plant may carry insurance on customers' property in the shop, or a person holding a mortgage on a building may insure the building although he doesn't own it.   ____ ____

5. When you sell property, you cannot assign the insurance policy along with the property unless you have permission from the insurance company.   ____ ____

6. Even if you have several policies on your property, you can still collect only the amount of your actual cash loss. All the insurers share the payment proportionately. Suppose, for example, that you are carrying two policies—one for \$20,000 and one for \$30,000—on a \$40,000 building, and fire causes damage to the building amounting to \$12,000. The \$20,000 policy will pay \$4,800; that is, $\frac{20,000}{50,000}$, or $\frac{2}{5}$, of \$12,000. The \$30,000 policy

will pay \$7,200; which is $\frac{30,000}{50,000}$, or $\frac{3}{5}$, of \$12,000.   ____ ____

7. Special protection other than the standard fire policy is needed to cover the loss by fire of accounts, bills, currency, deeds, evidences of debt, and money and securities.   ____ ____

8. If an insured building is vacant or unoccupied for more than 60 consecutive days, coverage is suspended unless you have a special endorsement to your policy canceling this provision.   ____ ____

9. If, either before or after a loss, you conceal or misrepresent to the insurer any material fact or circumstance concerning your insurance or the interest of the insured, the policy may be voided.   ____ ____

10. If you increase the hazard of fire, the insurance company may suspend your coverage even for losses not originating from the increased hazard. (An example of such a hazard might be renting part of your building to a drycleaning plant.)   ____ ____

	No action needed	Look into this

11. After a loss, you must use all reasonable means to protect the property from further loss or run the risk of having your coverage canceled. ____ ____

12. To recover your loss, you must furnish within 60 days (unless an extension is granted by the insurance company) a complete inventory of the damaged, destroyed, and undamaged property showing in detail quantities, costs, actual cash value, and amount of loss claimed. ____ ____

13. If you and the insurer disagree on the amount of loss, the question may be resolved through special appraisal procedures provided for in the fire insurance policy. ____ ____

14. You may cancel your policy without notice at any time and get part of the premium returned. The insurance company also may cancel at any time with a 5-day written notice to you. ____ ____

15. By accepting a coinsurance clause in your policy, you get a substantial reduction in premiums. A coinsurance clause states that you must carry insurance equal to 80 or 90 percent of the value of the insured property. If you carry less than this, you cannot collect the full amount of your loss, even if the loss is small. What percent of your loss you can collect will depend on what percent of the full value of the property you have insured it for. ____ ____

16. If your loss is caused by someone else's negligence, the insurer has the right to sue this negligent third party for the amount it has paid you under the policy. This is known as the insurer's right of subrogation. However, the insurer will usually waive this right upon request. For example, if you have leased your insured building to someone and have waived your right to recover from the tenant for any insured damages to your property, you should have your agent request the insurer to waive the subrogation clause in the fire policy on your leased building. ____ ____

17. A building under construction can be insured for fire, lightning, extended coverage, vandalism, and malicious mischief. ____ ____

Liability Insurance

1. Legal liability limits of $1 million are no longer considered high or unreasonable even for a small business. ____ ____

2. Most liability policies require you to notify the insurer immediately after an incident on your property that might cause a future claim. This holds true no matter how unimportant the incident may seem at the time it happens. ____ ____

3. Most liability policies, in addition, to *bodily* injuries, may now cover *personal* injuries (libel, slander, and so on) *if* these are specifically insured. ____ ____

	No action needed	Look into this

4. Under certain conditions, your business may be subject to damage claims even from trespassers.

5. You may be legally liable for damages even in cases where you used "reasonable care."

6. Even if the suit against you is false or fraudulent, the liability insurer pays court costs, legal fees, and interest on judgments *in addition to* the liability judgments themselves.

7. You can be liable for the acts of others under contracts you have signed with them. This liability is insurable.

8. In some cases you may be held liable for fire loss to property of others in your care. Yet, this property would normally not be covered by your fire or general liability insurance. This risk can be covered by fire legal liability insurance or through requesting subrogation waivers from insurers of owners of the property.

Automobile Insurance

1. When an employee or a subcontractor uses his own car on your behalf, you can be legally liable even if you don't own a car or truck yourself.

2. Five or more automobiles or motorcycles under one ownership and operated as a fleet for business purposes can generally be insured under a low-cost fleet policy against both material damage to your vehicle and liability to others for property damage or personal injury.

3. You can often get deductibles of almost any amount—say $250 or $500—and thereby reduce your premiums.

4. Automobile medical payments insurance pays for medical claims, including your own, arising from automobile accidents regardless of the question of negligence.

5. In most states, you must carry liability insurance or be prepared to provide other proof (surety bond) of financial responsibility when you are involved in an accident.

6. You can purchase uninsured motorist protection to cover your own bodily injury claims from someone who has no insurance.

7. Personal property stored in an automobile and not attached to it (for example, merchandise being delivered) is not covered under an automobile policy.

Workers' Compensation

1. Common law requires that an employer (1) provide his employees a safe place to work, (2) hire competent fellow employees, (3) provide safe tools, and (4) warn his employees of an existing danger.

2. If an employer fails to provide the above, under both common law and workers' compensation laws he is liable for damage suits brought by an employee.

	No action needed	Look into this

3. State law determines the level or type of benefits payable under workers' compensation policies.

4. Not all employees are covered by workers' compensation laws. The exceptions are determined by state law and therefore vary from state to state.

5. In nearly all states, you are now legally *required* to cover your workers under workers' compensation.

6. You can save money on workers' compensation insurance by seeing that your employees are properly classified.

7. Rates for workers' compensation insurance vary from 0.1 percent of the payroll for "safe" occupations to about 25 percent or more of the payroll for very hazardous occupations.

8. Most employers in most states can reduce their workers' compensation premium cost by reducing their accident rates below the average. They do this by using safety and loss-prevention measures.

Desirable Coverages

Some types of insurance coverage, while not absolutely essential, will add greatly to the security of your business. These coverages include business interruption insurance, crime insurance, glass insurance, and rent insurance.

Business Interruption Insurance

1. You can purchase insurance to cover fixed expenses that would continue if a fire shut down your business—such as salaries to key employees, taxes, interest, depreciation, and utilities—as well as the profits you would lose.

2. Under properly written contingent business interruption insurance, you can also collect if fire or other peril closes down the business of a supplier or customer and this interrupts your business.

3. The business interruption policy provides payments for amounts you spend to hasten the reopening of your business after a fire or other insured peril.

4. You can get coverage for the extra expenses you suffer if an insured peril, while not actually closing your business down, seriously disrupts it.

5. When the policy is properly endorsed, you can get business interruption insurance to indemnify you if your operations are suspended because of failure or interruption of the supply of power, light, heat, gas, or water furnished by a public utility company.

Crime Insurance

1. Burglary insurance excludes such property as accounts, fur articles in a showcase window, and manuscripts.

	No action needed	Look into this

2. Coverage is granted under burglary insurance only if there are visible marks of the burglar's forced entry.

3. Burglary insurance can be written to cover, in addition to money in a safe, inventoried merchandise and damage incurred in the course of a burglary.

4. Robbery insurance protects you from loss of property, money, and securities by force, trickery, or threat of violence on *or off* your premises.

5. A comprehensive crime policy written just for small businessmen is available. In addition to burglary and robbery, it covers other types of loss by theft, destruction, and disappearance of money and securities. It also covers thefts by your employees.

6. If you are in high-risk area and cannot get insurance through normal channels without paying excessive rates, you may be able to get help through the federal crime insurance plan. Your agent or state insurance commissioner can tell you where to get information about these plans.

Glass Insurance

1. You can purchase a special glass insurance policy that covers all risk to plate-glass windows, glass signs, motion picture screens, glass brick, glass doors, showcases, countertops, and insulated glass panels.

2. The glass insurance policy covers not only the glass itself, but also its lettering and ornamentation, if these are specifically insured, and the costs of temporary plates or boarding up when necessary.

3. After the glass has been replaced, full coverage is continued without any additional premium for the period covered.

Rent Insurance

1. You can buy rent insurance that will pay your rent if the property you lease becomes unusable because of fire or other insured perils and your lease calls for continued payments in such a situation.

2. If you own property and lease it to others, you can insure against loss if the lease is canceled because of fire and you have to rent the property again at a reduced rental.

Employee Benefit Coverages

Insurance coverages that can be used to provide employee benefits include group life insurance, group health insurance, disability insurance, and retirement income. Key man insurance protects the company against financial loss caused by the death of a valuable employee or partner.

Group Life Insurance

	No action needed	Look into this

1. If you pay group insurance premiums and cover all employees up to $50,000, the cost to you is deductible for Federal income tax purposes, and yet the value of the benefit is not taxable income to your employees.   ____   ____

2. Most insurers will provide group coverages at low rates even if there are 10 or fewer employees in your group.   ____   ____

3. If the employees pay part of the cost of the group insurance, state laws require that 75 percent of them must elect coverage for the plan to qualify as group insurance.   ____   ____

4. Group plans permit an employee leaving the company to convert his group insurance coverage to a private plan, at the rate for his age, without a medical exam if he does so within 30 days after leaving his job.   ____   ____

Group Health Insurance

1. Group health insurance cost much less and provides more generous benefits for the worker than individual contracts would.   ____   ____

2. If you pay the entire cost, individual employees cannot be dropped from a group plan unless the entire group policy is cancelled.   ____   ____

3. Generous programs of employee benefits, such as group health insurance, tend to reduce labor turnover.   ____   ____

Disability Insurance

1. Workers' compensation insurance pays an employee only for time lost because of work injuries and work-related sickness—not for time lost because of disabilities incurred off the job. But you can purchase, at a low premium, insurance to replace the lost income of workers who suffer short-term or long-term disability not related to their work.   ____   ____

2. You can get coverage that provides employees with an income for life in case of permanent disability resulting from work-related sickness or accident.   ____   ____

Retirement Income

1. If you are self-employed, you can get an income tax deduction for funds used for retirement for you and your employees through plans of insurance or annuities approved for use under the Employees Retirement Income Security Act of 1974 (ERISA).   ____   ____

2. Annuity contracts may provide for variable payments in the hope of giving the annuitants some protection against the effects of inflation. Whether fixed or variable, an annuity can provide retirement income that is guaranteed for life.   ____   ____

Key-Man Insurance

	No action needed	Look into this

1. One of the most serious setbacks that can come to a small company is the loss of a key man. But your key man can be insured with life insurance and disability insurance owned by and payable to your company.

2. Proceeds of a key-man policy are not subject to income tax, but premiums are not a deductible business expense.

3. The cash value of key-man insurance, which accumulates as an asset of the business, can be borrowed against and the interest and dividends are not subject to income tax as long as the policy remains in force.

SOURCES OF ADDITIONAL INFORMATION

Business Insurance, 4th edition, by Edwin H. White and H. Chasman, published by Prentice-Hall, Inc., Englewood Cliffs, NJ 07632.

General Insurance, 9th edition, by John H. Magee, published by Richard D. Irwin, Inc., 1818 Ridge Rd., Homewood, IL 60430.

General Insurance Guide, by B. G. Werbel, published by Werbel Publishing Co., 595 Old Willets Path, Smithtown, NY 11787.

Group Insurance Handbook, by Robert D. Eilers and Robert M. Crowe, editors, published by Richard D. Irwin, 1818 Ridge Road, Homewood, IL 60430.

Insurance and Risk Management for Small Business, by Mark R. Greene, published by the Small Business Administration, Superintendent of Documents, Washington, DC 20402.

Life and Health Insurance Handbook, 3rd edition, edited by Davis W. Gregg and Vane B. Lucas, published by Richard D. Irwin, Inc., 18181 Ridge Rd., Homewood, IL 60430.

Modern Life Insurance, 3rd edition, by Robert W. Osler, published by Macmillan Co., 866 Third Ave., New York, NY 10022.

Risk and Insurance, 3rd edition, by Mark R. Greene, published by Southwestern Publishing Co., 5101 Madison Rd., Cincinnati, OH 45227.

Risk Management and Insurance, 2nd edition, by C. Arthur Williams, Jr. and Richard M. Heins, published by McGraw-Hill Book Co., 1221 Avenue of the Americas, New York, NY 10020.

Risk Management: Concepts and Applications, by Robert I. Mehr and Bole A. Hedges, published by Richard D. Irwin, 1818 Ridge Rd., Homewood, IL 60430.

4

Business Planning

THE IMPORTANCE OF THE BUSINESS PLAN

Trying to be successful in a new business without a business plan is like trying to navigate a ship through perilous waters without a map and without a clear idea of your destination. Spending the time to develop a business plan allows you to visualize clearly where you want your business to go and what you want to accomplish. At the same time, the plan maps out the important steps necessary to get from where you are now to where you want to be at the conclusion of the plan period. Further, you will have a good idea of how long it will take to get where you want to go and what resources in money and personnel will be needed. The importance of the business plan is recognized by potential sources of financial assistance to such an extent that you will probably not be able to borrow money without completing a business plan for study by potential investors.

There are some firms which will develop business plans for you. They will change you from several hundred to several thousand dollars for their services. However, you are probably best qualified to develop a business plan for your business. Who knows better than you about your business, its resources, its relative strengths and weaknesses, and countless other critical factors? Therefore, this chapter will enable you to develop a superior business plan—and save a lot of money!

WHAT THE BUSINESS PLAN WILL DO FOR YOU

There are several things that the business plan will accomplish for you. These are as follows:

1. It will act as a road map.
2. It will assist you with management control.
3. It will help you in briefing new employees and other personnel.
4. It will help you to obtain financing.

A Business Plan as a Road Map

If you were traveling from point A to point B and you had never been there before, you would almost certainly consult a road map. If you didn't, you might drive around in circles for hours trying to locate the place where you wanted to be. In fact, many of us have done this very thing! However, with a map, everything is made simple. We can follow a precise route from where we are now to where we want to get. Of course, sometimes something occurs during our travel which our map did not warn us about; maybe a road is closed and so we have to take a detour. But regardless of this, the fact that we have a clear destination and a map which shows us how to get there assures us that we will eventually arrive.

A business plan works in the same fashion. Naturally, you want your business to succeed, and you want it to be profitable. However, it is possible to be much more specific in defining your goals in terms of sales, profits, or market share. A business plan which will show us how to reach our carefully defined goals serves the same function as the road map for the driver of a car. And the business plan enables you to reach your business goal much more quickly than you would without it.

Management Control

I said before that the driver of a vehicle, even if he has a road map, may find it necessary to take a detour. This may be because a road is being repaired, or because the weather makes the most direct route to his destination impassable. In the same way, as you are in the process of starting up and operating your business, you will encounter various problems which cannot be foreseen. In fact, it is almost certain that nothing will go exactly as planned. However, in thinking through your project and laying out a full and complete plan, you may very well see potential difficulties. Furthermore, inasmuch as you have a documented plan which leads directly to the goals that you have established, you will be able to see clearly the difference between what is happening during the planned-for period and what you had planned would happen. This gives you control over the situation and lets you see more clearly the corrective action needed to put yourself back on course.

Did you know that for almost every airplane flight, the pilot is required to submit a flight plan? This flight plan lays out all information, including the headings, distances, ground speed, fuel, time en route, and so on, for the specific destination that the pilot had decided upon. One major reason for this flight plan is constant control of the flight to its destination. The pilot can compare his actual course and progress with the course and progress he planned. He can analyze this information to make the best decisions. So important is this aspect of management control in flight planning that for some flights the air crew spends as much time planning for the flight on the ground as they do flying it in the air.

The business plan will give you management control over your business, just as the flight plan gives the pilot management control over his flight.

Briefing New Employees and Other Personnel

Many times you will want to inform other people regarding your business and its progress toward its goals, or about its objectives and how you intend on reaching them. For example, you may wish to brief new employees you have hired for your firm. This doesn't mean that you have to lay out the entire business plan with all its financial data. However, showing them the objectives that you have set for yourself, how and when you plan on reaching them, and where they fit into this big picture will not only motivate them but it will also help them to do a better job. Furthermore, once you organize and document this material in a business plan, you have it for all time. You will not need to run around to assemble all the information every time you wish to discuss your company in detail with someone.

Obtaining Financing

A potential loan source or someone interested in investing in your company will almost invariably wish to see your business plan, not only so he or she can understand exactly how the money will be used and how you plan on reaching your goals but also to be convinced that you have thought through your project, that you know what you are doing, that you have anticipated the obstacles that may arise, and that you have a plan for overcoming them. In fact, many sources of capital have indicated that the quality of the business plan is a major factor in their decision to fund a particular project or loan money.

THE STRUCTURE OF THE BUSINESS PLAN

A good business plan will contain the following sections:

1. Executive summary
2. Background and description of business
3. Organization of your company
4. Situation analysis
5. Problems and opportunities
6. Objectives
7. Marketing strategy
8. Budget
9. Financial plans
10. Strategy implementation time schedule

Let's look at each in turn.

Executive Summary

The executive summary is an overall view of your business and its potential, including what you want to do, how much money you need and how much money the business will make, return on investment, and how and when the investor will get his investment returned. The executive summary is important and should not be excluded. When they go through your business plan, financial investors will very frequently skip over parts of the plan which are not of interest to them and read only those sections which they specialize in. However, they will *always* read the executive summary, and therefore it is very important that you present the essence of your business plan in a few short paragraphs so that even if much of your plan goes unread, the thrust of what you are going to do, the objectives you intend to reach, and how you intend to reach them can be clear to the reader.

Background and Description of Business

In this paragraph, you should indicate details of your business, including what it is, how you are going to run it, the form of the business, why it will be successful, and anything in your background that gives your business a competitive edge over similar businesses. This section is important both for your investor and for you, for any business should have a perceived advantage over similar businesses.

Otherwise, why should your customer deal with you rather than with your established competitors? Such an advantage may be a unique product, lower costs, better service, closer location to your market, or any one of a thousand different things, including an expertise which is well known to your potential customers. Your competitive edge should be clearly identified and documented in this section.

The Organization of Your Company

In this section, you should detail exactly how your company will be organized, even if it is a sole proprietorship. You should also include, either here or perhaps in an appendix, detailed résumé of the principle officers in your company. These should *not* be generalized to include all experiences or background information that is not relevant. All facts in your résumé should be pointed to the position held in your firm. This would include not only education, but prior experience and other special qualifications which support the assertion that your business will be successful and win out over its competition.

Let me give you a specific example here. The fact that the owner of a business is multilingual and speaks three or four languages may be extremely important for an import/export company. However, if the business proposed is a retail business in an area where only English is spoken, a multilingual ability usually has no advantage. It is therefore irrelevant and should be omitted from the résumé.

The Situation Analysis

The situation analysis has several subsections which are important and should be included and discussed. These are: demand for your product or service, your target market, competition, unique advantages, legal restrictions, if any, and any other situational variables that you feel are important to your business.

Demand includes both the need for your product or service and the extent of this need. This need may be very basic; if your product is a food, for instance. On the other hand, your products or services may satisfy psychological needs that are not necessarily obvious. An example here is a brass case for business cards that has been on the market for several years. This brass case has sold for $20 or more. Now the question is: Is this brass case for business cards purchased to protect business cards or is it purchased primarily to promote the status of the owner? Inasmuch as cheap plastic cases to protect business cards are frequently used as premium giveaways or even supplied free with the cards, chances are this product is purchased primarily to satisfy status needs. Whatever the needs are for your product or service, they should be carefully considered and noted under this section. You should document the extent of the demand for this need, in other words, the strength of the need which is going to be fulfilled by your product or service. You should indicate whether the product is a repeat product which will be purchased again and again by your customers, or whether the product or service is a one-time need which is unlikely to be repeated; and, also, whether the product or service is likely to be sold over a long period of time or whether it is a short-lived fad. Finally, is the demand for the product or service growing, leveling off, or declining?

The *target market* is the market that you intend to seek for your product or your service. Naturally, the larger your potential market the better. But there are several different strategies that you might follow, and it might be advantageous to offer your product only to a certain segment of the total potential market. This is called a strategy of market segmentation, and it does offer a major advantage in certain situations in that you can concentrate all of your resources on satisfying the needs of this specific segment of the market and be stronger against this market segment than your competition can be if your competition spreads its resources and advertisements across the total potential market. Because of this strategy, and because of other possible strategies which we will discuss later in this chapter, you should note very carefully every single market segment that you intend to pursue, including how large this market segment is.

Regardless of the product or service that you offer, you will always have *competition,* even if the competition does not offer the exact same product or service. In some cases, your competition will be companies that offer other products or other services. However, they must be considered competition because their products or services fulfill the identical need that your product or service fulfills. Perhaps you sell burglar alarms. Is your competition only other firms selling burglar alarms? The answer is no. Other firms which fulfill the need for security are also competition. Other firms may offer iron bars which are to be installed over the windows. These are competitors. Security guards are also competition. Therefore, when you begin to analyze the competition for your product or service, be sure that you include all the potential competition and not just firms that are producing the identical product or service.

When you analyze your competition, you should also consider the fact that your competition will never remain static and will generally react to your business strategy if it is effective. If you introduce a new product into the marketplace which competes with some other firm that is already there, you can be assured that if your product is successful you will not be ignored. Your competition will then initiate some other strategy or action in order to try to overcome your success. You might expect your competition to do something with the price of its product, to change the product, or to change its advertising. Now, when you analyze your competition, think ahead, just as you would in a chess game.

Your firm is not the same as any other firm. You as an individual, as well as the owner of a company, offer certain *unique advantages* to your customers or potential customers. If you did not, then there would be no reason to deal with your firm. Some of these advantages have already been discussed, including specialized knowledge, lower prices, a totally unique product, additional services, and so forth. It is important to think through and write down these advantages in your business plan so that you will be certain not to overlook one, and so you can exploit them to the maximum extent at the same time that you emphasize them to potential investors who are looking through your business plan. Remember that although every firm and every individual have such advantages, if you do not document them and do not identify them, it will be as if they did not exist to a potential investor.

Legal restrictions should always be noted in your business plan if they are applicable. They don't always exist, but if they do, you must consider them and write them down, not only so you will not forget them, but also so you can let potential investors know that you are aware of them. For example, products concerned with drugs are closely regulated by a federal regulatory agency, the Food and Drug Administration. Many states license certain types of businesses such as advertising agencies, personnel agencies, and employment agencies. Every restriction should be carefully noted, along with licenses or other legal obligations that are necessary in order for you to do business. You should do the research necessary to be absolutely certain that you meet all your legal obligations. There is an additional advantage of documenting everything here. Sometimes someone going over your business plan will note something that you have forgotten, and this in itself can save you a great deal of time, money, and allocation of important company resources.

Other important situational variables should also be noted. These may be anything that you consider important to your business situation and the success of your business plan. Let us say that your product is seasonal and is only sold during the summer or during the Christmas holidays or during the winter. In such a case, there are special problems, including the expenses of overhead during the off-season, sales during peak periods, and so forth. Each of these should be noted as a situational variable.

Problems and Opportunities

Problems and opportunities are really different sides of the same coin. Many people make millions of dollars because when they note a problem, they also note within this problem an opportunity for success. Listerine is a mouthwash which has a rather harsh taste. In the words of the advertising of the competition, it tastes "mediciny." However, Listerine managed to make this problem an opportunity because the company realized that many people feel that if a mouthwash has a harsh taste, it must be harsher on germs, whereas a mouthwash that tastes sweet, or in the words of a Listerine advertisement, tastes "like soda pop," may not be killing germs nearly as well. Look for the opportunity in every problem that you note.

Objectives

Objectives should be clearly stated in your business plan. They may be identified or defined by stating the target market segments, the volume to be sold in dollars or perhaps in units, or they may include or be defined by a return on investment desired or other profitability analysis.

If more than one objective is stated, be certain that the two objectives do not conflict. For example, sometimes if a market share is specified as the objective, this can be reached only through a negative effect on short-term profitability. So, after specifying and clearly defining your objectives, check to be sure that it is not the case that one objective can only be achieved at the expense of another.

Marketing Strategy

Strategy for marketing your product or service can be conveniently categorized by the control of four different variables. These are: product variables, price variables, promotional variables, and distribution variables. Let's look at each in turn.

Product Variables. There are three basic things that you can do with any product. That is, you can introduce it, you can drop it, or you can change it. Each of these possibilities is in itself important and can have a tremendous impact on the profitability of your firm.

Most new products fail. Estimates of failure run as high as 90%. This means that 9 out of every 10 products that are introduced in the marketplace fail. Some failures can be avoided. Others cannot. For example, new products may fail because of lack of knowledge by the promoter, failure to develop a business plan, or failure to analyze properly whether or not there is a real demand for the product even before it is introduced. Other products fail even after extensive planning

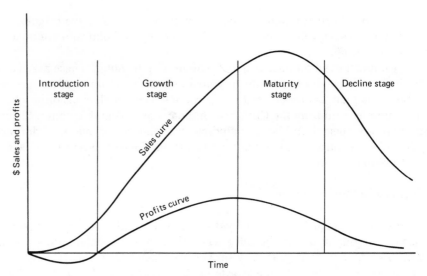

Figure 4.1. The product life cycle.

and research have been accomplished. The mistakes made are usually not discovered until the postmortems.

Even though most new products fail, for most firms it is essential to develop and offer new products or new services continually. This is because of the product's life cycle. Every product that is introduced goes through a number of stages until it finally drops out of the marketplace and is no longer offered. These stages are shown in Figure 4.1. First, a product goes through an introduction stage. Then, after being introduced, its use rapidly expands in a growth stage. Finally, the product becomes mature, and eventually the market becomes saturated as the product goes into decline. In Figure 4.1, you will see two different curves. One curve shows profits. You can see that as a product progresses from introduction to growth and maturity the profits are increasing. But at some time in the maturity stage profits begin to decline. The sales curve, however, does not follow the profit curve. The sales volume continues to rise, even as profit margins begin to decrease. Now, the reason for this phenomenon is well known. Even though sales are increasing, competition is being attracted to the market by the success of the product. At the same time, the product is obsolescent and newer similar products may be being introduced. Further, because of the competition, there will be increased price competition as the market becomes saturated with the product and the competitors endeavor to sell their product over their competition. Eventually, of course, the product becomes unprofitable and is discontinued. What the product life cycle means is that if you want your firm to continue to be profitable, you must continue to offer new products or new services. You cannot be satisfied with one winner.

The product life cycle also shows the need to drop products and why this may be a successful strategy. For example, we may drop a product by simply allowing it to sell out at the normal rate. Or, we could have a grand close-out sale. Or, we could simply withdraw the product from the market entirely and sell it as scrap. Each of these alternatives may have advantages under different situations. Whenever we drop a product, it always frees resources which we can use to pursue other endeavors such as developing or pushing new products.

We can also modify the product. If we modify the product and if it is done properly, this can serve to change the product life cycle and extend it. This is called a product extension strategy, and sometimes the product is not modified so much as is its use in the eyes of the customer. Arm & Hammer Baking Soda used a product extension strategy, not by changing its product or modifying it, but by modifying its use as perceived by the customer. For years people used baking soda for baking and for no other purpose. But, some years ago, Arm & Hammer extended the life cycle of the product by advertising the use of baking soda to absorb odors in refrigerators. Sometimes a product's life cycle can be extended by simply changing the packaging or the advertising. But, remember, regardless of how you extend the product's life cycle, the idea is that you want profit margins to be maintained while sales are increasing. You want to be on the most profitable part of the product's life cycle's profitability curve.

Another product strategy that you can employ is called product differentiation. With this strategy, although you continue to satisfy the needs of your customer with a product similar to that offered by your competition, you differentiate the product from his by playing up its unique advantages. Henry Ford was very successful in introducing the Model-T, but it was a standardized car which left the potential buyer no choice, not even with respect to color. It came only in black. Ford's competitor, General Motors, successfully countered Ford's mass marketing with a product differentiation strategy. They offered the customer a choice of color, type, engine, and so forth. The ways in which you can differentiate your product from the competition are almost limitless. The tack you take may have to do with special features or it may have to do with quality or reliability. What you are saying, basically, is that your product is different. Closely allied with a product differentiation strategy is a strategy known as positioning. Positioning refers to where you put your product in the marketplace in relation to other similar products. In this way, it impacts both marketing segmentation and product differentiation. This book, for example, is positioned as a problem-solving book for small businesspeople or entrepreneurs. Now, there are dozens of books on problem solving and dozens more on small business, but within these two classifications this book fills a special niche. It's positioned as a small business and entrepreneur's problem-solver and in this fashion is differentiated from other similar products.

Price Variables. Just as important as product variables, price variables frequently affect the other variables that you choose. If you choose one price, it positions your product automatically for one market and your product is perceived as one type of product. At a lower price or a higher price, the same product would be perceived entirely differently. Again, there are basic choices. You can price high, you can price low, or you can meet the competition's price. Pricing strategy has to be carefully considered because the price you select has an important effect on the image of the product or service that you are offering. This image helps to determine your market and whether your product will be successful or not. High price may sometimes be a price-skimming strategy. It is very effective if you are first in the marketplace with a new product because, in this situation, you can charge a higher price because you have no competition. As competition enters the marketplace, you can reduce your price to meet your competition and use the profits that you have obtained through your higher price to expand your advertising and maintain your market share. However, this is not the only strategy that you may decide upon when competition enters with a lower price. In some cases, it is possible actually to raise your price. This may position your product as being superior to your competitor's product.

A low price is usually used as a penetration strategy. That is, you use a low price when you are trying to penetrate a marketplace that is already established. In this case, your objective is to get in and take part of your competition's business away. To do this, you must give your potential customers a reason to buy from you rather than from him. If you cannot differentiate your product very much, you can differentiate the price, and with a lower price you will capture at least some customers on a trial basis. However, you should be aware that there are problems with low price. One of them should be clear from reading about the skimming strategy. You are now in a position of entering this market against the competition which has the financial resources to put up a good fight. Also, as you enter the market, even if you are successful you're going to split the market and thus the number of potential customers is much smaller than it would be with one less competitor.

Entering with a meet-the-competition price is simply going in at the same price as your competition with a similar or identical product or service. You can do this only in two situations: (1) if the market is so large and the demand so great that it's not currently being filled by the firms that are operating in this marketplace, and (2) if you can follow some sort of differentiation strategy and offer something that your competition does not. Otherwise, you must consider why your customers should turn from the competition and buy from you. If the competition is offering a good product and its service and other qualities are good, there is no reason for your potential customers to do this. In fact, you should always consider this question when you are entering business: Why should my customer buy from me? If you can think of no reason, then chances are he can't think of a reason, either, and you better stay out of the business.

Distribution Variables. You must decide in what geographical area you will market your product, the types of retail outlets you will use and their number, and also whether it is better to sell directly yourself, go to retail outlets, or go through wholesalers. These are distribution variables, and each has advantages and disadvantages. Sometimes through the use of a unique distribution system you can beat the competition or be far more profitable than through some other distributional option.

Choice of geographical area to market your product involves not only what your desires and total market potential are, but also the resources of your firm. Perhaps initially you have resources only to go into certain select geographical areas that are close to your area of manufacture or close to where your home business is located. Perhaps eventually you intend to market all over the United States or even internationally. Here you must consider the product life cycle and your competition. Expanding slowly because of limited financial resources may give an opportunity for your competition to get into and split your market. In other words, by the time you have the resources to go international or even national, your competition is already there and you are in the saturation or even the decline stage of the product life cycle. You must weigh this against your ability to get the necessary financial resources to go national or international distribution very quickly.

The types and numbers of retail outlets are important for many reasons, including image and your ability to sell the product. Sometimes selling through one channel of distribution precludes selling through another. Usually this is because of interchannel rivalry. If you sell your product to a retail outlet, the fact that your product is also sold down the street at a discount store will not be favorably perceived by the retailer. He doesn't need the competition. In the same way, a manufacturer's representative or agent who is selling your product may be less enthusiastic about pushing it to his customers if he knows that you are selling the same product to the same customers through another channel or through other representatives in his area. For this reason, some channels of distribution will insist upon the exclusive right to sell your product. Even if you are successful in getting multiple channels, their enthusiasm for pushing your product over other products that they handle may not be as great. To get established in the market quickly, you may want to use all channels and risk interservice rivalry and the problems associated with it. Once established in the marketplace, you may limit distribution and the outlets used in order to maximize long-run profitability.

Whether to sell direct or to sell through retail outlets or wholesale is another distribution strategy decision. Profitability, per se, may be maximized if you sell your product directly to the customer. On the other hand, you may not have the financial resources to do this. Or, if you do, you may not be able to reach the sales volume you could through an indirect channel. You may make $10 per product selling direct versus only $2 per product selling through a wholesaler or retailer outlet. But if the volume is ten times as high through a wholesale or retail outlet, you will make a lot more money overall by choosing one of these methods of distribution.

Promotional Variables. The promotional variable is frequently divided into advertising, personal selling, and sales promotion. Each of these has advantages and disadvantages.

Advertising includes not only the different media selected, that is, print, radio, television, and so forth, but also which specific magazines, radio stations, and TV channels. In addition, advertising strategy includes the different graphic or copy presentations that are used, as well as the different types of appeals that are made to the potential customers, and timing. All are discussed in detail elsewhere in this book.

Personal selling has a major advantage in that immediate feedback is available from the potential customer. It also has disadvantages since this strategy requires training a sales force, hiring a sales manager, and other expenses. A personal selling strategy is particularly effective and necessary when a product must be explained to be fully understood by the potential customer.

Sales promotion includes a number of different forms, among them window and interior displays, free samples, contests, and discounts. Like other strategies, it is not free, but costs certain amounts of your resources to use it. So the cost must be carefully weighed against the gain in sales for its use.

With some products, the use of sales promotion will be a major advantage. For others, the advantage is nonexistent.

Since all strategies may be followed to one extent or another in helping a product or a business to be successful, you may wonder why you shouldn't do everything. Why not have the perfect situation by having a product with unique features, low price, promoted advertising with salespeople, through sales promotion, and so forth? The answer is: allocation of resources. You cannot be strong everywhere. No one can, not your firm, not General Motors, not even the United States government. You cannot use every single possible strategic variable to help your product be successful because you simply do not have the resources. Therefore, you have to be selective. In some areas you may have to execute a holding action in order to allocate your resources in other areas. This, then, becomes your strategy. You may elect to continue a product which is already on the decline, but through allocating a great many resources to advertising still maintains acceptable profitability or more profitability than you might realize over the short term

Task	Weeks after Project Initiation and Amount Required												
	1	2	3	4	5	6	7	8	9	10	11	12	13
Place first ad		$300											
Order product for test		$50											
Order follow-on material			$75										
Place additional ads													$1,200
Order additional product													$200
Order additional follow-on material													$350

Figure 4.2.   Budget for business plan.

if you switched this money from advertising to new product development. The careful selection of the proper strategy for each situation will lead you to success.

Budget

As indicated previously, every single strategy costs some resources. It is very important to indicate exactly what these resources are in hard dollar amounts. For this reason, it is essential to establish a budget for your total strategic plan, indicating exactly how much each single task will cost and when these funds will be required. One way of doing this is indicated in Figure 4.2.

Financial Plans

The financial planning section should include not only the budget for the strategies, but also such items as a projected income statement as shown in Figure 4.3, a cash flow projection as shown in Figure 4.4, and a balance sheet as shown in Figure 4.5. Use of these forms is discussed in detail in Chapter 9 and Chapter 11. Financial planning gives the entire financial picture for your firm and will assist you not only directly with management control, but also in allowing potential investors to see your overall financial condition immediately.

Sometimes it is also useful to put a break-even analysis in this section. A break-even analysis is a method for evaluating relationships among sales revenues, fixed costs, and variable costs. The break-even point is the point at which the number of units sold covers all costs of developing, producing, and selling the product. Above this point, you will make money and below it you will lose money. The break-even analysis is also covered in detail in Chapter 11.

Strategy Implementation Time Schedule

The final section in your business plan should be a time schedule which shows an overview of your strategy implementation and the time when each task will be

Months after Starting Business

	1	2	3	4	5	6	7	8	9	10	11	12
Total net sales												
Cost of sales												
Gross profit												
Expenses (controllable)												
Salaries												
Payroll taxes												
Advertising												
Automobile												
Dues and subscriptions												
Entertainment												
Legal and accounting												
Office supplies												
Telephone												
Utilities												
Miscellaneous												
Total												
Expenses (fixed)												
Depreciation												
Insurance												
Rent												
Taxes and licenses												
Loan payments												
Total												
Net profit (loss) (before taxes)												

Figure 4.3. Project income statement.

completed. This is shown in Figure 4.6. The strategy implementation time schedule is extremely important in letting you know when you are supposed to do what will greatly assist you with management control, as well as showing potential investors that you really know what you're doing.

Below are some general comments about writing a business plan:

1. Always provide a table of contents. Most investors won't read every word, but rather specific areas that they are interested in. If you do not include a table of contents, they may overlook this area, feeling that you have eliminated it or omitted it from your business plan.

2. Establish your credibility. Remember that your firm and you have unique advantages—if not, you should not be in business. State these advantages clearly.

3. Documents supporting facts about new concepts or ideas. Remember that not everyone reading the plan has your knowledge or your experience. Therefore, new concepts or ideas should be carefully documented from established sources such as published reference works.

4. Establish your authority. Make certain that you emphasize why you personally have what it takes to succeed in this business.

	Start-up or prior to loan	1	2	3	4	5	6	7	8	9	10	11	12	Total
Months after Starting Business														
Cash (beginning of month) Cash on hand														
Cash in bank														
Cash in investments														
Total Cash														
Income (during month) Cash sales														
Credit sales payments														
Investment income														
Loans														
Other cash income														
Total Income														
Total cash and income														
Expenses (during month) Inventory or new material														
Wages (including owner's)														
Taxes														
Equipment expense														
Overhead														
Selling expense														
Transportation														
Loan repayment														
Other cash expenses														
Total expenses														
Cash flow excess (end of month)														
Cash flow cumulative (monthly)														

Figure 4.4. Cash flow projections.

5. Be optimistic, but truthful. Do not lie in your business plan. Rather, if there are disadvantages or problems that you anticipate, indicate them clearly, but also indicate how you will overcome them.

6. Emphasize your uniqueness. You have something that is different in some way from what everyone else has. Play up this difference.

7. Make sure your plan is workable. It is essential to have a business plan, but it is useless if it is not workable. After you've gone through and completed the plan, be sure that the plan fits together and that each part is reasonable and can work. Be especially critical of the cash flow and the financial aspects, as well as the anticipated sales. One of the biggest problems with business plans is sales realism. That is, the owner anticipates much higher sales than can realistically be expected. Analyze your plan by asking yourself what would happen if sales were 20%, 30%, 40%, or even 50% less than you have forecast. Analyze your costs to make sure they are also reasonable. Just as sales are frequently inflated during business planning, costs are sometimes deflated and listed too low for a successful business.

8. Update your plan. No business plan is good forever. Furthermore, the planning is never perfect and cannot foresee all circumstances that you will encounter. Therefore, as you put your plan into action, you will have to revise it to

	Year I	Year II
Current assets		
Cash	$ _____	$ _____
Accounts receivable	_____	_____
Inventory	_____	_____
Fixed assets		
Real estate	_____	_____
Fixture and equipment	_____	_____
Vehicles	_____	_____
Other assets		
License	_____	_____
Good will	_____	_____
Total assets	$ _____	$ _____
Current liabilities		
Notes payable (due within 1 year)	$ _____	$ _____
Accounts payable	_____	_____
Accrued expenses	_____	_____
Taxes owed	_____	_____
Long-term liabilities		
Notes payable (due after 1 year)	_____	_____
Other	_____	_____
Total liabilities	$ _____	$ _____
Net worth (assets minus liabilities)	$ _____	$ _____

Total liabilities plus net worth should equal assets

Figure 4.5. Balance sheet (project at start-up and after one year).

keep it up-to-date. This is true of all plans, not only business plans. In fact, the famous military writer and analyst, Von Clausewitz, called the difference between what actually happens once a war plan is implemented and the war plan itself "battle friction." This phenomenon is normal and will be encountered in every business. Therefore, to make sure that your plan is continually successful, you must keep alert and watch for changes on a day-to-day basis. This is not to say that your plan has to be changed daily; you should, however, be on top of conditions that are changing and adjust your plan accordingly when it is appropriate. To do this, you should: (a) be alert to the changes that come about in your industry, market, customers, competition, technology, and other important factors; (b) check your plan against these changes to make sure that the plan is still workable; (c) determine what revisions are necessary in your plan and make these if needed.

Weeks after Project Initiation

Task	1	2	3	4	5	6	7	8	9	10	11	12	13	14	15	16	17	18	19	20	21	22	23	24	25	26	27
Prepare classified copy	→																										
Place first ad		→																									
Order product for test		→																									
Prepare and order follow-on material			→																								
Product inventory received					→																						
Follow-on material received					→																						
First ad appears								→																			
Send follow-on material											→————————————————————————————→																
Profitability forecast											→—→																
Additional ads placed													→														
Additional product inventory ordered													→														
Additional follow-on material ordered													→														
Product inventory received															→												
Follow-on material received															→												
Additional ads appear																			——————→							
Send follow-on material																			——————————————————→						

Figure 4.6. Strategy implementation time schedule.

9. Get started. Your business plan is useless until you put it into action. You should make your plan as accurate as you can. However, no plan is perfect, so don't wait until every "i" is dotted and every "t" is crossed. When you are close enough that the plan is clearly workable, you should act upon it. Use your strategy implementation time schedule to help you. In this way, you will turn your business plan from a basic idea or concept which you have documented into a successful business.

Alternative Form for the Business Plan

Appendix VI is an alternative form of the business plan prepared by the SBA and used to qualify the small firm for special kinds of free SBA services.

SOURCES OF ADDITIONAL INFORMATION

How to Organize and Operate a Small Business, 5th edition, by Clifford M. Baumback, Kenneth Lawyer, and Pearce C. Kelley, published by Prentice-Hall, Inc., Englewood Cliffs, NJ 07632.

How to Run a Small Business, 4th edition, by the J. K. Lasser Tax Institute, published by McGraw-Hill Book Co., 1221 Avenue of the Americas, New York NY 10020.

How to Start, Finance, and Manage Your Own Small Business, by Joseph R. Mancuso, published by Prentice-Hall, Inc., Englewood Cliffs, NJ 07632.

Small Business Management Fundamentals, 2nd edition, by Dan Steinhoff, published by McGraw-Hill Book Co., 1221 Avenue of the Americas, New York, NY 10020.

Successful Marketing for Small Business, by William A. Cohen and Marshall E. Reddick, published by AMACOM, a division of the American Management Associations, 135 W. 50th St., New York, NY 10020.

The Entrepreneur's Manual, by Richard M. White, Jr., published by Chilton Book Co., Radnor, PA 19089.

Up Your Own Organization, by Donald M. Dible, published by The Entrepreneur Press, 3422 Astoria Circle, Fairfield, CA 94533.

Winning the Money Game, edited by Donald M. Dible, published by The Entrepreneur Press, 3422 Astoria Circle, Fairfield, CA 94533.

5

Recruiting Employees

Since recruiting can have a major impact on the future, effectiveness and efficiency of your firm, this activity is among the most important to which you can devote yourself as the head of your own company. This process can be divided into four basic steps:

1. Establishing personnel requirements
2. Establishing job specifications
3. Recruiting
4. Hiring

ESTABLISHING PERSONNEL REQUIREMENTS

The first step in the improvement process is to plan ahead for your company's needs. To do this, it is best to set a time period of from several months to a year and decide what your organization's objectives will be during this period and what the attainment of these objectives will involve. For example, if you are expanding, will you require more salespeople over the coming months or years? More production people? Are you going to develop a new product and will you need more technical people? Whatever future activities you plan, you must insure that you have the necessary personnel on board. Now is the time to start laying out your future personnel requirements.

The way to establish these personnel requirements is first to establish what your company is going to do and then to break down the overall objective into smaller steps or tasks. You then describe the kind of individual you will need to perform the task and estimate how many labor-hours will be needed from that person for each month over the period that you have selected. For additional details on how to accomplish this, see Chapter 10. If you already have individuals in your company who can do the job, you merely indicate this. But if you do have needs in the personnel area, the method shown in the chart in Figure 5.1 will enable you to lay them out clearly so that you will know exactly when you need new employees and the particular skills that they will need to have.

In some cases your need will be unforeseen, because of a termination, someone leaving, or unexpected new business. When this happens, you must readjust your forecasts, or in the case of new business, complete a new chart to help you determine the personnel requirements of the job. With the forecast chart, you will always know your requirements in detail.

Project/Task	Type of Individual Required	Hours of Work Estimated by Month											
		Jan.	Feb.	Mar.	Apr.	May	June	July	Aug.	Sep.	Oct.	Nov.	Dec.
Monthly Labor Requirements by Title (1)													
Current Labor Resources on Hand (2)													
Additional Labor Required (1) − (2)													

Figure 5.1. Chart for forecasting labor requirements.

ESTABLISHING JOB SPECIFICATIONS

At this point, you should have a list of individuals you need for the coming year as well as the month that they should be hired.

Your task now is to write a detailed description of the job you want these individuals to perform along with other factors that you consider important. For this purpose, you can use Figure 5.2, the job specification form, which details the job title, to whom the individual will report, the background on why you need the individual, the tasks that the individual will perform, desired prior experience, desired education, special problems, factors that would definitely exclude a candidate from consideration regardless of other qualifications or accomplishments, travel requirements, salary range, other compensation, and some ideas about why someone should take the job.

1. **Job title:** _____   2. **Required by:** _____

3. **Reporting to:** _____

4. **Background:** _____

_____

_____

Figure 5.2. Job specification form.

5. **Required Tasks:** _____

_____

_____

_____

_____

6. **Desired prior experience:** _____

_____

_____

_____

7. **Desired education:** _____

_____

_____

8. **Special problems:** _____

_____

_____

_____

9. **Factors that would definitely exclude a candidate from consideration:** _____

_____

_____

Figure 5.2. (Continued)

10. **Travel requirements:** _____

11. **Salary range:** _____

12. **Other compensation:** _____

_____

_____

13. **Why should someone take this job?** _____

_____

_____

_____

_____

Figure 5.2.   (Continued)

Figure 5.3 shows a completed job specification form. Note that even in the form the requirements are not cast in iron. You may change the job title at any time, and tasks can be added or reduced in number or in scope. Prior experience and education also should be flexible since it is what you want the individual to do and not what he or she has done already that is important. Past experience and education are important only as indicators of potential to perform work. For this reason, requirements such as a certain number of years of experience should always be flexible. The salary that you intend to pay should be noted as a range rather than as a specific value, but even the range should be considered only as a guideline, and as you interview and talk to various candidates, you can begin to narrow the salary range that you consider appropriate. Information about the advantages of taking the job is also very important, because it allows you to put yourself in the candidate's shoes and see things from his or her perspective. Why would the type of individual that you have specified here want to go to work for you? If there are few perceived advantages, you are not going to get the kind of individual you want. If you want good people, then there should be sufficient reasons motivating them to work for your company rather than going somewhere else or staying at their present place of employment. This section will be very useful for you in your recruiting, whether you do it yourself or go through someone else, such as a personnel agency, counselor, or headhunter.

1. **Job title:** Copywriter   2. **Required by:** Jan 1st, 1987

3. **Reporting to:** Creative Director

4. **Background:** The amount of copywriting required for ads for our client has

increased to such a degree that our one copyrwiter can no longer handle it

by himself. As a result, we are suffering delays up to 30 days causing

considerable dissatisfaction with our service. Therefore our need is urgent.

5. **Required tasks:** The individual will be responsible for all copywriting

having to do with industrial sales. This includes space advertising, direct

mail, telephone, and television.

6. **Desired prior experience:** This individual must have prior experience

with copywriting for industrial products and services. Two to five years would

probably be ideal, but if the individual is really talented, we could take

someone with only one year's experience.

7. **Desired education:** College graduate. Journalism,

english, marketing, communications, advertising,

business, or psychology. However, the field isn't important.

Figure 5.3. Completed job specification form.

8. **Special problems:** The creative director is sometimes hard to get along with.

We don't want any temperamental genius.

9. **Factors that would definitely exclude a candidate from consideration:**

No college degree. Less than one year's experience as a copywriter. Too sensitive

or temperamental.

10. **Travel requirements:** Maximum 5% of time.

11. **Salary range:** $25,000–30,000 per year.

12. **Other compensation:** Health and life insurance. Retirement plan.

21 days' paid vacation per year.

13. **Why should someone take this job?** As proved by this hire, we are a growing

company. Therefore there is an opportunity for growth into management. We are

giving more days of paid vacation than anyone else in the industry (standard

is 14 days). This will be our expert for industrial copywriting. The creative

director is a graphic designer, and the other copywriter will deal only with

consumer products.

Figure 5.3.   (Continued)

RECRUITING

Sources of Personnel

The following are all sources of personnel which you should consider:

1. Personnel currently in your own company
2. Personnel in other companies

3. Newly graduated individuals or students about to graduate from colleges or universities
4. Currently unemployed individuals
5. Job shop companies

Personnel Currently in Your Own Company. Staffing from within your own company is a good idea in many instances, and certainly when personnel for tasks required are currently available. This not only saves you money in recruiting but can also motivate all of your employees if the new job is a promotion and the individual within your company can handle the job. There are additional advantages. An individual recruited internally is already familiar with the practices, procedures, personnel, policy, special characteristics, and other employees of your company. Therefore, in general, there will be less time required to bring the individual up to speed for the job that you want him to perform. However, when recruiting from your own company, you must be concerned with who will take over the job that the individual was doing. You must also be sure that the change of job will create no problems. Does the individual really want the job? Do not automatically assume this to be the case, even if it means a promotion. Will other employees present problems that this individual must deal with in his or her new role? This is something else you must consider.

Personnel from Other Companies. In many instances, the necessary personnel do not exist within your own company and you must go outside the organization to recruit them. Going outside the organization has advantages. If you have sufficient time, you can hire an individual who has been successful in an identical or similar job with another company. This can increase his chances of success in the job that you have planned. In addition, bringing new people into your company will also bring in new ideas that they have picked up from other companies. Of course, there are disadvantages to recruiting outside of your company. These include the additional expense, the fact that the new personnel are unfamiliar with your company's way of operating, and possibly dissatisfaction on the part of current employees.

In our society, it is generally accepted that an individual can move from one company to another if the new company can offer a better job opportunity, and that any individual is free to go from one company to another for personal betterment. However, in considering individuals from other companies, you should attempt to ascertain his or her current state of mind, because it will affect the candidate's readiness to come to your company and it will also influence how you handle the employment interview. Remember, just because an executive recruiter is successful in going into a firm and pulling out an individual for a specific job, this does *not* mean that the individual was unhappy in his or her job. Quite the opposite may have been true. The individual may have been perfectly happy in his or her old job, and executive recruiters often argue that these individuals make the best new employees; if they were happy in their former employment they should be happy in your employ as well. With a job candidate who is currently happily employed, you need to present the job situation in its best light. This is where your reasons why someone should take this job are very important.

Newly Graduated Individuals or Students About to Graduate from Colleges or Universities. Most individuals newly graduated from institutions of higher learning go to larger companies, since larger companies offer training programs which initiate them into the industry and functional area they have chosen and can usually offer higher salaries. Also, because large companies send recruiters out all over the country in search of newly graduated talent, it is difficult for you as a small company to compete for this source of candidates. However, you can offer certain advantages to a college graduate that a larger company cannot offer. These include the possibility of rapid advancement, better visibility to top management, and more responsibility earlier. In fact, many individuals from college consider small companies more fun to work in and even seek them out. Further, if there are colleges or universities close by, you will not even have to bear a heavy travel expense to do this type of recruiting. All you need to do is to call the placement offices of colleges and universities in your geographical area. By emphasizing what you have to offer, you can successfully (and inexpensively) compete with larger companies for many top quality college graduates.

Currently Unemployed Individuals. A potential employee for your company may be currently unemployed because he or she was fired, quit, or was laid off from a previous job. None of these reasons need reflect unfavorably on your candidate. However, it should be routine to find out as much as you can about the former employment and why the individual left the former job. Many companies do not like to hire unemployed individuals, preferring individuals who are currently holding a job. However, this is a prejudice which has no validity. Many unemployed individuals are outstanding candidates, even for high-level jobs in your company.

Job Shop Companies. Job shop companies are known by various names, some less than flattering, but they are a source of skilled temporary help, even though in many large companies job shop individuals are used for periods as long as a year or more. What the job shop offers you is an individual who is rented out to you on an as-needed basis. The job shop company hires the individual and pays all fringe benefits concerned as well as salary. The advantage to the individual is that he or she is paid at a slightly higher rate than if he or she were working for one company and is guaranteed continued employment with less chance of a layoff from work than might otherwise be the case. To you, the advantage is that you will have personnel for short-term projects but you will not need to retain them when there is no more work for them. Of course, there is a disadvantage as well, and that is that it is difficult to make a "job shopper" an integral part of your company. He or she is unlikely to be as committed to your goals as your permanent employees since the term of employment is most definitely limited. Also, it is more difficult to control proprietary information with your company when you're using job shoppers. For more details on this, see Chapter 10.

Selection of the Right Recruiting Method

The recruiting methods that you should use will depend on many factors including your company, industry, the type of employee you seek, the job market at the time that you're doing your recruiting, and how long you are willing to look.

The methods discussed in the following paragraphs each have their own advantages and disadvantages. Some methods are very time consuming: advertising in certain magazines read by individuals owning the specialty for which you're looking, for example. The lead time for the ad to appear may be several months. Other methods may be very expensive: executive recruiting firms, for instance. You may be expected to pay as much as 30% of the annual compensation of the candidate in return for the firm's finding you a suitable candidate. Even employment agencies will require a fee of from 10 to 15% of annual compensation for their services. Some methods such as word of mouth which costs nothing are fine if you are not in a hurry, but may not be desirable at all if you need someone at once.

Word-of-Mouth Recruiting

Word of mouth is perhaps the easiest and the least expensive recruitment method. You or someone in your employ simply calls around to likely sources such as friends and professional associates and asks them if they would be interested in the position that you have, or if they know someone else who would be who meets the qualifications that you seek. This method has several advantages. As indicated before, it doesn't cost anything. It is also easy. There is no special procedure involved; anyone can do it. And either you know the individual yourself or your friends or associates know the individual. However, there are also disadvantages with this type of recruiting campaign. First, you will not reach as many potential candidates as you might otherwise. Also, if you are receiving recommendations from people who are friends of the candidate, the qualifications of the candidate may be somewhat colored by this relationship. If for one reason or another you want your hiring to be done without the knowledge of others, potential competitors or potential customers, you will not be able to use word of mouth. Finally, this process may not work very quickly.

Advertising for Candidates

Advertising for new candidates is expensive, but if your advertisement is reasonably well put together it will bring in applicants to fill the position for which you are advertising. If you are in a hurry, then you will probably run display or classified advertisements in the business section of your local paper or the *Wall Street Journal*. On the other hand, if you have time, then it may be wise to consider advertising in professional magazines that are read by individuals in the desired field. Such magazines may require a month to six weeks or more of lead time before the advertisement appears.

It is possible when you advertise to keep secret the fact that you are searching for new employees to fill certain designated positions. You can run a "blind ad" which gives a box number instead of the name of your company. The box number is provided by the newspaper or magazine that you have chosen. For a slight additional fee, they will collect all the responses to your ad and forward them to you. When considering a blind advertisement versus an open advertisement, however, you must also recognize that a blind advertisement will pull fewer responses than an open advertisement, since some potential candidates will be concerned about the identity of the advertiser. Needless to say, they have no desire for their present company to know that they have responded as a potential candidate for a new job.

If you are going to advertise, you should know what the competition is for the employees you seek to hire. This competition can be readily assessed by viewing the help wanted section of the Sunday edition of your local newspaper. Check the classified ads under the appropriate job description and also the display ads in the business section. By studying competitive ads you will get a general idea of what jobs are being offered in your geographical area. It is important once again for you to ask yourself the question: "Why should someone respond to my ad and go to work for me?'' Use the information that you've put together in your job specification form to construct an ad that's interesting and well written, one that will attract many qualified candidates for the job that you are seeking to fill. Use the AIDA formula. AIDA stands for attention, interest, desire, and action. You write your ad with a headline to attract attention. Elaborate on the headline with job benefits to arouse interest and then state more benefits and the qualifications you are seeking. Finally, invite the prospective job candidate to act by asking for his or her résumé and salary history.

One major advantage of advertising is that you will be able to locate candidates fairly rapidly for the position. Also, the method is reasonably certain. Unless the competition is overwhelming, your ad is really poorly constructed and written, or the terms that you advertise are just not competitive, you are going to get enough responses to enable you to fill the position.

The biggest disadvantage of advertising as a method of securing candidates is the cost. Even a single display ad can run a thousand dollars or more. Another disadvantage is the fact that you will only reach candidates who are seeking a position. This would appear to be an advantage—isn't that what you want, after all, individuals who are looking for work? However, for some positions, you may want to recruit individuals who are perfectly happy and content and performing well for other companies. This may be especially true for high-level jobs. You will not reach such individuals through advertising since they will not be looking in the employment section of newspapers. Also, even if by chance such an individual reads your ad, rarely will the information be sufficient an enticement to encourage this candidate to make up a résumé to send to you. Finally, if you are seeking a job specialty which is in great demand at the time of your search, you may not be able to find sufficient potential candidates or qualified candidates through advertising.

Government Employment Agencies

Government employment agencies, local and state, may be of assistance in finding suitable employees for your company. The quality of candidates that they provide varies widely from place to place and time to time. Candidates from government employment agencies generally appear to be somewhat less well qualified for professional positions than candidates from other sources. The reason for this is that many professionals do not register with government employment agencies except as a last resort. However, it is always worthwhile checking with government employment agencies. It costs you nothing and you may find just the right candidate.

Employment Agencies and Executive Recruiters

Although employment agencies and executive recruiters are collectively known as headhunters and in both cases you pay money for their services, the two differ in a number of ways.

Executive recruiters or executive search firms in general go after higher level candidates than do employment agencies. In theory, executive recruiters or search firms will actually go into other companies by telephone and find and recruit exactly the right candidate for you. For these services, you may pay 30% of the annual compensation or more. Many times these firms will operate only on retainer, and you must pay them a basic fee whether or not a candidate is sent to you that you ultimately hire. For this reason, this type of recruiter should be reserved for very top candidates and used only at a time when you can afford this special service.

Employment agencies may recruit from other companies as well, but they tend to rely primarily on applicants who register with them, and while some may require a retainer in the same way as search firms, most operate on contingency only. This means that you only pay the employment agency if you hire a candidate that the employment agency sends to you for an interview. Obviously this has major advantages for the small firm which cannot afford to finance a search which may not be successful. Each individual agency has its own fee schedule; they generally start at a low 10% and may go as high as 30%.

The difference today between an executive search firm and an agency is in some cases very blurred. Many executive search firms work on contingency as well as on retainer. Many employment agencies will recruit for very top level positions that pay $100,000 a year or more, even though the average employee that they place makes much less. However, many states require that any organization that recruits candidates compensated below a certain amount must obtain a state agency license, while above that amount an agency license is unnecessary.

There are also agencies around that collect fees from the individual job applicant. You must be much more careful with the candidates that you interview coming from this source because the agency is far more likely to try to sell you a candidate than to send you the best person available for the job.

If you are dealing with a professional recruiter, whether he is in a search firm or an agency, this source of candidates can offer a number of advantages to you. For one thing, you can be very precise in the requirements that you set for potential candidates. This can save you a great deal of time screening numerous résumés and interviewing applicants who are not qualified for the job. Also, if you yourself recruit from a competing firm, you can run into legal difficulties. However, if a search firm or employment agency does this for you, you are probably off the hook legally. Finally, there is usually some type of guarantee if you hire the candidate and he or she quits work after a short period of time, or for some reason proves to be unsatisfactory. This is something you most definitely should investigate prior to giving the okay to any type of headhunter. Guarantees may run up to as long as a year, with the firm required to return your money or to recruit a new candidate for you.

One final word of caution on using a headhunter or search firm. Get some idea before you pay a retainer as to how fast the recruiter is going to work and when you can expect to interview the first candidate.

You should expect any personnel agency, employment agency, or search firm that you deal with to screen the candidates for you. How much screening you get really depends upon the agency involved. On the low end, if you are paying something like 10%, probably all you're going to get is basic screening of résumés. On the high end, with an executive search firm on a retainer, you can expect many candidates to be approached, some candidates to be screened face to face, references to be checked, and three to five candidates, all of whom meet your qualifications, to be submitted to you for your consideration. Other firms' services will fall somewhere in the middle. Perhaps references will be checked, candidates will be talked to and screened, but the screening will not be done in as thorough a manner as would be the case if you were paying on a retainer basis.

Another organization that you should consider contacting is a national organization known as "Forty Plus." This is a self-help agency composed of individuals who have reached the age of 40 or older and who are currently unemployed. These individuals pay a small fee and may donate their time to helping out the organization. The result is that you will see qualified candidates, and even if you hire them, you pay nothing.

If you're going to use a headhunter, it is well to talk to other small business-people who have also used headhunters since the quality varies so much.

Recruiting Through the Schools

School recruiting is an excellent way for a small businessperson to acquire out-standing candidates for professional positions. For one thing, such candidates are frequently well trained, having received their bachelor's degree or an advanced degree, and eager to start work. They can be easily motivated to do a good job for you and yet their salaries are much lower than you would have to pay for a more experienced but perhaps less well qualified employee.

As pointed out earlier, you do not need to run around the country recruiting as does a major company. In fact, you need not do any face-to-face recruiting at all. If you are fortunate enough to live near a large city where there are many colleges and universities, place a telephone call to the career development office or to the department that teaches a subject likely to produce candidates for the job that you have open. This can produce very good results. Over the phone, you should indicate that you have a position open, what the qualifications are, some advan-tages for coming to work for you, and where you can be reached in order to set up an interview.

Depending upon how lucrative the position is and the job market in your area for these new graduates, you may or may not get a number of candidates for your job. However, this is a very easy way to recruit, and a very inexpensive one. You should not overlook it when seeking potential employees.

Professional Associations

Many professional associations will allow you to place recruiting advertisements in their newsletters or will act as a clearinghouse for job openings as a service to the members of the association. In many cases, this will cost you nothing—a major advantage for using this method. The disadvantage, as with many other low-cost methods, is that there are no assurances that you will get large numbers of candidates. In fact, you may not receive any applicants at all for the job. But you should consider professional associations as a supplemental source of job candidates.

Some Additional Recruiting Tips

1. Make sure you know exactly what you are looking for and the skills re-quired, and develop a complete job specification as on the form shown every time it's necessary for you to do recruiting.

2. Make certain that whoever answers the phone at your company has full information about the position so that he or she can answer inquiries about it if you are unavailable.

3. If your recruiting is going to bring in large numbers of résumés of candi-dates, then set minimum standards for these candidates and establish a list of these minimum standards so that someone else can screen these in-quiries for you.

4. Let your other employees know about the position and give them a brief

description from your job specification so that they can do free recruiting for you.

5. Select your recruiting methods based on your particular situation, but be certain to use all appropriate means of bringing in job candidates, especially those that are free.

6. If an advertisement under one heading fails to bring in an adequate number of qualified candidates, then try a different job heading or a slightly different job title.

7. If you decide to use a recruiter or an employment agency, visit the firm so that you can know better the headhunter who will be working for you. Also, ask if they can supply you with three names of clients not in your business who have been happy with their operation whom you may contact.

8. If you do a great deal of hiring, conduct an audit from time to time to see what your hiring costs are and which recruiting methods work best.

9. When you receive job applicants from organizations or associations which do not get paid, be certain to thank them for their time and effort in referring candidates or applicants to you.

HIRING

The hiring process consists of three steps: screening, interviewing, and making the offer. Let's look at each in turn.

Applicant Screening

If you used an employment agency or a search firm, the applicants have already been screened prior to the interview. In this case, you will be presented with a number of candidates and the amount of work that you will have to do along these lines is greatly reduced. On the other hand, if you've used any of the other methods, then you will have received résumés—sometimes quite a few. For example, a really good job at the professional level may bring in 500 to 800 résumés if you are located in a large urban area. Going through this number of résumés is a time-consuming and exacting task. However, if you establish basic requirements and communicate them to someone else, it may be easier and less expensive for a secretary or some other employee of yours to go through these résumés for you and reduce them to a reasonable amount. If the initial screening fails to weed out very many, then you can tighten up on the requirements and continue screening until you have a workable number. Remember that interviewing a candidate for a job also takes time. Therefore, the initial screening should pare the number of candidates down so that you see no more than 6 to 10. Some companies have the personnel manager do the initial screening, selecting 10 candidates from the résumés, and then the personnel manager sees these 10 himself or herself, and selects five candidates who will be interviewed by the executive doing the hiring. Use your own judgment in this, but don't spend all of your time interviewing, especially if it is not for a top-level job.

Opinions differ as to whether you should talk to references of the applicants prior to the interview. My feeling is not to do so until mutual interest has been established. Even if you only call three references for each candidate, when you are considering five candidates, that's 15 different telephone calls. Also, many candidates or applicants will not give you references until mutual interest is established as a result of the interview. The reason for this is that they do not want their references bothered by every single company with whom they interview. However, regardless of when you do a reference check, make certain that it is done prior to hiring. In fact, if you delay the reference check until after the offer, the offer should be contingent upon favorable references. Perhaps the best method is to interview the candidates and get permission to check references of one or two candidates you are seriously interested in. Assuming the references check out, you can extend the offer. Regardless of when the reference check is made, the following items should be checked:

1. How long the reference has known the candidate
2. Under what circumstances he or she has known the candidate
3. The candidate's personal qualities—honesty, reliability, dependability, and so forth
4. The candidate's general background
5. Specific items that you feel are relevant to this particular position, including years on the job, managerial experience if applicable, and what exactly the individual accomplished while working on the job.

Don't be surprised if occasionally a reference does not check out, even though the candidate appears outstanding for the job. Sometimes a reference that the candidate feels will be a good one turns out to be a negative one because of jealousy or some other reason. When that happens, look at the overall situation. If two out of three references are positive and only one is bad, you might want to get back and ask for additional references. On the other hand, if the general pattern of references is bad, you may wish to drop the candidate.

Another thing you must not overlook when checking references is questioning individuals who have supervised the candidate in the past. A candidate would have to be very foolish to give you the name of someone he knows will not give a good reference. However, he or she doesn't always have the same control when dealing with former employers.

Interviewing the Candidate

To get the maximum out of the interview, you must prepare for and plan the interview ahead of time.

One of the most important steps and one that is frequently overlooked is to be sure that you will not be continually interrupted during the interview. If you are, your train of thought will be broken, and the candidate will be impressed with your lack of consideration for him or her. It may cause the candidate to turn down the offer even though he or she is ideal for the job.

If you have time prior to the interview, mail out a job applicant's form about a week before the interview and ask the candidate to complete the form and return it to you. The job applicant's form is more valuable than a résumé in that it forces the candidate to list more complete information in some sort of chronological order. A clever applicant for a job can structure his or her résumé around your requirements and keep information that may negatively affect his or her chances at the job out of your reach. But it is to your advantage to get all the information that you can. A suitable form is shown in Figure 5.4.

Before the actual interview, you should review this application form and the

PROFESSIONAL EMPLOYMENT APPLICATION 1-93122 R7

PERSONAL RECORD

LAST NAME	FIRST NAME	MIDDLE OR MAIDEN NAME	SOCIAL SECURITY NUMBER	DATE

PRESENT ADDRESS: STREET NO. STREET APT.# CITY STATE ZIP | AREA CODE | PHONE | DATE OF BIRTH MO DAY YEAR

PERMANENT ADDRESS: STREET NO. STREET APT.# CITY STATE ZIP | AREA CODE | PHONE | MARITAL STATUS S M W D SEP

TYPE OF WORK DESIRED | DATE AVAIL. FOR EMPL | NO. DEPENDENTS

SECURITY CLEARANCE ☐ YES ☐ NO IF YES, SHOW: | LEVEL | ISSUING AUTHORITY | DATE | U.S. CITIZEN | BIRTH CERTIF. AVAILABLE? | WOULD YOU OBJECT TO A PHYS. EXAM. BY OUR DR.?

| NAME ANY PHYSICAL DISABILITIES | HEIGHT | WEIGHT | TIME LOST FROM WORK DURING LAST TWELVE MONTHS DUE TO ILLNESS | PRESENT DRAFT CLASSIFICATION | RESERVE STATUS ☐ ACTIVE ☐ INACTIVE ☐ READY ☐ STANDBY |

MILITARY SERVICE BRANCH	PRINCIPAL MILITARY EXPERIENCE	MILITARY RANK	MILITARY SERVICE DATES FROM TO	TYPE OF DISCHARGE
MILITARY SERVICE BRANCH	PRINCIPAL MILITARY EXPERIENCE	MILITARY RANK	MILITARY SERVICE DATES FROM TO	TYPE OF DISCHARGE
MILITARY SERVICE BRANCH	PRINCIPAL MILITARY EXPERIENCE	MILITARY RANK	MILITARY SERVICE DATES FROM TO	TYPE OF DISCHARGE

HAVE YOU EVER WORKED FOR ANY LTV COMPANY? ☐ YES ☐ NO | FROM | TO | WHAT DIVISION? | TYPE OF WORK

EDUCATION –

HIGH SCHOOL NAME	HIGH SCHOOL CITY	HIGH SCHOOL STATE	HIGH SCHOOL GRADUATION DAY MONTH YEAR	YEARS OF H.S. COMPLETED

COLLEGE/UNIVERSITY NAME	CITY AND STATE	YEARS ATTENDED FROM MO/YR	TO MO/YR	MAJOR FIELD OF EDUCATION	HOURS FOR DEGREE COMP.	REQ'D	OVERALL CUM GRD POINT (A-4.0)	YEAR GRADUATED	DEGREE

DID YOU GRADUATE FROM COLLEGE? ☐ YES ☐ NO | AVERAGE NUMBER HOURS WORKED DURING SCHOOLING ___ PER WEEK | PERCENTILE CLASS STANDING: UPPER ☐ 10% ☐ 25% ☐ 50% ☐ 75% | PERCENT COLLEGE EXPENSES EARNED

LIST ANY OTHER INFORMATION SUCH AS PUBLICATIONS, INVENTIONS, SCIENTIFIC AWARDS, FRATERNITIES, HONORARIES, ETC.
LIST ANY SPECIAL COURSES IN MATH OR SCIENCE WHICH YOU HAVE TAKEN THAT MAY OR MAY NOT BE RELATED TO YOUR BACKGROUND.

PROFESSIONAL ORGANIZATIONS NAME	FROM	TO	OFFICES HELD	LICENSE/PROF CERT. NUMBER	STATE	FIELD CODE

EMERGENCY NOTIFICATION NAME | STREET ADDRESS | CITY | STATE | ZIP | A/C | PHONE | RELATION

DO NOT WRITE BELOW THIS SPACE. SKIP TO REVERSE SIDE

HIRE TYPE CODE	MONTHS OF EXPER.	STARTED WORK	OCCUPATION GROUP AND DASH NUMBER	VETERAN CODE	NHR CODE	INTERVIEWER'S CODE	H/S CODE
SHIFT CODE	UNIT	JOB CODE	GRADE	LOC. CODE	RATE	EMPLOYEE NUMBER	

THE AGE DISCRIMINATION ACT OF 1967 PROHIBITS DISCRIMINATION ON THE BASIS OF AGE WITH RESPECT TO INDIVIDUALS WHO ARE AT LEAST 40 BUT LESS THAN 65 YEARS OF AGE.

Figure 5.4. Job applicant's form.

EMPLOYMENT RECORD
1-93122 R7 (BP)

THIS MUST BE COMPLETED EVEN IF A RESUME IS ATTACHED. START WITH YOUR MOST RECENT EMPLOYMENT AND LIST ALL JOBS YOU HAVE HELD, INCLUDING MILITARY SERVICE. COVER ALL YOUR TIME SINCE LEAVING SCHOOL, WHETHER EMPLOYED OR NOT. BE SURE TO GIVE CORRECT ADDRESSES OF PREVIOUS EMPLOYERS. ADDITIONAL INFORMATION MAY BE PLACED ON A SEPARATE SHEET AND ATTACHED.

MAY WE CONTACT YOUR PRESENT EMPLOYER? ☐ YES ☐ NO

EMPLOYER _____ PHONE NO. _____

ADDRESS _____

NAME AND TITLE OF SUPERVISOR _____

YOUR POSITION AND DUTIES _____

RATE OF PAY		EMPLOYED		TOTAL MONTHS
MONTHLY		FROM	TO	
STARTING	ENDING	MO	YR	MO	YR

REASON FOR LEAVING _____

NO. HRS/WK WORKED

EMPLOYER _____ PHONE NO. _____

ADDRESS _____

NAME AND TITLE OF SUPERVISOR _____

YOUR POSITION AND DUTIES _____

RATE OF PAY — MONTHLY — STARTING / ENDING | EMPLOYED FROM / TO — MO YR MO YR | TOTAL MONTHS

REASON FOR LEAVING _____

NO. HRS/WK WORKED

EMPLOYER _____ PHONE NO. _____

ADDRESS _____

NAME AND TITLE OF SUPERVISOR _____

YOUR POSITION AND DUTIES _____

RATE OF PAY — MONTHLY — STARTING / ENDING | EMPLOYED FROM / TO — MO YR MO YR | TOTAL MONTHS

REASON FOR LEAVING _____

NO. HRS/WK WORKED

EMPLOYER _____ PHONE NO. _____

ADDRESS _____

NAME AND TITLE OF SUPERVISOR _____

YOUR POSITION AND DUTIES _____

RATE OF PAY — MONTHLY — STARTING / ENDING | EMPLOYED FROM / TO — MO YR MO YR | TOTAL MONTHS

REASON FOR LEAVING _____

NO. HRS/WK WORKED

RELATIVES EMPLOYED BY LTV AEROSPACE CORPORATION

NAME	RELATIONSHIP	WHERE EMPLOYED

LIST FOUR REFERENCES OTHER THAN RELATIVES AND FORMER EMPLOYERS WHO HAVE KNOWN YOU FOR AT LEAST FIVE YEARS

NAME	ADDRESS (STREET, CITY, STATE, ZIP)	OCCUPATION	A/C	PHONE

CAN YOU TAKE SHORTHAND? _____ TYPE? _____ READ AIRCRAFT BLUEPRINTS? _____

WPM _____ WPM _____ READ SCHEMATICS? _____

SCORE _____ SCORE _____

LIST OFFICE AND FACTORY MACHINES YOU

CAN OPERATE _____

FOREIGN LANGUAGE ABILITY

LANGUAGE	SPEAK	UNDER-STAND	READ	WRITE
	☐	☐	☐	☐
	☐	☐	☐	☐
	☐	☐	☐	☐

STARTING SALARY EXPECTED

I CERTIFY THAT, TO THE BEST OF MY KNOWLEDGE AND BELIEF, THE ANSWERS AND STATEMENTS ON THIS FORM ARE CORRECT WITHOUT OMISSIONS OF ANY KIND. I UNDERSTAND THAT ANY FALSE INFORMATION CONTAINED IN THE APPLICATION IS CAUSE FOR DISCHARGE AT ANY TIME.

_____
APPLICANT'S SIGNATURE

Figure 5.4. (Continued)

résumé and other information you have about the candidate. Write down information that you feel is missing that you want to get from the candidate. Also, review the candidate's background against your job specification form very carefully and develop a list of questions you want to ask. Write down a syllabus for the candidate's interview. Also, put down things that you wish to explain about the job, or other events such as a plant tour that you might wish to take place. Doing this planning ahead of time will make the interview most fruitful for you and for the candidate. It will show your interest in seeing that he or she will be happy in the position, and he or she will learn something about the company and have an easier time making his or her decision to come to work for you.

If possible, arrange for the candidate to be interviewed by at least two other individuals in your company beside yourself. Select these individuals carefully—individuals who have a good understanding of what the job will require and what the company is looking for. Such multiple interviewing has many advantages. For one thing, it brings in someone else's opinion. Also, sometimes other interviewers will pick up things that you did not. Finally, it allows the candidate to meet other members of your company and gives the candidate a better idea of what your company is like and what's going to be required of him or her as a part of the job.

You want the candidate to relax as much as possible. Do not put the candidate under pressure unless being under pressure is part of the job. Here is the general procedure to follow. First, ask very general and open questions to get the candidate to talk. Also, note those aspects of the candidate that you would like to know more about and write these down. Then, ask the more specific and detailed questions you wrote down during your planning. Get the candidate to do most of the talking. At some point you should try to find out what you can about the candidate's current or former compensation and what salary figure he or she has in mind for the position. Finally, even if you do not have a company tour, let the candidate know that you are interested by telling him or her more about the job and its importance to the company, fringe benefits, and so forth. Promise that you will get back to the candidate as soon as a decision is made, but do not make an offer at this time, no matter how good the candidate seems. Always wait to think it over and if possible to compare notes with other interviewers.

If the candidate is a skilled interviewee, he or she will have done considerable homework and learned everything possible about your company and the job. The interviewee may even have made up a list of questions to ask you. The purpose of these questions is to exhibit his or her alertness and interest. The candidate may also wish to learn exactly what you want so that he or she can best answer your questions when you ask them. Do not allow yourself to be drawn into answering questions in detail until you have your own questions answered.

Here are some tips you should consider in any interview that you conduct to recruit new employees for your company.

1. Make the applicant feel comfortable and attempt to establish a friendly, personal relationship.
2. Make certain that you ask the questions that you have listed prior to the interview before the applicant asks questions of you.
3. Make certain the applicant has the necessary qualifications for the job.
4. Determine whether the applicant has the personal characteristics required for the job.
5. Try to discover what the applicant's attitude toward the position in your company is. Remember, you are looking for someone for a long-term rela-

5. tionship and do not want the person you hire to quit after a few weeks or a few months.

6. Always let the applicant do more talking than you do. In fact, a good way to start is to ask the candidate to tell you something about him- or herself.

7. Take notes on any information that you think is important or that you may wish to talk or ask about later.

8. Make sure you probe to get some idea of what the applicant is seeking in the way of compensation. This may affect your own tactics when making the offer later on.

9. Make sure any questions you ask conform with equal employment opportunity practices.

10. You should know and be able to explain everything about the job, including the basic duties, the salary range, the fringe benefits, any overtime hours expected, possibility of travel, and so forth.

Equal Employment Opportunity Laws

Equal employment opportunity laws state that you may not discriminate against an applicant on the basis of the applicant's race, religion, sex, national origin, or age. Some of the laws in the purview of equal opportunity employment are discussed below.

Equal Pay Act of 1963. This act prohibits employers from paying lower wages to an employee involved in producing, buying, or selling goods because of the sex of the employee. The act makes it illegal for employers to discriminate against employees on the basis of sex by paying lower wages to employees of one sex who within the same establishment perform equal work on a job requiring equal skill, effort, and responsibility, and who are performing under similar working conditions except where payment is based on:

1. The seniority system
2. A merit system
3. A system which measures earnings by quantity or quality of production
4. A differential based on any factor other than sex

Title VII, Civil Rights Act of 1964. This act is intended to eliminate any form of discrimination in employment based upon an individual's race, color, religion, sex, or national origin. Specifically, Title VII states that it shall be unlawful employment practice for an employer to:

1. Fail or refuse to hire or to discharge any individual or otherwise discriminate against any individual with respect to compensation, terms, conditions or privileges of employment because of such individual's race, color, religion, sex or national origin, or 2. Limit, segregate or classify employees (or applicants for employment) in any way which would deprive or tend to deprive any individual of employment opportunities or otherwise adversely affect his or her status as an employee because of such individual's race, color, religion, sex or national origin.

The Age Discrimination and Employment Act of 1967. This act prohibits discrimination on the basis of age against individuals who are between the ages of 40 and 64, inclusive, with the exception of cases in which age is a bona fide occupational qualification. For example, certain federal statutory and regulatory requirements impose compulsory age limitations on a few occupations for the safety of the public. Positions such as those requiring actors for youthful or elderly roles or persons who will advertise or promote products aimed toward youthful or elderly clientele often cannot be filled by individuals other than those in the appropriate age range.

The Equal Employment Opportunity Act of 1972. This act gives the Equal Employment Opportunity Commission the authority to file suits in federal courts against violators of the Civil Rights Act. The 1972 amendment also extends the coverage of the Title VII act to employment relationships in most government agencies, and states that employers who follow federally approved affirmative action plans for 12 months cannot be denied or suspended from a government contract without a special hearing.

How to Be an Equal Opportunity Employer. According to the Small Business Administration, to employ fairly you do not have to remember a lot of regulations. There's only one basic rule that you must keep in mind. The questions you ask, verbally or in writing on an employment form or in any other fashion, and any other test you administer must be relevant to the work for which the applicant is applying. Also, you must recognize that even if you do not intend to discriminate, if you ask the wrong questions you may cause an applicant to believe that you are prejudiced and the applicant may file a complaint against you. If you are found guilty of discrimination, even though you are a small business, size is no defense. You may be sued. Therefore, be very careful. To ask for the following information is considered discriminatory unless for some reason the information being gathered for employment is job related and essential for occupational qualification, or necessary for national or state security. Note that some of these questions may have been asked in the past, and you may consider them very innocent. Remember, they may be considered discriminatory.

1. Marital status
2. Birthplace
3. Age
4. Religion
5. How or when citizenship was attained
6. Extracurricular and nonprofessional affiliations or memberships in organizations
7. Wife's maiden name
8. Applicant's maiden name
9. Relatives [Note: After employment, you may request names of persons (do not specify relatives) who should be notified in case of an accident or emergency.]
10. How skill in foreign language was acquired
11. Arrests for crime (It is illegal to discharge or refuse to hire an employee who answers arrest record questions falsely. You may, however, ask questions regarding whether or not a person was ever *convicted* of a crime.)
12. Children
13. Physical size and weight

14. Garnishments of wages or salaries
15. Bond refusals
16. Possessions (whether applicant owns a home, car, etc.)
17. Spouse's job or father's/mother's job
18. Requesting a photograph of the applicant

Making the Offer

Once you have settled on a single candidate to make the offer to, state your offer either by telephone or in person. Generally, assuming the amount is fair, you should open at from 10 to 15% lower than what you think the person will accept. Some candidates will state a minimum figure which is really the maximum amount they feel they can get, and they may be perfectly willing to accept 10 to 15% less if this is a fair amount and not lower than the approximate going rate for the work. If the person is inflexible regarding the amount that he or she wants and you really wish to hire the candidate, then you can always allow yourself to be negotiated up to a higher figure in your predetermined range.

If the candidate asks for an unreasonably high figure which is well out of your range, you can explain to the candidate that while you want to hire him or her, the salary is too high and is not reasonable considering the going rate. Offer what you think the job is worth and emphasize other positive aspects of the job such as promotion opportunities, fringe benefits, and so forth.

Always keep in mind that your objective during negotiations is not to hire at the lowest figure possible, as even if you succeed in doing this it will probably make for an unhappy employee, and that you definitely don't want. Rather, your objective is to hire at the lowest fair price.

What to Do with Candidates You Do Not Hire

You should always endeavor to let unsuccessful candidates or applicants down gently. After all, they've gone to considerable trouble for you, submitting résumés, being interviewed, and allowing their references to be checked. Every candidate who has seen you in a face-to-face interview should be contacted after you have made your decision. You should explain to each that while he or she was an outstanding finalist for the job, you have made the decision to hire someone else. Thank him or her for coming for the interview. If the statement is true, tell the unsuccessful candidate that you would like to consider him or her for future positions with the company. In this way, you keep on good terms with everyone that you contact and can even use some of the unsuccessful candidates as potential candidates for future jobs. This could be extremely important if something went wrong with the deal you've already struck. If for any reason the candidate you hire cancels out prior to beginning work, you don't want to start from the beginning all over again.

SOURCES OF ADDITIONAL INFORMATION

Finding and Hiring the Right Employee, Small Marketers Aids No. 106, by Rudolph Raphelson, published by the Small Business Administration, Washington, DC 20402.

Hiring the Right Man, Small Marketers Aids No. 106 (no author listed), published by the Small Business Administration, Washington, DC 20402.

Management's Talent Search, by Paul W. Maloney, published by the American Management Association, New York, NY 10020.

Recruiting and Selecting Employees, A Self-Instruction Booklet (no author listed), published by the Small Business Administration, Washington, DC 20402.

The Selection Process, by M. M. Mandell, published by the American Management Association, New York, NY 10020.

6

Buying a Business

THE ADVANTAGES AND DISADVANTAGES OF BUYING A BUSINESS

Buying a business has both advantages and disadvantages when compared to starting your own business. Before deciding whether to buy a new business or to start one, it is important to consider all of the facts.

Advantages

1. Prior successful operation of a business increases your chances of success with the same business.
2. Prior successful operation provides the location of the business previously selected and in use.
3. If the business has been profitable or is headed toward profit, you will be profitable sooner than if you start up your own business.
4. The amount of planning that may be necessary for an ongoing business will probably be less than that for a new business.
5. You will already have established customers or clientele.
6. You will already have established suppliers and will not have to look for them.
7. You may already have inventory on hand and will not lose the time necessary for selecting, ordering, and waiting for the order to arrive before you can make your first sales.
8. Necessary equipment is probably already on hand.
9. Financing will be necessary for the single transaction of purchasing the business.
10. You may be able to buy the business at a bargain price.
11. You will acquire the benefit of the experience of the prior owner.
12. Much of the hard work of start-up is avoided, including finding the location, purchasing the equipment, and so forth.
13. If employees are on board, they are probably already experienced in the business.
14. You may be able to finance all or part of the purchase price through a note to the owner.
15. Existing records of the business may help you and guide you in running the business.

Disadvantages

1. You will inherit any bad will that exists because of the way the business has been managed.
2. The employees who are currently working for the company may not be the best or the best for you and the way you manage.
3. The image of the business is already established. This image will be difficult to change.
4. Precedents have already been set by the previous owners. They may be difficult to change.
5. Modernization may be needed.
6. The purchase price may create a burden on future cash flow and profitability.
7. It is possible that you can overpay due to misrepresentation or an inaccurate appraisal of what the business is worth.
8. The business location may be a drawback.

SOURCES OF OPPORTUNITIES TO PURCHASE A NEW BUSINESS

Before you can decide whether it is in your interest to buy a business or not, you have to look it over, and before you can do that, you must locate businesses for sale. Such businesses can be obtained from the following sources:

1. *Classified advertisements in newspapers.* The Sunday edition usually has a number of listings or try the *Wall Street Journal* under the classification "Business Opportunities."
2. *Classified or space advertisements in trade magazines.*
3. *Realtors.* You can find them in the yellow pages of the telephone directory.
4. *Business brokers.* They can also be found in the yellow pages of your telephone directory. (Note: When dealing with business brokers, check more than one. Some businesses may be handled on an exclusive basis and you will not be able to uncover all opportunities in your area by talking to one broker.)
5. *Chambers of commerce.* Some chambers of commerce maintain a buying and selling service for businesses in their area. Check with your local unit.
6. *Trade sources.* These include suppliers, distributors, manufacturers, trade associations, and so forth. Simply call up individuals who would be suppliers or distributors to the business which you would like to buy and ask if they know if the business is for sale.
7. *Professionals.* Check with attorneys, accountants, and bankers dealing with small business. They may know of a business of the type that you're interested in.
8. *Business owners.* Ask owners of the type of business in which you're interested. Small businesspeople are eager to help one another, sometimes even potential competitors, and they may know of a business that is for sale. Also, there is always the outside chance that the very businessperson you are talking with wishes to sell his or her business. Anyway, it never hurts to ask.

HOW TO SIZE UP BUSINESS BUY OPPORTUNITIES

The Screening Evaluation

The first step in evaluating a business buy opportunity is a screening evaluation. During the screening evaluation, you want to learn some basic facts about the new business that is for sale. The basic purpose of the screening evaluation is to decide not whether you will purchase the business, but whether you will look at it further.

Initial contact with the owner of the business that you wish to purchase can usually be by telephone. On the telephone you can ask some basic facts about the business: its location, annual sales, and such information. Make certain that you take good notes during this conversation. If anything said by the owner obviously disqualifies the business, then you should drop the matter right then and there and not waste additional time. But if the phone conversation seems to indicate to you that it is worthwhile to investigate further, then you should take the second step, which is to make an appointment for an initial visit with the owner.

Again, you are still in the screening stage, and even on an initial visit the purpose is simply to know whether to proceed or to scratch this business off your list. During this visit you should look around, assess how the business looks, the clientele or customers who may come in, the attitude of the owner, and especially his or her capabilities and personal integrity. Ask the history of the business, how it was established, and other background information.

It is extremely important that you determine the real reason for selling. Almost invariably the owner will give you one of two reasons: ill health or impending retirement. This may be the truth, but it is imperative that you check it out. Too many times these reasons are given to cover up a poor investment. For example, sales could be declining. There could be a major change in the neighborhood which is causing business to be lost or to be less favorable than it once was. There could be new competition or new technology on the scene. Perhaps the products are obsolete or a key employee has been lost. The business could have problems with creditors. It is essential that you really dig to find out the true facts. Sometimes you may be able to solve the problem and thus turn the whole situation around to your advantage. You will have a real bargain if you pay very little for the business and turn it around rapidly. This is far from fantasy. In fact, some individuals actually make a business of buying unprofitable businesses and turning them around. However, in order to be able to do this, you must identify the precise problems that are causing the business to go wrong and, of course, you must be absolutely confident that you can correct them.

The In-Depth Analysis

If the business still interests you, your real work begins. Now you must analyze the business much more carefully. You must study local conditions yourself to see exactly what is happening. This includes asking other businesspeople in the area their opinion of the business and their opinion of the owner; talking to suppliers and hearing about their experiences in dealing with this owner and the business; talking to customers; speaking with trade associations and executives about the business; talking to key employees and, if you have the opportunity, talking to former employees. This is sometimes your most valuable source of information since former employees may be more ready to give you information than present employees are. You should also talk to the bank, call the Better Business Bureau to see whether customers have complained about the business, talk to executives at the chamber of commerce, and contact Dun and Bradstreet who, for a fee, can give you their own intelligence estimate of the business. A local office of Dun and Bradstreet can be found in the white pages. If you are living in a small town or area that doesn't have a local office, then call or write to: Dun and Bradstreet, 99 Church St., New York, NY 10007.

Below we will discuss the aspects of the business you are considering buying that you will want to know *all* about before you decide.

Profits and Sales.   The main factor in analysis of profits and sales is not current or even past profits and sales, but what the future profit potential is. You can find out the owner's income from his business from federal or state income tax returns, records of bank deposits, and similar sources. You should also get actual figures on past profit sales, operating ratios, and other like information from the firm's books and auditor reports. You should go back at least five years, and the ratios obtained should be compared with industry ratios. It is advisable to have your accountant audit these business records for you.

If for any reason the seller cannot or will not supply records for your analysis, this should be a very clear warning signal to you that something is amiss.

Once these records have been obtained and audited, you should analyze for profitability with your improvements. But in doing this, don't dream. Be realistic. Your improvements can make a difference, but you won't be able to work miracles. You should also analyze expenses for the business and see whether they are in line for a business of this type. Once you have your figures and expenses straight, and your own plans for what you might do in order to increase profitability, you should project sales and profits forward for a period of one to two years. Then analyze these figures to see whether the investment that you must make will bring you a better return than would starting a similar business of your own from scratch.

When analyzing profits and sales, make good use of professional services including, as mentioned before, your accountant. But also bring in your lawyer, talk to your banker, and even consult your business insurance agent to make certain that the figures are factual and that your analyses are correct and realistic.

Inventory.   Look at the inventory and have an independent appraiser determine its value—examining the inventory for age, salability, quality, style, condition, and whether it is in line with the product line that you plan. These facts should determine the real value of the inventory to you. The questions you should ask yourself are: Can you sell this inventory? At what price? Do you have to clear out the inventory at a percentage of its supposed value at a loss to you? It's crucial to recognize exactly how much you will be able to receive for the inventory in dollars. You should also recognize that if the inventory is still being sold, this asset may not exist at the time you actually go to purchase. So, be sure that it does exist if you're going to pay for it.

Capital Equipment, Furniture, Fixtures, and the Building.   Again, the key is to find out the real market value of capital equipment. If it is old, must it be replaced? If it must be replaced, when must it be replaced? Is the equipment in good condition and modern? Can you actually make use of the equipment or will it just be sitting around taking up space? Will modifications to the equipment be needed? How much will they cost? It is important to inspect this equipment yourself and not just take the owner's word for or description of what you are getting.

Accounts Receivable.   You should check the accounts receivable closely. Look at how old each account is. The older the account is, the more difficult it will be to collect. Look for the credit standing of the accounts. Check the business to see how much is actually done on credit and what the credit collection rate is. If much business is done on credit with long payments, it will mean that you will have a shortage of working capital even if the accounts are eventually paid. Analyze the situation and think through the results if you employed a stricter credit policy. Would you lose some customers? What percentage of the customers and what percentage of sales could you be expected to lose?

Contracts.   These, including leases on rented equipment or buildings, have value. Be sure to check the transferability of the contract to you as the buyer and, if the contract can be renewed, the terms of renewal. Check how long the lease is for. Talk to the landlord and ascertain his or her attitude toward the business and the current owner. Check all the terms and options of the contract and lease. If the location is important, this becomes even more vital.

Clientele.   What kind of customers are you dealing with? Is it likely that these customers will stay with you once the business is transferred? Are key contracts transferable or will you lose them once you buy the business?

Customer Lists.   These lists can be extremely valuable and are most definitely so in any type of mail order business. In fact, in such a case, the customer list may constitute the major asset of the business. Make certain that you will own these lists yourself on purchase and that the seller will no longer have the right to use them.

Franchises.   Check the terms of the franchise. Note the exclusivity. Check also for the transferability of the franchise and note the original cost to the seller. All these are important factors in deciding the value of the franchise as an asset.

Good Will.   Good will has to do with the business's reputation, its established patronage, and its established image. Good will is worth something and should be considered an asset. But remember that an image cannot be readily changed no matter what it is, and that to be an asset "good will" must in fact be "good." Carefully evaluate this asset or lack of same based upon your investigation with the Better Business Bureau, suppliers, customers, and so forth.

Key Personnel.   Personnel who know the business well can be extremely valuable to you if they intend to stay with the business. You should check to ascertain whether or not they do. You should also analyze the situation to find out what the effect will be if key personnel leave the business. Talk to the former owner and size him up as a business person. He may be the guiding light who alone is able to make the business profitable. Once he leaves, the business may collapse. Is he willing to consult for you for a period of time to assure the business's continued success? Also, ask whether he is willing to sign a noncompeting agreement so that he cannot compete in the same business against you once he has sold this business to you.

Proprietary Items.   These items include copyrights, trademarks, patents, secret processes, and even a business name. Again, you must look at the situation closely to decide the real value of these items. A mechanical patent, for example, is only good for 17 years. How long has the patent been in force? Also, patents vary greatly in value even once granted. They can be designed around. They can even be invalidated in the courts, in which case the patent may be absolutely worthless. Are such items essential to the business or not?

Suppliers. Check business relations with suppliers. Make sure they will continue to supply you. You should also find out whether or not the business is committed to any supplier and how satisfactory each supplier has been in the past in supplying what was needed in a timely fashion.

Have your lawyer make sure that all assets claimed are written into and spelled out in the sale contract.

Liabilities. Every aspect of the business thus discussed can be either positive or negative; it can be either an asset or a liability. But it is particularly important that you identify every liability. Look for unpaid bills, back taxes owed, pending lawsuits, and so forth. Again, you must get the help of professionals for your investigation, including a lawyer and an accountant. This costs money, but the money that you save may save the business or save your investment for the future. Every liability that you will assume in the business should be put in writing (This goes for assets, too!) and a statement in the sales contract should indicate that all claims against the business not shown are assumed by the seller of the business.

Competition. It is extremely important to know what competition, both current and future, you may expect in this business. Again, you must do more than just talk to the current owner. Much can be revealed about competition by looking at sales trends over the past few years as well as talking to other businesses in your area or the trade association in which the business is a member.

The Market. Is the market, including the community that is being served, growing or has the growth leveled off? Is the market actually on the decline? Watch for things like traffic routing, new shopping centers, or regulations which may affect your business. A highway, freeway, or expressway going through the area can totally change the market that was formerly served by businesses in the area. Also, look for changing neighborhoods. A neighborhood that is being renovated may have a positive effect on the business, but it may have a negative effect instead, so you must check this carefully.

Circumstances Unique to Owner. Sometimes a business is based upon a particular owner, his family, his relations, his religion, ethnic group, or membership in certain social or political organizations. These may be the reasons his business and sales are at a certain level. You, coming into this business and not being of the same ethnic group, religion, family, social group, or whatever, may lose a great portion of his former sales. This is not always the case, but again you should be aware of the possibility.

Manpower. You should look not only at the key personnel discussed previously, but also at workers employed in this business. Are qualified people employed and will they stay? Should they leave, are there sources of additional manpower available in the local area?

Waste. Look for waste in the business. Sometimes this will help you purchase a real bargain. Is there unused machinery, for example? This is a waste. Are materials being wasted which could be resold or used in other manufacturing processes?

Location and Location History. Never buy a business without investigating the location and the location history of the business. Some locations are poor for almost any business, and a history over a period of time, say 5 or 10 years, will reveal that one business after another has been in that location and then failed. If some businesses have failed and some have not, find which ones did and which did not. Knowing what types have been successful and what types have not can be extremely helpful as an indicator of your chances of success. Use the checklist contained in Figure 6.1 to help you.

City or Town
1. Economic considerations
   Industry
      Farming
      Manufacturing
      Trading
   Trend
      Highly satisfactory
      Growing
      Stationary
      Declining
   Permanency
      Old and well established
      Old and reviving
      New and promising
      Recent and uncertain
   Diversification
      Many and varied industries
      Many of the same type
      Few but varied
      Dependent on one industry
   Stability
      Constant
      Satisfactory
      Average
      Subject to wide fluctuations
   Seasonality
      Little or no seasonal change
      Mild seasonal change
      Periodic—every few years
      Highly seasonal in nature
   Future
      Very promising
      Satisfactory
      Uncertain
      Poor outlook
2. Population
   Income distribution
      Mostly wealthy
      Well distributed
      Mostly middle income
      Poor
   Trend
      Growing
      Large and stable
      Small and stable
      Declining
   Living status
      Own homes

      Pay substantial rent
      Pay moderate rent
      Pay low rent
3. Competition
   Number of competing stores
      Few
      Average
      Many
      Too many
   Type of management
      Not progressive
      Average
      Above average
      Alert and progressive
   Presence of chains
      No chains
      Few chains
      Average number
      Many well established
   Type of competing stores
      Unattractive
      Average
      Old and well established
      Are many people shopping outside the community?
4. The town as a place to live
      Character of the city
      Are homes neat and clean, or run down and shabby?
      Are lawns, parks, streets, and so on neat, modern, and generally attractive?
      Are adequate facilities available?
         Banking
         Transportation
         Professional services
         Utilities
         Schools
         Churches
         Amusement centers
         Medical and dental services
      Is the climate satisfactory for the type of business you are considering?
The Site
1. Competition
      Number of independent stores of the same kind as yours
         Same block

Figure 6.1. Location checklist. [From *Buying and Selling a Small Business*, by Verne A. Bunn, Small Business Administration (1969).]

Same side of the street
Across the street
Number of chain stores
  In the same block
  Same side of the street
  Across the street
Kind of stores next door
Number of vacancies
  Same side of the street
  Across the street
  Next door
Dollar sales of your nearest competitor
2. Traffic flow
  Sex of pedestrians
  Age of pedestrians
  Destination of pedestrians
  Number of passersby
  Automobile traffic count
  Peak hours of traffic flow
3. Transportation
  Transfer points
  Highway
  Kind (bus, streetcar, auto, railroad)
4. Parking facilities
  Large and convenient
  Large enough but not convenient
  Convenient but too small
  Completely inadequate
5. Side of street

6. Plant
  Frontage and depth—in feet
  Shape of building
  Condition
  Heat—type, air conditioning
  Light
  Display space
  Front and back entrances
  Display windows
7. Corner location—if not, what is it?
8. Unfavorable characteristics
  Fire hazards
  Cemetery
  Hospital
  Industry
  Relief office
  Undertaker
  Vacant lot—without parking possibilities
  Garages
  Playground
  Smoke, dust, odors
  Poor sidewalks and pavement
  Unsightly neighborhood buildings
9. Professional men in block
  Medical doctors and dentists
  Lawyers
  Veterinarians
  Others
10. History of the site

Figure 6.1. (Continued)

Additional Projections. After your initial projections of sales and profits, you should project expenses and capital requirements for the next year. Include seasonal demands and, most important, include the amount that you must take out of the business for your own living expenses. No business can be successful if the owner cannot himself make a reasonable living.

Special Requirements. Check for licenses, permits, and other legal requirements for building, health, fire, and the like. This is especially important in some areas in which the local government will permit old businesses to operate under old laws, but upon sale they are considered new businesses and the new owners must abide by the new laws. Your attorney can help you out here.

Partnership Agreements. Be especially careful of partnership agreements. Read Chapter 1 of this book over again since all of this information applies. Insure that a new partnership agreement is signed which documents the obligations and liabilities of each partner, and know what you are getting into before you purchase the partnership.

HOW MUCH SHOULD YOU PAY?

In deciding how much to pay, of course, you must consider all the information that you have dug up about the business. Some businesses have special formulas for calculation of price which apply only to their industry. In order to discover these formulas for the business you are considering, check with business brokers. We discuss some general methods below.

Asset Appraisal

This is the valuation of the tangible assets with the help of an appraiser. Be careful here not to use replacement cost as a basis for determining value. Replacement cost is only valid in a very scarce supply situation. Only then would old assets have nearly the value of new assets. Usually the book value is used. This is the original cost less a reasonable depreciation amount. However, you should recognize that marginally useful equipment, equipment which is not useful at all, obsolete inventory, or other factors can further depreciate the book value of the asset. The value of intangible assets such as good will is negotiable. Usually in total they are priced at 10% to 20% of the value of the tangible assets, and almost always less than 50% of the tangible asset value. Don't forget to subtract liabilities in an asset appraisal method of determining price.

Future Earning Capitalization

Here, you estimate future profits over an agreed-upon period such as five years. Calculate a risk factor by comparison with the return for other known risks. Then divide the risk factor into the average yearly pretax profits. The result is the value of the business. For example, a bank may pay 10% interest. This represents a known return for a risk. If yearly pretax profits after deducting the owner's salary are $10,000, then you would divide $10,000 by 10%. This equals $100,000. If the business that you are considering purchasing is somewhat riskier, you may equate the risk factor with an investment having a return of 25%. In that case, you would divide $10,000 by 25% which would equal $40,000, which is considerably less.

Excess Earning Method

With the excess earning method, you would first value the tangible assets and then forecast annual profit. Next, you would estimate how many years it would take to establish a new and similar business and develop it to a similar level of profitability. Then you would determine a return on your investment. This return on investment can be either a return that you desire or a return that you can earn elsewhere. Now, multiply this return on investment by the value of the tangible assets. Add this to your salary. This gives you the total pretax profit that you expect. Subtract this sum from the annual profit forecast and multiply this times the number of years necessary to achieve similar profitability if you start a new business from scratch. This is the value of good will. Add this good will value to the tangible assets figure that you calculated in the beginning and this will result in the amount you should be willing to pay for the business. If subtraction from the annual profit forecast is a negative value, then you must subtract the good will figure from the tangible asset value that you've calculated. This means, of course, that the amount you should be willing to pay will be less than the tangible value of the assets that you calculated initially.

Let's look at an example. Assume that the value of tangible assets of the business is $100,000 and annual profit forecast is $40,000. To establish a similar business will take five years and you desire a return on your investment of 20%. Your annual salary is $28,000.

Step 1 $10,000 × 20\% = $2,000
Step 2 $28,000
        + 2,000
        $30,000 total expected pretax profit
Step 3 $40,000 − $30,000 = $10,000
        $10,000 × 5 years = $50,000 value of good will

In other words, regardless of other formulas used, if the seller must sell now, what will sophisticated buyers bid for this business? Clearly you would not want to spend more than that value.

NEGOTIATION

Rule 1 of negotiation is to get a lawyer for closing this important contract. Your agreement in writing should cover the following points: (1) a complete description of what is being sold including the assets fully described; (2) the liabilities that you will assume including the statement that all liabilities not spelled out in the contract will be assumed by the seller; (3) a statement of how adjustments are to be handled at the time of closing, including inventory sold up to this point, payroll, and similar items; (4) the seller's warranties to protect the buyer against inaccurate or false information; (5) the exact date that the buyer will take possession of the business; (6) who will pay legal fees; (7) an agreement by the seller not to compete (for a fixed period of time and/or limited to certain geographical locations depending on the situation and the business); (8) the exact purchase price; (9) the method of payment; (10) the seller's obligation and assumption of risk prior to closing; and (11) the time, place, and procedure of closing.

Once agreement is reached with the seller, it is best to close as soon as possible. In this way, inventory will not be depleted as much and problems caused by transition will be minimized.

If at all possible, try to get a note from the seller. This means that rather than borrowing money from someone else, you borrow it from him or her. It may be possible to negotiate a lower rate of interest this way. Also, the more willing the seller is to take a note, the less risk to you, since his or her willingness indicates confidence that you will be successful in this business.

Be careful of "buy-back" contracts. These are contracts to buy back the business if the business is unsuccessful or doesn't reach a certain level of sales or profits. These contracts are not risk free and can be absolutely worthless if the seller is dishonest and leaves town.

INITIAL FINANCIAL ESTIMATES

To estimate the first year's income, you can use Figure 4.3. To estimate the first year's cash requirements and expenses, use Figure 4.4. These estimates will help you in your decision whether to buy or not, and will also tell you your financial requirements and assist in your planning.

SOURCES OF ADDITIONAL INFORMATION

Buying and Selling a Small Business, by Verne A. Bunn, published by the Small Business Administration, U.S. Government Printing Office, Washington, DC 20402.

Guide to Buying or Selling a Business, by James M. Hanes, published by Prentice-Hall, Englewood Cliffs, NJ 07632.

How to Buy a Small Business, by Maxwell J. Mangold, published by Pilot Books, 347 Fifth Avenue, New York, NY 10016.

How to Organize and Operate a Small Business, 5th edition, by Clifford M. Baumback, Kenneth Lawyer, and Pearce C. Kelley, published by Prentice-Hall, Englewood Cliffs, NJ 07632.

Tax Guide for Buying and Selling a Business, 2nd edition, by Stanley Hagendorf, published by Prentice-Hall, Englewood Cliffs, NJ 07632.

7

Protecting Your Idea

This chapter discusses ways in which the small businessperson can protect him or herself from competitors and potential competitors. In some cases he or she may be able to get the exclusive right to some invention, product, service, or name which can be applied to his or her business and no other. Clearly this is of no small value for the small businessperson, and this chapter is one of the most important.

WHAT IS A PATENT?

A patent for an invention is a grant by the government to an inventor which permits him or her certain rights. In the United States, a patent is granted by the government acting through the Patent and Trademark Office. The patent is good for 17 years from the date on which it was issued, except for patents on ornamental designs which are granted for terms of 3½, 7, or 14 years. The term may be extended by a special act of Congress, but this occurs extremely rarely. Once the patent expires, the inventor has no control over his invention, and anyone has the free right to use it. You should also understand that the right inferred by the government to the patent grant extends only throughout the United States and its territories and possessions. That is, a U.S. patent does not give you protection in foreign countries. For such protection, you must obtain a separate patent in each country for which protection is desired. What you gain with a patent is the right to exclude others from making, using, or selling your invention.

WHAT CAN BE PATENTED

According to the patent law, which was first enacted in the United States in 1790, any person who "invents or discovers any new and usable process, machine, manufacture or composition of matter, or any new and useful improvements therefor, may obtain a patent."

Note that the statute refers to "composition of matter." This relates to chemical compositions and may include mixtures of ingredients as well as new chemical compounds. However, the Atomic Energy Act of 1954 excludes the patenting of inventions solely for the utilization of special nuclear material or atomic energy for atomic weapons.

The statute also specifies that the subject matter must be "useful." This means that whatever it is that you have invented must have a useful purpose and that it must be able to perform its intended purpose.

The courts have made various interpretations of this statute, and through these interpretations they have defined the limits of the subject matter which can be patented. The courts have ruled that methods of doing business, such as management by objectives, cannot be patented. Similarly, printed matter cannot be patented. Also, with regard to mixtures of ingredients, a patent cannot be granted unless there is more to the mixture than the effect of the individual components. Therefore, the combination of two or more components or ingredients in a single concoction cannot be patented unless the synergistic effect of the ingredients or components causes some greater or other benefit.

The statute says also that the invention must be new to be patentable. The invention cannot be patented if "(a) the invention was known or used by others in this country or patented or described in a printed publication in this or a foreign country before the invention thereof by the applicant for a patent, or, (b) the invention was patented or described in a printed publication in this or a foreign country or in public use or sale in this country more than one year prior to the application for a patent in the United States." This means that if the invention for which you seek a patent has been described in a printed publication anywhere in the world or if it has been in public use or on sale in this country before the date that the applicant made his invention, a patent cannot be issued. If the invention has been described in a printed publication anywhere or has been in public use or on sale in this country more than one year before the date on which an application for a patent is filed in this country, a valid patent cannot be obtained.

It is important to note here that it's immaterial when the invention was made or whether the printed publication or public use was by the inventor himself or by someone else. Therefore if you, the inventor, describe the invention in a printed publication such as a magazine, use the invention publicly, or place the invention on sale, you must apply for a patent before a year has gone by or your right to a patent will be lost.

Your invention must also be sufficiently different from a similar invention that has gone before. Even if what you seek to patent involves a few differences over a similar invention, a patent may be refused if the differences are "obvious." According to the Patent and Trademark Office, the subject matter which you seek to patent must be sufficiently different from what was described before or used before so that it may be said to amount to invention over the prior art, and small advances that would be obvious to a person having ordinary skill in the art are not considered inventions capable of being patented by this interpretation. For example, simply substituting one material for another material would not enable you to patent an idea as an invention.

WHO CAN APPLY FOR A PATENT

According to the law, only the inventor may apply for a patent on an object, with certain exceptions. If the inventor is dead, the application may be made by those who are legally authorized to represent him. If the inventor is insane or is otherwise under legal guardianship, his guardian may represent him. If an inventor is missing or refuses to apply for a patent, a joint inventor or a person having a proprietary interest in the invention may apply on behalf of the missing inventor. If a person who is not the inventor applies for a patent and is granted one, this patent would be void. Also, if an individual states that he is the inventor of an item and in fact he is not, he is subject to legal prosecution. If two or more persons make an invention jointly then they can apply as joint inventors.

Even though it is possible for an inventor to prepare the application for his own patent, this is not recommended. The procedures are very complex, and even if a patent is granted, it is unlikely that an untrained individual will secure all the rights he could to protect his invention through the patent. If you do decide to patent your invention by yourself, I would recommend reading one of the books available on this subject. One such is *Patent It Yourself,* by David Pressman, published by McGraw-Hill Book Co., 1221 Avenue of the Americas, New York, NY 10020.

Most inventors employ the services of persons known as patent attorneys or patent agents. Only certain patent attorneys and patent agents are authorized to practice before the Patent and Trademark Office, and this office maintains a register of these attorneys and agents. Those listed meet certain qualifications and demonstrate them by passing an examination. The difference between patent attorneys and patent agents is that patent attorneys are also attorneys at law. Patent agents are not. Both are fully qualified for preparing an application for a patent and conducting the prosecution in the Patent and Trademark Office. However, patent agents cannot conduct patent litigation in the courts or perform various other services which the local jurisdiction considers to be practicing law. You can get a complete list of those attorneys and agents registered to practice before the U.S. Patent and Trademark Office by sending $5 to the Superintendent of Documents, Washington, D.C. 20402, or through any district office of the U.S. Department of Commerce. You can also find a patent attorney through the yellow pages of your local phone book. Once you employ a patent attorney or an agent, you execute a power of attorney or authorization of agent. This must be filed in the Patent and Trademark Office, and is usually part of the application papers. Once an attorney has been appointed, the Patent and Trademark Office won't communicate with you directly, but will conduct all correspondence with your attorney, although, of course, you are free to contact the office concerning the status of your application. You can remove the attorney or agent from your patent case by revoking the power of attorney.

PROTECTING YOUR IDEA PRIOR TO PATENTING

How do you protect your idea prior to its patenting? One recommended method of protecting your invention is to get a close friend or someone who understands your invention to sign his or her name on a dated diagram or written description of the invention. In fact, you can do this during the process of your inventing. Every couple of days, as your work progresses, you can have someone sign as a witness to your notes. This will provide evidence of the time you came up with your idea or invention in case of a dispute with others as to who developed the invention first. Another way of protecting your invention prior to patenting is through a relatively new program established by the U.S. Patent and Trademark Office. This is known as the Disclosure Document Program. You file a disclosure document with the patent office which remains on file. This protects you for a two-year period. If you are interested in this program, you can get a copy of the pamphlet called *The U.S. Patent Office's Disclosure Document Program* by writing to the U.S. Department of Commerce, Patent and Trademark Office, Washington, D.C. 20231.

PATENT PROCEDURES

One of the first steps in patenting, before you begin to prepare the application, is to insure that you have established "novelty." According to the patent office, this is one of the most crucial and difficult determinations to make, and it involves two things. First, you must analyze your device according to standards specified by the patent office, and second, you must see whether or not anyone else has patented the device first. The only sure way of accomplishing the second requirement is to make a search of the patent office files.

Analyzing Your Device

You should analyze your device according to the standards of what is patentable. As pointed out earlier, for a device to be patentable, it must be (1) a new, useful, and unobvious process, machine, manufacture, or composition of matter, or a new, useful, and unobvious improvement thereof; (2) a new and unobvious original and ornamental design for an article manufacturer such as a new airplane design, (3) a distinct and new variety of plant, not propagated as tubes, which are asexually reproduced.

The following are not patentable: (1) an idea by itself; (2) a method of doing business; (3) printed matter; (4) an inoperable device; (5) an improvement in a device which is obvious or the result of mere mechanical skill.

Here are four government tests for novelty: (1) whether or not the device is known or used by others in this country before the invention of the applicant; (2) whether or not it was patented or described in a printed publication in this or a foreign country before the invention by the applicant; (3) whether or not it was described in a printed publication more than one year prior to the date of application for patent in the United States; (4) whether or not it was in public use or on sale in this country more than one year prior to the date of application for a patent in the United States.

Searching Existing Patents and Technical Literature

A search room is provided at the Scientific Library of the Patent and Trademark Office (the address is Crystal Plaza, 2021 Jefferson Davis Highway, Arlington, VA) where you may search and examine U.S. patents granted since 1836. In the search room, patents are arranged according to the Patent and Trademark Office classification system which includes over 300 subject classes and 64,000 subclasses. The search room also contains a set of U.S. patents arranged in numerical order and a complete set of the *Official Gazette,* the official journal relating to patents and trademarks which has been published weekly since January 1872. By searching in these classified patents, it is possible to determine whether an invention for the same or a similar device has already been granted before you actually file a patent application. It is also possible to obtain the information contained in patents relating to any field of endeavor that you desire.

However, it is not necessary for you or your attorney to travel personally to Virginia to make a search of Patent and Trademark Office files. Arrangements can be made with someone else in Arlington to do this for you. You may also order from the Patent and Trademark Office copies of lists of original patents or of cross-reference patents contained in the subclasses comprising the field of search, and inspect the printed copies of the patents in a library which has a numerically arranged set of patents. These libraries are: the University of the State of New

York in Albany, New York; the Georgia Tech Library in Atlanta, Georgia; the Public Library in Boston, Massachusetts; the Buffalo and Erie County Public Library in Buffalo, New York; the Public Library in Chicago, Illinois; the Public Library in Cincinnati, Ohio; the Public Library in Cleveland, Ohio; Ohio State University Library in Columbus, Ohio; the Public Library in Detroit, Michigan; the Linda Hall Library in Kansas City, Missouri; the Public Library in Los Angeles, California; the State Historical Society of Wisconsin in Madison, Wisconsin; the Public Library in Milwaukee, Wisconsin; the Public Library of Newark, New Jersey; the New York City Public Library; the Franklin Institute in Philadelphia, Pennsylvania; the Carnegie Library in Pittsburgh, Pennsylvania; the Public Library in Providence, Rhode Island; the Public Library in St. Louis, Missouri; the Oklahoma Agriculture and Mechanical College at Stillwater, Oklahoma; the Public Library in Sunnyvale, California; and the Public Library in Toledo, Ohio. The Patent and Trademark Office has also prepared a microfilm list of the numbers of the patents issued in each of the subclasses, and many libraries have purchased copies of these lists. If your library has these lists and a copy of the Manual of Classification, and also a set of patent copies or the *Official Gazette,* you can begin your search without communicating with the Patent and Trademark Office at all.

A patent search can save you a lot of time and trouble by letting you know beforehand whether or not your device is patentable. It will also indicate to you whether superior devices have been patented which may already be in production, or similar technologies which may be profitable to you or your company.

THE APPLICATION FOR A PATENT

The application for a patent is made to the commissioner of patents and trademarks. It includes the following: (1) a written document which comprises a specification of description and claims and an oath or declaration; (2) a drawing in those cases in which a drawing is possible; and (3) the filing fee.

There are some general requirements with regard to the form in which the application is submitted. The specification and oath of declaration must be in the English language and must be legibly written or printed in permanent ink on one side of the paper. The patent office prefers a typewritten application on legal-size paper, 8 to 8½ by 10½ to 13 inches, a line and a half or double spaced, with margins of one inch on the left-hand side and at the top. Various forms for patent applications are shown in Figure 7.1 through 7.11.

All applications are numbered in regular order and the applicant is informed of the serial number and filing date of the complete application by filing receipt. The filing date of the application is the date on which a complete and acceptable application is received at the Patent and Trademark Office, or the day on which the part completing such application is received if you have previously sent in an incomplete or a defective application.

The Specification

The specification must include a written description of the invention and of the manner and process of making and using it, and is required to be in such full, clear, concise, and exact terms as to enable any persons skilled in the art to which the invention pertains or with which it is most nearly connected to make and use the same invention. The specification must describe the precise invention for

To the Commissioner of Patents and Trademarks:

Your petitioner, ..., a citizen of the United States and a resident of ...., State of ...., whose post-office address is .... prays that letters patent may be granted to him for the improvement in ...., set forth in the following specification; and he hereby appoints ...., of ...., (Registration No. ....), his attorney (or agent) to prosecute this application and to transact all business in the Patent and Trademark Office connected therewith. (If no power of attorney is to be included in the application, omit the appointment of the attorney.)

[The specification, which includes the description of the invention and the claims, is written here.]

......................, the above-named petitioner, being sworn (or affirmed), deposes and says that he is a citizen of the United States and resident of ...., State of ...., that he verily believes himself to be the original, first and sole inventor of the improvement in .... described and claimed in the foregoing specification; that he does not know and does not believe that the same was ever known or used before his invention thereof, or patented or described in any printed publication in any country before his invention thereof, or more than one year prior to this application, or in public use or on sale in the United States more than one year prior to this application; that said invention has not been patented or made the subject of an inventor's certificate in any country foreign to the United States on an application filed by him or his legal representatives or assigns more than twelve months prior to this application; that he acknowledges his duty to disclose information of which he is aware which is material to the examination of this application; and that no application for patent or inventor's certificate on said invention has been filed by him or his representatives or assigns in any country foreign to the United States, except as follows: ....

....
(Inventor's full signature)

State of .... }
County of .... } ss:

Sworn to and subscribed before me this .... day of ...., 19.....

....
(Signature of notary or officer)

[SEAL]

....
(Official character)

Figure 7.1. Patent application, sole inventor; power of attorney, oath.

which a patent is being solicited, and it should be done in such a manner as to distinguish it from other inventions and from prior inventions. You must also describe the best method that you can think of for carrying out your invention. In the case of improvements, the specifications must particularly point out the part or parts of the process or device or whatever to which your improvement relates, and the description should be in such a form that the reader will have a complete understanding of it. The title of the invention should be as short and specific as possible, and it should appear as a heading on the first page of the specification, if it does not appear otherwise at the beginning of the application. Immediately following the claims, in a separate paragraph, it is necessary to write a brief abstract of the technical disclosure in the specification under the heading Abstract of the Disclosure. Before the detailed description, you write a brief summary of the invention indicating its nature and substance which may include a statement of the object of the invention. When there are drawings, each drawing should have a brief description of the several views, and your detailed description of your invention should refer to the different views by specifying numbers of the figures. You should conclude with one or more claims in which you point out very clearly the subject matter which you regard as your invention. These claims are the operative part of the patent. Both novelty and patentability are judged by the claims, and when a patent is granted, questions of infringement are judged by the courts on the basis of the claims.

To the Commissioner of Patents and Trademarks:

Your petitioners, ... and ...., citizens of the United States and residents, respectively, of ...., State of ...., and of ...., State of .... whose post-office addresses are, respectively, ... and .... pray that letters patent may be granted to them, as joint inventors, for the improvements in ...., set forth in the following specifications; and they hereby appoint ...., of .... (Registration No. ....), their attorney (or agent), to prosecute this application and to transact all business in the Patent and Trademark Office connected therewith. (If no power of attorney is to be included in the application, omit the appointment of the attorney.)

[The specification, which includes the description of the invention and the claims, is written here.]

.... and ...., the above-named petitioners, being sworn (or affirmed), depose and say that they are citizens of the United States and residents of ...., State of .... that they verily believe themselves to be the original, first and joint inventors of the improvement in .... described and claimed in the foregoing specification; that they do not know and do not believe that the same was ever known or used before their invention thereof, or patented or described in any printed publication in any country before their invention thereof, or more than one year prior to this application, or in public use or on sale in the United States for more than one year prior to this application; that said invention has not been patented or made the subject of an inventor's certificate in any country foreign to the United States on an application filed by them or their legal representatives or assigns more than 12 months prior to this application; that they acknowledge their duty to disclose information of which they are aware which is material to the examination of this application, and that no application for patent or inventor's certificate on said invention has been filed by them or their representatives or assigns in any country foreign to the United States, except as follows: ....

....
(Inventor's full signature)

State of.....................
County of..................... } ss:

Sworn to and subscribed before me this .... day of ...., 19.....

....
(Signature of notary or officer)

[SEAL]

....
(Official character)

Figure 7.2. Patent application, joint inventors; power of attorney, oath.

In summary, here is the order of arrangement for your specification: (1) title of invention (you may incorporate in this part the name, citizenship, and residence of the applicant and the title of the invention in one grouping); (2) cross-reference to related applications, if any; (3) a brief summary of the invention; (4) a brief description of the several views of the drawings, if you have included drawings as part of your invention; (5) a detailed description; (6) claim or claims; and (7) abstract of the disclosure.

Oath or Declaration and Signature

The oath or declaration from you as the applicant and inventor is required by statute. You must make an oath or declaration that you believe yourself to be the original and first inventor of the subject matter of the application, and must make various other allegations required by statute and various allegations required by the Patent and Trademark Office rules. Forms of oaths are shown in Figure 7.1, through 7.6 and in Figure 7.11. This oath will be sworn to by the inventor before a notary public or other officer authorized to administer oaths. A declaration may be used in lieu of an oath as part of the original application for a patent involving designs, plants, and other patentable inventions. This application must be signed by you as the inventor in person or by a person entitled by law to make applica-

To the Commissioner of Patents and Trademarks:

Your petitioner, A .... B ...., a citizen of the United States and a resident of ...., State of ...., whose post-office address is ...., administrator of the estate of C .... D ...., late a citizen of the United States and a resident of ...., State of ...., deceased (as by reference to the duly certified copy of letters of administration, hereto annexed, will more fully appear), prays that letters patent may be granted to him for the invention of the said C .... D .... for an improvement in .... set forth in the following specification; and he hereby appoints .... of .... (Rtgistration No. ....), his attorney (or agent), to prosecute this application and to transact all business in the Patent and Trademark Office connected therewith.

(If no power of attorney is to be included in the application, omit the appointment of the attorney.)

[The specification, which includes the description of the invention and the claims, is written here.]

A .... B ...., the above-named petitioner, being sworn (or affirmed), deposes and says that he is a citizen of the United States of America and a resident of ...., that he is the administrator of the estate (or executor of the last will and testament) of C .... D ...., deceased, late a citizen of the United States and resident of ...., that he verily believes the said C .... D .... to be the original, first and sole inventor of the improvement in .... described and claimed in the foregoing specification; that he does not know and does not believe that the same was ever known or used before the invention thereof by the said C .... D ...., or patented or described in any printed publication in any country before the said invention thereof, or more than one year prior to this application, or in public use or on sale in the United States for more than one year prior to this application; that said invention has not been patented or make the subject of an inventor's certificate in any country foreign to the United States on an application filed by the said C .... D .... or his legal representatives or assigns more than 12 months prior to this application; that he acknowledges his duty to disclose information of which he is aware which is material to the examination of this application, and that no application for patent or inventor's certificate on said invention has been filed by the said C .... D .... or his representatives or assigns in any country foreign to the United States, except as follows: ....

A....................... B.....................
                                     (Signature)
                        Administrator, etc.

State of ....⎰
County of ....⎰ ss:
Sworn to and subscribed before me this .... day of ...., 19....
[seal]

....
(Signature of notary or officer)

....
(Official character)

Figure 7.3. Patent application, administrator of estate of deceased inventor; power of attorney, oath.

tion on your behalf. A full first or middle name of each inventor without abbreviation, and a middle or first initial, if any, are required. Your mailing address is also required. Blank forms of applications are not supplied by the Patent and Trademark Office, but you can use those shown in the figures.

Drawings

In most cases you will have to furnish a drawing with your application. The drawing must show every feature of the invention specified in your claims, and is also required by the patent office to conform to a particular form. The patent office specifies the size of the sheet on which the drawing is made, the type of paper, the margins, and other details relating to the making of the drawing. They do this because the drawings are printed and published in a uniform, standard

STATE OF ....}
County of .... } ss:
........................., being sworn (or affirmed), deposes and says that he is a citizen of the United States of America and resident of ...., that on ...., 19..., he filed application for patent Serial No. .... in the United States Patent and Trademark Office, that he verily believes himself to be the original, first and sole inventor of the improvement in .... described and claimed in the specification of said application for patent; that he does not know and does not believe that the same was ever known or used before his invention thereof, or patented or described in any printed publication in any country before his invention thereof, or more than one year prior to the date of said application, or in public use or on sale in the United States for more than one year prior to the date of said application; that said invention has not been patented or made the subject of an inventor's certificate before the date of said application in any country foreign to the United States on an application filed by him or his legal representatives or assigns more than twelve months prior to the date of said application; that he acknowledges his duty to disclose information of which he is aware which is material to the examination of this application, and that no application for patent or inventor's certificate on said invention has been filed by him or his representatives or assigns in any country foreign to the United States, except as follows: ....

....
(Inventor's full signature)

Sworn to and subscribed before me this .... day of ...., 19...,

....
(Signature of notary or officer)

[SEAL]

....
(Official character)

Figure 7.4. Oath not accompanying application.

TO THE COMMISSIONER OF PATENTS AND TRADEMARKS:

Your petitioner, ..., a citizen of the United States and a resident of .... in the county of .... and State of ...., whose post-office address is ...., city of ...., State of ...., prays that letters patent may be granted to him for the new and original design for ...., set forth in the following specification; and he hereby appoints, ..., of ...., (Registration No. ....), his attorney (or agents), to prosecute this application and to transact all business in the Patent and Trademark Office connected therewith.

Be it known that I have invented a new, original, and ornamental design for .... of which the following is a specification, reference being had to the accompanying drawing, forming a part hereof.

The figure is a plan view of a ...., showing my new design.
I claim:

The ornamental design for a ...., as shown.

................., the above-named petitioner being sworn (or affirmed), deposes and says that he is a citizen of the United States and resident of county of ...., State of ...., that he verily believes himself to be the original, first, and sole inventor of the design for .... described and claimed in the foregoing specification; that he does not know and does not believe that the same was ever known or used before his invention thereof, or patented or described in any printed publication in any country before his invention thereof, or more than one year prior to this application, or in public use or on sale in the United States for more than one year prior to this application; that said design has not been patented or made the subject of an inventor's certificate in any country foreign to the United States on an application filed by him or his legal representatives or assigns more than 6 months prior to this application; that he acknowledges his duty to disclose information of which he is aware which is material to the examination of this application, and that no application for patent or inventor's certificate on said design has been filed by him or his representatives or assigns in any country foreign to the United States, except as follows: ....
....

....
(Inventor's full signature)

STATE OF ....}
County of .... } ss:
Sworn to and subscribed before me this .... day of ...., 19....
[SEAL]

....
(Signature of notary or officer)
....
(Official character)

Figure 7.5. Design specification, oath.

To the Commissioner of Patents and Trademarks:

Your petitioner, ..., a citizen of the United States and a resident of ...., in the State of ...., whose post-office address is ...., prays that letters patent may be granted to him for the new and distinct variety of ...., set forth in the following specification; and he hereby appoints .... of .... (Registration No. ....), his attorney (or agent), to prosecute this application and to transact all business in the Patent and Trademark Office connected therewith.

(If no power of attorney is to be included in the application, omit the appointment of the attorney.)

[The specification, which includes the description of the invention and the claims, is written here.]

................., the above-named petitioner, being sworn (or affirmed), deposes and says that he is a citizen of the United States of America and resident of ...., that he verily believes himself to be the original, first, and sole inventor of the new and distinct variety of .... described and claimed in the foregoing specification; that he has asexually reproduced the said new and distinct variety; that he does not know and does not believe that the same was ever known or used before his invention thereof, or patented or described in any printed publication in any country before his invention thereof, or more than one year prior to this application, or in public use or on sale in the United States for more than one year prior to this application; that said invention has not been patented or made the subject of an inventor's certificate in any country foreign to the United States on an application filed by him or his legal representatives or assigns more than 12 months prior to this application; that he acknowledges his duty to disclose information of which he is aware which is material to the examination of this application, and that no application for patent or inventor's certificate on said new and distinct variety of plant has been filed by him or his representatives or assigns in any country foreign to the United States, except as follow: ....

....
(Inventor's full signature)

State of .... } ss:
County of .... }

Sworn to and subscribed before me this .... day of ...., 19....,

....
(Signature of notary or officer)

[SEAL]

....
(Official character)

Figure 7.6. Plant patent application; power of attorney, oath.

To the Commissioner of Patents and Trademarks:

The undersigned having, on or about the .... day of ...., 19......, made application for letters patent for an improvement in ...., Serial Number ...., hereby appoints .... of ...., State of ...., Registration No. ...., his attorney (or agent), to prosecute said application, and to transact all business in the Patent and Trademark Office connected therewith.

....
(Signature)

Figure 7.7. Power of attorney or authorization of agent, not accompanying application.

style which the patent office issues, and also because the drawings must be readily understood by persons using the patent descriptions. The patent office publishes the following rules related to the standards for drawings.

1.84 *Standards for drawings.*

(a) *Paper and ink.* Drawings must be made upon paper which is flexible, strong, white, smooth, non-shiny and durable. Two-ply or three ply bristol board is preferred. The surface of the paper should be calendered and of a quality which will permit erasure and correction with India ink. India ink, or its equivalent in quality, is preferred for pen drawings to secure perfectly black solid lines. The use of white pigment to cover lines is not normally acceptable.

(b) *Size of sheet and margin.* The size of the sheets on which drawings are made may either be exactly 8½ by 14 inches (21.6 by 35.6 cm.) or exactly 21.0 by 29.7 cm.

To the Commissioner of Patents and Trademarks:

The undersigned having, on or about the .... day of ...., 19...., appointed ...., of ...., State of ...., his attorney (or agent) to prosecute an application for letters patent which application was filed on or about the .... day of ...., 19...., for an improvement in ...., Serial Number ...., hereby revokes the power of attorney (or authorization of agent) then given.

....
(Signature)

Figure 7.8. Revocation of power of attorney or authorization of agent.

(No special form is prescribed for assignments, which may contain various provisions depending upon the agreement of the parties. The following two forms are specimens of assignments which have been used in some cases.)

Whereas, I, ..., of ...., did obtain Letters Patent of the United States for an improvement in .... No. ...., dated ....; and whereas, I am now the sole owner of said patent; and,

Whereas, ..., of ...., whose post-office address is ...., City of ...., and State of ...., is desirous of acquiring the entire interest in the same;

Now, therefore, in consideration of the sum of .... dollars ($..........), the receipt of which is hereby acknowledged, and other good and valuable considerations, I, ..., by these presents do sell, assign, and transfer unto the said ...., the entire right, title, and interest in and to the said Letters Patent aforesaid; the same to be held and enjoyed by the said ...., for his own used and behoof, and for his legal representatives and assigns, to the full end of the term for which said Letters Patent are granted, as fully and entirely as the same would have been held by me had this assignment and sale not been made.

Executed, this .... day of ...., 19...., at ....

State ....⎱
County of ....⎰ *ss:*

Before me personally appeared said .... and acknowledged the foregoing instruments to be his free act and deed this .... day of ....,

....
(Notary Public)

[seal]

Figure 7.9. Assignment of patent.

(DIN size A4). All drawing sheets in a particular application must be the same size. One of the shorter sides of the sheet is regarded as its top. (1) On 8½ by 14 inch drawing sheets, the drawing must include a top margin of 2 inches (5.1 cm.) and bottom and side margins of ¼ inch (6.4 mm.) from the edges, thereby leaving a "sight" precisely 8 by 11¾ inches (20.3 by 29.8 cm.). Margin border lines are not permitted. All work must be included within the "sight." The sheets may be provided with two ¼ inch (6.4 mm.) diameter holes having their centerlines spaced $^{11}/_{16}$ inch (17.5 mm.) below the top edge and 2¾ inches (7.0 cm.) apart, said holes being equally spaced from the respective side edges. (2) On 21.0 by 29.7 cm. drawing sheets, the drawing must include a top margin of at least 2.5 cm., a left side margin of 2.5 cm., a right side margin of 1.5 cm., and a bottom margin of 1.0 cm. Margin border lines are not permitted. All work must be contained within a sight size not to exceed 17 by 26.2 cm.

(c) *Character of lines.* All drawings must be made with drafting instruments or by a process which will give them satisfactory reproduction characteristics. Every line and letter must be durable, black, sufficiently dense and dark, uniformly thick and well defined; the weight of all lines and letters must be heavy enough to permit adequate reproduction. This direction applies to all lines however fine, to shading, and to lines representing cut surfaces in sectional views. All lines must be clean, sharp, and solid. Fine or crowded lines should be avoided. Solid black should not be used for sectional or surface shading. Freehand work should be avoided wherever it is possible to do so.

WHEREAS, I, ..., of .... have invented certain new and useful Improvements in ...., for which an application for United States Letters Patent was filed on ...., Serial No. ...., [if the application has been prepared but not yet filed, state "for which an application for United States Letters Patent was executed on ....," instead] and

WHEREAS, ..., of ...., whose post-office address is ...., is desirous of acquiring the entire right, title and interest in the same;

Now, THEREFORE, in consideration of the sum of .... dollars ($.......), the receipt whereof is hereby acknowledged, and other good and valuable consideration, I, the said ...., by these presents do sell, assign and transfer unto said ...., the full and exclusive right to the said invention in the United States and the entire right, title, and interest in and to any and all Letters Patent which may be granted, therefore in the United States.

I hereby authorize and request the Commissioner of Patents and Trademarks to issue said Letters Patent to said ...., as the assignee of the entire right, title, and interest in and to the same, for his sole use and behoof; and for the use and behoof of his legal representatives, to the full end of the term for which said Letters Patent may be granted, as fully and entirely as the same would have been held by me had this assignment and sale not been made.

Executed this .... day of ...., 19...., at ....
....

STATE OF ....⎫
                              ⎬ ss:
County of ....⎭

Before me personally appeared said .... and acknowledged the foregoing instrument to be his free act and deed this ...... day of ...., 19....

....
(Notary Public)

[SEAL]

Figure 7.10. Assignment of application.

(Rules 65 and 68 of the Rules of Practice provide for a declaration in lieu of an oath in certain instances. The petition and specification preceded the declaration.) ...., the above-named petitioner .... declares that he is a citizen of the United States and resident of .... that he verily believes himself to be the original, first, and sole inventor of the improvement in .... described and claimed in the annexed specification; that he does not know and does not believe that the same was ever known or used before .... invention thereof, or patented or described in any printed publication in any country before his invention thereof, or more than one year prior to this application, or in public use or on sale in the United States more than one year prior to this application; that said invention has not been patented in any country foreign to the United States on an application filed by him or his legal representatives or assigns more than twelve months prior to this application; that he acknowledge his duty to disclose information of which he is aware is material to the examination of this application, and that no application for patent on said invention has been filed by him or his representatives or assigns in any country foreign to the United States, except as follows: ....

The undersigned petitioner .... declare .... further that all statements made herein of .... own knowledge are true and that all statements made on information and belief are believed to be true; and further that these statements were made with the knowledge that willful false statements and the like so made are punishable by fine or imprisonment, or both, under section 1001 of Title 18 of the United States Code and that such willful false statements may jeopardize the validity of the application or any patent issuing thereon.

Inventor's full name or names ....

....
(Signature)

Date ....

Figure 7.11. Declaration which may be included in an application in lieu of an oath.

(d) *Hatching and shading.* (1) Hatching should be made by oblique parallel lines spaced sufficiently apart to enable the lines to be distinguished without difficulty. (2) Heavy lines on the shade side of objects should preferably be used except where they tend to thicken the work and obscure reference characters. The light should come from the upper left-hand corner at an angle of 45°. Surface delineations should preferably be shown by proper shading, which should be open.

(e) *Scale.* The scale to which a drawing is made ought to be large enough to show the mechanism without crowding when the drawing is reduced in size to two-thirds in reproduction, and views of portions of the mechanism on a larger scale should be used when necessary to show details clearly; two or more sheets should be used if one does not give sufficient room to accomplish this end, but the number of sheets should not be more than is necessary.

(f) *Reference characters.* The different views should be consecutively numbered figures. Reference numerals (and letters, but numerals are preferred) must be plain, legible and carefully formed, and not be encircled. They should, if possible, measure at least one-eighth of an inch (3.2 mm.) in height so that they may bear reduction to one twenty-fourth of an inch (1.1 mm.); and they may be slightly larger when there is sufficient room. They should not be so placed in the close and complex parts of the drawing as to interfere with a thorough comprehension of the same, and therefore should rarely cross or mingle with the lines. When necessarily grouped around a certain part, they should be placed at a little distance, at the closest point where there is available space, and connected by lines with the parts to which they refer. They should not be placed upon hatched or shaded surfaces but when necessary, a blank space may be left in the hatching or shading where the character occurs so that is shall appear perfectly distinct and separate from the work. The same part of an invention appearing in more than one view of the drawing must always be designated by the same character, and the same character must never be used to designate different parts. Reference signs not mentioned in the description shall appear in the drawing, and vice versa.

(g) *Symbols, Legends.* Graphical drawing symbols and other labeled representations may be used for conventional elements when appropriate, subject to approval by the Office. The elements for which such symbols and labeled representations are used must be adequately identified in the specification. While descriptive matter on drawings is not permitted, suitable legends may be used, or may be required in proper cases, as in diagrammatic views and flow sheets or to show materials or where labeled representations are employed to illustrate conventional elements. Arrows may be required in proper cases, to show direction of movement. The lettering should be as large as, or larger than, the reference characters.

(i) *Views.* The drawings must contain as many figures as may be necessary to show the invention; the figures should be consecutively numbered if possible in the order in which they appear. The figures may be plain, elevation, section, or perspective views, and detail views of portions of elements, on a larger scale if necessary, may also be used. Exploded views, with the separated parts of the same figure embraced by a bracket, to show the relationship or order of assembly of various parts are permissible. When necessary, a view of a large machine or device in its entirety may be broken and extended over several sheets if there is no loss in facility of understanding the view. Where figures on two or more sheets form in effect a single complete figure, the figures on the several sheets should be so arranged that the complete figure can be understood by laying the drawing sheet adjacent to one another. The arrangement should be such that no part of any of the figures appearing on the various sheets are concealed and that the complete figure can be understood even though spaces will occur in the complete figure because of the margins on the drawing sheets. The plane upon which a sectional view is taken should be indicated on the general view by a broken line, the ends of which should be designated by numerals corresponding to the figure number of the sectional view and have arrows applied to indicate the direction in which the view is taken. A moved position may be shown by a broken line superimposed upon a suitable figure if this can be done without crowding, otherwise a separate figure must be used for this purpose. Modified forms of construction can only be shown in separate figures. Views should not be connected by projection lines nor should center lines be used.

(j) *Arrangements of views.* All views on the same sheet should stand in the same direction and, if possible, stand so that they can be read with the sheet held in an upright position. If views longer than the width of the sheet are necessary for the clearest illustration of the invention, the sheet may be turned on its side so that the top of the sheet with the appropriate top margin is on the right-hand side. One figure must not be placed upon another or within the outline of another.

(k) *Figure for Official Gazette.* The drawing should, as far as possible, be so planned that one of the views will be suitable for publication in the Official Gazette as the illustration of the invention.

(l) *Extraneous matter.* Identifying indicia (such as the attorney's docket number, inventor's name, number of sheets, etc.) not to exceed 2¾ inches (7.0 cm.) in width may be placed in a centered location between the side edges within three-fourths inch (19.1 mm.) of the top edge. Authorized security markings may be placed on the drawings provided they are outside the illustrations and are removed when the material is declassified. Other extraneous matter will not be permitted upon the face of the drawing.

(m) *Transmission of drawings.* Drawings transmitted to the Office should be sent flat, protected by a sheet of heavy binder's board, or may be rolled for transmission in a suitable mailing tube: but must never be folded. If received creased or mutilated new drawings will be required. (See rule 1.152 for design drawings, 1.165 for plant drawings, and 1.174 for reissue drawings.)

The requirements relating to these drawings are strictly enforced. However, a drawing which doesn't comply with all of the rules or regulations may be accepted for the purpose of examination with a new drawing required later. The patent office also advises all applicants to employ competent draftsmen to make the drawings. The patent office may furnish drawings at your expense, although the time required varies, if you can't otherwise procure them.

Filing Fees

The filing fee of an application for an original patent, except in design cases, consists of a basic fee and additional fees. The basic fee is currently $65 and entitles you to present 10 claims, including not more than one in independent form. For every additional independent form claim, you must pay an additional $10. You also pay an additional $2 per claim for every claim over 10.

A dependent form claim is a claim that refers back to and further restricts a single preceding claim. In other words, a claim is in dependent form if it incorporates by reference a single preceding claim and includes all the limitations of the claim incorporated by reference. Otherwise, the claim is considered to be in independent form.

Additional fees are also required on presentation of claims when an amendment is filed which presents additional claims over the total number already paid for, or additional independent claims over the number of independent claims already accounted for.

These filing fees are for the government only and do not include legal or attorney fees. You should understand up front that to obtain a patent in the limited state will cost several thousand dollars if you include attorney and other legal fees.

USE OF PATENT PENDING MARKING

If you make or sell patented articles, you are required to mark the articles with the word "patented" and the number of the patent. The penalty for failure to do this is that you may not recover damages from a patent infringer unless the infringer was notified of the infringement and continued to infringe after the notice. However, the marking of an article as patented when it is in fact not patented is against the law. Some inventors mark articles sold with the terms "patent applied for" or "patent pending." These phrases have no legal effect, but they warn that an application for a patent has been filed in the Patent and Trademark Office. Thus, a potential infringer knows that if he or she tools up to manufacture the item that has such a marking, when and if a patent is granted, he or she will be infringing on your patent and could be subject to a lawsuit. However, the protection afforded by a patent does not start until the actual grant of the patent.

LIMITATIONS AND DISADVANTAGES OF PROTECTION WITH PATENTS

There are disadvantages and limitations to the use of patents. Here are some that you should consider before you apply for a patent through the patent office.

First, your patent can be designed around. That is, if your patent shows how to accomplish a certain task, you're only being given a patent for that particular method of accomplishing that task. Someone else can then see what you are doing, think of a different way to do the same task which does not infringe on your patent, and patent the new invention himself.

Infringement of a patent consists in the unauthorized making, using, or selling of your patented invention within the territory of the United States during the term of the patent. However, if the patent is infringed, the government itself will not sue. That's your job. You may sue for relief in the appropriate federal court and you may ask the court for an injunction to prevent the continuation of the infringement, and award of damages because of the infringement. However, in such a suit, the defendant may raise the question of the validity of your patent. This is an important point. Your patent can be invalidated by the court even after it has already been granted to you. In fact, in one survey it was reported that 70% of patents that have been taken to court for infringement are actually invalidated. These inventors received nothing for their effort or for their expense in obtaining their patents, much less the court costs.

Another disadvantage of a patent is the cost. As stated, it will amount to several thousand dollars. And this only gets you a patent in the United States. Remember that a U.S. patent does not protect you in foreign countries, and each country has its own patent laws. While you can certainly obtain patents in foreign countries through your patent attorney, this will cost more money. Therefore, the cost of a patent must be weighed against its value prior to applying for it. Many inventors have the idea that it is possible to make a fortune simply by having a patent granted. This is not true.

Another disadvantage is the specifics on the invention required by the patent office. It is for this reason that many chemical processes, even though they can be patented, are not. It has been reported, for example, that the inventor of the paper which corrects typewriting mistakes made a gross error in patenting because the chemical would work over a large range of percentages of impregnation of the paper, whereas the patent office required a specific percentage to the nearest tenth. From the information in the patent itself, many others were able to copy the idea simply by impregnating the paper with other amounts of the chemical. To prevent this sort of infringement, the formula for Coca Cola has never been patented and still remains a secret. However, if you decide to proceed, the end result is the U.S. patent shown in Figure 7.12. To illustrate the differences, a foreign patent for the same device is shown in Figure 7.12A.

United States Patent [19]

Cohen

[11] **3,803,639**

[45] **Apr. 16, 1974**

[54] **BODY ARMOUR JACKET**

[76] Inventor: **William A. Cohen,** 1556 N. Sierra Madre Villa, Pasadena, Calif. 91107

[22] Filed: **July 11, 1973**

[21] Appl. No.: **378,207**

[30] **Foreign Application Priority Data**

Oct. 4, 1972 Israel.......................... 40502

[52] **U.S. Cl.** **2/2.5**
[51] **Int. Cl.** F41h 1/02
[58] **Field of Search** 2/2.5

[56] **References Cited**

UNITED STATES PATENTS

2,640,987	6/1903	Ehlers..	2/2.5
2,743,446	5/1956	Persico et al.	2/2.5
2,748,391	6/1956	Lewis et al..................................	2/2.5
2,954,563	10/1960	DeGrazio....................................	2/2.5
3,130,414	4/1964	Bailey et al.	2/2.5
3,392,406	7/1968	Pernini et al.	2/2.5

Primary Examiner—Alfred R. Guest
Attorney, Agent, or Firm—Benjamin J. Barish

[57] **ABSTRACT**

A body armour jacket, which may be easily donned and doffed and may be conveniently opened for purposes of comfort or ventilation, includes a front body assembly and a back body assembly, the front body assembly comprising a right armour section, a left armour section, and a center armour flap. The ends of the right and left armour sections are in abutting relationship and are fastened together by a fastener. The center armour flap is hinged to one of the sections along a line spaced from its abutting end and is fastenable by another fastener to the other section along a line spaced from its abutting end, such that the center armour flap, when closed, bridges the abutting ends of both sections.

7 Claims, 4 Drawing Figures

FIG.1 FIG.2 FIG.3 FIG.4

Figure 7.12. United States patent.

1

BODY ARMOUR JACKET

BACKGROUND OF THE INVENTION

The present invention relates to body armour jackets such as are used by soldiers and policemen to provide body protection against small arms fire, shrapnel, and the like.

A number of body armour jackets have been designed. In one type, the front assembly of the jacket includes a fabric carrier and a one-piece armour insert. Such a jacket, however, is not openable from the front and therefore is inconvenient to don and doff, sometimes uncomfortable to wear, and difficult to ventilate. Another known form of body armour jacket is made of flexible armour, such as ballistic nylon, and includes a front closure arrangement by overlapping the armour on the inside. Such an arrangement, however, would not be satisfactory with rigid armour, as distinguished from flexible armour, since rigid armour would produce undue discomfort in the chest and abdominal regions because of the armour rigidity.

Insofar as I am aware, a rigid armour body jacket having a front closure has not yet been devised. An object of the present invention is to provide such a body armour jacket.

SUMMARY OF THE INVENTION

According to the invention, there is provided a body armour jacket including a front body assembly and a back body assembly joined thereto, characterized in that the front body assembly comprises a right armour section, a left armour section, and a center armour flap.

The ends of the right and left armour sections are in abutting relationship and are fastened together by a first openable and closable fastener. The center armour flap is hinged to one of said sections along a line spaced from its abutting end and is fastenable by a second openable and closable fastener to the other of said sections along a line spaced from its abutting end, such that the center armour flap, when closed, bridges the abutting ends of both said armour sections.

According to another feature of the invention, the right and left armour sections and said center armour flap each comprises a fabric carrier and a rigid armour plate insert.

In the preferred embodiment of the invention described below, the center armour flap is hinged to one of these sections by stitching. Also, the first mentioned fastener is a slide-fastener, and the second-mentioned fastener comprises a series of snap-fasteners.

According to a further features, the front body assembly is joined to the back body assembly by adjustable shoulder and waist straps.

Such a body armour jacket, since it is provided with a front closure, may be easily donned and doffed, and may be conveniently opened when desired for purposes of comfort or ventilation.

Further features and advantages of the invention will be apparent from the description below.

BRIEF DESCRIPTION OF THE DRAWINGS

The invention is herein described, by way of example only, with reference to the accompanying drawings, wherein:

FIG. 1 is a front elevational view of a body armour jacket constructed in accordance with the invention;

2

FIG. 2 is a side elevational view of the body armour jacket of FIG. 1;

FIG. 3 is a rear elevational view of the body armour jacket of FIG. 1; and

FIG. 4 is a front elevational view corresponding to FIG. 1 but illustrating the center armour flap in its open position to permit opening and closing the front closure fastener.

DESCRIPTION OF THE PREFERRED EMBODIMENT

The body armour jacket illustrated in the drawings comprises a front assembly, generally designated 2, and a back assembly, generally designated 4, both joined together by adjustable shoulder straps 6 and adjustable waist straps 8. The straps are made adjustable by the provision of buckles 10 in the shoulder straps, and buckles 12 in the waist straps.

The back assembly, as shown in FIG. 3, comprises a single fabric carrier 14 and a single rigid armour plate insert 16 disposed within the fabric carrier. The shoulder straps 6 and waist straps 8 are fixed, as by stitching, to the fabric carrier 14.

Front assembly 2, is made of three parts, namely a right armour section 22, a left armour section 24, and a center armour flap 26. Each of the foregoing is also made of a fabric carrier (22a, 24a, 26a), and a rigid armour plate insert (22b, 24b, 26b) carried within its respective fabric carrier. If desired, the fabric carriers of the right and left sections may also be formed with pockets as shown at 28 and 30, respectively.

As shown particularly in FIG. 4 (wherein the center armour flap 26 is pivoted open), the ends of the right and left sections 2 and 4 are disposed in abutting relationship and are fastened together by an openable and closable slide-fastener 32, e.g., a zip-fastener. The center armour flap 26 is hingedly mounted, as by stitching, to the left armour section 24 along line 34, which line is spaced from the abutting end of that section. In addition, the center flap is fastenable to the right armour section by a line of snap fasteners 36, the female snaps 36 of which are located along a line on the fabric carrier 24a of the right section 24 spaced inwardly from its abutting end, and the male snaps 38 of which are located along a line on the fabric carrier 26a of the center armour flap 26 spaced slightly from the corresponding end of the flap.

The arrangement is such that when the center armour flap 26 is closed (FIG. 1), its rigid armour insert 26b completely bridges the abutting ends of the right and left armour inserts 22b, 24b of the sections. The armour insert 26b of the center flap thus provides armour portection for the region occupied by the front closure 32.

It will thus be seen that the body armour jacket illustrated may be opened from the front merely by detaching snaps 36, 38, thereby permitting the center armour flap to be pivoted open; and then opening the center slide-fastener 32 to open the jacket. To close the jacket, slide-fastener 32 is closed, and then fasteners 38 are snapped into fasteners 36 to close the center armour flap 26.

The armour inserts may be rigid reinforced fiberglass or ceramic. The invention could also be used with soft armour inserts, such as nylon.

It will thus be seen that the body armour jacket illustrated is provided with a front closure system which

Figure 7.12. (Continued)

3

permits the jacket to be conveniently donned, doffed and opened for purposes of comfort or ventilation.

Many modifications, variations, and other applications of the illustrated embodiment will be apparent.

What is claimed is:

1. A body armour jacket including a front body assembly and a back body assembly joined thereto, characterized in that the front body assembly comprises a right armour section, a left armour section, and a center armour flap, the end of the right and left armour sections being in abutting relationship and being fastened together by a first openable and closable fastener, the centre armour flap being hinged to one of said sections along a line spaced from its abutting end and being fastenable by a second openable and closable fastener to the other of said sections along a line spaced from its abutting end such that the center armour flap, when closed, bridges the abutting ends of both said armour sections.

4

2. A jacket according to claim 1, wherein said right and left armour sections and said center armour flap each comprises a fabric carrier and a rigid armour plate insert.

3. A jacket according to claim 1, wherein said center armour flap is hinged to said one section by stitching.

4. A jacket according to claim 1, wherein said first fastener is a slide-fastener.

5. A jacket according to claim 1, wherein said second fastener comprises a line of snap-fasteners.

6. A jacket according to claim 1, wherein said front body assembly is joined to the back body assembly by adjustable shoulder and waist straps.

7. A jacket according to claim 1, wherein said back body assembly comprises a fabric carrier and a rigid armour plate insert.

* * * * *

Figure 7.12. (Continued)

PATENT SPECIFICATION ⁽¹¹⁾ 1 378 609

1 378 609

(21) Application No. 40631/73 (22) Filed 29 Aug. 1973 (19)

(31) Convention Application No. 40502 (32) Filed 4 Oct. 1972 in

(33) Israel (IL)

(44) Complete Specification published 27 Dec. 1974

(51) International Classification F41H 1/02

(52) Index at acceptance

A3V 1A5A

(54) AN ARMOUR JACKET

(71) I, WILLIAM ALAN COHEN, of 1556 North Sierra Madre Villa, Pasadena, California, United States of America, do hereby declare the invention, for which I pray that a patent may be granted to me, and the method by which it is to be performed, to be particularly described in and by the following statement:—

The present invention relates to body armour jackets such as are used by soldiers and policemen to provide body protection against small arms fire, shrapnel, and the like.

A number of body armour jackets have been proposed. In one type, the front assembly of the jacket includes a fabric carrier and a one-piece armour insert. Such a jacket, however, is not openable from the front and therefore is inconvenient to put on and take off, sometimes uncomfortable to wear, and difficult to ventilate.

According to the present invention there is provided a body armour jacket including a front assembly and a back assembly joined thereto, the front assembly comprising a right armour section, a left armour section, and a centre armour flap, the free side edges of the right and left armour sections being intended to be disposed in mutually abutting relationship when the jacket is worn and being provided with a first openable and closable fastener to fasten together said abutting edges, and the centre armour flap being hinged to one of said sections along a line spaced from said free side edge of said one section and being fastenable by a second openable and closable fastener to the other of said sections along a line spaced from said free side edge of said other section such that the centre armour flap, when closed, bridges said free side edges of both said armour sections.

The right and left armour sections and the centre armour flap each comprise a fabric carrier and a rigid armour plate insert.

In the preferred embodiment of the invention described below, the centre armour flap is hinged to one of these sections by

[Price 25p]

stitching. Also, the first mentioned fastener is a sliding clasp fastener, and the second-mentioned fastener comprises a series of press-stud fasteners.

The front assembly may be joined to the back assembly by adjustable shoulder and waist straps.

Such a body armour jacket, since it is provided with a front closure, may be easily put on and taken off, and may be conveniently opened when desired for purposes of comfort or ventilation.

The invention will now be described in more detail, by way of example only, with reference to the accompanying drawings, in which:—

Fig. 1 is a front elevational view of a body armour jacket;

Fig. 2 is a side elevational view of the body armour jacket of Fig. 1;

Fig. 3 is a rear elevational view of the body armour jacket of Fig. 1; and

Fig. 4 is a front elevational view corresponding to Fig. 1 but illustrating the centre armour flap in its open position to permit opening and closing of the front closure fastener.

The body armour jacket illustrated in the drawings comprises a front assembly, generally designated 2, and a back assembly, generally designated 4, both joined together by adjustable shoulder straps 6 and adjustable waist straps 8. The straps are made adjustable by the provision of buckles 10 in the shoulder straps, and buckles 12 in the waist straps.

The back assembly, as shown in Fig. 3, comprises a single fabric carrier 14 and a single rigid armour plate insert 16 disposed within the fabric carrier. The shoulder straps 6 and waist straps 8 are fixed, as by stitching, to the fabric carrier 14.

Front assembly, 2, is made of three parts, namely a right armour section 22, a left armour section 24, and a centre armour flap 26. Each of the foregoing is also made of a fabric carrier 22a, 26a, and a rigid armour plate insert 22b, 24b, 26b, carried within its respective fabric carrier. If desired, the fabric carriers of the right

Figure 7.12A. Foreign patent.

155

and left sections may also be formed with pockets as shown at 28 and 30, respectively.

As shown particularly in Fig. 4 (wherein the centre armour flap 26 is pivoted open), the adjacent edges of the right and left sections 22 and 24 are disposed in abutting relationship and are fastened together by an openable and closable sliding clasp fastener 32, i.e. zip-fastener. The centre armour flap 26 is hingedly mounted, as by stitching, to the left armour section 24 along line 34, which line is spaced from said abutting side edge of that section. In addition, the centre flap is fastenable to the right armour section by a line of press-stud fasteners, the female members 36 of which are located along a line on the fabric carrier 22a of the right section 22 spaced inwardly from its abutting side edge, and the male members 38 of which are located along a line on the fabric carrier 26a of the centre armour flap 26 spaced slightly from the corresponding free side edge of the flap.

The arrangement is such that when the centre armour flap 26 is closed (Fig. 1), its rigid armour insert 26b completely bridges the abutting side edges of the right and left armour inserts 22b, 24b of the sections. The armour insert 26b of the centre flap thus provides armour protection for the region occupied by the front fastener 32.

It will thus be seen that the body armour jacket illustrated may be opened from the front merely by detaching press-stud fastener members 36, 38, thereby permitting the centre armour flap to be pivoted open; and then opening the centre sliding-clasp fastener 32 to open the jacket. To close the jacket, sliding-clasp fastener 32 is closed, and then fastener members 38 are snapped into fastener members 36 to close the centre armour flap 26.

The armour inserts may be of rigid reinforced fibre-glass or ceramic. The invention could also be used with soft armour inserts, such as nylon.

It will thus be seen that the body armour jacket illustrated is provided with a front closure system which permits the jacket to be conveniently put on and taken off and opened for purposes of comfort or ventilation.

WHAT I CLAIM IS:—

1. A body armour jacket including a front assembly and a back assembly joined thereto, the front assembly comprising a right armour section, a left armour section, and a centre armour flap, the free side edges of the right and left armour sections being intended to be disposed in mutually abutting relationship when the jacket is worn and being provided with a first openable and closable fastener to fasten together said abutting edges, and the centre armour flap being hinged to one of said sections along a line spaced from said free side edge of said one section and being fastenable by a second openable and closable fastener to the other of said sections along a line spaced from said free side edge of said other section such that the centre armour flap, when closed, bridges said free side edges of both said armour sections.

2. A jacket as claimed in claim 1, wherein the right and left armour sections and the centre armour flap each comprise a fabric carrier and a rigid armour plate insert.

3. A jacket as claimed in claim 1 or claim 2, wherein the centre armour flap is hinged to said one section by stitching.

4. A jacket as claimed in any one of claims 1 to 3, wherein said second fastener comprises a line of press-stud fasteners.

5. A jacket as claimed in any one of Claims 1 to 4, wherein said front assembly is joined to the back assembly by adjustable shoulder and waist straps.

6. A jacket as claimed in any one of Claims 1 to 5, wherein said back assembly comprises a fabric carrier and a rigid armour plate insert.

7. A body armour jacket substantially as herein described with reference to and as illustrated in the accompanying drawings.

MARKS & CLERK,
Chartered Patent Agents,
57 & 58 Lincoln's Inn Fields,
London WC1A 3LS.
Agents for the Applicant.

Printed for Her Majesty's Stationery Office by Burgess & Son (Abingdon), Ltd.—1974.
Published at The Patent Office, 25 Southampton Buildings, London, WC2A 1AY
from which copies may be obtained.

Figure 7.12A. (Continued)

Fig. 1.

Fig. 2.

Fig. 3.

Fig. 4.

Figure 7.12A.   (Continued)

QUESTIONS AND ANSWERS ABOUT PATENTS

Following are 40 frequently asked questions about patents and their responses published by the Patent and Trademark Office of the Department of Commerce.[1]

Nature and Duration of Patents

1. Q. **What is a patent?**

   A. A patent is a grant issued by the United States Government giving an inventor the right to exclude all others from making, using, or selling his invention within the United States, its territories and possessions.

2. Q. **For how long a term of years is a patent granted?**

   A. Seventeen years from the date on which it is issued; except for patents on ornamental designs, which are granted for terms of 3½, 7, or 14 years.

3. Q. **May the term of a patent be extended?**

   A. Only by special act of Congress, and this occurs very rarely and only in most exceptional circumstances

4. Q. **Does the patentee continue to have any control over use of the invention after his patent expires?**

   A. No. Anyone has the free right to use an invention covered in an expired patent, so long as he does not use features covered in other unexpired patents in doing so.

5. Q. **On what subject matter may a patent be granted?**

   A. A patent may be granted to the inventor or discoverer of any new and useful process, machine, manufacture, or composition of matter, or any new and useful improvement thereof, or on any distinct and new variety of plant, other than a tuber-propagated plant, which is asexually reproduced, or on any new, original, and ornamental design for an article of manufacture.

6. Q. **On what subject matter may a patent not be granted?**

   A. A patent may not be granted on a useless device, on printed matter, on a method of doing business, on an improvement in a device which would be obvious to a person skilled in the art, or on a machine which will not operate, particularly on an alleged perpetual motion machine.

Meaning of Words "Patent Pending"

7. Q. **What do the terms "patent pending" and "patent applied for" mean?**

   A. They are used by a manufacturer or seller of an article to inform the public that an application for patent on that article is on file in the Patent and Trademark Office. The law imposes a fine on those who use these terms falsely to deceive the public.

Patent Applications

8. Q. **I have made some changes and improvements in my invention after my patent application was filed in the Patent and Trademark Office. May I amend my patent application by adding description or illustration of these features?**

   A. No. The law specifically provides that new matter shall not be introduced into the disclosure of a patent application. However, you should call the attention of your attorney or agent promptly to any such changes you may make or plan to make, so that he may take or recommend any steps that may be necessary for your protection.

9. Q. **How does one apply for a patent?**

   A. By making the proper application to the Commissioner of Patents and Trademarks, Washington, D.C. 20231.

10. Q. **What is the best way to prepare an application?**

   A. As the preparation and prosecution of an application are highly complex proceedings they should preferably be conducted by an attorney trained in this specialized practice. The Patent and Trademark Office therefore advises inventors to employ a patent

[1] *Q and A About Patents*, U.S. Department of Commerce, Washington, D.C. (1979).

attorney or agent who is registered in the Patent and Trademark Office. No attorney or agent not registered in the Patent and Trademark Office may prosecute applications. The pamphlet entitled *Attorneys and Agents Registered to Practice Before the U.S. Patent and Trademark Office,* contains an alphabetical and geographical list of persons on the Patent and Trademark Office register.

See Question 40 for source and price.

11. Q. **Of what does a patent application consist?**

A. An application fee, a petition, a specification and claims describing and defining the invention, an oath or declaration, and a drawing if the invention can be illustrated.

12. Q. **What are the Patent and Trademark Office fees in connection with filing of an application for patent and issuance of the patent?**

A. A filing fee of $65 plus certain additional charges for claims depending on their number and the manner of their presentation are required when the application is filed. A final or issue fee of $100 plus certain printing charges are also required if the patent is to be granted. This final fee is not required until your application is allowed by the Patent and Trademark Office.

13. Q. **Are models required as part of the application?**

A. Only in the most exceptional cases. The Office has the power to require that a model be furnished, but rarely exercises it.

14. Q. **Is it necessary to go to the Patent and Trademark Office in Washington to transact business concerning patent matters?**

A. No; most business with the Patent and Trademark Office is conducted by correspondence. Interviews regarding pending applications can be arranged with examiners if necessary, however, and are often helpful.

15. Q. **Can the Patent and Trademark Office give advice as to whether an inventor should apply for a patent?**

A. No. It can only consider the patentability of an invention when this question comes regularly before it in the form of a patent application.

16. Q. **Is there any danger that the Patent and Trademark Office will give others information contained in my application while it is pending?**

A. No. All patent applications are maintained in the strictest secrecy until the patent is issued. After the patent is issued, however, the Patent and Trademark Office file containing the application and all correspondence leading up to issuance of the patent is made available in the Patent Search Room for inspection by anyone, and copies of these files may be purchased from the Patent and Trademark Office.

17. Q. **May I write to the Patent and Trademark Office directly about my application after it is filed?**

A. The Patent and Trademark Office will answer an applicant's inquiries as to the status of the application, and inform him whether his application has been rejected, allowed, or is awaiting action by the Patent and Trademark Office. However, if you have a patent attorney or agent the Patent and Trademark Office cannot correspond with both you and the attorney concerning the merits of your application. All comments concerning your invention should be forwarded through your patent attorney or agent.

18. Q. **What happens when two inventors apply separately for a patent for the same invention?**

A. An "interference" is declared and testimony may be submitted to the Patent and Trademark Office to determine which inventor is entitled to the patent. Your attorney or agent can give you further information about this if it becomes necessary.

19. Q. **Can the period allowed by the Patent and Trademark Office for response to an office action in a pending application be extended?**

A. No. This time period required by the examiner cannot be extended, but it may be reduced to not less than thirty days. The application will become abandoned unless proper response is received in the Patent and Trademark Office within the time allowed.

20. Q. **May applications be examined out of their regular order?**

A. No; all applications are examined in the order in which they are filed, except under certain very special conditions.

When to Apply for Patent

21. Q. **I have been making and selling my invention for the past 13 months and have not filed any patent application. Is it too late for me to apply for patent?**

A. Yes. A valid patent may not be obtained if the invention was in public use or on sale in this country for more than one year prior to the filing of your patent application. Your own use and sale of the invention for more than a year before your application is filed will bar your right to a patent just as effectively as though this use and sale had been done by someone else.

22. Q. **I published an article describing my invention in a magazine 13 months ago. Is it too late to apply for patent?**

A. Yes. The fact that you are the author of the article will not save your patent application. The law provides that the inventor is not entitled to a patent if the invention has been described in a printed publication anywhere in the world more than a year before his patent application is filed.

Who May Obtain a Patent

23. Q. **Is there any restriction as to persons who may obtain a United States patent?**

A. No. Any inventor may obtain a patent regardless of age or sex, by complying with the provisions of the law. A foreign citizen may obtain a patent under exactly the same conditions as a United States citizen.

24. Q. **If two or more persons work together to make an invention, to whom will the patent be granted?**

A. If each had a share in the ideas forming the invention, they are joint inventors and a patent will be issued to them jointly on the basis of a proper patent application filed by them jointly. If on the other hand one of these persons has provided all of the ideas of the invention, and the other has only followed instructions in making it, the person who contributed the ideas is the sole inventor and the patent application and patent should be in his name alone.

25. Q. **If one person furnishes all of the ideas to make an invention and another employs him or furnishes the money for building and testing the invention, should the patent application be filed by them jointly?**

A. No. The application must be signed, executed, sworn to, and filed in the Patent and Trademark Office, in the name of the true inventor. This is the person who furnishes the ideas, not the employer or the person who furnishes the money.

26. Q. **May a patent be granted if an inventor dies before filing his application?**

A. Yes; the application may be filed by the inventor's executor or administrator.

27. Q. **While in England this summer, I found an article on sale which was very ingenious and has not been introduced into the United States or patented or described. May I obtain a United States patent on this invention?**

A. No. A United States patent may be obtained only by the true inventor, not by someone who learns of an invention of another.

Ownership and Sale of Patent Rights

28. Q. **May the inventor sell or otherwise transfer his right to his patent or patent application to someone else?**

A. Yes. He may sell all or any part of his interest in the patent application or patent to anyone by a properly worded assignment. The application must be filed in the Patent and Trademark Office as the invention of the true inventor, however, and not as the invention of the person who has purchased the invention from him.

29. Q. **Is it advisable to conduct a search of patents and other records before applying for a patent?**

A. Yes; if it is found that the device is shown in some prior patent it is useless to make application. By making a search beforehand the expense involved in filing a needless application is often saved.

Patent Searching

30. Q. **Where can a search be conducted?**

   A. In the Search Room of the Patent and Trademark Office at Crystal Plaza, 2021 Jefferson Davis Highway, Arlington, Virginia. Classified and numerically arranged sets of United States and foreign patents are kept there for public use.

31. Q. **Will the Patent and Trademark Office make searches for individuals to help them decide whether to file patent applications?**

   A. No. But it will assist inventors who come to the Patent and Trademark Office by helping them to find the proper patent classes in which to make searches. For a reasonable fee it will furnish lists of patents in any class and subclass, and copies of these lists may be purchased for $1.00 each.

Technical Knowledge Available from Patents

32. Q. **I have not made an invention but have encountered a problem. Can I obtain knowledge through patents of what has been done by others to solve the problem?**

   A. The patents in the Patent Search Room contain a vast wealth of technical information and suggestions, organized in a manner which will enable you to review those most closely related to your field of interest. You may come to Arlington and review these patents, or engage a patent practitioner to do this for you and to send you copies of the patents most closely related to your problem.

33. Q. **Can I make a search or obtain technical information from patents at locations other than the Patent Search Room?**

   A. Yes. The libraries listed on page 14 have sets of patent copies numerically arranged in bound volumes, and these patents may be used for search or other information purposes as discussed in the answer to Question 34.

34. Q. **How can technical information be found in a library collection of patents arranged in bound volumes in numerical order?**

   A. You must first find out from the *Manual of Classification* in the library the Patent classes and subclasses which cover the field of your invention or interest. You can then, by referring to microfilm reels or volumes of the *Index of Patents* in the library identify the patents in these subclasses and, thence, look at them in the bound volumes. Further information on this subject may be found in the leaflet *Obtaining Information from Patents*, a copy of which may be requested from the Patent and Trademark Office.

Infringement of Others' Patents

35. Q. **If I obtain a patent on my invention, will that protect me against the claims of others who assert that I am infringing their patents when I make, use, or sell my own invention?**

   A. No. There may be a patent of a more basic nature on which your invention is an improvement. If your invention is a detailed refinement or feature of such a basically protected invention, you may not use it without the consent of the patentee, just as no one will have the right to use your patented improvement without your consent. You should seek competent legal advice before starting to make or sell or use your invention commercially, even though it is protected by a patent granted to you.

Enforcement of Patent Rights

36. Q. **Will the Patent and Trademark Office help me to prosecute others if they infringe the rights granted to me by my patent?**

   A. No. The Patent and Trademark Office has no jurisdiction over questions relating to the infringement of patent rights. If your patent is infringed you may sue the infringer in the appropriate United States court at your own expense.

Patent Protection in Foreign Countries

37. Q. **Does a United States patent give protection in foreign countries?**

A. No. The United States patent protects your invention only in this country. If you wish to protect your invention in foreign countries, you must file an application in the Patent Office of each such country within the time permitted by law. This may be quite expensive, both because of the cost of filing and prosecuting the individual patent applications, and because of the fact that most foreign countries require payment of taxes to maintain the patents in force. You should inquire of your practitioner about these costs before you decide to file in foreign countries.

How to Obtain Further Information

38. Q. **How does one obtain information as to patent applications, fees, and other details concerning patents?**

A. By ordering a pamphlet entitled *General Information Concerning Patents.* See Question 40 for sources and price.

39. Q. **How can I obtain information about the steps I should take in deciding whether to try to obtain a patent, in securing the best possible patent protection, and in developing and marketing my invention successfully?**

A. By ordering a pamphlet entitled *Patents and Inventions—An Information Aid to Inventors.* See Question 40 for source and price.

40. Q. **How can I obtain copies of the pamphlets mentioned in the answers to Questions 10, 38, and 39?**

A. These pamphlets may be purchased from the Superintendent of Documents, Washington, D.C. 20402, or through any district office of the U.S. Department of Commerce. The prices are subject to change without notice. The prices are:

Attorneys and Agents Registered to Practice Before the U.S. Patent and Trademark Office, $5.00; General Information Concerning Patents, $1.80; Patents and Inventions—An Information Aid to Inventors, $1.75.

WHAT IS A COPYRIGHT?

A copyright is a form of protection given to the authors of original works of authorship, be they literary, dramatic, musical, artistic, or even certain other types of intellectual works. Section 106 of the U.S. Copyright Act generally gives the owner of the copyright the exclusive rights to do and to authorize the following:

1. To reproduce a copyrighted work in copies or phono records
2. To prepare derivative works based upon the copyrighted work
3. To distribute copies of phonorecords of the copyrighted work to the public by sale or other transfer of ownership, or by rent or lease or lending
4. In the case of literary, musical, dramatic, and choreographic works, pantomimes, motion pictures, and other audiovisual works, to perform the copyrighted work publicly
5. In case of literary, musical, dramatic, choreographic, and sculptural works, including the individual images of motion picture or audiovisual works, to display the copyrighted work publicly

It is illegal for anyone to violate any of the rights provided to the owner by the copyright. However, these rights are not unlimited in their scope, and Sections 107 through 118 of the Copyright Act provide for limitations.

Typical of items which can be copyrighted are the following: literary works, musical works including any accompanying words; dramatic works including any accompanying music; pantomimes and choreographic works; pictorial, graphic and sculptural works; motion pictures and other audiovisual works; and sound recordings. This list is, however, not all-inclusive. For example, a computer program, software, is registerable as a literary work. Maps are also registerable as pictorial, graphic, or sculptural works, and so forth. All of these can be copyrighted.

WHAT CAN'T BE COPYRIGHTED

There are several categories of material that are not eligible for copyright protection. These include: (1) works that have not been fixed in a tangible form of expression, for example, works that have not been written down, recorded, or photographed; (2) titles, names, short phrases, and slogans, mere symbols or designs, mere variations of typographic ornamentation, lettering, or coloring, mere listings of ingredients or contents; (3) ideas, procedures, methods, systems, processes, concepts, principles, discoveries, or devices, as distinguished from a description, explanation, or illustration; (4) works consisting entirely of information that is common property and containing no original authorship. Examples here would include standard calendars, height and weight charts, tape measures and rules, schedules of sporting events, and lists of tables taken from public documents or other common sources.

WHO CAN COPYRIGHT

As with a patent, only the author or someone deriving his or her rights through the author can rightfully claim copyright. It is important to realize that, unlike a patent, a copyright is done automatically and does not require an attorney even for registration. The procedures for copyright registration are very simple. Copyright protection exists from the time the work is created in any fixed form. The copyright in the work of authorship immediately becomes the property of the author who created it. Now, there is an exception to this if you are working for someone else. In this case, it is the employer, not the employee, who is considered the author, as you come under a copyright statute defining "work for hire," which is work prepared by an employee within the scope of his or her employment, or a work specially ordered or commissioned for use as a contribution to a collective work.

If there are two or more authors of a joint work, all are co-owners of the copyright unless there are agreements to the contrary.

HOW TO APPLY FOR A COPYRIGHT

As we've said, a copyright is secured automatically upon creation. The way in which copyright protection is secured under a new law in the United States is sometimes confused with the way it worked under the old law. Under the old copyright law, copyright was secured by publication with the copyright notice or registration in the copyright office. However, under the new law, no publication or registration or other action in the copyright office is required to secure copyright. You should also recognize that this differs from a patent which must actually be granted by the Patent and Trademark Office.

Prior to 1978 when the new copyright law came into effect, copyright was secured by act of publication with the notice of copyright, publication meaning the distribution of copies of a work to the public by sale or other transfer of ownership, or by rental, lease, or lending. Even though publication is no longer required for copyright, the concept of publication is important in the copyright law because when a work is published, several important consequences follow:

1. Works that are published with a notice of copyright in the United States are subject to mandatory deposit with the Library of Congress.
2. Publication of a work can affect the limitations on the exclusive rights of the copyright owner that are set forth in the new law.
3. The year of publication is used in determining the length of the copyright protection for anonymous and pseudonymous works, when the author's identity is not in the records of the Copyright Office, and for works made for hire.
4. Deposit requirements of published works differ from those of registration of unpublished works.

Now, if you are publishing your work, let's talk first about the notice of copyright. The copyright notice should have three elements:

1. The symbol, a little "c" in a circle, ©, or the word "copyright" or the abbreviation "copr." (I would recommend the © plus the word "copyright," since in some countries this will give you additional international protection.)
2. The year of first publication of whatever it is you are publishing
3. The name of the owner of the copyright

Thus, a typical copyright would read as follows: © Copyright by William A. Cohen, 1982.

If you are copyrighting phonograph records or similar items, instead of ©, use this symbol: ℗ . In the same fashion, put down the year of first publication and the name of the owner of the copyright.

HOW TO REGISTER YOUR COPYRIGHT

Remember, you receive your copyright automatically. However, there are several advantages to registering your copyright with the U.S. Copyright Office. Here are a few:

1. There will be public record of your claim.
2. Registration may be necessary before infringement suits may be filed in court.
3. If made before or within five years of publication, registration will establish *prima facie* evidence in court of the validity of the copyright and facts stated on the copyright certificate.
4. If registration is made prior to an infringement of the work or registration is made within three months after publication of the work, the copyright owner will qualify in the courts for an award of statutory damages and attorney's fees. Otherwise, only an award of actual damages and profits is available to the copyright owner.

Under the new law, registration may be made at any time within the life of the copyright. It is highly recommended.

Unlike patenting, copyrighting can be done by yourself without professional help. It is also very inexpensive to do, costing at the present time no more than $10 per copyrighted work. Basically you need to submit only three things: (1) a completed application form, (2) the fee of $10 per application, and (3) a deposit of the work being registered. The copy requirements may vary in different situations. In general, they are as follows:

1. If the work is unpublished, one complete copy or phonorecord
2. If the work was first published in the United States on or after January 1, 1978, two complete copies or phonorecords of the best edition
3. If the work was first published in the United States before January 1, 1978, two complete copies or phonorecords of the work as first published
4. If the work was first published outside the United States, whenever published, one complete copy or phonorecord of the work as first published
5. If the work is a contribution to a collective work and published after January 1, 1978, one complete copy or phonorecord of the best edition of the collective work

To obtain copies of the application forms, write to the Register of Copyrights, Library of Congress, Washington, D.C. 20559. Sample forms are contained in Figures 7.14 through 7.17. However, do not submit these photocopied forms.

You should request Form TX if you are registering a published or unpublished nondramatic literary work. Form PA is for published and unpublished works of the performing arts, musical and dramatic works, pantomimes and choreographic works, motion pictures, and other audiovisual works. Form VA is for published and unpublished works of the visual arts, pictorial, graphic, and sculptural works. Form SR is for published and unpublished sound recordings. All of these forms are for original registrations.

HOW LONG IS THE COPYRIGHT GOOD?

Under the new law, a work that is created, that is, fixed and in tangible form for the first time on or after January 1, 1978, is automatically protected from the moment of its creation and is ordinarily given a term enduring for the author's life, plus an additional 50 years after the author's death. If the work is a joint work prepared by two or more authors who did not work for hire, the term lasts for 50 years after the last surviving author's death. For works made for hire and for anonymous and pseudonymous works, the duration of copyright will be 75 years from publication or 100 from creation, whichever is shorter.

Works that were created before the new law came into effect but have neither been published nor registered for copyright before January 1, 1978 have been automatically brought under the statute and are now given federal copyright protection. The duration of copyright for these works will generally be computed in the same way as for new works. However, all works in this category are guaranteed at least 25 years under statutory protection.

For works copyrighted before January 1, 1978, copyright was secured either on the date the work was published or on the date of registration if the work was registered in nonpublished form. In either case, a copyright lasted for a first term of

APPLICATION FOR COPYRIGHT REGISTRATION

for a
Nondramatic Literary Work

HOW TO APPLY FOR COPYRIGHT REGISTRATION:

- *First:* Read the information on this page to make sure Form TX is the correct application for your work.

- *Second:* Open out the form by pulling this page to the left. Read through the detailed instructions before starting to complete the form.

- *Third:* Complete spaces 1-4 of the application, then turn the entire form over and, after reading the instructions for spaces 5-11, complete the rest of your application. Use typewriter or print in dark ink. Be sure to sign the form at space 10.

- *Fourth:* Detach your completed application from these instructions and send it with the necessary deposit of the work (see below) to: Register of Copyrights, Library of Congress, Washington, D.C. 20559. Unless you have a Deposit Account in the Copyright Office, your application and deposit must be accompanied by a check or money order for $10, payable to: *Register of Copyrights.*

WHEN TO USE FORM TX: Form TX is the appropriate application to use for copyright registration covering nondramatic literary works, whether published or unpublished.

WHAT IS A "NONDRAMATIC LITERARY WORK"? The category of "nondramatic literary works" (Class TX) is very broad. Except for dramatic works and certain kinds of audiovisual works, Class TX includes all types of works written in words (or other verbal or numerical symbols). A few of the many examples of "nondramatic literary works" include fiction, nonfiction, poetry, periodicals, textbooks, reference works, directories, catalogs, advertising copy, and compilations of information.

DEPOSIT TO ACCOMPANY APPLICATION: An application for copyright registration must be accompanied by a deposit representing the entire work for which registration is to be made. The following are the general deposit requirements as set forth in the statute:

    Unpublished work: Deposit one complete copy (or phonorecord).

    Published work: Deposit two complete copies (or phonorecords) of the best edition.

    Work first published outside the United States: Deposit one complete copy (or phonorecord) of the first foreign edition.

    Contribution to a collective work: Deposit one complete copy (or phonorecord) of the best edition of the collective work.

These general deposit requirements may vary in particular situations. For further information about copyright deposit, write to the Copyright Office.

THE COPYRIGHT NOTICE: For published works, the law provides that a copyright notice in a specified form "shall be placed on all publicly distributed copies from which the work can be visually perceived." Use of the copyright notice is the responsibility of the copyright owner and does not require advance permission from the Copyright Office. The required form of the notice for copies generally consists of three elements: (1) the symbol "©", or the word "Copyright", or the abbreviation "Copr."; (2) the year of first publication; and (3) the name of the owner of copyright. For example: "© 1978 Constance Porter". The notice is to be affixed to the copies "in such manner and location as to give reasonable notice of the claim of copyright." Unlike the law in effect before 1978, the new copyright statute provides procedures for correcting errors in the copyright notice, and even for curing the omission of the notice. However, a failure to comply with the notice requirements may still result in the loss of some copyright protection and, unless corrected within five years, in the complete loss of copyright. For further information about the copyright notice and the procedures for correcting errors or omissions, write to the Copyright Office.

DURATION OF COPYRIGHT: For works that were created after the effective date of the new statute (January 1, 1978), the basic copyright term will be the life of the author and fifty years after the author's death. For works made for hire, and for certain anonymous and pseudonymous works, the duration of copyright will be 75 years from publication or 100 years from creation, whichever is shorter. These same terms of copyright will generally apply to works that had been created before 1978 but had not been published or copyrighted before that date. For further information about the duration of copyright, including the terms of copyrights already in existence before 1978, write for Circular R15a.

Figure 7.13. Copyright Form TX for Unpublished and Published Nondramatic Literary Works.

FORM TX

REGISTRATION NUMBER
TX   TXU

EFFECTIVE DATE OF REGISTRATION

. . . .
(Month)   (Day)   (Year)

DO NOT WRITE ABOVE THIS LINE. IF YOU NEED MORE SPACE, USE CONTINUATION SHEET (FORM TX/CON)

(1) Title

TITLE OF THIS WORK: **PREVIOUS OR ALTERNATIVE TITLES:**

If a periodical or serial give: Vol. . . . . . . No. . . . . . . Issue Date . . . .

PUBLICATION AS A CONTRIBUTION: (If this work was published as a contribution to a periodical, serial, or collection, give information about the collective work in which the contribution appeared.)

Title of Collective Work: . . . . Vol. . . . . . . No. . . . . . Date . . . . Pages . . . .

(2) Author(s)

IMPORTANT: Under the law, the "author" of a "work made for hire" is generally the employer, not the employee (see instructions). If any part of this work was "made for hire" check "Yes" in the space provided, give the employer (or other person for whom the work was prepared) as "Author" of that part, and leave the space for dates blank.

1

NAME OF AUTHOR: **DATES OF BIRTH AND DEATH:**

Was this author's contribution to the work a "work made for hire"?   Yes. . . . . .   No. . . . . .   Born . . . . Died . . . .
                                                       (Year)   (Year)

AUTHOR'S NATIONALITY OR DOMICILE: **WAS THIS AUTHOR'S CONTRIBUTION TO THE WORK:**

Citizen of . . . . } or { Domiciled in . . . .
         (Name of Country)   (Name of Country)   Anonymous?   Yes. . . . . . No. . . . . .
                                          Pseudonymous?   Yes. . . . . . No. . . . . .

AUTHOR OF: (Briefly describe nature of this author's contribution)   If the answer to either of these questions is "Yes," see detailed instructions attached.

2

NAME OF AUTHOR: **DATES OF BIRTH AND DEATH:**

Was this author's contribution to the work a "work made for hire"?   Yes. . . . . .   No. . . . . .   Born . . . . Died . . . .
                                                       (Year)   (Year)

AUTHOR'S NATIONALITY OR DOMICILE: **WAS THIS AUTHOR'S CONTRIBUTION TO THE WORK:**

Citizen of . . . . } or { Domiciled in . . . .
         (Name of Country)   (Name of Country)   Anonymous?   Yes. . . . . . No. . . . . .
                                          Pseudonymous?   Yes. . . . . . No. . . . . .

AUTHOR OF: (Briefly describe nature of this author's contribution)   If the answer to either of these questions is "Yes," see detailed instructions attached.

3

NAME OF AUTHOR: **DATES OF BIRTH AND DEATH:**

Was this author's contribution to the work a "work made for hire"?   Yes. . . . . .   No. . . . . .   Born . . . . Died . . . .
                                                       (Year)   (Year)

AUTHOR'S NATIONALITY OR DOMICILE: **WAS THIS AUTHOR'S CONTRIBUTION TO THE WORK:**

Citizen of . . . . } or { Domiciled in . . . .
         (Name of Country)   (Name of Country)   Anonymous?   Yes. . . . . . No. . . . . .
                                          Pseudonymous?   Yes. . . . . . No. . . . . .

AUTHOR OF: (Briefly describe nature of this author's contribution)   If the answer to either of these questions is "Yes," see detailed instructions attached.

(3) Creation and Publication

YEAR IN WHICH CREATION OF THIS WORK WAS COMPLETED: **DATE AND NATION OF FIRST PUBLICATION:**

Year. . . . .   Date. . . . .
                                       (Month)   (Day)   (Year)

(This information must be given in all cases.)   Nation . . . .
                                            (Name of Country)

(Complete this block ONLY if this work has been published.)

(4) Claimant(s)

NAME(S) AND ADDRESS(ES) OF COPYRIGHT CLAIMANT(S):

TRANSFER: (If the copyright claimant(s) named here in space 4 are different from the author(s) named in space 2, give a brief statement of how the claimant(s) obtained ownership of the copyright.)

• Complete all applicable spaces (numbers 5-11) on the reverse side of this page
• Follow detailed instructions attached   • Sign the form at line 10

DO NOT WRITE HERE
Page 1 of . . . . pages

Figure 7.13. (Continued)

HOW TO FILL OUT FORM TX

Specific Instructions for Spaces 1-4

- The line-by-line instructions on this page are keyed to the spaces on the first page of Form TX, printed opposite.
- Please read through these instructions before you start filling out your application, and refer to the specific instructions for each space as you go along.

SPACE 1: TITLE

- **Title of this Work:** Every work submitted for copyright registration must be given a title that is capable of identifying that particular work. If the copies or phonorecords of the work bear a title (or an identifying phrase that could serve as a title), transcribe its wording completely and exactly on the application. Remember that indexing of the registration and future identification of the work will depend on the information you give here.

- **Periodical or Serial Issue:** Periodicals and other serials are publications issued at intervals under a general title, such as newspapers, magazines, journals, newsletters, and annuals. If the work being registered is an entire issue of a periodical or serial, give the over-all title of the periodical or serial in the space headed "Title of this Work," and add the specific information about the issue in the spaces provided. If the work being registered is a contribution to a periodical or serial issue, follow the instructions for "Publication as a Contribution."

- **Previous or Alternative Titles:** Complete this space if there are any additional titles for the work under which someone searching for the registration might be likely to look, or under which a document pertaining to the work might be recorded.

- **Publication as a Contribution:** If the work being registered has been published as a contribution to a periodical, serial, or collection, give the title of the contribution in the space headed "Title of this Work." Then, in the line headed "Publication as a Contribution," give information about the larger work in which the contribution appeared.

SPACE 2: AUTHORS

- **General Instructions:** First decide, after reading these instructions, who are the "authors" of this work for copyright purposes. Then, unless the work is a "collective work" (see below), give the requested information about every "author" who contributed any appreciable amount of copyrightable matter to this version of the work. If you need further space, use the attached Continuation Sheet and, if necessary, request additional Continuation Sheets (Form TX/CON).

- **Who is the "Author"?** Unless the work was "made for hire," the individual who actually created the work is its "author." In the case of a work made for hire, the statute provides that "the employer or other person for whom the work was prepared is considered the author."

- **What is a "Work Made for Hire"?** A "work made for hire" is defined as: (1) "a work prepared by an employee within the scope of his or her employment"; or (2) "a work specially ordered or commissioned" for certain uses specified in the statute, but only if there is a written agreement to consider it a "work made for hire."

- **Collective Work:** In the case of a collective work, such as a periodical issue, anthology, collection of essays, or encyclopedia, it is sufficient to give information about the author of the collective work as a whole.

- **Author's Identity Not Revealed:** If an author's contribution is "anonymous" or "pseudonymous," it is not necessary to give the name and dates for that author. However, the citizenship or domicile of that author **must** be given in all cases, and information about the nature of that author's contribution to the work should be included.

- **Name of Author:** The fullest form of the author's name should be given. If you have checked "Yes" to indicate that the work was "made for hire," give the full legal name of the employer (or other person for whom the work was prepared). You may also include the name of the employee (for example, "Elster Publishing Co., employer for hire of John Ferguson"). If the work is "anonymous" you may: (1) leave the line blank, or (2) state "Anonymous" in the line, or (3) reveal the author's identity. If the work is "pseudonymous" you may (1) leave the line blank, or (2) give the pseudonym and identify it as such (for example: "Huntley Haverstock, pseudonym"), or (3) reveal the author's name, making clear which is the real name and which is the pseudonym (for example, "Judith Barton, whose pseudonym is Madeleine Elster").

- **Dates of Birth and Death:** If the author is dead, the statute requires that the year of death be included in the application unless the work is anonymous or pseudonymous. The author's birth date is optional, but is useful as a form of identification. Leave this space blank if the author's contribution was a "work made for hire."

- **"Anonymous" or "Pseudonymous" Work:** An author's contribution to a work is "anonymous" if that author is not identified on the copies or phonorecords of the work. An author's contribution to a work is "pseudonymous" if that author is identified on the copies or phonorecords under a fictitious name.

- **Author's Nationality or Domicile:** Give the country of which the author is a citizen, or the country in which the author is domiciled. The statute requires that either nationality or domicile be given in all cases.

- **Nature of Authorship:** After the words "Author of" give a brief general statement of the nature of this particular author's contribution to the work. Examples: "Entire text"; "Co-author of entire text"; "Chapters 11-14"; "Editorial revisions"; "Compilation and English translation"; "Illustrations."

SPACE 3: CREATION AND PUBLICATION

- **General Instructions:** Do not confuse "creation" with "publication." Every application for copyright registration must state "the year in which creation of the work was completed." Give the date and nation of first publication only if the work has been published.

- **Creation:** Under the statute, a work is "created" when it is fixed in a copy or phonorecord for the first time. Where a work has been prepared over a period of time, the part of the work existing in fixed form on a particular date constitutes the created work on that date. The date you give here should be the year in which the author completed the particular version for which registration is now being sought, even if other versions exist or if further changes or additions are planned.

- **Publication:** The statute defines "publication" as "the distribution of copies or phonorecords of a work to the public by sale or other transfer of ownership, or by rental, lease, or lending"; a work is also "published" if there has been an "offering to distribute copies or phonorecords to a group of persons for purposes of further distribution, public performance, or public display." Give the full date (month, day, year) when, and the country where, publication first occurred. If first publication took place simultaneously in the United States and other countries, it is sufficient to state "U.S.A."

SPACE 4: CLAIMANT(S)

- **Name(s) and Address(es) of Copyright Claimant(s):** Give the name(s) and address(es) of the copyright claimant(s) in this work. The statute provides that copyright in a work belongs initially to the author of the work (including, in the case of a work made for hire, the employer or other person for whom the work was prepared). The copyright claimant is either the author of the work or a person or organization that has obtained ownership of the copyright initially belonging to the author.

- **Transfer:** The statute provides that, if the copyright claimant is not the author, the application for registration must contain "a brief statement of how the claimant obtained ownership of the copyright." If any copyright claimant named in space 4 is not an author named in space 2, give a brief, general statement summarizing the means by which that claimant obtained ownership of the copyright.

Figure 7.13. (Continued)

CONTINUATION SHEET FOR FORM TX

FORM TX/CON
UNITED STATES COPYRIGHT OFFICE

- If at all possible, try to fit the information called for into the spaces provided on Form TX.
- If you do not have space enough for all of the information you need to give on Form TX, use this continuation sheet and submit it with Form TX.
- If you submit this continuation sheet, leave it attached to Form TX. Or, if it becomes detached, clip (do not tape or staple) and fold the two together before submitting them.
- **PART A** of this sheet is intended to identify the basic application. **PART B** is a continuation of Space 2. **PART C** is for the continuation of Spaces 1, 4, 6, or 7. The other spaces on Form TX call for specific items of information, and should not need continuation.

REGISTRATION NUMBER
TX   TXU
EFFECTIVE DATE OF REGISTRATION
. . . . (Month)   (Day)   (Year)
CONTINUATION SHEET RECEIVED
Page _____ of _____ pages

DO NOT WRITE ABOVE THIS LINE: FOR COPYRIGHT OFFICE USE ONLY

(A)

Identification of Application

IDENTIFICATION OF CONTINUATION SHEET: This sheet is a continuation of the application for copyright registration on Form TX, submitted for the following work.
- TITLE: (Give the title as given under the heading "Title of this Work" in Space 1 of Form TX.)

- NAME(S) AND ADDRESS(ES) OF COPYRIGHT CLAIMANT(S): (Give the name and address of at least one copyright claimant as given in Space 4 of Form TX.)

(B)

Continuation of Space 2

☐ **NAME OF AUTHOR:**
Was this author's contribution to the work a "work made for hire"?   Yes..... No.....

DATES OF BIRTH AND DEATH:
Born .... Died ....
(Year)   (Year)

AUTHOR'S NATIONALITY OR DOMICILE:
Citizen of .... } or { Domiciled in ....
(Name of Country)   (Name of Country)

WAS THIS AUTHOR'S CONTRIBUTION TO THE WORK:
Anonymous?   Yes...... No......
Pseudonymous?   Yes...... No......

AUTHOR OF: (Briefly describe nature of this author's contribution)
If the answer to either of these questions is "Yes," see detailed instructions attached.

☐ **NAME OF AUTHOR:**
Was this author's contribution to the work a "work made for hire"?   Yes...... No......

DATES OF BIRTH AND DEATH:
Born .... Died ....
(Year)   (Year)

AUTHOR'S NATIONALITY OR DOMICILE:
Citizen of .... } or { Domiciled in ....
(Name of Country)   (Name of Country)

WAS THIS AUTHOR'S CONTRIBUTION TO THE WORK:
Anonymous?   Yes...... No......
Pseudonymous?   Yes...... No......

AUTHOR OF: (Briefly describe nature of this author's contribution)
If the answer to either of these questions is "Yes," see detailed instructions attached.

☐ **NAME OF AUTHOR:**
Was this author's contribution to the work a "work made for hire"?   Yes...... No......

DATES OF BIRTH AND DEATH:
Born .... Died ....
(Year)   (Year)

AUTHOR'S NATIONALITY OR DOMICILE:
Citizen of .... } or { Domiciled in ....
(Name of Country)   (Name of Country)

WAS THIS AUTHOR'S CONTRIBUTION TO THE WORK:
Anonymous?   Yes...... No......
Pseudonymous?   Yes...... No......

AUTHOR OF: (Briefly describe nature of this author's contribution)
If the answer to either of these questions is "Yes," see detailed instructions attached.

(C)

Continuation of Other Spaces

CONTINUATION OF (Check which): ☐ Space 1   ☐ Space 4   ☐ Space 6   ☐ Space 7

Figure 7.13. (Continued)

<table>
<tr><td></td><td>EXAMINED BY: . . . .
CHECKED BY: . . . .</td><td>APPLICATION RECEIVED:</td><td rowspan="3">FOR
COPYRIGHT
OFFICE
USE
ONLY</td></tr>
<tr><td></td><td>CORRESPONDENCE:
☐ Yes</td><td>DEPOSIT RECEIVED:</td></tr>
<tr><td></td><td>DEPOSIT ACCOUNT
FUNDS USED:
☐</td><td>REMITTANCE NUMBER AND DATE:</td></tr>
</table>

DO NOT WRITE ABOVE THIS LINE. IF YOU NEED ADDITIONAL SPACE, USE CONTINUATION SHEET (FORM TX/CON)

PREVIOUS REGISTRATION:

- Has registration for this work, or for an earlier version of this work, already been made in the Copyright Office?   Yes . . . .   No . . . .
- If your answer is "Yes," why is another registration being sought? (Check appropriate box)
  - ☐ This is the first published edition of a work previously registered in unpublished form.
  - ☐ This is the first application submitted by this author as copyright claimant.
  - ☐ This is a changed version of the work, as shown by line 6 of this application.
- If your answer is "Yes," give: Previous Registration Number . . . . Year of Registration . . . .

(5) Previous Registration

COMPILATION OR DERIVATIVE WORK: (See instructions)

PREEXISTING MATERIAL. (Identify any preexisting work or works that this work is based on or incorporates.)

{ . . . .

MATERIAL ADDED TO THIS WORK. (Give a brief, general statement of the material that has been added to this work and in which copyright is claimed.)

{ . . . .

(6) Compilation or Derivative Work

MANUFACTURERS AND LOCATIONS: (If this is a published work consisting preponderantly of nondramatic literary material in English, the law may require that the copies be manufactured in the United States or Canada for full protection. If so, the names of the manufacturers who performed certain processes, and the places where these processes were performed *must* be given. See instructions for details.)

NAMES OF MANUFACTURERS	PLACES OF MANUFACTURE
. . . .	. . . .
. . . .	. . . .

(7) Manufacturing

REPRODUCTION FOR USE OF BLIND OR PHYSICALLY-HANDICAPPED PERSONS: (See instructions)

- Signature of this form at space 10, and a check in one of the boxes here in space 8, constitutes a non-exclusive grant of permission to the Library of Congress to reproduce and distribute solely for the blind and physically handicapped and under the conditions and limitations prescribed by the regulations of the Copyright Office: (1) copies of the work identified in space 1 of this application in Braille (or similar tactile symbols); or (2) phonorecords embodying a fixation of a reading of that work; or (3) both.

  a ☐ Copies and phonorecords   b ☐ Copies Only   c ☐ Phonorecords Only

(8) License For Handicapped

DEPOSIT ACCOUNT: (If the registration fee is to be charged to a Deposit Account established in the Copyright Office, give name and number of Account.)

Name: . . . .

Account Number . . . .

CORRESPONDENCE: (Give name and address to which correspondence about this application should be sent.)

Name: . . . .

Address: . . . .
. . . . (Apt.) . . . .

. . . .
(City)   (State)   (ZIP)

(9) Fee and Correspondence

CERTIFICATION: ✱ I, the undersigned, hereby certify that I am the: (Check one)

☐ author ☐ other copyright claimant ☐ owner of exclusive right(s) ☐ authorized agent of: . . . .
(Name of author or other copyright claimant, or owner of exclusive right(s))

of the work identified in this application and that the statements made by me in this application are correct to the best of my knowledge.

☞ Handwritten signature: (X) . . . .

Typed or printed name . . . . Date . . . .

(10) Certification (Application must be signed)

MAIL CERTIFICATE TO

(Certificate will be mailed in window envelope)

. . . .
(Name)

. . . .
(Number, Street and Apartment Number)

. . . .
(City)   (State)   (ZIP code)

(11) Address For Return of Certificate

✱ 17 U.S.C. § 506(e) Any person who knowingly makes a false representation of a material fact in the application for copyright registration provided for by section 409, or in any written statement filed in connection with the application, shall be fined not more than $2,500.

☆ U.S. GOVERNMENT PRINTING OFFICE: 1980: 341-278/1

Nov. 1980 — 500,000

Figure 7.13. (Continued)

INSTRUCTIONS FOR SPACES 5-9

SPACE 5: PREVIOUS REGISTRATION

• **General Instructions:** The questions in space 5 are intended to find out whether an earlier registration has been made for this work and, if so, whether there is any basis for a new registration. As a general rule, only one basic copyright registration can be made for the same version of a particular work.

• **Same Version:** If this version is substantially the same as the work covered by a previous registration, a second registration is not generally possible unless: (1) the work has been registered in unpublished form and a second registration is now being sought to cover the first published edition, or (2) someone other than the author is identified as copyright claimant in the earlier registration, and the author is now seeking registration in his or her own name. If either of these two exceptions apply, check the appropriate box and give the earlier registration number and date. Otherwise, do not submit Form VA; instead, write the Copyright Office for information about supplementary registration or recordation of transfer of copyright ownership.

• **Changed Version:** If the work has been changed, and you are now seeking registration to cover the additions or revisions, check the third box in space 5, give the earlier registration number and date, and complete both parts of space 6.

• **Previous Registration Number and Date:** If more than one previous registration has been made for the work, give the number and date of the latest registration.

SPACE 6: COMPILATION OR DERIVATIVE WORK

• **General Instructions:** Complete both parts of space 6 if this work is a "compilation," or "derivative work," or both, and if it is based on or incorporates one or more "preexisting works" that are not eligible for registration for one reason or another: works that have already been published or registered, or works that have fallen into the public domain. A "compilation" is defined as "a work formed by the collection and assembling of preexisting materials or of data that are selected, coordinated, or arranged in such a way that the resulting work as a whole constitutes an original work of authorship." A "derivative work" is "a work based on one or more preexisting works." In addition to various forms in which works may be "recast, transformed, or adapted," derivative works include works "consisting of editorial revisions, annotations, elaborations, or other modifications" if these changes, as a whole, represent an original work of authorship.

• **Preexisting Material:** If the work is a compilation, give a brief, general statement describing the nature of the material that has been compiled. Example: "Compilation of 19th Century political cartoons". In the case of a derivative work, identify the preexisting work that has been recast, transformed, or adapted. Examples: "Grünewald Altarpiece"; "19th Century quilt design."

• **Material Added to this Work:** The statute requires a "brief, general statement of the additional material covered by the copyright claim being registered." This statement should describe all of the material in this particular version of the work that: (1) represents an original work of authorship; (2) has not fallen into public domain; (3) has not been previously published; and (4) has not been previously registered for copyright in unpublished form. Examples: "Adaptation of design and additional artistic work"; "Reproduction of painting by photolithography"; "Additional cartographic material"; "Compilation of photographs."

SPACES 7, 8, 9: FEE, CORRESPONDENCE, CERTIFICATION, RETURN ADDRESS

• **Deposit Account and Mailing Instructions (Space 7):** If you maintain a Deposit Account in the Copyright Office, identify it in space 7. Otherwise you will need to send the registration fee of $10 with your application. The space headed "Correspondence" should contain the name and address of the person to be consulted if correspondence about this application becomes necessary.

• **Certification (Space 8):** The application is not acceptable unless it bears the handwritten signature of the author or other copyright claimant, or of the owner of exclusive right(s), or of the duly authorized agent of such author, claimant, or owner.

• **Address for Return of Certificate (Space 9):** The address box must be completed legibly, since the certificate will be returned in a window envelope.

MORE INFORMATION

THE COPYRIGHT NOTICE: For published works, the law provides that a copyright notice in a specified form "shall be placed on all publicly distributed copies from which the work can be visually perceived." Use of the copyright notice is the responsibility of the copyright owner, and does not require advance permission from the Copyright Office.

• **Form of the Notice:** The required form of the notice for copies generally consists of three elements: (1) the symbol "©", or the word "Copyright", or the abbreviation "Copr."; (2) the year of first publication; and (3) the name of the owner of copyright in the work, or an abbreviation by which the name can be recognized, or a generally known alternative designation of the owner. Example: "© 1978 Samuel Marlove." Under the statute, the year date may be omitted from the notice in cases "where a pictorial, graphic, or sculptural work, with accompanying text matter, if any, is reproduced in or on greeting cards, postcards, stationery, jewelry, dolls, toys, or any useful articles."

• **Position of the Notice:** The notice is to be affixed to the copies "in such manner and location as to give reasonable notice of the claim of copyright."

• **Errors or Omissions:** Unlike the law in effect before 1978, the new copyright statute provides procedures for correcting errors in the copyright notice, and even for curing the omission of the notice. However, a failure to comply with the notice requirements may still result in the loss of some copyright protection and, unless corrected within five years, in the complete loss of copyright. For further information about the copyright notice and the procedures for correcting errors or omissions, write to the Copyright Office.

FORM OF DEPOSIT FOR WORKS OF THE VISUAL ARTS

Exceptions to General Deposit Requirements: As explained on the reverse side of this page, the statutory deposit requirements (generally one copy for unpublished works and two copies for published works) will vary for particular kinds of works of the visual arts. The copyright law authorizes the Register of Copyrights to issue regulations specifying "the administrative classes into which works are to be placed for purposes of deposit and registration, and the nature of the copies or phonorecords to be deposited in the various classes specified." For particular classes, the regulations may require or permit "the deposit of identifying material instead of copies or phonorecords," or "the deposit of only one copy or phonorecord where two would normally be required."

What Should You Deposit? The detailed requirements with respect to the kind of deposit to accompany an application on Form VA are contained in the Copyright Office Regulations. The following does not cover all of the deposit requirements, but is intended to give you some general guidance.

• For an unpublished work, the material deposited should represent the entire copyrightable content of the work for which registration is being sought;

• For a published work, the material deposited should generally consist of two complete copies of the best edition. Exceptions:

—For certain types of works, one complete copy may be deposited instead of two. These include greeting cards, postcards, stationery, labels, advertisements, scientific drawings, and globes.

—For most three-dimensional sculptural works, and for certain two-dimensional works, the Copyright Office Regulations require the deposit of identifying material (photographs or drawings in a specified form) rather than copies.

—Under certain circumstances, for works published in five copies or less or in limited, numbered editions, the deposit may consist of one copy or of identifying reproductions.

Figure 7.13. (Continued)

APPLICATION FOR COPYRIGHT REGISTRATION

for a Sature Recording
for a Sound Recording

HOW TO APPLY FOR COPYRIGHT REGISTRATION:

- **First:** Read the information on this page to make sure Form SR is the correct application for your work.

- **Second:** Open out the form by pulling this page to the left. Read through the detailed instructions before starting to complete the form.

- **Third:** Complete spaces 1-4 of the application, then turn the entire form over and, after reading the instructions for spaces 5-9, complete the rest of your application. Use typewriter or print in dark ink. Be sure to sign the form at space 8.

- **Fourth:** Detach your completed application from these instructions and send it with the necessary deposit of the work (see below) to: Register of Copyrights, Library of Congress, Washington, D.C. 20559. Unless you have a Deposit Account in the Copyright Office, your application and deposit must be accompanied by a check or money order for $10, payable to: *Register of Copyrights.*

WHEN TO USE FORM SR: Form SR is the appropriate application to use for copyright registration covering a sound recording. It should be used where the copyright claim is limited to the sound recording itself, and it should also be used where the same copyright claimant is seeking to register not only the sound recording but also the musical, dramatic, or literary work embodied in the sound recording. Both published and unpublished works can be registered on Form SR.

WHAT IS A "SOUND RECORDING"? With one exception, "sound recordings" are works that result from the fixation of a series of musical, spoken, or other sounds. The exception is for the audio portions of audiovisual works, such as a motion picture soundtrack or an audio cassette accompanying a filmstrip; these are considered an integral part of the audiovisual work as a whole. For further information about "sound recordings," and the distinction between "sound recordings" and "phonorecords," see the reverse side of this sheet. For additional information about copyright in sound recordings, write to the Copyright Office.

DEPOSIT TO ACCOMPANY APPLICATION: An application for copyright registration must be accompanied by a deposit representing the entire work for which registration is to be made. For registration on Form SR, the following are the general deposit requirements:

Unpublished work: Deposit one complete phonorecord.

Published work: Deposit two complete phonorecords of the best edition, together with "any printed or other visually perceptible material" published with the phonorecords.

Work first published outside the United States: Deposit one complete phonorecord of the work as first published.

Contribution to a collective work: Deposit one complete phonorecord of the best edition of the collective work.

These general deposit requirements may vary in particular situations. For further information about the deposit requirements for sound recordings, see the reverse side of this sheet. For general information about copyright deposit, write to the Copyright Office.

THE COPYRIGHT NOTICE: For published sound recordings, the law provides that a copyright notice in a specified form "shall be placed on all publicly distributed phonorecords of the sound recording." Use of the copyright notice is the responsibility of the copyright owner and does not require advance permission from the Copyright Office. The required form of the notice for phonorecords generally consists of three elements: (1) the symbol "℗" (the letter P in a circle); (2) the year of first publication of the sound recording; and (3) the name of the owner of copyright. For example: " ℗ 1978 Rittenhouse Record Co." The notice is to be "placed on the surface of the phonorecord, or on the label or container, in such manner and location as to give reasonable notice of the claim of copyright." Unlike the law in effect before 1978, the new copyright statute provides procedures for correcting errors in the copyright notice, and even for curing the omission of the notice. However, a failure to comply with the notice requirements may still result in the loss of some copyright protection and, unless corrected within five years, in the complete loss of copyright. For further information about the copyright notice, see the reverse side of this sheet. For additional information concerning the copyright notice and the procedures for correcting errors or omissions, write to the Copyright Office.

DURATION OF COPYRIGHT: For works that were created after the effective date of the new statute (January 1, 1978), the basic copyright term will be the life of the author and fifty years after the author's death. For works made for hire, and for certain anonymous and pseudonymous works, the duration of copyright will be 75 years from publication or 100 years from creation, whichever is shorter. These same terms of copyright will generally apply to works that had been created before 1978 but had not been published or copyrighted before that date. Sound recordings fixed before February 15, 1972 are not eligible for registration, but may be protected by state law. For further information about the duration of copyright, including the terms of copyrights already in existence before 1978, write for Circular R15a.

Figure 7.14. Copyright Form PA for Published and Unpublished Works of the Performing Arts, Musical and Dramatic Works, Pantomimes and Choreographic Works, Motion Pictures, and Other Audiovisual Works.

FORM PA

UNITED STATES COPYRIGHT OFFICE

REGISTRATION NUMBER
PA   PAU

EFFECTIVE DATE OF REGISTRATION
. . . .
(Month)   (Day)   (Year)

DO NOT WRITE ABOVE THIS LINE. IF YOU NEED MORE SPACE, USE CONTINUATION SHEET (FORM PA/CON)

(1) Title

TITLE OF THIS WORK:

NATURE OF THIS WORK: (See instructions)

PREVIOUS OR ALTERNATIVE TITLES:

(2) Author(s)

IMPORTANT: Under the law, the "author" of a "work made for hire" is generally the employer, not the employee (see instructions). If any part of this work was "made for hire" check "Yes" in the space provided, give the employer (or other person for whom the work was prepared) as "Author" of that part, and leave the space for dates blank.

1

NAME OF AUTHOR:

Was this author's contribution to the work a "work made for hire"?   Yes......   No......

DATES OF BIRTH AND DEATH:
Born .... Died ....
(Year)   (Year)

AUTHOR'S NATIONALITY OR DOMICILE:
Citizen of .... } or { Domiciled in ....
(Name of Country)   (Name of Country)

AUTHOR OF: (Briefly describe nature of this author's contribution)

WAS THIS AUTHOR'S CONTRIBUTION TO THE WORK:
Anonymous?   Yes......   No......
Pseudonymous?   Yes......   No......
If the answer to either of these questions is "Yes," see detailed instructions attached.

2

NAME OF AUTHOR:

Was this author's contribution to the work a "work made for hire"?   Yes......   No......

DATES OF BIRTH AND DEATH:
Born .... Died ....
(Year)   (Year)

AUTHOR'S NATIONALITY OR DOMICILE:
Citizen of .... } or { Domiciled in ....
(Name of Country)   (Name of Country)

AUTHOR OF: (Briefly describe nature of this author's contribution)

WAS THIS AUTHOR'S CONTRIBUTION TO THE WORK:
Anonymous?   Yes......   No......
Pseudonymous?   Yes......   No......
If the answer to either of these questions is "Yes," see detailed instructions attached.

3

NAME OF AUTHOR:

Was this author's contribution to the work a "work made for hire"?   Yes......   No......

DATES OF BIRTH AND DEATH:
Born .... Died ....
(Year)   (Year)

AUTHOR'S NATIONALITY OR DOMICILE:
Citizen of .... } or { Domiciled in ....
(Name of Country)   (Name of Country)

AUTHOR OF: (Briefly describe nature of this author's contribution)

WAS THIS AUTHOR'S CONTRIBUTION TO THE WORK:
Anonymous?   Yes......   No......
Pseudonymous?   Yes......   No......
If the answer to either of these questions is "Yes," see detailed instructions attached.

(3) Creation and Publication

YEAR IN WHICH CREATION OF THIS WORK WAS COMPLETED:

Year...........

(This information must be given in all cases.)

DATE AND NATION OF FIRST PUBLICATION:

Date....................................
(Month)   (Day)   (Year)

Nation....................................
(Name of Country)

(Complete this block ONLY if this work has been published.)

(4) Claimant(s)

NAME(S) AND ADDRESS(ES) OF COPYRIGHT CLAIMANT(S):

TRANSFER: (If the copyright claimant(s) named here in space 4 are different from the author(s) named in space 2, give a brief statement of how the claimant(s) obtained ownership of the copyright.)

- Complete all applicable spaces (numbers 5-9) on the reverse side of this page
- Follow detailed instructions attached   • Sign the form at line 8

DO NOT WRITE HERE
Page 1 of .... pages

Figure 7.14. (Continued)

173

HOW TO FILL OUT FORM PA

Specific Instructions for Spaces 1-4

> - The line-by-line instructions on this page are keyed to the spaces on the first page of Form PA, printed opposite.
> - Please read through these instructions before you start filling out your application, and refer to the specific instructions for each space as you go along.

SPACE 1: TITLE

- **Title of this Work:** Every work submitted for copyright registration must be given a title that is capable of identifying that particular work. If the copies or phonorecords of the work bear a title (or an identifying phrase that could serve as a title), transcribe its wording completely and exactly on the application. Remember that indexing of the registration and future identification of the work will depend on the information you give here.

    If the work you are registering is an entire "collective work" (such as a collection of plays or songs), give the over-all title of the collection. If you are registering one or more individual contributions to a collective work, give the title of each contribution, followed by the title of the collection. Example: " 'A Song for Elinda' in *Old and New Ballads for Old and New People.*"

- **Nature of this Work:** Briefly describe the general nature or character of the work being registered for copyright. Examples: "Music"; "Song Lyrics"; "Words and Music"; "Drama"; "Musical Play"; "Choreography"; "Pantomime"; "Motion Picture"; "Audiovisual Work".

- **Previous or Alternative Titles:** Complete this space if there are any additional titles for the work under which someone searching for the registration might be likely to look, or under which a document pertaining to the work might be recorded.

SPACE 2: AUTHORS

- **General Instructions:** First decide, after reading these instructions, who are the "authors" of this work for copyright purposes. Then, unless the work is a "collective work" (see below), give the requested information about every "author" who contributed any appreciable amount of copyrightable matter to this version of the work. If you need further space, use the attached Continuation Sheet and, if necessary, request additional Continuation Sheets (Form PA/CON).

- **Who is the "Author"?** Unless the work was "made for hire," the individual who actually created the work is its "author." In the case of a work made for hire, the statute provides that "the employer or other person for whom the work was prepared is considered the author."

- **What is a "Work Made for Hire"?** A "work made for hire" is defined as: (1) "a work prepared by an employee within the scope of his or her employment"; or (2) "a work specially ordered or commissioned" for certain uses specified in the statute, but only if there is a written agreement to consider it a "work made for hire."

- **Collective Work:** In the case of a collective work, such as a song book or a collection of plays, it is sufficient to give information about the author of the collective work as a whole.

- **Author's Identity Not Revealed:** If an author's contribution is "anonymous" or "pseudonymous," it is not necessary to give the name and dates for that author. However, the citizenship or domicile of the author **must** be given in all cases, and information about the nature of that author's contribution to the work should be included.

- **Name of Author:** The fullest form of the author's name should be given. If you have checked "Yes" to indicate that the work was "made for hire," give the full legal name of the employer (or other person for whom the work was prepared). You may also include the name of the employee (for example: "Music Makers Publishing Co., employer for hire of Lila Crane"). If the work is "anonymous" you may: (1) leave the line blank, or (2) state "Anonymous" in the line, or (3) reveal the author's identity. If the work is "pseudonymous" you may (1) leave the line blank, or (2) give the seudonym and identify it as such (for example: "Huntley Haverstock, pseudonym"), or (3) reveal the author's name, making clear which is the real name and which is the pseudonym (for example, "Judith Barton, whose pseudonym is Madeleine Elster").

- **Dates of Birth and Death:** If the author is dead, the statute requires that the year of death be included in the application unless the work is anonymous or pseudonymous. The author's birth date is optional, but is useful as a form of identification. Leave this space blank if the author's contribution was a "work made for hire."

- **"Anonymous" or "Pseudonymous" Work:** An author's contribution to a work is "anonymous" if that author is not identified on the copies or phonorecords of the work. An author's contribution to a work is "pseudonymous" if that author is identified on the copies or phonorecords under a fictitious name.

- **Author's Nationality or Domicile:** Give the country of which the author is a citizen, or the country in which the author is domiciled. The statute requires that either nationality or domicile be given in all cases.

- **Nature of Authorship:** After the words "Author of" give a brief general statement of the nature of this particular author's contribution to the work. Examples: "Words"; "Co-Author of Music"; "Words and Music"; "Arrangement"; "Co-Author of Book and Lyrics"; "Dramatization"; "Entire Work"; "Compilation and English Translation"; "Editorial Revisions".

SPACE 3: CREATION AND PUBLICATION

- **General Instructions:** Do not confuse "creation" with "publication." Every application for copyright registration must state "the year in which creation of the work was completed." Give the date and nation of first publication only if the work has been published.

- **Creation:** Under the statute, a work is "created" when it is fixed in a copy or phonorecord for the first time. Where a work has been prepared over a period of time, the part of the work existing in fixed form on a particular date constitutes the created work on that date. The date you give here should be the year in which the author completed the particular version for which registration is now being sought, even if other versions exist or if further changes or additions are planned.

- **Publication:** The statute defines "publication" as "the distribution of copies or phonorecords of a work to the public by sale or other transfer of ownership, or by rental, lease, or lending"; a work is also "published" if there has been an "offering to distribute copies or phonorecords to a group of persons for purposes of further distribution, public performance, or public display." Give the full date (month, day, year) when, and the country where, publication first occurred. If first publication took place simultaneously in the United States and other countries, it is sufficient to state "U.S.A."

SPACE 4: CLAIMANT(S)

- **Name(s) and Address(es) of Copyright Claimant(s):** Give the name(s) and address(es) of the copyright claimant(s) in this work. The statute provides that copyright in a work belongs initially to the author of the work (including, in the case of a work made for hire, the employer or other person for whom the work was prepared). The copyright claimant is either the author of the work or a person or organization that has obtained ownership of the copyright initially belonging to the author.

- **Transfer:** The statute provides that, if the copyright claimant is not the author, the application for registration must contain "a brief statement of how the claimant obtained ownership of the copyright." If any copyright claimant named in space 4 is not an author named in space 2, give a brief, general statement summarizing the means by which that claimant obtained ownership of the copyright.

Figure 7.14. (Continued)

CONTINUATION SHEET FOR FORM PA

FORM PA/CON
UNITED STATES COPYRIGHT OFFICE

- If at all possible, try to fit the information called for into the spaces provided on Form PA.
- If you do not have space enough for all of the information you need to give on Form PA, use this continuation sheet and submit it with Form PA.
- If you submit this continuation sheet, leave it attached to Form PA. Or, if it becomes detached, clip (do not tape or staple) and fold the two together before submitting them.
- **PART A** of this sheet is intended to identify the basic application. **PART B** is a continuation of Space 2. **PART C** is for the continuation of Spaces 1, 4, or 6. The other spaces on Form PA call for specific items of information, and should not need continuation.

REGISTRATION NUMBER

PA   PAU

EFFECTIVE DATE OF REGISTRATION

. . . .
(Month)   (Day)   (Year)

CONTINUATION SHEET RECEIVED

Page _____ of _____ pages

DO NOT WRITE ABOVE THIS LINE. FOR COPYRIGHT OFFICE USE ONLY

(A)

Identification of Application

IDENTIFICATION OF CONTINUATION SHEET: This sheet is a continuation of the application for copyright registration on Form PA, submitted for the following work:
- TITLE: (Give the title as given under the heading "Title of this Work" in Space 1 of Form PA.)

. . . .

- NAME(S) AND ADDRESS(ES) OF COPYRIGHT CLAIMANT(S): (Give the name and address of at least one copyright claimant as given in Space 4 of Form PA.)

. . . .

(B)

Continuation of Space 2

NAME OF AUTHOR:

Was this author's contribution to the work a "work made for hire"?   Yes...... No......

DATES OF BIRTH AND DEATH:

Born .... Died ....
(Year)   (Year)

AUTHOR'S NATIONALITY OR DOMICILE:

Citizen of .... } or { Domiciled in ....
(Name of Country)   (Name of Country)

AUTHOR OF: (Briefly describe nature of this author's contribution)

WAS THIS AUTHOR'S CONTRIBUTION TO THE WORK:

Anonymous?   Yes ...... No ......
Pseudonymous?   Yes ...... No ......

If the answer to either of these questions is "Yes," see detailed instructions attached.

NAME OF AUTHOR:

Was this author's contribution to the work a "work made for hire"?   Yes...... No......

DATES OF BIRTH AND DEATH:

Born .... Died ....
(Year)   (Year)

AUTHOR'S NATIONALITY OR DOMICILE:

Citizen of .... } or { Domiciled in ....
(Name of Country)   (Name of Country)

AUTHOR OF: (Briefly describe nature of this author's contribution)

WAS THIS AUTHOR'S CONTRIBUTION TO THE WORK:

Anonymous?   Yes ...... No ......
Pseudonymous?   Yes ...... No ......

If the answer to either of these questions is "Yes," see detailed instructions attached.

NAME OF AUTHOR:

Was this author's contribution to the work a "work made for hire"?   Yes...... No......

DATES OF BIRTH AND DEATH:

Born .... Died ....
(Year)   (Year)

AUTHOR'S NATIONALITY OR DOMICILE:

Citizen of .... } or { Domiciled in ....
(Name of Country)   (Name of Country)

AUTHOR OF: (Briefly describe nature of this author's contribution)

WAS THIS AUTHOR'S CONTRIBUTION TO THE WORK:

Anonymous?   Yes ...... No ......
Pseudonymous?   Yes ...... No ......

If the answer to either of these questions is "Yes," see detailed instructions attached.

(C)

Continuation of Other Spaces

CONTINUATION OF (Check which):   ☐ Space 1   ☐ Space 4   ☐ Space 6

Figure 7.14.   (Continued)

175

EXAMINED BY:	APPLICATION RECEIVED:	
CHECKED BY:		FOR COPYRIGHT OFFICE USE ONLY
CORRESPONDENCE: ☐ Yes	DEPOSIT RECEIVED:	
DEPOSIT ACCOUNT FUNDS USED: ☐	REMITTANCE NUMBER AND DATE:	

DO NOT WRITE ABOVE THIS LINE. IF YOU NEED ADDITIONAL SPACE, USE CONTINUATION SHEET (FORM PA/CON)

PREVIOUS REGISTRATION:

⑤ **Previous Registration**

- Has registration for this work, or for an earlier version of this work, already been made in the Copyright Office? Yes . . . . No . . . .

- If your answer is "Yes," why is another registration being sought? (Check appropriate box)

  ☐ This is the first published edition of a work previously registered in unpublished form.
  ☐ This is the first application submitted by this author as copyright claimant.
  ☐ This is a changed version of the work, as shown by line 6 of the application.

- If your answer is "Yes," give: Previous Registration Number . . . . Year of Registration . . . .

COMPILATION OR DERIVATIVE WORK: (See instructions)

⑥ **Compilation or Derivative Work**

PREEXISTING MATERIAL: (Identify any preexisting work or works that the work is based on or incorporates.)
. . . .

MATERIAL ADDED TO THIS WORK: (Give a brief, general statement of the material that has been added to this work and in which copyright is claimed.)
. . . .

DEPOSIT ACCOUNT: (If the registration fee is to be charged to a Deposit Account established in the Copyright Office, give name and number of Account.)	**CORRESPONDENCE:** (Give name and address to which correspondence about this application should be sent.)	⑦ **Fee and Correspondence**
Name:	Name: . . . . Address: . . . . (Apt.)	
Account Number:	(City) (State) (ZIP)	

CERTIFICATION: ✱ I, the undersigned, hereby certify that I am the: (Check one)

⑧ **Certification (Application must be signed)**

☐ author ☐ other copyright claimant ☐ owner of exclusive right(s) ☐ authorized agent of: . . . .
(Name of author or other copyright claimant, or owner of exclusive right(s))

of the work identified in this application and that the statements made by me in this application are correct to the best of my knowledge.

Handwritten signature: (X) . . . .

Typed or printed name. . . . . Date . . . .

MAIL CERTIFICATE TO

⑨ **Address For Return of Certificate**

. . . .
(Name)
. . . .
(Number, Street and Apartment Number)
. . . .
(City)   (State)   (ZIP code)

(Certificate will be mailed in window envelope)

✱ 17 U.S.C. §506(e) FALSE REPRESENTATION—Any person who knowingly makes a false representation of a material fact in the application for copyright registration provided for by section 409, or in any written statement filed in connection with the application, shall be fined not more than $2,500.

☆ U.S.GOVERNMENT PRINTING OFFICE: 1981-341-278/2

DEC. 1980—500,800

Figure 7.14. (Continued)

INSTRUCTIONS FOR SPACES 5-9

SPACE 5: PREVIOUS REGISTRATION

• **General Instructions:** The questions in space 5 are intended to find out whether an earlier registration has been made for this work and, if so, whether there is any basis for a new registration. As a general rule, only one basic copyright registration can be made for the same version of a particular work.

• **Same Version:** If this version is substantially the same as the work covered by a previous registration, a second registration is not generally possible unless: (1) the work has been registered in unpublished form and a second registration is now being sought to cover the first published edition, or (2) someone other than the author is identified as copyright claimant in the earlier registration, and the author is now seeking registration in his or her own name. If either of these two exceptions apply, check the appropriate box and give the earlier registration number and date. Otherwise, do not submit Form PA; instead, write the Copyright Office for information about supplementary registration or recordation of transfers of copyright ownership.

• **Changed Version:** If the work has been changed, and you are now seeking registration to cover the additions or revisions, check the third box in space 5, give the earlier registration number and date, and complete both parts of space 6.

• **Previous Registration Number and Date:** If more than one previous registration has been made for the work, give the number and date of the latest registration.

SPACE 6: COMPILATION OR DERIVATIVE WORK

• **General Instructions:** Complete both parts of space 6 if this work is a "compilation," or "derivative work," or both, and if it incorporates one or more earlier works that have already been published or registered for copyright, or that have fallen into the public domain. A "compilation" is defined as "a work formed by the collection and assembling of preexisting materials or of data that are selected, coordinated, or arranged in such a way that the resulting work as a whole constitutes an original work of authorship." A "derivative work" is "a work based on one or more preexisting works." Examples of derivative works include musical arrangements, dramatizations, translations, abridgments, condensations, motion picture versions, or "any other form in which a work may be recast, transformed, or adapted." Derivative works also include works "consisting of editorial revisions, annotations, elaborations, or other modifications" if these changes, as a whole, represent an original work of authorship.

• **Preexisting Material:** If the work is a compilation, give a brief, general statement describing the nature of the material that has been compiled. Example: "Compilation of 19th Century military songs." In the case of a derivative work, identify the preexisting work that has been recast, transformed, or adapted. Example: "French version of Hugo's 'Le Roi s'amuse'."

• **Material Added to this Work:** The statute requires a "brief, general statement of the additional material covered by the copyright claim being registered." This statement should describe all of the material in this particular version of the work that: (1) represents an original work of authorship; and (2) has not fallen into the public domain; and (3) has not been previously published; and (4) has not been previously registered for copyright in unpublished form. Examples: "Arrangement for piano and orchestra"; "Dramatization for television"; "New film version"; "Revisions throughout: Act III completely new".

SPACES 7, 8, 9: FEE, CORRESPONDENCE, CERTIFICATION, RETURN ADDRESS

• **Deposit Account and Mailing Instructions (Space 7):** If you maintain a Deposit Account in the Copyright Office, identify it in space 7. Otherwise you will need to send the registration fee of $10 with your application. The space headed "Correspondence" should contain the name and address of the person to be consulted if correspondence about this application becomes necessary.

• **Certification (Space 8):** The application is not acceptable unless it bears the handwritten signature of the author or other copyright claimant, or of the owner of exclusive right(s), or of the duly authorized agent of such author, claimant, or owner.

• **Address for Return of Certificate (Space 9):** The address box must be completed legibly, since the certificate will be returned in a window envelope.

Figure 7.14. (Continued)

MORE INFORMATION

A NOTE ON TERMINOLOGY: The following are the meanings given to some of the terms used in the copyright statute:

• **"Works":** "Works" are the basic subject matter of copyright; they are what authors create and copyright protects. The statute draws a sharp distinction between the "work" and "any material object in which the work is embodied."

• **"Copies" and "Phonorecords":** These are the two types of material objects in which "works" are embodied. In general, **"copies"** are objects from which a work can be read or visually perceived, directly or with the aid of a machine or device, such as manuscripts, books, sheet music, film, and videotape. **"Phonorecords"** are objects embodying fixations of sounds, such as audio tapes and phonograph disks. For example, a song (the "work") can be reproduced in sheet music ("copies") or phonograph disks ("phonorecords"), or both.

• **"Sound Recordings":** These are "works," not "copies" or "phonorecords." With one exception, "sound recordings" are "works that result from the fixation of a series of musical, spoken, or other sounds." (The exception is for the audio portions of audiovisual works, including motion picture soundtracks; these are considered an integral part of the audiovisual work as a whole.) "Sound recordings" are registered on Form SR.

Example: When a record company issues a new release, the release will typically involve two distinct "works": the "musical work" that has been recorded, and the "sound recording" as a separate work in itself. The material objects that the record company sends out are "phonorecords": physical reproductions of both the "musical work" and the "sound recording."

FOR A MUSICAL OR DRAMATIC WORK, SHOULD YOU DEPOSIT COPIES OR PHONORECORDS WITH YOUR FORM PA?

• **For registration in unpublished form:**
(1) If the work exists only in one form or the other (copies or phonorecords, but not both), deposit the work in its existing form;
(2) If the work exists in both copies and phonorecords, deposit the form that best represents the musical or dramatic work in which copyright is being claimed.

• **For registration in published form:**
(1) If the work has been published in the form of copies but not phonorecords, deposit two copies of the best edition. If the work has been published in the form of phonorecords only, deposit two phonorecords of the best edition.
(2) If the work has been published in both forms, deposit two copies (**not phonorecords**) of the best edition.
(3) If the work has been first published outside the United States, deposit one copy or phonorecord as first published.

SHOULD YOU FILE FORM PA OR FORM SR? If the musical or dramatic work has been recorded, and both that "work," and the sound recording as a separate "work," are eligible for registration, the application form you should file depends on the following:

• **File only Form PA if:** You are seeking to register only the musical or dramatic work, not the sound recording.

• **File only Form SR if:** The copyright claimant for both the musical or dramatic work and the sound recording is the same, and you are seeking a single registration to cover both of these "works."

• **Separate applications on Forms PA and SR should be filed if:**
(1) The copyright claimant for the musical or dramatic work is different from the copyright claimant for the sound recording; or
(2) You prefer to have separate registrations for the musical or dramatic work **and** the sound recording.

FORM OF COPYRIGHT NOTICE ON PHONORECORDS:

For musical or dramatic works: The copyright notice for musical and dramatic works (for example: "© 1978 George Harvey Bone") is required to appear on "all publicly distributed copies from which the work can be visually perceived." There is no requirement that the notice for musical or dramatic works be placed on phonorecords reproducing them.

For sound recordings: The copyright statute provides that, whenever a sound recording is published, a special notice of copyright (for example: "℗1978 Miriam Haines") "shall be placed on all publicly distributed phonorecords of the sound recording." For further information about the requirements for copyright in sound recordings, write for Form SR.

FORM VA

UNITED STATES COPYRIGHT OFFICE
LIBRARY OF CONGRESS
WASHINGTON, D.C. 20559

APPLICATION FOR COPYRIGHT REGISTRATION

for a
Work of the Visual Arts

HOW TO APPLY FOR COPYRIGHT REGISTRATION:

- **First:** Read the information on this page to make sure Form VA is the correct application for your work.

- **Second:** Open out the form by pulling this page to the left. Read through the detailed instructions before starting to complete the form.

- **Third:** Complete spaces 1-4 of the application, then turn the entire form over and, after reading the instructions for spaces 5-9, complete the rest of your application. Use typewriter or print in dark ink. Be sure to sign the form at space 8.

- **Fourth:** Detach your completed application from these instructions and send it with the necessary deposit of the work (see below) to: Register of Copyrights, Library of Congress, Washington, D.C. 20559. Unless you have a Deposit Account in the Copyright Office, your application and deposit must be accompanied by a check or money order for $10, payable to: *Register of Copyrights.*

WHEN TO USE FORM VA: Form VA is the appropriate form to use for copyright registration covering works of the visual arts. Both published and unpublished works can be registered on Form VA.

WHAT IS A "WORK OF THE VISUAL ARTS"? This category consists of "pictorial, graphic, or sculptural works," including two-dimensional and three-dimensional works of fine, graphic, and applied art, photographs, prints and art reproductions, maps, globes, charts, technical drawings, diagrams, and models.

WHAT DOES COPYRIGHT PROTECT? Copyright in a work of the visual arts protects those pictorial, graphic, or sculptural elements that, either alone or in combination, represent an "original work of authorship." The statute declares: "In no case does copyright protection for an original work of authorship extend to any idea, procedure, process, system, method of operation, concept, principle, or discovery, regardless of the form in which it is described, explained, illustrated, or embodied in such work."

WORKS OF ARTISTIC CRAFTSMANSHIP AND DESIGNS: "Works of artistic craftsmanship" are registrable on Form VA, but the statute makes clear that protection extends to "their form" and not to "their mechanical or utilitarian aspects." The "design of a useful article" is considered copyrightable "only if, and only to the extent that, such design incorporates pictorial, graphic, or sculptural features that can be identified separately from, and are capable of existing independently of, the utilitarian aspects of the article."

LABELS AND ADVERTISEMENTS: Works prepared for use in connection with the sale or advertisement of goods and services are registrable if they contain "original work of authorship." Use Form VA if the copyrightable material in the work you are registering is mainly pictorial or graphic; use Form TX if it consists mainly of text. *NOTE:* Words and short phrases such as names, titles, and slogans cannot be protected by copyright, and the same is true of standard symbols, emblems, and other commonly-used graphic designs that are in the public domain. When used commercially, material of that sort can sometimes be protected under State laws of unfair competition or under the Federal trademark laws. For information about trademark registration, write to the Commissioner of Patents and Trademarks, Washington, D.C. 20231.

DEPOSIT TO ACCOMPANY APPLICATION: An application for copyright registration must be accompanied by a deposit representing the entire work for which registration is to be made. The following are the general deposit requirements for works of the visual arts, as set forth in the statute:

Unpublished work: Deposit one complete copy.

Published work: Deposit two complete copies of the best edition.

Work first published outside the United States: Deposit one complete copy of the first foreign edition.

Contribution to a collective work: Deposit one complete copy of the best edition of the collective work.

These general deposit requirements will vary in particular situations. In most cases, where the copies in which the work has been reproduced are three-dimensional, the Copyright Office Regulations provide for the deposit of identifying material (such as photographs or drawings) meeting certain requirements. For further information about the deposit requirements for works of the visual arts, see the reverse side of this sheet. For general information about copyright deposit, write to the Copyright Office.

DURATION OF COPYRIGHT: For works that were created after the effective date of the new statute (January 1, 1978), the basic copyright term will be the life of the author and fifty years after the author's death. For works made for hire, and for certain anonymous and pseudonymous works, the duration of copyright will be 75 years from publication or 100 years from creation, whichever is shorter. These same terms of copyright will generally apply to works that had been created before 1978 but had not been published or copyrighted before that date. For further information about the duration of copyright, including the terms of copyrights already in existence before 1978, write for Circular R15a.

Figure 7.15. Copyright Form Va for Published and Unpublished Works of the Visual Arts, Pictorial, Graphic, and Sculptural Works.

178

FORM VA
UNITED STATES COPYRIGHT OFFICE

REGISTRATION NUMBER
VA   VAU

EFFECTIVE DATE OF REGISTRATION
(Month)   (Day)   (Year)

DO NOT WRITE ABOVE THIS LINE. IF YOU NEED MORE SPACE, USE CONTINUATION SHEET (FORM VA/CON)

(1) Title

TITLE OF THIS WORK:

Previous or Alternative Titles:

NATURE OF THIS WORK: (See instructions)

PUBLICATION AS A CONTRIBUTION: (If this work was published as a contribution to a periodical, serial, or collection, give information about the collective work in which the contribution appeared.)

Title of Collective Work: .... Vol....... No....... Date................. Pages ....

(2) Author(s)

IMPORTANT: Under the law, the "author" of a "work made for hire" is generally the employer, not the employee (see instructions). If any part of this work was "made for hire" check "Yes" in the space provided, give the employer (or other person for whom the work was prepared) as "Author" of that part, and leave the space for dates blank.

1

NAME OF AUTHOR:

Was this author's contribution to the work a "work made for hire"?   Yes...... No......

AUTHOR'S NATIONALITY OR DOMICILE:
Citizen of .... } or { Domiciled in ....
(Name of Country)   (Name of Country)

AUTHOR OF: (Briefly describe nature of this author's contribution)

DATES OF BIRTH AND DEATH:
Born .... Died ....
(Year)   (Year)

WAS THIS AUTHOR'S CONTRIBUTION TO THE WORK:
Anonymous?   Yes ...... No ......
Pseudonymous?   Yes ...... No ......
If the answer to either of these questions is "Yes," see detailed instructions attached.

2

NAME OF AUTHOR:

Was this author's contribution to the work a "work made for hire"?   Yes...... No......

AUTHOR'S NATIONALITY OR DOMICILE:
Citizen of .... } or { Domiciled in ....
(Name of Country)   (Name of Country)

AUTHOR OF: (Briefly describe nature of this author's contribution)

DATES OF BIRTH AND DEATH:
Born .... Died ....
(Year)   (Year)

WAS THIS AUTHOR'S CONTRIBUTION TO THE WORK:
Anonymous?   Yes ...... No ......
Pseudonymous?   Yes ...... No ......
If the answer to either of these questions is "Yes," see detailed instructions attached.

3

NAME OF AUTHOR:

Was this author's contribution to the work a "work made for hire"?   Yes...... No......

AUTHOR'S NATIONALITY OR DOMICILE:
Citizen of .... } or { Domiciled in ....
(Name of Country)   (Name of Country)

AUTHOR OF: (Briefly describe nature of this author's contribution)

DATES OF BIRTH AND DEATH:
Born .... Died ....
(Year)   (Year)

WAS THIS AUTHOR'S CONTRIBUTION TO THE WORK:
Anonymous?   Yes ...... No ......
Pseudonymous?   Yes ...... No ......
If the answer to either of these questions is "Yes," see detailed instructions attached.

(3) Creation and Publication

YEAR IN WHICH CREATION OF THIS WORK WAS COMPLETED:

Year..........
(This information must be given in all cases.)

DATE AND NATION OF FIRST PUBLICATION:

Date..........................
(Month)   (Day)   (Year)

Nation ....
(Name of Country)
(Complete this block ONLY if this work has been published.)

(4) Claimant(s)

NAME(S) AND ADDRESS(ES) OF COPYRIGHT CLAIMANT(S):

TRANSFER: (If the copyright claimant(s) named here in space 4 are different from the author(s) named in space 2, give a brief statement of how the claimant(s) obtained ownership of the copyright.)

- Complete all applicable spaces (numbers 5-9) on the reverse side of this page
- Follow detailed instructions attached   • Sign the form at line 8

DO NOT WRITE HERE
Page 1 of .... pages

Figure 7.15. (Continued)

HOW TO FILL OUT FORM VA

Specific Instructions for Spaces 1-4

- The line-by-line instructions on this page are keyed to the spaces on the first page of Form VA, printed opposite.

- Please read through these instructions before you start filling out your application, and refer to the specific instructions for each space as you go along.

SPACE 1: TITLE

- **Title of this Work:** Every work submitted for copyright registration must be given a title that is capable of identifying that particular work. If the copies of the work bear a title (or an identifying phrase that could serve as a title), transcribe its wording completely and exactly on the application; otherwise give the work a short descriptive title, making it as explicit as possible. Remember that indexing of the registration and future identification of the work will depend on the information you give here.

- **Previous or Alternative Titles:** Complete this line if there are any additional titles for this work under which someone searching for the registration might be likely to look, or under which a document pertaining to the work might be recorded.

- **Publication as a Contribution:** If the work being registered has been published as a contribution to a periodical, serial, or collection, give the title of the contribution in the space headed "Title of this Work." Then, in the line headed "Publication as a Contribution," give information about the larger work in which the contribution appeared.

- **Nature of this Work:** Briefly describe the nature or character of the pictorial, graphic, or sculptural work being registered for copyright. Examples: "Oil Painting"; "Charcoal Drawing"; "Etching"; "Sculpture"; "Map"; "Photograph"; "Scale Model"; "Lithographic Print"; "Jewelry Design"; "Fabric Design".

SPACE 2: AUTHORS

- **General Instructions:** First decide, after reading these instructions, who are the "authors" of this work for copyright purposes. Then, unless the work is a "collective work" (see below), give the requested information about every "author" who contributed any appreciable amount of copyrightable matter to this version of the work. If you need further space, use the attached Continuation Sheet and, if necessary, request additional Continuation Sheets (Form VA/CON).

- **Who is the "Author"?** Unless the work was "made for hire," the individual who actually created the work is its "author." In the case of works of the visual arts, "authors" include artists, cartographers, sculptors, painters, photographers, printmakers, and all others who create pictorial, graphic, or sculptural material. Where a work is made for hire, the statute provides that "the employer or other person for whom the work was prepared is considered the author."

- **What is a "Work Made for Hire"?** A "work made for hire" is defined as: (1) "a work prepared by an employee within the scope of his or her employment"; or (2) "a work specially ordered or commissioned" for certain uses specified in the statute, but only if there is a written agreement to consider it a "work made for hire."

- **Collective Work:** In the case of a collective work, such as a catalog of paintings or a collection of cartoons by various artists, it is sufficient to give information about the author of the collective work as a whole.

- **Author's Identity Not Revealed:** If an author's contribution is "anonymous" or "pseudonymous," it is not necessary to give the name and dates for that author. However, the citizenship or domicile of the author **must** be given in all cases, and information about the nature of that author's contribution to the work should be included.

- **Name of Author:** The fullest form of the author's name should be given. If you have checked "Yes" to indicate that the work was "made for hire," give the full legal name of the employer (or other person for whom the work was prepared). You may also include the name of the employee (for example: "Fremont Enterprises, Inc., employer for hire of L.B. Jeffries"). If the work is "anonymous" you may: (1) leave the line blank, or (2) state "Anonymous" in the line, or (3) reveal the author's identity. If the work is "pseudonymous" you may (1) leave the line blank, or (2) give the pseudonym and identify it as such (for example: "Richard Heldar, pseudonym"), or (3) reveal the author's name, making clear which is the real name and which is the pseudonym (for example: "Henry Leek, whose pseudonym is Priam Farrel").

- **Dates of Birth and Death:** If the author is dead, the statute requires that the year of death be included in the application unless the work is anonymous or pseudonymous. The author's birth date is optional, but is useful as a form of identification. Leave this space blank if the author's contribution was a "work made for hire."

- **"Anonymous" or "Pseudonymous" Work:** An author's contribution to a work is "anonymous" if that author is not identified on the copies of the work. An author's contribution to a work is "pseudonymous" if that author is identified on the copies under a fictitious name.

- **Author's Nationality or Domicile:** Give the country of which the author is a citizen, or the country in which the author is domiciled. The statute requires that either nationality or domicile be given in all cases.

- **Nature of Authorship:** After the words "Author of" give a brief general statement of the nature of this particular author's contribution to the work. Examples: "Painting"; "Photograph"; "Silk Screen Reproduction"; "Co-author of Cartographic Material"; "Technical Drawing"; "Text and Artwork".

SPACE 3: CREATION AND PUBLICATION

- **General Instructions:** Do not confuse "creation" with "publication." Every application for copyright registration must state "the year in which creation of the work was completed." Give the date and nation of first publication only if the work has been published.

- **Creation:** Under the statute, a work of the visual arts is "created" when it is fixed in a copy for the first time. A work is "fixed" in a copy when its embodiment "is sufficiently permanent or stable to permit it to be perceived, reproduced, or otherwise communicated for a period of more than transitory duration." Where a work has been prepared over a period of time, the part of the work existing in fixed form on a particular date constitutes the created work on that date. The date you give here should be the year in which the author completed the particular version for which registration is now being sought, even if other versions exist or if further changes or additions are planned.

- **Publication:** "Publication" is defined as "the distribution of copies or phonorecords of a work to the public by sale or other transfer of ownership, or by rental, lease, or lending"; a work is also "published" if there has been an "offering to distribute copies or phonorecords to a group of persons for purposes of further distribution, public performance, or public display." The statute makes clear that public display of a work "does not of itself constitute publication." Give the full date (month, day, year) when, and the country where, publication first occurred. If first publication took place simultaneously in the United States and other countries, it is sufficient to state "U.S.A."

SPACE 4: CLAIMANT(S)

- **Name(s) and Address(es) of Copyright Claimant(s):** Give the name(s) and address(es) of the copyright claimant(s) in this work. The statute provides that copyright in a work belongs initially to the author of the work (including, in the case of a work made for hire, the employer or other person for whom the work was prepared). The copyright claimant is either the author of the work or a person or organization that has obtained ownership of the copyright initially belonging to the author.

- **Transfer:** The statute provides that, if the copyright claimant is not the author, the application for registration must contain "a brief statement of how the claimant obtained ownership of the copyright." If any copyright claimant named in space 4 is not an author named in space 2, give a brief, general statement summarizing the means by which that claimant obtained ownership of the copyright.

Figure 7.15. (Continued)

180

CONTINUATION SHEET FOR FORM VA

FORM VA/CON
UNITED STATES COPYRIGHT OFFICE

- If at all possible, try to fit the information called for into the spaces provided on Form VA.
- If you do not have space enough for all of the information you need to give on Form VA, use this continuation sheet and submit it with Form VA.
- If you submit this continuation sheet, leave it attached to Form VA. Or, if it becomes detached, clip (do not tape or staple) and fold the two together before submitting them.
- **PART A** of this sheet is intended to identify the basic application. **PART B** is a continuation of Space 2. **PART C** is for the continuation of Spaces 1, 4, or 6. The other spaces on Form VA call for specific items of information, and should not need continuation.

REGISTRATION NUMBER
VA   VAU
EFFECTIVE DATE OF REGISTRATION
(Month)   (Day)   (Year)
CONTINUATION SHEET RECEIVED
Page _____ of _____ pages

DO NOT WRITE ABOVE THIS LINE. FOR COPYRIGHT OFFICE USE ONLY

(A)
Identification of Application

IDENTIFICATION OF CONTINUATION SHEET: This sheet is a continuation of the application for copyright registration on Form VA, submitted for the following work:
- TITLE: (Give the title as given under the heading "Title of this Work" in Space 1 of Form VA.)

- NAME(S) AND ADDRESS(ES) OF COPYRIGHT CLAIMANT(S): (Give the name and address of at least one copyright claimant as given in Space 4 of Form VA.)

(B)
Continuation of Space 2

☐ **NAME OF AUTHOR:**
Was this author's contribution to the work a "work made for hire"?   Yes   No

DATES OF BIRTH AND DEATH:
Born _____ (Year)   Died _____ (Year)

AUTHOR'S NATIONALITY OR DOMICILE:
Citizen of _____ (Name of Country)   or   Domiciled in _____ (Name of Country)

WAS THIS AUTHOR'S CONTRIBUTION TO THE WORK:
Anonymous?   Yes   No
Pseudonymous?   Yes   No
If the answer to either of these questions is "Yes," see detailed instructions attached.

AUTHOR OF: (Briefly describe nature of this author's contribution)

☐ **NAME OF AUTHOR:**
Was this author's contribution to the work a "work made for hire"?   Yes   No

DATES OF BIRTH AND DEATH:
Born _____ (Year)   Died _____ (Year)

AUTHOR'S NATIONALITY OR DOMICILE:
Citizen of _____ (Name of Country)   or   Domiciled in _____ (Name of Country)

WAS THIS AUTHOR'S CONTRIBUTION TO THE WORK:
Anonymous?   Yes   No
Pseudonymous?   Yes   No
If the answer to either of these questions is "Yes," see detailed instructions attached

AUTHOR OF: (Briefly describe nature of this author's contribution)

☐ **NAME OF AUTHOR:**
Was this author's contribution to the work a "work made for hire"?   Yes   No

DATES OF BIRTH AND DEATH:
Born _____ (Year)   Died _____ (Year)

AUTHOR'S NATIONALITY OR DOMICILE:
Citizen of _____ (Name of Country)   or   Domiciled in _____ (Name of Country)

WAS THIS AUTHOR'S CONTRIBUTION TO THE WORK:
Anonymous?   Yes   No
Pseudonymous?   Yes   No
If the answer to either of these questions is "Yes," see detailed instructions attached

AUTHOR OF: (Briefly describe nature of this author's contribution)

(C)
Continuation of Other Spaces

CONTINUATION OF (Check which)   ☐ Space 1   ☐ Space 4   ☐ Space 6

Figure 7.15.   (Continued)

EXAMINED BY:	APPLICATION RECEIVED:	
CHECKED BY:		FOR COPYRIGHT OFFICE USE ONLY
CORRESPONDENCE: ☐ Yes	DEPOSIT RECEIVED:	
DEPOSIT ACCOUNT FUNDS USED: ☐	REMITTANCE NUMBER AND DATE:	

DO NOT WRITE ABOVE THIS LINE. IF YOU NEED ADDITIONAL SPACE, USE CONTINUATION SHEET (FORM VA/CON)

PREVIOUS REGISTRATION:

⑤ Previous Registration

- Has registration for this work, or for an earlier version of this work, already been made in the Copyright Office? Yes........ No ....

- If your answer is "Yes," why is another registration being sought? (Check appropriate box)
  - ☐ This is the first published edition of a work previously registered in unpublished form.
  - ☐ This is the first application submitted by this author as copyright claimant.
  - ☐ This is a changed version of the work, as shown by line 6 of the application.

- If your answer is "Yes," give: Previous Registration Number..................... Year of Registration.........................

COMPILATION OR DERIVATIVE WORK: (See instructions)

⑥ Compilation or Derivative Work

PREEXISTING MATERIAL. (Identify any preexisting work or works that this work is based on or incorporates.)
....
....
....
....

MATERIAL ADDED TO THIS WORK: (Give a brief, general statement of the material that has been added to this work and in which copyright is claimed.)
....
....
....
....

DEPOSIT ACCOUNT: (If the registration fee is to be charged to a Deposit Account established in the Copyright Office, give name and number of Account.)

Name:..............................

Account Number:..............................

CORRESPONDENCE: (Give name and address to which correspondence about this application should be sent.)

Name..............................

Address..............................

(Apt.)

(City)   (State)   (ZIP)

⑦ Fee and Correspondence

CERTIFICATION: ✱ I, the undersigned, hereby certify that I am the: (Check one)

☐ author ☐ other copyright claimant ☐ owner of exclusive right(s) ☐ authorized agent of
....
(Name of author or other copyright claimant, or owner of exclusive right(s))

of the work identified in this application and that the statements made by me in this application are correct to the best of my knowledge.

☞ Handwritten signature: (X)..............................

Typed or printed name..............................   Date..............................

⑧ Certification (Application must be signed)

MAIL CERTIFICATE TO

....
(Name)

....
(Number, Street and Apartment Number)

....
(City)   (State)   (ZIP code)

(Certificate will be mailed in window envelope)

⑨ Address For Return of Certificate

Jan. 1980—500,000

Figure 7.15. (Continued)

INSTRUCTIONS FOR SPACES 5-9

SPACE 5: PREVIOUS REGISTRATION

• **General Instructions:** The questions in space 5 are intended to find out whether an earlier registration has been made for this work and, if so, whether there is any basis for a new registration. As a general rule, only one basic copyright registration can be made for the same version of a particular work.

• **Same Version:** If this version is substantially the same as the work covered by a previous registration, a second registration is not generally possible unless: (1) the work has been registered in unpublished form and a second registration is now being sought to cover the first published edition, or (2) someone other than the author is identified as copyright claimant in the earlier registration, and the author is now seeking registration in his or her own name. If either of these two exceptions apply, check the appropriate box and give the earlier registration number and date. Otherwise, do not submit Form VA; instead, write the Copyright Office for information about supplementary registration or recordation of transfer of copyright ownership.

• **Changed Version:** If the work has been changed, and you are now seeking registration to cover the additions or revisions, check the third box in space 5, give the earlier registration number and date, and complete both parts of space 6.

• **Previous Registration Number and Date:** If more than one previous registration has been made for the work, give the number and date of the latest registration.

SPACE 6: COMPILATION OR DERIVATIVE WORK

• **General Instructions:** Complete both parts of space 6 if this work is a "compilation," or "derivative work," or both, and if it is based on or incorporates one or more "preexisting works" that are not eligible for registration for one reason or another: works that have already been published or registered, or works that have fallen into the public domain. A "compilation" is defined as "a work formed by the collection and assembling of preexisting materials or of data that are selected, coordinated, or arranged in such a way that the resulting work as a whole constitutes an original work of authorship." A "derivative work" is "a work based on one or more preexisting works." In addition to various forms in which works may be "recast, transformed, or adapted," derivative works include works "consisting of editorial revisions, annotations, elaborations, or other modifications" if these changes, as a whole, represent an original work of authorship.

• **Preexisting Material:** If the work is a compilation, give a brief, general statement describing the nature of the material that has been compiled. Example: "Compilation of 19th Century political cartoons". In the case of a derivative work, identify the preexisting work that has been recast, transformed, or adapted. Examples: "Grünewald Altarpiece"; "19th Century quilt design."

• **Material Added to this Work:** The statute requires a "brief, general statement of the additional material covered by the copyright claim being registered." This statement should describe all of the material in this particular version of the work that: (1) represents an original work of authorship; (2) has not fallen into public domain; (3) has not been previously published; and (4) has not been previously registered for copyright in unpublished form. Examples: "Adaptation of design and additional artistic work"; "Reproduction of painting by photolithography"; "Additional cartographic material"; "Compilation of photographs."

SPACES 7, 8, 9: FEE, CORRESPONDENCE, CERTIFICATION, RETURN ADDRESS

• **Deposit Account and Mailing Instructions (Space 7):** If you maintain a Deposit Account in the Copyright Office, identify it in space 7. Otherwise you will need to send the registration fee of $10 with your application. The space headed "Correspondence" should contain the name and address of the person to be consulted if correspondence about this application becomes necessary.

• **Certification (Space 8):** The application is not acceptable unless it bears the handwritten signature of the author or other copyright claimant, or of the owner of exclusive right(s), or of the duly authorized agent of such author, claimant, or owner.

• **Address for Return of Certificate (Space 9):** The address box must be completed legibly, since the certificate will be returned in a window envelope.

MORE INFORMATION

THE COPYRIGHT NOTICE: For published works, the law provides that a copyright notice in a specified form "shall be placed on all publicly distributed copies from which the work can be visually perceived." Use of the copyright notice is the responsibility of the copyright owner, and does not require advance permission from the Copyright Office.

• **Form of the Notice:** The required form of the notice for copies generally consists of three elements: (1) the symbol "©", or the word "Copyright", or the abbreviation "Copr."; (2) the year of first publication; and (3) the name of the owner of copyright in the work, or an abbreviation by which the name can be recognized, or a generally known alternative designation of the owner. Example: "© 1978 Samuel Marlove." Under the statute, the year date may be omitted from the notice in cases "where a pictorial, graphic, or sculptural work, with accompanying text matter, if any, is reproduced in or on greeting cards, postcards, stationery, jewelry, dolls, toys, or any useful articles."

• **Position of the Notice:** The notice is to be affixed to the copies "in such manner and location as to give reasonable notice of the claim of copyright."

• **Errors or Omissions:** Unlike the law in effect before 1978, the new copyright statute provides procedures for correcting errors in the copyright notice, and even for curing the omission of the notice. However, a failure to comply with the notice requirements may still result in the loss of some copyright protection and, unless corrected within five years, in the complete loss of copyright. For further information about the copyright notice and the procedures for correcting errors or omissions, write to the Copyright Office.

FORM OF DEPOSIT FOR WORKS OF THE VISUAL ARTS

Exceptions to General Deposit Requirements: As explained on the reverse side of this page, the statutory deposit requirements (generally one copy for unpublished works and two copies for published works) will vary for particular kinds of works of the visual arts. The copyright law authorizes the Register of Copyrights to issue regulations specifying "the administrative classes into which works are to be placed for purposes of deposit and registration, and the nature of the copies or phonorecords to be deposited in the various classes specified." For particular classes, the regulations may require or permit "the deposit of identifying material instead of copies or phonorecords," or "the deposit of only one copy or phonorecord where two would normally be required."

What Should You Deposit? The detailed requirements with respect to the kind of deposit to accompany an application on Form VA are contained in the Copyright Office Regulations. The following does not cover all of the deposit requirements, but is intended to give you some general guidance.

• For an unpublished work, the material deposited should represent the entire copyrightable content of the work for which registration is being sought;

• For a published work, the material deposited should generally consist of two complete copies of the best edition. Exceptions:

—For certain types of works, one complete copy may be deposited instead of two. These include greeting cards, postcards, stationery, labels, advertisements, scientific drawings, and globes.

—For most three-dimensional sculptural works, and for certain two-dimensional works, the Copyright Office Regulations require the deposit of identifying material (photographs or drawings in a specified form) rather than copies.

—Under certain circumstances, for works published in five copies or less or in limited, numbered editions, the deposit may consist of one copy or of identifying reproductions.

Figure 7.15. (Continued)

FORM SR

UNITED STATES COPYRIGHT OFFICE
LIBRARY OF CONGRESS
WASHINGTON, D.C. 20559

APPLICATION FOR COPYRIGHT REGISTRATION
for a
Sound Recording

HOW TO APPLY FOR COPYRIGHT REGISTRATION:

- ***First:*** Read the information on this page to make sure Form SR is the correct application for your work.

- ***Second:*** Open out the form by pulling this page to the left. Read through the detailed instructions before starting to complete the form.

- ***Third:*** Complete spaces 1-4 of the application, then turn the entire form over and, after reading the instructions for spaces 5-9, complete the rest of your application. Use typewriter or print in dark ink. Be sure to sign the form at space 8.

- ***Fourth:*** Detach your completed application from these instructions and send it with the necessary deposit of the work (see below) to: Register of Copyrights, Library of Congress, Washington, D.C. 20559. Unless you have a Deposit Account in the Copyright Office, your application and deposit must be accompanied by a check or money order for $10, payable to: *Register of Copyrights.*

WHEN TO USE FORM SR: Form SR is the appropriate application to use for copyright registration covering a sound recording. It should be used where the copyright claim is limited to the sound recording itself, and it should also be used where the same copyright claimant is seeking to register not only the sound recording but also the musical, dramatic, or literary work embodied in the sound recording. Both published and unpublished works can be registered on Form SR.

WHAT IS A "SOUND RECORDING"? With one exception, "sound recordings" are works that result from the fixation of a series of musical, spoken, or other sounds. The exception is for the audio portions of audiovisual works, such as a motion picture soundtrack or an audio cassette accompanying a filmstrip; these are considered an integral part of the audiovisual work as a whole. For further information about "sound recordings," and the distinction between "sound recordings" and "phonorecords," see the reverse side of this sheet. For additional information about copyright in sound recordings, write to the Copyright Office.

DEPOSIT TO ACCOMPANY APPLICATION: An application for copyright registration must be accompanied by a deposit representing the entire work for which registration is to be made. For registration on Form SR, the following are the general deposit requirements:

Unpublished work: Deposit one complete phonorecord.

Published work: Deposit two complete phonorecords of the best edition, together with "any printed or other visually perceptible material" published with the phonorecords.

Work first published outside the United States: Deposit one complete phonorecord of the work as first published.

Contribution to a collective work: Deposit one complete phonorecord of the best edition of the collective work.

These general deposit requirements may vary in particular situations. For further information about the deposit requirements for sound recordings, see the reverse side of this sheet. For general information about copyright deposit, write to the Copyright Office.

THE COPYRIGHT NOTICE: For published sound recordings, the law provides that a copyright notice in a specified form "shall be placed on all publicly distributed phonorecords of the sound recording." Use of the copyright notice is the responsibility of the copyright owner and does not require advance permission from the Copyright Office. The required form of the notice for phonorecords generally consists of three elements: (1) the symbol "℗" (the letter P in a circle); (2) the year of first publication of the sound recording; and (3) the name of the owner of copyright. For example: "℗ 1978 Rittenhouse Record Co." The notice is to be "placed on the surface of the phonorecord, or on the label or container, in such manner and location as to give reasonable notice of the claim of copyright." Unlike the law in effect before 1978, the new copyright statute provides procedures for correcting errors in the copyright notice, and even for curing the omission of the notice. However, a failure to comply with the notice requirements may still result in the loss of some copyright protection and, unless corrected within five years, in the complete loss of copyright. For further information about the copyright notice, see the reverse side of this sheet. For additional information concerning the copyright notice and the procedures for correcting errors or omissions, write to the Copyright Office.

DURATION OF COPYRIGHT: For works that were created after the effective date of the new statute (January 1, 1978), the basic copyright term will be the life of the author and fifty years after the author's death. For works made for hire, and for certain anonymous and pseudonymous works, the duration of copyright will be 75 years from publication or 100 years from creation, whichever is shorter. These same terms of copyright will generally apply to works that had been created before 1978 but had not been published or copyrighted before that date. Sound recordings fixed before February 15, 1972 are not eligible for registration, but may be protected by state law. For further information about the duration of copyright, including the terms of copyrights already in existence before 1978, write for Circular R15a.

Figure 7.16. Copyright Form SR for Published and Unpublished Sound Recordings.

HOW TO FILL OUT FORM SR
Specific Instructions for Spaces 1-4

> - The line-by-line instructions on this page are keyed to the spaces on the first page of Form SR, printed opposite.
> - Please read through these instructions before you start filling out your application, and refer to the specific instructions for each space as you go along.

SPACE 1: TITLE

- **Title of this Work:** Every work submitted for copyright registration must be given a title that is capable of identifying that particular work. If the phonorecords of the work bear a title (or an identifying phrase that could serve as a title), transcribe its wording completely and exactly on the application.

  If the work you are registering is an entire "collective work" (such as a compilation of previously-issued recordings), give the over-all title of the collection. If you are registering one or more individual contributions to a collective work, give the title of each contribution, followed by the title of the collection. Example: " 'Perpetual Motion' in *Croatian Folk Songs and Dances*."

- **Nature of Material Recorded:** Indicate the general type or character of the works or other material embodied in the recording. The box marked "Literary" should be checked for nondramatic spoken material of all sorts, including narration, interviews, panel discussions, and training material. If the material recorded is not musical, dramatic, or literary in nature, check "Other" and briefly describe the type of sounds fixed in the recording. For example: "Sound Effects"; "Bird Calls"; "Crowd Noises".

- **Previous or Alternative Titles:** Complete this space if there are any additional titles for the work under which someone searching for the registration might be likely to look, or under which a document pertaining to the work might be recorded.

SPACE 2: AUTHORS

- **General Instructions:** First decide, after reading these instructions, who are the "authors" of this work for copyright purposes. Then, unless the work is a "collective work" (see below), give the requested information about every "author" who contributed any appreciable amount of copyrightable matter to this version of the work.

- **Note:** As explained in more detail elsewhere on this application form, Form SR may be used to apply for a single registration to cover not only a sound recording but also the musical, dramatic, or literary work embodied in that recording, as long as the copyright claimant is the same for both. If you are submitting this Form SR to cover the recorded musical, dramatic, or literary work as well as the sound recording itself, it is important for space 2 to include full information about the various authors of all of the material covered by the copyright claim, making clear the nature of each author's contribution.

- **Who is the "Author"?** Unless the work was "made for hire," the individual who actually created the work is its "author." In the case of a work made for hire, the statute provides that "the employer or other person for whom the work was prepared is considered the author." Authorship of a sound recording may include the performance fixed in the recording, or the creative elements of the recording as such, or both.

- **What is a "Work Made for Hire"?** A "work made for hire" is defined as: (1) "a work prepared by an employee within the scope of his or her employment"; or (2) "a work specially ordered or commissioned" for certain uses specified in the statute, but only if there is a written agreement to consider it a "work made for hire."

- **Collective Work:** In the case of a collective work, such as a compilation of separately-made recordings, it is sufficient to give information about the author of the collective work as a whole.

- **Author's Identity Not Revealed:** If an author's contribution is "anonymous" or "pseudonymous," it is not *necessary* to give the name and dates for that author. However, the citizenship or domicile of the author **must** be given in all cases, and information about the nature of that author's contribution to the work should be included.

- **Name of Author:** The fullest form of the author's name should be given. If you have checked "Yes" to indicate that the work was "made for hire," give the full legal name of the employer (or other person for whom the work was prepared). You may also include the name of the employee (for example: "Music Makers Record Co., employer for hire of Lila Crane"). If the work is "anonymous" you may: (1) leave the line blank, or (2) state "Anonymous" in the line, or (3) reveal the author's identity. If the work is "pseudonymous" you may (1) leave the line blank, or (2) give the pseudonym and identify it as such (for example: "Huntley Haverstock, pseudonym"), or (3) reveal the author's name, making clear which is the real name and which is the pseudonym (for example: "Judith Barton, whose pseudonym is Madeleine Elster").

- **Dates of Birth and Death:** If the author is dead, the statute requires that the year of death be included in the application unless the work is anonymous or pseudonymous. The author's birth date is optional, but is useful as a form of identification. Leave this space blank if the author's contribution was a "work made for hire."

- **"Anonymous" or "Pseudonymous" Work:** An author's contribution to a work is "anonymous" if that author is not identified on the copies or phonorecords of the work. An author's contribution to a work is "pseudonymous" if that author is identified on the copies or phonorecords under a fictitious name.

- **Author's Nationality or Domicile:** Give the country of which the author is a citizen, or the country in which the author is domiciled. The statute requires that either nationality or domicile be given in all cases.

- **Nature of Authorship:** After the words "Author of" give a brief general statement of the nature of this particular author's contribution to the work. If you are submitting this Form SR to cover both the sound recording and the underlying musical, dramatic, or literary work, make sure that the precise nature of each author's contribution is reflected here. Examples where the authorship pertains to the recording: "Sound Recording"; "Performance and Recording"; "Recorded Reading"; "Compilation and Remixing of Sounds". Examples where the authorship relates to the underlying work: "Words and Music"; "Book and Lyrics"; "Co-author of Dialogue and Narration"; "Script of Speech". Examples where the authorship pertains to both: "Words, Music, Performance, Recording"; "Arrangement of Music and Recording"; "Compilation of Poems and Reading".

SPACE 3: CREATION AND PUBLICATION

- **General Instructions:** Do not confuse "creation" with "publication." Every application for copyright registration must state "the year in which creation of the work was completed." Give the date and nation of first publication only if the work has been published.

- **Creation:** Under the statute, a sound recording is "created" when it is fixed in a phonorecord for the first time. A work is "fixed" in a phonorecord when its embodiment "is sufficiently permanent or stable to permit it to be perceived, reproduced, or otherwise communicated for a period of more than transitory duration." Where a work has been prepared over a period of time, the part of the work existing in fixed form on a particular date constitutes the created work on that date. The date you give here should be the year in which the author completed the particular version for which registration is now being sought, even if other versions exist or if further changes or additions are planned.

- **Publication:** The statute defines "publication" as "the distribution of copies or phonorecords of a work to the public by sale or other transfer of ownership, or by rental, lease, or lending"; a work is also "published" if there has been an "offering to distribute copies or phonorecords to a group of persons for purposes of further distribution, public performance, or public display." Give the full date (month, day, year) when, and the country where, publication first occurred. If first publication took place simultaneously in the United States and other countries, it is sufficient to state "U.S.A."

SPACE 4: CLAIMANT(S)

- **Name(s) and Address(es) of Copyright Claimant(s):** Give the name(s) and address(es) of the copyright claimant(s) in this work. The statute provides that copyright in a work belongs initially to the author of the work (including, in the case of a work made for hire, the employer or other person for whom the work was prepared). The copyright claimant is either the author of the work or a person or organization that has obtained ownership of the copyright initially belonging to the author.

- **Transfer:** The statute provides that, if the copyright claimant is not the author, the application for registration must contain "a brief statement of how the claimant obtained ownership of the copyright." If any copyright claimant named in space 4 is not an author named in space 2, give a brief, general statement summarizing the means by which that claimant obtained ownership of the copyright.

Figure 7.16. (Continued)

185

INSTRUCTIONS FOR SPACES 5-9

SPACE 5: PREVIOUS REGISTRATION

• **General Instructions:** The questions in space 5 are intended to find out whether an earlier registration has been made for this work and, if so, whether there is any basis for a new registration. As a general rule, only one basic copyright registration can be made for the same version of a particular work.

• **Same Version:** If this version is substantially the same as the work covered by a previous registration, a second registration is not generally possible unless: (1) the work has been registered in unpublished form and a second registration is now being sought to cover the first published edition, or (2) someone other than the author is identified as copyright claimant in the earlier registration, and the author is now seeking registration in his or her own name. If either of these two exceptions apply, check the appropriate box and give the earlier registration number and date. Otherwise, do not submit Form SR; instead, write the Copyright Office for information about supplementary registration or recordation of transfer of copyright ownership.

• **Changed Version:** If the work has been changed, and you are now seeking registration to cover the additions or revisions, check the third box in space 5, give the earlier registration number and date, and complete both parts of space 6.

• **Previous Registration Number and Date:** If more than one previous registration has been made for the work, give the number and date of the latest registration.

SPACE 6: COMPILATION OR DERIVATIVE WORK

• **General Instructions:** Complete both parts of space 6 if this work is a "compilation," or "derivative work," or both, and if it is based on or incorporates one or more "preexisting works" not eligible for registration for one reason or another: works that have already been published or registered, or works that have fallen into the public domain, or sound recordings that were fixed before February 15, 1972. A "compilation" is defined as "a work formed by the collection and assembling of preexisting materials or of data that are selected, coordinated, or arranged in such a way that the resulting work as a whole constitutes an original work of authorship." A "derivative work" is "a work based on one or more preexisting works." In addition to various forms in which works may be "recast, transformed, or adapted," derivative works include works "consisting of editorial revisions, annotations, elaborations, or other modifications" if these changes, as a whole, represent an original work of authorship.

• **Preexisting Material:** If the work is a compilation, give a brief, general statement describing the nature of the material that has been compiled. Example: "Compilation of 1930 recordings by various Chicago jazz bands." In the case of a derivative work, identify the preexisting work that has been recast, transformed, or adapted. Example: "1945 recording by Sperryville Symphony of Bach Double Concerto."

• **Material Added to this Work:** The statute requires a "brief, general statement of the additional material covered by the copyright claim being registered." This statement should describe all of the material in this particular version of the work that: (1) represents an original work of authorship; (2) has not fallen into the public domain; (3) has not been previously published; (4) has not been previously registered for copyright in unpublished form; and (5) is not a sound recording fixed before February 15, 1972. Examples: "Recorded performances on bands 1 and 3"; "Remixed sounds from original multitrack sound sources"; "New words, arrangement, and additional sounds."

SPACES 7, 8, 9: FEE, CORRESPONDENCE, CERTIFICATION, RETURN ADDRESS

• **Deposit Account and Mailing Instructions (Space 7):** If you maintain a Deposit Account in the Copyright Office, identify it in space 7. Otherwise you will need to send the registration fee of $10 with your application. The space headed "Correspondence" should contain the name and address of the person to be consulted if correspondence about this application becomes necessary.

• **Certification (Space 8):** The application is not acceptable unless it bears the handwritten signature of the author or other copyright claimant, or of the owner of exclusive right(s), or of the duly authorized agent of such author, claimant, or owner

• **Address for Return of Certificate (Space 9):** The address box must be completed legibly, since the certificate will be returned in a window envelope.

MORE INFORMATION

A NOTE ON TERMINOLOGY: The following are the meanings given to some of the terms used in the copyright statute:

• **"Works":** "Works" are the basic subject matter of copyright: they are what authors create and copyright protects. The statute draws a sharp distinction between the "work" and "any material object in which the work is embodied."

• **"Copies" and "Phonorecords":** These are the two types of material objects in which "works" are embodied. In general, **"copies"** are objects from which a work can be read or visually perceived, directly or with the aid of a machine or device, such as manuscripts, books, sheet music, film, and videotape. **"Phonorecords"** are objects embodying fixations of sounds, such as audio tapes and phonograph disks. For example, a song (the "work") can be reproduced in sheet music ("copies") or phonograph disks ("phonorecords"), or both.

• **"Sound Recordings":** These are "works," not "copies" or "phonorecords." "Sound recordings" are "works that result from the fixation of a series of musical, spoken, or other sounds, but not including the sounds accompanying a motion picture or other audiovisual work."

Example: When a record company issues a new release, the release will typically involve two distinct "works": the "musical work" that has been recorded, and the "sound recording" as a separate work in itself. The material objects that the record company sends out are "phonorecords": physical reproductions of both the "musical work" and the "sound recording."

SHOULD YOU FILE MORE THAN ONE APPLICATION? If your work consists of a recorded musical, dramatic, or literary work, and both that "work," and the sound recording as a separate "work," are eligible for registration, the application form you should file depends on the following:

• **File only Form SR if:** The copyright claimant is the same for both the musical, dramatic, or literary work and for the sound recording, and you are seeking a single registration to cover both of these "works."

• **File only Form PA (or Form TX) if:** You are seeking to register only the musical, dramatic, or literary work, not the sound recording. Form PA is appropriate for works of the performing arts; Form TX is for nondramatic literary works.

• **Separate applications should be filed on Form PA (or Form TX) and on Form SR if:**

(1) The copyright claimant for the musical, dramatic, or literary work is different from the copyright claimant for the sound recording, or

(2) You prefer to have separate registrations for the musical, dramatic, or literary work and for the sound recording.

FORM OF COPYRIGHT NOTICE ON PHONORECORDS:

For sound recordings: The copyright statute provides that, whenever a sound recording is published, a special notice of copyright (for example: "℗ 1978 Miriam Haines") "shall be placed on all publicly distributed phonorecords of the sound recording."

For musical, dramatic, or literary works: The copyright notice for musical, dramatic, and literary works (for example: "© 1978 George Harvey Bone") is required to appear on "all publicly distributed copies from which the work can be visually perceived." There is no requirement that the notice for musical, dramatic, or literary works be placed on phonorecords reproducing them.

Figure 7.16. (Continued)

FORM SR
UNITED STATES COPYRIGHT OFFICE

REGISTRATION NUMBER
SR   SRU

EFFECTIVE DATE OF REGISTRATION
....
(Month)   (Day)   (Year)

DO NOT WRITE ABOVE THIS LINE. IF YOU NEED MORE SPACE, USE CONTINUATION SHEET (FORM SR/CON)

1 **Title**

TITLE OF THIS WORK:

Catalog number of sound recording, if any: ....

PREVIOUS OR ALTERNATIVE TITLES:

NATURE OF MATERIAL RECORDED: (Check Which)

☐ Musical   ☐ Musical-Dramatic
☐ Dramatic   ☐ Literary
☐ Other:...................................
....
....

2 **Author(s)**

IMPORTANT: Under the law, the "author" of a "work made for hire" is generally the employer, not the employee (see instructions). If any part of this work was "made for hire" check "Yes" in the space provided, give the employer (or other person for whom the work was prepared) as "Author" of that part, and leave the space for dates blank.

1

NAME OF AUTHOR:

Was this author's contribution to the work a "work made for hire"?   Yes...... No......

AUTHOR'S NATIONALITY OR DOMICILE:
Citizen of .... } or { Domiciled in ....
(Name of Country)   (Name of Country)

AUTHOR OF: (Briefly describe nature of this author's contribution)

DATES OF BIRTH AND DEATH:
Born......... Died.........
(Year)   (Year)

WAS THIS AUTHOR'S CONTRIBUTION TO THE WORK:
Anonymous?   Pseudonymous?

Yes..... No.....   Yes..... No.....
If the answer to either of these questions is "Yes," see detailed instructions attached.

2

NAME OF AUTHOR:

Was this author's contribution to the work a "work made for hire"?   Yes...... No......

AUTHOR'S NATIONALITY OR DOMICILE:
Citizen of .... } or { Domiciled in ....
(Name of Country)   (Name of Country)

AUTHOR OF: (Briefly describe nature of this author's contribution)

DATES OF BIRTH AND DEATH:
Born......... Died.........
(Year)   (Year)

WAS THIS AUTHOR'S CONTRIBUTION TO THE WORK:
Anonymous?   Pseudonymous?

Yes..... No.....   Yes..... No.....
If the answer to either of these questions is "Yes," see detailed instructions attached.

3

NAME OF AUTHOR:

Was this author's contribution to the work a "work made for hire"?   Yes...... No......

AUTHOR'S NATIONALITY OR DOMICILE:
Citizen of .... } or { Domiciled in ....
(Name of Country)   (Name of Country)

AUTHOR OF: (Briefly describe nature of this author's contribution)

DATES OF BIRTH AND DEATH:
Born......... Died.........
(Year)   (Year)

WAS THIS AUTHOR'S CONTRIBUTION TO THE WORK:
Anonymous?   Pseudonymous?

Yes..... No.....   Yes..... No.....
If the answer to either of these questions is "Yes," see detailed instructions attached.

3 **Creation and Publication**

YEAR IN WHICH CREATION OF THIS WORK WAS COMPLETED:

Year............
(This information must be given in all cases.)

DATE AND NATION OF FIRST PUBLICATION:

Date ....
(Month)   (Day)   (Year)

Nation...
(Name of Country)
(Complete this block ONLY if this work has been published.)

4 **Claimant(s)**

NAME(S) AND ADDRESS(ES) OF COPYRIGHT CLAIMANT(S):

TRANSFER: (If the copyright claimant(s) named here in space 4 are different from the author(s) named in space 2, give a brief statement of how the claimant(s) obtained ownership of the copyright.)

• Complete all applicable spaces (numbers 5-9) on the reverse side of this page
• Follow detailed instructions attached
• Sign the form at line 8

DO NOT WRITE HERE
Page 1 of ....pages

Figure 7.16. (Continued)

187

	EXAMINED BY:	APPLICATION RECEIVED:	FOR COPYRIGHT OFFICE USE ONLY
	CHECKED BY:		
	CORRESPONDENCE: ☐ Yes	DEPOSIT RECEIVED:	
	DEPOSIT ACCOUNT FUNDS USED: ☐	REMITTANCE NUMBER AND DATE:	

DO NOT WRITE ABOVE THIS LINE. IF YOU NEED ADDITIONAL SPACE, USE CONTINUATION SHEET (FORM SR/CON)

PREVIOUS REGISTRATION:

- Has registration for this work, or for an earlier version of this work, already been made in the Copyright Office? Yes .... No ....

- If your answer is "Yes," why is another registration being sought? (Check appropriate box)
  - ☐ This is the first published edition of a work previously registered in unpublished form.
  - ☐ This is the first application submitted by this author as copyright claimant.
  - ☐ This is a changed version of the work, as shown by line 6 of the application.

- If your answer is "Yes," give: Previous Registration Number .... Year of Registration ....

(5) Previous Registration

COMPILATION OR DERIVATIVE WORK: (See instructions)

PREEXISTING MATERIAL: (Identify any preexisting work or works that the work is based on or incorporates.)
....
....
....
....

MATERIAL ADDED TO THIS WORK: (Give a brief, general statement of the material that has been added to this work and in which copyright is claimed.)
....
....
....
....

(6) Compilation or Derivative Work

DEPOSIT ACCOUNT: (If the registration fee is to be charged to a Deposit Account established in the Copyright Office, give name and number of Account.)

Name: ....

Account Number: ....

CORRESPONDENCE: (Give name and address to which correspondence about this application should be sent.)

Name: ....

Address: ....
(Apt.)

(City)   (State)   (ZIP)

(7) Fee and Correspondence

CERTIFICATION: ✳ I, the undersigned, hereby certify that I am the: (Check one)
☐ author ☐ other copyright claimant ☐ owner of exclusive right(s) ☐ authorized agent of: ....
(Name of author or other copyright claimant, or owner of exclusive right(s))

of the work identified in this application and that the statements made by me in this application are correct to the best of my knowledge.

Handwritten signature: (X) ....

Typed or printed name: .... Date: ....

(8) Certification (Application must be signed)

....
(Name)

....
(Number, Street and Apartment Number)

....
(City)   (State)   (ZIP code)

MAIL CERTIFICATE TO

(Certificate will be mailed in window envelope)

(9) Address For Return of Certificate

May 1981—87,000

Figure 7.16. (Continued)

28 years from the first date that it was secured, and it was eligible for renewal once for an additional 28 years. Under the new copyright law, the renewal term has been extended from 28 to 47 years for copyrights that were subsisting on January 1, 1978. However, the copyright must be timely renewed to receive the 47-year period of added protection.

If you want a form for renewing a copyright which has already been registered, ask for Form RE. This is for claims to renew a copyright and for works copyrighted under the old law.

INTERNATIONAL COPYRIGHT PROTECTION

As with patents, there is no such thing as an international copyright that will automatically protect an author's writings throughout the entire world. However, most countries do offer protection to foreign works under certain conditions, and these conditions have been greatly simplified by international copyright treaties and conventions. The United States is a member of the Universal Copyright Convention (UCC) which came into force in 1955. Under this convention, a work by a national or domiciliary of a country that is a member of the Universal Copyright Convention or a work first published in a Universal Copyright Convention country may claim protection under the Universal Copyright Convention, as long as the work bears the notice of the copyright in the foreign position specified by the Universal Copyright Convention. It is for this reason that I advise that you use the word "copyright" as well as the symbol ©. However, any author who wants protection for his or her work in a particular country should find out about that specific country; if possible, he or she should do this before the work is published anywhere.

WHAT IS A TRADEMARK?

A trademark includes any word, name, symbol, device, or any combination thereof adopted and used by a manufacturer or merchant to identify his goods and distinguish them from those manufactured or sold by others. The primary function of the trademark is to indicate origin. However, it has other functions. Trademarks also guarantee the quality of the goods bearing the mark and through advertising help to create and maintain a demand for your product.

Rights in a trademark are acquired only by use, and the use must ordinarily continue if the rights so acquired are to be preserved. This means that although you may register a trademark in the Patent and Trademark Office, this by itself does not create or establish any exclusive right. Such registration is only recognition by the U.S. government of the right of the owner to use the mark in commerce to distinguish the mark from those of others.

TRADEMARKS YOU CANNOT REGISTER

Certain trademarks cannot be registered. This is so if the mark consists of or comprises:

1. Immoral, deceptive, or scandalous matter, or matter that may disparage or falsely suggest a connection with persons living or dead, institutions, beliefs, or national symbols, or bring them into contempt or disrepute

2.   The flag or coat of arms or other insignia of the United States or any state or municipality or of any foreign nation or any simulation thereof

3.   The name, portrait, or signature identifying a particular living individual, except by his written consent, or the name, signature, or portrait of a deceased president of the United States during the life of his widow, if any, except by the written consent of the widow

4.   A mark which so resembles a mark registered in the Patent and Trademark Office or a mark or trade name previously used in the United States or by another and not abandoned as to be likely when applied to the goods of another person to cause confusion or to cause mistake or to deceive

HOW TO REGISTER FOR A TRADEMARK

The application for registration for a trademark must be filed in the name of the owner of the mark. The owner may file and prosecute his own application for registration, or he or she may be represented by an attorney or other person authorized to practice in trademark cases.

There are four parts to the application for a trademark. They are as follows:

1.   A written application
2.   A drawing of the mark
3.   Five specimens or facsimiles
4.   The required filing fee

Let's look at each in turn.

The Written Application

The written application must be in the English language and plainly written on one side of the paper. The Patent and Trademark Office prefers legal-size paper, typewritten, double spaced with at least a one-and-one-half-inch margin on the left side and the top of the page.

The application must include a request for registration and must specify the following:

1.   The name of the applicant
2.   The citizenship of the applicant, or, if the applicant is a partnership, the name and the citizenship of the general partners, or, if the applicant is a corporation or association the state or union under the laws of which organized
3.   The domicile and post office address of the applicant
4.   That the applicant has adopted and is using the mark shown in the accompanying drawing
5.   The particular goods on or in connection with which the mark is used
6.   The class of merchandise according to the official classification if known to the applicant. The official classifications of goods and services are as follows:

GOODS

1. Chemical products used in industry, science, photography, agriculture, horticulture, forestry; artificial and synthetic resins; plastics in the form of powders, liquids or pastes, for industrial use; manures (natural and artificial); fire extinguishing compositions; tempering substances and chemical preparations for soldering; chemical substances for preserving foodstuffs; tanning substances; adhesive substances used in industry.

2. Paints, varnishes, lacquers; preservatives against rust and against deterioration of wood; coloring matters, dyestuffs; mordants; natural resins; metals in foil and powder form for painters and decorators.

3. Bleaching preparations and other substances for laundry use; cleaning, polishing, scouring and abrasive preparations; soaps; perfumery, essential oils, cosmetics, hair lotions; dentifrices.

4. Industrial oils and greases (other than oils and fats and essential oils); lubricants; dust laying and absorbing compositions; fuels (including motor spirit) and illuminants; candles, tapers, night lights and wicks.

5. Pharmaceutical, veterinary, and sanitary substances; infants' and invalids' foods; plasters, material for bandaging; material for stopping teeth, dental wax, disinfectants; preparations for killing weeds and destroying vermin.

6. Unwrought and partly wrought common metals and their alloys; anchors, anvils, bells, rolled and cast building materials; rails and other metallic materials for railway tracks; chains (except driving chains for vehicles); cables and wires (non-electric); locksmiths' work; metallic pipes and tubes; safes and cash boxes; steel balls; horseshoes; nails and screws; other goods in non-precious metal not included in other classes; ores.

7. Machines and machine tools; motors (except for land vehicles); machine couplings and belting (except for land vehicles); large size agricultural implements; incubators.

8. Hand tools and instruments; cutlery, forks, spoons; side arms.

9. Scientific, nautical, surveying and electrical apparatus and instruments (including wireless); photographic, cinematographic, optical, weighing, measuring, signalling, checking (supervision), lifesaving and teaching apparatus and instruments; coin or counter-freed apparatus; talking machines; cash registers; calculating machines; fire-extinguishing apparatus.

10. Surgical, medical, dental and veterinary instruments and apparatus (including artificial limbs, eyes, and teeth).

11. Installations for lighting, heating, steam generating, cooking, refrigerating, drying, ventilating, water supply and sanitary purposes.

12. Vehicles; apparatus for locomotion by land, air or water.

13. Firearms; ammunition and projectiles; explosive substances; fireworks.

14. Precious metals and their alloys and goods in precious metals or coated therewith (except cutlery, forks and spoons); jewellery, precious stones, horological and other chronometric instruments.

15. Musical instruments (other than talking machines and wireless apparatus).

16. Paper, cardboard, articles of paper or of cardboard (not included in other classes); printed matter, newspapers and periodicals, books; book-binding material; photographs; stationery; adhesive materials (stationery); artists' materials; paint brushes; typewriters and office requisites (other than furniture); instructional and teaching material (other than apparatus); playing cards; printers' type and cliches (stereotype).

17. Gutta percha, indiarubber, balata and substitutes, articles made from these substances and not included in other classes; plastics in the form of sheets, blocks and rods, being for use in manufacture; materials for packing, stopping or insulating; asbestos, mica and their products; hose pipes (non-metallic).

18. Leather and imitations of leather, and articles made from these materials and not included in other classes; skins, hides; trunks and travelling bags; umbrellas, parasols and walking sticks; whips, harness and saddlery.

19. Building materials, natural and artificial stone, cement, lime, mortar, plaster and gravel; pipes of earthenware or cement; roadmaking materials, asphalt, pitch and bitumen; portable buildings; stone monuments; chimney pots.

20. Furniture, mirrors, picture frames; articles (not included in other classes) of wood, cork, reeds, cane, wicker, horn, bone, ivory, whalebone, shell, amber, mother-of-pearl, meerschaum, celluloid, substitutes for all these materials, or of plastics.

21. Small domestic utensils and containers (not of precious metals, or coated therewith); combs and sponges; brushes (other than paint brushes); brush-making materials; instruments and material for cleaning purposes; steel wool; unworked or semi-worked glass (excluding glass used in building); glassware, porcelain and earthenware, not included in other classes.

22. Ropes, string, nets, tents, awnings, tarpaulins, sails, sacks; padding and stuffing materials (hair, kapok, feathers, seaweed, etc.); raw fibrous textile materials.

23. Yarns, threads.

24. Tissues (piece goods); bed and table covers; textile articles not included in other classes.

25. Clothing, including boots, shoes and slippers.

26. Lace and embroidery, ribands and braid; buttons, press buttons, hooks and eyes, pins and needles; artificial flowers.

27. Carpets, rugs, mats and matting; linoleums and other materials for covering existing floors; wall hangings (non-textile).

28. Games and playthings; gymnastic and sporting articles (except clothing); ornaments and decorations for Christmas trees.

29. Meats, fish, poultry and game; meat extracts, preserved, dried and cooked fruits and vegetables; jellies, jams; eggs, milk and other dairy products; edible oils and fats; preserves, pickles.

30. Coffee, tea, cocoa, sugar, rice, tapioca, sago, coffee substitutes; flour, and preparations made from cereals; bread, biscuits, cakes, pastry and confectionery, ices; honey, treacle; yeast, baking-powder; salt, mustard, pepper, vinegar, sauces, spices; ice.

31. Agricultural, horticultural and forestry products and grains not included in other classes; living animals; fresh fruits and vegetables; seeds; live plants and flowers; foodstuffs for animals, malt.

32. Beer, ale and porter; mineral and aerated waters and other non-alcoholic drinks; syrups and other preparations for making beverages.

33. Wines, spirits and liqueurs.

34. Tobacco, raw or manufactured; smokers' articles; matches.

SERVICES

35. Advertising and business.

36. Insurance and financial.

37. Construction and repair.

38. Communication.

39. Transportation and storage.

40. Material treatment.

41. Education and entertainment.

42. Miscellaneous.

Note: In the Trademark Search Room the prior U.S. classification numbers appear on registrations in addition to the international classification numbers.

Schedule for Certification Marks. In the case of certification marks, all goods and services are classified in two classes as follows:

A. Goods.

B. Services.

Schedule for Collective Membership Marks. All collective membership marks are classified as follows:

200 Collective Membership.

Use by Related Company. If the mark sought to be registered is not in fact being used by the applicant but is being used by one or more related companies whose use inures to the benefit of the applicant under section 5 of the Trademark Act, such facts must be indicated in the application.

7. The date of the applicant's first use of the mark as a trademark or in connection with goods specified in the application

8. The date of the applicant's first use of the mark as a trademark or in connection with goods specified in the application and in commerce which may lawfully be regulated by Congress, specifying the nature of such commerce

9. The mode or manner in which the mark is used on or in connection with the particular goods specified

The application must be signed and sworn to or include a declaration by the applicant or by a member of the firm or officer of the corporation or association that is applying. Trademark application forms are shown in Figures 7.18 through 7.21.

Drawings

The drawing must be a substantially exact representation of the mark as actually used in connection with the goods or services. The drawing of a service mark may be dispensed with if the mark cannot be represented by a drawing, but in such cases the written application must contain an adequate description. If the application you are making is for registration of a word, letter, or numeral, or some combination not depicted in special form, the drawing may be the mark typed in capital letters on paper, otherwise complying with the requirements.

The drawing must be made on pure white, durable paper, the surface of which must be calendered and smooth. A good grade of bond paper is suitable. India ink alone must be used for pen drawings to secure perfectly black, solid lines. The use of white pigment to cover lines is not acceptable.

The sheet on which your drawing is made must be 8 inches wide and 11 inches long. One of the shorter sides of the sheet should be regarded as its top. When the figure is longer than the width of the sheet, then the sheet should be turned on its side with the top at the right. The size of the mark must be such as to leave a margin of at least one inch on the sides and the bottom of the paper, and at least one inch between it and the heading.

Across the top of the drawing, beginning one inch from the top edge and not exceeding one-fourth of the sheet, there should be placed a heading listing in separate lines the applicant's name, the applicant's mailing address, the date of first use, and the goods or services recited in the application; or typical items of goods or services if a number are recited in the application.

All drawings except as otherwise provided must be made with a pen or by a process which will give them satisfactory reproduction characteristics. Every line and letter, names included, must be black. This direction applies to all lines, how-

Trademark application by an individual; Principal Register with oath.

Mark _____
(Identify the mark)

Class No. _____
(If known)

To the Commissioner of Patents and Trademarks:
(Name of applicant, and business trade name, if any)

_____ _____
(Business address)

_____
(Residence address)

_____
(Citizenship of applicant)

The above identified applicant has adopted and is using the trademark shown in the accompanying drawing (1) for the following goods:

_____,

and requests that said mark be registered in the United States Patent and Trademark Office on the Principal Register established by the act of July 5, 1946.

The trademark was first used on the goods (2) on _____; was
(Date)

first used in (3) _____ commerce on _____
(Type of commerce)

_____; and is now in use in such commerce. (4)

The mark is used by applying it to (5) _____ and five specimens showing the mark as actually used are presented herewith.

(6)

State of _____ }
                                  } ss.
County of _____ }

_____ states that he/she believes himself/herself to be the owner of the trademark sought to be registered; to the best of his/her knowledge and belief no other person, firm, corporation or association has the right to use said mark in commerce, either in the identical form or in such near resemblance thereto as to be likely, when applied to the goods of such other person, to cause confusion, or to cause mistake, or to deceive; and the facts set forth in this application are true.

JURAT:

_____
(Signature of applicant)

Subscribed and sworn to before me, this _____ day of _____

_____, _____.

_____ *

* The person who signs the jurat must be authorized to administer oaths by the law of the jurisdiction where executed, and the seal or stamp of the notary, or other evidence of authority in the jurisdiction of execution, must be affixed.

Figure 7.17. Trademark application by an individual; principal register with oath.

REPRESENTATION
(See form 4.2 and Note (7) below)

NOTES: (1) If registration is sought for a word or numeral mark not depicted in any special form, the drawing may be the mark typed in capital letters on letter-size bond paper; otherwise, the drawing shall comply with section 2.52.

(2) If more than one item in a class is set forth and the dates given for that class apply to only one of the items listed, insert the name of the item to which the dates apply.

(3) Type of commerce should be specified as "interstate," "territorial," "foreign," or other type of commerce which may lawfully be regulated by Congress. Foreign applicants relying upon use must specify commerce which Congress may regulate, using wording such as commerce with the United States or commerce between the United States and a foreign country.

(4) If the mark is other than a coined, arbitrary or fanciful mark, and the mark is believed to have acquired a secondary meaning, insert whichever of the following paragraphs is applicable:

(a) The mark has become distinctive of applicant's goods as a result of substantially exclusive and continuous use in _____
(Type of commerce)
commerce for the five years next preceding the date of filing of this application.

(b) The mark has become distinctive of applicant's goods as evidence by the showing submitted separately.

(5) Insert the manner or method of using the mark with the goods, i.e.,

"the goods," "the containers for the goods," "displays associated with the goods," "tags or labels affixed to the goods," or other method which may be in use.

(6) The required fee of $35.00 for each class must be submitted.

(7) If the applicant is not domiciled in the United States, a domestic representative must be designated. See form 4.4.

Figure 7.17. (Continued)

ever fine, and to shading. All lines must be clean, sharp, and solid, and they must not be too fine or crowded. Surface shading when used should be open. A photolithographic production or printer's proof copy may be used or otherwise suitable copy. Extraneous matter must not appear upon the face of the drawing.

Where color is a feature of the mark, the color or colors employed may be designated in the drawing by means of conventional linings as shown in the color chart in Figure 7.21.

Drawings transmitted to the Patent and Trademark Office other than type drawings should be sent flat, protected by a sheet of heavy binder's board or should be rolled for transmission in a suitable mailing tube.

A drawing not in conformity with the above requirements may be accepted for purposes of examination, but the drawing must be corrected or a new one furnished as required before the mark can be published or the application allowed. The necessary corrections will be made by the Patent and Trademark Office upon the applicant's request and his expense.

The Patent and Trademark Office, at the request of the applicant and at the applicant's expense, will make drawings if facilities permit.

Specimens

Five specimens are required. The five specimens must be duplicates of the real thing, but not larger than 8½ by 13 inches. Third-dimensional or bulky materials submitted as specimens won't be accepted and submission of such material may result in delay in receiving a filing date.

Trademark application by an individual; Principal Register with declaration.

Mark ------------------------------------
(Identify the mark)

Class No. -------------------------------
(If known)

To the Commissioner of Patents and Trademarks:

(Name of applicant, and business trade name, if any)

(Business address)

(Residence address)

---,
The above identified applicant has adopted and is using the trademark shown in the accompanying drawing (1) for the following goods: --------
---, and requests that said mark be registered in the United States Patent and Trademark Office on the Principal Register established by the act of July 5, 1946.

The trademark was first used on the goods (2) on --------------------;
(Date)

was first used in (3) ---------------------- commerce on -----------------;
(Type of commerce)   (Date)

and is now in use in such commerce. (4)

The mark is used in applying it to (5) -----------------------------------
and five specimens showing the mark as actually used are presented herewith. (6)

--- being hereby warned
(Name of Applicant)

that willful false statements and the like so made are punishable by fine or imprisonment, or both, under Section 1001 of Title 18 of the United States Code and that such willful false statements may jeopardize the validity of the application or any registration resulting therefrom,

declares: That he/she believes himself/herself to be the owner of the trademark sought to be registered; that to the best of his/her knowledge and belief no other person, firm, corporation, or association has the right to use said mark in commerce, either in the identical form or in such near resemblance thereto as may be likely, when applied to the goods of such other person, to cause confusion, or to cause mistake, or to deceive; that the facts set forth in this application are true; and that all statements made of his/her own knowledge are true and that all statements made on information and belief are believed to be true.

(Signature of applicant)

(Date)

REPRESENTATION
(See form 4.2 and Note (7) under form 4.1.)

NOTES: For Notes referred to in this form but not set out here, see same numbered Notes under form 4.1.

§ 4.2 Power of attorney at law (which may accompany application).*

Applicant hereby appoints (8) ---------------------------------------,
---------------------------------------, an attorney at law or attorneys
(Address)

at law, to prosecute this application to register, to transact all business in the Patent and Trademark Office in connection therewith, and to receive the certificate of registration.

NOTE: (8) An individual attorney at law or individual attorneys at law must be named here. If the name of a law firm is given, it will be regarded merely as a designation of address for correspondence.

* An attorney at law is not required to file a power of attorney; an attorney at law may represent a trademark applicant on the basis of being an attorney at law without presenting a power of attorney.

§4.4 Designation of domestic representative to accompany application. (9)

(Name of representative)

whose postal address is ---,
(Street, city and State)

is hereby designated applicant's representative upon whom notices or process in proceedings affecting the mark may be served.

NOTE: (9) The designation of domestic representative must be separate from a power of attorney at law or other authorization of representation.

Figure 7.18. Trademark application by an individual; principal register with declaration.

Trademark application by a partnership; Principal Register.

Mark ------------------------------------
(Identify the mark)

Class No. ------------------------------
(If known)

TO THE COMMISSIONER OF PATENTS AND TRADEMARKS:

(Name of partnership)

(Business address of partnership)

(Names of partners)

(Citizenship of partners)

(Body of application is same as in form 4.1).

State of ----------------------- ⎱
County of ----------------------- ⎰ s.s.

(Name of partner)

states that he/she is a partner of the applicant partnership; he/she believes
said partnership to be the owner of the trademark sought to be registered; to
the best of his/her knowledge and belief no other person, firm, corporation or
association has the right to use said mark in commerce, either in the identical form or in such near resemblance thereto as to be likely, when applied
to the goods of such other person, to cause confusion, or to cause mistake, or
to deceive; and the facts set forth in this application are true.

(Signature of partner)

JURAT:
Subscribed to and sworn to before me, this ------------------------- day of

-----------------------------, ---------.

----------------------------------- *

* The person who signs the jurat must be authorized to administer oaths by the law of the
jurisdiction where executed, and the seal or stamp of the notary, or other evidence of
authority in the jurisdiction of execution, must be affixed.

REPRESENTATION
(See form 4.2 and Note (7) under form 4.1.)

Figure 7.19. Trademark application by a partnership; principal register.

When due to the mode of applying or affixing the mark to the goods, or the
manner of using the mark on the goods, or the nature of the mark, specimens
cannot be furnished, five copies of a suitable photograph or other acceptable reproduction not larger than 8½ by 13 inches and clearly and legibly showing the
mark and how it is used are required.

The Filing Fee

The current cost of an application to register a trademark is $35.

Registering Your Trademark in Foreign Countries

As with patents and copyrights, there is no international trademark. Therefore, if
you are doing business or think that you may be doing business in foreign countries and you desire to protect your trademark, you must investigate the trademark laws of those countries in order to take the proper steps to protect your
rights. In some foreign countries, a resident may obtain a registration of trade-

Trademark application by a corporation; Principal Register.

Mark ------------------------------------

(Identify the mark)

Class No. ------------------------------------

(If known)

To the Commissioner of Patents and Trademarks:

(Corporate name and State or country of incorporation) (10)

(Business address)

(Body of application is same as in form 4.1.)

State of ------------------------ ⎫
County of ------------------------ ⎭ *ss.*

(Body of application is same as in form 4.1.)

-- states that

(Name of officer of corporation)

he/she is ------------------------ of applicant corporation (10) and is

(Official title)

authorized to execute this affidavit on behalf of said corporation; he/she believes said corporation to be the owner of the trademark sought to be registered; to the best of his/her knowledge and belief no other person, firm, corporation or association has the right to use said mark in commerce, either in the identical form or in such near resemblance thereto as to be likely, when applied to the goods of such other person, to cause confusion, or to cause mistake, or to deceive; and the facts set forth in this application are true.

By ------------------------------------

(Name of corporation)

By ------------------------------------

(Signature of officer of corporation
and official title of officer)

JURAT:

Subscribed to and sworn to before me, this ------------------------ day of

------------------------------------, ---------.

------------------------------------ *

Notary Public

* The person who signs the jurat must be authorized to administer oaths by the law of the jurisdiction where executed, and the seal or stamp of the notary, or other evidence of authority in the jurisdiction of execution, must be affixed.

REPRESENTATION

(See form 4.2 and Note (7) under form 4.1.)

Note: (10) If applicant is an association or other collective group, the word "association" or other appropriate designation should be substituted for "corporation" when referring to applicant.

Figure 7.20. Trademark application by a corporation; principal register.

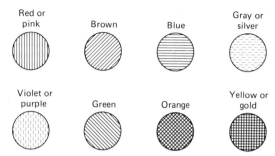

Figure 7.21. Color chart for trademark drawings.

mark without actually having used it in trade. Further, such a registration may be used to prevent the importation into that country of goods which bear that mark. Naturally, this may be of extreme importance to you.

RENEWAL OF TRADEMARKS

Trademarks are good for a 20-year period and may be renewed for periods of 20 years from the expiring period unless previously canceled or surrendered.

QUESTIONS AND ANSWERS ABOUT TRADEMARKS[2]

The Department of Commerce publishes the following answers to questions frequently asked about trademarks.

1. Q. **What is a trademark?**
    A. A trademark is a word, name, symbol, or device, or any combination of these, adopted and used by a manufacturer or merchant to identify his goods and distinguish them from those manufactured or sold by others. In short, it is a brand name used on goods moving in the channels of trade.
2. Q. **What is the function of a trademark?**
    A. The primary function of a trademark is to distinguish one person's goods from those of another; but a trademark also serves to indicate to purchasers that the quality of the goods bearing the mark remains constant, and it serves as the focal point of advertising to create and maintain a demand for the product.
3. Q. **How are trademark rights established?**
    A. Rights in a trademark are established by adoption and actual use of the mark on goods moving in trade, and use ordinarily must continue if the rights are to be maintained. No rights exist until there has been actual use; and a trademark may not be registered until the goods bearing the mark have been sold or shipped in interstate, foreign or Territorial commerce.
4. Q. **Who may own a trademark?**
    A. A trademark may be owned by an individual, a firm or partnership, a corporation, or an association or other collective group.
5. Q. **Is any provision made for the registration of trademarks under our federal laws?**
    A. Yes. Our first constitutional trademark registration act was passed in 1881. The present registration Act was passed on July 5, 1946, effective July 5, 1947, and is popularly known as the Lanham Act.
6. Q. **What other types of marks may be registered?**
    A. Service marks used in the sale or advertising of services; certification marks to certify regional origin, mode of manufacture, accuracy, quality, or other characteristics of the

[2] *Q and A about Trademarks*, U.S. Department of Commerce, Washington, D.C. (1979).

goods or services of someone, other than the certifier; and collective marks used by co-operatives or other collective groups or organizations.

7. Q. **What is a trade name?**
   A. Trade or commercial names are business names used by manufacturers, merchants, and others to identify their businesses or occupations, such as names of partnerships, companies, and other organizations. A trademark identifies a product, and a trade name identifies a producer.

8. Q. **May trade names be registered in the same manner as trademarks?**
   A. No provision is made in the present trademark law for the registration of trade or commercial names used merely to identify a business entity.

9. Q. **What Government agency has jurisdiction of the registration of trademarks under our federal laws?**
   A. The Patent and Trademark Office.

10. Q. **Is it necessary for the trademark owner to register his mark?**
    A. No. Trademark rights are protected under common law, but registration results in material advantages to the trademark owner. It constitutes notice of the registrant's claim of ownership; and it creates certain presumptions of ownership, validity and exclusive right to use the mark on the goods recited in the registration.

11. Q. **Is there any time limitation within which an application should be filed?**
    A. No. An application may be filed at any time after the mark has been used on the product and the product is sold or shipped in interstate, foreign or Territorial commerce.

12. Q. **What has to be done by the trademark owner in order to qualify for federal registration of a trademark?**
    A. The mark must be applied in some manner to goods or their containers and the goods sold or shipped in interstate, foreign or Territorial commerce.

13. Q. **How may information about the filing of a trademark application be obtained?**
    A. Order from the Government Printing Office the pamphlet "General Information Concerning Trademarks," price $1.60. If more information is desired, the "Trademark Rules of Practice of the Patent Office with Forms and Statutes" may be obtained from the Superintendent of Documents, Washington, D.C., 20402, for $5.00. Prices subject to change without advance notice.

14. Q. **Is it advisable to make a search of registered marks prior to the filing of an application?**
    A. Yes. A search may be made in the public Search Room of Trademark Examining Operation of the Patent and Trademark Office, located in Crystal Plaza Building No. 2, 2011 Jefferson Davis Highway, Arlington, Virginia.

15. Q. **Will the Patent and Trademark Office make a search?**
    A. No. The Patent and Trademark Office does not have personnel for making searches for the public.

16. Q. **How does the trademark owner apply for the registration of a trademark?**
    A. By making proper application to the Commissioner of Patents and Trademarks, Washington, D.C., 20231.

17. Q. **Are application forms available for distribution to the public?**
    A. Yes. Upon request forms for the registration of trademarks may be obtained from the Patent and Trademark Office for use in filing applications in the name of (a) an individual, (b) a firm or partnership, and (c) a corporation.

18. Q. **Must the applicant be represented by an attorney?**
    A. No. The application may be filed by the applicant, or an attorney may be appointed for this purpose.

19. Q. **Are all trademarks subject to registration?**
    A. No. A trademark may not be registered if it so resembles a mark previously registered in the Patent and Trademark Office, or a mark or trade name previously used in the United States by another and not abandoned, as to be likely, when applied to the applicant's goods, to cause confusion, mistake or deception. Other types of marks are prohibited registration by the statute, such as those comprising immoral or deceptive matter or those including the flag or insignia of the United States.

20. Q. **Can the Patent and Trademark Office give legal advice or advice as to the registrability of a specified mark prior to the filing of an application for registration?**
    A. No. The Patent and Trademark Office can give no assistance of this kind until a case comes regularly before it in an application duly filed

21. Q. **What comprises a complete application for the registration of a trademark?**

A. A complete application comprises (a) a written application properly notarized, (b) a drawing of the mark, (c) five specimens or facsimiles of the mark as actually in use in commerce, and (d) the filing fee of $35.00.

22. Q. **What is the term of a registration?**

A. Twenty years from the date of issue; and the registration may be renewed at the end of each twenty-year term so long as the mark is still in use in commerce.

23. Q. **May a trademark be assigned?**

A. Yes. A trademark may be assigned with the good will of the business with which it is used.

24. Q. **Does a U.S. registration give protection in foreign countries?**

A. No. A registration must be obtained in each country where protection is desired. A U.S. registration may, however, be used as the basis for obtaining registration in a number of foreign countries.

25. Q. **May a foreign trademark owner obtain a registration in this country?**

A. Yes. Application for registration may be based on use of the mark in commerce with this country, or on a registration previously obtained in the owner's country of origin in accordance with applicable international conventions and treaties.

26. Q. **Is it necessary to go to the Patent and Trademark Office to transact business concerning trademark matters?**

A. No. In general all business with the Patent and Trademark Office is conducted by correspondence.

SOURCES OF ADDITIONAL INFORMATION

General Information Concerning Patents, published by the Superintendent of Documents, U.S. Government Printing Office, Washington, D.C. 20402.

General Information Concerning Trademarks, published by the Superintendent of Documents, U.S. Government Printing Office, Washington, D.C. 20402.

Patent It Yourself, by David Pressman, published by McGraw-Hill Book Co., 1221 Avenue of the Americas, New York, NY 10020.

The Concise Guide to Patents, Trademarks, and Copyrights, edited by Solomon J. Schepps, published by Bell Publishing Co., a division of Crown Publishers, Inc., 1 Park Ave., New York, NY 10016.

The Inventors Patent Handbook, by Stacy V. Jones, published by The Dial Press, 1 Dag Hammarskjold Plaza, New York, NY 10017.

8

Leasing or Buying Equipment

LEASING, A VIABLE ALTERNATIVE TO PURCHASE

Leasing should always be considered as an alternative to purchase, if for no other reason than the fact that leasing does not require a large capital outlay. Because of this, more small businesses are leasing than ever before. Further, these small businesses are leasing all types of equipment, including motor vehicles, computers, furniture for the office, manufacturing machinery, testing equipment, and thousands of other items. But leasing is not always the answer, and in making a decision between leasing and buying equipment, you should understand the advantages and the disadvantages of leasing, and you should also make a thorough cash analysis. In this chapter, all aspects of the lease-or-buy question will be covered so that you may consider it from all angles and arrive at the correct decision for your situation. Bear in mind that the right choice can save you thousands and thousands of dollars.

LEASING TERMS AND WHAT THEY MEAN

Basically, a leasing is a long-term agreement to rent equipment, land, buildings, or any other assets. Although the terms "leasing" and "renting" are sometimes used interchangeably, there are differences between the two. "Rental" refers to short-term leasing, usually by the day, week, month, and generally for a year or less. And leasing may offer lower payments to you due to associated tax benefits. Also, leasing permits 100% financing. This allows your company to conserve its capital for other purposes. The small company which leases is known as a lessee. It makes periodic payments to the owner of this asset who is known as a lessor. Your payments cover the original cost of the equipment to the lessor and provide the lessor with a profit for this service. The period of the lease frequently approximates the depreciable life of the equipment that is leased.

TYPES OF LEASES

There are many different types of leases that you may encounter. Each possesses different advantages and disadvantages.

Conditional Sales Agreement

A conditional sales agreement can itself involve many different types of leases. With the basic type, the lessee is considered the owner, for tax purposes, from the very beginning of the lease. At the end of the conditional sale lease period, the terms of the contract are structured in such a fashion that the lessee's only practical option is to purchase the equipment at a predetermined price. This price is decided upon prior to initiating the lease through negotiations between the lessee and the lessor. It reflects both the residual value of the equipment and the size of the payments made by the lessee during the period of the lease. Some conditional sales agreement leases have "put and call" provisions in which the "put" is the minimum price that a lessee is obligated to pay for the leased equipment, and the "call" is a maximum price that the lessee may be obligated to pay for the equipment. The put and call provisions set limits for negotiation on the lessee's purchase price. The minimum price can protect the lessor if the equipment depreciates rapidly during the term of the lease. On the other hand, the maximum price protects the lessee from having to pay a purchase price much greater than the current fair market value of the equipment at the end of the lease.

Financial Lease

The financial lease is the most common. A financial lease is usually written for a term that does not exceed the economic life of the equipment. Typical provisions of the financial lease are: (1) that periodic payments must be made by the lessee; (2) that ownership of the equipment will revert to the lessor at the end of the lease term; (3) that the lease is noncancelable and the lessee has a legal obligation to continue payments to the end of the term, and (4) that the lessee agrees to maintain the equipment.

Gross Lease

Under a gross lease, the lessor is responsible for expenses such as maintenance, taxes, and insurance.

Leverage Lease

Under a leverage lease, the lessor puts up part of the purchase price of the equipment, usually 20 to 40%, and borrows the rest from other lenders. The tax benefits of ownership go to the lessor, not to the investors. The leverage lease is a type of "true lease" that will be discussed later. It is generally used for multimillion-dollar leases.

Net Lease

A net lease is the opposite of a gross lease. Under a net lease, the lessee is responsible for expenses such as those for maintenance, taxes, and insurance. The most common type of lease, the financial lease, is usually a net lease.

Nonpayout Lease

With the nonpayout lease, the lessor collects less than his equipment cost over the period of the lease. The nonpayout lease is not common, but it is sometimes used when asset durability is high and resale values are well established on the used equipment which is being leased. In the nonpayout lease, the lessor will take the equipment back and resell it or lease it again after the period of the lease.

Operating Lease

The operating lease or maintenance lease can usually be canceled under conditions spelled out in the lease contract. Maintenance of the asset is usually the responsibility of the lessor. Computer equipment is often leased using the operating or maintenance type of lease.

Payout Lease

The payout lease is the opposite of the nonpayout lease. Under the payout lease, the lessor does recover the original cost of the asset during the term of the lease.

Sale and Lease-Back Lease

The sale and lease-back lease is similar to the financial lease. With this type of lease, the owner of the equipment sells it to another party and simultaneously leases it back to use it for a specified term. This allows you to use the money normally tied up in an asset for other purposes. Buildings are typically leased with a sale and lease-back lease.

True Lease

A true lease is an agreement in which the leasing company owns the lease equipment at all times so that no equity is built up with the lease payments by the lessee. Therefore, if the lessee wants to buy the leased equipment at the end of the period of the lease, the purchase price is in addition to the scheduled payments.

Which Is Best?

To determine which type of lease is best for your situation, you should consider the following three questions for your business:

1. Does your business need the tax benefit of ownership to reduce current tax obligations? If so, then a conditional sales agreement may be the most cost-effective method of leasing.
2. Can the leasing company receive the tax benefits of ownership such as the investment tax credit, depreciation allowance, and interest deductions and in return reduce your lease payments?
3. What is the estimated residual value of the equipment at the end of the proposed lease term?

WHO LEASES

The majority of leasing is done by commercial banks, insurance companies, and finance companies. In fact, many of these types of organizations have subsidiaries which are primarily concerned with equipment leasing, and can make lease arrangements for almost any equipment that you may need. The growth of the leasing industry into a billion-dollar business has also caused companies to be founded which specialize only in leasing. Some may do general leasing with any type of equipment, while others may specialize in certain types of equipment such as computers or farm machinery. Many such leasing companies offer their services through trade magazines and newspapers. They may also work closely with manufacturers and provide training and outside financing to enable leasing directly from the manufacturers' sales. This leads us to a third kind of lessor: the manufacturer. Many manufacturers offer a lease plan to their customers. Naturally such firms usually lease only the equipment that they themselves manufacture. Finally, while not lessors, there are lease brokers which act as intermediaries between lessors and lessees and lessors and financing sources. The broker determines the need of the prospective lessee and solicits bids from banks, leasing companies, and other financing sources. His compensation usually comes from the organization furnishing the financing, although sometimes he may be paid as a consultant to the lessee.

THE ADVANTAGES AND DISADVANTAGES OF LEASING

As noted earlier, there are both advantages and disadvantages to leasing. Let's look at the advantages first:

1. *Use of an asset without a large initial cash outlay.*
2. *No down payment.* A loan may require 25% down where a lease is usually 100% financed requiring no down payment whatsoever.
3. *No restrictions on a company's financial operations.* By comparison, a loan may restrict your operation by its terms.
4. *Payments spread over a longer period.* With a lease, payments may be spread over periods of several years, and therefore you have lower payments than loans permit.
5. *Protection against equipment obsolescence.* A lease will protect you against the risk of the equipment's becoming obsolete since the lessee can get rid of the equipment at the end of the term of the lease.
6. *Tax benefits.* There are tax benefits in leasing, among them deductibility of lease payments as operating expenses if the arrangement is a true lease. Also, all the investment tax credit is usually taken by the lessor, but it may help the lessee as well since he or she may have reduced payments in return.
7. *Consulting advice from leasing firm.* Because the lessor has considerable experience with the equipment which it leases, it can provide expert technical advice.
8. *Flexible payment schedules.* Payment schedules for leases can be constructed so that they coincide with cash flow earnings of the company or various seasonal activities, depending upon the situation.
9. *Restriction on claims in the event of bankruptcy.* While all entrepreneurs should think positively, it is a fact that in the event of bankruptcy, the claims of a lessor to your assets are much more restricted than those of general creditors.

Now, let's look at some of the disadvantages of leasing:

1. *Loss of certain tax benefits.* Tax benefits that go with the ownership of an asset will not be available to you as a lessee. However, this may be no disadvantage if you don't have enough tax or liability for such tax benefits of ownership to come into force.

2. *No economic value of asset at end of lease term.* Since you do not own the asset as a lessee, in order to obtain the economic value of this asset at the end of the lease term you must purchase it. Frequently, the salvage value of a leased asset at the end of the lease term is much greater than you thought at the time of initiating the lease.

3. *Higher overall cost in purchase.* If you as lessee can currently use the tax benefits of ownership, including investment tax credit, depreciation tax allowance, and so forth, leasing may be more costly than purchase. It is for this reason that a thorough cash analysis must be performed.

4. *Difficulty in lease termination.* In general, you cannot terminate a lease without a penalty, and most leases for capital equipment are noncancelable contracts. Therefore, if you were to complete an operation that used leased equipment, you would have to pay as much as if the equipment were used during the full term of the lease.

5. *Senior debt obligation.* Although in the event of bankruptcy claims of a lessor to the assets of a firm are more restricted than those of general creditors, a lease may be one of the first debts that can be claimed by a creditor.

ANALYSIS OF COST OF LEASE VERSUS PURCHASE

It is extremely important to analyze the cash flow over the period of time of a lease versus a purchase in order to have an accurate comparison in hard figures. This analysis compares the cost of the two alternatives by considering the timing of the payments, the tax benefits, the interest rate on the loan, the lease rate, and other financial factors. To perform this analysis, you must know certain basic facts or make certain assumptions. These include information about the equipment cost, the estimated economic life, the lease terms, and the tax. Now let's look at an example.

Equipment cost. $40,000.

Estimated economic life. 10 years.

Lease terms. Eight annual payments of $7,000. First payment is due on delivery. Investment tax credit is taken by lessor. Lessee must maintain equipment.

Loan terms with purchase. Five years, 75% financing at 10% requiring five annual payments of $7,913.92. The first payment is due at the end of the first year.

Taxes. Lessee tax rate is 50%. Straight line depreciation is used.

Other facts. The equipment is needed for eight years. At the end of that period, if the decision has been made to purchase the equipment, it can be sold at a salvage value that is equal to the book value of the equipment (equipment cost less total depreciation). The average after-tax cost of capital to the lessee is 10%.

Before we begin the analysis, certain facts about this information should be noted. First, payments are usually made monthly. In this example, annual payments are used for simplification. However, exactly the same procedures would be used to analyze monthly payments.

Depreciation arises from recognition of the fact that, except for land, all capital assets have a finite life span after which they are worthless. When you do your taxes, depreciation expense is entered on your income statement, reducing reported profit. Thus, applying depreciation against profit represents a tax saving. Calculating depreciation of equipment involves estimating its life. Straight line depreciation means simply calculating the yearly depreciation by dividing the cost of the equipment by the number of years of its life. In this case, the equipment costs $4,000 per year. At the end of 10 years, the equipment would have a book value of zero. In theory, it would be worth nothing. In order to compare this lease with purchase, we must do our analysis over identical periods of time. Therefore, we will depreciate the equipment over a period of eight years. At $4,000 per year, that's $4,000 times 8 years or $32,000. Book value, which is salvage value of the equipment at this time, would be equal to the cost of the equipment minus the depreciation, $40,000 minus $32,000 or $8,000.

The actual tax rate depends on taxable income. In this case, it is assumed that this works out to be 50%.

Factors such as maintenance costs need not be included in the analysis, since in the example the lessee would pay these costs if leasing or if purchasing. If, however, the lessor were responsible for maintenance, then this fact would be taken into account by showing estimated annual maintenance costs as a savings in the cash flow evaluation of lease cost.

The concept of cost of capital is important as it allows you to calculate the present value of future costs. It refers to the fact that there is a time value of money. This time value can be seen if you consider receiving $1,000 today or $1,500 five years from now. At first glance, you may prefer the $1,500. But then you would probably remember that you can get a rather high rate of interest by depositing the $1,000 in a bank today. In fact, after five years, at 15% interest, your $1,000 would be worth $2,011. To allow for the time value of money, we discount each year's cash flow to the present, using Figure 8.1, Present Value of $1 Received at the End of n Number of Years.

Now, let's consider the cash flow evaluation of the loan. Note how the discount factors are extracted from Table 8.1 in column 9 and multiplied by the net cash flow in column 8 to result in the present value in column 10.

The appropriate interest rate or time value of money in this case is the after-tax cost of the loan. Since the loan cost is 10% and tax rate is 50%, 0.50 times 10% or 5% is the proper interest rate.

Now let's look at the cash flow evaluation of lease cost.

Cash Flow Evaluation of Lease Cost

(1) End of Year	(2) Lease Payment	(3) Tax Saving 50% × (2)	(4) Net Outlay (2) − (3)	(5) Discount Factor from Figure 8.1	(6) Present Value (4) × (5)
0	$7,000	$3,500	$3,500	1.0000	$ 3,500.00
1	7,000	3,500	3,500	0.9524	3,333.40
2	7,000	3,500	3,500	0.9070	3,174.50
3	7,000	3,500	3,500	0.8638	3,023.30
4	7,000	3,500	3,500	0.8227	2,879.45
5	7,000	3,500	3,500	0.7835	2,742.25
6	7,000	3,500	3,500	0.7462	2,611.70
7	7,000	3,500	3,500	0.7107	2,487.45
8	—	—	—	—	—
					$23,752.05

n/r	1%	2%	3%	4%	5%	6%	7%	8%	9%	10%	11%	12%	13%	14%	15%
1	.9901	.9804	.9709	.9615	.9524	.9434	.9346	.9259	.9174	.9091	.9009	.8929	.8850	.8772	.8696
2	.9803	.9612	.9426	.9246	.9070	.8900	.8734	.8573	.8417	.8264	.8116	.7972	.7831	.7695	.7561
3	.9706	.9423	.9151	.8890	.8638	.8396	.8163	.7938	.7722	.7513	.7312	.7118	.6931	.6750	.6575
4	.9610	.9238	.8885	.8548	.8227	.7921	.7629	.7350	.7084	.6830	.6587	.6355	.6133	.5921	.5718
5	.9515	.9057	.8626	.8219	.7835	.7473	.7130	.6806	.6499	.6209	.5935	.5674	.5428	.5194	.4972
6	.9420	.8880	.8375	.7903	.7462	.7050	.6663	.6302	.5963	.5645	.5346	.5066	.4803	.4556	.4323
7	.9327	.8706	.8131	.7599	.7107	.6651	.6627	.5835	.5470	.5132	.4817	.4523	.4251	.3996	.3759
8	.9235	.8535	.7894	.7307	.6768	.6274	.5820	.5403	.5019	.4665	.4339	.4039	.3762	.3506	.3269
9	.9143	.8368	.7664	.7026	.6446	.5919	.5439	.5002	.4604	.4241	.3909	.3606	.3329	.3075	.2843
10	.9053	.8203	.7441	.6756	.6139	.5584	.5083	.4632	.4224	.3855	.3522	.3220	.2946	.2697	.2472
11	.8963	.8043	.7224	.6496	.5847	.5268	.4751	.4289	.3875	.3505	.3173	.2875	.2607	.2366	.2149
12	.8874	.7885	.7014	.6246	.5568	.4970	.4440	.3971	.3555	.3186	.2858	.2567	.2307	.2076	.1869
13	.8787	.7730	.6810	.6006	.5303	.4688	.4150	.3677	.3262	.2897	.2575	.2292	.2042	.1821	.1625
14	.8700	.7579	.6611	.5775	.5051	.4423	.3878	.3405	.2992	.2633	.2320	.2046	.1807	.1597	.1413
15	.8613	.7430	.6419	.5553	.4810	.4173	.3624	.3152	.2745	.2394	.2090	.1827	.1599	.1401	.1229
16	.8528	.7284	.6232	.5339	.4581	.3936	.3387	.2919	.2519	.2176	.1883	.1631	.1415	.1229	.1069
17	.8444	.7142	.6050	.5134	.4363	.3714	.3166	.2703	.2311	.1978	.1696	.1456	.1252	.1078	.0929
18	.8360	.7002	.5874	.4936	.4155	.3503	.2959	.2502	.2120	.1799	.1528	.1300	.1108	.0946	.0808
19	.8277	.6864	.5703	.4746	.3957	.3305	.2765	.2317	.1945	.1635	.1377	.1161	.0981	.0829	.0703
20	.8195	.6730	.5537	.4564	.3769	.3118	.2584	.2145	.1784	.1486	.1240	.1037	.0868	.0728	.0611
21	.8114	.6598	.5375	.4388	.3589	.2942	.2415	.1987	.1637	.1351	.1117	.0926	.0768	.0638	.0531
22	.8034	.6468	.5219	.4220	.3418	.2775	.2257	.1839	.1502	.1228	.1007	.0826	.0680	.0560	.0462
23	.7954	.6342	.5067	.4057	.3256	.2618	.2109	.1703	.1378	.1117	.0907	.0738	.0601	.0491	.0402
24	.7876	.6217	.4919	.3901	.3101	.2470	.1971	.1577	.1264	.1015	.0817	.0659	.0532	.0431	.0349
25	.7798	.6095	.4776	.3751	.2953	.2330	.1842	.1460	.1160	.0923	.0736	.0588	.0471	.0378	.0304
26	.7720	.5976	.4637	.3607	.2812	.2198	.1722	.1352	.1064	.0839	.0663	.0525	.0417	.0331	.0264
27	.7644	.5859	.4502	.3468	.2678	.2074	.1609	.1252	.0976	.0763	.0597	.0469	.0369	.0291	.0230
28	.7568	.5744	.4371	.3335	.2551	.1956	.1504	.1159	.0895	.0693	.0538	.0419	.0326	.0255	.0200
29	.7493	.5631	.4243	.3207	.2429	.1846	.1406	.1073	.0822	.0630	.0485	.0374	.0289	.0224	.0174
30	.7419	.5521	.4120	.3083	.2314	.1741	.1314	.0994	.0754	.0573	.0437	.0334	.0256	.0196	.0151
35	.7059	.5000	.3554	.2534	.1813	.1301	.0937	.0676	.0490	.0356	.0259	.0189	.0139	.0102	.0075
40	.6717	.4529	.3066	.2083	.1420	.0972	.0668	.0460	.0318	.0221	.0154	.0107	.0075	.0053	.0037
45	.6391	.410	.2644	.1713	.1112	.0727	.0476	.0313	.0207	.0137	.0091	.0061	.0041	.0027	.0019
50	.6080	.3715	.2281	.1407	.0872	.0543	.0339	.0213	.0134	.0085	.0054	.0035	.0022	.0014	.0009

Figure 8.1. Present value of $1.

n/r	16%	18%	20%	22%	24%	26%	28%	30%	32%	34%	36%	38%	40%	45%	50%
1	.8621	.8475	.8333	.8197	.8065	.7937	.7813	.7692	.7576	.7463	.7353	.7246	.7143	.6897	.6667
2	.7432	.7182	.6944	.6719	.6504	.6299	.6104	.5917	.5739	.5569	.5407	.5251	.5102	.4756	.4444
3	.6407	.6086	.5787	.5507	.5245	.4999	.4768	.4552	.4348	.4155	.3975	.3805	.3644	.3280	.2963
4	.5523	.5158	.4823	.4514	.4230	.3968	.3725	.3501	.3294	.3102	.2923	.2757	.2603	.2262	.1975
5	.4761	.4371	.4019	.3700	.3411	.3149	.2910	.2693	.2495	.2315	.2149	.1998	.1859	.1560	.1317
6	.4104	.3704	.3349	.3033	.2751	.2499	.2274	.2072	.1890	.1727	.1580	.1448	.1328	.1076	.0878
7	.3538	.3139	.2791	.2486	.2218	.1983	.1776	.1594	.1432	.1289	.1162	.1049	.0949	.0742	.0585
8	.3050	.2660	.2326	.2038	.1789	.1574	.1388	.1226	.1085	.0962	.0854	.0760	.0678	.0512	.0390
9	.2630	.2255	.1938	.1670	.1443	.1249	.1084	.0943	.0822	.0718	.0628	.0551	.0484	.0353	.0260
10	.2267	.1911	.1615	.1369	.1164	.0992	.0847	.0725	.0623	.0536	.0462	.0399	.0346	.0243	.0173
11	.1954	.1619	.1346	.1122	.0938	.0787	.0662	.0558	.0472	.0400	.0340	.0289	.0247	.0168	.0116
12	.1685	.1372	.1122	.0920	.0757	.0625	.0517	.0429	.0357	.0298	.0250	.0210	.0176	.0116	.0077
13	.1452	.1163	.0935	.0754	.0610	.0496	.0404	.0330	.0271	.0223	.0184	.0152	.0126	.0080	.0051
14	.1252	.0985	.0779	.0618	.0492	.0393	.0316	.0253	.0205	.0166	.0135	.0110	.0090	.0055	.0034
15	.1079	.0835	.0649	.0507	.0397	.0312	.0247	.0195	.0155	.0124	.0099	.0080	.0064	.0038	.0023
16	.0930	.0708	.0541	.0415	.0320	.0248	.0193	.0150	.0118	.0093	.0073	.0058	.0046	.0026	.0015
17	.0802	.0600	.0451	.0340	.0258	.0197	.0150	.0116	.0089	.0069	.0054	.0042	.0033	.0018	.0010
18	.0691	.0508	.0376	.0279	.0208	.0156	.0118	.0089	.0068	.0052	.0039	.0030	.0023	.0012	.0007
19	.0596	.0431	.0313	.0229	.0168	.0124	.0092	.0068	.0051	.0038	.0029	.0022	.0017	.0009	.0005
20	.0514	.0365	.0261	.0187	.0135	.0098	.0072	.0053	.0039	.0029	.0021	.0016	.0012	.0006	.0003
21	.0443	.0309	.0217	.0154	.0109	.0078	.0056	.0040	.0029	.0021	.0016	.0012	.0009	.0004	.0002
22	.0382	.0262	.0181	.0126	.0088	.0062	.0044	.0031	.0022	.0016	.0012	.0008	.0006	.0003	.0001
23	.0329	.0222	.0151	.0103	.0071	.0049	.0034	.0024	.0017	.0012	.0008	.0006	.0004	.0002	.0001
24	.0284	.0188	.0126	.0085	.0057	.0039	.0027	.0018	.0013	.0009	.0006	.0004	.0003	.0001	.0001
25	.0245	.0160	.0105	.0069	.0046	.0031	.0021	.0014	.0010	.0007	.0005	.0003	.0002	.0001	.0000
26	.0211	.0135	.0087	.0057	.0037	.0025	.0016	.0011	.0007	.0005	.0003	.0002	.0002	.0001	
27	.0182	.0115	.0073	.0047	.0030	.0019	.0013	.0008	.0006	.0004	.0002	.0002	.0001	.0000	
28	.0157	.0097	.0061	.0038	.0024	.0015	.0010	.0006	.0004	.0003	.0002	.0001	.0001		
29	.0135	.0082	.0051	.0031	.0020	.0012	.0008	.0005	.0003	.0002	.0001	.0001	.0001		
30	.0116	.0070	.0042	.0026	.0016	.0010	.0006	.0004	.0002	.0002	.0001	.0001	.0000		
35	.0055	.0030	.0017	.0009	.0005	.0003	.0002	.0001	.0001	.0000					
40	.0026	.0013	.0007	.0004	.0002	.0001	.0001	.0000							
45	.0013	.0006	.0003	.0001	.0001	.0000									
50	.0006	.0003	.0001	.0000											

Figure 8.1. (Continued)

Table 8.1 Cash Flow Evaluation of Loan

(1) End of Year	(2) Payment	(3) Interest	(4) Principal Repayment (2) − (3)	(5) Outstanding Balance (5) − (4)	(6) Depreciation	(7) Tax Savings 50% × ((6) + (3))	(8) Net Cash Flow (2) − (7)	(9) Discount Factor from Figure 8.1	(10) Present Value (8) × (9)
0	$10,000.00			$30,000.00		$4,000.00[a]	$6,000.00	1.0000	$ 6,000.00
1	7,913.92	$3,000.00	$4,913.92	25,086.08	$4,000	3,500.00	4,413.92	0.9524	4,203.82
2	7,913.92	2,508.60	5,405.32	19,680.76	4,000	3,254.30	4,659.62	0.9070	4,226.28
3	7,913.92	1,968.07	5,945.85	13,734.91	4,000	2,984.03	4,929.89	0.8638	4,258.44
4	7,913.92	1,373.49	6,540.43	7,194.48	4,000	2,686.74	5,227.17	0.8227	4,300.97
5	7,913.92	719.44	7,194.48		4,000	2,359.72	5,554.20	0.7835	4,351.72
6					4,000	2,000.00	(2,000.00)	0.7462	(1,492.40)
7					4,000	2,000.00	(2,000.00)	0.7107	(1,421.40)
8	(8,000.00)[b]				4,000	2,000.00	(2,000.00)	0.6768	(1,353.60)
							(8,000.00)	0.4665[c]	(3,732.00)
									$19,341.83

[a] Investment credit tax = 10% × $40,000 purchase price = $4,000.

[b] Salvage value at the end of eight years.

[c] Discount factor calculated at the average after tax cost of capital of 10%.

Note: In the example, the interest portion of the loan payment is found by multiplying the loan interest rate of 10% by the outstanding loan balance for the previous period. Also that the outstanding balance is calculated by subtracting column 4 from column 5 of the preceding year. In the example, the net cost of leasing the equipment is $23,752.05 versus $19,341.83 if you buy the equipment by taking a loan. That's a net savings of $4,410.22 ($23,752.05 minus $19,341.83) if you purchase and take the loan. Clearly doing this analysis will more then pay for itself.

Figure 8.1. (Continued)

The final result of the analysis of leasing the equipment, $23,752.05, is the net present value of the costs of leasing. Now if we compare this with the net present value of purchasing, we will know whether leasing or purchasing will cost more money. In this case, purchasing the equipment, including the loan, results in a present value of $19,341.83. Since this is less than $23,752.05, it would be less expensive to purchase.

HOW TO CHOOSE A LEASING COMPANY

Leasing is a big business today. As pointed out earlier, the companies and firms, banks and manufacturers that make up this industry comprise a very diverse group. There is a major trade organization called the American Association of Equipment Lessors, located at 5635 Douglas Ave., Milwaukee, WI 53218. The association can provide you with membership rosters as well as other information on leases and leasing trends. You can also look in your Yellow Pages for the various types of companies that lease mentioned earlier. Because the industry is so competitive, you should definitely shop around. This means choosing several lessors that you may wish to deal with before making a decision to lease with one or another, or even before doing an analysis of a lease versus purchase. Look for two things:

1. The price or lease rate
2. The reputation of the lessor you may wish to deal with

The lease rate may vary greatly from company to company. Therefore, it is extremely important that you make this comparison with several potential lessors. Generally, the lease rate will depend upon the following factors:

1. The period of the lease
2. The equipment that you wish to lease
3. The use of the equipment
4. The equipment's residual value
5. Evaluation of your credit as the lessee
6. Who uses the investment tax credit

Equally important are the reputation and reliability of the lessor. These may be checked in several ways: by talking to individuals who have leased similar equipment from the firm, by asking for references from the company in question, and by checking with the Better Business Bureau in your area to see if any complaints have been made against the company.

TERMS OF THE LEASE CONTRACT

Don't forget that a lease contract is a legal document that carries a long-term obligation. Therefore, it's crucial that you know exactly what the terms of this contract are and that they cover all the points that are important to you. Naturally, lease contracts will differ depending upon the situation that is unique to your leasing arrangement. However, the major items that will be included in the contract are as follows:

1. The term of the lease (usually expressed as a period of months or years)
2. The rate (usually expressed in percentage of the total equipment cost paid on a monthly or quarterly basis)
3. The specific terms of the financial arrangement with the lessor
4. The disposition of the asset at the end of the term, as well as purchase options
5. The schedule of the value of the equipment for insurance and any special settlement terms in the event of damage or loss of the equipment
6. Who is responsible for maintenance and who is responsible for taxes
7. Who gets and is entitled to the investment tax credit
8. Substitution provisions if later designed equipment becomes available
9. Renewal options
10. Cancellation penalties
11. Any special terms and conditions (for example, a requirement that you keep the equipment in a certain location or other limitations pertaining to your use of the equipment leased)

HOW TO NEGOTIATE A LEASE

The general procedure in obtaining a lease is for the lessor to send a short, written proposal letter to the potential lessee after a verbal discussion. This proposal letter spells out the basic terms of the proposed lease. A sample proposal letter is shown in Figure 8.2. While negotiation really begins with the first verbal contact with the lessor, the receipt of a written document such as the proposal is a signal for more formal negotiations, and this document should be reviewed by both your attorney and your tax accountant to insure that the proposed terms are in your best interest. Based on the negotiations and assuming that you receive credit approval, the lessor will next send you a formal commitment letter which includes the detailed terms and the conditions of the proposed lease. Such an example is shown in Figure 8.3. Again, you should have these terms thoroughly reviewed by your accountant and your attorney. Assuming the terms in the lease commitment received are acceptable to you, you then sign this commitment. By your signature you accept the terms of the formal proposal contained in the commitment.

FINANCIAL TREATMENT OF LEASES

An important change has been made over the last several years regarding the financial and accounting treatment of leases. In previous years, financial leases were not included on the balance sheet. In fact, they were known as off-the-balance-sheet financing, even though they were listed in footnotes. However, not accounting for leases explicitly sometimes resulted in a failure to state operational assets and liabilities in a way that would convey a thorough understanding of the company's financial position. Accordingly, in 1977, the Financial Accounting Standards Board, which is the rule-making body for the accounting profession, changed its position and required that capital leases be recorded on the balance sheet directly and not as a footnote, and listed as both an asset and as a liability. Therefore, leasing is far more likely to affect your credit rating now than before this change in accounting procedures.

June 25, 1987

ABC Manufacturing Company
1055 Buffalo Street
Los Angeles, California 90009

Gentlemen:

Confirming the general terms of the leasing arrangement we discussed on June 18th, this letter contains a proposal covering the lease of a new plastic molding system with an approximate cost of $100,000. Please note that the figures are of rough order of magnitude only and should not be construed as a commitment on our part to lease for that amount.

	Option 1 (lessor retains investment tax credit)	Option 2 (lesser receives investment tax credit)	Option 3 (Conditional sale)
Term:	3 years	3 years	3 years
Depreciation:	Retained	Retained	Lessee
Investment tax credit:	Retained	Lessee	Lessee
Monthly payment (per $1000. of Cost):	$33.33	$38.89	$40.27
Renewal option:	At fair market value	At fair market value	None
Purchase option:	At fair market value	At fair market value	6% of cost

All options provide for 100% financing. Lessee is responsible for providing acceptable insurance coverage and maintaining equipment.
As with all lease proposals, this proposal is subject to credit approval.
If I can answer any questions regarding this proposal, please do not hesitate to call.

Sincerely,

John J. Smith
President

Figure 8.2. Sample proposal letter.

WHEN SHOULD YOU REPLACE EQUIPMENT?

Closely linked with the decision whether to lease or to buy is the decision to replace or not to replace older equipment that you are currently using. This decision depends mainly upon four major cost elements. These are:

1. Depreciation
2. Opportunity cost
3. Operating cost
4. Revenues

Let's look at each in turn.

Depreciation

As pointed out earlier, depreciation is the amount by which the asset decreases in value over the period of the life of the asset. The importance of depreciation as a

July 5, 1987

Mr. James C. Fite
President
ZKC Enterprises
150 N. Duke Street
Los Angeles, California   90009

Dear Mr. Fite:

In response to your invitation to submit a lease commitment on a Nutronic 521Z Computer, we are submitting this letter. On your request we agree to purchase for lease a Nutronic Model 521Z Computer if available as described below for amounts and terms as indicated.

1. Lessee: James C. Fite
            President
            ZKC Enterprises
            150 N. Duke Street
            Los Angeles, CA 90009

2. Lessor: ABC Leasing Company
            1151 Pasadena Ave.
            Los Angeles, CA 90032

3. Lease: Nutronic Model 521Z Computer with standard equipment as furnished by the manufacturer. Cost not in excess of $150,000.

4. Term: Lease term shall commence on delivery date of the computer and shall continue for 48 months from the lease scheduling date.

5. Lease payments:
    a. Interim rent will begin to accrue on the date the funds for purchase are advanced by the lessor until execution of the lease schedule. Daily rate will be $0.25 per $1,000 of cost, payable monthly.
    b. Beginning January 1, 1988, periodic rents are to be annually in arrears at $310.60 per $1,000 of lessors cost

6. Expiration of commitment: This commitment will expire unless it has been accepted on or before August 5, 1987.

7. Taxes and insurance: Lessee will pay all taxes except those which may be levied on the income of the lessor. Lessee will furnish physical damage and liability insurance in amounts acceptable to the lessor prior to the lessor's issuance of purchase orders.

8. Investment tax credit: Investment tax credit will be retained by lessor.

9. Renewal option: Lessee may renew lease at expiration of lease term for a period to be determined by agreement between both parties at the current lease term rental rate.

10. Purchase option: Lessee may purchase the equipment at the expiration of the lease term $30 per $1,000 of lessor's cost.

11. Security deposit: None required.
12. Warranties: None except furnished by manufacturer.
13. Delinquent charges: 12% per annum
14. Guarantors: None required.
15. Commitment fee: None required.

If the above terms are acceptable, and you agree to accept this proposal, acceptance is indicated by signing below, completing the required insurance information, and returning the letter.

Sincerely,

John J. Smith
President

JAMES C. FITE   INSURANCE INFORMATION
This proposal is accepted on _____ day of
_____, 1987.   _____
                                                                          agent
By: _____   _____
                                                                          address
Title: _____
                                                           _____
                                                                    telephone number

Figure 8.3.   Formal commitment letter.

cost element is the fact that you may deduct this depreciation from your tax. In a cost analysis it must be taken into consideration, as shown in the previous example comparing a lease and a purchase. Once the book value of old equipment reaches zero, you no longer may depreciate the equipment; thus, newly purchased equipment may be depreciated and may have a significant effect on your cost analysis. In order to do this analysis, including depreciation on the new equipment, you must know the initial cost of the equipment, its estimated service life, and its expected salvage value at the end of that period. The difference between the initial cost and the expected salvage value at the end of the estimated service life represents the amount which the equipment will depreciate during this service life.

Opportunity Cost

As pointed out earlier in this book, there is a time value to money, because you have alternative uses to which this money can be put. If you own an asset, the fact of ownership has tied up some of your capital. If you had to borrow this capital, you have to pay for the use of this money. But the same is true even if you use your own money and do not borrow. In this case, the amount involved is not available for other investments which could bring you a return. Therefore, this opportunity cost is one of the costs of owning the equipment. You allow for cost of capital by using the discount factor in Figure 8.1 as shown earlier in the comparison of the cash flow of leasing versus buying. The assumed percentage that you use for your opportunity cost depends upon what return you would obtain with an alternate investment. For example, if such an investment would bring you a return of 20%, then 20% is the figure that you should use in your calculations.

Operating Costs

Operating costs may include expenditures for labor, materials, supervision, maintenance, and power to run the equipment. These costs may tend to be higher with old equipment over new, due either to wear and tear on the equipment as it is used, or to the fact that new equipment is more sophisticated and therefore more efficient. Because of this, these costs must be considered in your analysis. Therefore, if you can save $5,000 in operating costs over your first year of use of a new piece of equipment replacing an old, this will most definitely affect your decision. There are two ways you can simplify your consideration of operating costs when doing your analysis. First, those costs that are the same for both the old and the new equipment can be ignored since they will cancel each other out in a comparison of the bottom line figure. Secondly, you can estimate only the differences between the operating costs of the old and those of the new equipment. In this way, your calculations for each type of equipment will be understated by the identical amount. Therefore, the difference between the total cost will remain the same and you will be able to make the comparison to recognize the more attractive economical alternative.

Revenues

Sometimes the revenues generated by the old equipment will be identical to those of the new equipment. If this is the case, then revenues may be ignored. However, in some cases, because of its improved capability, the new equipment can generate much greater revenues than the old. Let's say you calculate that new equipment output will result in an additional $5,000 from the sale of additional units manufactured for the same input over the old equipment. This $5,000 can be shown in your analysis in one of two ways: either the $5,000 is considered an additional cost which will be experienced when using the old equipment, or you can use the $5,000 as a negative annual expense with the new equipment. Either one of these two methods will work to give you an accurate bottom line comparison. However, be sure not to use both methods in the same analysis. If you do, they will cancel each other out and you will not have an accurate comparison.

Now let's look at an example of the economic analysis of the equipment replacement decision. Figure 8.4 shows the situation. Our current equipment has been fully depreciated so we have no depreciation. Also, the salvage value of our current equipment is zero. The new equipment that we wish to purchase will cost us $50,000, but it has a salvage value after 10 years of $5,000. Therefore, we can depreciate it over a 10-year period using the straight line method at $4,500 per year. There is also an operating cost savings over using the old equipment of $7,000 a year, and the new equipment will generate additional revenues without additional input of $1,000 per year. Finally, we have an investment tax credit of 10% of the $50,000 or $5,000 which we can take immediately the first year of purchase. In this case, we will assume that our company is in the 50% tax rate bracket and that the opportunity costs are 20%, which means that we can earn 20% on our money if we invest it in something other than the purchase of new equipment. For this analysis, we are going to use not only Figure 8.1, but also Figure 8.5. Look again at Figure 8.4. The cost of purchase for the current equipment is zero. Salvage value, if sold, is zero. Depreciation is zero. The operating cost savings over old equipment is zero, and the additional revenues with new equipment is zero. Of course, there is no investment tax credit, so this is zero as well. With the new equipment, we have the following information: As indicated, the equipment costs $50,000. Since this is the net outlay, we will assign this a negative value. The salvage value we said was $5,000 after 10 years. We will use a discount factor which

	Current Equipment	New Equipment	
Cost to purchase	0	$50,000	− $50,000.00
Salvage value if sold	0	$5,000 after 10 years × 0.1615 (discount factor = from Figure 8.1)	+ $ 807.50
Depreciation	0	$4,500/year (straight line method) × 50% × 4.1925 (discount factor from Figure 8.5)	+ 9,433.12
Operating cost savings over old equipment	0	$7,000/year × 4.1925 (discount factor from Figure 8.5)	+ 29,347.50
Additional revenues with new equipment	0	$1,000/year × 4.1925 (discount factor from Figure 8.5)	+ 4,192.50
Investment tax credit	0	$5,000 (10% × $50,000)	+ 5,000.00
Tax rate = 50%			
Opportunity costs = 20%			
	0		− $ 1,219.38

Figure 8.4. Examples of an economic analysis of the equipment replacement decision.

we obtained from Figure 8.1 just as we did in the earlier example of the lease versus purchase analysis. At 20% interest, after 10 years, the factor comes out 0.1615. We multiply this times $5,000 to arrive at a positive $807.50. Depreciation is $4,500 a year. Since our tax rate is 50%, we multiply this times 50% to get $2,250, and multiply this in turn by a discount factor of 4.1925. This we take not from Figure 8.1 but from Figure 8.5, since this amount is not in one lump sum after a number of years but rather every year. This comes out to be $9,433.12. We said the operating cost, if we use the old equipment, was $7,000 per year. Again, this is a savings that occurs every single year, so we use Table 8.5 and the same identical factor of 4.1925. Multiply it again and you get a positive $29,347.50. We also said there were additional revenues generated with new equipment of $1,000 per year, and again, since this is a yearly amount, we will use the 4.1925 figure to arrive at $4,192.50. Finally, we have the investment tax credit which we'll take at once which is 10% of the $50,000 or $5,000. We sum all of these figures algebraically. That is, there is one outlay and one outlay only, and that is the negative $50,000 which we will pay for the purchase price. All the other figures are summed together to give us a negative $1,219.38, which is less than the zero cost of the current equipment. This tells us that purchase of this new equipment is not in our interest at the present time. If the sum of these figures were positive, this would tell us to purchase the new equipment.

What might cause the situation to change in the future? It might do so if the cost of purchase were reduced. If the operating savings or additional revenues went up, that might cause the situation to change. And of course, the same might happen if the opportunity cost percentage changed for some reason. If any one of these possibilities occurred, we should reevaluate and do a new analysis to see whether we should buy new equipment.

OTHER FACTORS TO CONSIDER IN THE REPLACEMENT DECISION

In addition to the straight economic analysis discussed above, other factors must be taken into consideration when you are deciding whether to replace current equipment or not. These include the size of the investment required and whether you can manage it or not. You will note that in the above example it was assumed that cash was paid. Naturally, whether a loan would be required and what kind of loan could be obtained under what terms would also affect this decision. The safety and reliability of your current equipment must be considered. Equipment which is unsafe and which might cause injury to yourself or to your workers may be too much of a liability to continue with, even though a straight economic analysis might indicate that it is in your economic interest. In the same manner, reliability and down-time and how they might affect the flow of your goods and your customers' opinions of your company should also be considered. Interest and investment rates must always be considered, and so should what the trend is likely to be regarding such interest rates. Along the same lines, trends in development of equipment should be considered. It makes no sense to purchase a new piece of equipment if a similar amount of money will buy you much more in the not-too-distant future. Also, price and price trends should be considered. Additional features in the new equipment might also be weighed, even though there are no direct cost savings. Maybe the features just make it easier or more convenient to use. There is a value here to your business also, even though it may not be reasonable in economic terms.

n/r	1%	2%	3%	4%	5%	6%	7%	8%	9%	10%	11%	12%	13%	14%	15%
1	.9901	.9804	.9709	.9615	.9524	.9434	.9346	.9259	.9174	.9091	.9009	.8929	.8850	.8772	.8696
2	1.9704	1.9416	1.9135	1.8861	1.8594	1.8334	1.8080	1.7833	1.7591	1.7355	1.7125	1.6901	1.6681	1.6467	1.6257
3	2.9410	2.8839	2.8286	2.7751	2.7232	2.6730	2.6243	2.5771	2.5313	2.4869	2.4437	2.4018	2.3612	2.3216	2.2832
4	3.9020	3.8077	3.7171	3.6299	3.5459	3.4651	3.3872	3.3121	3.2397	3.1699	3.1024	3.0373	2.9745	2.9137	2.8550
5	4.8534	4.7135	4.5797	4.4518	4.3295	4.2124	4.1002	3.9927	3.8897	3.7908	3.6959	3.6048	3.5172	3.4331	3.3522
6	5.7955	5.6014	5.4172	5.2421	5.0757	4.9173	4.7665	4.6229	4.4859	4.3553	4.2305	4.1114	3.9975	3.8887	3.7845
7	6.7282	6.4720	6.2303	6.0020	5.7864	5.5824	5.3893	5.2064	5.0330	4.8684	4.7122	4.5638	4.4226	4.2883	4.1604
8	7.6517	7.3255	7.0197	6.7327	6.4632	6.2098	5.9713	5.7466	5.5348	5.3349	5.1461	4.9676	4.7988	4.6389	4.4873
9	8.5660	8.1622	7.7861	7.4353	7.1078	6.8017	6.5152	6.2469	5.9952	5.7590	5.5370	5.3282	5.1317	4.9464	4.7716
10	9.4713	8.9826	8.5302	8.1109	7.7217	7.3601	7.0236	6.7101	6.4177	6.1446	5.8892	5.6502	5.4262	5.2161	5.0188
11	10.3676	9.7868	9.2526	8.7605	8.3064	7.8869	7.4987	7.1390	6.8051	6.4951	6.2065	5.9377	5.6869	5.4527	5.2337
12	11.2551	10.5753	9.9540	9.3851	8.8632	8.3838	7.9427	7.5361	7.1607	6.8137	6.4924	6.1944	5.9176	5.6603	5.4206
13	12.1337	11.3484	10.6350	9.9856	9.3936	8.8527	8.3577	7.9038	7.4869	7.1034	6.7499	6.4235	6.1218	5.8424	5.5831
14	13.0037	12.1062	11.2961	10.5631	9.8986	9.2950	8.7455	8.2442	7.7862	7.3667	6.9819	6.6282	6.3025	6.0021	5.7245
15	13.8650	12.8493	11.9379	11.1184	10.3797	9.7122	9.1079	8.5595	8.0607	7.6061	7.1909	6.8109	6.4624	6.1422	5.8474
16	14.7179	13.5777	12.5611	11.6523	10.8378	10.1059	9.4466	8.8514	8.3126	7.8237	7.3792	6.9740	6.6039	6.2651	5.9542
17	15.5622	14.2919	13.1661	12.1657	11.2741	10.4773	9.7632	9.1216	8.5436	8.0216	7.5488	7.1196	6.7291	6.3729	6.0472
18	16.3983	14.9920	13.7535	12.6593	11.6896	10.8276	10.0591	9.3719	8.7556	8.2014	7.7016	7.2497	6.8399	6.4674	6.1280
19	17.2260	15.6785	14.3238	13.1339	12.0853	11.1581	10.3356	9.6036	8.9501	8.3649	7.8393	7.3658	6.9380	6.5504	6.1982
20	18.0455	16.3514	14.8775	13.5903	12.4622	11.4699	10.5940	9.8181	9.1285	8.5136	7.9633	7.4694	7.0248	6.6231	6.2593
21	18.8570	17.0112	15.4150	14.0292	12.8211	11.7641	10.8355	10.0168	9.2922	8.6487	8.0751	7.5620	7.1015	6.6870	6.3125
22	19.6604	17.6580	15.9369	14.4511	13.1630	12.0416	11.0612	10.2007	9.4424	8.7715	8.1757	7.6446	7.1695	6.7429	6.3587
23	20.4558	18.2922	16.4436	14.8568	13.4886	12.3034	11.2722	10.3711	9.5802	8.8832	8.2664	7.7184	7.2297	6.7921	6.3988
24	21.2434	18.9139	16.9355	15.2470	13.7986	12.5504	11.4693	10.5288	9.7066	8.9847	8.3481	7.7843	7.2829	6.8351	6.4338
25	22.0232	19.5235	17.4131	15.6221	14.0939	12.7834	11.6536	10.6748	9.8226	9.0770	8.4217	7.8431	7.3300	6.8729	6.4641
26	22.7952	20.1210	17.8768	15.9828	14.3752	13.0032	11.8258	10.8100	9.9290	9.1609	8.4881	7.8957	7.3717	6.9061	6.4906
27	23.5596	20.7069	18.3270	16.3296	14.6430	13.2105	11.9867	10.9352	10.0266	9.2372	8.5478	7.9426	7.4086	6.9352	6.5135
28	24.3164	21.2813	18.7641	16.6631	14.8981	13.4062	12.1371	11.0511	10.1161	9.3066	8.6016	7.9844	7.4412	6.9607	6.5335
29	25.0658	21.8444	19.1884	16.9837	15.1411	13.5907	12.2777	11.1584	10.1983	9.3696	8.6501	8.0218	7.4701	6.9830	6.5509
30	25.8077	22.3965	19.6004	17.2920	15.3724	13.7648	12.4090	11.2578	10.2737	9.4269	8.6938	8.0552	7.4957	7.0027	6.5660
31	26.5423	22.9377	20.0004	17.5885	15.5928	13.9291	12.5318	11.3498	10.3428	9.4790	8.7331	8.0850	7.5183	7.0199	6.5791
32	27.2696	23.4683	20.3888	17.8735	15.8027	14.0840	12.6466	11.4350	10.4062	9.5264	8.7686	8.1116	7.5383	7.0350	6.5905
33	27.9897	23.9886	20.7658	18.1476	16.0025	14.2302	12.7538	11.5139	10.4644	9.5694	8.8005	8.1354	7.5560	7.0482	6.6005
34	28.7027	24.4986	21.1318	18.4112	16.1929	14.3681	12.8540	11.5869	10.5178	9.6086	8.8293	8.1566	7.5717	7.0599	6.6091
35	29.4086	24.9986	21.4872	18.6646	16.3742	14.4982	12.9477	11.6546	10.5668	9.6442	8.8552	8.1755	7.5856	7.0700	6.6166
40	32.8347	27.3555	23.1148	19.7928	17.1591	15.0463	13.3317	11.9246	10.7574	9.7791	8.9511	8.2438	7.6344	7.1050	6.6418
45	36.0945	29.4902	24.5187	20.7200	17.7741	15.4558	13.6055	12.1084	10.8812	9.8628	9.0079	8.2825	7.6609	7.1232	6.6543
50	39.1961	31.4236	25.7298	21.4822	18.2559	15.7619	13.8007	12.2335	10.9617	9.9148	9.0417	8.3045	7.6752	7.1327	6.6605

Figure 8.5. Present value of $1 received annually.

n/r	16%	18%	20%	22%	24%	26%	28%	30%	32%	34%	36%	38%	40%	45%	50%
1	.8621	.8475	.8333	.8197	.8065	.7937	.7813	.7692	.7576	.7463	.7353	.7246	.7143	.6897	.6667
2	1.6052	1.5656	1.5278	1.4915	1.4568	1.4235	1.3916	1.3609	1.3315	1.3032	1.2760	1.2497	1.2245	1.1653	1.1111
3	2.2459	2.1743	2.1065	2.0422	1.9813	1.9234	1.8684	1.8161	1.7663	1.7188	1.6735	1.6302	1.5889	1.4933	1.4074
4	2.7982	2.6901	2.5887	2.4936	2.4043	2.3202	2.2410	2.1662	2.0957	2.0290	1.9658	1.9060	1.8492	1.7195	1.6049
5	3.2743	3.1272	2.9906	2.8636	2.7454	2.6351	2.5320	2.4356	2.3452	2.2604	2.1807	2.1058	2.0352	1.8755	1.7366
6	3.6847	3.4976	3.3255	3.1669	3.0205	2.8850	2.7594	2.6427	2.5342	2.4331	2.3388	2.2506	2.1680	1.9831	1.8244
7	4.0386	3.8115	3.6046	3.4155	3.2423	3.0833	2.9370	2.8021	2.6775	2.5620	2.4550	2.3555	2.2628	2.0573	1.8829
8	4.3436	4.0776	3.8372	3.6193	3.4212	3.2407	3.0758	2.9247	2.7860	2.6582	2.5404	2.4315	2.3306	2.1085	1.9220
9	4.6065	4.3030	4.0310	3.7863	3.5655	3.3657	3.1842	3.0190	2.8681	2.7300	2.6033	2.4866	2.3790	2.1438	1.9480
10	4.8332	4.4941	4.1925	3.9232	3.6819	3.4648	3.2689	3.0915	2.9304	2.7836	2.6495	2.5265	2.4136	2.1681	1.9653
11	5.0286	4.6560	4.3271	4.0354	3.7757	3.5435	3.3351	3.1473	2.9776	2.8236	2.6834	2.5555	2.4383	2.1849	1.9769
12	5.1971	4.7932	4.4392	4.1274	3.8514	3.6059	3.3868	3.1903	3.0133	2.8534	2.7084	2.5764	2.4559	2.1965	1.9845
13	5.3423	4.9095	4.5327	4.2028	3.9124	3.6555	3.4272	3.2233	3.0404	2.8757	2.7268	2.5916	2.4685	2.2045	1.9897
14	5.4675	5.0081	4.6106	4.2646	3.9616	3.6949	3.4587	3.2487	3.0609	2.8923	2.7403	2.6026	2.4775	2.2100	1.9931
15	5.5755	5.0916	4.6755	4.3152	4.0013	3.7261	3.4834	3.2682	3.0764	2.9047	2.7502	2.6106	2.4839	2.2138	1.9954
16	5.6685	5.1624	4.7296	4.3567	4.0333	3.7509	3.5026	3.2832	3.0882	2.9140	2.7575	2.6164	2.4885	2.2164	1.9970
17	5.7487	5.2223	4.7746	4.3908	4.0591	3.7705	3.5177	3.2948	3.0971	2.9209	2.7629	2.6206	2.4918	2.2182	1.9980
18	5.8178	5.2732	4.8122	4.4187	4.0799	3.7861	3.5294	3.3037	3.1039	2.9260	2.7668	2.6236	2.4941	2.2195	1.9986
19	5.8775	5.3162	4.8435	4.4415	4.0967	3.7985	3.5386	3.3105	3.1090	2.9299	2.7697	2.6258	2.4958	2.2203	1.9991
20	5.9288	5.3527	4.8696	4.4603	4.1103	3.8083	3.5458	3.3158	3.1129	2.9327	2.7718	2.6274	2.4970	2.2209	1.9994
21	5.9731	5.3837	4.8913	4.4756	4.1212	3.8161	3.5514	3.3198	3.1158	2.9349	2.7734	2.6285	2.4979	2.2213	1.9996
22	6.0113	5.4099	4.9094	4.4882	4.1300	3.8223	3.5558	3.3230	3.1180	2.9365	2.7746	2.6294	2.4985	2.2216	1.9997
23	6.0442	5.4321	4.9245	4.4985	4.1371	3.8273	3.5592	3.3253	3.1197	2.9377	2.7754	2.6300	2.4989	2.2218	1.9998
24	6.0726	5.4509	4.9371	4.5070	4.1428	3.8312	3.5619	3.3272	3.1210	2.9386	2.7760	2.6304	2.4992	2.2219	1.9999
25	6.0971	5.4669	4.9476	4.5139	4.1474	3.8342	3.5640	3.3286	3.1220	2.9392	2.7765	2.6307	2.4994	2.2220	1.9999
26	6.1182	5.4804	4.9563	4.5196	4.1511	3.8367	3.5656	3.3297	3.1227	2.9397	2.7768	2.6310	2.4996	2.2221	1.9999
27	6.1364	5.4919	4.9636	4.5243	4.1542	3.8387	3.5669	3.3305	3.1233	2.9401	2.7771	2.6311	2.4997	2.2221	2.0000
28	6.1520	5.5016	4.9697	4.5281	4.1566	3.8402	3.5679	3.3312	3.1237	2.9404	2.7773	2.6313	2.4998	2.2222	2.0000
29	6.1656	5.5098	4.9747	4.5312	4.1585	3.8414	3.5687	3.3316	3.1240	2.9406	2.7774	2.6313	2.4999	2.2222	2.0000
30	6.1772	5.5168	4.9789	4.5338	4.1601	3.8424	3.5693	3.3321	3.1242	2.9407	2.7775	2.6314	2.4999	2.2222	2.0000
31	6.1872	5.5227	4.9824	4.5359	4.1614	3.8432	3.5697	3.3324	3.1244	2.9408	2.7776	2.6315	2.4999	2.2222	2.0000
32	6.1959	5.5277	4.9854	4.5376	4.1624	3.8438	3.5701	3.3326	3.1246	2.9409	2.7776	2.6315	2.4999	2.2222	2.0000
33	6.2034	5.5320	4.9878	4.5390	4.1632	3.8443	3.5704	3.3328	3.1247	2.9410	2.7777	2.6315	2.5000	2.2222	2.0000
34	6.2098	5.5356	4.9898	4.5402	4.1639	3.8447	3.5706	3.3329	3.1248	2.9410	2.7777	2.6315	2.5000	2.2222	2.0000
35	6.2153	5.5386	4.9915	4.5411	4.1644	3.8450	3.5708	3.3330	3.1248	2.9411	2.7777	2.6315	2.5000	2.2222	2.0000
40	6.2335	5.5482	4.9966	4.5439	4.1659	3.8458	3.5712	3.3332	3.1250	2.9412	2.7778	2.6316	2.5000	2.2222	2.0000
45	6.2421	5.5523	4.9986	4.5449	4.1664	3.8460	3.5714	3.3333	3.1250	2.9412	2.7778	2.6316	2.5000	2.2222	2.0000
50	6.2463	5.5541	4.9995	4.5452	4.1666	3.8461	3.5714	3.3333	3.1250	2.9412	2.7778	2.6316	2.5000	2.2222	2.0000

Figure 8.5. (Continued)

SOURCES OF ADDITIONAL INFORMATION

Finance for the Nonfinancial Manager, by Herbert T. Spiro, published by John Wiley and Sons, Inc., 605 Third Ave., New York, NY 10058.

Should You Lease or Buy Equipment, Management Aid 249, by Paul Lerman, available free from the Small Business Administration, P.O. Box 15434, Fort Worth, TX 76119.

The Equipment Replacement Decision, by Raymond R. Mayer, available free from the Small Business Administration, P.O. Box 15434, Fort Worth, TX 76119.

9

Record Keeping

WHY RECORDS ARE VITAL

Records are crucial to the success of your business. Even if you are successful initially, it is unlikely that you will be able to sustain this success without good records, since you will not know what is making your business successful. You need records to insure that your business is profitable, and they should be kept from the very first day that you open your doors until such time as you sell your business to someone else or retire from it. Good records and record keeping are needed to make future plans for your company and to evolve strategies which will enable your business to grow rapidly and be successful in the future as well as to survive in the present. Without such records, your competition will eventually evolve strategies which you cannot counter since you will not know your position in the market or what is going wrong. Unfortunately, despite its importance, many small businesspeople use the shoebox approach to record keeping. That is, the only record of a sale or a purchase they make is a piece of paper tossed in a shoebox. At the end of the year, someone attempts to analyze the contents of the box. This isn't record keeping. It cannot enable a business to respond successfully to the day-to-day demands, problems, and opportunities that appear.

This chapter will help you avoid the shoebox approach and show you methods you can use not only to survive but also to make your business highly profitable. That these methods are made available to you does not mean that you shouldn't use the services of a good accountant. On the contrary, a good accountant can save you much additional money. A combination of using the methods described in this chapter and consulting an expert accountant will save you thousands and thousands of dollars throughout your business career, and may very well make the difference between mere survival and tremendous growth and success in your small business.

BASIC REQUIREMENTS

The basic requirements for your record-keeping system are four:

1. Your record system must be simple to use and to understand. If it's not simple to use, it will take much time and trouble to keep it updated, and if it is not easy to understand you will waste time as will your accountant trying to figure it out. Since time is money, make sure your system is comprehensible.

2. Your record-keeping system should be accurate and relevant. "Accurate" means free of errors and conforming to whatever standards you have set for your record-keeping system. "Relevant" means pertinent to your business; be sure you are not wasting time recording information that you do not need.

3. Your record-keeping system should be consistent throughout. This means that whatever standard and structure you decide upon should be adhered to throughout the system. This is not to say that if you find deficiencies in what you are doing you cannot change them. But it does mean that you should only deviate from your standard methods for good reasons and should maintain only one method of doing things.

4. Your system should insure that records are kept in a timely fashion. This means that you must keep them current. If you do not, you will not be able to use this information effectively.

THE FOUR BASIC RECORDS REQUIRED

Just as there are four basic requirements, there are four basic records that are required for any good small business record-keeping system. These are:

1. Sales records
2. Cash receipts
3. Cash disbursements
4. Accounts receivable.

Let's look at each in turn.

Sales Records

Sales records should be subdivided into convenient categories so that you can analyze them more easily later on. For example, you may subdivide your sales records into wholesale and retail sales, or you may subdivide them by geographical areas, or by some other market segmentation.

Cash Receipts

Cash receipts represent cash actually received in the form of sales as well as collection of accounts receivable from monies formerly owed to you.

Cash Disbursements

Cash disbursements are monies paid out by you for your business. In general, you should pay by check except for small items which you can pay out of a petty cash fund. In keeping track of cash disbursements, always list the date, the check number, the amount, and the purpose for which the disbursement was made. Also, you may break the heading into different categories, such as office supplies, advertising, rent, utilities, and so forth.

The petty cash fund is set up simply by drawing a check for a certain amount, say, $50. The check is cashed and logged under the general heading of checks for the petty cash fund. The money is then placed in some convenient location so that you can use it easily as required. As payments are made for small items such as postage, bus fares, small amounts of supplies, and so forth, each item is listed on a special form which again lists the date of expenditure, the amount, and the purpose for which the money was spent. When the fund is nearly spent, the items are summarized and a check is drawn to cover the exact amount. In this way, when the new check is cashed, the fund is replenished. Doing this also means that at all times the cash that you have on hand in the petty cash fund, plus listed expenditures, will equal the amount of the fund.

Accounts Receivable

Accounts receivable are monies owed to you for services or goods supplied for which you have not yet been paid. To control the accounts receivable, be sure that all bills are sent when goods are shipped or services rendered and that they are mailed to correct addresses. Be especially careful of the larger accounts in your accounts receivable ledger. At the end of every month, you will age your accounts receivable. This means that you list accounts and enter amounts that are current, those unpaid for 30 days, and those unpaid for 60 days and longer. For those that are unpaid for 60 days or longer, you must find out exactly why these accounts are unpaid. In this way your system will help you in account control and collection. You should also pay attention to customer complaints about bills that you have sent to him. If you feel the complaint is justified, perhaps you should negotiate and propose a special adjustment or in some other way reach agreement with your customer. Do not delay in doing this. If the customer has not paid and is delinquent in his or her payment, then try to get a promise of payment on a specific date. If the payment is not received by that date, then you should again contact the customer and ask the customer to explain why, and obtain a new promise if necessary. If funds are still not forthcoming, many states have provisions for a small claims court for which a lawyer is not required and through which it is fairly easy to take a delinquent to task for nonpayment. You may try other means of intimidating the customer and getting him or her to pay, depending on the situation, the size of the account, future business anticipated with the same customer despite slowness in payment, whether you feel that you will ultimately be paid, and various other factors.

You should establish a definite figure below which you will not bother going after monies owed. Let us say you have decided that this figure is $10, and so you ask twice for the amount from the individual owing this to you and then you drop it. You do this because the trouble and time spent collecting are worth more than this amount. On the other hand, if letting one customer get away with nonpayment may lead others to expect they can do the same thing, then maybe even a small account will have to be gone after. Large accounts, of course, should be pursued vigorously to obtain payment.

Sometimes a new customer whom you do not know asks for credit. In this case, have your customer complete a simple form such as that shown in Figure 9.1 which lists the name, address, telephone number, place of employment, bank, and credit references of the individual who would like this credit. Make sure that the credit is warranted before you grant it, especially with larger amounts. Obviously if the customer is an old customer of yours and has not paid his bill promptly, then you should think twice before granting credit or require a substantial amount up front.

GENERAL RULES FOR KEEPING TRACK OF YOUR FINANCES AND YOUR BOOKKEEPING SYSTEM

Here are some general rules you should always follow no matter what system you adopt.

Always pay your business bills by check or through your petty cash fund. Never make disbursements out of your daily cash receipts.

Be certain that all incoming cash is recorded along with amounts, where the money came from, and the dates.

Never take money out of your daily cash receipts for your personal use, but instead, pay yourself a salary

Use a business bank account for all your business funds and deposit all cash receipts in the account day by day as you receive them. Do not use your personal bank account for your business bank account, and keep your personal cash separate from cash generated from the business.

Periodically have your record keeping system checked over by a certified public accountant (CPA).

SHOULD YOU USE CASH OR ACCRUAL BASIS FOR RECORDS?

Many small businesses will use a simple cash basis for bookkeeping. Which basis is used will depend on whether or not credit is granted to customers and the amount of inventory that is required. For example, if you are selling hamburgers, probably a credit system is not required, nor is inventory extensive. In this situation, you would probably use a cash basis for your records. On the other hand, with credit granted to customers and a more extensive inventory, the accrual basis would probably be better. With the accrual basis, each item is entered as earned or as the expense is incurred without regard to when the actual payments are made or received. This means that sales that are made on credit are written down at once in your books as sales and also in your accounts receivable records. At such time as the bills are actually collected, then your accounts receivable records are adjusted. Accruals are also made for expense items that are payable at times in the future. An example is yearly or periodic interest rates on loans. These accruals are made by entries explained later in this chapter.

Name _____

Address _____   Years at this address _____

Place of employment _____   Years at this employment _____

Telephone _____

                    Name   Address   Telephone

Bank references _____

                 _____

                 _____

                    Name   Address   Telephone

Credit references _____

                 _____

                 _____

                 _____

                 _____

Former employment _____

                 _____

                 _____

                 _____

                 _____

Figure 9.1. Sample credit form.

WHICH METHOD OF DEPRECIATION SHOULD YOU ADOPT?

Depreciation is an expense of the business just as are rent, utilities, and salaries. Therefore, a charge to expenses should be made to cover depreciation of fixed assets other than land, which does not depreciate. Fixed assets may be defined as items that are normally in use for one year or longer. These may include buildings, equipment, tools, furniture, and other similar items. Most small businesses charge depreciation at the end of their fiscal year. However, if you have very substantial fixed assets such as a motel or hotel, you may want to calculate depreciation on a monthly basis. There are two basic methods of depreciation which you may use: (1) straight line depreciation, and (2) the declining balance method of depreciation.

Straight Line Depreciation

Straight line depreciation is based on the expected life of the items for book purposes. Therefore, it is first necessary to estimate the total life of the item being depreciated. Let us say that you own a new building. A reasonable period of depreciation for a building is 20 years. This means that to depreciate the building 100%, you would depreciate it 5% a year. Other assets may have shorter periods of depreciation. Machinery may have an estimated life of five years. In this case, the item should be depreciated at 20% per year. An example of depreciations in a depreciation chart using the straight line method is shown in Figure 9.2.

Declining Balance Method of Depreciation

The declining balance method of depreciation is used whenever quicker recovery of the investment is desirable. Using this method, your asset is depreciated by a certain percentage of the balance each year. However, if you use the declining

Item	Date Purchased	Cost	Estimated Life	Yearly Depreciation	Accumulated Prior Depreciation	This Year's Depreciation	Total Accumulated Depreciation
Office	Jan. 1980	$100,000	20 years	5%	$25,000	$5,000	$30,000
Automobile	Jan. 1982	$10,000	5 years	20%	$6,000	$2,000	$8,000
Printing press	Mar. 1982	$5,000	10 years	10%	$1,416.67	$500	$1,916.67
Computer	July 1983	$2,000	4 years	25%	$750	$500	$1,250

Figure 9.2. Sample form for depreciation of assets using straight line method (year 1985). *Note 1:* To find yearly depreciation divide the estimated life into 1.0. Example: Estimated life = 20 years. 1.0/20 = 5%. *Note 2:* If purchase date is other than January, first year depreciation will be less than the full amount. Example: Purchase in March, 1982 (therefore, only 10 months depreciation in 1982). To adjust, if yearly depreciation is $500, then depreciation in 1982 would be 10/12 × $500. = $416.67.

	Straight Line	Declining Balance	
Year	Depreciation	Remaining Value	Depreciation
1	(20% × $1,000) = $ 200	$1,000	(40% × $1,000) = $400
2	(20% × $1,000) = $ 200	$ 600	(40% × $ 600) = $240
3	(20% × $1,000) = $ 200	$ 360	(40% × $ 340) = $144
4	(20% × $1,000) = $ 200	$ 216	(40% × $ 216) = $ 86.40
5	(20% × $1,000) = $ 200	$ 129.60	(40% × $ 129.60) = $ 51.84
	$1,000		$922.24

Asset cost = $1,000   Estimated life = 5 years
Yearly depreciation (straight line) = 1/5 = 20%
Yearly depreciation (declining balance) = 40% of remaining value each year

Figure 9.3.   Depreciation: declining balance method versus straight line method.

balance method for tax-paying purposes, the Internal Revenue Service will not allow the rate of depreciation using the declining balance method to be greater than double the straight line rate of depreciation. This means that if yearly depreciation using the straight line method is computed at 5%, the asset would be depreciated at an annual rate of 10% using the declining balance method. If the yearly depreciation was 20%, then, using the declining balance method, 40% would be the figure. The difference in using the declining balance method is that the yearly depreciation is taken not of the total cost of the asset but rather of the remaining value.

A comparison of the two methods is shown in Figure 9.3. Note that using the declining balance method, the remaining value approach never reaches zero. In the example, in both cases the asset cost $1,000 and the estimated year life is five years. This means that yearly depreciation using the straight line method is 20%, or, using the declining balance method, 40% of the remaining value of each year. The total depreciation after five years using the straight line method is $1,000, but since in the declining balance method it never will quite reach $1,000 and the remaining value will approach but will never equal zero, in this case it actually equals $922.24. In order to allow for this, the small businessperson should switch to the straight line depreciation method near the end of the asset's useful life. Therefore, in the example shown (the fourth and fifth year of life depreciating at $86.40 and $51.84, respectively), the $216 remaining value in the fourth year should be split up to $108 each, and therefore at the end of the period the depreciation would be $1,000 instead of the $922.24 shown.

The declining balance method permits the businessperson to take a heavy depreciation in the early years of the equipment's life. This is very desirable when the asset has a high rate of obsolescence and its market value accordingly decreases very rapidly.

Up to now, we've assumed the salvage value of any equipment to be zero. However, this is usually not the case. That is, at the end of the depreciable period, the equipment is probably worth something either for resale, trade-in, or scrap. This salvage value should be estimated at the time that the estimated life figure is established. This scrap or salvage value is then subtracted from the original cost of the equipment to give the amount to be depreciated over the estimated life. For example, if the automobile shown in Figure 9.2 had a salvage value of $5,000 after the five-year period of estimated life, then only $5,000 should be depreciated rather than the $10,000 shown in the figure. If you fail to use a salvage value in your depreciation calculations, then this amount is recoverable by the IRS at such time as you do receive money for trade-in, scrap, or salvage.

WHICH BOOKKEEPING SYSTEM SHOULD YOU ADOPT?

Specialized bookkeeping systems are available for almost every business and industry. In order to see what is available in your area of interest, you should contact the trade organization that serves your business. You may also check with stationery and office supply stores. Usually either a general bookkeeping system or even one designed especially for your business will be available. The Small Business Administration has compiled a list of bookkeeping systems in two categories: systems designed for use in any retail or service establishment and systems designed for use in specific retail and service trades. This list will be found at the end of this chapter, along with a description of each system. You can also use the forms provided in Figures 1.2 to 1.6.

THE NEED FOR GENERAL BOOKS AND JOURNALS

In addition to the basic records I've already discussed, you will need books for different journal entries. These are called general books. General entries of this type are used to record business transactions which do not involve cash. Examples would be accruals for depreciation and expenses that are due in the future.

Another book you should keep is called the general ledger. The general ledger is kept to record balances of assets, liabilities, and capital, and to accumulate sales and expense items. At the end of each fiscal year, your accounts are balanced and closed. Sales and expense account balances are transferred to the profit and loss account. The remaining asset, liability, and capital accounts provide the figures for the balance sheet. We will discuss this shortly. A typical classification of accounts for the general ledger follows:

1. Assets
2. Cash in banks
3. Petty cash fund
4. Accounts receivable
5. Materials and supplies
6. Prepaid expenses
7. Deposits
8. Land
9. Buildings
10. Tools and equipment
11. Automotive equipment
12. Furniture and fixtures
13. Reserve for depreciation (The reserve for depreciation is subtracted from the asset account. Technically this is known as a "credit" against the asset account.)
14. Liabilities
15. Accounts payable
16. Notes payable
17. Sales taxes payable
18. FICA taxes payable
19. Federal withholding taxes

20. State withholding taxes
21. Unemployment taxes
22. Long-term debt and mortgages payable
23. Long-term debt SBA loan
24. Miscellaneous accruals
25. Capital accounts
26. Common capital stock
27. Preferred capital stock (for corporations only)
28. Proprietorship accounts (for a proprietorship)
29. Proprietorship withdrawals (for a proprietorship)
30. Retained earnings
31. Sales accounts
32. Retail sales
33. Wholesale sales
34. Sales services
35. Miscellaneous income
36. Expenses
37. Salaries and wages
38. Contract labor
39. Payroll taxes
40. Utilities
41. Telephone
42. Rent
43. Office supplies
44. Postage
45. Maintenance expense
46. Insurance
47. Interest
48. Depreciation
49. Travel expense
50. Entertainment
51. Advertising
52. Dues and contributions
53. Auto expense
54. Contributions
55. Electricity
56. Heat
57. Trade dues

Do not use too many different accounts, although you should tailor which accounts are used to your particular business. Sales should be broken down in a sufficient number of categories to provide a clear indication of your business. Different expense accounts should be used depending upon the frequency of the individual expenses. Miscellaneous expenses are used for small unrelated expense items.

OTHER IMPORTANT RECORDS

Several other important records should be maintained by your business. These include an equipment list, insurance records, and payroll records.

Equipment List

An equipment list consists of all the permanent equipment used in the business. Don't bother keeping track of the small items, but do keep track of any item that is useful for a period of a year or longer and has some appreciable value to it. On your list you should show date purchased, the name of the supplier, description of the item, the number of the check with which the equipment was paid for, and the amount. This list is very useful for calculating depreciation as described earlier, as well as for reorder information, insurance preparation, and business functions.

Insurance Records

Insurance records are an absolute must. See Chapter 3 concerning business insurance for more details.

Payroll Records

Use Figure 1.5 to assist you in preparing payroll records. Yearly and quarterly reports of individual payroll payments must be made to state and federal governments. You must supply each individual employee a W-2 Form at the year's end showing total withholding payments made for the employee during that calendar year. A special employment card should be kept for each individual employee showing the individual's Social Security number, as well as name, address, telephone number, name of next of kin, and current address. Also on the form you should indicate whether the employee is married and the number of exemptions claimed. In this same file a W-4 Form should be on record which is completed earlier by the employee, as explained earlier in this book. A summary payroll should also be maintained showing the names, employee numbers, the rate of pay, hours worked, overtime hours if any, total pay, and the amount of deductions for FICA, withholding taxes and deductions for insurance, pension, and/or savings plan. Use Figure 1.5 to maintain the records on individual employees including rate of pay, Social Security number, and other information previously described. Enter the amounts for each pay period covering hours worked, gross pay, and the various deductions. At the end of each quarter, add up the amounts and the balance. These forms provide the needed information for quarterly and annual reports.

PREPARATION OF FINANCIAL STATEMENTS

There are two basic financial statements which you must either prepare yourself or have an accountant prepare. These statements are most important. One study showed that less than 7% of a group of failed businesses prepared these statements. These statements are (1) the balance sheet, and (2) the profit and loss statement. Both forms are prepared using the records which you've already accumulated.

The Balance Sheet

The balance sheet records the condition of your company at a single point in time. Therefore, the information contained on it is true on one specific date and on one specific date only. It is prepared usually at the close of the last day of the month and it answers the question: How does your company stand financially at this point in time? The balance sheet has two main sections. One section shows the assets, and the other shows the liabilities and owner's equity, which together represent claims against the assets. On the balance sheet, the total assets always equal the combined total of the liabilities and the owner's equity. It is from this fact that this particular financial statement gets its name.

A sample balance sheet is shown in Figure 9.4. Note that the assets are grouped into various subsections. These include current assets, long-term assets, fixed assets, and other assets. Current assets are cash and resources that can be converted into cash within 12 months of the date of the balance sheet. These include cash which is both money on hand and deposits in the bank, accounts receivable, inventory, temporary investments expected to be converted into cash within a year, and prepaid expenses. Long-term assets, which are also called long-term investments, are holdings that the business intends to keep for a year or longer, and

Balance Sheet		December 31, 19___
Current assets:		
Cash	$ 35,000.00	
Accounts receivable	55,000.00	
Inventory	60,000.00	
Temporary investments	3,000.00	
Prepaid expenses	2,000.00	
Total current assets		$155,000.00
Fixed assets:		
Machinery and equipment	$ 35,000.00	
Buildings	42,000.00	
Land	40,000.00	
Total fixed assets		117,000.00
Other assets:		
None		
Total other assets		0
Total assets		$272,000.00
Current liabilities:		
Accounts payable	$ 36,000.00	
Notes payable	44,000.00	
Current portion of long-term notes	4,000.00	
Interest payable	1,000.00	
Taxes payable	3,000.00	
Accrued payroll	2,000.00	
Total current liabilities		$ 90,000.00
Long-term liabilities:		
Notes payable	$ 25,000.00	
Total long-term liabilities		$ 25,000.00
Equity:		
Owner's equity	$115,000.00	
Total equity		$115,000.00
Total liabilities and equity		$272,000.00

Figure 9.4.   Sample balance sheet for the XYZ Company.

typically yield interest for dividends including stocks, bonds, and savings accounts of a special type which are not to be touched for a term greater than a year. Fixed assets include the plant and equipment. These are the resources a business owns or acquires and uses in its operations, and are not intended for resale. Finally, we have other assets. These are resources that are not listed in any of the above categories. These include intangibles such as outdated equipment which is salable for scrap and trademarks or patents.

Now let's look at the liability section. Current liabilities are debts and obligations that are payable within 12 months. Typically they include accounts payable, (amounts owed to suppliers for goods and services rendered in connection with business); notes payable (the balance of the principal due to pay off short-term debts for borrowed funds); interest payable; taxes payable; the current portion of long-term notes that are payable; and payroll (salaries and wages currently owed). Long-term liabilities are those notes or other liabilities due over a period exceeding 12 months. The amount listed is the outstanding balance less the current portion which is shown under current liabilities. Equity, which is also called net worth, is the claim of the owners on the assets of the business. In a proprietorship or partnership, equity is each of the owners' original investment plus any earnings after withdrawal. Of course, in a corporation, the owners are the shareholders. The corporation's equity is the sum of the contributions plus earnings retained after paying dividends. The breakdown of equity includes capital stock, which is the total amount invested in the business in exchange for shares of stock, and retained earnings, which is the total accumulated net income less the total accumulated dividends declared since the corporation's founding. As noted earlier, the sum of the liabilities and equity must equal that of the assets. Note how this is true in Figure 9.4.

The Income Statement

The income statement, also known as the profit and loss statement, measures costs and expenses against sales revenues over a definite period of time, such as a month or a year, to show the net profit or loss of the business for the entire period covered by the statement. A sample income statement is shown in Figure 9.5. The first entry is net sales or revenue. This is all the income coming into a business for services rendered or for goods sold. In addition to actual cash transactions, it reflects the amounts due from customers on accounts receivable, as well as equivalent cash values for merchandise or other tangible items if used as a payment. From this figure is subtracted the value of returned merchandise and allowances made for defective goods. The result is net sales. The next major column is cost of sales. Cost of sales equals the total amount of goods available less the inventory remaining at the end of the accounting period for which the income statement is constructed. Generally, service businesses such as a medical practice or a consultancy have no cost of sales. From the foregoing, the gross profit or gross margin is calculated. It is the difference between the cost of goods sold and the net sales. It is the business's profit before expenses and before taxes.

Operating expenses are the expenses of doing business. They generally fall into two major categories: (1) selling, and (2) general and administrative expenses. Selling may include such things as salaries and wages, commissions, advertising, depreciation, and so forth. General and administrative expenses include salaries and wages of owners or senior managers, employee benefits, insurance, depreciation, and similar items.

Income Statement		For the year ended December 31, 19___
Sales or revenue:	$1,040,000.00	
Less returns and allowances	5,000.00	
Net sales		$1,035,000.00
Cost of sales:		
Beginning inventory, Jan 1, 19___	250,000.00	
Merchandise purchases	500,000.00	
Cost of goods available for sale	750,000.00	
Less ending inventory, Dec 31, 19___	225,000.00	
Total cost of goods sold		525,000.00
Gross profit		$ 510,000.00
Operating expenses:		
Selling and general and administrative		
Salaries and wages	180,000.00	
Advertising	200,000.00	
Rent	10,000.00	
Utilities	5,000.00	
Other expenses	10,000.00	
Total operating expenses		405,000.00
Total operating income		$ 105,000.00
Other revenue and expenses		0
Pretax income:		$ 105,000.00
Taxes on income	50,000.00	
Income after taxes but before extraordinary gain		
or loss		$ 55,000.00
Extraordinary gain or loss		0
Net income (or loss)		$ 55,000.00

Figure 9.5.   Sample income statement for the XYZ Company.

The total operating expenses just calculated are now subtracted from the gross margin to show what the business earned before financial revenue and expenses, taxes, and extraordinary items.

Other revenue and expenses are income and expenses that are not generated by usual operations of the business. Typical items in this category are interest from investments and various financial expenses.

Total financial revenue less the expenses is now added to the total operating income. The result is pretax income. Taxes are then subtracted to develop income after taxes but before extraordinary items.

Extraordinary items are listed separately on the income statement. These are occurrences that are extremely unusual, cannot be foreseen, and are not generally expected to recur, which generate either an income or a loss. Damage due to a storm or an earthquake, for example, might be considered an extraordinary loss.

Adding in this final item results in the net income or net loss for the period of the income statement.

The balance sheet and the income statement are extremely important tools for you as a small businessperson. They are intended to represent a true and fair picture of the condition of your company for the period which they represent. However, because they are drawn up under conditions of uncertainty and some transactions are not complete at the time they are prepared, they should be used with caution and the judgment of both yourself and your accountant who may prepare them. You should bear this in mind when you use some of the financial tools presented in a later chapter.

SMALL BUSINESS FINANCIAL STATUS CHECKLIST

The following is a checklist of what every owner/manager should know on a daily, weekly, and monthly basis. It was developed by John Cotton, a retired utility executive in Albuquerque, New Mexico.[1]

Small Business Financial Status Checklist
(What an Owner-Manager Should Know)

Daily

1. Cash on hand.
2. Bank balance (keep business and personal funds separate).
3. Daily Summary of sales and cash receipts (see attached).
4. That all errors in recording collections on accounts are corrected.
5. That a record of all monies paid out, by cash or check, is maintained.

Weekly

1. Accounts Receivable (take action on slow payers).
2. Accounts Payable (take advantage of discounts).
3. Payroll (records should include name and address of employee, Social Security number, number of exemptions, date ending the pay period, hours worked, rate of pay, total wages, deductions, net pay, check number).
4. Taxes and reports to State and Federal Government (sales, withholding, social security, etc.).

Monthly

1. That all Journal entries are classified according to like elements (these should be generally accepted and standardized for both income and expense) and posted to General Ledger.
2. That a Profit and Loss Statement for the month is available within a reasonable time, usually 10 to 15 days following the close of the month. This shows the income of the business for the month, the expense incurred in obtaining the income, and the profit or loss resulting. From this, take action to eliminate loss (adjust mark-up? reduce overhead expense? pilferage? incorrect tax reporting? incorrect buying procedures? failure to take advantage of cash discounts?).
3. That a Balance Sheet accompanies the Profit and Loss Statement. This shows assets (what the business has), liabilities (what the business owes), and the investment of the owner.
4. The Bank Statement is reconciled. (That is, the owner's books are in agreement with the bank's record of the cash balance.)
5. The Petty Cash Account is in balance. (The actual cash in the Petty Cash Box plus the total of the paid-out slips that have not been charged to expense total the amount set aside as petty cash.)

[1] John Cotton, *Keeping Records in Small Business,* The Small Business Administration (1976).

6. That all Federal Tax Deposits, Withheld Income and FICA Taxes (Form 501) and State Taxes are made.

7. That Accounts Receivable are aged, i.e., 30, 60, 90 days, etc., past due. (Work all bad and slow accounts.)

8. That Inventory Control is worked to remove dead stock and order new stock. (What moves slowly? Reduce. What moves fast? Increase.)

SPECIALIZED RECORD-KEEPING SYSTEMS

Here is the list of specialized record-keeping systems compiled by staff members of the Office of Management Information and Training:

I. Systems Designed for Use in Any Retail or Service Establishment

Most of the recordkeeping systems listed below are available from local stationery stores. If a particular system is not available from your local retail store, you may contact the publisher at the address given with each entry.

Blackbourn's General Business Bookkeeping System. Blackbourn Systems, Inc., 1821 University Ave., St. Paul, Minn. 55104. Provides for accounting inventory and personal records in quick, easy entries. Lists merchandise payments, record of sales and receipts on one side of the book, and operating expenses on the opposite page. Shows monthly record of sales; monthly balance sheets, showing cash on hand, amounts owed and due. Other sections include Accounts Payable, complete with discount columns: Inventory Sheets; Employee Social Security and Income Tax Records; Sales Record by Departments; Notes Receivable and Payable; Depreciation Schedule. Includes a list of suggested allowable tax deductions.

Binex Automated Business Systems, 3102 "O" St., Sacramento, Calif. 95816. A complete computer based report system able to provide an income statement, balance sheet, cash flow analysis, vendor analysis, and a variety of other information. BINEX also produces W-2 forms, provides the data for Federal and State employment taxes, sales taxes, and provides a complete employee payroll history. Other systems include a customer follow-up for service station owners, a complete Accounts Receivable System, and address label system, and other analytic programs. Local BINEX users or franchises can assist with a complete business service. Because the family of computer programs is so complete and flexible, BINEX is able to provide to the small business owner the exact information desired at a price the business owner can afford.

Dome Simplified Monthly Bookkeeping Record, #612; Dome Simplified Weekly Bookkeeping Record #600. Price $5.45. Dome Publishing Company, Dome Building, Providence, R.I. 02903. Available in stationery stores and chain stores. Contains the following forms sufficient for recording the results of one year's business: monthly record of income and expenses; annual summary sheet of income and expenditures; weekly payroll records covering 15 employees; individual employee compensation records. Also contains general instructions, specimen filled-in monthly record of income and expenses and list of 276 expenses which are "legal deductions" for Federal Income Tax purposes. This record was designed by a CPA and fits every type and kind of business.

General Business System.   General Business Services, Inc., (51 Monroe Street, Rockville, Md. 20850). Locally authorized business counselors provide complete, easy-to-maintain, preprinted manual, one-write or computerized record-keeping systems; custom designed for sole proprietors, partnerships and corporations including a *monthly profit and loss statement* and proof of accuracy, meeting requirements of Internal Revenue Service. Service includes: review and analysis of particular recordkeeping requirements; furnishing a complete set of records; personal instructions on use and maintenance of records; analysis of records and financial statements with guidance throughout the year; preparation of Federal and State income tax returns, both business and personal, with guarantee of accuracy by professional staff at national office; tax advisory service by tax specialists for research and answers to income tax questions; monthly tax bulletin with money-saving ideas; and supplementary services by local business counselors as required. Also offers on an optional basis: accounts receivable, computerized monthly billings, collection system for delinquent accounts, and tax preparation service for employed individuals.

Greenwood's Approved Business and Income Tax Record.   The Greenwood Company, 712 South Federal St., Chicago, Ill. 60605. System No. 212. Permanently bound book $10.95; looseleaf style, with two and a half times more sheets, $19.85. Contains the following forms: daily record of cash payments for month; monthly totals; yearly balance sheet; yearly profit and loss statements. Also includes filled-in specimen sheets. Individual and weekly payroll records are also available. Write for samples.

Ideal System: General Bookkeeping and Tax Record #3611. Dymo Visual Systems, Inc., P.O. Box 1568, Augusta, Ga. 30903. $11.95. Designed for any business operating primarily on a cash basis. Sufficient forms for recording the results of one years' business.

Ideal System: Business Service Bookkeeping and Tax Record #3621. Dymo Visual Systems, Inc., P.O. Box 1568, Augusta, Ga. 30903. $11.95. Designed for every type of business primarily offering a service (as opposed to merchandise). Examples would be Acting, Advertising, Clubs, Associations and Fraternal Organizations.

Ideal System: Merchants Bookkeeping and Tax Record #3021, Dymo Visual Systems, Inc., P.O. Box 1568, Augusta, Ga. 30903. $11.95. Designed for any retailer or wholesaler, for anyone buying at one price and reselling at another.

Ideal System: Weekly Bookkeeping and Tax Record #M-2025. Dymo Visual Systems, Inc., P.O. Box 1568, Augusta, Ga. 30903. $4.95. For every business, profession, trade, farm or ranch. Can be started any time. Pages for sample entries plus 52 sheets for weekly entries.

Ideal System: Payroll Record 1 to 25 Employees #M 1812. $3.95. Payroll Record 1 to 50 Employees #M 2812, $4.95. Dymo Visual Systems, Inc., P.O. Box 1568, Augusta, Ga. 30903. Both books provide one sheet for each employee. Column headings for both hourly-wage and salaried employees, all taxes and other withholdings.

Ideal System: Payroll Record #5812, Dymo Visual Systems, Inc., P.O. Box 1568, Augusta, Ga. 30903. $9.95. For use with any bookkeeping system. Sheets for 50 employees. Can be expanded with additional sheets.

Ideal System: Double Entry Combined Journal #5831. Dymo Visual Systems, Inc., P.O. Box 1568, Augusta, Ga. 30903. $9.95. This simplified Journal Ledger, used in conjunction with General Ledger, provides for distribution of Sales, Cash, Purchases, Disbursements and Journal entries.

Ideal System: Double Entry General Ledger #5836. Dymo Visual Systems, Inc., P.O. Box 1568, Augusta, Ga. 30903. $9.95. Used in conjunction with Combined Journal, provides all necessary records for any business, trade, profession, farm, or ranch.

Ideal System: Inventory Management System #5900. Dymo Visual Systems, Inc., P.O. Box 1568, Augusta, Ga. 30903. $9.95. Shows at a glance your inventory position by item, what to order and when, its value, prime and alternate supplier.

Kolor-Key. Moore Business Forms, Inc., Post Office Box 5252, Eastmont Station, Oakland, CA 94605. May be ordered through local Moore Business Forms representatives. System includes basic business forms (sales slip, invoice, statement, voucher check, purchase order, daily cash control, duplicate deposit slip); instructions for preparations and filing of forms; recordkeeping aids. The System is adaptable to a wide range of businesses and can be easily modified as the business grows and forms need change.

Modern Merchant Simplified Bookkeeping. The Johnson Systems, 828 North Broadway, Milwaukee, Wis. 53202. $6.25. Contains the following forms sufficient for recording the results of two years' business: daily sales; expenses.

Practical Bookkeeping for the Small Business. Henry Regnery Company, 180 North Michigan Ave., Chicago, Ill. $5.95. Every aspect of business bookkeeping is presented and explained in detail: basic accounting reasoning and terms; the entire bookkeeping cycle, from the initial entry to closing the books; the correct uses of checking accounts and petty cash; making out payrolls, providing for deductions, and maintaining necessary payroll records; the IRS-approved cash-basis and accrual-basis bookkeeping methods; and how to figure State sales tax. Summary problems coordinate chapter information to facilitate complete understanding of this simple and accurate bookkeeping system.

Safeguard Business Systems, Inc. Eric R. Haymen, General Market Mgr., 470 Maryland Drive, Fort Washington, Pa. 19034. Offers a number of one-write systems designed to save time and assist the small business owner with recordkeeping activities. Systems are installed and serviced by local representatives. Also available are computerized financial reports through the business owner's accountant. All services and products are detailed in the "Business Systems Reference Manual," free on request.

Simplified Master System. Simplified Business Services, Inc., 233 East Lancaster Avenue, Ardmore, Pa. 19003. Includes personalized business consultation services and preparation of Federal and State Income Tax Returns, also Business Advisory and Tax Questioning and Answering Service. Available through authorized local distributors or directly from the company. Monthly Financial Statements prepared and forwarded by mail for businesses wishing such services. Contains the following forms sufficient for recordkeeping: current business expenses; total employee weekly salaries; cash withdrawn for personal use by the owners or partners; daily cash receipts; summary of current business expenses; payments for notes, fixtures, and equipment; summary of monthly cash payments; payments for merchandise on everything bought to resell; summary of daily sales including charge sales; work sheets; income tax information sheet; balance sheet and statement of net worth on a comparative basis; monthly and accumulated profit and loss statements; stock and bond records; record of sales of business real estate or personal property; record of income from estates; record of real estate and property expenses and income; personal deduction records; real estate mortgage records; equipment and property inventory and depreciation records; inventory; notes payable; notes receivable; insurance records. Available in different editions for individuals, partnerships, and corporations. Includes (in addition to both forms and services) a Business Advisory Service; business bulletins and instructions; business improvement ideas; management techniques and ideas and instructions on their use. See individual business listings on following pages for availability of specialized systems.

Marcoin—Busco Division—Business Management Services. MARCOIN, INC. 1924 Cliff Valley Way, N.E., Atlanta, Ga. 30329, phone: 404-325-1200. MARCOIN "Daily Record System" with User's Guide. One year supply of daily sheets with ring binders—$25.

National organization provides local and personal business counseling service. Trained counselors design and install a tailorized recordkeeping system to fit individual business needs. At owner's option, all Federal, State and local taxes are prepared by competent MARCOIN representatives for the client. The Basic Management Service includes a *monthly* departmentalized Operating (Profit) Statement, Financial Statement and written analysis of each month's operation. In addition, MARCOIN'S Professional Counselor representatives each month discuss client's own business, review problems, and offer suggestions to improve operations, sales income, employee performance, and profits.

Whitehill Systems—Division of Small Business Advisors, Inc. 48 West 48th St., New York, N.Y. 10036, phone 212-869-9642. A nationwide organization devoted to counseling small and medium sizes businesses with emphasis on recordkeeping systems, computerized programs, and tax service. The programs include complete, easy to maintain, preprinted manual, one-write or computerized recordkeeping system, custom designed to provide a monthly profit and loss statement and proof of accuracy, meeting requirements of the Internal Revenue Service. Locally authorized business counselors review and analyze recordkeeping requirements; furnish a complete set of records; provide personal instructions on use and maintenance of records; analyze records and financial statements; provide guidance throughout the year. Federal and State income tax returns are prepared with a guarantee of accuracy by professional staff at the national office. Tax specialists in national office provide tax advisory service and answer income tax questions, publish a monthly tax bulletin including up to date tax information and money-saving ideas.

II. Systems Designed for Use in Specific Retail and Service Trades

Companies listed under this heading offer services for use in specific retail and service trades. Some of these systems are provided by trade associations. For example, see "Appliance Dealers." When an entry lacks a listing, such as General Business System, Safeguard Business Systems, Inc., and others, the listing can be found under Part I, SYSTEMS DESIGNED FOR USE IN ANY RETAIL OR SERVICE ESTABLISHMENT.

Appliance Dealers

NARDA Simplified Bookkeeping System Instructions for Dealer Participants. National Appliance & Radio TV Dealers Assn., 2 North Riverside Plaza, Chicago, Ill. 60606. To get started in the program, dealer must supply the beginning balances of each balance sheet account as of the date to begin the program. If dealer is starting up at any time other than the beginning of fiscal year, the beginning balances of all Profit and Loss Statement Accounts must be supplied. From then on, the dealer will record information in the four journals used as source documents for this program. These are: Cash Receipts Journal, Sales Journal, Purchase Journal, and Cash Disbursements Journal. Program also includes a manual containing step-by-step directions with illustrated entries. A revised fee for participating in the program is .002 of the dealer's monthly volume if a member of the association. Non-members are charged an additional 25 percent per month.

General Business System for Appliance Dealers.

Safeguard Business Systems, Inc. for Appliance Dealers.

Automobile Dealers

General Business System for Automobile Dealers.

Barber Shops

Binex Automated Business Systems for Barber Shops

Dome Simplified Weekly Bookkeeping Record #600; Dome Simplified Monthly Bookkeeping Record #612.

General Business System for Barber Shops.

Ideal System: Barber Shop Bookkeeping and Tax Record.

Modern Merchant Simplified Bookkeeping for Barber Shops.

Bars and Restaurants

Easy Bookkeeping Tax System: Bars and Restaurants.   Eric J. Engelhardt. Each retails for $60. Hampton Management Inc., P.O. Box 224, Greenville L.I., N.Y. 11548. An elementary bookkeeping system which stresses daily and monthly analyses and business controls with the goal of increased profits through better business management. It is a do-it-yourself business kit, containing the following business forms and tax records: daily income and expenses; daily checks issued; summary of monthly income and expenses; the investment in fixtures, equipment, furniture; insurance, business and personal; ready-made financial reports, such as balance sheets and profit-and-loss statements; loan and note records; payroll book and record; personal tax deduction elementary tax guide, and ready-made envelopes to Internal Revenue Service; social security information; illustrated sample worksheets; monthly inventory controls; capital gains and investments; gross-profit chart; schedule of interest and dividend income; schedule of assets and depreciation records; personal instructions; preparation of Federal and State Tax returns with guarantee of accuracy—all of the above meeting the requirements of Internal Revenue Service.

Dome Simplified Weekly Bookkeeping Record #600; Dome Simplified Monthly Bookkeeping Record #612. $5.45.

General Business System for Bars and Restaurants.

Ideal Systems Tavern & Cafe Bookkeeping and Tax Record.

Modern Merchant Simplified Bookkeeping for Bars and Restaurants.

Safeguard Business Systems, Inc. for Bars and Restaurants.

Beauty Salons

Beautician Simplified Bookkeeping.   The Johnson Systems, 828 North Broadway, Milwaukee, Wis. 53202. $6.25. The Johnson Systems are simplified journals, designed especially for the small business owner. Easy to keep, the journal enables the business owner to prepare and to maintain accounting records, and prepare monthly Balance Sheet and Profit and Loss Statements. It is also an approved U.S. Federal and State Income Tax record and assists in the preparation of all quarterly and annual Tax Returns.

Dome Simplified Weekly Bookkeeping Record #600; Dome Simplified Monthly Bookkeeping Record #612. $5.45.

Easy Bookkeeping Tax System for Beauty Salons. (See Bars and Restaurants).

General Business System for Beauty Salons.

Ideal System: Beauty Shops.

Modern Merchant Simplified Bookkeeping for Beauty Salons.

NHCA Simplified Weekly Business Record. Dome Publishing Company, Inc., The Dome Bldg. Providence, R.I. 02903. Design for National Hairdressers and Cosmetologists Assoc., Inc. 3510 Olive St., St. Louis, MO. 63103.

Safeguard Business Systems, Inc. for Beauty Salons.

Simplified Master System—Beauty Shop. Simplified Business Services, Inc.

Building Contractors

Binex Automated Business Systems for Building Contractors. In addition to complete control of the financial statements listed in the general section, BINEX provides a report which allows a contractor to manage the sequence of expenses in a building project. Budgeted amounts can be compared with actual expenses as the project proceeds to help keep the costs under control. The job-cost program can be the difference between profit and loss on a project.

General Business System for Building Contractors.

Safeguard Business Systems, Inc. for Building Contractors.

Simplified Master System—Contractor. Simplified Business Services, Inc.

Practical Accounting and Cost Keeping for Contractors. Frank R. Walker Co., 5030 North Harlem Ave., Chicago, Ill. 60656. 7th ed. 1975. $12.95. Includes estimating, job organization, time keeping and cost keeping methods, bookkeeping and accounting, social security records, etc.

Practical Bookkeeping and Accounting Systems for Contractors. Frank R. Walker Co., 5030 North Harlem Ave., Chicago, Ill. 60656. Send for complete illustrated catalog with prices. A complete line of bookkeeping and accounting systems for contractors; also time sheets, payroll forms, estimate sheets, cost systems, etc.

Blackbourn Systems for Contractors' Job Analysis Pad No. 257, $2.90; Job Cost Pad No. 155, $2.90

Credit Control and Billing System

American Billing Corp. National Headquarters, 4014 North 7th St., Phoenix, AZ. 85014. A simple four-step third party system for controlling accounts receivable, that is effective and easy to run. The ABC System is a time saver which increases cash flow, helps maintain business-like relations with credit clientele, increases efficiency in billing and credit operations, and is completely controlled by each user at point of use with no communications gaps or time delays. Low price of the System ($1.50 per account for 20 accounts, or $1.10 per account for 100 accounts) consistently produces a very low, cost/effective ratio, and it can be obtained in carbon sets for typing or in continuous format for computerized operations. The System is applicable wherever credit is extended, in both retail and whole establishments. It is being successfully used in animal hospitals, appliance stores, automobile dealers, auto parts dealers, camera stores, caterers, cleaners, clinics, clothing stores, contractors, dairies, dentists, doctors, employment agencies, floor covering stores, florists, fuel oil dealers, funeral homes, furniture stores, garages, glass shops, hardware stores, home improvement shops, hospitals, hotels, interior decorators, laundries, lawyers, lumber and building supply companies, newspapers, plumbers, printers, service stations, tool rental shops, TV sales and service, sporting goods shops, universities, upholsterers, veterinarians, and wholesalers.

Safeguard Business Systems, Inc. for Credit Control and Billing.

Credit Control and Receivable Billing System

American Accounting Credit Control Systems, Inc. (Western office) 1055 East Tropicana Ave., Las Vegas, Nev. 89109 (702) 736-6660. Yearly membership $89.50. AACC is a complete self-contained credit control system which places direct control to the member. *A time saving method* that will apply overall efficiency to credit operation. The system recovers and increases cash flow while maintaining customer relations, using the *third party intervention method* which gives the businessperson an effective system to properly extend credit, billing and follow-up procedure, generates prompt payment of accounts receivable. Includes a collection system proven throughout the collection industry without excessive commissions or charges. Letter forms are provided on an unlimited basis to members throughout the year. American Accounting guarantees the system. This fully tax deductible system is designed for every type of business in existence today. Among our members are doctors, dentists, vets, chiropractors, plumbers, electricians, printers, drug stores, appliance stores, TV repair-sales, builder-contractors, hardware, florists, auto repair, service stations, carpet and drapery stores, photography studios, grocery, hotel-motels, furniture stores, and many other businesses.

Mail inquiries for Eastern and Central time zones should go to P.O. Box 17149, Nashville, Tenn. All States in the Mountain and Pacific time zones should forward mail to P.O. Box 11311, Las Vegas, Nev. 89111.

Dairy Farm

General Business System for Dairy Farm.

Johnson Systems, The. 828 North Broadway, Milwaukee, WI. $6.25. All necessary records for two years' business.

Safeguard Business Systems, Inc. for Dairy Farm.

Simplified Master System for Dairy Farm. Simplified Business Services, Inc.

Drug Stores

Easy Bookkeeping Tax System for Drug Stores. (See Bars and Restaurants.)

General Business System for Drug Stores.

Safeguard Business Systems, Inc. for Drug Stores.

Blackbourn Systems for Drug Stores. $7. (No. 170P)

Dry Cleaner, Tailor and Dyers

Easy Bookkeeping Tax System: Cleaners and Dyers. For general information see entry under Bars and Restaurants.

General Master Systems: Dry Cleaner or Tailor.

Simplified Master System for Dry Cleaner or Tailor. Simplified Business Services, Inc.

Farm and Ranch

Blackbourn Systems for Farmers and Ranchers. $9 (No. 715X).

Easy Bookkeeping Tax System: Farm and Ranch. For general information, see entry under Bars and Restaurants.

Johnson Systems for Farm & Ranch. See entry under Beauty Salons.

Safeguard Business Systems, Inc. for Farm and Ranch.

Florists

Guide to the FTDA Uniform Accounting System. Florists' Transworld Delivery Association, 29200 Northwestern Hwy., P.O. Box 2227, Southfield, MI 48037. A guide to simplified recordkeeping with sample forms. Available to members only.

Dome Simplified Weekly Bookkeeping Record #600; Dome Simplified Monthly Bookkeeping Record #612.

Easy Bookkeeping Tax System for Florists. See entry under Bars and Restaurants.

General Business System for Florists.

Safeguard Business Systems, Inc. for Florists.

Funeral Director

General Business System for Funeral Director.

Safeguard Business Systems, Inc. for Funeral Director.

Simplified Master Systems: Funeral Director. Simplified Business Services, Inc.

Furniture Stores

NRFA Uniform Accounting System. National Home Furnishings Association, 405 Merchandise Mart, Chicago, Ill. 60654. $75 to members; $112.50 to nonmembers. Contains the following forms sufficient for recording the results of one years' business: cash disbursements journal; cash receipts and sales journal; general journal; special analysis forms designed for specific secondary records. Also a "Guide to the System," containing step-by-step directions, with illustrated entries.

Safeguard Business Systems, Inc. for Furniture Stores.

Garage or Auto Repair

Dome Simplified Weekly Bookkeeping Record #600; Dome Simplified Monthly Bookkeeping Record #612.

General Business System for Garage or Auto Repair.

Safeguard Business Systems, Inc. for Garage or Auto Repair.

Simplified Master Systems: Garage or Auto Repair. Simplified Business Services.

Gift Shops

General Business Systems for Gift Shops.

Safeguard Business Systems, Inc. for Gift Shops.

Grocery and Meat Stores

Blackbourn Systems for Grocery and Market Bkkpg. No. 160 X, $16.75; No. 160P, $7.

General Business Systems for Grocery and Meat Stores.

Modern Merchant Simplified Bookkeeping. The Johnson Systems, 828 North Broadway, Milwaukee, Wis. 53202. $4.94. Contains forms sufficient for recording results of two years' business.

Safeguard Business Systems, Inc. for Grocery and Meat Stores.

Hardware Stores

Blackbourn Systems for Hardlines Bkkpg. No. 130P, $7.

General Business System for Hardware Stores.

NRHA. Better Business Records. National Retail Hardware Association, 964 North Pennsylvania St., Indianapolis, Ind. 46204. Price list available from Association; sale confined to members of State or National Associations. Contains the following forms: Daily record: expense distribution—cost of doing business; invoice and margin register, monthly and annual summary; profit-and-loss and financial statements; profit planning for business control forms. Also available: duplicate customers' ledger system and ledger sheets; sales books; envelopes; receipt books; order books; etc.; and *How To Keep Books Without Being a Bookkeeper,* $2, an instruction manual covering recommended accounting system for retail hardware stores.

NRHA Departmental Accounting System. National Retail Hardware Association, 964 North Pennsylvania St., Indianapolis, Ind. 46204. Price list available from Association. Sale confined to members of State or National Associations. Contains the following: System setup for eight departments: daily record; expense distribution; invoice and accounts payable record; monthly summary; monthly estimated profit and loss; year-end profit and loss and financial statements; profit planning and control sheets; instruction manual—*How To Keep Books Departmentally,* $2—instruction manual on departmental system.

Safeguard Business Systems, Inc. for Hardware Stores.

Hotels

Blackbourn Systems for Hotel Guest Register, No. 703X. $15; Hotel Guest Register No. 703P. $6.25.

Simplified Master Systems for Hotels. Simplified Business Services, Inc.

Uniform System of Accounts for Hotels. Hotel Association of New York City, Inc., 141 West 51st St., New York, N.Y. 10019. 1977. $10. A 128-page book containing the basic information required in establishing an accounting system in any hotel, large or small. The book contains a format for preparing a balance sheet and profit and loss statement and detailed explanations for recording financial transactions within the framework of these statements. Using the system will enable a hotel's operation to be compared with one of a similar size also using the system.

Jewelers and Watchmakers

General Business Systems for Jewelers and Watchmakers.

Safeguard Business Systems, Inc. for Jewelers and Watchmakers.

Modern Merchant Simplified Bookkeeping for Jewelers and Watchmakers. $6.35.

Laundries

Easy Bookkeeping Tax System for Dry Cleaning and Coin-Op Laundries.

General Business System for Laundries.

Safeguard Business Systems, Inc. for Laundries.

Liquor Package Stores

Blackbourn Bookkeeping Systems for Liquor Store No. 91P. $5.75.

General Business System for Liquor Package Stores.

Safeguard Business Systems, Inc. for Liquor Package Stores.

Simplified Master Systems. Simplified Business Services, Inc.

Men's Clothing and Furnishing Stores

Inventory System: Store Supply Catalog pp. 72–107. National Clothier Corp., 1727 W. Devon, Chicago, Ill. 60660. 1977. Minimum order $10. Prices subject to change. Contains monitor stock status with systems designed for specific items; control various departments with the aid of systems and publications covering different aspects of retail operations; financial and accounting procedures compiled by the financial and operations group of MRA and presented in manual form; operating experiences collected from nationwide sources and presented in our annual business survey.

General Business System for Men's Clothing and Furnishing Stores.

Safeguard Business Systems, Inc. for Men's Clothing and Furnishing Stores.

Motels and Motor Hotels

An Account Book for Small Tourist and Resort Businesses. No. R-604. Robert W. McIntosh, 1953. 48 pp. Michigan State University, Tourist and Resort Service. $1. A simplified account book for the use of motel operators. Instructions for use included. This book may be obtained from the Bulletin Office, P.O. Box 231, East Lansing, Mich. 48824. Use number R-604 when ordering.

Blackbourn Motel & Resort Bookkeeping No. 450P. $7.

General Business Systems for Motels and Motor Hotels.

Safeguard Business Systems, Inc. for Motels and Motor Hotels.

Simplified Master Systems—Motels. Simplified Business Services, Inc.

Music Stores

NAMM Standard Accounting Manual for Music Stores. National Association of Music Merchants, Inc., 35 East Wacker Dr., Chicago, Ill. 60601. $35 postpaid. The aim of this manual is flexibility. The owner-manager may choose the accounts needed; use whichever forms desired; prepare reports and statements as often and as detailed as desired, and adopt segments of this system when convenient. Contains the following illustrations: general ledger; cash receipts journal; cash disbursements journal; accounts receivable ledger; accounts payable ledger; payroll journal; sales journal; purchase journal; property and equipment ledger; insurance register; general journal; and "railroaded" general ledger accounts.

General Business System for Music Stores.

Safeguard Business Systems, Inc. for Music Stores.

Nursing Homes

Blackbourn Nursing Homes & Hospitals. Book No. 270X. $16.75.

Safeguard Business Systems, Inc. for Nursing Homes.

Simplified Master Systems—Nursing Homes. Simplified Business Services, Inc.

General Business System for Nursing Homes.

Office Supply and Stationery Stores

General Business System for Office Supply and Stationery Stores.

Safeguard Business Systems, Inc. for Office Supply and Stationery Stores.

Pest Control

Uniform Accounting Manual for Pest Control. National Pest Control Association. 8150 Leesburg Pike, Vienna, Va. 22180. 1965. 32 pp. $2.50 to members; $4 to non-members. Complete with chart of accounts, descriptions of the accounts by four size classifications.

Basic Bookkeeping System for Pest Control. National Pest Control Association, 8150 Leesburg Pike, Vienna, Va. 22180. 316—8½ × 11 pre-printed loose leaf pages including income sheets, expense sheets, payroll records, general journal sheets, and profit and loss statements. Designed for the small firm (1–5 employees). Price $15 to members; $25 to non-members.

General Business System for Pest Control.

Safeguard Business Systems, Inc. for Pest Control.

Real Estate Business

Binex Automated Business System. Binex provides a report which can be used by a realtor to control rental properties which the realtor handles for others. This report tracks expenses, revenues, and computes the payment due the owner.

Blackbourn Real Estate Bookkeeping. No. 100X. $16.75

General Business System for Real Estate Business.

Ideal System: Real Estate Business Bookkeeping and Tax Record #3311. Dymo Visual Systems, Inc., P.O. Box 1568, Augusta, Ga. 30903. $11.95. Designed for Agents and Brokers with special columns for Sales, Sales Commission, Rental Commission, Insurance Commission, etc.

Income Property. The Johnson Systems, 828 North Broadway, Milwaukee, Wis. 53202. Contains the following forms sufficient for recording the results of two years' business: tenants' records; disbursements and expenses.

Safeguard Business Systems, Inc. for Real Estate Business.

Resorts and Tourist Business

Account Book for Small Tourist and Resort Business. See listing under Motels and Motor Hotels.

Blackbourn Motel and Resort Bookkeeping No. 450P. $7.

General Business System for Resorts and Tourist Business.

Safeguard Business Systems, Inc. for Resorts and Tourist Business.

Restaurants and Taverns (see also Bars and Restaurants)

Cafe and Restaurant Record. The Greenwood Company, 712 South Federal St., Chicago, Ill. 60605. Price available from Publisher. Contains the following forms: daily purchase and expenses for months; record of daily sales; record of daily cash receipts; record of daily payments.

Restaurant Simplified Bookkeeping. The Johnson Systems, 828 North Broadway, Milwaukee, Wis. 53202. $4.95. Contains the following forms sufficient for recording the results of two years' business: daily sales; daily food purchases; general overhead expense.

Simplified Master Systems—Restaurants. Simplified Business Services, Inc.

Tavern and Buffet Record. The Greenwood Company, 712 South Federal St., Chicago, Ill. 60605. Form 70A. Price available from publisher. Contains the following forms: daily purchases and expenses for month; record of daily sales; record of daily cash receipts; record of daily payments.

Uniform Systems of Accounts for Restaurants. National Restaurant Association. One IBM Plaza, Suite 2600, Chicago, Ill. 60611. A manual containing a system for all classifications of restaurants with detailed explanation of accounts and procedures.

Retail Stores and Service Firms

Easy Bookkeeping Tax System: General Retail and Service Firm. For general information, see entry under Bars and Restaurants.

General Business System for Retail Stores and Service Firms.

Safeguard Business System, Inc. for Retail Stores and Service Firms.

Service Stations and Garages

Binex Automated Business Systems for Service Stations and Garages. A complete computer prepared analysis of a service station is available from the local BINEX user or franchise. The report includes a monthly and year-to-date analysis of income and expenses, a complete statement of financial position, control of inventory, comparison with industry averages, complete payroll history including W-2 forms. All tax reports for Federal and State employment taxes and State sales taxes can be prepared. In addition, the BINEX customer follow-up system mails post cards to customers thanking them for coming in to have their car serviced or reminding them to do so. The combination of these two systems gives a service station owner the best information available to run his business.

Easy Bookkeeping Tax System: Service Stations. For general information, see entry under Bars and Restaurants.

Garage and Gas Station Record. The Greenwood Company, 210 South Federal St., Chicago, Ill. 60605. Form 50. Price available from publisher. Contains the following forms: daily purchases and expenses for month; record of daily sales; record of daily cash receipts; record of daily payments.

Safeguard Business Systems, Inc. for Service Stations and Garages.

Simplified Master Systems—Service Station. Simplified Business Services, Inc.

Service Station Simplified Bookkeeping. The Johnson Systems, 828 North Broadway, Milwaukee, Wis. 53202. $4.95. Contains daily sales and expense forms sufficient for recording the results of two years' business.

Dome Simplified Monthly Bookkeeping Record, #612, and Dome Simplified Weekly Bookkeeping Record #600 for Service Stations and Garages. $5.45.

Shoe Repair Shops

Shoe Service Shop Bookkeeping System. Shoe Service Institute of America, 222 West Adams St., Chicago, Ill. 60606. $2. Contains the following forms sufficient for recording the results of one years' business: daily sales, purchases of materials and merchandise; operating expenses; monthly profit-and-loss statements; purchase of equipment and fixtures. Instructions included.

Safeguard Business Systems, Inc. for Shoe Repair Shops.

General Business System for Shoe Repair Shops.

Smaller Stores

Merchandise Control & Budgeting (M44566). National Retail Merchants Association, 100 West 31st St., New York, N.Y. 10001. $7.25/non-members $10.50. Explains the fundamentals of merchandise control planning and budgeting. Includes formulas to maintain proper ratios between stocks and customer demand. Illustrated with all necessary forms for maintaining profitable inventories and shows how to figure open-to-buy.

Retail Accounting Manual—Revised (C13276). National Retail Merchants Association, 100 West 31st St., New York, N.Y. 10001. 1976. $25.75/non-members $40.75. A new publication with an updated chart of accounts flexible enough to accommodate the needs of multi-unit companies as well as individual single unit retail stores. In addition to serving the industry as a guide in the area of expense accounting and reporting, the revised manual places emphasis on merchandise accounting and management reporting. Separate chapters on the determination of gross margin, return on investment, and workroom accounting is covered in detail. A looseleaf reference book of 196 pages.

Retail Inventory Method Made Practical (C14370). National Retail Merchants Association, 100 West 31st St., New York, N.Y. 10001. 1971. $4.75/non-members $6.75. Presents the fundamental operation involved in establishing and maintaining accurate inventories. Chapters clearly explain what the Retail Method of Inventory is and how it differs from the cost method, its advantages and disadvantages. Includes sample forms for recording merchandise transfers, sales, price changes, departmental merchandise statements, open-to-buy and many more. Soft cover, 70 pages.

Blackbourn Smaller Varied Business Bookkeeping No. 19X. $13.25.

Safeguard Business Systems, Inc. for Smaller Stores.

General Business Systems for Smaller Stores.

Sporting Goods Dealers

NSGA Annual Cost of Doing Business Survey. $10. National Sporting Goods Association, 717 North Michigan Ave., Chicago, Ill. 60611. A 40-page compilation of sales, inventory and operating ratios for a variety of sporting goods retailers, and institutional team distributors. Most data includes average, median and hi-lo ratios, with separate compilations based on volume, size of outlets, regional locations, and makeup of retailers (pure retail or combination of retail-and-team). Selected composite balance sheet ratios are included.

General Business System for Sporting Goods Dealers.

Safeguard Business Systems, Inc. for Sporting Goods Dealers.

Television and Radio

General Business System for Television and Radio.

Safeguard Business System, Inc. for Television and Radio.

Television-Radio Sales & Service Record.   The Johnson Systems, 828 North Broadway, Milwaukee, Wis. 53202. $4.95. Contains space and forms to record the following information sufficient to record two years' business: sales of new and used television and radio sets; daily charges of servicing and repairing of television and radio sets; merchandise purchases; repair parts; general overhead expenses.

Truckers and Motor Carriers

Blackbourn Truckers' Bookkeeping No. 350X. $16.75.

General Business System for Truckers and Motor Carriers.

Safeguard Business Systems, Inc. for Truckers and Motor Carriers.

Simplified Master Systems—Trucking. Simplified Business Services, Inc.

SOURCES OF ADDITIONAL INFORMATION

Financial Recordkeeping for Small Stores, Small Business Management Series No. 32, by Robert C. Ragan, published by the Small Business Administration, Washington, D.C. 20402.

Keeping Record in Small Business, Small Marketers Aids No. 155, by John Cotton, published by the Small Business Administration, Washington, D.C. 20402.

Record Keeping Systems Small Stores and Service Trade, Small Business Bibliography No. 15, by Nathan H. Olshan and Office of Management Information and Training staff, SBA, published by the Small Business Administration, Washington, D.C. 20402.

10

Personnel Management

Personnel management is the management of people, and people, you will find, are the most important resource in your business. Chapter 5 covered how to find and hire new personnel. This chapter discusses developing job descriptions, wage scales, and compensation plans, doing performance appraisal and counseling your employees, dealing with disciplinary problems, motivating employees, terminating employees, and using temporary help services. Finally, it covers the major labor laws which affect your business.

PERFORMING A JOB ANALYSIS AND DEVELOPING JOB DESCRIPTIONS

Good job descriptions will assist you in hiring, in establishing wage scales and compensation, in constructing your performance appraisal, and in hiring temporary help services. In fact, good job descriptions are the basis of most actions that you must take in personnel management. The job description itself is based on a good prior job analysis. Job analysis is really a methodology for discovering the most important factors concerning a job in your company. The analysis answers the four major questions for the job description and job specification:

1. What physical and/or mental tasks does the worker perform? These may include cleaning, fabricating, planning, judging, managing, and numerous other functions.
2. How does the worker do the job—what methods are used and what equipment or machinery, if any, is involved? For example, does the job require use of a lathe, a cash register, a computer, and if a lathe is used, for what purpose is it used?
3. Why is the job done? In this part of the analysis, you should develop a short explanation of the objective of the job and how it relates to other jobs that are done in your company. Here you may indicate that your copywriter writes copy which is used in space and direct mail advertisements.
4. What qualifications are needed to perform this job? List knowledge, skills, training, personal characteristics, and so forth that are required of the worker. For example, a sales engineer may need a bachelor's degree in engineering, ability to get along with people, a pleasing personality, persuasiveness, and energy.

In summary, the job analysis provides a complete picture of the job that you want performed, including what the worker does, how he does it, his job's relationship to other jobs that must be performed, and knowledge, skills, training, and education that the worker must have in order to do the job.

Conducting a job analysis is not difficult. The easiest way is simply to sit down and think through the various aspects of the job as mentioned previously. If you already have an employee in the job and you wish to redefine it, you may speak with him or her and his or her supervisor. If not, you could talk with people in other companies who have similar jobs. You could also ask the employee or supervisor to list the duties and responsibilities and qualifications he or she feels are important in performing the job. You can then modify this information as appropriate. To assist you in doing this, use the job analysis outline shown in Figure 10.1. A completed example of this form is shown in Figure 10.2

Job title_____ Reporting to_____

What tasks will the employee perform?_____

_____

_____

_____

How will the employee accomplish the work?_____

_____

_____

_____

Why will this job be done?_____

_____

_____

_____

Figure 10.1. Job analysis form.

What qualifications are needed to perform this work?_____

_____

_____

_____

With whom inside and outside the organization will this employee interface?_____

_____

_____

_____

Special problems_____

_____

_____

Figure 10.1. (Continued)

Job title Buyer, Office Supplies _____   Reporting to Chief Buyer _____

What tasks will the employee perform? 1. Maintain a complete file of vendors _____

for office supplies. 2. Place purchase orders for office supplies. 3. Meet _____

with office supplies salespersons. Disseminate information about new types of supplies _____

that are available. 4. Negotiate lowest prices possible for office supplies bought. _____

How will the employee accomplish the work? Employee will have private office _____

Figure 10.2.   Completed job analysis form.

and share secretary with two other buyers. Appointments and proposals will be

solicited by mail and/or telephone. Small budget will be available for purchase

of basic directories of office supply vendors and manufacturers.

Why will this job be done? Office supplies are needed to support

$20-million-a-year engineering consultant company.

What qualifications are needed to perform this work? Prior experience

as a buyer of office supplies. Knowledge of accounting procedures. Persuasiveness

and good negotiating abilities.

With whom inside and outside the organization will this employee interface?

Inside the organization, this employee will interface with all functional and

staff division chiefs. Outside the organization, with sales representatives of

the various office supply companies.

Special problems None

Figure 10.2.   (Continued)

Now that you have completed the job analysis, you have the material necessary to develop a job description and job specification. There is a small distinction between job descriptions and job specifications. A job description is part of the job analysis which describes the responsibilities of the job, how the job is done, and how it ties in with other jobs in your business. The job specification part, which is used directly in your recruiting efforts, is that part of the analysis which describes those qualifications required of someone in order to do the job properly. Therefore, to prepare a job description, simply summarize the important facts about the job which you have analyzed. Write down in a clear, concise way the important information, including a job title that is descriptive of the position, a brief summary of the work to be performed, major responsibilities of the job including knowledge of equipment that may be necessary, decision making, and scheduling, minor job duties that are performed only occasionally, and the relationship of the job to other positions in your firm, including whom the employee would supervise and to whom the employee would report. To assist you with this, use the outline for writing a job description contained in Figure 10.3. An example of this use is shown in Figure 10.4.

Title _____

Supervisor _____

Duties _____

_____

_____

Background requirements _____

_____

_____

Personal requirements _____

_____

_____

_____

Figure 10.3. Outline for writing a job description.

Title <u>Office Supplies Buyer</u>

Supervisor <u>Chief Buyer</u>

Duties <u>Purchase office supplies for $20-million engineering consultant company.</u>

<u>Involves maintaining file of sources, contacting and meeting with salespeople</u>

<u>representing office supply companies, negotiating prices, and placing orders</u>

<u>for office supplies.</u>

Background requirements <u>Prior experience as a buyer of office supplies</u>

<u>and knowledge of accounting procedures.</u>

Personal requirements <u>Should be a persuasive person and a good</u>

<u>negotiator.</u>

Figure 10.4.   Completed outline for writing a job description.

Figure 5.2 in Chapter 5 shows an outline for writing a job specification. This is especially necessary for your hiring and recruiting effort. Figure 5.3 shows a simple job specification form completed.

WAGE SCALES AND COMPENSATION

How much to pay your employee for a particular job is very important. Unfortunately, the question has no simple answer. If you pay too little, your better employees will leave to do the same work elsewhere or to work on their own, and only the poorer, less motivated, and less able employees will remain to work for you for lower pay. On the other hand, overpaying has a drawback. You can be less competitive in the price you charge for the product or the service which you are offering.

Also, an important consideration is the fact that compensation is measured in more than mere dollars, and many compensation programs fail because the business does not recognize this as a fact. Back in the 1880s, Congress, in a serious cost reduction effort, failed to appropriate money for the salaries of army officers. Thus, army officers received no compensation whatsoever for such services as they rendered, and they were able to support their families at the subsistence level only because they were granted government quarters and were able to eat at government mess facilities. Yet, despite this drastic effort, there were no mass resignations. Clearly, the compensation that was received was other than in dollars, for these officers continued to work without pay for almost two years.

Compensation obviously does consist of elements other than salary. These include working environment, terms of employment, status, and fringe benefits. We'll come back to salary, but, because of their importance, let's look at these other elements first.

Working Environment

Working environment is an extremely important element of compensation. It encompasses a wide range of factors. These include working conditions, the facilities in which your workers work, and the *esprit de corps* that you as the president of a company are able to develop in the group of employees that work for you.

Terms of Employment

Terms of employment also include many different aspects, both tangible and intangible. These can include the security that your company offers, the hours of work, the number of holidays and vacation days and their length, sick days, and many similar items.

Status

Status may come from your company and its relative position in the industry as well as from the title which you give the job that the employee holds. If yours is a small company, it may at first appear unlikely that you have anything to offer in the way of status. However, imaginative titles for the various jobs that people do for you as employees can create status. In fact, it can be a major portion of the compensation which you pay to your employees.

Fringe Benefits

There are basically two types of fringe benefits. There are those that everyone who works for you will receive and those that are reserved for key personnel. Certain fringe benefits have become very common with many companies, even small ones. These include life insurance policies, retirement plans, medical and hospital insurance, and the like. In many cases such supplements to salary will be expected. If you are trying to recruit someone who already has one or more of these benefits at his or her current place of employment, you will find that it will be difficult to hire this person if you cannot duplicate the benefits offered. Fringe benefits for key personnel include stock options, use of a car, club memberships, and so on. These fringe benefits for key personnel can be even larger than the salary element of compensation.

Bonuses

Bonuses are an addition to the normal salary. For maximum benefit to you, they should be tied in some way to the performance of the individual as well as to the performance of your company. You must be very careful with bonuses. Used correctly, a bonus element of compensation can help motivate maximum performance. Used incorrectly, it can cause frustration and hurt your personnel policies and the performance of your company.

The Salary Component of Compensation

In determining the salary component, consider the following principles:

1. Higher pay should be given for work requiring more knowledge, skill, or physical exertion.
2. Pay should be competitive with that given for similar work in other companies.
3. Total earnings should reflect the employee's contribution to the performance of your company.
4. So far as possible, pay scales should be known to all employees.
5. Overqualified employees should not be paid more or at least not very much more than fully qualified employees for the same position and same work.
6. You should strive to be as fair as possible in the application of these basic principles of salary compensation, as well as in compensation in general for your employees.

DEVELOPING A COMPENSATION PACKAGE

The first step in developing a total compensation package for a position is to document all the nonsalary elements including insurance, unique things about your company, the title you have given the job, and others. You should also endeavor to find out what compensation other firms are paying for similar work. You can obtain such data from professional organizations and associations, industrial organizations, your local chamber of commerce, the U.S. Bureau of Labor Statistics, independent management consultants, and executive recruiters. Once you have gotten these data, you can list them on a form such as that shown in Figure 10.5. You should endeavor to quantify in dollars those factors that are quantifiable. Naturally, some intangibles cannot be quantified, such as stability of employment, the reputation of your company in the industry, or a job title. But you should document these factors as shown in Figure 10.6. The final result of this work should be a range of quantitative compensation figures along with a list of important intangible variables that you are offering.

You should develop the compensation package for every position in your organization. Do not finalize any until all have been analyzed. In this way, you will insure that the system that you're putting together for your firm will be cohesive, make sense, and be fair to all. One way of making sure that the various positions in your company do hang together is to categorize them: professional, skilled worker, and unskilled worker. Then, within these general groupings, a point

Job title

Company	Salary	Bonus	Life Insurance	Health insurance	Retirement plan	Other Quantitative	Total Quantitative	Non-quantifiable

Figure 10.5. Form for compensation comparisons.

Job title

Company	Salary	Bonus	Life Insurance	Health Insurance	Retirement Plan	Other Quantitative	Total Quantitative	Non-quantifiable
A	$18–30 K	—	$1,000	$1,000	$1,500	2 weeks vacation (.7–1.1 K)	$22.2–34.6 K	Very stable employment situation
B	$17–32 K	—	$1,000	$1,000	$1,500	Auto = $2 K 2 weeks vacation (.7–1.2 K)	$21.2–38.7 K	Frequent layoffs and turnover
C	$16–26 K	—	$1,000	$1,000	$1,500	2 weeks vacation (.6–1 K)	$20.1–30.5 K	Best reputation in industry
D	$17–30 K	5–10% of base salary	$1,000	$1,000	$2,000	Savings plan: 5% of salary 2 weeks vacation (.7–1.1 K)	$23.4–39.6 K	Company will fund additional schooling
E	$18–25 K	.5–1.0 K	$1,000	$1,000	$2,000	2 weeks vacation (.7–1 K)	$23.2–31 K	Traditionally rapid promotion
F	$18–30 K	—	$1,000	$1,000	$1,000	2 weeks vacation (.7–1 K)	$21.7–34 K	Outstanding location
Survey of 200 firms in industry	$15–36 K	80 unknown	Unknown	Unknown	Unknown	Unknown	$15–36 K	—

Figure 10.6. Completed form for compensation comparisons.

system can be used to establish these relationships using the following four steps:

1. *Select the relevant factors.* In this case, you select factors which are applicable to your particular situation, including your objectives, type of work being performed, and other factors. Each factor should represent a characteristic of the work which you feel is significant. In rating professional individuals for your company, you may consider education, experience, leadership ability required, level of responsibility, and number of individuals supervised.

2. *Define the factors by points.* Whatever factors you have established must now be defined by points. One way of doing this is to use 100 points as maximum and break down various levels of achievement for whatever factors you are analyzing. If you are analyzing the education factor, a doctorate may be worth 100 points; a master's degree required, 75 points; bachelor's degree required, 50 points; or no degree required for the position, 25 points. Other factors might be point-defined as shown in Figure 10.7.

3. *Weight the factors.* After you have defined the number of points for each factor, you must weight them to help you decide on the relative importance of each of these factors for performing the work. No matter how many factors are

Note: These point definitions are for examples only. You must break down whatever factors you are analyzing to assign points for various levels of achievement in the same way, but the point assignment break down you use depends on your particular situation.

EDUCATION	Points	LEADERSHIP ABILITY	Points
No degree required	25	No leadership ability required	25
Bachelor's Degree requrired	50	Little leadership ability re'd	50
Master's Degree required	75	Some leadership ability req'd	75
Doctor's Degree required	100	Much leadership ability req'd	100

EXPERIENCE		LEVEL OF JOB RESPONSIBILITY	
Less than 5 years req'd	25	Responsible for less than $250,000	25
Less than 10 years req'd	50	Responsible for less than $500,000	50
Less than 20 years req'd	75	Responsible for less than $ 1 mil	75
20 or more years req'd	100	Responsible for $1 mil or more	100

TECHNICAL ABILITY		NUMBER OF INDIVIDUAL SUPERVISED	
No technical ability req'd	25	No personnel supervised	25
Little technical ability req'd	50	1-50 personnel supervised	50
Some technical ability req'd	75	51-100 personnel supervised	75
Much technical ability req'd	100	More than 100 personnel supervised	100

Figure 10.7. Point method for salary/compensation evaluation: point definitions.

considered or their relative weighting by percentage, the total number must equal 100%. Therefore, with the factors described previously, you might decide on a weighting for a specific professional job as follows:

Education required	5%
Experience required	25%
Leadership ability required	30%
Level of responsibility for the job	30%
Number of people supervised	10%
Total	100%

4. *Perform the necessary calculations.* The final step necessary is to make calculations for each position. You do this by reviewing the job specifications that you developed earlier, applying points for each factor, and multiplying the number of points by the factor weighting. Let's look at an example here using the weighting we have established for the factors in item 3 above. If we have specified a bachelor's degree, it is worth 50 points (Figure 10.7). In the weighting given in item 3 above, education is 5%. Therefore, 50 points times 5% is 2.5 points. If the experience required is less than five years, Figure 10.7 gives us 20 points. Again, referring above to our weighting, we see that experience is worth 25%, so 20 points times 25% is 5 points. We will say that little leadership ability is required for this job. This, according to Figure 10.7, is worth 50 points. Fifty points times the 30% weighting found above equals 15 points. The level of job responsibility is less than $1 million per year. Figure 10.7 says this is 25 points. The weighting for this is 30%, which times the 25 points equals 6 points. Finally, we will assume that this position is nonsupervisory. According to Figure 10.7, no individuals supervised equals 20 points and in our weighting this is 10%. So, the result is 2 points. The grand total of the above is:

$$
\begin{array}{r}
2.5 \\
5.0 \\
15.0 \\
6.0 \\
\underline{2.0} \\
30.5 \text{ points}
\end{array}
$$

This would therefore be considered a 30.5-point professional position. This total is recorded and will be compared with totals for other positions that you calculate. You can make final adjustments among the compensation packages based on these point differences.

HOW TO ADMINISTER YOUR COMPENSATION SYSTEM

If you administer your compensation system in a fair and effective way, you will obtain and keep good employees. To do this, consider the following as reasons to increase salary:

1. Merit increases to recognize performance and contribution
2. Tenure increases for time spent working at your company
3. Increases for market and economic conditions depending upon supply and demand for certain types of employees
4. Promotion increases for employees assigned to higher level jobs

To allow for these increases, a planned and scheduled review should be accomplished for all your employees, generally on a yearly basis, either all at one time or on anniversary of hire. This annual review should consider all of these factors regarding a pay and salary increase. However, salary increases should not be automatic or tied to a cost of living benefit. Further, merit increases should not be made unless performance actually warrants it. To do otherwise will demotivate your employees for high performance and eventually make the prices that you must charge for your goods or services noncompetitive.

PERFORMANCE APPRAISAL AND COUNSELING

Performance appraisal and counseling are essential for your company, and a well-designed performance appraisal system will enable you to do the following:

1. Select individuals for promotion fairly and wisely
2. Determine merit increases fairly
3. Identify individual needs for special training
4. Provide an opportunity for a complete discussion of performance, career goals, progress, organizational policies, and other areas of interest to you and your employees
5. Obtain feedback from your employees

Performance appraisal systems can be rather informal, especially for the small company. However, they should always be documented, both for reference in the future and to enable you to compare different employees and their performance.

There are seven basic methods for performance appraisal. These are:

1. Graphic rating scale
2. Forced distribution
3. Forced choice
4. Critical incidents
5. Ranking
6. Essay appraisals
7. Management by objectives

The Graphic Rating Scale

The graphic rating scale is a scale which can be either numerical or descriptive in which an individual is rated on a variety of attributes which you feel are important for the particular job. Because it can be numerical, the method allows for a total score and therefore easy comparison if you have large numbers of personnel. Since each factor has a score, it is easy to identify those areas in which an individual may be doing well or may need to improve. An example of a graphic rating scale is shown in Figure 10.8.

Forced Distribution

In the forced distribution method, whoever is doing the performance appraisal must rate a certain number of individuals and place each number into a different

III. PERFORMANCE FACTORS *Specific example of performance required*	NOT OBSERVED OR NOT RELEVANT	FAR* BELOW STANDARD	BELOW* STANDARD	MEETS STANDARD	ABOVE* STANDARD	WELL* ABOVE STANDARD
1. JOB KNOWLEDGE *(Depth, currency, breadth)*	O	☐	☐	☐	☐	☐
2. JUDGMENT AND DECISIONS *(Consistent, accurate, effective)*	O	☐	☐	☐	☐	☐
3. PLAN AND ORGANIZE WORK *(Timely, creative)*	O	☐	☐	☐	☐	☐
4. MANAGEMENT OF RESOURCES *(Manpower and material)*	O	☐	☐	☐	☐	☐
5. LEADERSHIP *(Initiative, accept responsibility)*	O	☐	☐	☐	☐	☐
6. ADAPTABILITY TO STRESS *(Stable, flexible, dependable)*	O	☐	☐	☐	☐	☐
7. ORAL COMMUNICATION *(Clear, concise, confident)*	O	☐	☐	☐	☐	☐
8. WRITTEN COMMUNICATION *(Clear, concise, organized)*	O	☐	☐	☐	☐	☐
9. PROFESSIONAL QUALITIES *(Attitude, dress, cooperation, bearing)*	O	☐	☐	☐	☐	☐
10. HUMAN RELATIONS *(Equal opportunity participation, sensitivity)*		☐	☐	☐	☐	☐

Figure 10.8. Example of the graphic rating scale.

percentage category—for example, upper 25%, middle 50%, lower 25%—according to some criteria. The forced distribution scale is also used when there are large numbers of people to be rated. One advantage of the forced distribution system over the graphic rating scale by itself is that it eliminates the danger that the rater will be either too severe or too lenient, since he or she must place everyone in one category or another. However, forced distribution also has a major disadvantage in that it assumes that all groups have identical percentages of poor, fair, or outstanding performance, which is, of course, highly unlikely.

Forced Choice

The forced choice method of rating forces the appraiser to choose a most and least descriptive statement about the individual being rated out of several statements that are listed together in the same group. A number of these groups make up a rating form. A typical forced choice group is shown in Figure 10.9.

In using this method, some of the raters' choices are disregarded by whoever is analyzing the results. These include those descriptions that are not highly rele-

	Most	Least
1. Exhibits a high degree of technical knowledge	( )	( )
2. Carries out assignment reliably	( )	( )
3. Demonstrates good judgment	( )	( )
4. Knows how to deal with people	( )	( )

Figure 10.9. Forced choice group.

vant to the job which the individual is performing. The main advantage in forced choice rating is that it also minimizes the rate of bias. Research has also shown some evidence that forced choice rating correlates better with productivity than many other types of ratings. However, forced choice does have serious drawbacks. It is expensive, and the forms must be specially prepared and specially administered.

Critical Incidents

With the critical incidents method, the appraiser begins by making up a list of requirements that are considered critical to the performance of the job. This can be done with the assistance of the job description and job specification which you prepared earlier. Once the list of critical requirements is prepared, the rater notes incidents during the rating period, both positive and negative, which pertain to each of the critical requirements listed. The main advantage of this system is that it provides specific examples of performance rather than generalities to discuss during the counseling period of performance appraisal. The difficulty is trying to compare the ratings of one individual and another based solely on such nonquantitative data. However, the critical incident method does adapt very well to the purposes of a small company.

Ranking

The ranking method is very easy, especially if you have a small number of employees. You simply rank the individuals reporting to you, starting with your best individual and proceeding down the list to your worst. Clearly, ranking is very valuable in determining such things as promotions, raises, layoffs and the like. However, it is of very little use during an interview or during the annual salary review, and the question of fairness may be raised regarding comparing individuals performing totally different jobs and having totally different functions within your company.

Essay Appraisals

With the essay appraisal, the rater simply writes a descriptive essay on the individual performance during the period of rating. Essays may make use of critical incidents, and they are very useful because of this for the evaluation interview and for documenting recommendations for promotion and other personnel actions. Again, the problem is one of making comparisons among different performances; also, these essays may be time consuming to accomplish.

Management by Objectives

Management by objectives (MBO) is both a performance rating method and a style of management. It provides for specific quantifiable performance goals that are decided upon by you and the individual rated at the beginning of the performance rating period. At the end of the performance rating period, which is usually a year, you sit down with the employee and review these agreed-upon goals. In doing this, you are also critiquing actual performance.

There are clearly advantages to using MBO. These include a closer relationship between you and your employees, the fact that your subordinates have the opportunity to discuss problems with you that otherwise they might not bring up for discussion, and the focus on future performance rather than the past. However, there are also serious problems in using MBO. These include the facts that the goal may be set too low, that MBO stresses those things that are quantifiable when many goals that you wish the employee to reach during the oncoming year may not be quantifiable, and that MBO does not encourage flexibility. Therefore, if company goals are changed during the period of rating, MBO goals must be changed as well. If you don't do this, then the MBO goals may bear no relationship to the direction that you want to see your company take.

Any of the above methods of performance appraisal can work for your company. However, you should be sure that the method of performance appraisal adopted is spelled out clearly to all your employees and also that you use a standard appraisal form for use on all your employees and by managers who may be doing appraisals. A typical form, regardless of which performance appraisal method is used, should include such job performance factors as dependability, initiative, job knowledge, volume of work accomplished, the quality of performance, results achieved, ability to work with others in your firm, and effectiveness in dealing with others outside of your company, including customers, suppliers and so forth.

While the annual, semiannual, or biannual performance appraisal is an excellent time to sit down with your employee and discuss past performance, counseling should never be reserved for such occasions. Of course, you should see your employees if you are dissatisfied with the job they are doing, and counsel them one-on-one as to what you expect and why they are not performing up to your expectations. In fact, to keep communications open and your organization running smoothly, you may want to have periodic talks with key employees whether or not you have something specific to say. That is, a one-on-one meeting is useful just to review their problems, how they feel about their job and the way they are doing it, and what can be done and what you can do in order for them to be able to do it better. We might conclude that although the performance appraisal is an excellent tool and your employees should be counseled whenever you use it, do not make this the only counseling you ever have with your employees.

DEALING WITH DISCIPLINARY PROBLEMS

You may not like confrontations with employees over disciplinary problems. Few do. But, in a way, it is a cost of doing business. You can minimize disciplinary problems by creating an atmosphere of mutual trust and understanding and common purpose in which all of your employees know your company rules, as well as the reasons for them, and therefore do everything possible to support them.

Now, some rules may be common to all firms, including those pertaining to absenteeism, tardiness, drunkenness, theft, and so forth. However, above and beyond this, here are a few guidelines for establishing company rules which will help foster the positive climate of discipline which you are seeking.

1. The rules and standards which you establish must be reasonable and perceived to be reasonable by your employees.

2. Whatever rules you establish, they should be communicated so they are known and they are understood by all employees. This means not only that the words are understood, but that the reasoning behind them and why they are essential are understood as well.

3. There should be no favoritism. What is expected of one employee should be expected of all employees.

4. Even though you have established rules which all employees are expected to adhere to, if some extenuating circumstances exist which make a rule either extraordinarily harsh or unreasonable, it should be modified for that specific instance.

5. Your employees should be aware of the fact that they can and should tell you if they are dissatisfied with rules they consider unfair or unreasonable, and that you will consider modification of these rules or elimination if the rule is in fact as they perceive it to be.

6. The punishment for breaking certain important rules should be spelled out and should be understood by your employees.

7. When you are developing these rules, you should consult your employees before adopting them.

8. There should always be an appeals procedure available so that an employee who feels that you have made an unfair decision in applying the rule can be heard.

HOW TO MOTIVATE YOUR EMPLOYEES

The Importance of Motivation

Motivation is extremely important. Nonmotivated employees can have several negative effects on your business. These include friction on the job, substandard output in quality, a high turnover of employees, absenteeism, tardiness, and many of the disciplinary problems which you wish to avoid. It is a fact that motivated employees are the most productive and will produce to their maximum abilities for your company.

Over the years, researchers have developed different theories regarding motivation. Among these are Frederick Taylor, who felt that motivation should be primarily through economic means, and Frederick Hertzberg, who discovered a number of job satisfiers and dissatisfiers and developed the theory that motivation could be achieved primarily through something called "job enrichment." Other theories would have employees participate more in the management of the company and in general decision making, or would have motivation depend primarily upon management style. A summary of the various means of motivation discussed above indicate that there are 15 things you can do to promote motivation among employees in your company. You should practice them as much as possible in your day-to-day management.

Fifteen Ways to Promote Motivation in Your Company

1. Care about the people who work for you. The people who work for you don't have to become friends, but they are people and you should recognize them as such. You should be concerned with their problems and their opportunities both on the job and off.

2. Take responsibility for your actions. This means that when you make a mistake, you should acknowledge it freely and don't try to blame it on an employee.

3. Be tactful with your employees. They are not pieces of machinery. They have feelings, thoughts, and ambitions. Therefore, they deserve respect and to be treated with tact.

4. Give praise when a job is well done. If your employee does something good, show that you appreciate it by your public recognition.

5. So far as possible, foster independence in your employees. Let them have as much authority and responsibility as they can handle.

6. Be willing to learn from your employees. You are not an expert on everything. Acknowledge expertise of those who work for you.

7. Always exhibit enthusiasm and confidence. Enthusiasm and confidence are catching, and if you are enthusiastic and confident, your employees will be also.

8. Keep open lines of communication to your employees so they can express their opinions, even if they disagree with you.

9. If your employee has a problem doing his or her job, don't just give orders. Give as much help as you can in order to allow your employee to do the job as best as he or she can.

10. Set standards for yourself and your company. Communicate these standards to your employees.

11. Always let your employees know where they stand—when you are happy with them and when you are unhappy. Never let them be in doubt.

12. Keep your employees informed about what's going on in the way of future plans in your company. If your employees can understand "the big picture," they can help you better by orienting their jobs to your overall objectives.

13. Encourage initiative, innovation, and ingenuity in your employees. Don't turn off ideas submitted by someone who works for you simply because he or she is not supposed to come up with ideas. Good ideas are hard to come by, and you want all you can get.

14. Be aware of your own prejudices and biases toward certain people. Do not allow these prejudices or biases to interfere with the way you treat them or your evaluation of their performance.

15. Always be flexible. The fact that you have done something one way since you started your business does not mean that it has been done right. Always be ready to change for something better.

If you will follow these 15 pieces of advice, you will have better motivation and higher performance from your employees.

TERMINATION

Sometimes it will be necessary to terminate employees for cause. This should never be taken lightly. Remember that in hiring an individual you have invested considerable time and effort. You have invested further effort in training your employee to do the job. If possible, prior to dismissal, a warning and a second chance should be given. However, sometimes dismissal is absolutely required. To keep some employees, either because of violation of rules or their low level of performance, will pull down the performance of other employees and cause problems with morale and motivation.

In terminating an employee, you should have an exit interview in which you inform them forthrightly but tactfully why they are being released. Don't be angry or unpleasant. Remember that this employee, even though he or she may not work for you again, will probably work for someone else in the future. Further, regardless of his or her performance for you, this person may work for someone else quite satisfactorily.

Here is some further guidance on termination:

1. Warn and counsel an employee whose dismissal is contemplated prior to the dismissal decision.
2. Once it is definitely decided to dismiss an employee, do not delay.
3. Hold a termination interview with the employee, explaining tactfully but straightforwardly the reasons for termination.
4. Be sure that you have the employee's correct forwarding address and telephone number.
5. Pay all wages that are due to the employee.
6. If severance pay is part of the contract, be sure that it is paid.
7. Maintain a file on terminated employees which includes the reasons for termination.
8. Respond to any requests for information from the Workers' Compensation Disability Insurance or Unemployment Insurance Board if your terminated employee applies for any of these benefits.

USING TEMPORARY HELP SERVICES

Sometimes it is better for your company to use temporary labor rather than permanent labor. Such services may be necessary when a rush order comes in or the work load suddenly increases but you know that it will drop back to a normal level after the rush order is completed. Temporary help may be necessary during time of sickness of many of your employees or when a key employee is ill, or a special project or seasonal demand must be fulfilled. Under these circumstances, bringing in temporary help is far better than hiring and then having to fire, lay off, or pay for services which are not being fully utilized.

TEMPORARY HELP VERSUS HIRING YOUR OWN TEMPORARY HELP

Before considering temporary help of any kind, you should consider paying overtime for additional work from your present employees. However, sometimes this isn't possible, either because they are already working overtime, or for some other reason. Once you decide on temporary help, you have two choices. One choice is to hire your own temporary help. The problems are having to find this help and the expense for hiring. If you go to a temporary help service, you avoid these difficulties. A temporary help service has already hired these individuals as its own employees. Therefore, they are fully covered by insurance and generally understand the specific types of jobs that you may have for them. In essence, you are relieved of any problems with recruiting, interviewing, screening, testing, and training. Of course, there are some disadvantages. These include the fact that although the individual may be competent for the type of work being done, he or she does not know your particular company and some orientation may be necessary before the job will be done exactly as you want.

There are about a thousand firms in the temporary help industry in the United States. They are usually located near large population centers. You can generally find these firms in the yellow pages of your telephone book. Look under employment—temporary, or employment—contractors, temporary help. The cost will vary depending upon the firm, the location, and other relevant factors. It will be higher than the basic salary or wage you would pay for a similar permanent employee. This is because for this one price you are paying not only for the hours worked but for other things such as payroll taxes, Social Security, workers' compensation, and, of course, the expenses and profits of the temporary help firm. William Olsten, president of the Olsten Corp. of New York, recommends planning early for successful use of temporary help. He gives the following three general planning procedures if you decide that temporary help is necessary.[1]

1. What to do when the time comes
2. Preparing for the temporary employee
3. The work begins

What to Do When the Time Comes

When the time comes that you need extra help and you want to place an order with a temporary-help service, take these steps:

ONE—*Estimate your needs.*   Decide what the specific requirements of the job are. Exactly what talents do you need? How long will you need the employee?

Don't ask for someone with higher qualifications than the work calls for—the cost will be unnecessarily high. On the other hand, don't try to economize by getting underqualified help and then expecting the worker to carry out tasks that he or she isn't prepared to handle.

TWO—*Give the temporary-help service full information.*   If the temporary-personnel firm is to help you get the best results at the lowest possible cost, you must give its people detailed information about the work to be done. Tell them the nature of your business, the working hours, when and how long you'll need help, the skills required, the types of equipment to be operated. You may want to send samples of the work to be done, if it is feasible, for example, with various clerical tasks. Be sure to give the exact location of your business, transportation available, parking information, and the name and title of the person to whom the temporary employee is to report.

[1] *Pointers on Using Temporary-Help Services,* Small Business Administration (1979).

Preparing for the Temporary Employee

A few steps taken before the temporary employee reports for work will do much to make the association a success, both for the employee and for you.

ONE—Arrange for supervision.   Appoint one of your permanent employees to supervise the temporary employee and check on the progress of the work from time to time. Be sure this supervisor understands the job to be done and just what his own responsibility is.

TWO—Tell your permanent employees.   It's a good idea to let your staff know that you are taking on extra help and that it will be temporary. Explain why the extra help is needed and ask them to cooperate with the new employee in any way possible.

THREE—Prepare the physical facilities.   Have everything ready before the temporary worker arrives. The work to be done should be organized and laid out so that the employee can begin producing with a minimum of time spent in adjusting to the job and the surroundings. See that the materials needed are available and the equipment is in place and in good working order.

FOUR—Plan the workload.   Don't set up schedules that are impossible to complete within the time you allot. Try to stay within the time limits you gave the temporary-help service, but plan to extend the time period, if necessary, rather than crowd the employee. Rushing and overwork can result in costly mistakes.

FIVE—Prepare detailed instructions.   Describe your type of business, the products you manufacture or the services you offer. Be specific in outlining the procedures your company follows. Most employees of temporary-help services adjust quickly to the methods of an individual firm because of their varied experience.

The Work Begins

You've made all the preparations. The employee has arrived and is ready to start work. What now? How do you get a temporary worker started? What should you expect? What if you're not satisfied.

This is the crucial stage of the relation between your company and the temporary employee. Get off to a good start and the rest will go smoothly.

ONE—Help the employee settle in.   Receive the temporary employee as you would receive one hired on a permanent basis. Make him feel like a member of your team. Explain where to hang coats, the location of the washroom, the lunch hour, coffee breaks, and so on.

Introduce the temporary employee to the permanent employee who will supervise the work.

Introduce the temporary employee also to permanent employees in the same department. Explain that "Miss Jones will be here for a few days to help out." Or, "John will be here this week to help get out the rush job."

TWO—Explain the job.   Go over the work assignment and the instructions. Explain company routines. Make your directions as simple as possible and provide samples of the work to be done. If the work is complex, explain it clearly and make certain that your explanation is understood. Assure the temporary employee of your staff's cooperation and willingness to help, and show your own interest and concern.

THREE—Don't expect the impossible.   How much can you expect from a temporary employee? Fully as much as you contracted for with the service firm. Most employees of temporary-personnel services perform well. They are experienced and versatile. Because they have worked for a variety of businesses, they have learned to adapt quickly to a new situation, and they know that future assignments depend on their doing satisfactory work.

But don't expect the impossible. Don't overload temporary employees—make a slight allowance for the fact that they are not familiar with your business and its operations. Check the work occasionally, ask for any questions, never leave the employee feeling stranded or left out. At the same time, don't make him nervous by hovering over him. And don't push or prod too much.

MAJOR LABOR LAWS THAT AFFECT YOUR BUSINESS

It is important that you know and obey the major labor laws that can affect your business. Following is a list compiled by the U.S. Department of Labor.

Age Discrimination in Employment Act of 1967, as Amended (ADEA)

When Passed and Amended.   The Age Discrimination in Employment Act was passed in 1967 and amended in 1974 to bring most federal, state, and local government workers under its protection.

A Brief Explanation.   ADEA prohibits arbitrary age discrimination against persons 40 to 65 in matters of employment such as hiring, discharge, leave, compensation, and promotions. The law applies to employers of 20 or more persons, employment agencies serving covered employers, labor organizations with 25 or more members or which represent employees of covered employers, and all federal, state, and local government employees without regard to the 20-employee requirement. The regulations cited below contain specific exemptions for programs designed exclusively to provide employment to persons with special job problems.

Regulations.   29 CFR 850 and 860 (CFR means Code of Federal Regulations).

Administration of the Law.   ADEA is administered by the Wage-Hour Division of the Employment Standards Administration (ESA), except for its application to federal employees. The Civil Service Commission is responsible for federal employees.

Relationship with Other Laws or Agencies.   ADEA was amended by the Fair Labor Standards Act Amendments of 1974 (Public Law 93-259), effective May 1, 1974 (see first paragraph). The Civil Service Commission administers the law's application to federal employees.

For information see the list of offices at the end of this section.

Alien Certification

When Passed and Amended.   The Immigration and Nationality Act governs the immigration of aliens to the United States.

A Brief Explanation.   Under the Immigration and Nationality Act, any alien who seeks to immigrate to the United States for the purpose of employment is allowed to enter the country only after the Department of Labor has determined and certified to the Department of State and to the Immigration and Naturalization Service that qualified U.S. workers are not available and that the alien's employment will not adversely affect wages and working conditions of the workers in the U.S. who hold similar jobs. This certification by the Department of Labor is popularly referred to as "labor certification."

Regulations. 29 CFR Part 60 (CFR means Code of Federal Regulations).

Administration of the Law. The Immigration and Nationality Act authorizes the Labor Department to issue a labor certification.

Relationship with Other Laws or Agencies. Tied in with the Immigration and Nationality Act, as noted above. Other agencies which have jurisdiction under the act are the Immigration and Naturalization Service and the Department of State.

For Information. For additional information, contact the nearest office of your state employment service. You may also contact the Employment and Training Administration in Region 9:

> Employment and Training Administration
> U.S. Department of Labor
> Alien Certification Unit
> P.O. BOX 36084
> 450 Golden Gate Avenue, 9th floor
> San Francisco, CA 94102
> (415) 556-5624

Black Lung Benefits Act of 1972
(Title IV, Federal Coal Mine Health and Safety Act)

When Passed and Amended. This law was enacted in 1972 as Title IV of the Federal Coal Mine Health and Safety Act.

A Brief Explanation. The Black Lung Benefits Act authorizes medical treatment and monthly payments to coal miners totally disabled from pneumoconiosis (black lung) arising from employment in the nation's coal mines. The Act also provides benefits to certain survivors of miners who died due to pneumoconiosis, or while totally disabled from it.

Regulations. 20 CFR 715, 717, 718, 720, 722, 725, and 726 (CFR means Code of Federal Regulations).

Administration of the Law. The Black Lung Benefits Act is administered by the Office of Workers' Compensation Programs (Division of Coal Mine Workers' Compensation) of our Employment Standards Administration (ESA).

Relationship with Other Laws or Agencies. As noted above, the law is Title IV of the Federal Coal Mine Health and Safety Act.

For Information. Contact specialists in our national office in Washington, D.C. for information and assistance on the Black Lung Benefits of 1972. You may write:

> Division of Coal Mine Workers' Compensation
> Washington, D.C. 20210
> Telephone (202) 523-6755

Comprehensive Employment and Training Act (CETA)

When Passed and Amended. "CETA" was passed in 1973 to establish a flexible, decentralized system of federal, state, and local manpower activities. The law brings the local control concept to the administration of federally funded employment and training programs.

A Brief Explanation. The major purpose of the Comprehensive Employment and Training Act is to provide the economically disadvantaged, the unemployed, and the underemployed with the assistance they need to compete for, secure, and hold jobs challenging their fullest capabilities. The bulk of CETA funds are distributed to state and local governments acting as prime sponsors to operate their manpower programs. These funds are distributed under three major titles. Title I allows prime sponsors to establish programs of comprehensive manpower services, including job training, counseling, transitional public employment jobs, and supportive services such as child care. Title II provides for transitional public employment programs in areas with substantial—6.5 percent or more—unemployment. Up to 20 percent of CETA funds may also be set aside for national manpower programs, including Job Corps and programs designed to benefit special target groups, such as senior citizens, migrant farm workers, Indians and ex-offenders.

Regulations. 29 CFR Part II (CFR means Code of Federal Regulations).

Administration of the Law. CETA is administered by the Employment and Training Administration (formerly Manpower Administration).

Relationship with Other Laws or Agencies. CETA is one of the major programs administered by the Employment and Training Administration to help people who are out of work or who seek new work. The act is administered in cooperation with participating State, county and local governments designated as prime sponsors, as noted above.

For Information. For information about CETA programs in your home town, contact your city hall. For additional information, contact the Employment and Training Administration in Region 9:

> Employment and Training Administration
> U.S. Department of Labor
> CETA Unit
> 450 Golden Gate Avenue, 9th floor
> P.O. BOX 36084
> San Francisco, CA 94102
> (415) 556-6172

Consumer Credit Protection Act—Title III
(Federal Wage-Garnishment Law)

When Passed and Amended.   Title III of the act, known as the Federal Wage-Garnishment Law, became effective in 1970. It puts limitations on withholding wages to satisfy creditors, one of which is tied in with the Fair Labor Standards Act, last amended in 1974.

A Brief Explanation.   The Federal Wage-Garnishment Law limits the amount of an employee's disposable earnings that can be withheld in any one week by an employer to satisfy creditors. "Disposable earnings" means that part of an employee's earnings remaining after deduction of any amount required by law to be withheld. Restrictions on the amount that can be garnished in a week do not apply to court orders for support of a person, bankruptcy court orders, and debts for state or federal taxes. The law also prohibits an employer from discharging an employee whose earnings have been subjected to garnishment for any one indebtedness.

Regulations.   20 CFR Part 870 (CFR means Code of Federal Regulations).

Administration of the Law.   The Federal Wage-Garnishment Law is administered by the Wage-Hour Division of our Employment Standards Administration (ESA).

Relationship with Other Laws or Agencies.   See paragraph 1 above. The Federal Wage-Garnishment Law doesn't annul, alter, affect, or exempt any person from complying with state laws that prohibit garnishments or provide for more limited garnishments than are allowed under the federal law. Nor does the federal law prohibit the discharge of any employee because his earnings have been subject to garnishment for more than one indebtedness. Any applicable provision of a state *law* that subjects *less* of an individual's earnings to garnishment than the federal law is the one to be applied under a garnishment order. On the other hand, the federal restrictions apply when they result in a *smaller* amount of wages withheld because of garnishment.

For Information.   Contact local Wage-Hour Area Offices of our Employment Standards Administration listed at the end of this section.

Contract Work Hours and Safety Standards Act

When Passed.   This law, first passed as the Work Hours Act of 1962, replaces the former Eight Hour Laws. In 1969 it was amended to include safety provisions for construction work.

A Brief Explanation.   The law requires overtime pay for laborers and mechanics working on certain federal contracts and subcontracts. These workers are entitled to time and one-half their basic rate of pay for all hours worked over 8 in a calendar day or 40 in a work week, whichever is the greater. Since 1969 the law has contained health and safety standards for covered construction contracts. Federal contractors and subcontractors are subject to the act if they have contracts or subcontracts equalling or exceeding the following dollar amounts:

$2,000 on federal construction contracts

$2,500 on federal service contracts

$2,500 on federal supply contracts (supply contracts over $10,000 are subject to the Public Contracts Act)

Regulations. 41 CFR 1–12.3; 41 CFR 1–18.7; 29 CFR Part 5 (CFR means Code of Federal Regulations).

Administration of the Law. The Contract Work Hours and Safety Standards Act is administered by the Wage-Hour Division of our Employment Standards Administration (ESA). Safety and health requirements are administered by our Occupational Safety and Health Administration (OSHA).

Relationship with Other Laws or Agencies. As stated above, our Occupational Safety and Health Administration handles safety and health requirements of the act; our Wage-Hour Division administers the remainder of the act.

For Information. Contact local Wage-Hour Area Offices and Occupational Safety and Health Area Offices listed at the end of this section.

Davis-Bacon Act

When Passed and Amended. The law was enacted in 1931 to set wage-standards for construction. The law was amended, 40 U.S.C. 276 (a) et seq. as affected by the "Portal-to-Portal Act" of 1947, 29 U.S.C. 251 et seq., and Reorganization Plan No. 14 of 1950 (15 F.R. 3176, 64 Stat. 1267).

A Brief Explanation. Davis-Bacon applies to all federal and federally assisted contracts in excess of $2,000 for the construction, alteration, or repair (including painting and decoration) of public buildings or public works. The law provides that all laborers and mechanics employed under such contracts must be paid the wage rates and fringe benefits found by the Department of Labor to be prevailing in the locality and included in a wage decision in the contract. Such contracts also require the submission of certified payroll records on a weekly basis to the contracting agency.

Regulations. 41 CFR 1–18.7; 29 CFR Parts 1, 3, and 5 (CFR means Code of Federal Regulations).

Administration of the Law. The Wage-Hour Division of the Employment Standards Administration is responsible for determining prevailing wage rates and fringe benefits. Reorganization Plan No. 14 of 1950 assigns primary enforcement responsibility to the contracting agency although in some instances investigations are made by the Wage-Hour Division.

Relationship with Other Laws or Agencies. A contract that is subject to the Davis-Bacon Act or most of the related acts is also subject to the Copeland (Anti-Kickback) Act. This law prohibits illegal deductions or kickbacks of wages.

For Information. Contact the local Wage-Hour Office listed at the end of this section.

Employee Retirement Income Security Act of 1974

When Passed and Amended. The Employee Retirement and Income Security Act (ERISA) was passed in 1974.

A Brief Explanation. ERISA was enacted to protect the interests of participants and beneficiaries in employee pension and welfare benefit plans. ERISA requires reporting of plan and financial information to the Department of Labor, as well as plan participants and beneficiaries. ERISA safeguards plan assets through establishment of fiduciary and funding standards. ERISA safeguards benefits through establishment of vesting and participation standards and by requiring plan termination insurance for certain pension plans. The act applies to employee pension and welfare benefit plans, regardless of size, maintained by employers engaged in commerce or in an industry or activity affecting commerce—or by employee organizations representing employees so engaged, except those plans specifically exempted.

Regulations. 26 CFR 420; 29 CFR Ch XXV (CFR means Code of Federal Regulations).

Administration. ERISA is administered by the Office of Employee Benefits Security of our Labor Management Services Administration (LMSA).

For Information. For information, contact local LMSA Area Offices listed at the end of this section.

Equal Pay Act

When Passed and Amended. The Equal Pay Act was passed in 1963, incorporated into the Fair Labor Standards Act by the 1966 amendments to that act, and again amended by the National Education Act of 1972.

A Brief Explanation. The Equal Pay Act prohibits a wage differential based on sex between employees employed in the same establishment on jobs requiring equal skill, effort, and responsibility and performed under similar working conditions.

Regulations. 29 CFR 800 (CFR means Code of Federal Regulations).

Administration of the Law. The Equal Pay Act is administered by the Wage-Hour Division of the Employment Standards Administration.

Relationship with Other Laws or Agencies. As noted above, the Equal Pay Act is part of the Fair Labor Standards Act.

For Information. Contact the local Wage-Hour Area Offices listed at the end of this section.

Executive Order 11246, as Amended by Executive Order 11375 (Parts II, III and IV)

When Passed and Amended. EO 11246 on Equal Employment Opportunity was issued in 1965 and amended by Titles, II, III and IV of EO 11375 in 1968.

A Brief Explanation. The Order requires that equal opportunity be provided for all persons without regard to race, color, religion, sex, or national origin, who are employed or seeking employment with government contractors, or with contractors performing under federally assisted construction. The Order also applies to programs involving federal financial assistance that may include a construction project, and to all contractors and subcontractors performing under construction contracts related to the assistance program.

Regulations. 41 CFR 1–12.8; 41 CFR 60 (CFR means Code of Federal Regulations).

Administration of the Law. The Order is administered by the Office of Federal Contract Compliance Programs (OFCCP) of our Employment Standards Administration (ESA).

Relationship with Other Laws and Agencies. As noted above, Executive Order 11246 was amended by Executive Order 11375, Parts II, III and IV.

For Information. For additional information, contact the local specialist in Region 9:

> Office of Federal Contract Compliance Programs
> Employment Standards Administration
> U.S. Department of Labor
> 450 Golden Gate Avenue, Room 10341
> San Francisco, CA 94102
> Telephone (415) 556-3597

The Fair Labor Standards Act of 1938, as Amended

When Passed and Amended. The Fair Labor Standards Act (FLSA), also known as the Federal Wage-Hour Law, was passed in 1938. It has been amended several times; most recently in 1974. The Act was amended by the Equal Pay Act of 1963 to require that employers pay equal wages for equal work regardless of sex.

A Brief Explanation. FLSA sets minimum wage, overtime, record-keeping, and child labor standards. It covers employees individually engaged in interstate commerce, producing goods for interstate commerce, or employed in certain enterprises engaged in interstate commerce, unless a specific exemption applies. Employers must meet the standards set by the Act regardless of the number of employees or whether the employee works full or part-time. The 1974 amendments extended minimum wage and overtime protection to some domestic (household) employees. The 1974 amendments also extended the act's protection to federal, state and local government employees.

Regulations. 41 CFR 1–12.7; 7 29 CFR 518-800 (CFR means Code of Federal Regulations).

Administration of the Law. FLSA is administered by the Wage-Hour Division of the Employment Standards Administration. The Civil Service Commission is responsible for administering the FLSA to federal employees.

Relationship with Other Laws or Agencies. As noted above in paragraphs 1 and 4.

For Information. Contact local Wage-Hour Area Offices listed at the end of this section.

Farm Labor Contractor Registration Act as Amended December, 1974

When Passed and Amended. The law was passed in 1963 to improve conditions for migrant farm workers. It was amended by Public Law 93-518, as enacted December 7, 1974.

A Brief Explanation. This act now requires farm labor contractors, their full-time employees, and users of migrant farm workers, to observe certain rules with reference to the employment of migrant farm workers. Farm labor contractors covered by the Act must register with the U.S. Department of Labor and obtain a certificate of registration. Such contractors must also clearly inform workers as to their rights, working conditions, pay, etc. when recruiting—in writing and in a language in which they are fluent. Records must be kept, and certain automobile insurance is required for vehicles transporting migrant farm workers. Discrimination is prohibited against any person filing a complaint under this act, and legal penalties are available against persons who fail to comply with the law.

Regulations. 29 CFR Parts 40 and 41 (CFR means Code of Federal Regulations).

Administration of the Law. The Farm Labor Contractor Registration Act is administered by the Wage-Hour Division of our Employment Standards Administration.

Relationship with Other Laws or Agencies. Some states have passed laws to the federal statute. It would be well to check state labor departments for information on state laws of this kind.

For Information. Contact the local Wage-Hour Area Office listed at the end of this section.

Federal Employees' Compensation Act, as Amended

When Passed and Amended. The Federal Employees' Compensation Act (FECA), first passed in 1916, has been amended many times, most recently in 1974.

A Brief Explanation. This law authorized payment of workers' compensation benefits to civil officers and employees of all branches of the federal government, and to specific categories of other workers and of enrollees under certain programs—including some programs under the Comprehensive Employment and Training Act (CETA) of 1973, as amended, as specified in applicable regulations.

Regulations. 20 CFR 10 (CFR means Code of Federal Regulations).

Administration of the Law. FECA is administered by the Office of Workers' Compensation Programs (OWCP) of our Employment Standards Administration.

Relationship with Other Laws or Agencies. FECA ties in with CETA (see above), the War Hazards Compensation Act, and the War Claims Act. Two related federal compensation laws explained elsewhere in this section are the Longshoremen's and Harbor Workers' Compensation Act, and the so-called Black Lung Law.

For Information. Contact local specialists in Region 9 for additional information:

> Office of Workers' Compensation Programs
> (Federal Employees' Compensation)
> Employment Standards Administration
> U.S. Department of Labor
> 450 Golden Gate Avenue, Room 10017
> San Francisco, CA 94102
> Telephone (415) 556-5757

Longshoremen's and Harbor Workers' Compensation Act

When Passed and Amended. This law, originally passed in 1927, has been amended several times, most recently in 1972.

A Brief Explanation. This law offers workers' compensation benefits to employees disabled from injuries that occurred on the navigable waters of the United States, or on an adjoining area customarily used by employees in loading, unloading, repairing, or building a vessel. The act also offers benefits to dependents if the injury causes the employee's death. The law contains safety and health provisions.

Regulations. 20 CFR 701–704 (CFR means Code of Federal Regulations).

Administration of the Law. The Longshoremen's and Harborworkers' Compensation Act is administered by the Office of Workers' Compensation Programs of our Employment Standards Administration (ESA). Compliance with the Act's safety and health provisions is administered by our Occupational Safety and Health Administration (OSHA).

Relationship with Other Laws or Agencies. Extensions of the act include the Defense Base Act; Outer Continental Shelf Act; the District of Columbia Workmen's Compensation Act, which provides for benefits for employees in private industry in the District of Columbia; and the Nonappropriated Fund Instrumentalities Act, which provides for benefits for civilian employees in post exchanges and commissaries.

For Information. For information about Safety and Health provisions of the Act contact the Area Office of the Occupational Safety and Health Administration, listed at the end of this section. For information about all other aspects of the act contact the:

> Office of Workers' Compensation Programs
> Longshore & Harbor Workers' Compensation
> Employment Standards Administration
> U.S. Department of Labor
> 450 Golden Gate Avenue
> P.O. Box 36066
> San Francisco, CA 94102
> Telephone (415) 556-6297

Section 503, Rehabilitation Act of 1973, as Amended

When Passed and Amended. This law was passed in 1973 and amended in 1974.

A Brief Explanation. Section 503 requires government contractors and subcontractors to take affirmative action to employ and advance in employment qualified handicapped individuals. Section 503 applies to all contracts and subcontracts in excess of $2,500.

Regulations. 41 CFR 1-12; 20 CFR 741 (CFR means Code of Federal Regulations).

Administration of the Law. Section 503 is administered by the Office of Federal Contract Compliance Programs (OFCCP). The Department of Health, Education and Welfare is responsible for the administration of the Rehabilitation Act of 1973 other than Section 503.

Relationship with Other Laws or Agencies. As noted above. In addition, some states have passed similar laws. Information concerning state laws can be obtained from state departments of industrial relations.

For Information. Contact the local specialist in Region 9:

> Office of Federal Contract Compliance Programs
> Employment Standards Administration
> U.S. Department of Labor
> 450 Golden Gate Avenue, Room 10341
> San Francisco, CA 94102
> Telephone (415) 556-7472

Service Contract Act of 1965, as Amended

When Passed and Amended. The Service Contract Act (SCA) was passed in 1965 and amended in 1972.

A Brief Explanation. SCA established wage standards for service employees doing work on federal contracts and subcontracts that are principally for services. It requires:

(1) Payment of not less than the minimum wage provided in Section 6(a) (1) of the Fair Labor Standards Act if the contract is for $2,500 or less.

(2) Payment of not less than the wage rates and fringe benefits found by the Department of Labor to be prevailing in the locality, or in certain cases, wage rates and fringe benefits contained in a predecessor-contractor's collective bargaining agreement, if the contract exceeds $2,500. Compliance with Section 6(a) (1) of the Fair Labor Standards Act is also required.

Wage determinations are included in covered contracts. The law also contains record-keeping and safety and health requirements.

Regulations. 41 CFR 1-12.9; 29 CFR Part 4 (CFR means Code of Federal Regulations).

Administration of the Law.   SCA is administered by the Wage-Hour Division of our Employment Standards Administration.

Relationship with Other Laws or Agencies.   As noted above, a relationship with the Fair Labor Standards Act.

For Information.   For information contact the local Wage-Hour Area Office and the Occupation Safety and Health Area Office listed at the end of this section.

Trade Act of 1974

When Passed and Amended.   The Trade Act of 1974 became law in 1975. It provides special income protection for American workers who lose their jobs or whose hours of work and wages are reduced as a result of trade with other countries.

A Brief Explanation.   Under the Trade Act of 1974, workers whose employment is adversely affected by increased imports may apply for Worker Adjustment Assistance. This includes trade adjustment allowances that provide weekly income for them to live on while they are unemployed or on reduced work schedules. It also includes a variety of help in preparing them for and obtaining new jobs. They may be eligible for allowances to enable them to take training away from home when it is not available locally; to search for work in other towns and cities; and to move to a new job. To apply for adjustment assistance, you petition the Labor Department. Any group of three or more workers of a firm or subdivision of a firm, their union, or their duly authorized representative, who feel that competition from increased imports has contributed importantly to the workers' unemployment or reduced workweek may petition the Labor Department for a determination of eligibility to apply for adjustment assistance. Workers who are denied eligibility may appeal the decision to the U.S. Court of Appeals that has jurisdiction in the area of your place of employment. There are time limits for each step in the process. A determination must be issued within 60 days after a worker petition is filed. Workers have 60 days to appeal the determination.

Regulations.   29 CFR 90; 29 CFR 91 (CFR means Code of Federal Regulations).

Administration of the Law.   The Trade Act of 1974 is administered by the Bureau of International Labor Affairs and the Employment and Training Administration through State employment service offices.

Relationship with Other Laws or Agencies.   Tied-in with the Federal-State Employment Service system, as noted above.

For Information.   For more information, contact the nearest local office of your state employment service. You may also obtain additional information from the regional Employment and Training Administration, 450 Golden Gate Avenue, San Francisco, California 94102. Telephone (415) 556-1416.

Unemployment Insurance

When Passed and Amended.   The nation's unemployment insurance system was born of the Great Depression. It is an income maintenance program that offers a measure of financial protection to workers who are involuntarily unemployed and looking for work.

A Brief Explanation.   The Unemployment Insurance System is a cooperative Federal-State program. Each state has its own unemployment insurance law and is responsible for determining who is eligible for benefits, how much they receive, and for how long. The benefits are of limited duration and are based on an individual's insured wages and not upon need. An unemployed worker files a claim for benefits at the nearest state unemployment service office. The unemployment insurance system is funded by employers covered under the law who pay unemployment insurance taxes on the wages of their employees. The taxes go into a state fund and are used solely for paying benefits to eligible workers. Employers covered under the Federal Unemployment Tax Act also pay a tax to the federal government. The federal tax is used to finance the administrative costs of the employment security program, including the unemployment insurance program, and to pay for one-half of Federal-State extended benefits.

Regulations.   20 CFR Part 600 and following (CFR means Code of Federal Regulations).

Administration of the Law.   The Federal Unemployment Tax Act is administered by the Unemployment Insurance Service in our Employment and Training Administration.

Relationship with Other Laws and Agencies.   Administered in cooperation with each state's unemployment insurance law, as noted above.

For Information.   For more information contact your local state unemployment insurance office. Information may also be obtained from the Employment and Training Administration in Region 9:

> Employment and Training Administration
> U.S. Department of Labor
> P.O. Box 36084
> 450 Golden Gate Avenue, 9th floor
> San Francisco, CA 94102
> (415) 556-1416

Veterans' Reemployment Rights

When Passed and Amended.   The law is technically Chapter 43, Title 38 U.S. Code, Sections 2021 and following. It was passed in 1967 to protect the reemployment rights of veterans and amended December 3, 1974.

A Brief Explanation.   Under this law, any employee enlisting in or inducted into the armed services of the United States who leaves a position (other than temporary) in order to perform military service, receives a certificate of satisfactory service, and makes application for reemployment within 90 days of leaving the service shall be restored to the position that the individual otherwise would have achieved but for military service, with attendant seniority, status, and pay if still qualified to perform.

If by reason of disability sustained during service, the individual is unable to perform in the job, the person shall be offered another appropriate position. If there are complaints, the Department of Labor investigates and attempts to resolve the problem.

Under somewhat similar provisions, it also provides statutory protection to employees who leave their positions to perform training duty with the National Guard or Reserves.

The law applies to all employers in private industry regardless of size or number of employees (and all state or local governments) if the employee was released from military service after December 3, 1974.

Administration of the Law.   The law is administered by the Office of Veterans' Reemployment Rights of our Labor-Management Services Administration (LMSA).

Relationships with Other Laws and Agencies.   The U.S. Department of Labor has established close working liaison with the Armed Service agencies to help ensure that military personnel nearing separation are aware of their rights under the law.

Information.   Contact the local Area Office of the Labor-Management Services Administration listed at the end of this section.

Vietnam Era Veterans' Readjustment Assistance Act of 1974

When Passed and Amended.   The law is technically Chapter 42, Title 38, U.S. Code, Section 2012, passed in 1974 to emphasize the employment and advancement of veterans by Government contractors and subcontractors.

A Brief Explanation.   This law requires that Government contractors and subcontractors take affirmative action to employ and advance in employment qualified disabled and Vietnam Era veterans. Each contractor or subcontractor is required to list all suitable employment openings with the local office of the State Employment Service, which must give veterans priority referral to these openings.

A veterans' employment representative is located in each State Employment Service office to give employment advice and assistance to veterans. A veteran to whom the requirements apply may contact the veterans' employment representative or the regional office of our Employment Standards Administration if it appears that a contractor or subcontractor has failed to comply. The law applies to all government contracts and subcontracts of $10,000 or more for procurement of personal property or nonpersonal services.

Regulations.   Not yet published.

Administration of the Law.   The law is administered by two Department of Labor agencies:

> Employment Standards Administration
> Office of Federal Contract Compliance Programs
> Employment and Training Administration
> Veterans' Employment Service

For Information. Contact local specialists in Region 9:

> Office of Federal Contract Compliance Programs
> Employment Standards Administration
> U.S. Department of Labor
> 450 Golden Gate Avenue, Room 10341
> San Francisco, CA 94102
> Telephone (415) 556-7472

Walsh-Healey Public Contracts Act

When Passed and Amended. "Walsh-Healey" was passed in 1938 to set wage standards for workers on certain federal contracts. The law now also contains safety and health provisions.

A Brief Explanation. The Walsh-Healey Public Contracts Act applies to federal contracts over $10,000 for the manufacture or furnishing of materials, supplies, articles, and equipment unless exempted by regulations. (See below.) Walsh-Healey requires that contractors be either manufacturers or regular dealers, and that they pay their employees performing on covered contracts minimum wages that shall be not less than the rate provided in Section 6(a) (1) of the Fair Labor Standards Act; and overtime compensation at rates not less than one and one-half times the employees' regular rate of pay for all hours worked in excess of 8 in a day or 40 in a work week, whichever is greater. The act also prohibits the employment of minors under 16 years of age and convict labor, and contains safety and health provisions.

Regulations. 41 CFR 1–12.6; 41 CFR 50-201 (CFR means Code of Federal Regulations).

Administration of the Law. Walsh-Healey is administered by the Wage-Hour Division of our Employment Standards Administration.

Relationship with Other Laws or Agencies. Tied in with the Fair Labor Standards Act, as noted above. Safety and Health provisions are administered by the federal Occupational Safety and Health Agency (OSHA).

For Information. For additional information, contact the Wage-Hour Area Office and the Area Office of our Occupational Safety and Health Administration (OSHA) listed at the end of this section.

"Williams-Steiger" Occupational Safety and Health Act (OSHA)

When Passed and Amended. The "Williams-Steiger" Occupational Safety and Health Act was passed in 1970 to assure safe and healthful conditions in the workplace.

A Brief Explanation. This law, abbreviated to OSHA, covers all employers engaged in business affecting commerce and who have one or more employees. However, to avoid duplication of effort among agencies, OSHA is not applicable to those particular hazards which may be reduced or eliminated under regulations issued by other federal agencies. State and local government employees are also exempted.

OSHA requires covered employers to furnish their employees a safe and healthful workplace. Employers must comply with standards and applicable record-keeping and reporting requirements specified in regulations issued by the Labor Department agency that administers OSHA—our Occupational Safety and Health Administration, also known for short as "OSHA." Some states, operating OSHA-approved State plans in accordance with the federal law, have their own occupational safety and health programs which may gradually replace federal programs. The law provides that a small business may request loans through the Small Business Administration (SBA) when it can show that substantial economic injury is likely to result from a requirement to comply with standards issued by either federal programs or by approved state programs. In many states, both with and without plans, small businessmen and women may request the services of state personnel who provide consultation on applicable standards. These state consultants are not inspectors and they do not issue citations when they visit employers for consultations, except when they encounter imminent danger situations.

Regulations.   29 CFR 1900 (CFR means Code of Federal Regulations).

Administration of the Law.   The Occupational Safety and Health Act is administered by the Occupational Safety and Health Administration, an agency of the U.S. Department of Labor.

Relationship with Other Laws and Agencies.   See explanation above.

For Information.   Contact local OSHA area office listed at the end of this section.

Work Incentive Program (WIN II)

When Passed and Amended.   The "WIN II" program was established under 1971 amendments to the Social Security Act. It is a national program to help welfare recipients obtain suitable employment.

A Brief Explanation.   Under the WIN II program, all persons receiving Aid to Families with Dependent Children (AFDC), except those in exempt categories, are required to register for WIN and accept jobs or job training. The program contains incentives for both AFDC recipients and employers who hire them. For persons on AFDC, WIN makes working more profitable than receiving AFDC benefits alone. For employers, the program offers a sizeable tax credit on the wages paid workers hired through WIN, a fast tax writeoff on training and child-care facilities, and in certain cases reimbursement for training costs and loss of productivity, WIN II also requires state welfare agencies to provide participants with a variety of supportive services, such as child care and medical aid for three months after employment, and special arrangements to help participants adjust to working.

Regulations.   29 CFR 56; 45–2 CFR 224 (CFR means Code of Federal Regulations).

Administration of the Law.   The WIN II program is conducted by our Employment and Training Administration in cooperation with the U.S. Department of Health, Education and Welfare (HEW).

Relationship with Other Laws or Agencies. As part of the Social Security Act the program is administered in conjunction with HEW, as noted above.

For Information. For additional information about the WIN project in your area, contact the nearest office of your state employment service.

Area Offices
Labor-Management Services Administration
U.S. Department of Labor

California
Labor-Management Services Administration[2]
U.S. Department of Labor
Federal Building, Room 7730
300 North Los Angeles Street
Los Angeles, California 90012
Telephone: (213) 688-4975

Labor-Management Services Administration
U.S. Department of Labor
100 McAllister Street, Room 1604
San Francisco, California 94102
Telephone: (415) 556-2030

Hawaii
Labor-Management Services Administration
U.S. Department of Labor
1833 Kalakaua Avenue, Room 601
Honolulu, Hawaii 96815
Telephone: (808) 955-0259

Area Offices
Occupational Safety and Health Administration
U.S. Department of Labor

Arizona
U.S. Department of Labor—OSHA
Amerco Towers—Suite 318
2721 North Central Avenue
Phoenix, Arizona 85004
Telephone: (602) 261-4857

California
U.S. Department of Labor—OSHA
Hartwell Building—Room 401
19 Pine Avenue
Long Beach, California 90802
Telephone: (213) 796-2431

U.S. Department of Labor—OSHA
100 McAllister Street, Room 1706
San Francisco, California 94102
Telephone: (415) 556-7260

Hawaii
U.S. Department of Labor—OSHA
333 Queen Street—Suite 505
Honolulu, Hawaii 96813
Telephone: (808) 546-3157

Nevada
U.S. Department of Labor—OSHA
1100 East William Street, Suite 222
Carson City, Nevada 89701
Telephone: (702) 883-1226

Wage-Hour Area Offices
U.S. Department of Labor
Employment Standards Administration

California
Wage-Hour Area Office
U.S. Department of Labor
Hollywood First National Bank Building
6777 Hollywood Blvd., Room 504
Hollywood, California 90028

Wage-Hour Area Office
U.S. Department of Labor
Federal Building
300 N. Los Angeles St., Room 3251
Los Angeles, California 90012
Telephone: (213) 688-4957

Wage-Hour Area Office[3]
U.S. Department of Labor
Federal Building
650 Capitol Mall, Room 8410
Sacramento, California 95814
Telephone: (916) 449-2346

Wage-Hour Area Office
U.S. Department of Labor
760 Market Street, Room 409
San Francisco, California 94102
Telephone: (415) 556-6815

Wage-Hour Area Office
U.S. Department of Labor
1600 North Broadway, Suite 440
Santa Ana, California 92706
Telephone: (714) 836-2156

Arizona
Wage-Hour Area Office[4]
U.S. Department of Labor
Park Plaza Building
1306 North 1st Street
Phoenix, Arizona 85004
Telephone: (602) 261-4224

Hawaii
Wage-Hour Area Office
U.S. Department of Labor
1833 Kalakaua Avenue, Room 614
Honolulu, Hawaii 96815
Telephone: (808) 588-0264

SOURCES OF ADDITIONAL INFORMATION

Affirmative Action and Equal Employment: A Guide Book, published by U.S. Government Printing Office, Washington, D.C. 20402.

Compensation, by Robert E. Sibson, published by American Management Associations, 135 West 50th St., New York, NY 10020.

Effective Psychology for Managers, by Mortimer R. Feinberg, published by Prentice-Hall, Inc., Englewood Cliffs, NJ 07632.

Grievance Handling: 101 Guides for Supervisors, by Walter E. Baer, published by American Management Associations, 135 West 50th St., New York, NY 10020.

Handbook of Modern Personnel Administration, edited by Joseph J. Famularo, published by McGraw-Hill Book Co., 1221 Avenue of the Americas, New York, NY 10036.

Handbook of Wage and Salary Administration, by Milton L. Rock, published by McGraw-Hill Book Co., 1221 Avenue of the Americas, New York, NY 10036.

Personnel Management, by Michael J. Jucius, published by Richard Irwin, Inc., 1818 Ridge Rd., Homewood, IL 60430.

Personnel, The Human Problems of Management, 3rd edition, by George Strauss and Leonard R. Sayles, published by Prentice-Hall, Inc., Englewood Cliffs, NJ 07632.

The OSHA Compliance Manual, by Donald C. Petersen, published by McGraw-Hill Book Co., 1221 Avenue of the Americas, New York, NY 10036.

[4] Southern Nevada residents contact the Wage-Hour Area Office in Phoenix.

11

Financial Management

FINANCIAL MANAGEMENT—WHAT IT IS AND WHY IT IS IMPORTANT

Financial management includes a number of different functions:

1. Managing old and new assets so that every single asset contributes to the maximum extent possible toward the profitable operation of your business
2. Insuring that the assets that you have are used in such a manner as to bring the maximum return possible on the money that you invest
3. Obtaining funds to finance additional assets
4. Evaluating the need for new assets
5. Repaying borrowed monies from profits that the same money has generated

These functions impact on your profitability and your survivability. For this reason, they are extremely important. One reason for owning and operating your own business is to make a good profit for yourself, and you will need good financial management to reach this goal.

Methods to help you with these functions are discussed throughout the book, not only in this chapter. However, in this chapter we will focus on items of particular concern for the small businessperson in handling his or her financial management responsibilities. These include the definition and components of working capital, the tools of financial management necessary to accomplish any of the functions listed, analysis methods needed to find out whether or not you are performing adequately financially, and the break-even analysis which must be used for many of your business decisions prior to an investment. This chapter is one that you will refer to again and again, and using it in conjunction with other chapters such as that on record keeping will enable you to analyze what is going on in your business at all times. This will help you correct deficiencies and make your business increasingly more profitable.

WORKING CAPITAL

Small businesspersons are particularly concerned with the term "working capital." It is the difference between your current assets and your current liabilities. It is the circulating lifeblood of your business. Research has shown that lack of control of this lifeblood is a primary cause of business failure in firms of all sizes. For this reason, you must understand the components of working capital. This understanding will allow you to be alert for change or the opportunity for change. A change in your business implies a change in the financial health of your company, either for better or for worse. Monitor these components to insure that the end result in your company is for the better.

1. *Cash and cash equivalents.* This is the most liquid form of current assets. This means it is the easiest to convert in form and to use. Cash equivalents are usually marketable securities or short-term certificates of deposit. You must maintain a well-planned cash budgeting system so that you will know whether the cash on hand in the form of cash and equivalents is adequate to meet current expenses as you must pay them—whether the timing relationship between cash inflow and outflow is favorable. Remember, it is fine that at the end of the year you would make a big profit, but if at any time during the year you have a sufficiently large negative cash flow, you could end up bankrupt. You should also know when peak cash needs may occur and the magnitude of borrowing that might be required to meet cash shortfalls. And, of course, your system should enable you to see when and how repayment will be accomplished.

2. *Accounts receivable.* As explained in an earlier chapter, in many cases your business will be required to extend credit to your customers or clients. However, this account must be closely watched, and you should note whether the amounts of accounts receivable are reasonable in relationship to your overall sales and the age of these accounts, and, of course, what action you can take to speed up collections and whether such accounts should be eliminated in the future. It may be of little help if sales are extremely high if most of your sales are in accounts receivable. Everyone may owe you money, but no one is paying!

3. *Inventories.* Frequently your inventory may make up better than 50% of your current assets. This is a significant amount and means that you must keep a close watch on this account. You should know whether the amount of inventory is reasonable in relation to sales and other operational characteristics of your business. A rapidity of turnover of inventory is important here and should be compared with that of other firms in your industry. Also, you should note whether any amount of inventory is invested in items which are not moving or are slow to move. On the other hand, are you losing sales due to an inadequate supply of inventory? Either situation implies action that you must take either to increase or to decrease your inventory.

4. *Accounts payable and trade notes payable.* One source of credit is trade credit. We talked about this earlier, and about how money you owe to suppliers actually is a form of loan. But unlimited amounts of credit are not good for your business, even if you could obtain them. In this respect, you should note the amount of credit and how it compares with your purchases. What is your payment policy and how does it affect your credit rating? This could be extremely important to you in the future, even if it is not now. Also, note the possible advantages of discount, such as the 2% if paid within 10 days discussed in an earlier chapter. Also of interest are the possible timing relationships between the payments on accounts payable and collections that you receive on accounts receivable.

5. *Notes payable.* Notes payable to banks or perhaps even to individual lenders or the former owner of your business are a major source of possible financing, and one that we discussed in Chapter 2. You must know whether the

debt amount is reasonable in relationship to other types of financing such as equity financing of your firm. Also, you must know when various payments will fall due and whether funds are available to meet these payments on time.

6. *Accrued expenses and taxes payable.* Accrued expenses and taxes payable represent obligations of the firm as of the date that you prepare the balance sheet. These accrued expenses represent items such as salaries, interest payable, bank notes, insurance premiums payable, and so forth. Taxes payable are self-evident. But in both cases, it is extremely important that the magnitude, timing, and availability of funds be looked into very carefully. Taxes not paid on time, for example, can result in your firm's being closed down by the government until the taxes are paid.

To help you keep track of some of the items which are necessary in monitoring the elements of your working capital listed above, various ratio analyses have been developed and used over the years. These will be discussed shortly.

THE TOOLS OF FINANCIAL MANAGEMENT

Certain tools are available for you in accomplishing the functions needed in financial management of your firm. These tools are as follows:

1. *Accounting records.* These records are the basis of your financial management. At this point you may feel that keeping track of your business on a day-to-day basis and accounting for all transactions is too time consuming. Overall, you will save time and money doing this. Methods of keeping accurate and precise records are contained in Chapter 9.

2. *Financial records and reports.* These records and reports are also of great help in financial management. They include the balance sheet and the profit and loss statement as discussed earlier in Chapter 4 on Business Planning and Chapter 9 on Record Keeping. These two financial statements are the basis for all financial analyses and are used by bankers and other investors in making loan evaluations and investment decisions. For this reason, you must understand these two documents and be able to explain each item that may appear in them. State and federal laws pertaining to taxation also require reports that can be put together only from the use of profit and loss and balance sheets. Finally, these two documents will be very helpful in accomplishing your financial analyses.

3. *Analysis techniques.* Techniques of analysis developed for financial management are the third set of tools that you will use in accomplishing this task. These tools include ratio analyses, return-on-investment guides, and break-even analysis. They will be discussed next.

RATIO ANALYSES

Ratio analyses are indicators that have been developed to help you to determine the state of health of various financial aspects of your business. They provide indications as to weaknesses and strengths in your financial operation as well as clues as to where and how to develop better financial performance. Such ratios also permit you to compare how you are doing with the performance of other similar businesses in your industry.

However, even with their importance and the considerable insight they provide, there are limitations to the use of ratio analyses. You must also consider the following limitations during your analysis:

1. The ratios are based on past performance. Therefore, you must balance their indications with what is happening now and what is likely to happen in your business in the future.
2. Ratios are frequently calculated for specific dates. If your business is seasonal, this factor must be considered.
3. Businesses are not perfectly comparable. Different items may be stated in different ways on financial statements. As a result, the financial ratios computed for your business may differ from those of the average in your industry for reasons other than performance.

Despite these limitations, financial ratios and ratio analyses may be of great help to you. Let's look at some of those available.

Measures of Liquidity

Liquidity is the ability to use the money available in your business. In general, the more liquid the better the state of financial health. However, this is a bit oversimplified as I will show you later. The ratios intended to measure liquidity in your business will tell you whether you have enough cash on hand plus assets that can be readily turned into cash to pay debts that may fall due during any given period. They will also tell you about how quickly they can be turned into cash.

The Current Ratio

The current ratio is possibly the best-known measure of financial health. It answers this question: Does your business have sufficient current assets to meet current debts with a margin of safety for possible losses due to uncollectible accounts receivable and other factors?

The current ratio is computed by using information on your balance sheet. You simply divide current assets by current liabilities. For example, if we consider the sample balance sheet in Figure 9.4, current assets are $155,000, and current liabilities are $90,000. $155,000 divided by $90,000 equals a current ratio of 1.7.

Now you may ask: Is this a good current ratio or is it not? You cannot determine this from the numerical value of 1.7 by itself, even though there is a popular rule of thumb which says that a current ratio of at least two to one is okay. The current ratio very much depends on your business and the specific characteristics of your current assets and liabilities. However, one major indication is a comparison with other companies in your industry. I'll give you sources for this information later in the chapter.

If after analysis and comparison you decide that your current ratio is too low, you may be able to raise it by the following actions:

1. Increase your current assets by new equity contributions.
2. Try converting noncurrent assets into current assets.
3. Pay some of your debts.
4. Increase your current assets from loans or other types of borrowing which have a maturity of at least a year in the future.
5. Put some of the profits back into the business.

The Acid Test or "Quick" Ratio

The "quick" ratio or acid test ratio is also an outstanding measure of liquidity. You calculate this ratio as follows: cash plus government securities plus receivables divided by current liabilities.

The company shown in Figure 9.4 has no government securities. Therefore, the numerator of this figure becomes $35,000 cash plus $55,000 in accounts receivable or $90,000. This is divided by current liabilities on the same balance sheet of $90,-000 to result in an acid test ratio of 1.0

The quick ratio concentrates on really liquid assets whose values are definite and well known. Therefore, the quick ratio will answer this question: If all your sales revenue disappears tomorrow, can you meet current obligations with your cash or quick funds on hand? Usually an acid test ratio of approximately 1.0 is considered satisfactory. However, you must also make this decision conditional on the following:

1. There should be nothing in the offing to slow up the collection of your accounts receivable.
2. The receipt of accounts receivable collections should not trail the due schedule for paying your current liabilities. In checking out this timing, you should consider payment of your creditors sufficiently early to take advantage of any discounts which are offered.

If these two conditions are not met, then you will need an acid test ratio higher than 1.0. However, it is erroneous to believe that either the current or the acid test ratio should always be as high as possible. Only those from whom you have borrowed money would say this is so. Naturally, they are interested in the greatest possible safety of their loan. However, you do not want to have large sums of money lying idle and not earning you additional profits. If you do have idle cash balances and receivables and inventories which are out of proportion to your needs, you should reduce them. The key here is to be conservative enough to keep a safety pad and yet bold enough to take advantage of the fact that you have these resources which can be used to earn additional profits for you. Before you make this decision as to the right amount of liquidity, you should consider the two ratios discussed next, average collection period and inventory turnover.

Average Collection Period

The average collection period is the number of days that sales are tied up in accounts receivable. This number can be calculated by using your profit and loss statement or income statement as shown in Figure 9.5. First, take your net sales which in Figure 9.5 are $1,035,000, and divide this figure by the days in your accounting period or 365. This equals $2,836, the average sales per day in the accounting period. Next, take your accounts receivable which you obtain from the balance sheet, Figure 9.4. Accounts receivable are $55,000. Divide $55,000 by the figure you just calculated ($2,836). $55,000 divided by $2,836 equals 19. This is the average number of days sales are tied up in receivables. It is also your average collection period.

This tells you how promptly your accounts are being collected considering whatever credit terms you are extending. It tells you two other things: (1) the quality of your accounts and notes receivable, that is, whether you are really getting paid rapidly or not, and (2) how good a job your credit department is doing in collecting these accounts.

Now the question is: Is the figure of 19 days good or not good? There is a rule of thumb that says the average collection period should not exceed one and one-third times the credit terms offered. Therefore, if your company offers 30 days to pay and the average collection period is only 19 days, you are doing very well. On the other hand, anything in excess of 40 days (1⅓ × 30 = 40) would show that you may have a problem.

Inventory Turnover

Inventory turnover will show you how rapidly your merchandise is moving. It will also show you how much capital you had tied up in inventory to support the level of your company's operations for the period that you are analyzing. To calculate inventory turnover, simply divide the cost of goods sold that you obtain from your income statement, Figure 9.5, by your average inventory. According to Figure 9.5, your income or profit and loss statement, the cost of goods sold equals $525,000. You cannot calculate your average inventory from Figure 9.4. You only know that for the period for which the inventory is stated, it equals $60,000. Let's assume that the previous balance sheet indicated that your inventory was $50,-000. Then, the average inventory for the two periods would be $60,000 plus $50,-000 divided by 2, or $55,000. Now, let's see what inventory turnover is: Cost of goods sold again was $525,000 divided by $55,000 equals 9.5.

This means that you turned your inventory 9.5 times during the year. Put another way, through your business operations you used up merchandise which total 9.5 times the average inventory investment. Under most circumstances, the higher the turnover of inventory, the better, because it means that you are able to operate with a relatively small sum of money invested in this inventory. Another implication is that your inventory is the right inventory. That is, it is salable and has not been in stock too long. But, even here, you must consider that too high a figure may be a sign of a problem. Very high inventory may mean that you have inventory shortages, and inventory shortages soon lead to customer dissatisfaction and may mean a loss of customers to the competition in the long run.

Is 9.5 a satisfactory inventory turnover or not? Again, the desirable rate depends on your business, your industry, your method of valuing inventories, and numerous other factors that are unique to your situation. And, once again, it is helpful to study and compare your turnover rate with that of similar businesses of your size in your industry. Once you have been working and operating for some time, past experiences with inventory turnover will indicate what is good and what is not with less reliance on inventory comparisons.

Very frequently it is helpful to analyze not just your total inventory but specific inventory turnover for different products or even groups of products or product lines. This will show you which items are doing well and which are not. You may also prepare turnover analyses for much more frequent periods than a year. Even monthly or weekly periods may be necessary or required for perishable items or items that become obsolete very quickly. Thus, you will know to reorder those items which are truly "hot" items early and in plenty of time, and you will also know which items you should not order and which items you must order before their value goes down to a point where you can no longer sell them at all.

PROFITABILITY MEASURES

Measures of profitability are essential in your business if you are to know how much money you are making, whether you are making as much as you can, or whether you are making money at all. There are several different ratios which will assist you in determining this. These are the asset earning power, return on owner's equity, net profit on sales, investment turnover, and finally, return on investment (ROI).

Asset Earning Power

Asset earning power is determined by the ratio of earnings before interest and taxes to total assets. From the income statement in Figure 9.5 we can see that total operating profit or income is $105,000. Total assets from the balance sheet, Figure 9.4, are $272,000. Therefore, $105,000 divided by $272,000 equals 0.39 or 39%.

Return on the Owner's Equity

Return on the owner's equity shows the return that you received in exchange for your investment in your business. To compute this ratio you will usually use the average equity for 12 months, if it is available, or, if not, the average of figures from two different balance sheets, your latest and the one prior. Return on the owner's equity equals net profit divided by equity. Net profit from Figure 9.5 is $55,000. Equity from Figure 9.4 is $115,000. Assuming the equity from the period before is also $115,000, we will use this as an average. Therefore, return on the owner's equity equals $55,000 divided by $115,000, which equals 0.48 or 48%.

You can calculate a similar ratio by using tangible net worth in lieu of equity. Tangible net worth equals equity less any intangible assets such as patents and good will. If no intangible assets exist, then, of course, the two will be equal.

Net Profit on Sales

The net profit on sales ratio measures the difference between what you take in and what you spend in the process of doing business. Again, net profit was determined to be $55,000. Net sales from Figure 9.5 is $1,035,000. Therefore, net profit on sales equals 0.053 or 5.3%.

This means that for every dollar of sales the company has made a profit of 5.3¢.

The net profit on sales ratio depends mainly on these two factors: (1) operating costs, and (2) pricing policies. Therefore, if this figure goes down, it could be because you have lowered prices or it could be because costs have been increasing at the same time that prices have remained stable.

Again, this ratio should be compared with figures from other similar businesses, and you should consider trends over a period of time. It is also useful to compare net profit on sales ratios for individual products to show which products or product lines should be given additional emphasis and which should be eliminated.

Investment Turnover

This ratio is annual net sales to total assets. In this case, net sales of $1,035,000, divided by total assets of $272,000 from Figure 9.4, equals 3.8.

Again, investment turnover should be compared and watched for trends.

Return on Investment (ROI)

There are several different ways of calculating return on investment. It is a very useful method of measuring profitability. One simple way is simply to take net profit and divide it by total assets. In this case, the net profit equals $55,000. Total assets are $272,000. Therefore, $55,000 divided by $272,000 equals 0.20 or 20%.

It is desirable here to have the highest net profit for the smallest amount of total assets invested. You can use this rate of return on investment for intercompany and interindustry comparisons, as well as pricing costs, inventory and investment decisions, and many other measurements of efficiency and profitability. However you use it, always be sure that you are consistent in making your comparisons; that is, be sure that you use the same definitions of net profit and assets invested.

Here are some additional measures of profitability using ROI:

1. *Rate of earnings on total capital employed equals net income plus interest and taxes divided by total liabilities and capital.* This ratio serves as an index of productivity of capital as well as a measure of earning power in operating efficiency.

2. *Rate of earnings on invested capital equals net income plus income taxes divided by proprietary equity and fixed liabilities.* This ratio is used as a measure of earning power of the borrowed invested capital.

3. *Rate of earnings on proprietary equity equals net income divided by total capital including surplus reserves.* This ratio is used as a measure of the yield on the owner's investment.

4. *Rate of earnings on stock equity equals net income divided by total capital including surplus reserves.* This ratio is used as a measure of the attractiveness of common stock as an investment.

5. *Rate of dividends on common stock equity equals common stock dividends divided by common stock equity.* This ratio is used to indicate the desirability of common stock as a source of income.

6. *Rate of dividends on common stock equity equals common stock dividend per share divided by market value per share of common stock.* This ratio is used as a measure of the current yield on investment in a particular stock.

SOURCES OF RATIO ANALYSES FROM ALL INDUSTRIES

In order to be able to compare your business with other businesses in your industry, it is necessary to obtain pertinent data on other businesses. Here are different sources for such information:

1. Dun and Bradstreet, Inc., Business Information Systems, 99 Church St., New York, NY 10007. This firm publishes key business ratios in 125 lines annually. Legal copies can be obtained free on request.

2. Accounting Corporation of America, 1929 First Ave., San Diego, CA 92101. This organization publishes *Parameter of Small Businesses* which classifies its operating ratios for various industry groups on the basis of gross volume.

3. National Cash Register Co., Marketing Services Department, Dayton, OH 45409. This firm publishes *Expenses in Retail Businesses* which examines the cost of operations in over 50 kinds of businesses obtained from primary sources, most of which are trade associations.

4. Robert Morris Associates, Philadelphia National Bank Building, Philadel-

phia, PA 19107. Robert Morris has developed and published ratio studies for over 225 lines of businesses.

5. The Small Business Administration. The SBA has a new series of reports which provide expenses as a percentage of sales for many industries. While the reports do not provide strict ratio information, a comparison of percentage expenses will be very useful for your financial management.

6. Trade Associations. Many national trade associations publish ratio studies, including the following:

Air-Conditioning & Refrigeration Wholesalers, 22371 Newman Avenue, Dearborn, MI 48124

Air Transport Association of America, 1000 Connecticut Avenue NW, Washington, D.C. 20036

American Bankers Association, 90 Park Avenue, New York, NY 10016

American Book Publishers Council, One Park Avenue, New York, NY 10016

American Booksellers Association, 175 Fifth Avenue, New York, NY 10010

American Carpet Institute, 350 Fifth Avenue, New York, NY 10001

American Institute of Laundering, Doris and Chicago Avenues, Joliet, IL 60433

American Institute of Supply Associations, 1505 22d Street NW, Washington, D.C. 20037

American Meat Institute, 59 East Van Buren Street, Chicago, IL 60605

American Paper Institute, 260 Madison Avenue, New York, NY 10016

American Society of Association Executives, 2000 K Street, NW, Washington, D.C. 20006

American Electric Association, 16223 Meyers Street, Detroit, MI 48235

American Supply Association, 221 North LaSalle Street, Chicago, IL 60601

Automotive Service Industry Association, 230 North Michigan Avenue, Chicago, IL 60601

Bowling Proprietors' Association of America, Inc., West Higgins Road, Hoffman Estates, IL 60172

Florists' Telegraph Delivery Association, 900 West Lafayette Boulevard, Detroit, MI 48226

Food Service Equipment Industry, Inc., 332 South Michigan Avenue, Chicago, IL 60604

Laundry and Cleaners Allied Trades Association, 1180 Raymond Boulevard, Newark, NJ 07102

Material Handling Equipment Distributors Association, 20 North Wacker Drive, Chicago, IL 60616

Mechanical Contractors Association of America, 666 Third Avenue, Suite 1464, New York, NY 10017

Menswear Retailers of America, 390 National Press Building, Washington, D.C. 20004

Motor and Equipment Manufacturers Association, 250 West 57th Street, New York, NY 10019

National-American Wholesale Lumber Association, 180 Madison Avenue, New York, NY 10016

National Appliance and Radio-TV Dealers Association, 1319 Merchandise Mart, Chicago, IL 60654

National Association of Accountants, 525 Park Avenue, New York, NY 10022

National Association of Building Owners and Managers, 134 South LaSalle Street, Chicago, IL 60603

National Association of Electrical Distributors, 600 Madison Avenue, New York, NY 10022

National Association of Food Chains, 1725 Eye Street, NW, Washington, D.C. 20006

National Association of Furniture Manufacturers, 666 North Lake Shore Drive, Chicago, IL 60611

National Association of Insurance Agents, 96 Fulton Street, New York, NY 10038

National Association of Music Merchants, Inc., 222 West Adams Street, Chicago, IL 60606

National Association of Plastic Distributors, 2217 Tribune Tower, Chicago, IL 60611

National Association of Retail Grocers of the United States, 360 North Michigan Avenue, Chicago IL 60601

National Association of Textile and Apparel Wholesalers, 350 Fifth Avenue, New York, NY 10001

National Association of Tobacco Distributors, 360 Lexington Avenue, New York, NY 10017

National Automatic Merchandising Association, Seven South Dearborn Street, Chicago, IL 60603

National Beer Wholesalers' Association of America, 6310 North Cicero Avenue, Chicago IL 60646

National Builders' Hardware Association, 1290 Avenue of the Americas, New York, NY 10019

National Electrical Contractors Association, 1200 18th Street, NW, Washington, D.C. 20036

National Electrical Manufacturers Association, 155 East 44th Street, New York, NY 10017

National Farm and Power Equipment Dealers Association, 2340 Hampton Avenue, St. Louis, MO 63130

National Home Furnishing Association, 1150 Merchandise Mart, Chicago, IL 60654

National Kitchen Cabinet Association, 918 Commonwealth Building, 674 South 4th Street, Louisville, KY 40204

National Lumber and Building Material Dealers Association, Ring Building, Washington, D.C. 20036

National Office Products Association, Investment Building, 1511 K Street, NW, Washington, D.C. 20015

National Machine Tool Builders Association, 2071 East 102d Street, Cleveland, OH 44106

National Oil Jobbers Council, 1001 Connecticut Avenue, NW, Washington, D.C. 20036

National Paper Box Manufacturers Association, 121 North Bread Street, Suite 910, Philadelphia, PA 19107

National Paper Trade Association, 220 East 42d Street, New York, NY 10017

National Parking Association, 1101 17th Street, NW, Washington, D.C. 20036

National Restaurant Association, 1530 North Lake Shore Drive, Chicago, IL 60610

National Retail Furniture Association, 1150 Merchandise Mart Plaza, Chicago, IL 60654

National Retail Hardware Association, 964 North Pennsylvania Avenue, Indianapolis IN 46204

National Retail Merchants Association, 100 West 31st Street, New York, NY 10001

National Shoe Retailers Association, 200 Madison Avenue, New York, NY 10016

National Sporting Goods Association, 23 East Jackson Boulevard, Chicago, IL 60604

National Stationery and Office Equipment Association, Investment Building, 1511 K Street, NW, Washington, D.C. 20005

National Tire Dealers and Retreaders Association, 1343 L Street, NW, Washington, D.C. 20005

National Wholesale Druggists' Association, 220 East 42d Street, New York, NY 10017

National Wholesale Jewelers Association, 1900 Arch Street, Philadelphia, PA 19103

National Wholesale Hardware Association, 1900 Arch Street, Philadelphia, PA 19103

Northamerican Heating & Airconditioning Wholesalers Association, 1200 West 5th Avenue, Columbus, OH 43212

Optical Wholesalers Association, 222 West Adams Street, Chicago, IL 60606

Paint and Wallpaper Association of America, 7935 Clayton Road, St. Louis, MO 63117

Petroleum Equipment Institute, 525 Dowell Building, Tulsa, OK 74114

Printing Industries of America, 711 14th Street, NW, Washington, D.C. 20005

Robert Morris Association, Philadelphia National Bank Building, Philadelphia, PA 19107

Scientific Apparatus Makers Associates, 20 North Wacker Drive, Chicago, IL 60606

Shoe Service Institute of America, 222 West Adams Street, Chicago, IL 60606

Super Market Institute, Inc., 200 East Ontario Street, Chicago, IL 60611

United Fresh Fruit and Vegetable Association, 777 14th Street, NW, Washington, D.C. 20005

United States Wholesale Grocers' Association, 1511 K Street, NW, Washington, D.C. 20005

Urban Land Institute, 1200 18th Street, NW, Washington, D.C. 20036

Wine and Spirits Wholesalers of America, 319 North Fourth Street, St. Louis, MO 63102

BREAK-EVEN ANALYSIS

The break-even analysis is an excellent technique for determining the ultimate success of any project even before you begin. The break-even analysis will tell you the following:

1. How many units you must sell in order to start making money
2. How much profit you will make at any given level of sales

3. How changing your price will affect profitability
4. How expense reductions of different types will affect profitability

To accomplish a break-even analysis, you must first separate the costs associated with your project into two types: fixed costs and variable costs.

Fixed costs are those expenses associated with the project that you would have to pay whether you sold one unit or 10,000 units or for that matter sold no units at all. For example, if you rented a garage to use in your business and the owner of the garage charged you $500 to rent the garage for the period of the project, then this would be a fixed cost for that period. You would have to pay the $500 whether or not you sold any products or many of your products. Research and development costs for a project or a product would also be considered a fixed cost, since this money would have to be paid whether or not you sold any of the product.

Variable costs vary directly with the number of units that you sell. If it costs you $1.80 to manufacture a unit, then that $1.80 is a variable cost. If postage for mailing your product to a ccustomer is $1, then $1 is a variable cost. If you sell 10 units, then your postage cost will be 10 times $1 or $10. If you sell 100 units, your total variable cost for postage will be 100 times $1 or $100.

It is difficult to decide whether to consider some costs fixed or to consider them variable, and very frequently there is no single right answer. You must make this decision by yourself as the owner of the business. As a general guideline, if there is a direct relationship between cost and number of units sold, consider the cost variable. If you can find no relationship, then consider the cost fixed.

Total cost of your project will always equal total fixed costs plus total variable costs. Consider the following example for an item which you are going to sell. Fixed costs:

Utility expense at $100 per month for 36 months, $3,600
Telephone at $200 per year for 3 years, $600
Product development, $1,000
Patenting expense, $2,500
Total fixed costs, $7,700

Variable costs:

Cost of product, $1 per unit
Cost of postage and packaging, 50¢ per unit
Cost of advertising, $3 per unit
Total variable cost, $4.50 per unit

To calculate break-even, we start with profit. Profit is the number of units sold multiplied by the profit at which we are selling them less the number of units sold multiplied by the total variable cost minus the total fixed cost. Let's use an equation to make this a little easier to follow.

Let P equal profit, p equal price, U equal number of units sold, V equal variable cost, and F equal fixed cost. Then our equation becomes:

$$P = (U \times p) - (U \times V) - F$$

Or, we can simplify this to:

$$P = (U \times p - V) - F$$

Substituting the values we have in our sample, we have:

$$P = (\$1{,}000 \times \$10 - \$4.50) - \$7{,}700 = \$55{,}000 - \$7{,}700 = -\$2{,}200$$

What is the significance of the minus number? This means that instead of making a profit, we have lost money, $2,200 to be exact. Now, we may want to know how many units we must sell in order to make money, or at what point we will stop losing money. This point at which we will either make money or lose money is called break-even. Beginning at this point, we will begin to show a profit. In order to calculate this, we use the break-even formula. In the break-even formula, using the same variables as above:

$$\text{Break-even} = F \div p - V$$

Since we know that F equals $7,700 and P equals $10 and V equals $4.50,

$$\text{Break-even} = \$7{,}700 \div \$610 - \$4.50 = 1{,}400 \text{ units}$$

This means if we don't change price or reduce expenses in any other way, we need to sell 1,400 units of this product before we start making any money.

However, there is an easier way to calculate this; we can use a break-even chart as shown in Figure 11.1. A break-even chart has a major advantage over the break-even and profit formulas. It shows us graphically the relationship of fixed and variable costs and total expenses to sales at all volumes of sales. This means that we can calculate profits at any level of sales right away.

Figure 11.1. Break-even analysis.

To construct a break-even chart, follow the following five steps:

Step 1: Get some graph paper and label the horizontal line on the bottom *Units Sold.* Label the vertical line at the left of the graph *Dollars (sales and expenses).* Divide each line into equal parts of dollars and units and label them appropriately.

Step 2: Analyze all of your costs for the project and decide whether each is fixed or variable. Decide on the period of sales for your project. Total your fixed variable costs.

Step 3: Draw a horizontal line to intersect the proper point on the vertical line to represent fixed costs, as at point A in Figure 11.1.

Step 4: Calculate the dollar value of sales for any unit number. For example, if you sell 2,000 units, how much is this in sales dollars? For the example, total sales volume would be 2,000 times $10 or $20,000. Plot this point at 2,000 units at $20,000 on the chart as point "a." Put one end of a ruler at the zero point in the lower left corner of the chart and the other end at the point you have just plotted. This is total sales line B in Figure 11.1.

Step 5: Calculate the dollar value for variable costs for any unit number. For example, in this case variable cost is $4.50 per unit. At 2,000 units, total variable cost is 2,000 times $4.50 or $9,000. Add $9,000 to the fixed cost, in this case $7,700, to come up with $16,700. Plot this on the chart as "b" in Figure 11.1. Lay one end of the ruler at the point where the fixed cost line, B, intersects with the vertical dollar scale, and the other at the point you just plotted. Draw a line to form the variable cost line, C, in Figure 11.1.

Now your break-even chart is complete. The point at which the total sales line or variable cost line intersects is a break-even point which you read on the horizontal unit scale at the bottom of the chart in Figure 11.1 as 1,400 units, just as we calculated before using the equation.

To calculate profit for any number of units you want, simply subtract the dollar value read opposite the profit point on the variable cost line, C, from the dollar value read opposite the profit point on the total sales line, B. For example, to calculate the profit if you sell 2,000 units, read right up from 2,000 units on the unit scale to point "b" on the variable cost line. Read straight across from point "b" to $16,700 on the vertical dollar scale. Now read straight out from 2,000 units on the unit scale to a point on the total sales line. Read straight across from point "a" to $20,000 on the vertical dollar scale. $20,000 minus $16,700 equals $3,300 if you sell 2,000 units. Do the same thing for any number of units to calculate profit.

Use break-even analysis any time you want to calculate the profit or how many units you must sell before you begin to make money.

There are some limitations to break-even analysis. These are as follows:

1. Break-even analysis shows profit at various levels of sales, but does not show profitability. Since there are always alternative uses for your firm's financial resources, it is impossible to compare products for profitability solely based on break-even, whereas profitability should be one of the major points of consideration. For a profitability comparison, you must use one of the ratio analyses given to you earlier.

2. Break-even analysis does not allow you examination of cash flows, and it is generally accepted that the appropriate way to make investment or capital budgeting decisions is to consider the value of cash flows over a period of time and to discount this value using the cost of capital concept explained to you in an earlier chapter. This cannot be done with break-even analysis, either.

CHECKLIST FOR PROFIT WATCHING

Financial management boils down to one major consideration. Are you making a profit or are you not? To assist you with this calculation, the Small Business Administration has published a checklist for profit watching, developed by Narendra C. Bhandari, associate professor of management, and Charles S. McCubbin, Jr., both of the University of Baltimore.[1] Use this checklist to be sure that you are doing everything possible to manage the financial resources of your firm effectively and efficiently.

Are You Making a Profit?

Analysis of Revenues and Expenses.   Since profit is revenues less expenses, to determine what your profit is you must first identify all revenues and expenses for the period under study.

	Yes	**No**

1. Have you chosen an appropriate period for profit determination?

For accounting purposes firms generally use a twelve month period, such as January 1 to December 31 or July 1 to June 30. The accounting year you select doesn't have to be a calendar year (January to December); a seasonal business, for example, might close its year after the end of the season. The selection depends upon the nature of your business, your personal preference, or possible tax considerations.

2. Have you determined your total revenues for the accounting period?

In order to answer this question, consider the following questions:

What is the amount of gross revenue from sales of your goods or service? **(Gross Sales)**

What is the amount of goods returned by your customers and credited? **(Returns and Rejects)**

What is the amount of discounts given to your customers and employees? **(Discounts)**

What is the amount of net sales from goods and services? **(Net Sales = Gross Sales −[Returns and Rejects + Discounts])**

What is the amount of income from other sources, such as interest on bank deposits, dividends from securities, rent on property leased to others? **(Nonoperating Income)**

What is the amount of total revenue? **(Total Revenue = Net Sales + Nonoperating Income)**

3. Do you know what your total expenses are?

Expenses are the cost of goods sold and services used in the process of selling goods or services. Some common expenses for all businesses are:

---

[1] Narendra C. Bhandari and Charles S. McCubbin, Jr., *Checklist to Profit Watching*, Small Business Administration (1980).

Yes   No

Cost of goods sold (Cost of Goods Sold = Beginning Inventory + Purchases − Ending Inventory)

Wages and salaries (Don't forget to include your own—at the actual rate you'd have to pay someone else to do your job.)

Rent

Utilities (electricity, gas, telephone, water, etc.)

Supplies (office, cleaning, and the like)

Delivery expenses

Insurance

Advertising and promotional costs

Maintenance and upkeep

Depreciation (Here you need to make sure your depreciation policies are realistic and that all depreciable items are included.)

Taxes and licenses

Interest

Bad debts

Professional assistance (accountant, attorney, etc.)

There are, of course, many other types of expenses, but the point is that *every* expense must be recorded and deducted from your revenues before you know what your profit is. Understanding your expenses is the first step toward *controlling them* and *increasing* your *profit*.

Financial Ratios

A **financial ratio** is an expression of the relationship between two items selected from the income statement or the balance sheet. Ratio analysis helps you evaluate the weak and strong points in your financial and managerial performance.

4. Do you know your current ratio?

The **current ratio** (current assets divided by current debts) is a measure of the cash or near cash position (liquidity) of the firm. It tells you if you have enough cash to pay your firm's current creditors. The higher the ratio, the more liquid the firm's position is and, hence, the higher the credibility of the firm. Cash, receivables, marketable securities, and inventory are current assets. Naturally, you need to be realistic in valuing receivables and inventory for a true picture of your liquidity, since some debts may be uncollectable and some stock obsolete. Current liabilities are those which must be paid in one year.

5. Do you know your quick ratio?

Quick assets are current assets minus inventory. The **quick ratio** (or acid-test ratio) is found by dividing quick assets by current liabilities. The purpose, again, is to test the firm's ability to meet its current obligations. This test doesn't include inventory to make it a stiffer test of the company's liquidity. It tells you if the business could meet its current obligations with quickly convertible assets should sales revenues suddenly cease.

	Yes	No

6. Do you know your total debt to net worth ratio?

This ratio (the result of total debt divided by net worth then multiplied by 100) is a measure of how the company can meet its total obligations from equity. The lower the ratio, the higher the proportion of equity relative to debt and the better the firm's credit rating will be.

7. Do you know your average collection period?

You find this ratio by dividing accounts receivable by daily credit sales. (Daily credit sales = annual credit sales divided by 360.) This ratio tells you the length of time it takes the firm to get its cash after making a sale on credit. The shorter this period the quicker the cash inflow is. A longer than normal* period may mean overdue and uncollectable bills. If you extend credit for a specific period (say, 30 days), this ratio should be very close to the same number of days. If it's much longer than the established period, you may need to alter your credit policies. It's wise to develop an aging schedule to gauge the trend of collections and identify slow payers. Slow collections (without adequate financing charges) hurt your profit, since you could be doing something much more useful with your money, such as taking advantage of discounts on your own payables.

8. Do you know your ratio of net sales to total assets?

This ratio (net sales divided by total assets) measures the efficiency with which you are using your assets. A higher than normal ratio indicates that the firm is able to generate sales from its assets faster (and better) than the average concern.

9. Do you know your operating profit to net sales ratio?

This ratio (the result of dividing operating profit by net sales and multiplying by 100) is most often used to determine the profit position relative to sales. A higher than normal ratio indicates that your sales are good, that your expenses are low, or both. Interest income and interest expense should not be included in calculating this ratio.

10. Do you know your net profit to total assets ratio?

This ratio (found by multiplying by 100 the result of dividing net profit by total assets) is often called return on investment or ROI. It focuses on the profitability of the overall operation of the firm. Thus, it allows management to measure the effects of its policies on the firm's profitability. The ROI is the single most important measure of a firm's financial position. You might say it's the bottom line for the bottom line.

11. Do you know your net profit to net worth ratio?

This ratio is found by dividing net profit by net worth and multiplying the result by 100. It provides information on the productivity of the resources the owners have committed to the firm's operations.

All ratios measuring profitability can be computed either before or after taxes, depending on the purpose of the computations. Ratios have limitations. Since the information used to derive ratios is itself based on accounting rules and personal

Yes No

judgments, as well as facts, the ratios cannot be considered absolute indicators of a firm's financial position. Ratios are only one means of assessing the performance of the firm and must be considered in perspective with many other measures. They should be used as a point of departure for further analysis and not as an end in themselves.

Sufficiency of Profit

The following questions are designed to help you measure the adequacy of the profit your firm is making. Making a profit is only the first step; making enough profit to survive and *grow* is really what business is all about.

12. Have you compared your profit with your profit goals? ⎯⎯ ⎯⎯

13. Is it possible your goals are too high or too low? ⎯⎯ ⎯⎯

14. Have you compared your present profits (absolute and ratios) with the profits made in the last one to three years? ⎯⎯ ⎯⎯

15. Have you compared your profits (absolute and ratios) with profits made by similar firms in your line? ⎯⎯ ⎯⎯

A number of organizations publish financial ratios for various businesses, among them Dun & Bradstreet, Robert Morris Associates, the Accounting Corporation of America, NCR Corporation, and the Bank of America. Your own trade association may also publish such studies. Remember, these published ratios are only averages. You probably want to be better than average.

Trend of Profit

16. Have you analyzed the direction your profits have been taking? ⎯⎯ ⎯⎯

The preceding analyses, with all their merits, report on a firm only at a single time in the past. It is not possible to use these isolated moments to indicate the trend of your firm's performance. To do a trend analysis performance indicators (absolute amounts or ratios) should be computed for several time periods (yearly for several years, for example) and the results laid out in columns side by side for easy comparison. You can then evaluate your performance, see the direction it's taking, and make initial forecasts of where it will go.

Mix of Profit

17. Does your firm sell more than one major product line or provide several distinct services? ⎯⎯ ⎯⎯

If it does, a separate profit and ratio analysis of each should be made:

To show the relative contribution by each product line or service;

To show the relative burden of expenses by each product or service;

To show which items are most profitable, which are less so, and which are losing money; and

To show which are slow and fast moving.

The profit and ratio analyses of each major item help you find out the strong and weak areas of your operations. They can help you to make profit-increasing decisions to drop a product line or service or to place particular emphasis behind one or another.

Records

Good records are essential. Without them a firm doesn't know where it's been, where it is, or where it's heading. Keeping records that are accurate, up-to-date, and easy to use is one of the most important functions of the owner-manager, his or her staff, and his or her outside counselors (lawyer, accountant, banker).

Basic Records

18. Do you have a general journal and/or special journals, such as one for cash receipts and disbursements?   _____   _____

A general journal is the basic record of the firm. Every monetary event in the life of the firm is entered in the general journal or in one of the special journals.

19. Do you prepare a sales report or analysis?   _____   _____

(a) Do you have sales goals by product, department, and accounting period (month, quarter, year)?   _____   _____

(b) Are your goals reasonable?   _____   _____

(c) Are you meeting your goals?   _____   _____

If you aren't meeting your goals, try to list the likely reasons on a sheet of paper. Such a study might include areas such as general business climate, competition, pricing, advertising, sales promotion, credit policies, and the like. Once you've identified the apparent causes you can take steps to increase sales (and profits).

Buying and Inventory System

20. Do you have a buying and inventory system?   _____   _____

The buying and inventory systems are two critical areas of a firm's operation that can affect profitability.

21. Do you keep records on the quality, service, price, and promptness of delivery of your sources of supply?   _____   _____

22. Have you analyzed the advantages and disadvantages of:

(a) Buying from suppliers,   _____   _____

(b) Buying from a minimum number of suppliers?   _____   _____

23. Have you analyzed the advantages and disadvantages of buying through cooperatives or other such systems?   _____   _____

24. Do you know:

(a) How long it usually takes to receive each order?   _____   _____

(b) How much inventory cushion (usually called safety

	Yes	No

stock) to have so you can maintain normal sales while you wait for the order to arrive?

25. Have you ever suffered because you were out of stock?

26. Do you know the optimum order quantity for each item you need?

27. Do you (or can you) take advantage of quantity discounts for large size single purchases?

28. Do you know your costs of ordering inventory and carrying inventory?

The more frequently you buy (smaller quantities per order), the higher your average ordering costs (clerical costs, postage, telephone costs, etc.) will be, and the lower the average carrying costs (storage, loss through pilferage, obsolescence, etc.) will be. On the other hand, the larger the quantity per order, the lower the average ordering cost and the higher the carrying costs. A balance should be struck so that the minimum cost overall for ordering and carrying inventory can be achieved.

29. Do you keep records of inventory for each item?

These records should be kept current by making entries whenever items are added to or removed from inventory. Simple records on 3 × 5 or 5 × 7 cards can be used with each item being listed on a separate card. Proper records will show for each item: quantity in stock, quantity on order, date of order, slow or fast seller, and valuations (which are important for taxes and your own analyses).

Other Financial Records

30. Do you have an accounts payable ledger?

This ledger will show what, whom, and why you owe. Such records should help you make your payments on schedule. Any expense not paid on time could adversely affect your credit, but even more importantly such records should help you take advantage of discounts which can help boost your profits.

31. Do you have an accounts receivable ledger?

This ledger will show who owes money to your firm. It shows how much is owed, how long it has been outstanding, and why the money is owed. Overdue accounts could indicate that your credit granting policy needs to be reviewed and that you may not be getting the cash into the firm quickly enough to pay your own bills at the optimum time.

32. Do you have a cash receipts journal?

This journal records the cash received by source, day, and amount.

33. Do you have a cash payments journal?

This journal will be similar to the cash receipts journal but will show cash paid out instead of cash received. The two cash journals can be combined, if convenient.

	Yes	No

34. Do you prepare an income (profit and loss or P & L) statement and a balance sheet?

These are statements about the condition of your firm at a specific time and show the income, expenses, assets, and liabilities of the firm. They are absolutely essential.

35. Do you prepare a budget?

You could think of a budget as a "record in advance," projecting "future" inflows and outflows for your business. A budget is usually prepared for a single year, generally to correspond with the accounting year. It is then, however, broken down into quarterly and monthly projections.

There are different kinds of budgets: cash, production, sales, etc. A cash budget, for example, will show the estimate of sales and expenses for a particular period of time. The cash budget forces the firm to think ahead by estimating its income and expenses. Once reasonable projections are made for every important produce line or department, the owner-manager has set targets for employees to meet for sales and expenses. You must plan to assure a profit. And you must prepare a budget to plan.

SOURCES OF ADDITIONAL INFORMATION

Accounting Handbook for Non-Accountants, by Clarence B. Nickerson, published by Cahners Books International, Inc., 221 Columbus Ave., Boston, MA 02116.

Finance for the Nonfinancial Manager, by Herbert T. Spiro, published by John Wiley and Sons, Inc., 605 Third Ave., New York, NY 10058.

Financial Handbook, edited by Jules I. Bogen, published by John Wiley and Sons, Inc., 605 Third Ave., New York, NY 10058.

Managerial Finance, 5th ed., by J. Fred Weston and Eugene F. Brigham, published by The Dryden Press, Hinsdale, IL 60521.

Profit Strategies for Business, by Robert Rachlin, published by Marr Publications, P.O. Box 1421, Radio City Station, New York, NY 10019.

12

Preventing Burglary, Robbery, Shoplifting, Internal Theft, and Bad Checks

Unfortunately, crime is rising in the United States. In fact, in just five years losses due to crime in small business have risen more than 100%, and this percentage is based on official figures, which involve only reported crimes. Probably, in actuality, the number of crimes is even higher. The subject of crime is very important to a small business. In fact, the Small Business Administration says that crime contributes to 30 to 40% of business failures. Furthermore, a small business is 35 times as likely to be a victim of crime as is a large business.

In this chapter, we are going to cover the methods of preventing major crimes for small business owners. These crimes include:

1. Burglary
2. Robbery
3. Shoplifting
4. Internal theft
5. Bad checks

BURGLARY

Burglary is any unlawful entry to commit a felony or a theft, whether or not force was used to gain entrance. Statistics show that burglaries have doubled in the past several years, and so it is a major crime with which small business must contend.

Prevention of Burglary

There are methods that can prevent burglary in your small business. These include: locks, alarm systems, key control, lighting, burglar-resistant windows, window screens, safes, guards or patrols, watchdogs, and frequent cash deposits. Let's look at each in turn.

Locks. Locks are important because even if they fail to keep a burglar out, the burglar must force his or her way onto your premises. This is important because in many standard burglary insurance policies, you must have evidence of a forced entry in order to collect.

According to the Small Business Administration, most experts on locks consider the pin-tumbler cylinder lock to provide the best security. Such a lock has a variable number of pins. You should consider a lock with at least five pins, as burglars can easily pick one with fewer pins. It is also wise to utilize dead-bolt locks. A dead-bolt lock is one having a lock bolt that must be moved positively by turning the knob or key without action of a spring. It cannot be opened by sliding a piece of flexible material or tool between the door edge and door jamb. If you use a double cylinder dead-bolt lock, the door cannot be opened without a key on either side. This is important, especially in the case of glass doors, because if the burglar breaks the glass and attempts to open the door merely by reaching through, he or she will not be able to do so. A double cylinder dead-bolt lock also provides protection in the case where a thief remains concealed during the day and then attempts to break out with his loot (your goods) after closing time. It is advisable to be particularly careful about the rear door in a store since burglars tend to favor rear doors. You may consider barring it in addition to locking it. All locks should be installed by a competent locksmith; even the best lock available will not be effective in preventing burglaries if it is not installed properly.

Alarm Systems. A silent central station burglar alarm generally is better protection than a local alarm such as a siren or a bell. This is because a silent alarm will alert only the specialist who knows how to handle the burglary and will not notify the burglar of his detection as will a loud local alarm system. On the other hand, if your intention is to frighten the burglar off prior to his entrance, it is the better type of protection.

Regardless of whether you want a silent alarm or a local alarm, there is a wide choice of sensory devices available for the system that you adopt. These include: ultrasonic detectors, photo beams, radar motion detectors, vibration detectors, and auxiliary equipment such as an automatic phone dialer which notifies the police when the alarm system has been triggered.

Each type of alarm has advantages and disadvantages, depending on your situation. Therefore, it is recommended that you have professional guidance in determining which alarm is best for you. For example, local alarms may be useless in areas that are not frequently patrolled or in secluded neighborhoods.

Key Control. Key control is as important as the lock the key opens. You should avoid key duplication by having the key stamped, "Do not duplicate." You should caution employees who have access to keys not to leave store keys with parking lot attendants or anywhere else where someone may gain access to them. You should keep a record of each of your keys and who has custody of it at any given time. When employees leave your employ or if a key is lost, you should install new locks and issue new keys. Don't use the same key for outside doors as for the door to your office. Remember that if you use a master key, it will weaken your security system since one key will open all locks. Do not have your keys plainly marked as to specific store or specific lock. Use a code with key numbers. Do everything possible to make it tougher for a potential burglar.

Lighting. Burglars prefer the darkness because of the protection that it offers. Therefore, illuminating exterior and interior parts of your premises at night will discourage burglars. In addition, indoor lighting allows police or patrol cars to see silhouettes in your store. Silhouettes help them to spot something amiss.

It is possible to control lighting with a photoelectric eye system which will turn on your lights automatically at dusk and turn them off at dawn. This saves you a trip on weekends, and means one less thing for you to remember to do.

Burglar-Resistant Windows. Windows, especially storefront windows that offer a burglar access to the store's interior, are very vulnerable to hit-and-run attacks by burglars who will break the glass, enter the store or perhaps open the window only, steal something, and leave immediately. The likelihood of such an attack's occurring can be reduced by using tempered glass, laminated glass, or impact-resistant plastic windows.

Window Screens. Steel mesh screens or bars are available to give added protection to windows, transom skylights, ventilator shafts, air vents, and manholes. Such protection is particularly important in screening areas that are not in view, as they are an excellent route of entry and exit for burglars. Heavy window screens or gratings are also available to protect show windows. After closing time, these screens are shut and locked into place and allow no room for entry of an object that could break your window.

Safes. Many safes are available which can provide excellent protection for your money and other valuables. Along these lines, you should recognize that a fire-resistant safe is not necessarily burglar resistant. In fact, being made of fire-retardant materials may make it easy to break open if it is not also burglar resistant. Note that the word is "resistant." Any safe can be broken open if the burglar has enough time. Because of this, many burglars will attempt to carry a small safe off rather than try to open it on your premises.

While many types of burglar-resistant safes are available, the "E" safe is considered adequate under most situations. "E" safes are more expensive; however, many insurance companies will give a reduction in premiums for use of this type of safe.

Four precautions regarding your safe will help to reduce burglaries.

1. Bolt the safe to the building structure. As noted earlier, burglars may attempt to carry your safe off. Surprisingly, even some very heavy safes have been carted off by enterprising thieves. Beware!
2. In the case of a store, put the safe where it can be seen from the street, if possible. Also, make sure that the safe is well lighted at night.
3. Never leave the combination to your safe on store premises.
4. When an employee who knows your safe combination leaves your employ, always change the combination to your safe.

Guards on Patrols. Special and private guards and private police patrols can be hired to stay on your premises during certain hours or check your store at regular intervals. Such private help may also assist you in training your employees and auditing your store for areas which may give easy access to potential burglaries.

Although the cost of private guards and police patrols is not low and may be prohibitive for a particularly small operation, you may be able to get around this by banding together with several stores, all of you contributing to a common fund for this purpose. Private guards and police patrols can be located in the yellow pages of your telephone book.

Watchdogs. Watchdogs are very valuable in preventing burglaries since they confront the potential burglar with an immediate physical threat. Also, word of your watchdog soon gets around and may even deter the attempt. You need not own your own watchdog; you may be able to rent them for a monthly rate of several hundred dollars. Again, check the yellow pages of your telephone book.

Frequent Cash Deposits.   One sure way to minimize losses is to make frequent bank deposits. In fact, having little cash on hand provides little motivation for a burglar to take the risk of attempting to burglarize your business.

ROBBERY

Technically, robbery is stealing or taking anything of value by force, violence, or the use of fear. Robbery is the fastest growing crime in the United States. Also, the greatest increase has been found in retail stores where holdups alone have increased 75% in recent times. Note that robbery is a violent crime and in the majority of cases the robber uses a weapon. As a result, robbery victims are frequently hurt. So it is naturally in your interest to do everything possible to prevent robbery.

Prevention of Robbery

Some of the means to prevent burglaries will also prevent robberies. For example, frequent cash deposits will remove some of the motivation, but you must be very careful here. The sight of the money may trigger a robbery. Therefore, it is wise to vary your hours and routes to the bank if possible, and not carry your deposits in obvious money containers. An armored car service may be of value here. Such services offer a safe alternative with pickup times scheduled to meet your needs with guaranteed delivery. Special safes may also be available in conjunction with an armored car service. These special safes, known as dual control safes, can only be unlocked jointly by the armored car guard and the store owner.

Another unique safe which is helpful in preventing robberies is a safe with an inner compartment, with a special drop slot for cash deposits. Such a safe works on the same principle as a dual control safe—the advantage being that only the manager or owner of the store as opposed to the cashier has access to the second compartment once the cash has been deposited.

The Importance of Opening and Closing Routines.   Special routines for opening and closing your store may be of great assistance in preventing robberies. This should be a two-man job. When you open the store, the second man observes your actions as you open, enter, and check the burglar alarm. If you do not reappear at a prearranged time, this should be the signal for your "second man" to call the police. If everything is all right, the owner would reappear and signal to the assistant. The closing routine at night should be similar, with the assistant again waiting outside and observing.

A trained guard dog can be of value in preventing robbery. A guard dog would be in your presence at all times and would be trained to attack anyone who threatens you. These guard dogs can't be rented because of the personal nature of the defense—they usually must be owned by the store owner.

Physical Deterrents.   Certain devices will assist you in minimizing the effect of robberies once they take place. One is a surveillance camera which, if robbers know it exists, may also act as a deterrent. Other types of silent alarms, including footrail switches, cash door contacts, and holdup buttons, can also be of great assistance in catching robbers once the act has taken place. A handgun may also be of use during a robbery, if it is legal and *if you are trained in its use*. On the other hand, you must be aware of the risk that if you use your handgun the robber will probably use his as well.

Cautions on Night Calls.   You should be particularly cautious if you are called at night to return to your business for some purpose. If the reason given is a malfunction of your burglar alarm system, you should phone the police department and ask that someone meet you at your place of business. If the problem is some sort of repair that must be done, make sure to phone the repair company and ask that the service truck meet you. Call before you leave your home, not from the store. If you arrive at your store and do not see the police car or the repair truck, don't park near your store or enter it. Verify all phone calls you receive after store hours.

SHOPLIFTING

Shoplifting is the most commonplace of all small business crimes, and currently shoplifters are stealing more than $2 billion worth of merchandise annually. Everything that you can do to spot, deter, apprehend, prosecute, and prevent shoplifting is much to the advantage of your business and other businesses across the country.

Types of Shoplifters

If you can learn to spot a shoplifter, it will help a great deal in shoplifting prevention. Addison H. Verrill, chairman of Dale System, Inc., Garden City, New York, describes shoplifters as falling into five categories.

Juvenile Offenders.   Juvenile offenders account for approximately 50% of all shoplifters. They usually steal on a dare or simply for a thrill, and often they expect store owners and the courts not to prosecute fully because of their age. Sometimes they enter stores in groups or gangs in an attempt to intimidate the owner. The best prevention here is to prosecute, remembering that this usually is the first type of theft committed by youngsters who later commit much more serious crimes.

Impulse Shoplifters.   Impulse shoplifters may appear to be perfectly respectable people. The theft is not premeditated, but occurs upon the sudden presentation of an opportunity, at which time the shoplifter falls to the temptation provided. The best prevention here is to insure that you have structured deterrents into your store to remove opportunities and temptations for shoplifting.

Alcoholics, Vagrants, and Drug Addicts.   In this category fall people whose physiological dependency requires them to commit theft. Because of their other problems, very frequently these criminals are clumsy or erratic in their behavior, and for this reason they may be easier to detect than other types of shoplifters. However, at the same time, you must remember that such people may be under the influence of drugs and may be armed as well as violent. It is best to leave the apprehension of such people to the police.

Kleptomaniacs.   Persons suffering from kleptomania have a driving psychological need to steal. Frequently they have little or no use for the items they steal and could easily afford to pay for the items. However, unless you are a psychologist or a psychiatrist, you can probably do nothing special to prevent theft by this group.

Professionals.   Professionals make up the final category of shoplifters. These individuals are usually highly skilled and may be difficult to spot. They tend to steal items which can be quickly resold, such as high-demand consumer goods including televisions, stereos, and other smaller appliances. Shoplifting professionals may case a store well in advance of the actual theft. Again, your most effective defense is proper deterrence with the layout of your store and alert, well-trained personnel.

Tactics of Shoplifters

Another way to help prevent shoplifting and be able to spot shoplifters is to know what tactics they use in accomplishing their theft. Basic shoplifter tactics include putting on clothes and simply walking out wearing them. Another common tactic is for two or more shoplifters to work as a team; while one or more use some tactic to distract the store owner or salesperson, the other or others commit the theft. Another tactic is simply to switch price tags and in this way to pay lower prices for more expensive items. Many shoplifters will use a palming tactic whereby the merchandise to be taken is placed under a handkerchief, between the folds of a newspaper, or with some similar item used to cover the item which is shoplifted. Common items such as pocketbooks, umbrellas, baby strollers, briefcases, are also used as depositories for items that are shoplifted, or the shoplifter may slip the item into a pocket of a jacket or within a dress. Professionals are a little more sophisticated, using items known as booster boxes, which are empty cartons disguised in gift wrappings. These booster boxes have hidden openings which allow shoplifters to pick up the item quickly without being observed. Professionals may also use hooker belts, which are worn around the waist. These hooker belts support hooks on which stolen items can be attached. You should be aware of all of these tactics and similar tactics used by shoplifters.

Deterring Shoplifters

To deter shoplifters, you must take four basic actions. These are: educating your employees as to what to expect or what to do, planning your store keeping shoplifters in mind, using protective equipment, and using protective personnel.

Educating Your Employees. You should brief your employees regarding shoplifter tactics as well as the various types of shoplifters. You should also instruct them to watch for suspicious-looking shoppers and shoppers carrying possible concealing devices such as those described. If you operate a clothing store, your salespeople should keep careful count of the number of items carried into and out of dressing rooms. Employees should be especially aware of groups of shoppers who enter the store together and who may be trying diversionary tactics. The salespeople should also be watchful of individuals who handle a great deal of merchandise, but take an especially long time to make the decision. Watch for loitering of customers in any one area and customers who only shop during certain hours when sales personnel on duty are few. Individual employees accepting payment for goods such as cashiers should be careful of switched price labels and purchased items which can be containers for stolen goods, such as garbage cans or tool boxes.

Frequently, local police conduct training seminars for store personnel. Such courses can be very helpful in showing you and your personnel how to spot shoplifters, and teaching you the latest methods of prevention. To find out if such training is available, contact your local police.

Planning Store Layout. It is unfortunate that you must consider shoplifters when you are planning the layout of your store. But this is a fact, and not to do so would be a terrible mistake which would cost you dearly in lost merchandise. Therefore, do plan your store with deterrents in mind. Some of these are: maintaining adequate lighting in all areas of the store, maintaining merchandise displayed in standard groups of three or four items per display so that your salespeople will notice when something is missing, keeping small items of high value behind a counter or in a locked case with sales personnel on duty, keeping your displays neat (it is easier to spot an item missing from an orderly display than from one in disarray), positioning your cash register so that it provides complete and unobstructed views of aisles of goods, and having your display cases which contain all of your expensive items locked. Finally, if fire regulations permit, you should lock all exits which are not to be used by your customers. Those exits which are not locked should have alarm systems attached to them which make a noise when someone enters or leaves. Close and block off unused checkout aisles.

Using Protective Equipment.   These devices can greatly decrease the amount of shoplifting to which your store is subjected. It includes two-way mirrors, one-way viewing mirrors, peepholes, closed circuit television, and convex wall mirrors. The use of special electronic tags will prevent much shoplifting. If someone attempts to leave when electronic tags are not removed or rendered inoperative, an alarm goes off. Other tags are almost tamper-proof because they are either attached to hard-to-break plastic string or constructed in such a fashion that they cannot easily be removed or switched. Price labels marked by rubber stamps or pricing machines are also very useful in preventing removal and switching, and are better than either felt-marked or pencil-marked price tags since they cannot be switched, or the amount altered. You can also institute a system to alert your employees as to whether a package has been paid for or not. For example, you can instruct your cashiers or salespeople to staple receipts to the outside of all packages that have been paid for. A simple system, but it works.

Protective Personnel.   Another method of preventing or deterring shoplifting is using protective personnel. These include detectives disguised as customers who can better observe what is going on in your store than your salespeople can, and uniformed guards who stand as visual deterrents to shoplifting.

Apprehending Shoplifters

Apprehension of shoplifters is very critical. It must be done with some finesse, because you certainly don't want to disturb your regular customers or collar an innocent person. Not only will you lose future sales, but you could be sued. Therefore, apprehension should be carefully thought out and policies established beforehand. In general, in order to make shoplifting charges stick, you must do the following:

1. See the shoplifter take or conceal store merchandise
2. Positively identify the merchandise as belonging to you
3. Testify that it was taken by the shoplifter with the intent to steal
4. Prove that the merchandise was not paid for

Failure to meet these basic criteria leaves you open to counter-charges of false arrest. You must remember that false arrest does not necessarily mean arrest by police, but may simply mean that you have prevented a customer from conducting normal activities. Therefore, you should be extremely careful about this point and check regarding laws pertaining to shoplifting in your state with your lawyer or your local police or both. Be especially careful that the shoplifter is not able to dump the merchandise after you have decided to arrest him. In fact, a good rule is: if you lose sight of the shoplifter for even an instant, forget it. If the shoplifter succeeded in getting rid of the merchandise, you could be in for a lot of trouble.

INTERNAL THEFT

According to the SBA, loss due to theft amounts to between 1 and 7% of sales, of which dishonest employees account for two-thirds. The Department of Commerce further estimates that dishonest employees are responsible for 75 to 80% of all retail shortages. The most common type of internal theft is embezzlement in which cash is received and your employee merely pockets it without making a record of the sale. A slightly more complicated type of internal theft or embezzlement is called "lapping." With this type of theft, the embezzler withholds receipts such as payments on accounts receivable temporarily, perhaps with the intent to repay. The amount withheld is eventually paid by "borrowing" from yet another account which is intended to be a payment on accounts receivable. In this way, borrowing may increase and the amounts grow larger and larger; in fact, sometimes this type of fraud may run on for years and years, and when it is finally detected the amount is in the tens or even hundreds of thousands of dollars.

Internal theft is frequently concealed, and therefore you must look for clues to the fact that it is going on. Here are six different occurrences which should lead to an investigation to see if an embezzler is ripping you off.

1. *Decline or unusually small increase in cash or credit sales.* This could mean that some sales are not being recorded.
2. *Increase in overall sales returns.* This might mean a concealment of accounts receivable payments.
3. *Inventory shortages.* This could be caused by fictitious purchases, unrecorded sales, or some other means of theft.
4. *Profit declines and expense increases.* This could be a sign that cash is being taken from your accounts in some way.
5. *Slow collection.* This could be a device concealing lapping mentioned previously.
6. *Unusual bad debt writeoffs.* This could cover some sort of internal theft scheme.

In general, there are two major ways to cut down on internal theft. These are:

1. Screening your employees
2. Controlling your business operations and removing theft hazards

Screening employees we have talked about before, especially as it pertains to your hiring practices as discussed in an earlier chapter. Five areas for potential theft and ways to prevent this theft are recommended by Saul D. Astor, president of Management Safeguards, Inc., of New York City.[1]

---

[1] Saul D. Astor, *Preventing Retail Theft*, Small Business Administration (1978).

Pricing

Loosely controlled pricing procedures constitute a major cause of inventory "shrinkage."

Case in Point. Items in a thrift store were ticketed in pencil. Moreover, some tickets were unmarked. Since the store was inadequately staffed, many customers marked down prices, switched tickets, or wrote in their own prices.

Antitheft Pointers

Price items by machine or rubber stamp, not by handwriting.

Permit only authorized employees to set prices and mark merchandise.

Make *unannounced* spot checks to be sure that actual prices agree with authorized prices and price charge records.

Refunds

Refunds provide dishonest employees an easy means to ply their trade. There are more ways to lose money on returns or refunds than the average retailer dreams possible.

Case in Point. In one store, many returned items were marked down to a fraction of cost because of damage. It was easy for clerks to get authorization to buy "as is" merchandise. When they were armed with an okay, they substituted first-grade items for "as is" stock.

Antitheft Pointers

Insist on a merchandise inspection by someone other than the person who made the sale.

Match items to the return vouchers and then return the merchandise back into stock as quickly as possible.

Keep a tight control on all credit documents. Spot check customers by mail or telephone to make sure they got their refunds.

Popular Salespeople

The popular salesperson is a great asset—providing he or she is popular for the right reasons. However, many salespeople win "fans" because of the deals they swing and the favors they grant.

Case in Point. Customers stood in line to wait for one veteran saleswoman. They refused to be served by anyone else. And no wonder! She switched tickets for many "special" customers, giving them substantial markdowns. Store losses amounted to about $300 a week—not including $25 a week in increased commissions for the crook.

Antitheft Pointers

The popular salesperson may be your biggest asset. But don't take it for granted. Find out for yourself *why* he or she is so well liked.

Pay special attention to the salesperson who is visited by too many personal friends. To discourage such socializing, some retailers hire people who live outside the immediate store vicinity.

Cash Handling

The cashier's post is particularly vulnerable to theft. The experienced cash handler with larceny on his or her mind can rob a store blind in a hundred and one ways.

Case in Point. A store owner's sales were high, but his profits were dragging. The cause was traced to a cashier who rang up only some of the items bought by his "customers." In most cases, he didn't ring "put-downs" at all. (A "put-down" is the right amount of cash which a customer leaves on the counter when he rushes out without waiting for his tape.)

Antitheft Pointers

Keep a sharp eye open for signals—nods, winks, and so on—between cashiers and customers.

Pay special attention to cashiers when they are surrounded by clusters of people.

Be alert to the use of over-ring slips to cover up shortages.

Watch for items bypassed when ringing up sales.

Check personal checks to make sure they are not being used to cover up shortages.

Use a professional shopper to check for violations of cash register and related procedures.

Backdoor Thefts

Large-scale theft is carried on more often through the back than the front door. Hundreds, even thousands, of dollars worth of merchandise can be stolen within a few seconds.

Case in Point. A stock clerk parked his car at the receiving dock. He kept his trunk closed but unlocked. At 12:30 P.M., when the shipping-receiving manager was at lunch, the stock clerk threw full cartons of shoes into his trunk and then slammed it locked. Elapsed time: 18 seconds.

Antitheft Pointers

Have a secondary check by a worker or salesperson on all incoming shipments.

Insist on flattening all trash cartons and make spot checks of trash after hours.

Prohibit employees from parking near receiving door or dock.

Keep receiving door *locked* when not in use. Make sure locked door cannot be raised a few inches. A receiving door should be opened only by a supervisor who remains in area until it's relocked.

Alarm on door should ring until turned off with key held by store manager. Distribute door keys carefully and change lock cylinders periodically.

The Bank of America, in its excellent booklet "Crime Prevention for Small Business," recommends instituting several control measures to reduce the danger of internal theft. First, key job cross-checks in which one person orders the merchandise while another records hours worked and a third makes out payroll checks. This may be difficult or impractical for all small businesses, but you could divide duties so that employees do not have excessive control over your operations. Cash register controls are important since it is here that employees have direct access to incoming cash. Therefore, each checker should be responsible for his or her own cash drawer, counting all cash receipts at the beginning of the shift and signing the register tape. The customer should receive a sales receipt for every transaction. In this way, individuals at the cashier's station are prevented from pocketing cash or underringing a sale and pocketing the difference, since the customer would notice this and call attention to the incorrect ring-up. You must be sure that whoever is operating the cash register immediately replaces tape, since it is possible to ring up with no tape in the machine and in that way not record any sales. Checking all incoming merchandise against purchase invoices insures that quantities, prices, shipping charges, and other conditions are correct. Keeping storage rooms locked and allowing access only under supervision will eliminate the opportunities for theft through this quarter. Paying by serially numbered checks will control disbursements. Keeping checks under lock and key, along with check-writing equipment, will help control this source of possible theft. Voiding all paid bills or invoices will insure that they can't be used a second time, and if you establish firm price and discount policies, unauthorized discounts will be unlikely.

Christopher J. Moran, CPA, a partner in A. M. Pullen and Company of Greensboro, North Carolina, recommends the following 16 precautions.[2]

Ounces of Prevention

There are many steps an owner-manager can take to cut down on the possibility of losses through embezzlement. Do you take the following precautions?

1. Check the background of prospective employees. Sometimes you can satisfy yourself by making a few telephone calls or writing a few letters. In other cases, you may want to turn the matter over to a credit bureau or similar agency to run a background check. (Keep in mind that the rights of individuals must be preserved in furnishing, receiving, and using background information.)

2. Know your employees to the extent that you may be able to detect signs of financial or other personal problems. Build up rapport so that they feel free to discuss such things with you in confidence.

3. See that no one is placed on the payroll without authorization from you or a responsible official of the company. If you have a personnel department, require that it approve additions to the payroll as a double check.

[2] Christopher J. Moran, *Preventing Embezzlement*, Small Business Administration (1977).

4. Have the company mail addressed to a post office box rather than your place of business. In smaller cities, the owner-manager may want to go to the post office himself to collect the mail. In any event, you or your designated keyman should personally open the mail and make a record at that time of cash and checks received. Don't delude yourself that checks or money orders payable to your company can't be converted into cash by an enterprising embezzler.

5. Either personally prepare the daily cash deposits or compare the deposits made by employees with the record of cash and checks received. Make sure you get a copy of the duplicate deposit slip or other documentation from the bank. Make it a habit to go to the bank and make the daily deposit yourself as often as you can. If you delegate these jobs, make an occasional spot check to see that nothing is amiss.

6. Arrange for bank statements and other correspondence from banks to be sent to the same post office box, and personally reconcile all bank statements with your company's books and records. The owner-manager who has not reconciled the statements for some time may want to get oriented by the firm's outside accountant.

7. Personally examine all canceled checks and endorsements to see if there is anything unusual. This also applies to payroll checks.

8. Make sure that an employee in a position to mishandle funds is adequately bonded. Let him know that fidelity coverage is a matter of company policy rather than any feeling of mistrust on your part. If a would-be embezzler knows that a bonding company also has an interest in what he does, he may think twice before helping himself to your funds.

9. Spot check your accounting records and assets to satisfy yourself that all is well and that your plan of internal control is being carried out.

10. Personally approve unusual discounts and bad-debt writeoffs. Approve or spot check credit memos and other documentation for sales returns and allowances.

11. Don't delegate the signing of checks and approval of cash disbursements unless absolutely necessary and never approve any payment without sufficient documentation or prior knowledge of the transaction.

12. Examine all invoices and supporting data before signing checks. Make sure that all merchandise was actually received and the price seems reasonable. In many false purchase schemes, the embezzler neglects to make up receiving forms or other records purporting to show receipt of merchandise.

13. Personally cancel all invoices at the time you sign the checks to prevent double payment through error or otherwise.

14. Don't sign blank checks. Don't leave a supply of signed blank checks when you go on vacation.

15. Inspect all prenumbered checkbooks and other prenumbered forms from time to time to insure that checks or forms from the backs of the books have not been removed and possibly used in a fraudulent scheme.

16. Have the preparation of the payroll and the actual paying of employees handled by different persons, especially when cash is involved.

BAD CHECKS

The Department of Commerce estimates that more than $2 billion worth of losses a year can be attributed solely to bad checks. It's worth your effort to prevent a portion of this huge amount from coming out of your pocket. You will be a lot less likely to accept bad checks if you (1) require identification, and (2) consider certain key points before you hand over the cash.

Require Identification

You should always require identification to make sure that the person presenting you with a check is the same person whose name is printed on the check. It is better to require at least two pieces of identification. Usually, these should be a driver's license and a major credit card. Recording information such as the serial number from the driver's license and the number from the credit card will help to deter the person from passing the bad check, and it will also help locate the individual if the check turns out to be bad.

Of course, identification is not foolproof. Any identification can be forged. However, some pieces of identification are more difficult to forge than others. The following types of identification are more difficult and are therefore better for check cashing purposes: automobile operator's license, automobile registration card, credit cards, government passes, and identification cards issued by companies that carry a photograph, description, and signature.

The following cards are not good identification because they are easily forged: Social Security cards, business cards, club organization cards, bank books, work permits, insurance cards, learner's permits, letters, birth certificates, library cards, and voter registration cards.

Check Key Points

The following key points should be considered when the check and pieces of identification are presented.

1. Compare signature from the check with signature on the identification.
2. If the check is written for a nonlocal bank, make sure the customer's out-of-town as well as his local address and telephone are written on the back of the check.
3. Check the date, including day, month, and year. Do not accept checks that are not dated or postdated, or checks on which the date is more than 30 days past.
4. Be sure that the numerical amount agrees with the amount written in in numerals.
5. Be sure that the check is legibly written, signed in ink, and does not have any erasures or written-over amounts.
6. Be sure that you are the payee, or your firm is. If a check is a two-party check, that is, a check which is written to the individual presenting you with the check and is to be endorsed over to you, be sure that you get full information and take special care.
7. It is safer to take personal checks only for the exact amount of purchase. Of course, whether you do this or not is your decision.

8. Set a limit on the amount that you will cash a check for. Post the amount for your customers to see and accept none beyond that amount except for amount of purchase.

9. Statistically, checks with low serial numbers are returned more often than checks with higher numbers. Therefore, be especially cautious about low numbers.

10. Statistically, bad checks tend to be in the $25 to $35 range, according to the Small Business Administration. Be particularly careful of checks around this amount or under $50.

11. Look for lack of concern about the price of the merchandise purchased. Lack of concern may indicate that the check is no good.

Bad Check Protection Services and Equipment

Certain devices and services will assist you in minimizing bad checks. You can photograph the individual who cashes the check with a Polaroid camera. This procedure is definitely a deterrent since bad check passers do not want to be photographed. There is a check verification service available in many states for a small monthly fee. A central computer contains only negative information about check passers. You can get this information as a participating businessperson by calling a central number and giving the customer's driver's license number. Another mechanical deterrent available is a fingerprint register. This fingerprint register works without the traditional black, messy ink. It involves only one thumbprint on the back of the check which is registered by the machine. Obviously, bad check passers do not wish to be fingerprinted either.

You can find out more about check protection equipment by checking in the yellow pages of your telephone directory and also by talking with other merchants who are using similar devices.

You Are Under No Obligation to Take a Check

Never forget that you are not obligated to take anyone's check, even if the individual presents identification and all of the key points described above are positive. Naturally, you may wish to do so in order to make a sale and for good will. However, Leonard Kolodny, who is the manager of the Retail Bureau of the Metropolitan Washington Board of Trade, Washington, D.C., recommends that you not accept a check if:

1. The person presenting it appears to be intoxicated
2. The customer acts at all suspiciously
3. The check has an old date
4. The check is dated in advance

Kolodny also recommends that you not tell a customer that you cannot acccept his check because he is a college student or lives in a bad neighborhood, or give a similar response. If you respond in such a way as to appear to discriminate when refusing to cash a check, you may be in violation of a state or federal law on discrimination.

SOURCES OF ADDITIONAL INFORMATION

Mind Your Own Business, by Norman Jaspen, published by Prentice-Hall, Inc., Englewood Cliffs, N.J. 07632

Protect Your Business Against Crime—A Guide for the Small Businessman, published by Drake Publishers, Inc., New York, N.Y. 10017.

Shop Lifting and Shrinkage Protection for Stores, by Loren E. Edwards, published by Charles C. Thomas, 301 East Lawrence Ave., Springfield, Ill. 62717

Sticky Fingers, by William W. McCullough, published by AMACOM, a division of the American Management Associations, 135 W. 50th St., New York, N.Y. 10020

13

Credit and Credit Collection

CREDIT IN TODAY'S ECONOMY

It is a fact of life in today's economy that credit is necessary in most situations and for most businesses. This means that the basic problem is usually not whether or not to give credit, but how to manage the credit in such a fashion that the following objectives are achieved:

1. You have fewer dollars tied up in accounts receivable, allowing profitable application elsewhere in your business.
2. Your credit losses are minimized.
3. You have increased and maximized profits.
4. Customers or clients will be encouraged to use your services or buy your goods.
5. Your company's investment in accounts receivable will be protected to the maximum extent possible.

CREDIT POLICY

To achieve the objectives outlined above, you must have a credit policy. This credit policy may either be written down or not, but it must be communicated to your employees and your customers or clients. Cooke O'Neal, who is vice president of the National Association of Credit Management, notes the following factors which will influence your company's credit policy.

1. Nature and size of business
2. Overall business objectives
3. General policy of business
4. Product or service requirements
5. Channels of distribution
6. Classes of customers
7. Conditions of competition
8. Price of product or service
9. Expectations of customers

Your credit policy may be characterized by liberal extension of credit or strict extension of credit, liberal collection or strict collection, or your policy may fall somewhere between these two sets of extremes. You have to decide by weighing stimulation of sales on one hand and failure to collect or exposure to a larger bad debt loss on the other. You must also consider the amounts in your accounts receivable and the working capital position of your business.

THE BASIC ELEMENTS OF YOUR CREDIT POLICY PROGRAM

The basic elements of your credit policy program are as follows:

1. To whom credit will be extended
2. Credit terms
3. Problem detection
4. Collection procedures

To Whom Credit Will Be Extended

The extension of credit depends on several considerations, including personal judgment and investigation, credit applications, evaluation factors, the application evaluation, information verification, and applicant stability. Let's look at each in turn.

Judgment. Clearly, judgment plays an important part in determining whether you should grant credit or not, and many potential problems can be eliminated simply by exercising good judgment. For example, if an individual or a firm owes you a great deal of money and has been slow to pay in the past, or has not paid, it doesn't take any special insight to know that it is probably wise to refuse to give credit. If a firm or an individual appears low on cash, simply exercising good judgment may prevent a loss due to bad debt. Remember that the need for sales alone may not solve cash flow problems that you have in your business. In fact, building up sales but not collecting money may worsen your situation. Therefore, when making a credit decision, consider your likelihood of getting paid. If the likelihood is small, don't grant credit.

Investigation. Before making a decision on credit, you should get all of the facts. This means that for any sizable amount of credit you should do a thorough investigation. This will help protect you from an individual or a firm which really has no intention of paying at all, as well as those which are slow in paying. This may range from simply checking on a credit card number to be sure that the credit card has not been stolen and is still in force to a much more thorough probe involving the areas discussed in the following paragraphs.

Credit Applications. Much information can be gained from a credit application, and for any sizable amount of credit an application such as that shown in Figure 13.1 should be required—and the information contained in it should be verified. In many cases, specific information may be required due to your situation, location, or industry. In that case the information shown in Figure 13.1 can be supplemented by additional information needed.

DATE_____

NAME_____ AGE_____

ADDRESS_____ HOW LONG?_____

HOME PHONE_____ BUSINESS PHONE_____ SINGLE____
MARRIED____
DIVORCED____

NUMBER OF DEPENDENTS_____

FORMER ADDRESS_____ HOW LONG?_____

EMPLOYER_____ PHONE NO._____

ADDRESS_____ HOW LONG?_____

POSITION_____ MONTHLY INCOME_____ OTHER INCOME_____

PREVIOUS EMPLOYER_____ PHONE NO._____

ADDRESS_____HOW LONG?_____

BANK ACCOUNT (SAVINGS)_____ PHONE NO._____

ADDRESS_____

BANK ACCOUNT (CHECKING)_____ PHONE NO._____

ADDRESS_____

NAME OF SPOUSE_____ WHERE EMPLOYED?_____ MONTHLY INCOME_____

DO YOU OWN AN AUTOMOBILE?_____YEAR AND MODEL_____ WHEN PURCHASED_____

NEAREST RELATIVE WITH WHOM YOU ARE NOT LIVING_____

ADDRESS_____RELATIONSHIP_____

REAL ESTATE OWNED (OTHER THAN HOME)_____

CREDIT REFERENCES
_____

TYPE	REFERENCE	ADDRESS	MONTHLY PAYMENT	BALANCE OWED
HOME				
AUTOMOBILE				
CREDIT CARD				
CREDIT CARD				
~~OTHER~~				
OTHER				

IF GRANTED CREDIT, I AGREE TO PAY ALL BILLS IN ACCORDANCE WITH THE FOLLOWING TERMS:
_____
_____

SIGNED:_____

Figure 13.1. Credit application form.

COMPANY_____PHONE NO._____

ADDRESS_____

TYPES OF BUSINESS AND ORGANIZATION _____
_____

BANK_____ PHONE NO._____
ADDRESS _____

TRADE REFERENCES
(Note: Do not use oil companies,credit cards, IBM, Xerox, or public utilities
since these organizations will not confirm credit information.)

1. _____
_____
2._____
_____
3._____
_____

OWNERS AND/OR OFFICERS OF YOUR COMPANY

1. NAME_____ TITLE _____

2. NAME_____ TITLE_____

3. NAME_____ TITLE+_____

PERSON TO BE CONTACTED WITH REGARD TO FINANCIAL COMMITMENTS

1. NAME _____ TITLE _____

It is understood that all purchases made during a given month are payable in thirty
(30) days or no later than the end of the following month. Accounts not paid
in accordance with these terms will be charged a 133/4% monthly service charge
equivalent to 20% annual interest.

DATE_____   AUTHORIZED SIGNATURE_____

AUTHORIZATION FOR BANK CREDIT INQUIRY
I hereby authorize _____ to disclose credit information to _____
for consideration of the establishment of trade credit.

NAME OF ACCOUNT_____ ACCOUNT NO. _____ AUTHORIZED SIGNATURE_____

ESTIMATED MONTHLY CREDIT REQUIREMENTS_____

SALES TAX STATUS ____TAXABLE ____EXEMPT,RESALE PERMIT NO._____

INDIVIDUALS IN YOUR COMPANY AUTHORIZED TO PLACE ORDERS

NAME_____ TITLE_____ NAME_____ TITLE _____

NAME _____ TITLE_____ NAME _____ TITLE_____

NAME _____ TITLE _____ NAME_____ TITLE_____

Figure 13.1. (Continued)

Evaluation Factors for Credit.   Experts say that there are three basic factors to consider in evaluating a credit application. These are:

1. The applicant's ability to pay. This is based upon income and obligations.
2. The applicant's willingness to pay. This is determined from past credit history.
3. The potential profitability of the account.

Remember that you will lose the cost of your product or the service if you do not collect on any account where credit is granted. When the cost is very high relative to the selling price, you must be particularly careful and assess such risk with great care.

Evaluating the Application.   In order to evaluate these factors, consider the following:

1. Amount of credit desired
2. The bank balances of the applicant
3. Current credit standing
4. Current income
5. Current position
6. Employment history
7. Job security
8. Other obligations, including loan payments, rent, and so forth
9. Personal assets
10. Time on the job

Verifying Information.   Whether you are dealing with an individual or a firm, the information contained on credit applications must be thoroughly verified or it is worthless. You must be sure that it is current, that it is correct, and that it is complete and nothing has been left out. For individuals, places of employment, and other personal references regarding income, time on the job, and so forth can be verified fairly easily by a letter or telephone request. Bank references can be verified in the same manner, even though banks may be somewhat restrictive in the information they provide. However, they will usually confirm the existence of an account and give a broad, general range of the average balance. A bank may also indicate whether or not the account has been satisfactory. However, when checking out the facts concerning firms as opposed to individuals, other sources may be necessary. The following sources of credit information are useful for both firms and individuals depending upon the situation.

1. *Mercantile credit agencies.*   These are agencies which are privately owned and operated, and on a continuous basis they collect, analyze, and evaluate credit information on business firms. For a fee, they provide credit ratings based upon their observations. Perhaps the best known mercantile credit agency is Dun and Bradstreet. Dun and Bradstreet covers many fields and provides a reference book, credit reports, and other specific information to firms using its services. Information provided includes credit ratings, evaluation of financial strength, and other important credit information. Other mercantile agencies work in specialized areas; for example, the Lyon Furniture Mercantile

Agency works the furniture industry, and the Jeweler's Board of Trade in that industry. In addition, the National Credit Office reports on several different trades including textiles, banking, metals, electronics, leather, furniture, paint, rubber, and chemicals.

2. *Credit bureaus.* Many credit bureaus are available for firms that need to check credit information on a frequent basis. Most local credit bureaus are affiliated with other national bureaus including the International Consumer Credit Association of the Associated Credit Bureaus of America. In this way, even if the individuals have moved into your area recently, frequently credit information is available on them. Credit bureaus will supply information including checks on newcomers in your area, written and telephone credit information on individuals, data on changes in customers' credit risk status, assistance in tracing customers who leave your area without providing forwarding information, and collection of poor risk accounts.

3. *Suppliers.* Suppliers in credit departments will frequently be willing to exchange information with you. This interchange can be extremely valuable to update your own records and warn you of situations where credit may negatively affect your business. You should also keep in touch with competitors and other firms which may be dealing with your customers. Frequently, an exchange of credit information can help out both sides, especially in a fluid situation where a customer's credit position may be changing rapidly.

4. *Department of Commerce.* The Department of Commerce will frequently provide assistance in checking out foreign firms that you may want to do business with. Check with the local office of the Department of Commerce which can be located under the heading "U.S. Government" in your telephone book.

CREDIT TERMS

The credit terms which you extend may have a significant effect on your sales as well as your profits. You should be familiar with the terms used in business sales contained in Figure 13.2. You should also consider the following points:

1. Insist on all or a portion of the money up front before you provide the goods or the services. In some industries this will be impossible. In others, such as consulting, it may be fully acceptable. If you have an extremely poor credit risk, it may be the only way to protect yourself from severe financial losses.

2. The use of credit cards is an excellent way to protect yourself, whether you are dealing with other firms or with individuals. Essentially, the credit card company, such as Visa or Master Charge or others, grants the credit, and you get your money at once. The customer or client will have his credit needs met without your having to take any risk. Of course, you will pay a percentage of your sales for this service, and it is a factor you must consider. However, a lot of grief can be saved through the use of credit cards, and it is well worth taking the time to see if you can use them.

3. Remember that you are not obligated to grant credit at any time. Therefore, never fool yourself into building up false sales when the chances of your getting paid are poor. If you're not going to get paid later on or if the time when you'll get paid is way down the road, the only solution is to refuse credit.

Term	Explanation
3/10, 1/15, n/60	3 percent discount for first 10 days; 1 percent discount for 15 days; bill due net on 60th day.
M.O.M. (Middle of month)	Billing will be on the 15th of the month (middle of the month), including all purchases made since the middle of the previous month.
E.O.M. (End of month)	Billing at end of month, covering all credit purchases of that month.
C.W.O. or C.I.A. (Cash with order, or Cash in advance)	Orders received are not processed until advanced payment is received.
C.B.D. (Cash before delivery)	Merchandise may be prepared and packaged by the seller, but shipment is not made until payment is received.
C.O.D. (Cash on delivery)	Amount of bill will be collected upon delivery of goods.
S.D. — B.L. (Sight draft—Bill of lading)	A negotiable bill of lading, accompanied by the invoice and a sight draft drawn on the buyer, is forwarded by the seller to the customer's bank. The bill of lading is released by the bank to the customer only upon his honoring the draft.
2/10, n/30, *R.O.G. (Receipt of goods)	2 percent discount for 10 days; bill due net on 30th day—but both discount period and 30 days start from the date of receipt of the goods, not from the date of the sale.
2/10, n/30, M.O.M.	2 percent discount for 10 days; bill due net on 30th day—but both periods start from the 15th of the month following the sales date.
2/10, n/30, E.O.M.	2 percent discount for 10 days; bill due net on 30th day—but both periods start from the end of the month in which the sale was made.
8/10, E.O.M.	8 percent discount for 10 days; bill due net on 30th day—but both periods start from the end of the month following the sales date.

Sales date is the day that the shipment was made. It will generally be the same date shown on the invoice. In consumer credit, the sales date is the day the sale was made and may or may not coincide with the date of shipment.

*The owner-manager should keep in mind that 2%/10, n/30 amounts to 36.5 percent in annual interest calculation:

$$\frac{2\%}{30-10} \times 365 = 36.5\%$$

Figure 13.2. Common business credit sales terms. [From Harvey C. Krentzman, *Managing for Profit*, Small Business Administration (1968).]

4. Detecting problems must be an essential part of your credit and credit collection program. One way to do this is to calculate the average collection period. The average collection period is calculated by dividing your accounts receivable by the average daily credit sales. Let us say that your current outstanding accounts receivable are $10,000, and on the average your monthly credit sales are $3,000. First, you must calculate the average daily credit sales. This would be the monthly sales of $3,000 divided by 30 days or $100. Now, divide the accounts receivable of $10,000 by the average daily credit sales of $100. This equals the average collection period in days. In this example, we would have $10,000 divided by $100 equals 100 days. This means that on the average your customers are taking about 100 days to pay for their accounts. There is anther way of calculating the average collection period using net credit sales which are determined by subtracting an estimated allowance for bad debts from your total annual sales.

Now that you have the average collection period for your accounts receivable, what do you do with it? You can make the following comparisons to determine whether or not a problem exists.

1. *Payment terms.* How does the average collection period compare with the terms of sale which you offer? If you request payment within 100 days and the average collection period is not greater than this, it indicates that your creditors are complying with your terms. If, on the other hand, the average collection period is greater than 100 days, they are not.

2. *Past history.* How does your current average collection period compare with that that you had in the past? Are things getting better or getting worse?

3. *Industry averages.* How does your average collection period compare with those of other companies in your industry? This will indicate whether your credit and collection policies are as effective as those of other companies and your competitors in your industry.

How Much of a Problem Do You Have?

If the three above comparisons using your average collection period indicate that you do have a problem, your next step is to determine how *much* of a problem you have. This can be accomplished by comparing your actual receivables with a target level. Let us say that your terms of sale specify payment within 30 days, which compares with your industry average as well. This, then, would make a suitable target for your receivables. If your average daily credit sales are $100 as in the previous example, you could then calculate a target for your receivables by multiplying your average daily credit sales by the collection period of 30 days, in this case $100 times 30 days equals $3,000.

You would then compare this with your actual receivables. In the case above, actual receivables are $10,000. You then know that you have a problem which amounts to $10,000 minus $3,000 or $7,000.

The implication of problem detection is problem solving. That is, you take immediate action to reduce the collection period, the speed of conversion of your receivables to cash, to minimize the capital that you have tied up in accounts receivable and reduce the risk of uncollectible accounts.

COLLECTION PROCEDURES

The Fundamental Rule of Collection

The fundamental rule of collection is to minimize the time between the sale or performance of the service and the collection of the money. For example, Dr. Robert Kelley, a consultant and teacher, states in his book, *Consulting*, that a former graduate student of his conducted research having to do with the billing practices of professionals, doctors, dentists, and lawyers. This student found that professionals who request payment before the client leaves the office have 90 to 100% collection rates, and those who send monthly statements average 65% collection rates. Therefore, to increase your collection, minimize this time span.[1]

Invoices

Invoice preparation is crucial to your collection procedures. Your invoices should be prepared promptly and accurately. Time is essential to eliminate one source of delay. Accuracy is necessary to eliminate another source: customer disputes with the information about which you have invoiced him or her. An invoice should clearly state the credit terms you have decided upon as described earlier.

Statements

Statements keep customers advised of their account balances, and monthly statements should be submitted to all creditors with open accounts. The statement should summarize the amount owed previously as well as any additional activity in the account during the month. Figure 13.3 shows a properly prepared invoice, and Figure 13.4, a statement.

Delinquency Charges

In some types of businesses, delinquency charges are applied against late payments in order to discourage customers from allowing their accounts to become overdue. This normally involves a finance or service charge of between 1 and 1½% per month on all balances more than 30 days past due. However, in recent times of high inflation, many companies have raised these percentages.

Lateness Followup

When your customers or clients do not pay, you should initiate a followup immediately. The longer an account becomes dated the less the chance of a collection. Never be afraid to initiate these follow-up actions. Some people are afraid to do so because they feel that a strict followup and harassment of their customers will hurt their business. Again, remember that you have no business without payment, and a good customer is not a good customer unless he or she actually pays. Some individuals are also afraid of pursuing a rigid collection policy for fear that this will hurt their reputation. It is highly unlikely that an individual who owes you money will spread the word around town that you are harassing him for late payment.

A standard follow-up procedure for lateness in paying overdue or past due ac-

[1] Robert E. Kelley, *Consulting*, Charles Scribner's Sons, New York (1981).

XYZ Manufacturing Company
1200 N. Applewood Dr. Fairview, California 90076
Telephone: (805)789-6781

Terms: 2% Discount for payment in 10 days. Total amount due in 30 days. There is a finance charge for amounts outstanding at 30 days or more of 1.5% per month (annual rate 18%).

Package No.	Quantity	Description	Unit Price	Total Price

Figure 13.3. Invoice.

XYZ Manufacturing Company
1200 N. Applewood Dr. Fairview, California 90076
Telephone: (805)789-6781

Previous Charges and Credits

Balance from previous bill		$189.00	
Payments applied as of this date		100.00	
	Balance	$ 89.00	$ 89.00

Current Charges and Credits

P.O. No. 1876 1000 envelopes		$ 55.00	
P.O. No. 1891 1000 business cards		15.00	
	Current Charges	$ 70.00	$ 70.00
	Total amount due		$159.00

TERMS: 2% discount for payment in 10 days. Total amount of current charges due in 30 days. There is a finance charge for amount outstanding at 30 days or more of 1.5% per month (annual rate 18%).

Figure 13.4. Statement.

counts is generally a good idea. Such a policy makes it easier to implement the action required in an expeditious manner.

A typical follow-up procedure will be a telephone call, a letter or series of letters, or some combination of these two instruments, usually with the letters coming first.

Initial Collection Letter

An initial collection letter should be used when the account becomes approximately 15 days past due. At this time, the account is not considered seriously delinquent; therefore the tone of the letter, while firm, should be moderate. If this letter is unsuccessful, a second letter should be sent approximately one month later. If this letter is unsuccessful as well, a third and stronger letter should be sent.

Figures 13.5, 13.6, amd 13.7 show an initial collection letter, a second collection letter, and a third collection letter. Note how the tone grows progressively

---

Dear _____:

We know that it is probably an oversight, but the amount of $400 owed us for consulting services performed for your company is overdue. Please send us your check immediately so we can update our records and mark you "paid in full . . . credit good."

Sincerely,

_____

Senior Partner

Figure 13.5.   Initial collection letter.

Dear _____:

Unfortunately, our Senior Partner, _____, tells me that your account is in arrears in the amount of $400 for consulting services performed for your firm, also that a previous letter was sent to you pointing out this fact.

We would like to maintain you as a client and for you to maintain your good standing. However, your past due bill must be paid immediately or further action will be taken in accordance with our policy.

Sincerely,

_____

President

Figure 13.6.   Follow-up collection letter.

Dear _____:

This is the final notice we intend to send you before initiating legal action. Your account is in arrears $400 for consulting services performed for your company. If this amount is not received within ten days to clear your account, we intend to initiate proceedings to recover this amount.

Sincerely,

_____

President

Figure 13.7.   Second follow-up collection letter.

stronger. The implication of action of a more serious nature is introduced as the letters progress. The exact wording that you use depends on the situation in which you find yourself, including your relationship with this particular customer, your industry, and so forth. But the basics are clear. Send the letters as indicated 15 days after the account becomes due, and then at intervals of 30 days. A standard format can be adopted which will greatly reduce the time you spend doing this.

Use of the Telephone

The telephone can be used either with the letters or by itself. It can be even more persuasive since you will get immediate feedback and can respond directly to the information given by the individual. However, the basic methodology is the same, and if you make more than one call, each call should be firmer than the last. The disadvantages of a telephone call are that it consumes your time and that it is a direct confrontation and can sometimes be tricky.

If you use the telephone technique, you should again attempt to find out what the problem is. If the entire amount cannot be paid, find out how much can be paid over a reasonable period and how soon the initial payment of the amount can be expected.

Again, your telephone call should indicate to the creditor that you are aware that the payment has not been made, and that you do not intend that the creditor will get away with nonpayment.

External Collection Procedures

There are two external collection procedures that are available to you should the letter or telephone calls fail. These are collection agencies and courts of law.

Collection Agencies.   These agencies will collect past due accounts receivable for you. The advantages they offer are their experience, knowledge of persuasive collection techniques, and the additional emphasis that an outside agency gives to the collection procedure. While at first glance this may appear an easy way to take care of your problems, you should be aware of the fact that collection agencies usually will insist upon 25 to 50% of the amount that they succeed in collecting. Further, once you agree to work with a collection agency, you must make this percentage payment fee whether the debt is collected by you or through the agency.

Courts of Law.   A court of law is the final recourse for collection. If the amount is small enough, you may be able to go through a small claims court which, except for your time, will cost you nothing. However, for large amounts, you will have to sue for collection. This will take considerable money as well as time. Before making such a decision, you should consider both your chances of collection and the cost in time and money. Check with your attorney on this.

Credit Insurance

Credit insurance is available, but it is available only to manufacturers and wholesalers that sell to other business firms. This is because it is difficult to analyze the risk involved in selling to ultimate consumers, and because a retailer's need for credit insurance is not as great since the retailer's risk is spread among a greater number of customers. It is possible to insure some specific business accounts rather than getting general coverage. This is desirable since higher percentages of coinsurance are required for accounts which are considered to be high risk in order to discourage reckless credit by firms that are insured. Accounts are usually classified according to rating by Dun and Bradstreet or similar agencies, and the premiums will vary depending upon the account ratings assigned by these firms. For export accounts, credit insurance is available from the Foreign Credit Insurance Association. Check with your local Department of Commerce office.

Use of a Factor

If you are using the services of a factor as described in Chapter 2, you can avoid maintaining credit and collection systems. This is because a factor establishes a working procedure for clearing credit for new customers and setting up credit limits for old customers, and for collecting accounts receivable; then the factor buys the accounts receivable outright from you. Naturally, this is going to cost you something, so once again, you must consider the costs as well as the benefits.

CREDIT AND COLLECTION POLICIES CHECKLIST

The establishment of credit and collection policies which work well for your firm can be a major factor in your business's profitability and survivability. But, like any procedures, they must be reevaluated periodically in order to determine their effectiveness. To assist you in reviewing your current policies or in formulating new policies, the following credit and collection policies checklist is provided.

	Yes	No	Not Applicable
Credit Approval			
Is a written application required with every credit request?	___	___	___
Do you have a standard form for credit applications?	___	___	___
Is it completed personally by the applicant?	___	___	___
Is it reviewed for completeness?	___	___	___
Is all information verified for accuracy and timeliness?	___	___	___
Are applicants checked out with a credit bureau?	___	___	___
Does your evaluation consider income?	___	___	___
Does your evaluation consider fixed obligations?	___	___	___
Does your evaluation consider job stability?	___	___	___
Does your evaluation consider residential stability?	___	___	___
Does your evaluation consider credit history?	___	___	___
Does your evaluation consider bank balances?	___	___	___
Does your evaluation consider other assets?	___	___	___

	Yes	No	Not Applicable

Invoices

Are invoices prepared promptly?

Is invoice preparation always accurate?

Are payment terms clearly stated?

Are customers' special instructions followed carefully?

Terms of Sale

Do you offer a cash discount?

Do you use a late payment penalty?

Is the time limit for payment clearly stated?

Statements

Are monthly statements submitted to all open accounts?

Are statements prompt and accurate?

Problems of Identification

Do you determine your average collection period on a regular basis?

Do you compare your collection period with industry averages?

Do you compare your current collection period with your previous experience?

Do you compare your collection period with your payment terms?

Do you have a monthly aging of all outstanding accounts?

When a problem is identified, is corrective action prompt and firm?

Follow-up

Do you have a systematic procedure for follow-up on slow accounts?

Is there a standard sequence of follow-up letters?

Is the tone of these letters progressively stronger?

Do you use the telephone to contact delinquent accounts?

Is your telephone technique effective?

Do you offer special arrangements for collecting past-due accounts?

Do you have a late-payment penalty?

Do you put delinquent accounts on a C.O.D. basis?

	Yes	No	Not Applicable
External Resources			
Do you have a working relationship with a collection agency?	____	____	____
Are accounts turned over automatically after a specific time period?	____	____	____
Do you refer the most serious delinquencies to an attorney?	____	____	____

SOURCES OF ADDITIONAL INFORMATION

Credit and Credit Collection for Small Business, by Donald R. Kitzing, published by AMACOM, a division of the American Management Association, 135 W. 50th Street, New York, NY 10020.

Credit Management Handbook, edited by William B. Abbott *et al.,* published by Credit Research Foundation, 3000 Marcus Ave., Lake Success, NY 11040.

Credits and Collections: Management and Theory, 8th edition, by Theodore N. Beckman and Ronald S. Foster, published by McGraw-Hill Book Co., 1221 Avenue of the Americas, New York, NY 10020.

The Dun and Bradstreet Handbook of Credit and Collections, by Harold T. Redding and Guyon H. Knight III, published by Thomas Y. Crowell Co., 666 Fifth Ave., New York, NY 10003.

14

Advertising and Public Relations

THE IMPORTANCE OF ADVERTISING

Millions of dollars are spent on advertising every single year. In fact, you were exposed to about two million advertising messages from the time you were born until you reached the age of 21. To prove the strength of these messages, see if you can answer these questions. What is a Bulova? What is a Bic? What is Bayer? What is Rinso? What is Ivory? What is a Mustang? What is Prell? What is Lowenbrau? Unless you neither read, watch television, nor listen to the radio, you probably answered the majority of these questions without difficulty. Now, let's try one a little more difficult. What do the letters "LSMFT" stand for? Research has shown that a significant number of people can answer this question, even among those who are now in their early twenties. Yet, the advertising message which gave these letters has not been used for more than 20 years. "LSMFT" stands for "Lucky Strike Means Fine Tobacco," and the message hasn't been on the air since 1958!

Advertising is used for three basic purposes. These are:

1. To promote awareness of a business and its product or service
2. To stimulate sales directly
3. To establish a firm's image or modify a firm's image

YOU CAN COMPETE WITH THE BIG COMPANIES

Amazingly, even though some firms spend millions of dollars on their advertising every year, you can compete with them, and you can beat them if you get your money's worth for your advertising dollar. Why is this so? It is so because many firms, even large firms, do not advertise in a very efficient manner.

Let's look at some examples. For years, cigarette manufacturers fought to keep television advertising. When cigarettes were finally banned from advertising on television, tobacco companies predicted doom and stocks plunged. Yet, what happened to cigarette sales without television advertising? Sales went up! This showed that for more than 50 years, the million dollars that had been spent had largely been wasted through ineffective television advertising.

Some years ago a major company, Lestoil, developed a new spray cleaner. This new cleaner was a disinfectant that cleaned so well that household germs were killed instantly. In order to convey this message, this new product was advertised under the name "Clean and Kill." The result, however, was that the product was killed before the household germs. The advertising campaign was totally ineffective. Why? Possibly housewives, the buying agent for this product, thought that the product was some type of poison.

Just as there have been major disasters in advertising, there have been tremendously successful campaigns. Can you imagine a company bragging about not being first? Well, that's what Avis Rent-A-Car did some years ago. Their message was, "We're No. 2," and therefore, "We try harder." This made it very difficult for Hertz. How could Hertz retaliate without appearing to be the villain? The campaign was tremendously effective, and Hertz lost much of the power that it should have had from being in first place.

Some years ago, Mercedes Benz produced its first diesel car of modern times. This was long before the time of the energy crunch. In fact, the diesel engine seemed to offer very few advantages since gasoline was relatively cheap. Even today, diesel fuel cannot be purchased everywhere, and then, some 15 years ago, diesel fuel was even more difficult to find. Also, diesel engines are very noisy compared with the standard gasoline engine. In despair, Mercedes Benz prepared to junk the production of the diesel engine car. But as a last resort, they turned the project over to a direct marketing expert by the name of Ed McLean. Ed McLean wrote a direct sales letter targeted to individuals who had the money and might be persuaded to buy a Mercedes Benz. This sales letter turned the supposed disadvantages of the diesel engine around and made them advantages. The fact that diesel fuel couldn't be found everywhere meant that the automobile was exclusive. The noise of the engine was promoted as positive evidence that the engine was running. This letter was sent out to consumers on well-chosen mailing lists. The campaign was so successful that Mercedes Benz actually had to reopen the production line and manufacture more diesel engine automobiles! This advertising success won Ed McLean the Golden Mailbox Award from the Direct Mail Marketing Association.

HOW TO DEVELOP AN ADVERTISING PROGRAM

Advertising will work as well for a small firm as for a major multimillion-dollar corporation, if you use it correctly. To use advertising correctly, you must have an advertising program. To develop an advertising program, you must take the following steps:

1. Analyze the market.
2. Set concrete goals and objectives.
3. Set a budget.
4. Develop a creative strategy.
5. Choose your medium or media.
6. Evaluate the results.

Analyze the Market

To analyze the market, you've got to view your own product or service in terms of who can use it. That "who," whether it be male or female, child or senior citizen (or all of the above), is your target consumer. Now, how are you going to reach him and/or her?

Along these lines, marketing and advertising experts have developed a very useful concept called *market segmentation*. If you use the market segmentation concept, instead of trying to sell to the entire market, you zero in on a specific segment of the population who are most interested and can best be served by buying your product or service. The segmentation concept makes sense. You cannot satisfy the entire market with one specific item, and further, you will always have limited resources with which to advertise and promote your products or services.

Advertisers use segmentation through their application of strategy: positioning strategy, media strategy, and creative strategy. *Positioning strategy* refers to how your product is positioned in comparison to the competition. For example, Colonel Sanders' Kentucky Fried Chicken was successful when aimed at buyers who are mainly housewives with a contemporary state of mind, busy, active, finding it hard to prepare meals for their family on a daily basis. Yet, at first, Kentucky Fried Chicken was a failure when positioned mainly as a countrified, folksy product.

Use of *media strategy* by advertising means selecting the appropriate medium or media to reach the segment that is most interested or would be most interested in buying your product. For example, why are beer, razors, and similar male-oriented products advertised on television during sporting events? Clearly because this is when and where the main user of these products is available as an audience for the advertising.

Creative strategy concerns the copy (writing) in the advertisement, the graphics, pictures, or photographs, and the ideas that combine these into an effective ad. For example, Mark O. Haroldsen wrote a book called *How to Wake Up the Financial Genius Within You*. His message for the opportunity-seeker's market in magazines such as *Salesman Opportunity, Spare Time Opportunities,* and the like used the title of the book as the headline. Yet, in advertising in the *Wall Street Journal*, Haroldsen used an entirely different advertisement; the headline read: "How to Avoid Paying Taxes Legally." Why did he use this different creative strategy for the *Wall Street Journal*? In the first case he was appealing to individuals who wanted to grasp an opportunity to make money. In the *Wall Street Journal* he was appealing to professional managers and entrepreneurs who were already making money and were interested in reducing their considerable taxes.

Nowadays, advertisers segment the market in many ways. Here are just a few categories that you might consider for your product or service.

Age. Advertisers tend to spend the most money trying to gain the attention of individuals in the age group 18 to 34. Why do they do this? Because, statistically, this is the group that spends the most money on consumer products. However, this is certainly not true for all types of products or services. For example, record manufacturers go primarily to the age group 12 to 19, and those who sell luxury items appeal to the age group 34 to 49.

Sex. Here again you can see a segmentation. Mennen's Speed Stick underarm deodorant is sold to men. But women will buy an entirely different brand, although the chemical composition may be almost identical to that of Mennen's Speed Stick. Or, more obviously, men buy *Playboy;* women buy *Playgirl.*

Income, Education, and Occupation. Income, education, and occupation are frequently considered together because they are related. For instance, a medical doctor generally has a high income and a considerable education. However, this is not always true. Many blue-collar workers earn as much as or more than their white-collar counterparts. In fact, one of the problems that Robert Oppenheimer had when he headed the Manhatten Project which developed the atom bomb was that his electricians made as much as his scientists and engineers, and when his professionals discovered this they complained bitterly about this "inequity." Many tradesmen such as plumbers, certain mechanics, and others may make high salaries. And, of course, if you are self-employed you have the potential for making much more money than salaried professionals.

Geographic Location.   Here again, cold weather implies heavy clothing. Winter weather implies certain types of products just as sunny Miami or California implies other types of products. If you are selling disco clothes, your product would direct you to the location of your potential sales.

Marital Status and Family Size.   Here again, certain types of products and services will segment according to these factors. Video dating services, travel and tour services, singles bars, nightclubs, will all segment the market in advertising depending on marital status. Certain types of products are segmented by family size when a giant economy size is offered.

Ethnic Group.   Segmentation is accomplished by ethnic group because some groups prefer certain types of products over others. Soybean products, for example, such as tofu or soybean milk, are sold mainly to Asian communities. Certain types of delicatessen products are sold mainly to Jewish, Italian, or German communities. Other types of foods, cosmetic products, or luxury items must also be segmented by ethnic group.

Subculture.   Subcultures such as "disco youth" or "over 65" can also be effectively segmented from the mass market and therefore advertised to. For example, for the over-65 group, market research has shown a greater tendency to do comparison shopping, to buy mainly nationally known name brands, and to shy away from shops that are felt to cater exclusively to older customers. In fact, some years ago, a nationally known baby food company lost millions of dollars in sales because it introduced a special line of senior foods which was ignored by its intended market.

Social Class.   Different social classes tend to prefer and read different types of publications. For example, *Reader's Digest* and *Ladies' Home Journal* are in one class; *Time* and *Sports Illustrated* in another; *New Yorker* and *Vogue* magazine in yet another.

Of the categories previously discussed, age, sex, marital status, family size, income, education, and occupation, and geographical location are all known as *demographic* factors. Subculture, ethnic group, and social class are known as social culture factors. There is also more and more segmentation done for advertising in psychographics and life style categories. These include activities, interests, and opinions, product usage, new product adoption behavior, and family decision making. To accomplish segmentation by psychographics or life style factors, special research is done which measures aspects of human behavior including what products or services are consumed, the activities, interests, and opinions of respondents, special value systems, personality traits and conception of self, and attitudes toward various product classes.

Recently, additional special groups have been identified as being especially good targets for segmentation. Some of these new groups are as follows.

College Students.   There are more than 11 million college students. Individuals selling to this market have made millions of dollars, going back to computer dating which itself originated with a college student in 1966. This student became a millionaire prior to graduation through market segmentation.

The Hispanic Market. This is a viable market which has become so strong that special courses in marketing to this segment have been offered at some of the nation's largest universities. It includes more than 15 million people.

Divorces. While divorce may not be desirable in any society, it is a fact in ours. The average marriage today lasts only six years. As a result, divorcees today are one-half of the single population.

Individuals Living Together. Today, individuals who are living together constitute a segment in themselves. Their number approaches two million.

The Working Woman. Today, two-thirds of women are working, and more than 50% of mothers are working; this is a truly gigantic segment.

Health. There's a tremendous interest in health in the United States. Vitamin sales have doubled in 10 years. The readership of magazines pertaining to health, such as *Prevention,* is steadily growing, with new magazines and newsletters appearing every day. There are 60 million individuals in the United States who are overweight, and two-thirds of these individuals are women. As a result, diet books and other products and services are of continual interest to this segment. There is almost always at least one diet book on *The New York Times* Best Seller List.

Children with Money. Today, children ages 6 through 11 receive allowances the average of which approaches more than $100 a year. The result is $2.5 billion dollars in spendable income, making this segment a tremendous buying force.

Sports Enthusiasts. Jogging, tennis, bicycling, swimming, and even the martial arts are nosing out more traditional sports such as football and basketball in popularity. There is a tremendous interest in all sports and a tremendous market segment to be served.

Spiritual and Mind Power. Recent popular interest in such subjects as yoga, mysticism, Transcendental Meditation, Scientology, and Silva Mind Control has made this a leading and increasingly large segment of the population. Further, this group constitutes a segment which is completely separate from religion in the traditional sense.

In order to learn how best to reach your customer, some sort of market research will be necessary. One way of doing this is with your own survey of your customers or potential customers. A form for you to use is shown in Figure 14.1, a consumer profile questionnaire.

A book which will help you is *Do It Yourself Marketing Research,* by George Edward Breen, published by McGraw-Hill Book Co., 1221 Avenue of the Americas, New York, N.Y. 10020.

Set Concrete Goals and Objectives

Once your analysis is completed, your job is to establish the goals and objectives of your advertising program. What do you want to happen? You should answer the question in precise, concrete terms so that you can measure your results at a

CONSUMER PROFILE QUESTIONNAIRE

PERSONAL DEMOGRAPHIC INFORMATION

Mark the boxes that describe you.

1. Sex:
   - ☐ Male
   - ☐ Female

2. Age:
   - ☐ Under 6
   - ☐ 6 to 11
   - ☐ 12 to 17
   - ☐ 18 to 24
   - ☐ 25 to 34
   - ☐ 35 to 44
   - ☐ 45 to 54
   - ☐ 55 to 64
   - ☐ 65 & over

3. Martial Status:
   - ☐ Married
   - ☐ Single (never married)
   - ☐ Widowed
   - ☐ Divorced or separated

4. Education:
   - ☐ Grade school or less (grades 1–8)
   - ☐ Some high school
   - ☐ Graduated from high school (grades 9–12)
   - ☐ Some colleges
   - ☐ Graduated from college
   - ☐ Some postgraduate college work

5. Principal Language Spoken at Home:
   - ☐ English
   - ☐ Spanish
   - ☐ Other

6. Color:
   - ☐ White
   - ☐ Nonwhite

7. Employment:
   - ☐ Not employed outside the home
   - ☐ Employed outside the home
   - ☐ Employed full time (30 hours per week or more)
   - ☐ Employed part time (less than 30 hours per week)
   - ☐ Not employed—looking for work

8. Occupation:
   - ☐ Professional and technical
   - ☐ Managers, officials, and proprietors, except farm
   - ☐ Clerical
   - ☐ Sales
   - ☐ Craftsman
   - ☐ Foreman
   - ☐ Nonfarm laborers
   - ☐ Service workers
   - ☐ Private household workers
   - ☐ Farm managers
   - ☐ Farm laborers
   - ☐ Farm foreman
   - ☐ Armed services
   - ☐ Retired
   - ☐ Student
   - ☐ Other

9. Geographic Region:
   - ☐ Northeast
   - ☐ Metropolitan New York
   - ☐ Mid-Atlantic
   - ☐ East Central
   - ☐ Metropolitan Chicago
   - ☐ West Central
   - ☐ Southeast
   - ☐ Southwest
   - ☐ Metropolitan Los Angeles
   - ☐ Remaining Pacific

10. Geographic Area:
    - ☐ Central City
    - ☐ Urban Fringe (suburbs)
    - ☐ Town
    - ☐ Rural

Population of city or town:
   - ☐ 4 million or over
   - ☐ Between 4 and 1 million
   - ☐ Between 1 million and 500 thousand
   - ☐ Between 500 thousand and 250 thousand
   - ☐ Between 250 thousand and 50 thousand
   - ☐ Between 50 thousand and 35 thousand
   - ☐ Under 35 thousand

11. County Size:
    - ☐ A county—one of the largest markets
    - ☐ B county—not included in A but area over 150,000 population
    - ☐ C county—not included in A or B but area over 35,000
    - ☐ D county—all remaining counties under 35,000

HOUSEHOLD DEMOGRAPHIC INFORMATION

Answer these statements about your family:

12. Household Sizes:
    - ☐ 1 or 2 members
    - ☐ 2 or 3 members
    - ☐ 3 or 4 members
    - ☐ 5 or more members

13. Number of Children:
    - ☐ None
    - ☐ Two
    - ☐ Three or more

14. Ages of Youngest Child:
    - ☐ No child under 18
    - ☐ Youngest child 12 to 17
    - ☐ Youngest child 6 to 11
    - ☐ Youngest child 2 to 5
    - ☐ Youngest child under 2

15. Household income:
    - ☐ Under $5,000
    - ☐ $5,000 to $7,999
    - ☐ $8,000 to $9,999
    - ☐ $10,000 to $14,999
    - ☐ $15,000 to $24,999
    - ☐ $25,000 and over

16. Wage Earners in the Family:
    - ☐ Male head of household
    - ☐ Female head of household
    - ☐ Wife (non-head of household)
    - ☐ One child
    - ☐ Two children
    - ☐ Over three children

17. Home Ownership:
    - ☐ Own home
    - ☐ Rent home

Five years prior to survey date:
    - ☐ Lived in same home
    - ☐ Lived in different house
    - ☐ in same county
    - ☐ in different county

18. Dwelling Characteristics:
    - ☐ House (unattached)
    - ☐ Attached home
    - ☐ Apartment
    - ☐ Mobile home or trailer
    - ☐ Single family dwelling unit
    - ☐ Multiple family dwelling unit

SOCIAL CLASS INFORMATION

Mark the group your family belongs to.

19. ☐ The local elite with inherited wealth and family tradition.
20. ☐ Top executive or professional manager or owner.
21. ☐ Business, industrial, or professional manager or owner.
22. ☐ White-collar worker in industry or government and small business owner.
23. ☐ Semi-skilled worker in con-

Figure 14.1. Consumer profile questionnaire.

From *Advertising Today* by J. Douglas Johnson. © 1978, J. Douglas Johnson. Reprinted by permission of the publisher, Science Research Associates, Inc.

struction or industry. Probably blue-collar union member.

24. ☐ Unskilled worker, perhaps unemployed.

PSYCHOGRAPHIC INFORMATION

Personality indicators

Mark the accurate statements about yourself.

It is my nature to:

25. ☐ Want to rival and surpass others.
26. ☐ Accept leadership and follow willingly.
27. ☐ Want things arranged, organized, secure, and predictable.
28. ☐ Want to be the center of attention.
29. ☐ Seek freedom, resist influence, and do things my own way.
30. ☐ Form friendships and participate in groups.
31. ☐ Want to understand others, examine their motives and my own.
32. ☐ Seek aid, help, and advice from others.
33. ☐ Want to control others and be the leader of groups.
34. ☐ Feel inferior, guilty, and accept blame easily.
35. ☐ Want to help others, be sympathetic and protective.
36. ☐ Look for new and different things to do.
37. ☐ Stick to a task and work hard to complete a job.
38. ☐ Am attracted by the opposite sex, go out and enjoy company.
39. ☐ Belittle, blame, attack, and want to punish people.
40. ☐ Have frequent daydreams and fantasies.
41. ☐ Experience times of tenseness, self-pity, and am restless or excitable.
42. ☐ Am self-confident in social, professional, and personal dealings.

LIFE-STYLE PREFERENCES AND ATTITUDES

Mark the answers that fit you best.

Leisure

43. ☐ Enjoy entertaining formally and going to movies, concerts, plays, dances, or dinner.
44. ☐ Habitually read newspapers, magazines, and books.
45. ☐ Spend a lot of time listening to music (not just as a background).
46. ☐ Think I have the right to do absolutely nothing some of the time.
47. ☐ Anxious to be busy, go out and see people, participate in sports and other activities.
48. ☐ Would rather study or work than "waste time" playing.

Cooking

49. ☐ Want to prepare good, healthy meals and think I am good at it.
50. ☐ Like convenience foods that are frozen, in cans, or packaged as mixes.
51. ☐ Judge my achievement on the basis of compliments I receive for enjoyable meals.
52. ☐ Try to stay out of the kitchen as much as possible and hate the drudgery of cooking.
53. ☐ Enjoy preparing fancy, exotic, or unusual dishes "from scratch" and serving them in an unusual way.

Family

54. ☐ Think the man should be the boss and run the family.
55. ☐ Think the woman should be the boss and run the family.
56. ☐ Believe marriage should be a partnership with no bosses.
57. ☐ Think children should be considered in most family decisions.
58. ☐ Believe parents should make an effort to teach children and spend time with them.

Dress

59. ☐ Like to wear casual, comfortable clothes.
60. ☐ Want to look fashionable and stylish.

Physical Condition

61. ☐ Am in very good health.
62. ☐ Have an overweight problem.
63. ☐ Always on some kind of a diet.
64. ☐ Watch the scale, eat intelligently, and exercise.
65. ☐ Feel sickly much of the time.
66. ☐ Use over-the-counter drugs for minor ailments.
67. ☐ Seldon take anything for a headache or an upset stomach.

Finances

68. ☐ Have money in the bank and feel secure.
69. ☐ Just about break even every month.
70. ☐ Am in debt but believe the bills can be paid.
71. ☐ Am not optimistic about the financial future.

Risk

72. ☐ Am conservative and do not take chances.
73. ☐ Will take a calculated risk.
74. ☐ Take chances just to see what will happen.

Buying Style

75. ☐ Pick the same brand of products habitually.
76. ☐ Think about the products I buy and select them because they satisfy.
77. ☐ Look for bargains, deals, premiums, and usually compare prices.
78. ☐ Want quality in a product and will pay extra to get it.
79. ☐ Choose advertised brands and do not take chances on unknown products or manufacturers.
80. ☐ Keep trying new products to see what they are like.
81. ☐ Buy what I need when I need it and when a store is handy.
82. ☐ Plan shopping carefully with a list of needs and make an excursion out of the trip.
83. ☐ Judge brands on the basis of ingredients, weight, and package size.
84. ☐ Never read the information on a package to find out what it contains.
85. ☐ Am attracted to a brand by its name, color of the package, and its design.
86. ☐ Usually buy what friends say is good.
87. ☐ Pay attention to advertisements and study them to make up my mind about what to buy.
88. ☐ Do not check into low-cost items much, but do shop intelligently and compare prices for high-priced products.
89. Respond to advertisements in:
    - ☐ Newspaper
    - ☐ Radio
    - ☐ Magazine
    - ☐ Television

Figure 14.1. (Continued)

MEDIA USE AND INTEREST

I use media at these times:

	Newspaper		Magazines		Radio		Television	
	Day	Wkend	Day	Wkend	Day	Wkend	Day	Wkend
90. 6 A.M. to 10:00 A.M.	☐	☐	☐	☐	☐	☐	☐	☐
91. 10:00 A.M. to 3:00 P.M.	☐	☐	☐	☐	☐	☐	☐	☐
92. 3:00 P.M. to 7:00 P.M.	☐	☐	☐	☐	☐	☐	☐	☐
93. 7:00 P.M. to midnight	☐	☐	☐	☐	☐	☐	☐	☐
94. Midnight to 6:00 A.M.	☐	☐	☐	☐	☐	☐	☐	☐

I pay attention to these types of stories or programs:

	Newspaper	Magazine	Radio	Television
95. Local news	☐	☐	☐	☐
96. National news	☐	☐	☐	☐
97. Weather	☐	☐	☐	☐
98. Sports	☐	☐	☐	☐
99. Business and finance	☐	☐	☐	☐
100. Editorials and interviews	☐	☐	☐	☐
101. Classified	☐	☐	☐	☐
102. Daytime serials	☐	☐	☐	☐
103. Comics or comedy shows	☐	☐	☐	☐
104. Crime news or programs	☐	☐	☐	☐
105. Adventure	☐	☐	☐	☐
106. Quizzes or, game shows	☐	☐	☐	☐
107. Movies	☐	☐	☐	☐
108. Self-help stories	☐	☐	☐	☐
109. How-to-do-it	☐	☐	☐	☐
110. Theater arts, and entertainment	☐	☐	☐	☐
111. Editorials	☐	☐	☐	☐
112. Interviews	☐	☐	☐	☐
113. Travel	☐	☐	☐	☐
114. Police shows	☐	☐	☐	☐
115. Romantic programs	☐	☐	☐	☐
116. Sexy stories and pictures	☐	☐	☐	☐
117. Cooking programs and stories	☐	☐	☐	☐

USE OF A PARTICULAR PRODUCT OR SERVICE

(Statements must be adapted)

118. I am a
light _____
medium _____
heavy _____
or nonuser _____
119. I use your product/service daily _____
once a week _____
once a month _____
once a year _____
120. I have used your product for a
short time _____
many years _____
121. I have tried similar products. The names are

_____

_____

122. I use your product in combination with

_____

_____

123. I buy your product at a supermarket _____
drugstore _____
department store _____
discount store _____
hardware store _____
or other store _____
124. The quantity I buy at one time is
a single package _____
several packages _____
many packages _____

TRADE WITH A PARTICULAR STORE

125. I shop in your store
more than once a week _____
at least once a week _____
every two weeks _____
once a month _____
once a year _____
126. The distance from my home to your store is
less than five blocks _____
one mile away _____

two or three miles _____
five miles _____
over ten miles _____
127. I usually buy these types of products at your store:

_____

_____

_____

_____

128. The part of my shopping I do with your store is:
All _____
Most _____
129. My favorite stores that are similar to yours (and including it) are:
First choice _____
Second choice _____
Third choice _____
130. Each year I spend this amount in your store $_____

Figure 14.1. (Continued)

later time. And by when do you want it to happen? Give a specific time frame. For example, a suitable advertising objective might be to increase the number of males ages 15 to 25 who walk into your retail establishment and make a purchase by 20% over the next three months. That says precisely who, what, and when.

The Advertising Budget

Once goals and objectives have been established, you must look to your advertising budget. In some cases your budget will be established before goals and objectives due to your limited resources. It will be a given, and you may have to modify your goals and objectives. If money is available, you can work the other way around and see how much money it will take to reach the goals and objectives you have established.

The professionals use different methods of establishing an advertising budget. These are as follows:

Quantitative models
The objective and task method
Percentage of anticipated sales
Percentage of past year's sales
Affordable approach
Arbitrary approach

Of these methods, a recent survey shows that the most popular method used today is that of *percentage of anticipated sales*. This means that you must forecast your sales for the future period and then allocate a fixed percentage. This fixed percentage is usually found by comparing other firms advertising in your industry that are of your size and have a similar product. Obviously, this method has an advantage over taking a fixed percentage of a past year's sales since you are looking to the future. On the other hand, it says little about the advertising program and has nothing to do with the objectives and goals that you have established.

The *arbitrary approach* means simply that you pull a figure out of the air and decide that this is how much money will be devoted to advertising. This method has little to recommend it.

Quantitative models can be extremely sophisticated. However, their complexity and the fact that so many factors must be considered mean that it is little used and probably not desirable or even workable for a small firm. As a matter of fact, even by major firms the quantitative model method is little used.

With the *objective and task* approach, you relate your budget to the goals and objectives you have established. While the percentage of sales or profits or percentage of any approach first determines how much you'll spend without much consideration of what you want to accomplish, this method establishes what you must do in order to meet your objectives—only then do you calculate its cost. For a small firm, it must frequently be used with the affordable approach since in some cases, and as mentioned previously, you may set objectives which can only be reached at a much higher budget than you can afford. In this case, you must scale down your objectives.

In order to use the objective and task method, you break down the cost of your budget by calendar periods, by media, and perhaps by sales areas. Breakdown by calendar periods means that you divide the advertising plan on a monthly or

Account	Month		Year to Date	
	Budget	Actual	Budget	Actual

Media
  Newspapers
  Radio
  TV
  Literature
  Direct Mail
  Other
Promotions
  Exhibits
  Displays
  Contests
  Sweepstakes
Advertising Expense
  Salaries
  Supplies
  Stationery
  Travel
  Postage
  Subscriptions
  Entertainment
  Dues				

Totals				

Figure 14.2. Advertising budget. [Adapted from *Advertising Guidelines for Small Retail Firms*, by Ovid Riso, SMA 160, Small Business Administration (1980).]

weekly basis. Media breakdown denotes how much money you will place in each advertising medium, such as television, radio, newspaper, direct mail, and so forth. Sales areas are the areas in which you will spend your advertising budget. That is, if you are going after different market segments simultaneously under one advertising program, you have to decide how much money each market segment will get. Use the form in Figure 14.2 to assist you in preparing your advertising budget.

Creative Strategy

Creative strategy involves what you will say in your advertising message, how you will say it, and any artwork that is included. Unless you are professional in this area, or your ad is very simple, it is better to get expert, professional help in preparing creative work. You can find these professionals fairly easily in your phone book. For artwork, look under Artists—Commercial or Advertising Artists. Do the same for photography and for copywriters.

If you intend to write your own copy, I would recommend the book *How to Write a Good Advertisement*, by Victor O. Schwab. This is published by the Wilshire Book Co., 12015 Sherman Rd., North Hollywood, CA 91605.

If you are going to write your own copy, follow the following guidelines.

First, make the headline appeal to self-interest, offer exciting news, or rouse interest in your consumer. The headline should be positive, not negative. The headline should suggest that the reader can obtain something easily and quickly. Make the headline stress the most important benefit of your product or your service, and write it so that it grabs the reader's attention and causes him or her to read further. Also, be sure that the headline is believable and, of course, when you begin to write the body of the copy, make sure that the headline does in fact tie in with what you write later.

In the copy content itself, you should try to gain interest immediately. If you have enough room in your copy, use a story or a startling or unusual statement or quote; use news if you don't have enough room. Show the benefits and advantages that appeal to emotional needs to such an extent that your offer and what you say are made irresistible. If you can, add credibility to your copy through the use of testimonials. These are statements made by other people who have used your product or service and are happy with it.

Always remember when you are writing copy that you are writing to communicate, and therefore write it in a conversational tone and keep your copy moving right along. Use short words, short sentences, and short paragraphs, and lots of subheadings throughout. If you want your copy to be read, make it interesting and make it easy to read. I have found that Rudolf Flesch's book, *The Art of Readable Writing*, published by Harper and Row Publishers, Inc., to be of considerable help here.

These principles in copywriting should apply whether your advertisement is to appear in print or on radio or television. Only minor modifications should be necessary depending on limitations of these different media.

Medium and Vehicle Selection

Each of the different advertising *media* categories (print, television, radio, etc.) has several vehicles: magazine or newspaper, and which type; what sort of radio television show, and so on. There are four major considerations when you make your selection of medium (assuming you're using just one) and vehicle. These are as follows:

1. *Budget match.* Which medium and vehicle you use must be consistent with the money that you have available for use in your budget.

2. *Medium and vehicle and target consumer match.* The medium and vehicle that you select must be seen, heard, or read by your target consumer market.

3. *Medium and vehicle market mix relationship.* Which medium and vehicle you select also must be reflected in the emphasis that you give to the marketing mix. The marketing mix is made up of various inputs of product, price, the distribution method that you use, and promotional factors. What is the relationship between medium and vehicle and market mix? Let's take a new product. With a new product you may choose to use TV as your medium because with TV you can reach the most people in the shortest amount of time. Also, the product must fit the medium or vehicle. Some years ago, entrepreneur Joe Cossman sold over one million plastic shrunken heads. Obviously *Vogue* magazine was never considered a vehicle for this particular product. In the same way, high price denotes a certain medium and vehicle, as does low price. Similar matching must be followed with distribution and promotional factors.

4. *Creative medium and vehicle marriage.* Certain appeals are best for certain media and vehicles, as mentioned previously using the example of Mark O. Haroldsen's book, *How to Wake Up the Financial Genius Within You.* To reach those interested in getting rich quick, the vehicle selected was *Specialty Salesmen* and similar magazines. To reach those interested in tax shelters, the vehicle selected was the *Wall Street Journal.*

The Categories of Media. The categories of media should all be considered as you plan for your advertising campaign. These include:

1. Print (newspapers, magazines)
2. Broadcasts (radio, TV)
3. Direct mail (letters addressed directly to lists of potential buyers in your target consumer market group)
4. Specialty items (pens, pencils, or other gadgets with the name of your firm embossed on them)
5. Directories (yellow pages advertisements, advertisements in association membership directories, and so forth)
6. Outdoor (billboards, transit posters)
7. Movie theater advertisements
8. Various others, such as matchbook covers

Audience. One publication that will greatly assist you in planning your campaign is the *Standard Rate and Data Service* or SRDS. The SRDS publishes a set of periodically updated volumes concerning the following items:

1. Consumer magazines
2. Farm publications
3. Business publications
4. Newspapers
5. Weekly newspapers
6. Network radio and TV
7. Spot radio and TV
8. Transit

While major advertisers and advertising agencies may subscribe to SRDS, many libraries carry these volumes. You will find them extremely useful in matching your target audience and selecting the media and vehicles that you can use.

Making Intermediate Comparisons. Each medium has its advantages and its disadvantages for your particular situation. For example, television, which has a broad reach and offers opportunities for a dynamic demonstration, is expensive and does not allow for demographic selectivity to any great extent. Newspapers may be relatively cheap; however, they offer little secondary readership, limited color facilities, and little demographic selectivity possibilities. To assist you in making intermedia comparisons, consider Figure 14.3, the advertising media comparison chart developed by the Bank of America.

Advertising Planning Concepts. Some of the concepts that you should consider in your planning, in addition to cost, are reach versus frequency; continuity; target market, marketing and advertising objectives; the marketing mix of product, price, promotion and distribution, and promotional variables; competitive advertising activity; the size of your budget; and your creative strategy.

All of these have been discussed previously except for reach versus frequency and continuity.

Reach versus Frequency.   Reach is the total number of households that will be exposed to an advertising message in a particular vehicle or medium over a certain period of time. It is expressed as a percentage of the total universe of households. Frequency is the number of exposures to the same message each household receives. Therefore, average frequency would equal the total exposures for all households sampled, divided by the reach. Even at tremendous expense, you cannot reach 100% of your target market. Therefore, the key is trying to estimate the point at which additional dollars should go into frequency after the optimal reach has been achieved. Some pointers that will assist you in making this decision are as follows:

Go for greater reach

1. . . . when you're introducing a new product to a mass market and want as many people as possible to know about it.
2. . . . when your advertising message is so compelling that most people will react to the initial exposure.
3. . . . when your product or service message is in itself newsworthy and will itself demand attention.

Go for higher frequency

1. . . . when your competitor is going for high frequency against the same segment as you.
2. . . . when you are seeking direct response; that is, when you want individuals to order the product or respond to the service directly from the ad.
3. . . . when you want your target consumer to act within a certain limited time period.
4. . . . when there isn't too much to differentiate what you are offering from what your competition is selling.

Continuity.   Continuity has to do with the length of time that your medium schedule should run. Obviously, you can run a medium schedule continuously or periodically; once a day, once a week, or even more infrequently. Here again, you should consider the various factors that may influence success as a trade-off against cost and limited resources. For funding optimal frequency, experts have developed something called the "three-hit theory." The basis of the theory is that there is an optimal range after which you are wasting money. This range, according to the theory, is three receipts of your message or "hits." Three hits will insure that the customer learns of your product or service through your advertising message. To get the three hits, you need 11 to 12 potential advertising exposures. Therefore, the average potential frequency should be 11 to 12 times.

Once you have decided upon the medium (or media), you must then decide upon the vehicle(s). To do this, you should use demographics, that is, the demographic research that you have done against that supplied by the vehicle in question. And in this regard, you should know that every magazine or television or radio show can offer a current demographic profile of its readership or listenership. It is therefore a question of matching up their information with your research of your target customer.

ADVERTISING MEDIA

Medium	Market Coverage	Type of Audience	Sample Time/Space Costs
Daily Newspaper	Single community or entire metro area; zoned editions sometimes available.	General; tends more toward men, older age group, slightly higher income and education.	Per agate line, weekday; open rate: Circ: 8,700: $ .20 19,600: $ .35 46,200: $ .60 203,800: $ 1.60
Weekly Newspaper	Single community usually; sometimes a metro area.	General; usually residents of a smaller community.	Per agate line; open rate: Circ: 3,000: $ .35 8,900: $ .50 17,100: $ .75
Shopper	Most households in a single community; chain shoppers can cover a metro area.	Consumer households.	Per agate line; open rate: Circ: 10,000: $ .20 147,000: $ 2.00 300,000: $ 3.20
Telephone Directories	Geographic area or occupational field served by the directory.	Active shoppers for goods or services.	Yellow Pages, per half column; per month: Pop: 14-18,000: $ 15.00 110-135,000: $ 35.00 700-950,000: $ 100.00
Direct Mail	Controlled by the advertiser.	Controlled by the advertiser through use of demographic lists.	Production and mailing cost of an 8½″ × 11″ 2-color brochure; 4-page, 2-color letter; order card and reply envelope; label addressed; third class mail: $.33 each in quantities of 50,000.
Radio	Definable market area surrounding the station's location.	Selected audiences provided by stations with distinct programming formats.	Per 60-second morning drive-time spot; one time: Pop: 400,000: $ 35.00 1,100,000: $ 90.00 3,500,000: $ 150.00 13,000,000: $ 300.00
Television	Definable market area surrounding the station's location.	Varies with the time of day; tends toward younger age group, less print-oriented.	Per 30-second daytime spot; one time; nonpreemptible status: Pop: 400,000: $100.00 1,100,000: $300.00 3,500,000: $500.00 13,000,000: $600.00
Transit	Urban or metro community served by transit system; may be limited to a few transit routes.	Transit riders, especially wage earners and shoppers; pedestrians.	Inside 11″ × 28″ cards; per month: 50 buses: $ 125.00 400 buses: $1,000.00 Outside 21″ × 88″ posters; per month: 25 buses: $1,850.00 100 buses: $7,400.00
Outdoor	Entire metro area or single neighborhood.	General; especially auto drivers.	Per 12′ × 25′ poster; 100 GRP* per month: Pop: 21,800: $ 125.00 386,000: $ 135.00 628,900: $ 150.00
Local Magazine	Entire metro area or region; zoned editions sometimes available.	General; tends toward better educated, more affluent.	Per one-sixth page, black and white; open rate: Circ: 25,000: $ 310.00 80,000: $ 520.00

*Several boards must be purchased for these GRPs.

Figure 14.3. Advertising media comparison chart. (Reprinted with permission from Bank of America, NT & SA, "Advertising Small Business," *Small Business Reporter*, Vol. 15 No. 2, Copyright 1976, 1978, 1981.)

COMPARISON CHART

Particular Suitability	Major Advantage	Major Disadvantage
All general retailers.	Wide circulation.	Nonselective audience.
Retailers who service a strictly local market.	Local identification.	Limited readership.
Neighborhood retailers and service businesses.	Consumer orientation.	A giveaway and not always read.
Services, retailers of brand-name items, highly specialized retailers.	Users are in the market for goods or services.	Limited to active shoppers.
New and expanding businesses; those using coupon returns or catalogs.	Personalized approach to an audience of good prospects.	High CPM.
Businesses catering to identifiable groups; teens, commuters, housewives.	Market selectivity, wide market coverage.	Must be bought consistently to be of value.
Sellers of products or services with wide appeal.	Dramatic impact, wide market coverage.	High cost of time and production.
Businesses along transit routes, especially those appealing to wage earners.	Repetition and length of exposure.	Limited audience.
Amusements, tourist businesses, brand-name retailers.	Dominant size, frequency of exposure.	Clutter of many signs reduces effectiveness of each one.
Restaurants, entertainments, specialty shops, mail-order businesses.	Delivery of a loyal, special-interest audience.	Limited audience.

Figure 14.3. (Continued)

Negotiating and Special Discounts.   Many small business advertisers don't realize that they could advertise for much less than they are doing now if they knew about the special negotiating possibilities and discounts which are offered. These include the following:

1. Mail order discounts
2. PI (per inquiry) deals
3. Frequency discounts
4. Stand-by rates
5. Help if necessary
6. Remnants and regional editions
7. Barter
8. Bulk buyers
9. Seasonal discounts
10. Spread discounts
11. An in-house agency
12. Cost discounts

If you are a mail order advertiser, many magazines realize that you must make money directly from your ad or you cannot stay in business and will not advertise again. In addition to this, with this type of advertising, it is easy to know immediately whether you are doing well and whether it made money for you. Accordingly, many magazines will give special *mail order discounts*, sometimes up to 40%, to mail order advertisers. Therefore, if the advertisement normally costs you $200, you need only pay $120. This is a big discount and certainly nothing to pass by. Even for many national mail order advertisers, it may spell the difference between a profitable ad and failure.

A *PI deal* is one in which you agree to pay the publication only for those inquiries or sales that the ad itself brings in. This may be on the radio, television, or in a magazine. As a result, in return for this agreement, the magazine will run your advertisement with no money from you up front. Certainly this is a major advantage for a small businessperson. Usually the mail is sent to the vehicle which will sort it and keep the records for you. At other times the ad is keyed and the mail sent directly to you. You must turn a percentage of each order over to the vehicle at fixed periods that you agree upon. If the orders go to the vehicle, they will send you the names of those who order so that you can respond and send the product to the customer. They will also send that amount owed you for each product. A typical PI deal will usually cost something like 50% of the selling price to the publication vehicle.

Frequently it is difficult to locate PI deals, and you need to talk to the salesperson representing the vehicle. Few magazines, radio stations, or television stations like their regular advertisers to know that they accept PI deals, so don't expect them to be advertised as such. They are not easy to find, but they are worth the trouble of looking for them.

Most media will offer *frequency discounts*. Therefore, if you advertise more than once or more than what is standard, you can expect a lower cost than what you might otherwise achieve. Be careful, however, in committing yourself to long-range advertising programs until you know whether or not the campaign is going to work.

Most vehicles are committed to publication or broadcast on a regular basis. At certain times, all advertising may not be sold outright up to the last minute. The vehicle therefore has a choice: it can either sell this advertising at a greatly reduced amount—*stand-by rate*—or put in some sort of editorial content which does not generate additional profits. To get the stand-by rate, you must first let the different vehicles know that you are interested in this type of a deal, and they must be able to get hold of you quickly by telephone. Sometimes a stand-by rate is available only after you advertise with this publication or station for some time. Then, the people know you and trust you. This is important since the deal is closed verbally—no money from you in advance. The advantage of the stand-by rate is well worth it. Again, you may pay as little as 40 to 50% of the normal cost of advertising.

Help if necessary, is applicable usually to mail order advertisers and again, is in recognition of the fact that the mail order advertiser must make money from the ad in order to stay in business. What it means is that if the ad is not profitable, the publication may agree to run the ad again and repeat it if necessary until you at least break even. Help may not assist you in making additional money, but it sure can prevent you from losing a lot of money. Therefore, you should always check into the possibility of help-if-necessary deals if you are a mail order advertiser.

Many national magazines today will allow advertisers to buy space only in certain regional editions rather than in every edition which appears nationally. This situation works to your advantage in reduced advertising costs, and sometimes the regional editions will not be sold out in advertising and space may go begging. You can get *remnants in regional editions* at a discount of as much as 50%. To locate remnant advertising possibilities, talk to salespeople representing the advertising vehicle.

Sometimes a publication or station may be willing to *barter*, that is, to take products or services in exchange for advertising. This occurs where the vehicle has an interest other than publishing or broadcasting. Barter is a great way to go since it allows you to increase sales without using up capital resources.

Bulk Buyers are purchasers of huge amounts of advertising from advertising media. Because of the quantity in which it is bought, they pay much less. The bulk buyer then resells the advertising space. The price you pay to a bulk buyer will vary greatly and it will be negotiable. Toward the end of the advertising period, if this space isn't sold, you may be able to get discounts as large as 50% of what you would normally pay.

Certain media do not do well during certain seasons of the year. As a result, during these periods they offer substantial *seasonal discounts* over their normal rate. If your product or service sells well during that season, you should seriously consider seasonal discounts in your advertising. On the same principle, your product may cost a great deal to sell during prime time on television or radio. However, there may be no need to sell during prime time. In fact, your product may sell better in other than prime time. Therefore, you should consider nonprime time discounts much in the line of seasonal discounts.

If you are a big advertiser and advertise on two or three pages or more of a particular issue of a magazine, you may be able to get a special *spread discount*. This may or may not be on the vehicle's rate card which describes its advertising costs, so you must ask about it. Again, discounts can run as high as 50% of the normal cost.

Advertising agencies get an automatic 15% discount from any vehicle in which they place your ad. This is one way they have of making their money. As a result, many small businesspeople form their own *in-house agency* to take advantage of the 15% discount for themselves. Most vehicles say they will not deal with in-house agencies and will not accept advertising from them at the 15% discount. However, what they are really saying is that they will do this as long as you're not obvious about the fact that you are an in-house agency. Therefore, for the cost of registration of a name other than that of your regular company, and some specially printed stationery with this name, you can get a 15% discount every single time you advertise. To recapitulate:

1. Select a name for your in-hour advertising agency which is different from the name of your regular firm.
2. Have special stationery printed up with the in-house agency's name.
3. Do not volunteer the fact that you are an in-house agency. Merely indicate that you're placing the ad for the company indicated and give other instructions in accordance with the rate card or the *Standard Rate and Data Service* publication.

Many advertisers overlook the fact that most vehicles will give a 2% *cash discount* for payment of cash within the first ten days. However, if you do not take this discount, very few vehicles will automatically return your money. So, look for this information in materials supplied in the information on the rate card which you request from the vehicle. If you can get a 2% discount, you can save a lot of money. Even small firms are saving as much as $50,000 a year this way, once they become large advertisers.

Evaluation of Results

Unless you know how well your advertising is doing, much or all of your money could be totally wasted. Therefore, it is important to establish some measurements of the effectiveness of your advertising. There are several methods of doing this. They are:

1. Direct response
2. Involuntary methods
3. Recognition and awareness tests
4. Recall tests
5. Focus group tests

Direct Response.   This is probably the best means of measuring the effectiveness of your advertising, because you measure actual responses to your ad. In order to do this, all you need do is code the advertisement so that you'll know which response is from which advertisement. A typical code uses "Suite," "Room," "Drawer," or sometimes even different initials before the name of the company, or different initials after the box number. For example, a letter can stand for the vehicle in which the advertisement appears, and a digit following the letter can denote the month. Let us say that you advertised in *Outdoor Life* magazine in January. "A" could stand for *Outdoor Life,* and the digit "1" could stand for advertisement in January. The simple addition to your address of "Suite A-1" or "Room A-1" would tell you immediately the vehicle and the exact advertisement.

Involuntary Methods.   These methods of measuring advertisement effectiveness are usually pretesting methods. They record involuntary responses over which neither the subject nor the researcher has control. They are objective, but they are also expensive. They are also done in an unnatural setting. One device, called a pupilometer, measures the dilation of the pupil while the individual is observing advertising. The device is unwieldy and uncomfortable, and it certainly isn't the way that the reader usually sees advertising. One very simple involuntary method is called the "down the chute" test. It consists of having someone read advertising copy while you watch his eyes. If there are no problems with comprehension or readability, it is presumed that the individual's eyes will keep moving from left to right, left to right, as he goes line by line down the page. But if the pupils stop moving, there could be a problem, and at this point you should ask the reader what he is reading. You note the problem and then continue the procedure.

Recognition and Awareness Tests. In recognition and awareness tests, consumers who have read or seen an advertisement are asked whether they remember the ad. One limitation is the possibility of confusion of your ad with similar ads, and the sample size used is usually small compared to the total number of readers.

The oldest type of recognition test is a readership test called the "Starch." In the Starch system, the interviewer shows the magazine to the subject, and if the subject says he or she has read it, the interviewer goes through the magazine ad by ad with the subject indicating whether he or she has "noted the ad," which means has seen it; "associated it," which means he or she remembers the brand name; or "read most," which means that he or she has read at least half of the copy. The Starch system reports the percentage of ads "noted," "associated," and "read most" for each subject.

Awareness tests measure the cumulative effect of advertising. Test subjects are consumers in the target consumer group for the ad. First, demographic information is gathered to determine if they are likely customers. Then, they are asked the question: "Have you seen the ads lately for (name of product)? The problem with this type of test is that there are too many variables which can affect the response.

Recall Tests. In a typical recall test, the prospects are first screened and asked questions about their attitude. They are then asked to watch a program, while those in a control group are asked similar questions but do not watch. The effectiveness of recall is determined later when brand awareness is measured in both groups and the results are compared.

Focus Group Tests. The focus group has grown as a method of pretesting in recent years. It is relatively low budget in that 8 to 10 representative consumers are invited in. It is therefore not a quantitative measure but rather a qualitative measure of reactions to help you decide whether to run one ad or another.

The small businessperson can adopt many of these methods to help in determining the effectiveness of advertising. The key is to keep your methods simple, hold down costs, and be careful about drawing inferences if you use a very small sample size.

SHOULD YOU EMPLOY AN ADVERTISING AGENCY?

Whether or not to employ an advertising agency depends a great deal on how large a company you have and what an advertising agency can do for you. Many of the things that an advertising agency can do, such as media selection, copy-writing, supplying artwork, and so forth, you may do for yourself, in which case it may be better to establish your own in-house agency as described earlier and save 15%. On the other hand, all these activities take up your resources, and an agency can tie everything together and can probably do a more professional job for you. The problem here is that many of the best agencies will only work for your firm when you become a major advertiser. If you are big enough, the services provided by an agency may cost you nothing since the agency receives 15% commission from the medium or media used. If you are not a major advertiser, the agency will bill you for services rendered on an hourly, daily, or project basis.

If you do decide to employ an advertising firm, do not engage the first one that you contact. First, talk to the principals of the agency and get some definite information about them. This should include: the size of the agency, that is, last year's billing, how long the principals have been with the agency, their general philosophy of positioning, whether they deal mainly with industrial accounts or with consumer accounts, and what some of their accounts are. You should also query them to find out in which areas of your business they would like to become involved. Some agencies will handle everything for you. Others will develop and place your ads, and that's it. Ask who at the agency would be working directly on your account and his or her title, and who would be responsible for supervision on a day-to-day basis. You should also ask for representative accounts, accounts similar to yours with which the advertising agency has experience so that you may contact those firms. Naturally, you should ask about compensation arrangements. If you are going to be doing a considerable amount of advertising, it is perfectly legitimate to ask for a speculative presentation by the agency. In fact, you should ask for a proposal from several different agencies. During these speculative presentations, you can get a feel for what the agency can do and whether you like or do not like the people and services you will be paying for. There are, however, certain disadvantages to asking several agencies for proposals. They will have competitive information on your firm, and some agencies will see this as exploitive inasmuch as they obviously must pay for this proposal whether or not they get your business. In general, it is better not to ask for a speculative proposal unless the agency is a serious candidate.

Consider the following factors in making your decision to "hire" an agency:

1. Is the agency size consistent with your needs and growth plans?
2. Is the agency's philosophy of positioning compatible with your own?
3. Is the agency's management strength compatible with your firm?
4. Is the agency's ability to offer overall marketing counsel good?
5. Is there a similarity among the agency's other accounts and your firm?
6. Do you have a good opinion of the account team assigned from the agency to be responsible for working with you and doing your advertising?
7. Does the agency have a good research capability?
8. Does the agency have a good creative capability?
9. Does the agency have a good media planning capability?
10. Is the agency in good financial shape?
11. How did the references check out?

Of course, as mentioned earlier, one of the problems that you will have as a small firm is interesting an agency in working with you. One way to do this is to stress your tremendous growth potential. If you don't have much cash, try barter. That is, trade your product or services for their services. Finally, you could offer stock in your company in exchange for their services.

HOW TO GET FREE ADVERTISING THROUGH A PUBLICITY RELEASE

Every magazine is constantly looking for new ideas, new news, and new information to tell its readers. So, whenever you have a new product or service or something different happens with regard to your current product or service that might be of interest to a magazine's readers, many magazines will be happy to publicize it for you and will charge you nothing. This has an additional advantage. Editorial coverage of your product or service is usually more effective than your own advertising. You should understand that magazines will not run every single idea or product publicity release which you submit. In order to reach those that will, you must run a direct mail campaign. Your campaign package should consist of three basic elements:

1. A sales letter to the editor
2. Suggested editorial material about your new product or service (called the "release")
3. Either the product itself or a 4-by-5-inch glossy photograph of the product (Generally a photograph is just as good, unless your product is a book or a booklet.)

Figure 14.4 is a letter to the editor for free advertising for a body armor product I sold several years ago. Follow this general format when asking for free advertis-

---

Mr. A. B. Jones
Editor
World Military Gazette
101 New State Drive
New York NY 10065

Dear Mr. Jones:

I am writing to you because my company, Global Associates, has just developed a new product which will have a tremendous effect on casualty reduction in military operations. This new product is a personal protective body armor which is half the weight of current models but gives slightly more than double the level of protection.

This amazing armor is called "KPC Composite," and it is soft and flexible although it has five times the tensile strength of steel. A special patented carrier has been developed for the KPC Composite material. The whole unit is called "The Commando MK III Armor Jacket."

I know that your readers will be interested in knowing not only of the existence of this life-saving garment, but also that individual soldiers can order their own Commando MK III Armor Jackets directly from Global Associates at $300 per unit, insurance and postage costs included. I have enclosed a publicity release along with a photograph for your use if desired.

Sincerely,

President
GLOBAL ASSOCIATES

Figure 14.4. Letter to the editor for a publicity release.

New Body Armor Announced

Global Associates, a body armor company, announced the development of a new personal protective body armor today. The new armor, known as KPC Composite, is half the weight of current body armor, but offers twice the level of protection. The armor also has the unusual properties of being soft and flexible although it displays five times the tensile strength of steel. The armor has defeated projectiles travelling as fast as 2000 feet per second. It has also been tested against and has stopped various small-arm ammunition, including .38 caliber, .45 caliber, .22 magnum, 9mm, .41 magnum, and .44 magnum. A special patented carrier has been designed for the armor and designated the Commando MK III Armor Jacket. This garment itself has many unusual features. It is worn like a jacket, with a closure in the front. This permits increased ventilation during use and allows the armor to be donned or doffed without removing the helmet or other headgear. In addition, a special lockstrap suspension system has been developed. Although the straps cannot be pulled apart, under emergency conditions the armor can be completely jettisoned in less than three seconds. For normal armor closure, a protected slide fastener is provided. The entire ensemble comes in three sizes—small, medium, and large. It weighs just 4½ pounds. Interested buyers can purchase the Commando MK III Armor Jacket by sending $300 to Global Associates, P.O. Box 1975, Sierra, California 91076.

Figure 14.5. Publicity release.

Figure 14.6.

ing in a letter. Do not mention that you may become a paid advertiser later. If you are sending money to the magazine for a paid advertisement, do not send it with a letter to the editor requesting free editorial mention. Do not mention whether you're currently an advertiser in the magazine.

Figure 14.5 shows a typical publicity release that might accompany a letter such as the one shown in Figure 14.4. Note that the publicity release is typed and need not be printed. Figure 14.6 shows a photograph of the product. Photographs can be reproduced in quantity rather cheaply, although usually not by a standard commercial photographer. For example, a 4-by-5-inch glossy in quantities of 100 can be obtained for as little as 20¢ a copy by a duplicate photograph service which you can find in your yellow pages. One that I have used and recommend is Duplicate Photo Laboratories, Inc., P.O. Box 2670, 1522 North Highland Ave., Hollywood, CA 90028.

SOURCES OF ADDITIONAL INFORMATION

How to Advertise—A Handbook for Small Business, by Sandra Linville Dean, published by Enterprise Publishing, Inc., 725 Market St., Wilmington, DE 19801.

How to Advertise and Promote Your Business, by Gonnie McClung Siegel, published by John Wiley and Sons, Inc., 605 Third Ave., New York, NY 10058.

How to Be Your Own Advertising Agency, by Herbert J. Holtje, published by AMACOM, a division of the American Management Associations, 135 West 50th St., New York, NY 10020.

How to Get Big Results from a Small Advertising Budget, by Cynthia S. Smith, published by Hawthorne Books, Inc., 260 Madison Ave., New York, NY 10016.

How to Write a Good Advertisement, by Victor O. Schwab, published by Wilshire Book Co., 12015 Sherman Rd., North Hollywood, CA 91605.

Risk Free Advertising, by Victor Wademan, published by John Wiley and Sons, Inc., 605 Third Ave., New York, NY 10058.

Tested Advertising Methods, by John Caples, published by Reward Books, Englewood Cliffs, NJ 07632.

The Successful Promoter, by Ted Schwarz, published by Contemporary Books, Inc., 180 N. Michigan, Chicago, IL 60601.

15

Marketing Research

MARKETING RESEARCH—WHAT IT IS AND HOW IT CAN MAKE MONEY FOR YOU

Marketing research is the gathering, recording, and analyzing of information about problems relating to marketing. It will help you to identify who your market is as well as which methods will best satisfy the needs of your market. But it encompasses many other aspects of marketing, including new product introductions, prices, advertising, consumer behavior, and so on. So important is marketing research that certain basic marketing strategies such as market segmentation, in which you identify a specific portion of the market and concentrate your resources on selling to that one segment, or product differentiation, in which you differentiate your product from that of a competitor in such a fashion as to best appeal to potential buyers, would be absolutely impossible without it.

Among the many things that marketing research will tell you are the following:

1. Who are your customers and who are your potential customers?
2. What kinds of people are your customers? (This includes demographic categories, such as age, income, and education, and psychographic categories such as interests and preferences.)
3. Where do your customers live?
4. Why do your customers buy?
5. Do they have the ability to pay?
6. Are you offering the kinds of goods and services that your customers want?
7. Are you offering your products or services at the best place, at the best time, and in the correct amounts?
8. Are your prices consistent with the value your customers place on the product or service that you are selling?
9. How are your promotional programs working?
10. What do your customers think of your business and its image?
11. How do your business and your business procedures compare with those of your competitors?

Correct use of marketing research can mean amazing profits for your business and tremendous advantages over your competitors. A famous example of correct use of marketing research took place in the early 1960s. Ford, along with two other major American motor companies, had developed cars to compete with foreign cars such as the Volkswagen. Ford's entry had been the Falcon, introduced in 1959. As the years passed, the numbers of Ford Falcons that were sold began to decrease as a percentage of Ford's total sales. This was also true for the competing cars offered by the two other American companies. Ford might simply have concluded that American small cars were no longer wanted. Instead, Ford did marketing research to find out more about the falling off of Falcon sales. During this research, Ford discovered an interesting and important fact: while sales of the Falcon were declining, sales of sporty options such as bucket seats and a special interior were increasing. This was due primarily to the greater numbers of young adults who were purchasing the vehicle. Ford's careful study of the market research findings led the company to put out the Ford Mustang, introduced in 1965. This sporty vehicle demolished all previous records for sales and developed a new market after which competitors followed as best they could, some two to three years behind.

But successful use of marketing research is not limited to major companies such as Ford. Thousands of small firms and entrepreneurs have used marketing research successfully to carve out huge shares of their respective markets. An optical firm totally turned its company around and doubled sales within a year by identifying its customers. A mail order entrepreneur sold $10 million worth of a single product through marketing research techniques. A small computer firm successfully took on IBM for a segment of the total computer market and won through the correct application of marketing research.

In this chapter you will learn the same techniques used by these and other firms so successfully.

THREE IMPORTANT CATEGORIES OF MARKETING RESEARCH

Here are three categories of marketing research important to any small business: internal information, secondary research, and primary research. Let's look at each in turn.

Internal Information

Internal information is extremely useful because it is generally close at hand and costs you little or nothing to obtain. Therefore, before thinking about expensive field experiments or surveys, look at your own records and files. These include: sales records, receipts, complaints, all of the records noted in the record-keeping section of this book, and anything else which shows and tells about your customers and what they are interested in and what they buy. One source of information is your customers' addresses. This alone will tell a great deal about your customers, including where they live, their income, and their life styles. This information can be of great assistance to you in determining what your customers will be interested in buying.

Secondary Research

Secondary research concerns information already available outside your company. The key here is its availability. It has already been put together by someone else. This information may have been collected by other firms, by government agencies, and may be found in books, newspapers, and a host of other sources. But the important fact is that this information is already available. Someone else has done the work; that's why it's called "secondary" research. It costs you little or nothing to obtain. You don't have to design the survey method. You don't have to do the interviewing. And you don't have to spend time and resources collecting this information yourself. Where can you find this information? At the end of this chapter you will find over 100 sources of statistics, studies accomplished, and secondary research that you can analyze to obtain more facts regarding your customers.

Primary Research

Perhaps you have already looked at the cheaper and easier research methods—your internal records and secondary sources of information—and found that the specific information that you need simply isn't available. In this case, you must do the research yourself or hire someone else to do it for you. The means of getting this information, specifically tailored to your needs, is called primary research.

EXPLORATORY VERSUS SPECIFIC RESEARCH

There are two basic types of research that you should consider once the decision is made that primary research is necessary. One type is called *exploratory research* and the other is called *specific research*. Exploratory research is aimed at helping you to define the problem. It is typically done through in-depth interviews with a relatively small number of people. It tends to be open-ended. Questions are asked which invite detailed, lengthy answers from the respondents. These interviews tend to be nonstructured and freewheeling. One example of exploratory research was accomplished by a soup company sometime ago. A promotion for a new soup product had failed. The basic promotion had been a free pair of nylons if the customer would try the soup. The general question was: Why had the soup failed? In-depth interviews were conducted with a limited number of customers to discover the answer. From this limited research, the result was found that an image of "feet in soup" had resulted. This error in consumer behavior psychology had caused the promotion for the new product to fail.

Specific research is used when the basic problem has already been defined. It focuses on ways of solving the problem. Specific research typically uses much larger samples than exploratory research, and because of this it tends to be much more expensive. The interviews used with specific research are very structured, complete, and of formal design. Using the example of the soup, specific research would be conducted to find out what to do about the soup promotion, that is, what premium, if any, should be given to consumers for trying the new soup, and the respondent might be given a number of choices from which to select his or her preference.

THE MARKETING RESEARCH PROCESS

The marketing research process can be divided into certain steps. These steps are as follows:

1. Define the problem
2. Decide whether marketing research is needed
3. Identify objectives

4. State specific data to be obtained
5. Design the research instrument
6. Decide on the sample
7. Collect the data
8. Tabulate and analyze
9. Draw conclusions and decide on courses of action

Define the Problems

You cannot proceed until you have a good definition of what your problem is, whether it be a new product introduction, identification of customers for a certain market, or whatever. This first step of the research process seems obvious and for this reason many people tend to overlook it. Yet, experts tell us that it is the most important step. When defining the problem, look beyond symptoms. Symptoms may be declining sales, declining profits, and so on. But you must ask yourself: Why are sales declining? Why are profits down? List every possible reason. Could your customers be changing? Is there new competition? List all possibilities, but focus on those that can be measured. These are the ones that you can do your marketing research on. Problems that cannot be measured are not candidates for marketing research.

Decide Whether Marketing Research Is Needed

As noted in the last section, if you cannot measure the influence on the problem, you cannot do marketing research. But even if measurement is possible, before you decide to invest your time and treasure in marketing research, you should consider several factors: (1) Is internal or secondary research available? (2) What in general will it cost in money, resources, and time to do the research?

If the research has already been done and is available free, it makes little sense to do it over. If the research can be obtained, but at too high a cost, higher than the increase in sales or profits that may result, the research is clearly not worthwhile. The same thing is true if it will take so long to get the information that you will not be able to use it. Therefore, always recognize that doing marketing research may not be the answer to the problem that you have defined. However, if thinking through the situation shows that you can accomplish research which will be of assistance in solving the problem, then proceed to the next step.

Identify Objectives

You should understand everything you can about the problem and the information you are seeking before proceeding. This will enable you to specify clearly the objective or objectives of the study that you are undertaking. You may have a single objective or you may have several. But, either way, you must state it or them in the clearest possible terms. For example: "The objective of this study is to determine who is buying memberships in health clubs within 10 miles of my location."

State Specific Data to Be Obtained

Now, you must decide on exactly what information you want to obtain. If you want to know who is purchsing memberships in health clubs in a 10-mile area, you may wish to know them by (1) income, (2) education, (3) age, (4) sex, (5) occupation, (6) employment, (7) precise geographical location, (8) what type of media they read, see, or listen to, and so forth. All of this information should be specified in this section.

Design the Research Instrument to Be Used

Now, you must decide how you will do the research. First, you must decide whether you wish to do exploratory or specific research. Then, you must decide where and how the information is to be obtained. Your questionnaire must motivate the respondents to supply the information you want, sometimes concealing the reasons for obtaining it so as not to introduce extraneous factors into the results. It can have several different forms: it may be a set of questions designed to be asked over the telephone or in a personal interview, or a survey going through the mail. Each form has advantages and disadvantages, and which one to use depends on your situation. For example, a mail survey must be as short as possible, or people won't respond. The same is true for the telephone interview. But a personal, face-to-face interview can be as long as an hour or more. You must also consider the complexity of the questions you will ask. For most complex questions, a personal interview is necessary. If you are handling a touchy subject, the telephone interview may be extremely difficult because the respondent may hang up. Also, the personal interview may be risky because the individual making the interview may bias the reply. In a mail interview, since you are not there to obtain feedback, you must strongly motivate the individual to answer. A self-addressed, stamped envelope is almost a necessity, to enable the respondent to send the survey back to you easily. But you don't use a postage stamp. You would waste your money if the person did not answer. Instead, use a special reply permit indicia which you can obtain at your local post office. Even with this the respondents by mail will be far fewer than with other survey means. In some surveys the response has been as low as 2% or 3%. You must allow for this in the number of samples that you attempt to obtain. One survey gives a comparison in maximum response of the three methods as follows: mail, 15%; telephone survey, 70%; and personal interview, 80%. There are also tradeoffs regarding cost. Mail is probably the cheapest, followed by telephone. Personal interview is generally three times as costly as phone since an individual must go from place to place and must be compensated for his time. Use Figure 15.1 for a means of comparing the three methods in detail.

Once you've decided which type of questionnaire to construct, you must then begin to design it. Usually the questionnaire should be divided into several sections. The first section contains the basic classification data, including the name of the respondent, the address, and so forth. Frequently this information can be filled in by the interviewer prior to the interview.

The introductory statement is usually the second section. It establishes rapport with the interviewee. Although it may be structured into the questionnaire section itself, if this is a personal or phone interview it should be put in the interviewer's own words so as not to sound stilted. Establishing this early rapport will make the difference between success or failure of the interview.

The next section may describe the product or service if the research has to do with your wares directly. Be careful of overselling the product here so as not to bias the results. The description should be complete and it should be factual. Generally, initial impression questions should appear first. They should be non-

Survey Aspect	Mail	Telephone	Personal Interview
Questionnaire			
Length of interview	The shorter the better	Short (half-hour or less)	Longer (one hour or more; plus possible mail back)
Complexity of questions	May be moderately complex	Must be simple	Can be more complex; can use cards or props.
Flexibility (skipping)	Poor skipping dangerous	Excellent	Excellent
Probing	Poor	Better	Best
Getting at reasons (determining "why")	Poor	Better	Best
Handling touchy subject.	Relatively good	Risky: R may hang up	Risky: may bias replies
Control of question order	R may read ahead	Excellent	Excellent
Sample			
Sample bias	A real problem. R's usually higher in education and interest. Other biases uncertain.	Under-represents low income (no phone) and high income and others (not listed, especially in urban areas. But note random dialing)	Best. But occasionally a problem.
Sample of nonrespondents	Often necessary	Usually not necessary	Usually not necessary
List Availability	Must provide list of addresses.	Free, renewed annually	Area sampling a problem. Must get maps, population estimates by sub-areas.
Georgraphic clustering		Sometimes (but usually not dangerous number of clusters).	Often if reasonably large.
Stratifying information	May have	Usually not available.	May have income, race, etc., by area (from Census, etc.).
Interviewing			
Response rate	Low: 15% or so for a single mailing to general public, higher for special groups, especially professionals, and for several mailings.	Good: about 70%	Good: about 80%
Interviewing bias and cheating	None	Can occur. But supervisor can counteract to a considerable extent.	Can occur. Can telephone a sample of R's to check cheating.
Identity of R	Not certain	Known	Known
Administration and Cost			
Cost	Low, especially if response rate is high and telephone sample of nonresidents not necessary.	Low	High: three or more times cost of mail or telephone.
Administrative load	Light	Heavier: must hire, train and supervise telephoners.	Heaviest: must hire train, supervise, check and pay at a distance.

Figure 15.1.   Comparison of mail, telephone, and personal interview data collection.

Figure 15.2. Example of measuring attitude intensity using scales.

complicated and nonpersonal. If the questionnaire is exploratory in nature, the questions should be open-ended without leading to any specific answers. If specific, the questions should give the respondent a c'oice of alternative answers. You may use attitude scales to determine the intensity of the respondents' feelings as in Figure 15.2.

It is important with products to determine buying intentions, because sometimes individuals will like a product but will not want to purchase it. If you can determine the reasons for this attitude, you may be able to make the changes necessary to make the product or service successful. Product appeals are necessary to determine how to promote the product effectively. This information will help you to determine what is important to emphasize and what is important to deemphasize. Pricing is also a very important aspect, and here you should attempt to determine a selective demand curve for your product or your service. That is, by asking your potential customers about the likelihood of their purchase of the product at different prices, you can later tabulate the results and know at which price the product is demanded more than at any other. It may be difficult to get exact answers for this question, but it will certainly help to give you a general idea of the price range. You should also determine distribution channels by asking the consumer where he or she would expect to find the product. Determine the advertising medium in which he or she would expect to see, hear, or read about the product or service advertised.

Certain information of a personal nature such as age, education, income, and the like should be left to the end of the questionnaire. You should be careful never to ask for a person's specific age or income or other information of this type, but rather indicate a range. Finally, at the end of the interview, deliver a friendly thank you. Your subjects are deserving of this.

Be certain that the information that you want is contained in your questionnaire. As mentioned previously, in some cases it may be necessary to conceal what you are actually after in order to obtain unbiased responses. For example, if you are trying to determine which one of a number of products is favored by the consumer and your product is one of these, it may be important to conceal the fact that you are representing one of the products indicated in the survey.

Always consider:

Whether your respondent has the information that you're asking

Whether he or she has the necessary experience to provide you with an accurate answer

Whether it is likely that he or she will remember in order to provide you with an accurate answer

Whether he or she will have to work hard to get the information

Whether he or she is likely to give you the information

Whether he or she is likely to give you the *true* information

There are many different types of questions that you may use in your questionnaire. Some which you may find useful are:

1. *Open-ended.* This is where you ask the question and allow the respondent to talk at some length. The question is not structured and there is no one specific answer.

2. *Multiple choice.* Here you give a number of different choices to your respondent. Each choice may be a different product or a different description of some information that you are trying to obtain. Or, in the case of demographics, it may simply be a different age group.

3. *Forced choice.* Forced choice means that you give two choices, one or the other. Sometimes it is very difficult for a respondent to give a specific answer, but you may wish to have him or her choose one or two. An example is, "Do you primarily eat ice cream (1) at home, or (2) at an ice cream parlor?"

4. *Semantic differential.* A semantic differential allows for an intensity of feelings about some statement. For example, if we are talking about ice cream, you might ask a question such as this: "The XYZ brand of ice cream is. . . ." You would then have an adjective scale ranging from "delicious" to "terrible." In between these two extreme points would be other adjectives such as "fair," and there would be different points on the scale such as in Figure 15.2.

By analyzing a number of responses, you can come up with an average for each question.

Sequencing of your questions is extremely important. In general, your opening questions should motivate and not challenge your respondents psychologically. As pointed out earlier, identification items fit easily into this classification. Think of easing your respondent into the questionnaire.

Difficult questions should come in the body or at the end of the questionnaire. Why? First, your respondents are more at ease after they've answered some of the questions. Second, they are more accustomed to answering your questions and are less likely to hesitate in answering.

Another important point is that earlier questions will influence questions that follow. For example, the mention of a product in one question may influence the answer to a following question. Consider this question: "ABC Soap has recently changed its formulation to be even more cleansing. Have you used this new formulation?" Let's say your next question is: "What do you think of the new ABC Soap?" You can see how the first question will influence the next question.

A summary of these guides to questionnaire preparation is provided in Figure 15.3. Figure 14.1 is a consumer profile questionnaire which has a number of different questions which you may want to ask regarding demographics, psychographics, life style, social class, media use and interest, and other information. You can extract from this questionnaire when you design your own.

Very basic classification data can usually be filled in by the interviewer before the interview. Complicated or very personal classification data should go at the end of the questionnaire.

Name of respondent _____ Name of Interviewer _____
Address _____ Date _____
Phone _____ Time _____
Other (nonpersonal) relevant data _____

The introductory statement establishes rapport with the interviewee. It should not be read, but rather put in the interviewer's own words. This introduction will make the difference between success and failure for the interview.

Good morning, my name is _____, and I am conducting a marketing study for a new product (service) called _____ The answers you give to the following questions will help determine whether or not to introduce this new product (service) idea, and what features to incorporate into the product. May I have a few minutes of your time?

Product description tells the interviewee about the product or service. It should be a complete description of the product. Do not try to oversell the product; that may bias the results.

The name of this product is _____. It is a _____, and its functions/purposes are _____

The benefits of this product are _____

Initial impression questions should appear first. They should be noncomplicated, nonpersonal, closed-end questions. Attitude scales are used to determine the intensity of the respondents' feelings.

1. What is your immediate reaction to this idea?

Positive	*So-so*	*Negative*
Great ___		I do not particularly like it ___
Like it very much ___		I do not like it at all ___
Like it somewhat ___		

Open-end questions are useful for determining why the person feels the way he or she does.

Why do you say that? Explain.

_____
_____

Buying intentions are important to determine. A person may like the idea, but not want to buy it. If one can determine why they would not, perhaps the product can be revised to meet more with their demands.

2. Which of the following best expresses your feeling about buying this product if it were available to you?

Positive	*Negative*
I'm absolutely sure I would buy it ___	I probably would not buy it ___
I'm almost sure I would buy it ___	I am almost sure I would not buy it ___
I probably would buy it ___	I am absolutely sure I would not buy it ___

Why do you say that?

_____
_____

3. Tell me, all things considered, what is there about this product idea that appeals to you most. What do you consider its most important advantages?

Appeal to Most | Advantages

1. _____ 1. _____

2. _____ 2. _____

3. _____ 3. _____

Product appeals must be determine, so as to be able to effectively promote the product. Such information will indicate what to emphasize and what to de-emphasize.

4. How much do you think such a product would cost? _____

Pricing is an important aspect. Here one can determine a relative demand curve for the product. It is difficult for the consuner to answer this question precisely, but it should at least give the entrepreneur an idea of the price range.

5. Where would you expect to buy such a product? _____

The *retail outlet*, where the product would be most likely to be found, is important.

6. Where would you expect such a product to be advertised? _____

The *advertising medium* to use must also be determined. Sometimes consumers do not like a product for minor reasons, and when these reasons are elevated, they will buy it. The more difficult, tiring questions should be placed at the end of the interview.

7. Are there any suggestions you would care to make that you think might improve this product? _____

Classification data of a personal nature should be asked at the end of the interview. Never ask for a person's specific age or income, because they will become suspicious of you and may become mad.

Classification data:
1. In what category does your age fall:

below 15 ____
16–21 ____
22–29 ____
30–49 ____
50–60 ____
over 60 ____

2. Please tell me where your total family income falls:

below $5,000 ____
$5,000–9,999 ____
10,000–14,999 ____
15,000–19,999 ____
above 20,000 ____

3. Check one:
Female; single ____ married ____
Male; single ____ married ____

Thank you for your cooperation!

Always close with a friendly thank you. You may wish to interview them again.

Figure 15.3. Designing a questionnaire—summary of rules.

Deciding on the Sample

Deciding on the sample means defining whom you will survey as well as how many people. Whom you survey will depend on your objectives and on the method of selection of your sample subjects. For example, you may use either random sampling or nonrandom sampling. If you use random sampling, every individual from the population surveyed has an equal chance at being selected. If you use nonrandom sampling, you may include groups containing certain specific individuals you wish to be sampled or surveyed, or you may simply obtain respondence by means of availability.

The sample size decision depends upon how much confidence you have or wish to have in your results. For 100% confidence you would need to sample everyone. But, of course, this isn't always possible or desirable. If you can't sample randomly or sample everyone, you may try systematic sampling. That means you sample every nth element in the total population. Let's say that you are sampling customers. Perhaps you talk to every 25th or every 50th customer. Another way of handling this problem is to subdivide the total universe of people that you want sampled into a few groups that are mutually exclusive. You would then randomly sample these smaller groups. Or, you could divide the total number of people into many groups and randomly choose some of the groups for sampling. Determining how many responses you need in order to reflect the nature of the total universe of individuals you are sampling depends upon the standard deviation or dispersion of the responses the consumer may give. If you are going to use a random sampling, one way of determining sample size is with the following method.

Let us say you have a new product on the market and have introduced it into your area in which there are 2,000 stores that are selling the product. The reports on the new product won't be in for a month, but you want to know how well this product is doing immediately in order to make investment and inventory decisions. One way, of course, is to survey all 2,000 stores. However, this would be needlessly expensive and time consuming. Another is to survey a certain number of stores at random. This would give us an answer which would be useful for decisions that we have to make.

The first step is to look at a few samples of the stores and calculate an average. Let us say we looked at five stores and they sold the following numbers of our new product: Store No. 1, 10 units; Store No, 2, 18 units; Store No. 3, 30 units; Store No. 4, 42 units; Store No. 5, 50 units. Added together, 150 units were sold, divided by 5 equals an average of 30 units.

The second step is to decide how much accuracy we want. Let's say the accuracy that we're happy with is plus or minus 10%. This is an arbitrary figure. We could have decided on plus or minus 5% or plus or minus 15%.

The third step is to calculate an acceptable limit based on an accuracy that we calculated in the previous step. Plus or minus 10% times 30 units equals plus or minus 3 units. Therefore, acceptable units of accuracy in our case are plus or minus 3 units.

The fourth step is to estimate the standard deviation of our sample. Of any normal distribution, 68% of the units will fall within one standard deviation. We've looked at five stores. Therefore, 68% times 5 is 3.4. Since we can't use a partial store, we will say that 68% times 5 stores equals 3 stores. Now, let's look at Figure 15.4 with the stores noted on it. Figure 15.4 shows that on the left, Store No. 1 is 10 units. The next in the line is Store 2 with 18 units. Then comes Store No. 3 with 30, Store No. 4 with 42, and Store No. 5 with 50. The 3 units we're looking at would be stores in the center, Stores 2, 3, and 4; 18, 30, and 42 units, respectively.

Figure 15.4. Calculating the standard deviation.

We can see that the difference between 18 and 30 is 12, and the difference between 30 and 42 is 12 as well. Therefore, the standard deviation would be 12.

For the fifth step, we calculate the required sample size using the following formula, which will provide the answer at a 95% confidence level:

$$n = \left(\frac{S}{I/1.96} \right)^2 + 1$$

where: n = sample size
S = standard deviation of sample
I = acceptable limits

In our example,

$$n = \left(\frac{12}{3/1.96} \right)^2 + 1 = 64 \text{ stores}$$

What will we do if we wished accuracy of 15% instead of 10%? In that case, the acceptable limits would be 15% times 30 equals plus or minus 4.5 instead of plus or minus 3.

This approach is good only if our answer, 64 stores divided by the total number of stores, 2,000, is less than 5%. In our case, 64 divided by 2,000 equals 0.032, or 3.2%, which is less than 5%, so we're all right. But, let's say that instead of 2,000 stores, there were only 200 stores. What should we do then? In this case, we just adjust our answer. We do so using the following formula:

$$n^1 = \frac{n}{1 + \dfrac{n}{N}}$$

where n is our sample size, N is the total number of units surveyed, and n^1 is our adjusted sample size. In this case:

$$n^1 = \frac{n}{1 + \dfrac{n}{N}} = \frac{64}{1 + \dfrac{64}{200}} = 48.48 = \text{approx. } 48$$

If we had 200 stores selling the product instead of 2,000, we would sample 48 stores.

Collecting Data

Once the sample size has been decided upon, we can then begin to utilize the research tool that we have designed actually to collect data. Remember to be neat, courteous, and professional if you are doing this either in person or by telephone.

Tabulation and Analysis

In this step, the data that have been collected should be tabulated according to the specific questions that we have constructed to find information that we seek. This data can then be analyzed on a percentage basis to tell us the answers to our questions. For example, our demographic analysis may show us that the majority of our customers are ages 18 to 24, and that they are single. It may also show that most of our customers have graduated from high school and taken some college courses, and that they are mostly white-collar workers. This information can be extremely important. One local record shop had been carrying large stocks of classical records for years when most of its buyers were teenagers. A dress shop which was doing poorly was offering racks of expensive dresses which most of its customers could not afford.

Conclusions and Decisions on Courses of Action

At this point, conclusions should be drawn based on your analysis of the data as to your customers, the product, or whatever you were researching. You shouldn't stop with conclusions, but should make changes to increase your profits based on these conclusions.

Examples of Research You Can Do

The kind of marketing research you do is really limited only by your imagination. Some research can be done, even of the primary type, at very little cost except for your time. Here are some examples of simple research done by small businesses which greatly increased sales. These ideas were suggested by J. Ford Laumer, Jr., James R. Harris, and Hugh J. Guffey, Jr., all professors of marketing at Auburn University of Auburn, Alabama.

1. *License plate analysis.* In many states, license plates give you information about where car owners live. Therefore, simply by taking down the numbers of cars parked in your location and contacting the appropriate state agency, you can estimate the area from which you draw business. Knowing where your customers live can help you in your advertising or in targeting your approach to promotion. Through the same method you can find who your competitors' customers are.

2. *Telephone number analysis.* Telephone numbers can also tell you the areas in which people live. You can obtain customers' telephone numbers from sales slips or credit card slips or checks. Again, knowing where they live will give you excellent information about their life styles.

3. *Coded coupons.* The effectiveness of your advertising vehicle can easily be checked by coding coupons which can be used for discounts or inquiries about products. You can find out the areas that your customers come from, as well as which vehicle brought them your message.

4. *People watching.* Simply looking at your customers can tell you a great deal about them. How are they dressed? How old are they? Are they married or single? Do they have children or not? Many owners use this method intuitively to get a feel about their customers. However, a little sophistication with a tally sheet for a week can provide you much more accurate information simply, easily, and without cost. It may confirm what you've known all along, or it may change your picture of your typical customer completely.

CHECKLIST FOR APPRAISAL OF YOUR RESEARCH STUDY

Figure 15.5 is a complete checklist for appraisal of your research study. If you use it, your research should provide you with excellent results.

---

1. Review of research objectives
   a. In relation to the problem.
   b. In relation to previous research.
   c. In relation to developments subsequent to initiation of research.

2. Overall study design
   a. Are the hypotheses relevant? Consistent?
   b. Is the terminology relevant and unambiguous?
   c. Is the design a logical bridge from problem to solution?
   d. Are there any biases in the design that may have influenced the results?
   e. Was care taken to preserve anonymity, if needed?
   f. Were proper ethical considerations taken into account?
   g. Was the study well-administered?

3. Methods used
   a. Were the right sources used (populations sampled)?
   b. Do any of the data collection methods appear to be biased?
   c. What precautions were taken to avoid errors or mistakes in data collection?
   d. If sampling was used, how representative is the sample? With what margin of error?
   e. Were the data processed with due care? What precautions were taken to assure good coding?
   f. Are the categories used in tabulation meaningful?
   g. Were any pertinent tabulations or cross classifications overlooked? On the other hand, are the tabulations so detailed as to obscure some of the main points?
   h. Do the analytical (statistical) methods appear to be appropriate?
   i. Is the report well-executed in terms of organization, style, appearance, etc.?

4. Review of interpretations and recommendations
   a. Do they follow from the data? Are they well-supported?
   b. Are they comprehensive? Do they relate to the whole problem or only part of it?
   c. Are they consistent with the data? With existing information—other studies, executives' experiences, etc.?
   d. Were any relevant interpretations overlooked?

5. Responsibility for action and follow-up
   a. Will information receive due consideration from all those concerned?
   b. What are the implications of the results for action? Will all action possibilities be considered? (How do the results affect aspects of total operation outside the scope of the report?)
   c. Is an action program necessary? Will it be formulated?
   d. Is further information needed? If so, along what lines?
   e. Is responsibility for follow-up clearly assigned?
   f. Should a time be set for re-evaluation of the action program, e.g., to re-evaluate an innovation, or test a new package after introduction.

Figure 15.5. Checklist for appraisal of your research study.

SOURCES OF SECONDARY RESEARCH

Following are more than 100 sources based on bibliographies put together by Lloyd M. DeBoer, Dean of the School of Business Administration at George Mason University, Fairfax, Virginia, and the Office of Management and Training of the SBA and published by the Small Business Administration as a part of two booklets, *Marketing Research Procedure, SBB 9,* and *National Directories for Use in Marketing, SBB 13.*

Preliminary Sources

This section lists a wider range of reference sources to help locate pertinent materials for specific data. It is a good idea to consult one or more of them before investing substantial time or effort in any kind of market analysis.

> *Basic Library Reference Sources.* SBB-18. SBA. Free. Contains a section on marketing information and guides to research.
>
> *Bureau of the Census Catalog.* Bureau of the Census, U.S. Department of Commerce. Quarterly, cumulative to annual, with monthly supplements. GPO. Part I lists all publications issued by the Bureau of the Census. Part II lists available data files, special tabulations, and other unpublished materials. Both indexed.
>
> *Bureau of the Census Guide to Programs and Publications, Subjects and Areas, 1973.* Bureau of the Census, Department of Commerce. 1974. GPO. Stock Number 0324-00196. On charts, describes the statistical information available in Census Bureau publications since 1968; defines geographic areas covered; outlines programs and activities. Indexed.

Note: Census data is issued initially in separate, paperbound reports. Publication order forms are issued for reports as they become available and may be obtained from the Subscriber Service Section (Publications), Bureau of Census, Washington, D.C. 20233, or any U.S. Department of Commerce field office.

> *Directory of Federal Statistics for Local Areas: A Guide to Sources, 1976.* Bureau of Census, U.S. Department of Commerce. 1978. GPO. Stock No. 003-024-01553-6. $5.50. Spanning the period 1966–1976, gives detailed table-by-table descriptions of subjects for almost all types of areas smaller than States. Covers the whole range of local data—social, economic, technical—published by the U.S. Government. Bibliography with names and addresses of source agencies. Appendixes. Indexed.
>
> *Industrial Market Information Guide.* Regular monthly column appearing in every issue. $1.50 a copy. Crain Communications, Inc., 740 North Rush St., Chicago, Ill. 60611. Lists, in 32 market categories, over 600 items of market data annually. Most items available from business publications, Government agencies, and other publishers; some material for a limited period.
>
> *Measuring Markets: A Guide to the Use of Federal and State Statistical Data.* Bureau of Domestic and International Business Administration, Department of Commerce. Revised periodically. August 1974. GPO. $1.35. Stock No. 003-025-00031. This is an excellent reference which not only describes Federal and State Government publications useful for measuring markets but also demonstrates the use of Federal statistics in market measurement.
>
> *Statistical Abstract of the United States.* Bureau of Census, Department of Commerce. Annual. 1977. GPO. This is the most comprehensive and authoritative data book on the social, economic, and governmental characteristics of the United States. Special features include sections on recent national trends and an appendix on statistical methodology and reliability. Indexed. Appendix IV, *Guide to Sources of Statistics,* is arranged alphabetically by major subjects listing Government and private sources.

Statistics Sources: A Subject Guide to Data on Industrial, Business, Social, Educational, Financial, and Other Topics for the United States and Selected Foreign Countries. 5th ed., 1977. Gale Research Co., Book Tower, Detroit, Mich. 48226. Provides thousands of sources of statistics on about 12,000 subjects with 22,000 citations. $58.

Consumer Market Information

This section lists references which provide information on products and services bought by individuals or households for home or personal use.

General Data

County and City Data Book. Bureau of Census, Department of Commerce. 1977. GPO. A total of 195 statistical items tabulated for the U.S., its regions, and each county and State; 190 items for each city; and 161 items for 277 Standard Metropolitan Statistical Areas. Information is derived from latest available censuses of population, housing, governments, mineral industries, agriculture, manufactures, retail and wholesale trade, and selected services. Also includes data on health, vital statistics, public assistance programs, bank deposits, vote cast for President, and crime.

Statistics for States and Metropolitan Areas. (A preprint from *County and City Data Book, 1977*). Bureau of Census, Department of Commerce. $2.75. GPO. Presents data for 195 statistical items for the U.S., its regions, and each State, and 161 items for 277 Standard Metropolitan Statistical Areas.

Statistical Abstract of the United States. Bureau of Census, Department of Commerce, GPO. Includes many consumer market statistics such as income, employment, communications, retail and wholesale trade and services, housing, population characteristics by State and for large cities and standard metropolitan areas. The 1977 edition carries 131 new tables on such topics as gambling, daytime care for children, households with TV sets, Federal R&D obligations for energy development, franchised businesses, among others.

A Guide to Consumer Markets, 1977/78. Annual. 1977. $30.00. The Conference Board, Inc., Information Services, 845 Third Ave., New York, N.Y. 10022. Presents a detailed statistical profile of U.S. consumers and the consumer market. Contains data on population growth and mobility, employment, income, consumer spending patterns, production and sales, and prices.

E&P Market Guide. 1978. Published annually in Fall. $30. Editor & Publisher Company, 575 Lexington Ave., New York, N.Y. 10022. Tabulates current estimates of population, households, retail sales and for nine major sales classifications, income for States, counties, metropolitan areas, and 1,500 daily newspaper markets. Also lists specific information on major manufacturing, retailing, and business firms, transportation and utilities, local newspapers, climate, and employment, for newspaper markets. Includes State maps.

S&MM's Survey of Buying Power. Revised annually in July. $30. *Sales and Marketing Management*, 633 Third Ave., New York, N.Y. 10017. Information includes current estimates of population and households by income groups, total effective buying income, retail sales for major retail lines, and market quality indexes; given for all regions, States, counties, and metropolitan areas.

S&MM's Survey of Buying Power—Part II. Revised annually in October. $15. *Sales and Marketing Management*, 633 Third Ave., New York, N.Y. 10017. Gives population, income, retail sales, and buying income figures for television

and newspaper markets in the United States and Canada. The data for televi
sion markets outlines the areas of dominant influence, while the newspaper
markets information identifies both dominant and effective coverage areas.

Specific Data

Each of the reference sources listed above under *General Data* includes at least
some *specific* market data. In addition, there are sources of data useful only for
the appraisal and management of specific markets. Examples of some of these
important market types are listed below.

> *Automotive Marketing Guide.* 9th ed., 1976. $100. *Motor Age,* Chilton Way,
> Radnor, Pa. 19089. Number and relative importance (shown as percentage of
> U.S. total) of automotive wholesalers, franchised car dealers, repair shops, and
> service stations for counties, marketing areas, and States.

> *The New Yorker Guide to Selective Marketing.* 1974. $5. Market Research
> Department, 25 West 43d St., New York, N.Y. 10036. Identifies and ranks mar-
> kets for quality and premium-priced products and services available in the
> United States. Includes maps and statistics for 40 top-tier areas of best poten-
> tial to sell premium-priced products. Gives statistics on high-income families,
> high-priced car registrations, expensive homes and various retail sales indices
> for top 40 and next 20 U.S. markets.

> *Survey of Industrial Purchasing Power.* Revised annually in April. $12. *Sales
> and Marketing Management,* 633 Third Ave., New York, N.Y. 10017. A com-
> prehensive look at the nation's key industrial markets. Included are a sales
> road map for the industrial marketer, an evaluation of the top 50 manufactur-
> ing counties, and statistics showing manufacturing activity by State, county,
> and 4-digit SIC code.

> *Sales and Marketing Management Survey of Selling Costs.* Revised annually
> in February. $12. *Sales and Marketing Management,* 633 Third Ave., New
> York, N.Y. 10017. Contains data on costs of sales meetings and sales training,
> Metro sales costs for major U.S. markets, compensation, sales-support activi-
> ties and transportation. There is also some cost information in the interna-
> tional area.

Business Market Information

This section lists references for all types of markets other than the consumer (individuals or household for personal use) markets. Some of the sources described
in the *Consumer Market* sections of this *SBB* also provide data for *business* markets, such as commercial, farm, industrial, institutional, and Federal and State
governments.

General Data

> *County Business Patterns.* Department of Commerce. Annual. GPO. Sepa-
> rate book for each State, District of Columbia, and a U.S. Summary. Reports
> provide figures on first quarter employment, first quarter payroll, annual pay-
> roll, number of establishments and number of establishments by employment
> size class for some 700 different U.S. business and industries by each county in
> the United States.

County and City Data Book. Bureau of Census, Department of Commerce. 1977. GPO. Presents data on housing, population, income, local government financing, elections, agriculture, crime, etc., for States, cities, counties, and 277 Standard Metropolitan Statistical Areas.

Statistics for State and Metropolitan Areas. (A preprint from County and City Data Book, 1977). Bureau of Census, Department of Commerce. 1977. $2.75. GPO. Presents data for 195 statistical items for the U.S., its regions, and each State, and 161 items for 277 Standard Metropolitan Statistical Areas.

Statistical Abstract of the United States. Bureau of Census, Department of Commerce. Annual. GPO. Includes national and State data relating to business, industry, and institutional markets, as well as agriculture.

Specific Data

Automotive Marketing Guide. 9th ed., 1976. $100. *Motor Age,* Chilton Way, Radnor, Pa. 19089. Number and relative importance (shown as a percentage of U.S. total) of automotive wholesalers, franchised car dealers, repair shops, and service stations for counties, marketing areas, and States.

Mechandising: Statistical Issue and Marketing Report. Annual. 1978. $20. Billboard Publications, 1 Astor Plaza, New York, N.Y. 10036. Gives retail sales of major appliance types and number of appliance dealers by State and public utility service areas; also gives number of residential utility customers, and housing starts by State.

Maps

This section lists (1) maps that serve merely as a base for market analysis by providing geographic information, and (2) maps that themselves display marketing statistics. For ready reference, the maps are listed by publisher's name. Prices are shown when available.

American Map Company, Inc., 1926 Broadway, New York, N.Y. 10023. *Catalog of Cleartype and Colorprint Maps.* Free. The catalog describes the types of maps (including plastic-surfaced maps for crayon presentations and maps on steel to accommodate magnetic markers). Company publishes U.S. base maps for depicting sales, markets, territories, distribution, statistics, and traffic data; detailed State, county, zip codes and township maps; and several types of atlases for use in analyzing national markets.

Rand McNally & Company, P.O. Box 7600, Chicago, Ill. 60680. Publishes a variety of maps and atlases. This publisher leases at $110 a year, a *Commercial Atlas and Marketing Guide* which contains maps showing counties and cities, a road atlas, and statistical data on manufacturing, retail sales, and population. Standard metropolitan areas are shown. Includes a city index with information on transportation facilities, banks, and posted volume and an international section.

Sales Builders, 633 Third Ave., New York, N.Y. 10017. Publishes two sets of nine regional maps (11″ × 17″) which cover the 50 States and depict either retail sales or industrial sales information. Also publishes two 50-State Wall Maps (24½″ × 38″) which have county outlines and depict either the consumer or manufacturing data. For list of prices and order blank, write Sales Builders Division, *Sales and Marketing Management.*

U.S. Geological Survey, Department of the Interior, Washington, D.C. 20402. Publishes a variety of maps that show State and city areas. The following maps and a list (free) of other available maps may be ordered from the DISTRIBUTION SECTION, U.S. GEOLOGICAL SURVEY, 1200 South Eads St., Arlington, Va. 22202.

Map 2-A (54″ × 80″) $2. Shows State and county boundaries and names. State capitals, and county seats in black, water features in blue.

Map 2-B (42″ × 65″) $2. Same as above, without land tint background.

Map 3-A (42″ × 65″) $1.50. Shows State boundaries and names. State capitals and principal cities in black, water features in blue.

Map 5-A (24½″ × 38″) 75 cents. Shows State and county boundaries and names, water features in black.

Map 7-A (20″ × 30″) 50 cents. Shows State boundaries and principal cities in black, water features in blue.

Map 11-A (13½″ × 20″) 20 cents. Shows State boundaries and principal cities in black, water features in blue.

Map 16-A (9½″ × 13″) 10 cents. Shows State boundaries and principal cities in black, water features in blue.

Contour Map—Map 7-B (20″ × 30″) $1.25. State boundaries and principal cities in black, water features in blue, contours in brown.

Outline Map—Map 5-D (24½″ × 38″) 50 cents. State boundaries and names only.

Physical Divisions Map—Map 7-C (28″ × 32″) 50 cents. Physical divisions are outlined in red on the base map. Subdivisions and characteristics of each division are listed on the margin.

Locating Sources of National Lists

Other directories, new publications or revisions, may be located in one of the six following sources. Some of the selected directories, as well as the locating guides, are available for reference in public and university libraries.

1. *Mailing lists.* A major use of directories is in the compilation of mailing lists. Attention, therefore, is directed to another SBA Bibliography (SBB 29), "National Mailing-List Houses," which includes a selected compilation of both general line and limited line mailing-list houses that are national in scope. Also, consult Klein's *Directory of Mailing List Houses*—see listings under "Mailing-List Houses" for further description of these two publications.

2. *Trade associations and national organizations.* For those trades or industries where directories are not available, membership lists of trade associations, both national and local, are often useful. For names and addresses of trade associations, consult the following directory source—available at most business reference libraries: *Encyclopedia of Associations, Vol I., National Organizations of the United States,* Gale Research Co., Book Tower, Detroit, Mich. 48226. Published annually, 13th edition, 1979, $80. Lists trade, business, professional, labor, scientific, educational, fraternal, and social organizations of the United States, includes historical data.

3. *Business periodicals.* Many business publications, particularly industrial magazines, develop comprehensive specialized directories of manufacturers in their respective fields. Names and addresses of business periodicals are listed (indexed by name of magazine and by business fields covered) in the

Business Publication Rates and Data published monthly by Standard Rate and Data Service, 5201 Old Orchard Road, Skokie, Ill. 60077. Also, for listings of periodicals by subject index, consult the *Standard Periodical Directory* and for a listing by geographical areas, refer to *Ayer Directory of Publications.* Most libraries have one or more of these directories for reference.

4. *American directories.* Another source is *Guide to American Directories,* 10th edition, 1979, $45 a copy. Published by B. Klein Publications, P.O. Box 8503, Coral Springs, Fla. 33065.

5. *F & S Index of Corporations and Industries.* It is available in most libraries. Indexes over 750 financial, trade, and business publications by corporate name and by SIC code. Published by Predicasts, Inc., 200 University Circle Research Center, 11001 Cedar Ave., Cleveland, Ohio 44106.

6. *The Public Affairs Information Service.* Available in many libraries, is published weekly, compiled five times a year and put into an annual edition. This is a selective subject list of the latest books, Government publications, reports, and periodical articles, relating to economic conditions, public conditions, public administration and international relations. Published by Public Affairs Information Service, Inc., 11 West 40th St., New York, N.Y. 10018.

Directories

The selected national directories are listed under categories of specific business or general marketing areas in an alphabetical subject index.

When the type of directory is not easily found under the alphabetical listing of a general marketing category, such as "jewelry," look for a specific type of industry or outlet, for example, "department stores."

Apparel

Fur Source Directory, Classified, 1979-80. Annually in June. 1979. $5. Alphabetical directory of fur manufacturers in New York City area classified by type of fur; names, addresses, and telephone numbers for each. Also, lists pelt dealers, fur cleaners, fur designers, resident buyers and brokers and those engaged in fur repairing, processing, and remodeling. Fur Vogue Publishing Co., 127 West 30th St., New York, N.Y. 10001.

Hat Life Year Book (Men's). Annual. 1979. $4. Includes classified list of manufacturers and wholesalers of men's headwear. Hat Life Year Book, 551 Summit Ave., Jersey City, N.J. 07306.

Knit Goods Trade, Davison's. Annual. 88th Edition, July 1979. $35 postage prepaid. Lists manufacturers of knitted products, manufacturers' agents, New York salesrooms, knit goods wholesalers, chain store organizations, department stores with names of buyers, discount chains, brokers and dealers, and rack jobbers. Davison Publishing Co., P.O. Drawer 477, Ridgewood, N.J. 07451.

Men's & Boys' Wear Buyers, Nation-Wide Directory of (Exclusive of New York Metropolitan Area). Annually in November. 1980. $60. More than 20,000 buyers and merchandise managers for 5,000 top department, family clothing and men's and boys' wear specialty stores. Telephone number, buying office, and postal zip code given for each firm. Also available in individual State editions. The Salesman's Guide, Inc., 1140 Broadway, New York, N.Y. 10001. Also publishes *Metropolitan New York Directory of Men's and Boys' Wear Buyers.* Semiannually in May and November $15 for both. (Lists same information for the metropolitan New York area as the nationwide directory.)

Teens' & Boys' Outfitter Directory. Semiannually in April and October. (Pocket size.) $2 per issue. Lists manufacturers of all types of apparel for boys and students by category, including their New York City addresses and phone numbers; also lists resident buying firms for out-of-town stores, and all trade associations related to boys' wear. The Boys' Outfitter Co., Inc., 71 West 35th St., New York, N.Y. 10001.

Women's & Children's Wear & Accessories Buyers, Nationwide Directory of (Exclusive of New York Metropolitan Area). Annually in February. 1980. $60. Lists more than 25,000 buyers and divisional merchandise managers for about 5,000 leading department, family clothing and specialty stores. Telephone number and mail zip code given for each store. Also available in individual State editions. The Salesman's Guide, Inc., 1140 Broadway, New York, N.Y. 10001.

Appliances, Household

National Buyer's Guide 1980. Annual. $25. Lists manufacturers and distributors in home electronics, appliances, kitchens. Gives the products they handle, the territories they cover, and complete addresses for each distributor. Dealerscope, 115 Second Avenue Waltham, Ma. 02154.

Arts and Antiques

American Art and Antique Dealers, Mastai's Classified, Directory of. Lists 20,000 art museums, with names of directories and curators; art and antique dealers; art galleries; coin, armor, tapestry and china dealers in the United States and Canada. Mastai Publishing Co., 21 E 57th St., New York, N.Y. 10022.

Automatic Merchandising (Vending)

NAMA Directory of Members. Annually in July. 1979. $75 nonmembers. Organized by State and by city, lists vending service companies who are NAMA members. Gives mailing address, telephone number, and products vended. Also includes machine manufacturers and suppliers. National Automatic Merchandising Association, 7 South Dearborn St., Chicago, Ill. 60603.

Automotive

Automotive Affiliated Representatives, Membership Roster. Annual. 1979. Free to firms seeking representation. Alpha-geographical listing of about 400 member firms including name, address, telephone number, territories covered, and lines carried. Automotive Affiliated Representatives, 625 South Michigan Ave., Chicago, Ill. 60611.

Automotive Directory of Manufacturers and Their Sales Representatives, National. Annual. 1980. $15. Alphabetical arrangement of manufacturers serving automotive replacement market. Where available, includes names and addresses of each manufacturers' representative showing territory covered. W. R. C. Smith Publishing Co., 1760 Peachtree Rd. N.W., Atlanta, Ga. 30357.

Automotive Warehouse Distributors Association Membership Directory. Annually. $50. Includes listing of manufacturers, warehouse distributors, their products, personnel and territories. Automotive Warehouse Distributors Association, 1719 W. 91st Place, Kansas City, Mo. 64114.

Auto Trim Resource Directory. Nov. edition; annual issue of *Auto Trim News* (monthly; $7.50 a year; $1.00 a copy; Directory $5.) Alphabetical listing of name, address, and telephone number of auto trim resources and wholesalers who service auto trim shops. Has directory of product sources—listed by product supplied—with name and address of firm. Auto Trim News, 1623 Grand Ave., Baldwin, N.Y. 11510.

Credit and Sales Reference Directory. Three times annually. Available only to supplier-manufacturers on annual fee basis. Contains listings of 17,000 automotive distributors in the United States and Canada. Data include name and address of companies, and other pertinent information. Motor and Equipment Manufacturers Assn., MEMA Service Corp., 222 Cedar Lane, Teaneck, N.J. 07666.

Home Center, Hardware, Auto Supply Chains. Annually. 1979. $92. Lists headquarter addresses, telephone numbers, number and types of stores and locations, annual sales volume, names of executives and buyers. Chain Store Guide Publications, 425 Park Ave., New York, N.Y. 10022.

Jobber Topics Automotive Aftermarket Directory. Annual. Lists 7,000 automotive warehouse distributors automotive rebuilders, manufacturers agents, automotive jobbers, associations, and manufacturers. The Irving-Cloud Publishing Co., 7300 N. Cicero Ave., Lincolnwood, Chicago, Ill. 60646.

Aviation

World Aviation Directory. Published twice a year. Spring and Fall. 79–80 edition. $50 per copy in U.S. and Canada. Other countries $55. Gives administrative and operating personnel of airlines, aircraft, and engine manufacturers and component manufacturers and distributors, organizations, and schools. Indexed by companies, activities, products, and individuals. Ziff-Davis Aviation Division, 1156 15th St., N.W., Washington, D.C. 20005.

Bookstores

Book Trade Directory, American. Annual. Updated bimonthly. 1979. Lists retail and wholesale booksellers in the United States and Canada. Entries alphabetized by state (or province), and then by city and business name. Each listing gives address, telephone numbers, key personnel, types of books sold, subject specialties carried, sidelines and services offered and general characteristics. For wholesale entries give types of accounts, import-export information and territory limitations. Edited by the Jaques Cattell Press. R. R. Bowker Company, 1180 Avenue of the Americas, New York, N.Y. 10036.

Multiple Book Store Owners, Directory of. Annually. $25. Lists over 1,000 chains of book stores by state, city, and alphabetically by store within each city. Oldden Mercantile Corp., 560 Northern Blvd., Great Neck, N.Y. 11021.

Building Supplies

Building Supply News Buyers Guide. Annually. Classified directory of manufacturers of lumber, building materials, equipment, and supplies. Cahners Publishing Co., 5 S. Wabash Ave., Chicago, Ill. 60603.

Business Firms

Dun & Bradstreet Middle Market Directory. Annually in October. 1979. Lists about 31,000 businesses with net worth between $500,000 and $1,000,000. Arranged in three sections; alphabetically, geographically, and product classification. Gives business name, state of incorporation, address, telephone number, SIC numbers, function, sales volume, number of employees, and name of officers and directors. Marketing Services Division, Dun & Bradstreet, Inc., 99 Church St., New York, N.Y. 10007.

Dun & Bradstreet Million Dollar Directory.   Annually in January. 1979. Lists about 46,000 businesses with a net worth of $1 million or more. Arranged in four sections; alphabetically, geographically, line of business, and officers and directors with the same information as detailed in the preceding entry. Marketing Services Division, Dun & Bradstreet, Inc., 99 Church St., New York, N.Y. 10007.

Buying Offices

Buying Offices and Accounts, Directory of.   Annually in March. 1980. $30. Approximately 230 New York, Chicago, Los Angeles, Dallas and Miami Resident Buying Offices, Corporate Offices and Merchandise Brokers together with 11,-000 accounts listed under its own Buying Office complete with local address and alphabetically by address and buying office. The Salesman's Guide, Inc., 1140 Broadway, New York, N.Y. 10001.

China and Glassware

American Glass Review.   Glass Factory Directory Issue. Annually. Issued as part of subscription (13th issue) to *American Glass Review:* $15 a year. Lists companies manufacturing flat glass, tableware glass and fiber glass, giving corporate and plant addresses, executives, type of equipment used. Ebel-Doctorow Publications, Inc., 1115 Clifton Ave., Clifton, N.J. 07013.

China Glass & Tableware Red Book Directory Issue.   Annually. Issued as part of subscription (13th issue) to *China Glass & Tableware.* $12 a year. Lists about 1,000 manufacturers, importers, and national distributors of china, glass, and other table appointments, giving corporate addresses and executives. Ebel-Doctorow Publications, Inc., 1115 Clifton Ave., Clifton, N.J. 07013.

City Directories Catalog

Municipal Year Book.   Annual. $29.50. Contains a review of municipal events of the year, analyses of city operations, and a directory of city officials in all the States. International City Management Association, 1140 Connecticut Ave., N.W., Washington, D.C. 20036.

College Stores

College Stores, Directory of, 1980.   Published every two years. $35. Lists about 3,500 college stores, geographically with manager's name, kinds of goods sold, college name, number of students, whether men, women, or both, whether the store is college owned or privately owned. B. Klein Publications, P.O. Box 8503, Coral Springs, Fla. 33065.

Confectionery

Candy Buyers' Directory.   Annually in January. $25. Lists candy manufacturers; importers and United States representatives, and confectionery brokers.

The Manufacturing Confectionery Publishing Co., 175 Rock Rd., Glen Rock, N.J. 07452.

Construction Equipment

Construction Equipment Buyer's Guide, AED Edition. Annual. Summer, 1979. $20. Lists U.S. and Canadian construction equipment distributors and manufacturers; includes company names, names of key personnel, addresses, telephone numbers, branch locations, and lines handled or type of equipment produced. Associated Equipment Distributors, 615 West 22d St., Oak Brook, Ill. 60521.

Conventions and Trade Shows

Directory of Conventions. Annually in January. 1980. $60 a year, includes July supplement. Contains about 21,000 cross-indexed listings of annual events, gives dates, locations, names and addresses of executives in charge and type of group two years in advance. Successful Meetings Magazine, Directory Dept., 633 Third Ave., New York, N.Y. 10017.

Exhibits Schedule. Annually in January with supplement in July. 1980. $65 a year. Lists over 10,000 exhibits, trade shows, expositions, and fairs held throughout the world with dates given two years in advance. Listings run according to industrial classification covering all industries and professions; full information on dates, city, sponsoring organization, number of exhibits, attendance, gives title and address of executive in charge. Successful Meetings Magazine, Directory Dept., 633 Third Ave., New York, N.Y. 10017.

Dental Supply

Dental Supply Houses, Hayes Directory of. Annually in August. 1979–80 Edition. $33. Lists wholesalers of dental supplies and equipment with addresses, telephone numbers, financial standing and credit rating. Edward N. Hayes, Publisher, 4229 Birch St., Newport Beach, Calif. 92660.

Department Stores

Department Stores. Annually. 1979. $97. Lists headquarters address and branch locations, telephone numbers, number of stores, resident buying office, names of executives and buyers for independent and chain operators. Chain Store Guide Publications, 425 Park Ave., New York, N.Y. 10022.

Sheldon's Retail. Annual. 96th Edition, 1980. $60. Lists 1,700 large independent department stores, 446 large junior deartment store chains, 190 large independent and chain home-furnishing stores, 694 large independent women's specialty stores, and 270 large women's specialty store chains alphabetically by States and also major Canadian stores. Gives all department buyers with lines bought by each buyer, and addresses and telephone numbers of merchandise executives. Also gives all New York, Chicago, or Los Angeles buying offices, the number and locations of branch stores, and an index of all store/chain headquarters. Phelon, Sheldon & Marsar, Inc., 32 Union Sq., New York, N.Y. 10003.

Discount Stores

Discount Department Stores, Phelon's. 1980–81. $60. Gives buying headquarters for about 2,000 discount stores, chains, drug chains, catalog showrooms, major jobbers and wholesalers; lines of merchandise bought, buyers' names, leased departments, addresses of leasees, executives, number of stores and price range. Includes leased department operators with lines and buyers' names. Phelon, Sheldon & Marsar, Inc., 32 Union Sq., New York, N.Y. 10003.

Discount Department Stores. Annually. 1979. $102. Lists headquarters address, telephone number, location, square footage of each store, lines carried, leased operators, names of executives and buyers (includes Canada). Also special section on leased department operators. Chain Store Guide Publications, 425 Park Ave., New York, N.Y. 10022.

Drug Outlets—Retail and Wholesale

Drug Stores, Chain. Annually. 1979. $92. Lists headquarters address, telephone numbers, number and location of units, names of executives and buyers, wholesale drug distributors (includes Canada). Chain Store Guide Publications, 425 Park Ave., New York, N.Y. 10022.

Druggists—Wholesale. Annually in March. $14. Wholesale druggists in United States with full-line wholesalers specially indicated as taken from the *Hayes Druggist Directory.* Edward N. Hayes, Publisher, 4229 Birch St., Newport Beach, Calif. 92660.

Druggist Directory, Hayes. Annually in March. 1979. $80. Lists all the retail druggists in the United States, giving addresses, financial standing, and credit rating. Also publishes regional editions for one or more States. Computerized mailing labels available. Edward N. Hayes, Publisher, 4229 Birch St., Newport Beach, Calif. 92660.

Drug Topics Buyers' Guide. 1979. Gives information on wholesale drug companies, chain drug stores headquarters, department stores maintaining toilet goods or drug departments, manufacturers' sales agents, and discount houses operating toilet goods, cosmetic, proprietary medicine or prescription departments. Drug Topics, Medical Economics Company, Oradell, N.J. 07649.

National Wholesale Druggists' Association Membership and Executive Directory. Annually. Lists 800 American and foreign wholesalers and manufacturers of drugs and allied products. National Wholesale Druggists' Association, 670 White Plains Rd., Scarsadle, N.Y. 10583.

Electrical and Electronics

Electronic Industry Telephone Directory. Annual. 1980. $21.75, with order. Contains over 80,000 listings in White and Yellow Page sections. White pages: name, address, and telephone number of manufacturers, representatives, distributors, government agencies, contracting agencies, and others. Yellow Pages: alphabetic listings by 600 basic product headings and 3,000 sub-product headings. Harris Publishing Co., 2057-2 Aurora Rd., Twinsburg, Ohio 44087.

Electrical Wholesale Distributors, Directory of. 1978. $265. Detailed information on almost 5,000 listings, including name, address, telephone number, branch and affiliated houses, products handled, etc. Electrical Wholesaling,

McGraw-Hill Publications Co., Dept. ECCC Services, 1221 Avenue of the Americas, New York, N.Y. 10020.

Who's Who in Electronics, including Electronic Representatives Directory. Annual. 1980. $52 postpaid. Detailed information (name, address, telephone number, products handled, territories, etc.) on 7,500 electronic manufacturers, 500 suppliers, 3,500 independent sales representatives, and 2,500 industrial electronic distributors and branch outlets. Purchasing index with 1,600 product breakdowns for buyers and purchasing agents. Harris Publishing Co., 2057-2 Aurora Rd., Twinsburg, Ohio 44087.

Electrical Utilities

Electric Utilities, Electrical World Directory of. Annually in October. $125. Complete listings of electric utilities (investor-owned, municipal, and government agencies in U.S. and Canada) giving their addresses and personnel, and selected data on operations. McGraw-Hill Publications Co., Inc., Directory of Electric Utilities, 1221 Avenue of the Americas, New York, N.Y. 10020.

Embroidery

Embroidery Directory. Annually in October–November. 1979. $5. Alphabetical listing with addresses and telephone numbers of manufacturers, merchandisers, designers, cutters, bleacheries, yarn dealers, machine suppliers and other suppliers to the Schiffli lace and embroidery industry. Schiffli Lace and Embroidery Manufacturers Assn., Inc., 512 23d St., Union City, N.J. 07087.

Export and Import

American Register of Exporters and Importers. Annually. $50 prepaid. Includes over 30,000 importers and exporters and products handled. American Register of Exporters and Importers, Inc., 15 Park Row, New York, N.Y. 10038.

Canadian Trade Directory, Fraser's. June. 1979. Write directly for price. Contains more than 12,000 product classifications with over 400,000 listings from 38,000 Canadian companies. Also lists over 10,000 foreign companies who have Canadian representatives. Fraser's Trade Directories, 481 University Ave., Toronto M5W 1A4, Ontario, Canada.

Flooring

Flooring Directory. Annually in November. 1979. $5. Reference to sources of supply, giving their products and brand names, leading distributors, manufacturers' representatives, and associations. Flooring Directory, Harcourt Brace Jovanovich Publications, 1 East First St., Duluth, Minn. 55802.

Food Dealers—Retail and Wholesale

Co-ops, Voluntary Chains and Wholesale Grocers. Annually. 1979. $86. Lists headquarters address, telephone number, number of accounts served, all branch operations, executives, buyers, annual sales volume (includes Canada and special "rack merchandiser" section). Chain Store Guide Publications, 425 Park Ave., New York, N.Y. 10022.

Food Brokers Association, National Directory of Members. Annually in July. Free to business firms writing on their letterhead. Arranged by States and cities, lists member food brokers in the United States and Europe, giving names and addresses, products they handle, and services they perform. National Food Brokers Association, 1916 M St., N.W., Washington, D.C. 20036.

Food Service Distributors. Annually. 1979. $82. Lists headquarters address, telephone number, number of accounts served, branch operations, executives and buyers for distributors serving the restaurant and institutional market. Chain Store Guide Publications, 425 Park Ave., New York, N.Y. 10022.

Fresh Fruit and Vegetable Dealers, The Blue Book of Credit Book and Marketing Guide. Semiannually in April and October. (Kept up to date by Weekly Credit Sheets and Monthly Supplements.) $225 a year. Lists shippers, buyers, jobbers, brokers, wholesale and retail grocers, importers and exporters in the United States and Canada that handle fresh fruits and vegetables in carlot and trucklot quantities. Also lists truckers, truck brokers of exempt perishables with "customs and rules" covering both produce trading and truck transportation. Produce Reporter Co., 315 West Wesley St., Wheaton, Ill. 60187.

Frozen Food Fact Book and Directory. Annual. 1980. $50 to nonmembers, free to Association members. Lists packers, distributors, suppliers, refrigerated warehouses, wholesalers, and brokers; includes names and addresses of each firm and their key officials. Contains statistical marketing data. National Frozen Food Association, Inc., P.O. Box 398, 1 Chocolate Ave., Hershey, Pa. 17033.

Grocery Register, Thomas'. Annual. 1979. 3 vols. $60/set. $45. Vol. 1 & 3 or Vol. 2 & 3. Volume 1: Lists supermarket chains, wholesalers, brokers, frozen food brokers, exporters, warehouses. Volume 2: Contains information on products and services; manufacturers, sources of supplies, importers. Volume 3: A–Z index of 56,000 companies. Also, a brand name/trademark index. Thomas Publishing Co., One Penn Plaza, New York, N.Y. 10001.

Quick Frozen Foods Directory of Wholesale Distributors. Biennially. Lists distributors of frozen foods. Quick Frozen Foods, P.O. Box 6128, Duluth, Minn. 55806.

Supermarket, Grocery & Convenience Store Chains. Annually. 1979. $97. Lists headquarters address, telephone number, location and type of unit, annual sales volume, executives and buyers, cartographic display of 267 Standard Metropolitan Statistical Areas (includes Canada). Chain Store Guide Publications, 425 Park Ave., New York, N.Y. 10022.

Tea and Coffee Buyers' Guide, Ukers' International. Biennial. 1978–79. Includes revised and updated lists of participants in the tea and coffee and allied trades. The Tea and Coffee Trade Journal, 18–15 Francis Lewis Blvd., Whitestone, N.Y. 11357.

Gas Companies

Gas Companies, Brown's Directory of International. Annually in August. 1979. $95 plus $1.50 handling. Includes information on every known gas utility company and holding company worldwide. Brown's Directory, Harcourt Brace Jovanovich Publications, 1 East First St., Duluth, Minn. 55802.

LP/Gas. Annually in March. $5. Lists suppliers, supplies, and distributors. Harcourt Brace Jovanovich Publications, 1 East First St., Duluth, Minn. 55802.

Gift and Art

Gift and Decorative Accessory Buyers Directory. Annually in August. Included in subscription price of monthly magazine. *Gifts and Decorative Accessories,* $17 a year. Alphabetical listing of manufacturers, importers, jobbers, and representatives in the gift field. Listing of trade names, trademarks, brand names, and trade associations. Geyer-McAllister Publications, 51 Madison Ave., New York, N.Y. 10010.

Gift and Housewares Buyers, Nationwide Directory. Annually with semiannual supplement. $90. 1979–80. For 4,673 different types of retail firms lists store name, address, type of store, number of stores, names of president, merchandise managers, and buyers, etc., for giftwares and housewares. State editions also available. The Salesman's Guide, Inc., 1140 Broadway, New York, N.Y. 10001.

Gift & Tableware Reporter Directory Issue. Annual. August 1979. Alphabetical listing by category of each (manufacturer, representative, importer, distributor, or jobber). Includes identification of trade names and trademarks, and statistics for imports, manufacturing, and retail sales. Gift & Tableware Reporter, 1 Astor Place, New York, N.Y. 10036.

Gift Shop Directory. Biennially. Lists 900 gift shops in the U.S. Resourceful Research, Box 642, F.D.R. Station, New York, N.Y. 10022.

Hardware

Hardware Wholesalers Guide, National. Annual. 1980. $7.50. Alphabetical listing of manufacturers of hardware and building supplies. Where available, includes names and addresses of each manufacturer's representative showing territory covered. W.R.C. Smith Publishing Co., 1760 Peachtree Rd. N.W., Atlanta, Ga. 30357.

Hardware Wholesalers, Verified List of. 1979. Lists distributors (wholesale general hardware houses and hardware chain stores) serving the United States and Canada. Also lists manufacturers' agents handling hardware and allied lines. Chilton Co., Chilton Way, Radnor, Pa. 19089.

Home Furnishings

The Antiques Dealer. Annual Directory Issue. Issued in September as part of subscription. $12 a year. Lists major wholesale sources by geographical section. Includes special listing for show managers, auctioneers, appraisers, reproductions, supplies and services. Ebel-Doctorow Publications, Inc., 115 Clifton Ave., Clifton, N.J. 07013.

Home Lighting & Accessories Suppliers. Directory issues. Semiannual. Issued in March and October as part of subscription. $12 a year. Lists names and addresses of suppliers to the lamp and lighting industry. Ebel-Doctorow Publications, Inc., 1115 Clifton Ave., Clifton, N.J. 07013.

Interior Decorator's Handbook. Semiannually. To trade only, $12 a year (2 issues). Published expressly for decorators and designers, interior decorating staff of department and furniture stores. Lists firms handling items used in interior decoration. Columbia Communications, Inc., 370 Lexington Ave., New York, N.Y. 10017.

Hospitals

American Hospital Association Guide to the Health Care Field. 1979 edition. Annually in August. $43.75. Lists registered hospitals, with selected data as well as listings of nursing homes, health related organizations, and professional schools. Includes international, national, regional, and state organizations and agencies. American Hospital Association, 840 North Lake Shore Dr., Chicago, Ill. 60611.

Hotels and Motels

Hotel-Motel Guide and Travel Atlas, Leahy's. Annually. 1979. $20. Lists more than 47,000 hotels and motels in the United States, Canada, and Mexico; includes room rates, number of rooms, and plan of operation. Also has extensive maps. American Hotel Register Co., 2775 Shermer Road, Northbrook, Ill. 60062.

Hotel Red Book. Annually in May. 1979. $25. Lists hotels in the United States, Canada, Caribbean, Mexico, Central and South America. Includes a section covering Europe, Asia, and Africa. Gives detailed information for each hotel. American Hotel Association Directory Corporation, 888 Seventh Ave., New York, N.Y. 10019.

Hotels Systems, Directory of. Annually in July. 1979. $15. Lists approximately 300 hotel systems in the Western Hemisphere. American Hotel Association Directory Corporation, 888 Seventh Ave., New York, N.Y. 10019.

Housewares

Housewares Reps Registry. Annually in May. 1979. (Included with subscription to Housewares, $8 a year U.S.A.) Compilation of resources of the housewares trade, includes listing of their products, trade names, and a registry of manufacturers' representatives. Housewares Directory, Harcourt Brace Jovanovich Publications, 1 East First St., Duluth, Minn. 55802.

Jewelry

The Jewelers Board of Trade Confidential Reference Book. Semiannually in March and September. Supplied only to members subscribing to the agency service. Write directly for prices. Lists manufacturers, importers, distributors and retailers of jewelry; diamonds; precious, semiprecious, and imitation stones; watches; silverware; and kindred articles. Includes credit ratings. The Jewelers Board of Trade, 70 Catamore Blvd., East Providence, R.I. 02914.

Liquor

Wine and Spirits Wholesalers, Blue Book of. Annually in December. 1979. Lists names of member companies; includes parent house and branches, addresses, and names of managers. Also, has register of suppliers, and gives State liquor control administrators, national associations, and trade press directory. Wine and Spirits Wholesalers of America, Inc., 2033 M St., N.W., Suite 400, Washington, D.C. 20036.

Mailing List Houses

Mailing List Houses, Directory of. 1980. $35. Lists more than 3,000 list firms, brokers, compilers, and firms offering their own lists for rent; includes the specialties of each firm. Arranged geographically. B. Klein Publications, P.O. Box 8503, Coral Springs, Fla. 33065.

National Mailing-List Houses. (Small Business Bibliography 29). Free. Lists selected national mailing list houses; includes both general line and limited line houses. Small Business Administration, P.O. Box 15434, Ft. Worth, Tex. 76119.

Mail Order Businesses

Mail Order Business Directory. 1980. $45. Lists more than 6,300 names or mail order firms with buyers' names, and lines carried. Arranged geographically. B. Klein Publications, P.O. Box 8503, Coral Springs, Fla. 33065.

Manufacturers

MacRae's Blue Book. Annual. 1979. $69.25. In five volumes: Volume 1—Corporate Index lists company names and addresses alphabetically, with 60,000 branch and/or sales office telephone numbers. Volumes 2, 3, and 4—companies listed by 40,000 product classifications. Volume 5—company product catalogs. MacRae's Blue Book, 100 Shore Drive, Hinsdale, Ill. 60521.

Manufacturers, Thomas' Register of American. Annual. 1979. $85 post-paid. In 14 volumes, Volume 1–7—products and services; suppliers of each product category grouped by State and city. Vols. 9–14—manufacturers' catalogs. Thomas Publishing Co., One Penn Plaza, New York, N.Y. 10001.

Manufacturers' Sales Representatives

Manufacturers & Agents National Association Directory of Members. Annually in July. $35 per copy—includes 12 monthly issues of *Agency Sales.* Contains individual listings of manufacturers' agents throughout the United States, Canada and several foreign countries. Listings cross-referenced by alphabetical, geographical and product classification. Manufacturers' Agents National Association, P.O. Box 16878. Irvine, Calif. 92713.

Mass Merchandisers

Major Mass Market Merchandisers, Nationwide Directory of. (Exclusive of New York, Metropolitan Area). Annually. 1980. $55. Lists men's, women's, and children's wear buyers who buy for over 175,000 units—top discount, variety, supermarket and drug chains; factory outlet stores; leased department operators. The Salesman's Guide, Inc., 1140 Broadway, New York, N.Y. 10001.

Mass Retailing Merchandiser Buyers Directory. Annually. Lists 7,000 manufacturers, mass retail chains, manufacturers' representatives, jobbers and wholesalers serving the mass retailing field. Merchandiser Publishing Co., Inc. 222 West Adams, Chicago, Ill. 60606.

Metalworking

Metalworking Directory, Dun & Bradstreet. Annually in May. Published in one national and five sectional editions. 1979. Retail price available upon request. Lists about 44,000 metalworking and metal producing plants with 20 or more production employees. Arranged in four sections: geographically, line of business, alphabetically, and statistical courts summary. Marketing Services Division, Dun & Bradstreet, Inc., 99 Church St., New York, N.Y. 10007.

Military Market

Buyers' Guide. Annually. 1979. $2.50. Listings grouped by systems served of suppliers names and addresses, military representatives and civilian brokerage firms that specialize in serving military stores are given. Military Market, 475 School St., S.W., Washington, D.C. 20024.

Non-Food Products

Non-Food Buyers, National Directory Of. Annually. Alpha-geographical listing of 9,000 buyers of non-food merchandise for over 336,000 outlets. United Publishing Co., 1372 Peachtree St., N.E., Atlanta, Ga. 30309.

Paper Products

Sources of Supply Buyers' Guide. 1980. $40. Lists mills and converters of paper, film, foil and allied products, and paper merchants in the United States alphabetically with addresses, principal personnel, and products manufactured. Also lists trade associations, brand names, and manufacturers' representatives. Advertisers and Publishers Service, Inc., P.O. Drawer 795, 300 N. Prospect Ave., Park Ridge, Ill. 60068.

Physicians and Medical Supply Houses

Medical Directory, American. 27th Ed. 1979. Price U.S.A., possessions, Canada, and Mexico, $225 for 5 volumes. Volumes 1–4 gives complete information about all physicians in the United States and possessions—alphabetical and geographical listings. Volume 5—Directory of Women Physicians. American Medical Associations, 535 North Dearborn St., Chicago, Ill. 60610.

Physician and Hospital Supply Houses, Hayes' Directory of. Annually in August. 1979–80. $44. Listings of 1,850 U.S. wholesalers doing business in physician, hospital and surgical supplies and equipment; includes addresses, telephone numbers, financial standing, and credit ratings. Edward N. Hayes, Publisher, 4229 Birch St., Newport Beach, Calif. 92660.

Plumbing

Manufacturers' Representatives, Directory of. Annually as a special section of the February issue of *The Wholesaler* magazine, currently $20 a copy ... 1980 will be $25. Write directly for subscription price. Lists representatives of manufacturers selling plumbing, heating and cooling equipment, components, tools and related products, to this industry through wholesaler channels with detailed information on each. Scott Periodicals Corp., 135 Addison Avenue, Elmhurst, Ill. 60126.

Premium Sources

Premium and Incentive Buyers, Directory of.   Annual in September. 1980, $110. Lists over 16,000 executives for 12,000 firms with title, telephone number, address, and merchandise executive desires to buy in the premium, incentive and travel fields. The Salesman's Guide, 1140 Broadway, New York, N.Y. 10001.

Incentive Marketing/Incorporating Incentive Travel: Supply Sources Directory.   Annual in January. $2 a copy. Contains classified directory of suppliers, and list of manufacturers' representatives serving the premium field. Also, lists associations and clubs, and trade shows. Incentive Marketing, 633 Third Ave., New York, N.Y. 10017.

Purchasing, Government

U.S. Government Purchasing and Sales Directory.   Booklet by Small Business Administration. Sept. 1977. Designed to help small business receive an equitable share of Government contracts. Lists types of purchases for both military and civilian needs, catalogs procurement offices by State. Lists SBA regional and branch offices. Order from Superintendent of Documents, U.S. Government Printing Office, Washington, D.C. 20402.

Refrigeration and Air-Conditioning

Air Conditioning, Heating & Refrigeration News.   Dec. 31, 1979 issue. $10 a copy. Lists alphabetically and by products, the names of refrigeration, heating and air-conditioning manufacturers, trade names, wholesalers, and associations in the United States. Business News Publishing Co., P.O. Box 2600, Troy, Mich. 48084.

Air-Conditioning & Refrigeration Wholesalers Directory.   Annually. $5. Lists alphabetically 950 member air-conditioning and refrigeration wholesalers with their addresses, telephone numbers, and official representatives by region, state, and city. Air-conditioning and Refrigeration Wholesalers, 22371 Newman Ave., Dearborn, Mich. 48124.

Restaurants

Restaurant Operators.   (Chain). Annually, 1979. $94. Lists headquarters address, telephone number, number and location of units, trade names used, whether unit is company-operated or franchised, executives and buyers, annual sales volume for chains of restaurants, cafeterias, drive-ins, hotel and motel food operators, industrial caterers, etc. Chain Store Guide Publications, 425 Park Ave., New York, N.Y. 10022.

Roofing and Siding

RSI Trade Directory.   Annually in April. 1979. $5 a copy or with subscription ($9 a year in U.S.A.) to *Roof Siding and Insulation,* monthly. Has listing guide to products and equipment manufacturers, jobbers and distributors, and associations in the roofing, siding, and home improvement industries. RSI Directory, Harcourt Brace Jovanovich Publications, 1 East First St., Duluth, Minn. 55802.

Selling, Direct

Direct Selling Companies/1979–80, A Supplier's Guide to. $100 ($25 for members). Information supplied by member companies of the Direct Selling Association includes names of contact persons, company product line, method of distribution, etc. Direct Selling Association, 1730 M Street, N.W., Washington, D.C. 20036.

Direct Selling Directory.   Annually in February issue of *Specialty Salesman and Business Opportunities Magazine.* 1979. $1 a copy. Alphabetical listing of name and address under product and service classifications of specialty sales firms and their products. Specialty Salesmen, 307 North Michican Ave., Chicago, Ill. 60601.

Who's Who in Direct Selling.   Membership roster of the Direct Selling Association. No charge for single copies. Active members classified by type of product or service. Alphabetical listing gives name, address and telephone of firm, along with managing official. Direct Selling Association, 1730 M Street, N.W., Washington, D.C. 20036.

Shoes

Chain Shoe Stores Directory.   Lists chain shoe stores at their headquarters including officers, buyers, lines carried, trading names of stores, number of operating units. The Rumpf Publishing Co., Div. of Nickerson & Collins Co., 1800 Oakton St., Des Plaines, Ill. 60018.

Shopping Centers

Shopping Centers in the United States and Canada, Directory of.   Annual. Alphabetical listing of 16,000 American and Canadian shopping centers, location, owner/developer, manager, physical plant (number of stores, square feet), and leasing agent. National Research Bureau, Inc., 424 North Third St., Burlington, Iowa 52601.

Specialty Stores

Women's Specialty Stores, Phelon's.   7th Edition, 1980–81. $60. Lists over 18,-000 women's apparel and accessory shops with store headquarters name and address, number of shops operated, New York City buying headquarters or representatives, lines of merchandise bought and sold, name of principal and buyers, store size, and price range. Phelon, Sheldon, & Marsar, Inc. 32 Union Sq., New York, N.Y. 10003.

Sporting Goods

Sporting Goods Buyers, Nationwide Directory of.   1979–80. $75. Including semi-annual supplements. Lists over 4,500 top retail stores (23 different types) with names of buyers and executives, for all types of sporting goods, athletic apparel and athletic footwear, hunting and fishing, and outdoor equipment. The Salesman's Guide, Inc., 1140 Broadway, New York, N.Y. 10001.

The Sporting Goods Register.   (Including jobbers, manufacturers' representatives and importers). Annual. 1980. $20. Geographical listing of firms (name, address, buyers, types of goods sold, etc.) doing wholesale business in sporting goods merchandise and equipment. Similar data for Canadian firms. Alphabetical grouping of manufacturers' representatives and importers. The Sporting Goods Dealer, 1212 North Lindbergh Blvd., St. Louis, Mo. 63132.

The Sporting Goods Dealer's Directory. Annual. 1980. $5 a copy. Lists about 5,000 manufacturers and suppliers. Also includes names of manufacturers agents, wholesalers and sporting goods associations and governing bodies of sports. The Sporting Goods Dealer, 1212 North Lindbergh Blvd., St. Louis, Mo. 63132.

Trailer Parks

Campground Directory, Woodall's North American Canadian Edition. Annually. 1980. $8.95. Lists and star rates public and private campgrounds in North American continent alphabetically by town with location and description of facilities. Also lists more than 1,000 RV service locations. Regional editions available. Woodall Publishing Company, 500 Hyachinth Place, Highland Park, Ill. 60035.

Trucking

Trinc's Blue Book of the Trucking Industry and Trinc's Five Year Red Book. Retail price upon request. Together these two directories furnish comprehensive statistics on the trucking industry and individual truckers represented by about 3,500 Class I and Class II U.S. motor carriers of property. TRINC Transportation Consultants, P.O. Box 23091, Washington, D.C. 20024.

Variety Stores

General Merchandise, Variety and Junior Department Stores. Annually. 1979. $86. Lists headquarters address, telephone number, number of units and locations, executives and buyers (includes Canada). Chain Store Guide Publications, 425 Park Ave., New York, N.Y. 10022.

Warehouses

Distribution Services, Guide to. Annually in July. $15. Lists leading public warehouses in U.S. and Canada, as well as major truck lines, airlines, steamship lines, liquid and dry bulk terminals, material handling equipment suppliers, ports of the world and railroad piggyback services and routes. Distribution Magazine, Chilton Way, Radnor, Pa. 19089.

Public Refrigerated Warehouses, Directory of. Annually. Free to concerns in perishable food business. Geographical listing of over 750 public refrigerated warehouse members. International Associations of Refrigerated Warehouses, 7315 Wisconsin Ave., N.W., Washington, D.C. 20014.

Stationers

Wholesale Stationers' Association Membership Roster. Annually. $15. Alphabetical listing by company of over 300 wholesaler companies. Wholesale Stationers Assn., 3166 Des Plaines Ave., Des Plaines, Ill. 60018.

Textiles

Textile Blue Book, Davison's. Annual. 1979. $50 postpaid. Contains over 18,-000 separate company listings (name, address, etc.) for U.S. and Canada. Firms included are cotton, wool, synthetic mills, knitting mills, cordage, twine, and duck manufacturers, dry goods commission merchants, converters, yarn dealers, cordage manufacturers' agents, wool dealers and merchants, cotton merchants, exporter, brokers, and others. Davison Publishing Co., P.O. Drawer 477, Ridgewood, N.J. 07451.

Toys and Novelties

Toys, Hobbies & Crafts Directory. Annually in June. 1979. $5. Lists manufacturers, products, trade names, suppliers to manufacturers, supplier products, character licensors, manufacturers' representatives, toy trade associations, and trade show managements. Toys Directory, Harcourt Brace Jovanovich Publications, 1 East First St., Duluth, Minn. 55802.

Wholesalers and Manufacturers, Directory of. Contains information on wholesalers, manufacturers, manufacturers' representatives of toys, games, hobby, art, school, party, and office supply products. Toy Wholesalers' Association of America, 1514 Elmwood Ave., Evanston, Ill. 60201.

Other Important Directories

The following business directories are helpful to those persons doing marketing research. Most of these directories are available for reference at the larger libraries. For additional listings, consult the *Guide To American Directories* at local libraries.

AUBER Bibliography of 1977 Publications of University Bureaus of Business and Economic Research. Leyden, Dennis R. et al. eds. 1977. Vol. 22. $12.50. Lists studies published by Bureaus of Business and Economic Research affiliated with American colleges and universities. Done for the Association for University Bureaus of Business and Economic Research. Issued annually. Previous volumes available, Bureau of Business Research, College of Business and Economics, West Virginia University, Morgantown, W.Va. 26506.

Bradford's Directory of Marketing Research Agencies and Management Consultants in the United States and the World. 13th ed. 1978. $25.50. Gives names and addresses of over 350 marketing research agencies in the United States, Canada, and abroad. Lists service offered by agency, along with other pertinent data, such as date established, names of principal officers, and size of staff. Bradford's Directory Of Marketing Research Agencies, P.O. Box 276, Department B-15, Fairfax, VA 22030.

Consultants and Consulting Organizations Directory. 2nd ed. $45. Contains 5,041 entries. Guides reader to right organization for a given consulting assignment. Entries include names, addresses, phone numbers, and data on services performed. Gale Research Company, Book Tower, Detroit, Mich. 48226.

Research Centers Directory. Palmer, Archie M., editor. 1974. 4th ed. $47.50. Lists more than 5,500 nonprofit research organizations. Descriptive information provided for each center, including address, telephone number, name of director, data on staff, funds, publications, and a statement concerning its principal fields of research. Has special indexes. Gale Research Company, Book Tower, Detroit, Mich. 48226.

MacRae's Blue Book—Materials, Equipment, Supplies, Components. Annual. 1979. $55. In five volumes: Vol. 1 is an index by corporations; Vols. 2–4 are a classification by products showing under each classification manufacturers of that item; Vol. 5 contains company catalogs. MacRae's Blue Book Company, 100 Shore Drive, Hinsdale, Ill. 60521.

Thomas' Grocery Register. Annual. $30. Lists wholesale grocers; chain store organizations; voluntary buying groups; food brokers; exporters and importers of food products; frozen food brokers; distributors and related products distributed through grocery chains. Thomas Publishing Company, One Penn Plaza, New York, N.Y. 10001.

Thomas' Register of American Manufacturers. Annual. 1979. $85. In 14 volumes: Vols. 1–7 contain manufacturers arranged geographically under each product, and capitalization or size rating for each manufacturer, Vol. 7 also lists brands names and their owners; Vol. 8 lists company addresses, phone numbers, and local offices; Vols. 9–14 contain company catalogs. Thomas Publishing Company, One Penn Plaza, New York, N.Y. 10001.

Other Sources

U.S. Small Business Administration, Washington, D.C. 20416. SBA issues a wide range of management and technical publications designed to help owner-managers and prospective owners of small business. (For general information about SBA, its policies and assistance programs, ask for *SBA—What It Is,* free on request to nearest SBA office.) Listings of currently available publications (free and for-sale) may be requested from SBA, P.O. Box 15434, Ft. Worth, Tx. 76119, or any of SBA's field offices. Ask for: SBA 115A—*Free Management Assistance Publications* and *SBA 115B—For-Sale booklets.* The lists are free and may be used for ordering the particular series listed, either the free series from SBA, or the for-sale series from the Superintendent of Documents (GPO).

Small Business Bibliography (8- to 12-page pamphlet). Each title in this series deals with a specific kind of business or business function, giving reference sources. It consists of an introduction that gives a description of the operation, listing of references applicable to the subject covered. Free.

> *Statistics and Maps for National Market Analysis* (SBB 12)
> *National Directories For Use in Marketing* (SBB 13)
> *Basic Library Reference Sources* (SBB 18)
> *Advertising-Retail Store* (SBB 20)

Management Aids for Small Manufacturers (4- 8-page leaflet). Each title in this series discusses a specific management practice to help the owner-manager of small manufacturing firms with their management problems. Free.

> *Using Census Data In Small Plant Marketing* (MA 187)
> *Locating or Relocating Your Business* (MA 201)
> *Finding a New Product for Your Company* (MA 216)

Small Marketers Aids (4- to 8-page leaflet). Each title in this series gives guidance on a specific subject for owners of small retail, wholesale, and service business. Free.

Measuring The Results Of Advertising (SMA 121)
Factors in Considering A Shopping Center Location (SMA 143)
Using a Traffic Study To Select A Retail Site (SMA 152)
Using Census Data to Select a Store Site (SMA 154)
Advertising Guidelines for Small Retail Firms (SMA 160)

Small Business Management Series. Each booklet in this series discusses in depth the application of a specific management practice. The Series covers a wide range of small business subjects. Prices vary. GPO.

Office of Management and Budget, Executive Office Building, Washington, D.C. 20503.

Standard Industrial Classification Manual. 1972 (with a 1977 supplement). GPO. Gives the definitions of the classifications of industrial establishments by the type of activity in which each is engaged and the resulting Industrial Classification Code. Very useful in classifying data collected from industrial firms so its classification is comparable to data reported by Government sources.

Bureau of the Census, Commerce Department, Suitland, MD 20233. Request list of publications from the Census Bureau. Publication order forms are issued for reports as they become available.

Census Of Business For 1972: Retail-Area Statistics—U.S. Summary. GPO. Final figures from the 1972 Census of Retail Trade, includes statistical totals for each region, State, city and standard metropolitan area—tabulated by type of establishment.

County Business Patterns. GPO. A series of publications presenting first quarter employment and payroll statistics, by county and by industry. Separate reports issued for each of the 50 States, the District of Columbia, Puerto Rico and outlying areas of the United States.

County and City Data Book. VTGB. GPO. Contains data for 50 States, 3141 counties or county equivalents, 243 SMSAs, 840 cities of 25,000 inhabitants or more, among others.

Directory Of Federal Statistics For Local Areas, A Guide To Sources. 1966. GPO. Guide to local area socio-economic data contained in 182 publications of 33 Federal agencies.

Directory of Federal Statistics Of States, A Guide To Sources. 1967. GPO. Guide to State socio-economic data contained in more than 750 publications of Federal agencies.

Directory of Non-Federal Statistics For State And Local Areas. 1968. GPO. Guide to non-federal sources of current statistics on social, political, and economic subjects for 50 States, the District of Columbia, Guam, Puerto Rico, and the Virgin Islands.

Standard Metropolitan Statistical Areas. 1967. GPO. Gives the criteria followed in establishing standard metropolitan statistical areas. Changes after 1967 issued periodically as amendments. Eight issued to date.

Department of Commerce, Domestic and International Business Administration, Washington, D.C. 20230.

Measuring Markets: A Guide To The Use Of Federal and State Statistical Data. 1974. GPO. Presents features and measurements of markets, types of useful data published by Federal and State Governments, case examples of market measurement by use of government data, and bibliographies.

SOURCES OF ADDITIONAL INFORMATION

A Manager's Guide to Marketing Research, by Paul E. Green and Donald E. Frank, published by John Wiley and Sons, Inc., 605 Third Ave., New York, NY 10058.

Business Research: Concept and Practice, by Robert G. Murdick, published by Richard D. Irin, Inc., 1818 Ridge Rd., Homewood, IL 60430.

Do-It-Yourself Marketing Research, by George E. Breen, published by McGraw-Hill Book Co., 1221 Avenue of the Americas, New York, NY 10020.

Market and Sales Forecasting, by F. Keay, published by John Wiley and Sons, Inc., 605 Third Avenue, New York, NY 10058.

Marketing Research: A Management Overview, by Evelyn Konrad and Rod Erickson, published by AMACOM, a division of the American Management Associations, 135 West 50th St., New York, NY 10020.

Research for Marketing Decisions, by Paul E. Green and Donald S. Tull, published by Prentice-Hall, Inc., Englewood Cliffs, NJ 07632.

16

Personal Selling

THE IMPORTANCE OF PERSONAL SELLING

As a method of promotion, personal selling of your product should have major consideration. Unlike other methods of promotion, including advertising, publicity releases, contests, and sweepstakes, personal selling involves face-to-face communication, and that gives it a tremendous edge.

THE ADVANTAGES OF PERSONAL SELLING

There are six major advantages that personal selling has over other promotional methods. These are as follows:

1. *More flexibility.* Your salespeople can vary and tailor the sales presentations they make depending upon the customers' needs, behavior, motives, and special situations.

2. *Immediate feedback.* Salespeople can vary their presentation and approach depending upon the reaction as they proceed.

3. *Market pinpointing.* Much advertising is wasted because you pay for sending your message to individuals who may be readers or viewers of a vehicle but are not real prospects for your goods or service. With face-to-face, personal selling, greater pinpointing of the target consumer is possible than with any other means of promotion.

4. *On-the-spot sales.* Personal selling is the only method of promotion with which you can sell the product and receive money immediately.

5. *Not just sales.* Your salespeople can perform other necessary services while making sales calls. For instance, they can do customer research, relay customer complaints, develop credit information, and verify the reality of customer prospects.

6. *No time limit.* An advertisement gets read. It either does its work or is disregarded. But until they get thrown out, your salespeople can keep trying to make the sale.

THE SINGLE DISADVANTAGE OF PERSONAL SELLING

Face-to-face selling has one single disadvantage, and it is a big one. That is: its high cost. The cost of recruiting, motivating, training, and operating a sales force is not low. Finding the caliber of people necessary to do the job may be extremely expensive. As energy costs have skyrocketed, so has the cost of each individual sales call. In many parts of the country today, a single sales call costs $150 or even more.

Because of this major limitation, sales forces and face-to-face selling must be used wisely and efficiently. This chapter will show you how to accomplish this.

WHAT DIFFERENT SALES JOBS DO SALESPEOPLE DO?

Salespeople do a variety of different types of sales jobs. Some sales jobs simply require order taking rather than actually persuading an individual to buy something. Others require the sale of complicated, sophisticated, and expensive machinery. The different sales jobs are sometimes placed into seven groups.

Group 1: Product delivery persons. With this type of sales position, selling is actually secondary to delivering the product, be it milk, fuel oil, soft drinks, or whatever. This type of salesperson rarely originates sales. Therefore, a persuasive personality is not required, although an individual who performs good service and is reasonably pleasant may ultimately increase sales over a period of time.

Group 2: Inside order-takers. Inside order-takers are salespeople who generally work inside, behind retail counters. In this case, and in the majority of situations, the customer has already entered the store in order to buy. These salespeople primarily service the customer. Sales can be increased by the order-taker's helpful attitude, but usually not significantly so.

Group 3: Outside order-takers. Outside order-takers are salespeople who work in the field outside of the store. Their job generally involves calling on retail food establishments. They do little or no selling, but, like the salespeople in the first group, are primarily delivery people.

Group 4: Missionary salespeople. The primary job of missionary salespeople is to build good will while performing promotional activities or providing other services to a customer. Examples of these types of salespeople are those detail men and women who service physicians and the pharmaceutical industry. They may or may not be expected or even permitted to solicit orders.

Group 5: Technical salespeople. Technical salespeople such as sales engineers don't need persuasive powers so much as they need technical, in-depth knowledge of the product or service which they can display when dealing with the customer. No matter how persuasive, a technical salesperson cannot be successful without this technical background. Therefore, technical knowledge is the foremost trait required for salespeople in this group.

Group 6: Creative sellers of tangibles. These are salespeople that must sell tangible products through creative selling. That is, they must actually persuade people to purchase. Now, we are getting into a more difficult sales job since the customer may not be aware of a need for the product or how the product can satisfy his or her needs better than other products or services he or she is currently using. The creative seller may sell a product which is also technical; however, in this case persuasiveness and other sales traits are as important as or more important than the technical knowledge. Sellers of tangible products sell everything from encyclopedias to airplanes.

Group 7:   Creative sellers of intangibles.   This is probably the most difficult of sales positions. Not only must the salesperson be persuasive and be able to sell, but he or she must sell a product which is not easily demonstrated and cannot be shown to or touched by the customer. Products that fall into the intangibles category include such items as insurance, consulting services, and advertising.

Knowing what kind of salesperson you want is very important. If you get the wrong type for your sales job, you will either fail to get sales or waste money on qualifications you do not need.

THREE KEYS TO IMPROVING SALES BY DEVELOPING A SUPERIOR SALES FORCE

Your sales force can do a poor, mediocre, or terrific job in selling for you. It all depends on you and your ability to develop your sales force. Here are three keys to success:

   1. *Selection.*   You've got to find the best salespeople. It is a challenging problem, but if you succeed, it will make a major contribution to the overall sales ability of your organization.

   2. *Training.*   Once you have superior people, your superior people must be given the correct training to enable them to maximize their sales ability.

   3. *Compensation.*   Compensation plans depend on many factors. They are critical in sales because compensation is what motivates your salespeople and makes them perform. Performance cannot be measured simply in terms of sales volume. While the importance of sales volume cannot be overemphasized, other factors may be very important to your organization. These factors may include service, providing information to customers and creating good will.

Selecting Salespeople

To begin the selection process, you must identify what type of salesperson you need. Next, you must establish a job description and specification (see chapters 5 and 10). Armed with a job description and specification, you can search for sources of available salespeople and finally implement your selection system.

Sources of Salespeople.   While you can use sources described earlier in your recruiting and selection of a sales force, salespeople fall into a special category. For example, a research study in the insurance industry revealed that there were four primary sources for prospective insurance salespeople:

   1.   Salespeople personally known by the hiring sales manager

   2.   Individuals with influence

   3.   Individuals selected from the present sales force and given new geographical territories or sent to new locations

   4.   Salespeople recruited through direct mail advertising

Which of these groups do you think did best? Those recruited from the present sales force did five times as much business the first month as those recruited cold through direct mail advertising. Also of interest is the fact that it took six times as long to complete negotiations and start the new sales recruits doing business from groups 3 and 4 as it did to start those from groups 1 and 2.

Other sources of salespeople which you should consider in your sales force recruiting are as follows:

1. *Those working for you who are not currently in sales.* Be alert for the bright, persuasive individual with a "sales-type personality" who is interested in selling. Such an individual may be moved from another position in your company to become very effective for you in a sales position.

2. *Word of mouth from present customers.* Your current customers may assist you by recommending effective salespeople.

3. *Local schools and universities.* New graduates are always looking for opportunities, and sales is a great way to start. If you have such an opportunity, schools and colleges will assist you in finding candidates from among their students.

4. *Recommendations from your present sales force.* Your present sales force frequently comes in contact with other salespeople from other companies and in other industries. They may have some excellent recommendations for new recruits.

The Six Elements of a Sales Force Selection System. The six elements of your selection system are as follows:

1. Application forms
2. References
3. The interview
4. Intelligence and aptitude tests
5. Physical examination
6. Field observations of candidates

While application forms, references, and interviewing have all been discussed in an earlier chapter, it is important to realize that here the most important qualities in a candidate are his or her readiness and ability to sell. Therefore, you should not hesitate to emphasize this aspect, especially in checking on references and in the personal, face-to-face interview.

In fact, in order to make the personal interview more objective, some interviewers of potential salespeople use a form having a semantic differential intensity scale to note differences. In this manner, various attributes can be more or less objectively rated immediately through judgment. A typical judgment chart is shown in Figure 16.1.

As recommended in an earlier chapter, the prospective candidate should be interviewed by more than one individual in your firm so that opinions can be compared. This is especially true when seeking salespeople who must have considerable persuasive abilities, who must actually inform and persuade people regarding their needs and wants and the ability of the product or the service to fulfill them. First, you want some objective opinion about this ability. But second, if the candidate has it, you don't want to miss some key point because of his or her ability to persuade *you*.

Tests, physical examinations, and field observations have not been discussed previously for other types of jobs. They are particularly important, however, for

1. General appearance		6. Imagination	
poor 1 2 3 4 5 6 7 8 9 excellent		poor 1 2 3 4 5 6 7 8 9 excellent	
2. Dress		7. Attitude toward work	
poor 1 2 3 4 5 6 7 8 9 excellent		poor 1 2 3 4 5 6 7 8 9 excellent	
3. Verbal communication		8. Intelligence	
poor 1 2 3 4 5 6 7 8 9 excellent		poor 1 2 3 4 5 6 7 8 9 excellent	
4. Manners		9. Ability to sell himself or herself	
poor 1 2 3 4 5 6 7 8 9 excellent		poor 1 2 3 4 5 6 7 8 9 excellent	
5. Persuasiveness		10. Overall handling of interview	
poor 1 2 3 4 5 6 7 8 9 excellent		poor 1 2 3 4 5 6 7 8 9 excellent	

Figure 16.1. A semantic differential intensity scale for use in interviewing potential sales personnel.

sales positions. Because the sales job itself may require considerable field work, good health and personal appearance may have a direct bearing on success or failure. Therefore, if the job is at all demanding physically, a physical examination should be required prior to hiring. There are types of intelligence and aptitude tests for selling that were extremely popular in the late 1950s and early 1960s. They are currently controversial since they are far from perfect and many eliminate a few excellent candidates while allowing some poor candidates to get through. However, psychological testing will eliminate candidates who are totally unsuited for selling. Administering these tests has one additional advantage. It will impress the potential employee of the importance that you place on the sales position. This can have a motivational effect on the candidates you hire.

Remember, be very careful with psychological testing. Have a professional evaluate the results. You can find such psychological testers listed in your yellow pages of the telephone book under Aptitude and Employment Testing. Do not attempt to purchase the test and evaluate the results on your own. One firm that did this eventually discovered that candidates it hired who got top scores on a test were much poorer performers than those who scored less well.

For some very important positions, on-the-job observation may be necessary to determine whether the salesperson is suitable or not. This can be done through a conditional hire. An acceptable performance under personal observation is made one of the criteria for permanent hire.

Do's and Don't's of Salespeople Selection

Kenneth Grubb, president of Kenneth Grubb Associates of Princeton, New Jersey, developed the following list of do's and don't's for selection of salespeople.[1]

In thinking about tips on selecting salesmen, look first at the "Do's."

[1] Kenneth Grubb, *Tips on Selecting Salesman MA No. 196*, Small Business Administration (1976).

Do—Write a Job Description

The starting point in selecting salespeople is a job description. You should, if you haven't already done so, spell out the duties and responsibilities required for your selling job.

This description should define the type of selling that the job requires. Do you sell a product, a service, or a combination of the two? Selling a service, or a product and its related service, often requires your salesman to have a technical background or an aptitude for absorbing technical information.

As a counterpart to the job description, man specifications should also be prepared. Spell out in as much detail as you can the abilities and qualities which an applicant needs to be successful in selling your product or service. There is no substitute for knowing what you are looking for.

Do—Select for Initiative and Perseverance

Initiative and perseverance are vital to successful selling. Salespeople have to be self-starters because they are among the least supervisable of employees whether "on the road" or on the sales floor.

They either make themselves work, or they don't. At best, evaluation and incentive plans are a poor substitute for spontaneous self-drive, and self-policing. You or your sales manager, if you have one, cannot generate initiative in a dead battery.

How much of a self-starter you need depends on the job to be done. If your salespeople check into the office each morning, for example, they can be reminded, if necessary, to call on particular accounts. But if they are on the road all week, they have to remind themselves.

Do—Look for Reliability

An applicant salesman must be reliable because you will have to trust him to do his job. He also will have to gain the confidence of customers. The test of his reliability is their reactions to him. It boils down to his being a "straight shooter."

"Straight shooting" starts at home. In encouraging salesmen to do the right thing, three rules of thumb may be useful. First, the owner-manager should not fool himself about what his policies are. For example, if he has to withhold certain information for competitive reasons from his salesmen, he should not kid himself or them by pretending that they have all the information.

Second, the owner-manager should keep in mind that any failures in ethics which a salesman possesses will usually be turned first against his employer. If a company condones shady practices when they favor the company, the salesman is likely to use this attitude as license to put his own interests above those of the company.

Third, to many customers and to the public, almost the only "picture" they get of a company is the salesman whom they see. Moreover, they often see through a salesman more quickly than either the salesman or his company may believe. If he is not reliable, customers may realize it before the owner-manager does.

Do—Seek Mental Ability

The amount of brainpower which a salesman needs depends on the selling job. Some jobs require only enough mentality to memorize sales talks and put one foot in the door. Other jobs require a high degree of imagination, intelligence, and sometimes technical education.

In many small companies, the difference between a large and a small sales volume lies in the salesman's ability to understand quickly the key points in a customer's problem and to come up with an imaginative solution. Other small companies build a big sales volume on the salesman's ability to see new ways to redesign particular products. Such ingenuity enables the owner-manager to get a jump on his competitors. In selecting a salesman, make sure his mental ability matches the requirements of selling your product.

Do—Look for Willingness to Travel

If extensive travel is part of your selling job, make sure that the applicant is willing to travel. If he doesn't know it already, make him aware that the comforts and pleasures of normal home and social life are often impossible in a travelling job.

Your objective is to forestall trouble. If the wife wants her husband at home, or he wants to be with his family, all sorts of problems ensue.

On the other hand, some men like travel. They don't like the routine of calling on the same customers over short periods. They like to be away because it's so nice to come back. They like the attention they get from their families when they return from their trips.

When this is the case, you're lucky. This type of "travel-happy" salesman doesn't need the "diversions of the road" which can tarnish a company's reputation.

Do—Look for Willingness to Take Punishment

Many salesmen are paid to take punishment from which other employees would shrink. They receive rough and even rude treatment from the hard-to-see prospect, not to mention his secretary and other office help with instructions to keep salesmen away from his door.

Sometimes a salesmanager hands out, in a different way, as much punishment as the salesman receives from customers. At best, the push for large quotas turns into a battle of wits between the salesman and his boss.

In some companies, the punishment includes the risk of alcoholism. The owner-manager feels—not always correctly—that his salesmen must drink freely with all customers. When, and if, this is part of the selling job, applicants should be told.

Do—Select Emotionally Balanced Men

Selling is often a sort of schizophrenic job. The demands and pressures split some men in two.

Most salesmen have to appear cheerful and unworried during frequent discouragements. For example, they have to be polite to a rude prospect when they prefer not to be.

Even with the most pleasant customers, the salesman often has to repress his desires in their favor. He may have to lean over backwards to satisfy some customers. Often he has to listen when he prefers to talk. A liking for people helps to cushion the pressures. When a salesman likes people, it is easier for him to put his preferences in the background when he needs to.

The pressures on salesmen are bad enough when times are good. They can become terrific when there is a temporary drought in sales. The boss may blame him and push for sales—sometimes where none are to be had. To add insult to injury, sometimes the factory may let him down on delivery dates he has promised customers. In addition, some customers—often big volume accounts—may jump on the bandwagon. They seem to sense that the salesman is "down" and try to browbeat him.

Under such topsy-turvy pressures, only an emotionally balanced person can survive. If a salesman is inclined to be upset easily, he may start acting less than rationally. Or he may quit his job, and you lose your investment in him.

Whether the pressures are heavy or light, the effective salesman has to surmount them. Preoccupation with his own problems make him insensitive to the unspoken shifts in attitudes and interests of his customers. Also he needs to be emotionally mature to handle success—to resist the temptation to coast during good times.

In selecting salesmen, the "don't's" are as important as the "do's." A few of the negative aspects follows. They may remind you of others that are peculiar to your situation.

Don't—Pick Only for Selling Skills

Contrary to folklore, skills and experience in selling may be the last thing to look for in selecting a salesman. If you already have a successful sales organization, your best bet is probably to select people who can be trained in your methods. When the candidate's other qualifications (for example, he knows your industry and the needs of customers) are sound, he can usually be taught the necessary selling techniques fairly quickly.

On the other hand, when you hire an "experienced" salesman, you may be buying trouble. He may have to unlearn old ways before learning new ones. "Experience" includes bad practices, tricks, habits, and abuses which may handicap him in learning your ways of selling. For example, he may be in the habit of over-stocking customers.

In a fairly new company, the owner-manager may have to hire experienced salesmen because no one in his company really knows how to sell. If such is your case, make sure that you select salesmen whose skills and experience are sound for your type of selling job.

Don't—Pick for Control of Accounts

Some owner-managers are tempted to hire men from competitors on the theory that such salesmen bring business with them. If you are thinking in that direction, keep in mind that there is a strong tendency to exaggerate the extent to which salesmen can "take customers with them" and hold such business.

Don't—Pick for Trade Secrets

Some companies hire a competitor's salesman for the information they hope to gain rather than for the selling the man can do.

The owner-manager who hires with the expectation of gaining trade secrets or accounts should keep one fact in mind. That fact is: Benedict Arnolds are always available to the highest bidder. Money draws them from one company to another.

Don't—Pick Only for Wide Acquaintance

The owner-manager who hires a salesman because he is widely known among potential customers may be kidding himself. He may be the kind of salesman from whom customers run if they see him coming. His faults may outweigh the advantages of knowing the prospects you are trying to reach. Worthwhile prospects are ready to listen to salesmen who show promise of helping *them* to have fewer headaches and make more money.

Don't—Expect the Impossible

Some owner-managers expect their salesmen to do the impossible. They do little planning and preparation and expect the salesman to "steam roll" his way to a large sales volume. Even the best salesman is handicapped when the home office makes faulty marketing plans, such as insufficient advertising or a tight billing policy.

Often, when an owner-manager expects to get by with little or no planning, he picks men who have strong compulsions to get ahead fast. "We pay a high commission," he says, "and expect top results." The salesman drives himself, often sacrificing his personal life, to make such big money. Some individuals crack under such pressure. Addicted to big money, others change jobs for greener pastures.

In this same vein, an owner-manager should not expect his salesmen to do what he wouldn't do himself. For example, he would not himself be a doormat for customers to wipe their feet on. Nor would be deliberately lie to customers.

It is important also to caution your men about leading customers to expect the impossible. For example, a salesman should not sell more than you can ship. Nor should he "oversell" a customer on the benefits of your products.

Finally, in not expecting the impossible, if you hire a relative as a salesman, do it with your eyes open. It is one thing if he has proved his ability by selling for another company. It is another thing if his most prominent talent is kinship with you.

Intentionally Suggestive

These do's and don't's are suggestive. You may think of others that are pertinent to your situation.

Keep in mind the importance of doing your own thinking about the kind of salesmen you need. They develop procedures that will help in selecting individuals who meet the requirements of your situation.

In selecting salesmen, there is always the question: How do you tell whether the candidate is qualified? How does the owner-manager determine whether the candidate has: initiative, reliability, mental ability, and other requirements for the job?

You have to make a judgment based on what you can learn about the candidate. His application blank gives you some information. You get additional facts and impressions about his past performance by talking at length with him. Sometimes you may test him by asking critical questions about your industry and its customers. Or you might use tests which are prepared by firms that specialize in their preparation.

Above all, it is important to check his references before making a decision. Use the telephone or a face-to-face contact because a former employer may be too busy, or reluctant, to express himself freely in writing.

Training Salespeople

There are four main areas in which training will contribute to success of your sales force regardless of the type of selling in which they are engaged. These four main areas are as follows:

1. Knowledge
2. Work habits
3. Selling skills
4. Attitude

Knowledge.   A salesperson must have knowledge of the product, knowledge of the company, knowledge of the customer, knowledge of the sales environment, and knowledge of the entire environmental situation in which he or she is operating. Only with knowledge can the sales individual best explain the product or the service to the customer.

Work Habits.   The salesperson's work habits are responsible for great success stories as well as great failures. An individual's work habits can also spell the difference between sales success and failure in your company. With sales calls as expensive as they are, a salesperson who makes few calls a day can ruin you in short order. Making calls is a matter of mental attitude and selling work habits.

Selling Skills.   There are so-called "natural salespeople." But, while some individuals may be naturally better suited for selling than others, sales skills can be learned and mastered by many people. These skills include establishing rapport and empathy, making effective presentations, handling objections, closing, and so forth.

Attitude.   A critical factor in performance in selling is attitude. In fact, it is so important that many books by successful salespersons emphasize this one factor. Elmer G. Leterman, who sold over $300 million worth of life insurance policies more than 25 years ago, said in his book, *The New Art of Selling,*[2] that the first law of creative success is to quit looking outside ourselves for solutions to our problems. In other words, it is the salesperson's attitude that spells success or failure.

Methods of Training Salespeople.   There are several methods which you can use to train your salespeople to become sales "superstars."

   1. *Indoctrination training.*   With indoctrination training, you give your salespeople basic orientation on the sales job and how it is done. In many cases, your sales manager will accompany the new salesperson to help him learn the job through observation. As the salesperson gets more and more experience, he or she takes over more and more of the job, and finally the manager backs off entirely and the salesperson is on his or her own.

   2. *Job rotation training.*   Job rotation training is generally for larger companies. A salesperson spends a certain amount of time in a variety of jobs which may include positions in the factory, in production, in research and development, in the office, and in a sales branch. This way he or she gets a better idea of how the salesperson's job fits into other company operations.

   3. *In-class training.*   When field experience cannot be easily given, or sometimes even if it is, classes can be conducted to train salespeople how to do their job. This training is particularly effective for providing new information on products, the company, the market, and so forth. The classroom can also be used for motivation. Also, selling skills can be taught and experienced through various types of role-playing. However, in-class training is time consuming. In a very small company, extensive classroom training may take too many of your resources. Even so, one multimillion-dollar executive recruiting operation started with a solid week of training for everyone hired and maintains this policy to this day.

   4. *Sales meetings.*   Sales meetings act as a training ground for new employees who are salespeople as well as older ones. In sales meetings, they can trade

---

[2] Elmer G. Leterman, *The New Art of Selling,* Harper and Brothers, New York (1957).

experiences and build friendly competition. You can also give additional or new training to help salespeople increase their job effectiveness.

5. *Seminars.* Many training companies around the country have training programs especially designed to train new salespeople. There are many training organizations, both national and local, which can provide training needs for your salespeople. These companies can be located in your telephone book in the yellow pages under Training—Sales or Sales Training headings. An investment of this type can pay off tremendously in the effectiveness of your new sales employees.

Compensating the Salesperson

The compensation plan for salespeople is particularly important, and it has definite aims. These aims include encouraging the highest volume of sales for your most profitable items while at the same time providing motivation and incentive for your salespeople to work harder. Specifically, your compensation plan must have objectives both for your company and for your salespeople.
Objectives for your salespeople:

1. To receive compensation in direct proportion to sales accomplishments
2. To be compensated for time spent with the customer which does not directly result in sales, such as "missionary" work and service to the customer
3. To have provisions for security, retirement, and possible seasonal or other slumps in selling
4. To receive compensation on a par with what could be earned selling for other companies or for other lines of products or services
5. To have a sense of *esprit de corps*, not only in the sales force but with other employees

Objectives for your company:

1. To motivate and inspire your salespeople to increase sales
2. To encourage your salespeople to sell high-profit items
3. To enable your firm to maintain the maximum of profit consistent with other factors including compensation for your salespeople which meet all criteria listed as objectives
4. To maintain the maximum control possible over your sales force and your salespeople's activities
5. To encourage cooperation among your salespeople and with other functional areas and people in your company
6. To encourage company *esprit de corps*

The Three Basic Means of Compensating a Sales Force. There are three basic means of compensating a sales force. These are: (1) salary, (2) commission, and (3) combination plans. Each has its advantages and its disadvantages.

With a *salary* plan, you have an arrangement whereby you pay a defined amount of money, weekly, monthly, or annually, in return for whatever work is required by the sales force. Such a plan is as discussed in Chapter 10 "Personnel Management." It has the following advantages:

1. It is easy for the company to budget and administer.
2. Since the compensation is guaranteed so long as the salesperson works for you, it allows for the greatest amount of control over your sales force.
3. It is generally easier to recruit salespeople for this type of compensation plan.
4. Since compensation is guaranteed, extravagant promises or overselling by your salespeople will be discouraged.
5. It is easier to arrange for your salespeople to accomplish nonselling activities since their "time is not money."
6. The system encourages the maximum cooperation among salespeople and other members of your company.
7. It is easier to transfer salespeople to other territories using this plan.

However, this compensation plan also has disadvantages:

1. There is a lack of incentive for high sales.
2. Salary is a fixed cost unrelated to sales revenue.
3. So-called "super" salespeople are rarely attracted by a straight salary since they can make much more money on a commission system.
4. If business activity is declining, it is very difficult to adjust salaries. You generally are forced to discharge some of your salespeople. This means morale problems and additional costs for training and hiring when business conditions improve.
5. Salaries must be paid whether or not there are sales.

Straight salary plans are usually most useful under any of four conditions:

1. For compensating new salespeople who are not yet ready to assume their full responsibilities
2. For compensating missionary salespeople whose duties are not to make an immediate sale, but whose work eventually leads to sales over a period of months or even years
3. For opening new territories in which you have not formerly been selling
4. For sales of sophisticated or technical products requiring lengthy negotiations

A compensation plan using sales *commissions* is simply an agreement on your part to pay the salesperson a percentage of each dollar of a product or service sold. In such a plan, the salesperson is usually entirely on his or her own. A successful salesperson can make a lot of money. An unsuccessful salesperson makes nothing. In some states the straight commission plan has been modified since minimum wages must be paid. However, the basic principle is the same. The amount earned is directly related to sales made.
Advantages of the commission plan are as follows:

1. A company with limited capital can fully staff its sales force without high overhead commitments.
2. This method provides direct incentive for high sales.
3. A commission plan attracts more aggressive and persuasive salespeople since these are the only ones that can make it work successfully.
4. The costs of sales are automatically reduced if and when sales decline.

Naturally, the commission plan has its disadvantages, although at first it may appear that the system is absolutely ideal for any company. The disadvantages of the commission system of compensation are as follows:

1. There is a great deal of difficulty getting salespeople to devote time to sales tasks which may be important to your company but for which no commission is paid.

2. There is great danger in overselling the customer and possibly incurring customer ill will.

3. There is a great deal of bookkeeping involved.

4. There is potentially greater difficulty in recruiting.

5. There is less cooperation within the company among salespeople and among other functional areas.

Because of the potential difficulties with straight commission plans, modifications have been made. Here are the primary changes that have been introduced.

With the *commission against draw* modification of the straight commission, a salesperson is allowed to draw a certain amount of money ahead of his or her sales against commissions that will be earned later. This sales advance or draw allows the salesperson to have living expenses even during a slump. As soon as the first commissions are earned, they are used to pay the draw that the salesperson has already been advanced.

With the *modified commission scale,* a commission rate is established by a series of steps. It is frequently used with the draw in order to help the salesperson pay off the money advanced as rapidly as possible. In order to do this, a higher commission may be paid on the first sales until the money advanced is covered; then the commission rate may drop to lower levels or steps depending upon the scale that is constructed. Of course, this is also advantageous to the company if sales are greater than anticipated since the commission will be less on the higher amount of sales. The approach, however, does have a disadvantage; some companies take the opposite tactic and increase commission percentage for higher amounts of sales. In some cases this increase is effected through a bonus plan, a bonus being paid for effort resulting in increased sales or sales above a certain set goal or quota. Let us say that you are paying 10% commission and have established the quota for salespeople of $20,000 in sales per month. The bonus would come into play if this $20,000 per month were exceeded. Perhaps you would offer an additional 5% bonus for sales exceeding the quota. Thus, if a salesperson only met this quota, he or she would receive $20,000 times 10% or $2,000 commission. But for sales of $30,000 a month, your salesperson would receive $30,000 times 10% or $3,000, plus an additional 5% of the $10,000 difference between $20,000 and $30,000, or an additional $500. Therefore, the total amount of compensation would be $3,000 plus $500 or $3,500.

Commission plans work well under the following circumstances:

1. Where considerable incentive and motivation are needed to get high sales

2. Where very little missionary work or other sales assistance that does not have to do with closing out a sale is required

3. Where the company is not so strong financially that is can afford large amounts of overhead to compensate salespeople whether or not sales are made

4. Where salespeople can operate independently

Combination plans offer a fixed compensation element plus a variable element made up of a commission on sales or a bonus based on volume. In combination plans, the fixed portion is a salary. The variable portion is used to motivate sales and to achieve many of the benefits of the commission type of compensation plan. The variable element of the combination plan may include payments on sales volume, payments on a performance evaluation, a combination of volume and a performance evaluation, or some type of bonus.

The advantages of combination plans are:

1. Flexibility in dealing with the overall job of selling the company's product or service
2. Flexibility in making changes in territory assignment or assignment of customers
3. Choice among the various factors that will motivate the salespeople to work independently to achieve high sales
4. Ability to group salespeople for team selling situations of major products while applying direct incentive as well as salary compensation to motivate this performance

The disadvantages of combination plans are:

1. Complexity in construction of the plan
2. Amount of time required for administration and bookkeeping
3. Difficulty of explaining the plan to salespeople
4. The need for constant review to be sure that the factors that are being used as part of the overall compensation are doing what they are supposed to be doing

The combination plan can work well for many companies, but in order to use it you must balance the best features of the salary plan and the commission plan while at the same time trying to eliminate their disadvantages. This isn't always easy and requires considerable thinking and planning ahead of time. It should be used when (1) a complex selling task is to be rewarded, and (2) factors other than volume are considered important and yet an incentive element is definitely required.

HOW TO MEASURE THE PERFORMANCE OF YOUR SALES PERSONNEL

Until you know how your sales force is performing, you have no way of making meaningful changes which will improve performance. Therefore, it is necessary to develop means of evaluation. In general, this is done through two means: judging quantitative factors and judging qualitative factors. Quantitative factors generally are easier since they are specific and objective. Sales volume either goes up or it does not. You see the results in black and white. Qualitative factors must rely much on subjective judgment. However, in many types of sales operations, qualitative factors must be considered because of the importance of their influence on company objectives.

Quantitative Factors

The following are factors in sales that are useful in comparing quantitative performance:

1. Sales volume segmented as to areas, products, customer groups, and so forth
2. Sales volume as a percentage of a predetermined quota or calculated territorial potential
3. Gross profit
4. Sales that may be segmented by number of orders, average size, or similar factors
5. Closing ratio (a ratio of the number of sales closes divided by the number of calls made)
6. Percentage of new accounts sold
7. Number of new accounts sold
8. Number of new accounts sold divided by number of new accounts called on

Qualitative Factors

The following are factors which should be considered in evaluating your sales force on a qualitative basis:

1. Analytical ability
2. Company knowledge
3. Competition knowledge
4. Customer relations
5. Decision-making ability
6. General attitude
7. General knowledge of sales environment, the customer, legal aspects, and the product
8. Health
9. Organization and management of time
10. Personal appearance
11. Personality
12. Preparation for presentations and sales calls
13. Product knowledge

IMPROVING A SALES REPRESENTATIVE'S PERFORMANCE

Raymond O. Loen of R. O. Loen Company, Management Consultants of Lake Oswego, Oregon, developed the following guide to bringing about improvements in sales performance in three steps.[3] These three steps are planning, measuring, and correcting. Use this to help you improve your salesperson's performance.

[3] Raymond O. Loen, *Measuring Sales Performance MA 190*, Small Business Administration (1978).

Planning

Get the sales representative's agreement about goals to attain or exceed for the next year:

1. Total profit contribution in dollars.
2. Profit contribution in dollars for:
   Each major profit line.
   Each major market (by industry or geographical area).
   Each of 10–20 target accounts (for significant new and additional business).

Get the sales representative's agreement about expenses to stay within for the next year:

1. Total sales expense budget in dollars.
2. Budget in dollars for: travel, customer entertainment, telephone, and other expenses.

Measuring

Review at least monthly the sales representative's record for:

1. Year-to-date progress toward 12-month profit contribution goals.
2. Year-to-date budget compliance.

Correcting

Meet with sales representatives if his or her record is 10 percent or more off target. Review the number of calls made on each significant account plus what he or she feels are his or her problems and accomplishments. In addition, you may need to do some of the following to help improve performance:

—Give more day-to-day help and direction.
—Accompany on calls to provide coaching.
—Conduct regular meetings on subjects which representatives want covered.
—Increase sales promotion activities.
—Transfer accounts to other sales representatives if there is insufficient effort or progress.
—Establish tighter control over price variances allowed.
—Increase or reduce selling prices.
—Add new products or services.
—Increase financial incentives.
—Transfer, replace, or discharge.

WHETHER TO USE SALES TERRITORIES

A sales territory is a geographical area in which a salesperson does his or her business. His or her activities may be limited in certain areas or may not be. Further, he or she may or may not have an exclusive over a certain area. Establishing sales territories has the following advantages:

1. It fixes precise performance responsibilities.
2. It helps a salesperson to organize his time.
3. It helps maximize customer service.
4. It cuts down on overlapping of sales efforts.
5. It fosters competition and comparison among salespeople in different territories.
6. It helps equalize opportunities in various territories among different salespeople.
7. It makes for adaptation of certain background personality factors and desires of salespeople to their customers.
8. It helps control the overall sales operation.
9. It ensures that all of your salespeople have ample opportunities to sell.
10. It helps maintain total and efficient coverage of your entire market.

However, in certain circumstances, it is better not to limit your salespeople to distinct territories. This may be true if you don't have sufficient salespeople to cover all the territories that might be available, or if certain of your salespeople seem to operate better when they are freewheeling, and maybe you can get best results out of all of them if you do not establish territorial rights. Sometimes you will not be able to establish territory divisions fairly. In this case it is better not to establish them at all. And in some industries, such as executive recruiting, for example, it may make sense not to establish territories in a geographical sense but rather to group your salespeople depending upon the functions of the various individuals whom they are trying to recruit. Finally, if you are introducing a new product and you want to saturate the market as quickly as possible, the restrictions of sales territories may slow some of your people down.

HOW TO ESTABLISH SALES TERRITORIES

1. If you're going to establish sales territories, it is important first to establish them in a fair fashion. Therefore, there must be some basis of comparison. Usually, a market index or indices relating to the product or the service that you are selling are selected. These indices are usually based on one or more demographic factors, such as income, which would represent buying power or segments of the population which would be interested in the product or the service. For example, if you were selling a high-priced automobile, how many families in the area or the potential area which would constitute a geographical territory could afford such a car? Or, if you had a product that went in the home, how many homes are in the territory which uses such a product? Sometimes a combination of different factors is used with a weighting system applied depending upon the relative importance of the factor. In this fashion, territories are divided with indices resulting in approximately the same sales potential.

2. The next problem is to determine how wide an area a salesperson can handle. Factors such as distance, call frequency, as well as numbers that a salesperson can process must all be considered. This will impact on the size of the dif-

ferent territories that are divided, and will also let you know how many salespeople you will need to cover a particular area.

3. At this point you may begin allotting the various territories based on market potential to salesmen. Various adjustments may be necessary depending upon local conditions, demand, competition, transportation factors, the product, and other of the strategic and environmental variables that we discussed in Chapter 4. For example, if a newer product is being sold, the territory may be expanded to give the salesperson having to sell this new product greater opportunity to sell a profitable volume. Each factor for adjustment should be considered on an individual basis so that the net result is territories which have essentially identical market potential and number of accounts that can be serviced by the salesperson. Territory allotment should be done so that the servicing of the territories will be profitable to you and profitable to the individual doing the selling.

WHETHER TO USE A SALES REPRESENTATIVE

A sales representative is a special type of sales agent who is independent and sells for a number of different companies for the commission that he or she is paid. Selling using a sales representative has some particular advantages for a small firm with a limited product line. First, you don't have to pay money up front to hire salespeople to sell your product. You pay only the commission after the product is sold. Second, you do not have to recruit except to locate the sales representative. And third, with a limited product line and your own salespeople, you must amortize the cost of selling over a limited line of products. Each call is therefore that much more costly and less profitable. There are other advantages to using a sales representative. These include:

1. Immediate entry into a specific territory or a more general market
2. Regular calls on your customers and prospects
3. Quality salesmanship with no need for you to train
4. The fact that cost is a predetermined selling expense, a percentage of sales as their commission

However, there are also advantages that you must consider if you are going to use a sales representative:

1. You have limited control over a sales agent as opposed to a salesperson, who is your own employee, who reports to you, whom you train, and who is dependent directly upon you for compensation.
2. On very large volumes of sales, the selling expense will be large, much larger than it would be with your own employees.
3. An independent agent's allegiance to your products and your company is not total since he or she also serves other clients who are selling similar (but noncompeting) products or services. Therefore, such individuals must have special incentives to push your products over others.
4. If and when you terminate a contract with a sales representative, the sales representative may take your customers with him or her to a new client who is a competitor.

HOW TO SELECT A SALES REPRESENTATIVE

If you do decide that a sales representative is worthwhile employing for your business, you must get someone who is right for you, right for your company, and will build profits. Therefore, selecting a sales representative should not be done hastily. Edwin E. Bobrow, of Bobrow-Lewell Associates, Inc. of New York, recommends that you ask yourself the following questions in matching an agent to your company's character and image.[4]

What sort of selling skills are necessary for selling my products? Does the agent need technical knowledge and experience in addition to personal selling ability?

What marketing functions, if any, do I need in addition to selling?

Must the agent service my product as well as sell it?

Do I need a one-man or one-woman agency or an organization? If the latter, how large an organization?

What is the agent's record of success in products and territories similar to mine?

How long has the agent been in business? What is the agent's reputation? How well can I trade on it?

Are the other lines carried by the agent compatible with mine? Will the agent's contract for his or her existing lines help gain entry for my line?

Is the trade the agent specializes in the one I want to reach?

Does the agent cover the geographic area I need covered and in what depth?

Do the character, personality, values, and integrity of our two organizations correspond?

Can the "reps" who are the employees of the sales agent sales manage their own territories or will they need management and guidance from the agent? Or from me?

Is the agent the type who merely follows instructions or does the agent have a reputation for offering constructive suggestions? Which type do I need?

Is the chemistry right? Will we enjoy working together?

In my own businesses I have employed a special form that all potential manufacturers' representatives or sales representatives are required to complete. This is shown in Figure 16.2. You may incorporate it or design a similar one for your own firm.

SOURCES FOR FINDING SALES REPRESENTATIVES

The following are sources of sales representatives for your company:

1. The Manufacturers and Agents National Association (P.O. Box 16878, Irvine, CA 92713) publishes a directory which may be available in your public library. It is called *The Manufacturers and Agents National Association Directory of Members.*

---

[4] Edwin E. Bobrow, *Is the Independent Sales Agent for You?* MA 200, U.S. Small Business Administration (1978).

GLOBAL ASSOCIATES
Protective Armor Systems
1556 N. SIERRA MADRE VILLA
PASADENA, CALIFORNIA 91107
U. S. A.

Representative's Application Form

This application is for sales representatives of Global Associates' armor product lines on a commission basis for the territory indicated.

Name of firm _____

Address _____

_____

_____

Year established _____ Number of salespeople _____ Annual sales _____

Managers' or partners' names _____

_____

Territory covered _____

Territory desired _____

References _____

_____

Firms now represented/products

_____

_____

_____

_____

_____

Figure 16.2. Form for evaluating potential sales representative.

2. *The Directory of Manufacturers Agents* is published by McGraw-Hill Book Co., 330 West 42nd St., New York, NY 10036.

3. Recommendations from customers, sales managers of noncompeting companies, as well as editors, salesmen, and trade magazines can all be useful.

4. If you are exporting, contact the Department of Commerce. They may be able to find a manufacturer's representative for you abroad through their computerized system.

5. You can place classified ads in trade magazines whose readership includes the type of manufacturers' representatives that you are seeking.

GENERAL ADVICE ABOUT WORKING WITH AN AGENT

It's better to have a written contract with an agent so that both sides know exactly what they are going to do. Typically, this contract should spell out that either side may terminate the relationship with the other given 30 days' notice.

When dealing with a new sales representative, you should also be very choosy about granting wide territories. Unfortunately, a few sales representatives will take many more territories than they actually can service well, and some that they do not work in at all. But remember that under the terms of the contract, any sales made in any of those territories, whether directly or indirectly by the sales representative, will ensure him or her of a commission. Therefore, until you understand the situation fully, it is better to limist sales to those territories in which the sales representative has accomplished sales in the past, so that you can be reasonably sure he or she will be able to do so for you in the future.

Even after you have begun a relationship with a sales representative, look for ways to maximize the relationship. Seek ways that you can promote your products or your service with the agent. Remember that you are dealing with a human being, and it is not simply a matter of dropping the whole thing in the agent's lap and letting him or her run. You must give encouragement and reason to excel. You must motivate this individual who is selling for you. Never forget that his or her prime incentive is to build his or her own company. Your sales representative cannot afford to push your products or your services if they are unprofitable. Therefore, you must do what you can to insure that these products or services are profitable. Get feedback regarding customer relations and what features are liked and what features are not, and how your products and services can be improved.

Always involve the sales representative in all phases of your marketing. Invite him or her back for meetings either annually or semiannually at your company. Take his or her suggestions regarding packaging, promotion, and marketing. Make your manufacturer's representative or sales agent a part of your team.

However, with all of this information, do not burden your sales agent with confusing details. He or she must go out and make the sale. So, make your instructions and your aids clear-cut in order to make it easier for your representative to achieve this goal.

SOURCES OF ADDITIONAL INFORMATION

How I Raised Myself from Failure to Success in Selling, by Frank Bettger, published by Prentice-Hall, Englewood Cliffs, NJ 07632.

How to Develop Successful Salesmen, by Kenneth B. Haas, published by McGraw-Hill Book Co., 1221 Avenue of the Americas, New York, NY 10020.

How to Sell Well, by James F. Bender, published by McGraw-Hill Book Co., 1221 Avenue of the Americas, New York, NY 10020.

Management of the Sales Force, by William J. Stanton and Richard H. Buskirk, published by Richard D. Irwin, Inc., 1818 Ridge Rd., Homewood, IL 60430.

Sales Planning and Control, by Richard D. Crisp, published by McGraw-Hill Book Co., 1221 Avenue of the Americas, New York, NY 10020.

The Lacy Techniques of Salesmanship, by Paul J. Micali, published by Hawthorne Books, Inc., 260 Madison Ave., New York, NY 10016.

The New Art of Selling, by Elmer G. Leterman, published by Bantam Books, Inc., 666 Fifth Ave., New York, NY 10019.

The Sales Managers Handbook, 13th edition, edited by John C. Aspley, published by The Dartnell Corp., 4660 Ravenswood Ave., Chicago, IL 60640.

17

How to Make Money
with Trade Shows

WHAT IS A TRADE SHOW?

Trade shows have been held since medieval times, providing sellers with an opportunity to get together to display their products. It has been estimated that there are over 35,000 trade events in the United States alone every year, and more than 7,800 trade shows. Taking proper advantage of the unique potential offered by a trade show can make a great deal of extra money for you by boosting your sales. On the other hand, incorrect use of this promotional opportunity will waste your money, time, and resources.

ADVANTAGES OF TRADE SHOWS

Trade shows offer unique advantages over other means of promotion. Here are a few:

1. You can meet with many of your customers and potential customers at one time. You can demonstrate your products and give your customers an opportunity to see and handle them.
2. You can meet with your sales representatives and bring them up to date on your latest products, techniques, and plans, and you can also locate new sales representatives.
3. You can promote your company image in a certain business or industry.
4. Because the trade show itself will be promoted to interest a certain target group of potential customers, you will be furnished with a preselected audience having interests matched with your products or services.
5. You can rapidly test new products to see whether there is interest from customers and sales representatives.
6. You can distribute additional information regarding your products or services to qualified buyers, potential buyers, sales representatives, and other interested people.
7. You will be able to reach some people who ordinarily are not accessible.
8. Other companies in your industry, both competitors and suppliers, will often be demonstrating their products at the same trade show. This gives you a look at your competition as well as the opportunity to talk to the top people in firms important to your business.

9. You will be able to develop inquiries and leads for expanding your mailing list into new markets which you haven't yet entered.

10. You will be able to make large numbers of potential contacts in a relatively short interval of time.

11. You will complement your other promotional activities through your trade show participation.

SETTING OBJECTIVES FOR YOUR PARTICIPATION

In order to maximize the benefits that you will receive, it is necessary that you set definite objectives prior to your participation. That is, you should sit down and work out exactly what you wish to accomplish by your participation in the trade show. Study the list below and consider which objectives are applicable in your case.

1. To test market a new product
2. To recruit new sales personnel or new sales representatives or dealers
3. To develop new sales territories or new distribution channels
4. To encourage your customers to bring their technical problems to you for solutions
5. To introduce new products or new services or policies
6. To make sales
7. To demonstrate equipment which could not otherwise be shown easily to a customer
8. To bring together your representatives, internal sales and marketing people, and other key executives for conferences during the trade show
9. To expand your list of potential customers
10. To check on your competition and what they are offering
11. To increase the morale of your sales personnel and representatives and encourage them to work together
12. To build your company's image in the industry
13. To demonstrate your interest in and support of the sponsoring association

Please note that this list of objectives is not all-inclusive. There may be other goals or objectives which are unique to your situation, and which you should identify prior to trade show participation.

HOW TO DECIDE WHICH TRADE SHOWS TO ATTEND

With the large number of trade shows being held worldwide every year, it is clear that you cannot attend them all. It is therefore extremely important that those that you do attend are the most beneficial in boosting your sales and accomplishing others of the objectives that you establish. In order to make your plans, you must first know what shows are going to be held. The following are sources of information:

1. *Successful Meetings Magazine*, 1422 Chestnut St., Philadelphia, PA 19102, publishes an annual exhibit schedule.

2. A *Trade Show Convention Guide* is available from Budd Publications, Box 7, New York, NY 10004.

3. *World Meetings, United States and Canada,* and *World Meetings Outside the United States and Canada* are directories available from the MacMillan Publishing Co., 866 Third Ave., New York, NY 10022.

4. *Exhibits Schedule* is published by Bill Communications, Inc., 633 Third Ave., New York, NY 10017.

5. Check your trade or industry magazine. Frequently a calendar of upcoming trade shows and conventions is furnished.

From any of these sources, make a list of shows that interest you and seem to be for your business. Then, write the management of each show and ask for the literature that it has prepared. Specifically, you are interested in obtaining answers to the following questions:

1. Who has attended in the past and who are the people that these shows attract

2. How many attend

3. The geographical areas from which the attendees come

4. The industries and markets the attendees represent

5. The job titles and responsibilities held by the attendees

6. The topics of seminars, workshops, and events that may be offered at the show

7. The physical location of various exhibit booths available and the location relative to other events going on, entrances, exits, and so forth

8. Other services provided by the show sponsors

You should keep in mind that the information provided to you is a sales document and will therefore present everything in the best possible light. Therefore, one additional source of information obtained from this document which you can and must put to use is the list of prior exhibitors. If you contact these individuals, you can ask directly whether they were able to reach their objectives and whether they think your needs will be met by the trade show in question. Ask a lot of questions. The more you can learn about the show, the more information you have to make your decision.

HOW TO CALCULATE THE SPACE YOU WILL NEED FOR YOUR EXHIBIT

In order to calculate how much space you will need, you must consider your objectives and what will go into your exhibit. Every display, exhibit, or piece of furniture will require a certain amount of square footage. In addition, you will probably have salespeople on duty in the booth, and they too will require space. Therefore, you must decide how many salespeople you should have and how much footage you should allow for this.

Robert B. Konikow, public relations counsel for the Trade Show Bureau in New York City, recommends finding out first how many of the people visiting the trade show are likely prospects. You do this using the prospectus that you received in the mail from the trade show. Try to ascertain the number of visitors with meaningful titles or groups that you would be interested in talking with. Clearly, you won't be able to get all of these people to your booth, but you should be able to fit at least half of them. Take the total number of prospects of the type you are seeking and divide by two. Divide this number by the total number of hours the show will be open. From this calculation you can obtain the average number of visitors per hour.

A salesperson can typically handle approximately 15 prospects per hour. This is a good figure to use for your next calculation unless your own experience has shown that your salespeople handle more or less. Take the hourly visitor rate you have calculated previously and divide it by 15. From this you will get the average number of salespeople you should have on duty in your booth to handle the number of visitors you expect.

For each sales representative you have on duty, you must allow approximately 50 square feet of space. With less than 50 feet of space, the visitor will have a feeling of being crowded. But with more space, the visitor gets a feeling of loneliness and is unwilling to intrude on your salespeople! So, multiply the number of salespeople that you have calculated by 50 and you will get the amount of clear space that you will need. Add this to the space that you've calculated previously for your demonstration equipment and furniture and you will come up with how large a booth you are likely to need in square feet.

Let's look at an example of this. Let's assume that your furniture and equipment which you are going to display occupy 5 square feet of space. Let us say that you have decided from the prospectus that 1,200 prospects are likely to attend the show. Dividing this figure by 2 gives you 600, the number likely to visit your booth. Further, the show will be open a total of 20 hours. Dividing 600 by 20 gives you 30 visitors per hour. Dividing the 30 visitors per hour by the 15 prospects that a salesperson can see per hour on the average gives us 2 salespeople who should be on duty. Multiply 50 by 2 to get 100 square feet of space necessary for your salespeople. 100 plus 5 for the furniture and equipment you're going to display equals a total of 105 square feet necessary. Now, as it happens, most standard booths are 10 by 10, or 100 square feet. The extra 5 square feet can be easily absorbed and a standard booth will fill your bill. On the other hand, if the amount of space you need is much larger then the standard size, perhaps you should consider either two standard booths or an irregularly sized booth, if available.

HOW TO DESIGN YOUR DISPLAY

You must design your display to meet your own requirements as well as to conform to the requirements of the trade show. You should also consider the following factors:

1. You cannot show more than your budget will allow.
2. You want to attract only good prospects who will meet the objectives you have established.
3. You want to demonstrate the uniqueness of whatever it is that you are selling.

You must consider your booth just as you would an advertisement. That is, it must first attract attention, then gain interest, then create a desire to step in, and finally encourage action by your prospects, whether he or she is a potential customer, potential sales representative or whatever.

Remember that just as the headline in a good display or space advertisement attracts a reader to a specific ad, your trade show booth should, through its appearance, attract the people you want to see to your booth. It is best to use live demonstrations and other displays that are different from those of your competition and demonstrate benefits to your customers or to the prospects you are trying to attract. Participation demonstrations will gain added interest and are much better than static exhibits or presentations which prospects merely watch.

Demonstrations can be very simple and yet still carry the message across to the audience you wish to reach. A manufacturer of a new safety lens, much more protective than the ordinary safety lens, developed a simple but highly effective demonstration. He arranged a table like a small shooting gallery with a pellet gun mounted in a transparent, protective case. The handle and trigger of the gun were exposed so that it could be fired. A regular safety lens and this manufacturer's lens could be shot by interested prospects. The regular safety lens shattered easily. This manufacturer's new safety lens did not. This was the hit of this particular trade show and resulted in numerous sales. Go to other trade shows in your area even if you are not exhibiting and check out the exhibits which are attracting large numbers of prospects. This will give you many good ideas when you design your own exhibit.

THINGS TO DO BEFORE THE SHOW

After you have selected your trade show or (shows), designed your exhibit, and made other arrangements, you can greatly increase your ability to capitalize on a trade show's advantages if you venture into some of the following preshow activities:

1. Feature a unique item. Focus the activities around this unique item, brought in especially for the show. Naturally, the unique item should support the objectives that you have established previously.

2. Contact local media for publicity. Write letters to newspapers, radio and television stations, and other media in the city where the trade event will be held. With the letter, send a publicity release as described in Chapter 14. Feature the unique item you have developed for the show and ask to have your publicity release printed. Make yourself available for personal interviews.

3. Publicize to your industry. Send the publicity release that you have developed on your unique item for the show to all trade magazines in your field. Again, promote this unique product or service to the maximum extent possible and ask to have your publicity release printed.

4. Mail special letters with the publicity release to your regular customers, sales representatives, and others who may be interested. Give them a special invitation to see you at your booth and see your new item or the item you are promoting. Be sure that you indicate the exact location of your booth.

5. Send letters with the publicity release and with your invitation to other interested parties who might not normally attend a trade show for your particular industry or association. For example, if you were a small book publisher and exhibiting a special health food diet cookbook at a certain exhibit, you might also do a mailing to all the health food stores in the city in which the show is being held. These individuals might not normally attend a book or publisher's trade show, but a special invitation promoting an item they are interested in might get them there and to your booth.

6. Obtain and prepare additional promotional material, such as posters in your show windows or stickers to affix to your normal correspondence, which announce the fact that you will be in a certain trade show. This will have the additional advantage of promoting your image to your customers and suppliers even if they do not go to the show.

7. Prepare brochures or other information about your products or services to distribute to prospects at the show. Make sure this information is to the point, directly relates to what you are selling, and, of course, is interesting. However, unless your product is highly technical and is an expensively priced item, do not go overboard on this. Remember that there are many show attendees who do nothing more than collect brochures and throw them away later.

You should also be concerned with the following tasks, many of the details of which were probably covered in the prospectus sent to you by the trade organization. They are important, so don't neglect them.

1. Be sure that you have insurance covering your trade show activities.

2. Prepare and prefabricate as much of your booth as possible prior to shipping. Labor costs at shows for doing this are expensive.

3. Be sure you've timed your packing and shipping so everything arrives well ahead of time.

4. Select your booth location. The better locations sometimes cost more money. However, many experts say that the location of the booth is a major factor in trade show success.

5. Be sure that you have your hotel reservations and also a rental car reserved if you will need it.

6. Have an emergency plan concocted in case your booth is lost or delayed in shipment. You might be able to fall back on displays put up through your local representatives or other equipment that you might carry with you. Always remember, "Expect the best but be prepared for the worst."

7. Have certain items duplicated and carry them with you in case they are lost or damaged in shipment, and have a tool kit for emergency repairs.

THINGS TO DO DURING THE SHOW

In order to maximize the benefits of a trade show, you should not simply go and have a good time. You should make a list of specific things which you intend to do and then do them. Your list may include the following:

1. Contact the local media if they haven't already contacted you after a mailing. Try to get additional exposure through interviews, appearing on television and radio talk shows, and so forth.

2. Contact local customers, suppliers, and other interested prospects. If you cannot do this face to face, use your telephone. Personal contact while you are in town will be of considerable assistance to your business.

3. Meet and talk with other exhibitors. Sell to them, if possible. Think creatively about ways in which other exhibitors may help you in your business. One exhibitor made thousands of dollars in sales simply by noting that his product fit naturally as a lead-in item to a higher-priced item sold by another exhibitor. His proposal was to give this other exhibitor exclusive sales rights in his industry, which was totally different from the industry for which the product was usually sold. Be alert to opportunities at exhibits.

4. Use your local sales representatives to the maximum extent possible. They will be able to profit heavily from the fact that you are exhibiting in their city. They can help you prepare your booth and be your local contact point.

During the exhibit, you will meet many people and will obtain sales cards from many. It is a sad fact that when you talk to many people, one after the other, you will not remember later what these business cards are for. One way of dealing with this problem is to write what the individual wants on the back of the business card as soon as you receive it. An even better way is to use a pocket tape recorder and record this information.

THINGS TO DO AFTER THE SHOW

The trade show itself will generate many potential sources of business for you. But you must follow up immediately in order that all this potential business does not grow cold. Consider the following suggestions:

1. Write up another publicity release and mail it to all prospects that you met during the show. If the show provides a registration list of the names of companies and other persons attending the show, use this and add it to your mailing list.

2. Mail a publicity release to all your sales representatives throughout the country and promote your participation at the show to them. If you got good results during the trade show, let your sales representatives know about it. It will stimulate them to do more and better work for you.

3. Go over the business cards that you obtained and make certain that each one is individually handled and that what the prospect wanted is furnished.

4. Go over the objectives you established for the trade show and ask yourself whether these objectives were met. This will provide you with important information as to whether the trade show was worthwhile and whether you should attend next year. If you decide that this trade show was worthwhile, start planning immediately. Make reservations right away.

SOURCES OF ADDITIONAL INFORMATION

Creative Selling Through Trade Shows, by Al Hanlon, published by Hawthorne Books, Inc., 260 Madison Ave., New York, NY 10016.

How to Get Big Results from a Small Advertising Budget, by Cynthia S. Smith, published by Hawthorne Books, Inc., 260 Madison Ave., New York, NY 10016.

How to Participate Profitably in Trade Shows, by Robert B. Konikow, published by Dartnell Corp., 4660 Ravenswood Ave., Chicago, IL 60640.

The Exhibit Medium, by David Maxwell, published by *Successful Meetings Magazine,* 1422 Chestnut St., Philadelphia, PA 19102.

Trade Show Exhibit Planning Guide, published by Guideline Publishing Co., 5 Holmes Rd., Lexington, MA 02173.

18

How to Price Your Products and Services

COST VERSUS PRICE

It is important to realize right from the start that it is the market, not your costs, that determines the price at which you can sell your product or service. Your costs only establish a floor below which you cannot sell your product or service and make any money. Therefore, in determining the price for your product or service, you should recognize that the relevant price is the price between the price floor that you established with your cost data and the price ceiling that is the maximum amount for which you could possibly sell your product or service.

THE IMPORTANCE OF THE PRICING DECISION

The decision on what price to ask for your product or service has a major influence in several important areas. These include the following:

1. *Profit.* The price you select determines how much profit you will make.

2. *Recouping your investment.* The price at which you decide to sell your product or service will determine how quickly you will be able to recover the investment you made in developing and marketing your product or service.

3. *Resources available for promotion.* Your price will help determine the amount of financial resources you have at any given time to compete in the marketplace.

4. *Ability to penetrate a new market.* The price you select will determine whether or not you will be successful in getting into a new market.

5. *Image.* The price you select creates an image of the product and of your business. A high price may imply status and quality. A low price may imply economy.

THE EMPHASIS ON NONPRICE COMPETITION

With the considerable importance of price in determining the success of your business, you would think that every single business owner and manager devotes a great deal of thought to pricing. However, this is not true. One reason is that, even in today's economy, many consumers have much larger disposable incomes than in the past. Therefore, price may be of less importance, depending upon what you are selling. Also, with the many sophisticated marketing techniques that are available today, many marketers feel that they don't need to use price as a means of attracting consumers. Some businesspeople give little thought to price because they are simply unaware of the sensitivity of demand in the marketplace to making changes in price, either upward or downward.

Perhaps those most aware are those dealing in direct response marketing. In this case, testing of all types, including the testing of different prices, is a must. Along these lines, I've had some experiences of my own. I once sold a four-volume set of booklets on how to become published as a writer for $19.95. During testing I reduced the price to $14.95, wondering whether the increased number of sales would make up for the loss in contribution of each individual set sold. Note that I assumed that sales would go up as price was reduced. The results were quite surprising. Not only did I lose money because of the $5 differential in price for each unit sold, but the total number of sales actually went down. When I increased the price to $19.95, sales went up to their former level.

Some businessmen avoid serious pricing decisions because they feel there are fewer worries if they maintain a single stable price. They don't have to change the prices of the items in their literature or catalog, they don't have to reevaluate inventories for accounting, they don't have to renegotiate contracts. To them, price just isn't worth the worry. I hope to convince you in this chapter that this is not a good way to handle pricing.

The fact that many business owners do not seriously price their products or services gives you an opportunity to make a great deal of money and win out over your competition by doing so.

WHEN SHOULD YOU CONSIDER PRICING OR REPRICING?

You should consider pricing or repricing what you are selling at any time, but especially in the following circumstances:

1. When you are introducing a new product or products
2. When there is an interrelated addition to your product line which may affect the pricing of older items already in the line
3. When you wish to penetrate a new market
4. When the competition has changed its price
5. During periods of inflation
6. During periods of depression
7. When you are about to change your strategy
8. When you are testing to find the "correct price"
9. When the product is in a different part of its life cycle (we'll be talking more about this in the next chapter

THE ECONOMIC THEORY OF PRICING

According to economic theory, price is determined according to the downward-sloping demand curve as shown in Figure 18.1. As prices increase, a smaller quantity of the product or service is demanded by your customer. The implication of the downward slope of the demand curve is that it takes a lower price to sell

Figure 18.1. Downward-sloping demand curve.

more. However, note that according to a new demand curve, D+1, which is higher than the other demand curve, D, in Figure 18.1, for the same price you can sell more products. The implication of this higher demand curve is that in order to shift the demand from D to D+1 you must take additional action, such as increased advertising or a sweepstakes or some other form of promotion. However, at the same price you may also sell fewer products if the demand curve shifts to D+1 as shown in Figure 18.1. This can happen as technology causes obsolescence of your product. When the slide rule was first replaced by the hand-held calculator, the demand curve shifted downward, and eventually the slide rule could no longer be sold. This shift could also be caused by a product failure such as the crash of a certain model of aircraft. Now, at the same price, less of that model of aircraft will be sold.

Now, even though this is true, a firm can sometimes charge more and sell more product; this is what happened with the mail order product I mentioned earlier. This is true because of selective demand for a specific product and the way the product is perceived. Some factors here are distinctive features, perceived value, and status.

HOW TO PRICE A NEW PRODUCT

Let's look first at perhaps one of the most difficult pricing tasks that any manager of a small business or even a giant business faces: the pricing of a new product which is not yet in the market. To price a new product, there are three steps that you must take. These are as follows:

1. Determine your objective.
2. Find the demand versus the price.
3. Determine your basic pricing strategy.

Determining Your Objective

In any pricing decision that you make, you should think about what your overall objective is. Research in the United States showed that pricing decisions were made primarily for the following five business objectives:

1. To see a return on investment
2. To stabilize price and profit margin
3. To capture a target market share
4. To meet or prevent competition
5. To maximize profit

These pricing objectives show that your pricing decision should be based on a combination of goals which are internal to your company and the external market environment.

How to Estimate Demand versus Price

Now that your basic objectives have been established, you must find some way to estimate the demand versus the price. The following methods have all been found effective in estimating this demand.

1. *Ask customers.* From asking a sufficient number of customers about various potential prices, you will get some idea of how much of your product can be sold at each price. You may also learn the percentages of your potential customers that will buy at each price. For example, a survey may show that 80% of your customers would buy the product if the price were $5, 20% if $7, and 10% if $10. This information will also give you some indication of the profits that you might expect. The drawback here is that people will now always respond truthfully. (See the chapter on marketing research for more details about this.)

2. *Comparison with close substitutes or a replacement item.* We may compare the item that we are going to introduce with similar items that are on the market today—what their prices are and how many are selling at those prices. If the product is totally new, then we may try to find a product which it is replacing. For example, if we are introducing a new type of electronic watch, we may derive some initial price demand curves from the old design.

3. *Cost savings.* Sometimes, especially with industrial products, a price can be calculated based on the cost savings possible with the adoption of a new product. If you are going to price in this fashion, it will be important for you to promote the cost savings to your prospective customers.

4. *Test marketing.* Test marketing of the product is an outstanding way to derive demand versus product price. All that is necessary is that the product be offered at various prices to the same market. Since this type of testing requires the customer actually to put money on the barrel head for the product, it is much more accurate than simply asking the potential customer whether he or she would or would not purchase.

Once quantitative figures can be established for demand at various prices that we may set, we will consider the various pricing strategies that may be adopted.

Pricing Strategies for a New Product

For a new product, there are three basic pricing strategies. These are:

1. A high price strategy known as skimming strategy
2. A low price strategy known as a penetration strategy
3. A meet-the-competition price strategy

Skimming Price Strategy. This strategy is used when the product is so new that basically there is no competition, or when you wish to give the product status through the price. You can skim the market using the high price, and later on, when competition enters the market, you can reduce the price to meet the competition. Such a strategy also enables you to have more resources available to meet the competition when that day comes.

Penetration Strategy. This strategy is used to get yourself into a new market by going in at a very low price. Some people will try your product simply because your price is significantly lower than the price that the competition is charging. Naturally, you must be very careful when using this strategy because of the implications regarding quality and the possibility of getting stuck with a low status image. Also, maintaining the low price with a lower contribution to profit margin means very, very high volume sales which cannot always be achieved. Many companies using this strategy do so only to get the product tried by prospective customers, and once it has been adopted by a sufficient number the price is raised and the strategy changed to a meet-the-competition price or an even higher price.

A Meet-the-Competition Strategy. According to this strategy, you are going to price your product or service at the same price as the competition's. If you are going to do this, you must have something else unique or people will not switch from the competition to your company unless they are thoroughly dissatisfied with the competition for some other reason. For example, perhaps you set the same price as your competition, but the quality of your product is mugh higher; or the reliability of your product is better; or your service is better and your employees more friendly. The point is that you must offer something different, something more than your competition, or people will have no reason to switch.

SECOND PHASE PRICING

After you have introduced a new product or service, you may or may not wish to maintain the same pricing that you used to introduce the product into the market. Perhaps you introduced a product that was totally new and for which you have no patent or other protection. After some time, the competition will enter the market with its new products which are similar to yours. Perhaps they will be using a penetration price, or some price which is lower than the one that you are offering. How do you react to this, a potential loss of your market? As mentioned earlier, perhaps your product has gone rapidly through the life cycle. Let us say you are selling an electronic calculator which technology has now rendered obsolete. In this case you may make the decision to do a remainder sale and sell everything out at a fraction of its initial high price, perhaps even at or below your cost. Whatever second phase strategy you will work out, you must begin to think ahead even as you introduce a new product.

Here is an excellent example of a second phase strategy. The individual who used it actually increased his price when the competition entered with a penetration price. During one summer season, marketing genius Joe Cossman introduced the now common sprinkler hose with hundreds of tiny holes placed in a flexible tubing to allow water to sprinkle the grass or flowers in any desired pattern. This unique plastic hose was easily duplicated and no patent protection was possible. Therefore, Cossman expected and had many competitors during the second summer season. However, Cossman's method of distribution was not to sell direct but instead to sell through grocery stores to which he gave an approximate 50% discount from retail price. Instead of reducing his price when the competition came in, Joe actually increased his retail price. He passed the increased profit margin on to his distributors, the grocery stores. This increased their profits, and at the same time the image of the Cossman sprinkler was that it was of higher quality than the products of the competition. Cossman's innovative price strategy extended his control of the market, and he made more profit the second year with competition than he did the first year without.

Always think through your situation regarding distribution and other important factors in developing an innovative pricing decision.

WHAT TO DO IF NO ONE BUYS

If the market will not take your product or your service at the price you have established, to cover your costs and to allow you to make a desired profit, you have five alternatives:

1. *Lower the price.* This means you are accepting less profit in the hope that more of your product or service will be purchased.

2. *Increase the price.* This means that you are repositioning your product as compared with that of the competition so your product will be perceived by your potential customers as being of higher quality or better in some other fashion.

3. *Reduce your costs.* In this way you can maintain the price and still be profitable with the amount of product that you are selling.

4. *Drop the product completely.* This may sound drastic, but sometimes it is the wisest course.

5. *Differentiate your product from that of your competition.* This is the same sort of thing you must do if you establish a meet-the-competition price for a new product. That is, you emphasize quality, service, product performance, delivery time, financing arrangements, discounting, or some other aspect of importance to your customer.

PRICING POLICIES

There are three basic pricing policy categories. These are:

1. *Single price.* You have one price for all buyers regardless of timing, quantity purchase, and other factors

2. *Variable price.* Price is always open to negotiation

3. *Nonvariable price.* You offer the same price to all under similar conditions. Of course, under different conditions a different price is offered.

A single price has few advantages. The single price policy is used frequently in the consumer field or when selling to other small-purchase customers. The policy, of course, is easy to administer, and the emphasis then is always on nonprice appeals including all types of promotion such as face-to-face salesmen. Clearly, this policy will not be very attractive to individuals who buy in large quantity.

When selling to customers who make larger purchases, it is important to understand when it is best to have a nonvariable pricing policy or a variable pricing policy.

As noted earlier, a variable price can be negotiated. This has the following advantages. First, you can make adjustments to your price instantly during the process of negotiation. Secondly, you can be flexible in your dealings. Whatever the competition does can be countered immediately, and you can easily respond to other changes in the marketplace during the negotiation process. Finally, you can vary your appeal to be based on price or nonprice promotionals according to the situation.

However, a variable pricing policy also has many disadvantages. Since the resulting price charged will be different from one customer to another, the potential exists for bad feelings on the part of those customers who pay more for the same product or service. Also, for very large contracts, it will take time to negotiate. It is often said that time is money, and when your own time or the time of valuable people resources in your firm is spent, costs will not be insignificant. Sometimes having a variable price means that you will not be able to negotiate yourself, in which cases you must delegate the pricing decision to someone working for you. This means loss of your control over the pricing in your firm to a certain degree. The potential also exists for abuse in this delegation since some of your people may resort to what amounts to price cutting instead of actually "selling." Finally, there are some legal complications which may result, growing out of a law known as the Robinson-Patman Act. We will discuss the implications of this act for a variable pricing policy shortly.

A *nonvariable price* has advantages as well. Clearly, it simplifies the selling process since no one except you has any authority to vary the prices. There is an ease of administering such a policy, and it is clearly fair to all buyers. Naturally, you will avoid any legal complications of having a variable price, and you, of course, maintain control over the pricing decision.

DISCOUNT POLICIES

Discount policies can also affect sales in a very dramatic fashion. One entrepreneur, the inventor of a unique item used by pilots, lost thousands of dollars in potential orders from the government simply because he had no discount policy. Discount policy may be classified in the following ways:

1. *A promotional discount.* This means special discounts to the consumer or perhaps within your distribution or organization to promote your product or your service.

2. *A trade discount.* This is a discount on the basis of the position in the distribution channel, such as a discount offered to a retailer or a wholesaler if you are a manufacturer, or anyone between you and the ultimate consumer of your product or service.

3. *A quantity discount to encourage large orders.* There are two types of quantity discounts. One is a noncumulative type which is based purely on the quantity ordered at a specific period of time. Another is the cumulative discount which is increased depending on quantities ordered by the same buyer over an indefinite period of time. Cumulative discounts tend to tie the buyer to the seller.

THE ROBINSON-PATMAN ACT OF 1936

The Robinson-Patman Act deals with price discrimination. Its intent is to regulate any tendency to injure competition. The implication is clear for any of your pricing policy decisions, and either the Federal Trade Commission or a private complainant can initiate action against you for your pricing policies if you sell at different prices to two or more competing customers engaged in interstate commerce and your acts have a tendency to injure competition. Now, there are certain defenses against these accusations. For example, it is not a violation of the act if you are selling at different prices because of cost differences, or if you have to lower the price to one customer to meet the competition, or if you have to lower the price because of changing market conditions. When in doubt, consult your attorney.

TWO CHECKLISTS FOR PRICING

The following checklists are provided to assist you in pricing. The first is a general pricing checklist for managers developed by Joseph D. O'Brien, associate professor of marketing at the College of Business Administration, Boston College, Boston, Massachusetts.[1] The second checklist is a special pricing checklist for small retailers developed by Bruce J. Walker, associate professor of marketing at Arizona State University, Tempe, Arizona.[2]

Checklist One: Examining Costs, Sales Volume, and Profits

The questions in this part should be helpful when you look at prices from the viewpoint of costs, sales volume, and profits.

Costs and Prices

The small retailer who sets the price for an item by applying a standard markup may be overlooking certain cost factors which are connected with that item. The following questions are designed to help you gather information which should be helpful when you are determining prices on specific types of items.

		Yes	No
1.	Do you know which of your operating costs remain the same regardless of sales volume?	____	____
2.	Do you know which of your operating costs decrease percentage-wise as your sales volume increases?	____	____
3.	Have you ever figured out the breakeven point for your items selling at varying price levels?	____	____
4.	Do you look behind high gross margin percentages? (For example, a product with a high gross margin, may also be a slow turnover item with high handling costs. Thus is may be less profitable than lower margin items which turn over fast.)	____	____

[1] Joseph D. O'Brien, *A Pricing Checklist for Managers*, Small Business Administration (1972).
[2] Bruce J. Walker, *A Pricing Checklist for Small Retailers*, Small Business Administration (1979).

Yes   No

5. When you select items for price reductions, do you project the effects on profits? (For example, if a food marketer considers whether to run canned ham or rump steak on sale, an important cost factor is labor. Practically none is involved in featuring canned ham; however, a rump steak sale requires the skill of a meat-cutter and this labor cost might mean little or no profits.)   _____ _____

Pricing and Sales Volume

An effective pricing program should also consider sales volume. For example, high prices might limit your sales volume while low prices might result in a large, but unprofitable volume. The following questions should be helpful in determining what is right for your situation.

6. Have you considered setting a sales volume goal and then studying to see if your prices will help you reach it?   _____ _____

7. Have you set a target of a certain number of new customers for next year? (If so, how can pricing help you to get them?)   _____ _____

8. Should you limit the quantities of low-margin items which any one customer can buy when they are on sale? (If so, will you advertise this policy?)   _____ _____

9. What is your policy when a sale item is sold out before the end of the advertised period? Do you allow disappointed customers to buy the item later at the sale price?   _____ _____

Pricing and Profits

Prices should help bring in sales which are profitable over the long pull. The following questions are designed to help you think about pricing policies and their effect on your annual profits.

10. Do you have all the facts on costs, sales, and competitive behavior?   _____ _____

11. Do you set prices with the hope of accomplishing definite objectives, such as a 1-percent profit increase over last year?   _____ _____

12. Have you set a given level of profits in dollars and in percent of sales?   _____ _____

13. Do you keep records which will give you the needed facts on profits, losses, and prices?   _____ _____

14. Do you review your pricing practices periodically to make sure that they are helping to achieve your profit goals?   _____ _____

Judging the Buyer, Timing, and Competitors

The questions in this part are designed to help you check your practices for judging the buyer (your customers), your timing, and your competitors.

The Buyer and Pricing Strategy

After you have your facts on costs, the next point must be the CUSTOMER—whether you are changing a price, putting in a new item, or checking out your present price practices. Knowledge of your customers helps you to determine how to vary prices in order to get the average gross margin you need for making a profit. (For example, to get an average gross margin of 35 percent, some retailers put a low markup—10 percent, for instance—on items which they promote as traffic builders and use high markup—sometimes as much as 60 percent—on slow-moving items.) The following questions should be helpful in checking your knowledge about your customers.

		Yes	No
15.	Do you know whether your customers shop around and for what items?	_____	_____
16.	Do you know how your customers make their comparisons? By reading newspaper ads? Store shopping? Hearsay?	_____	_____
17.	Are you trying to appeal to customers who buy on price alone? To those who buy on quality alone? To those who combine the two?	_____	_____
18.	Do any of your customers tell you that your prices are in line with those of your competitors? Higher? Lower?	_____	_____
19.	Do you know which item (or types of items) your customers call for even though you raise the price?	_____	_____
20.	Do you know which items (or types of items) your customers leave on your shelves when you raise the price?	_____	_____
21.	Do certain items seem to appeal to customers more than others when you run weekend, clearance, or special-day sales?	_____	_____
22.	Have you used your individual sales records to classify your present customers according to the volume of their purchases?	_____	_____
23.	Will your customers buy more if you use multiple pricing? (For example, 3 for 39 cents for products with rapid turnover.)	_____	_____
24.	Do your customers respond to odd prices more readily than even prices, for example, 99 cents rather than $1?	_____	_____
25.	Have you decided on a pricing strategy to create a favorable price image with your customers? (For example, a retailer with 8,000 different items might decide to make a full margin on all medium or slow movers while featuring—at low price levels—the remaining fast movers.)	_____	_____
26.	If you are trying to build a quality price image, do your individual customer records, such as charge account statements, show that you are selling a larger number of higher priced items than you were 12 months ago?	_____	_____
27.	Do your records of individual customer accounts and your observations of customer behavior in the store show price as the important factor in their buying? Service? Assortments? Some other consideration?	_____	_____

Time and Pricing

Effective merchandising means that you have the right product, at the right place, at the right price, and at the *right time*. All are important, but timing is the critical element for the small retailer. The following questions should be helpful in determining what is the right time for you to adjust prices.

		Yes	No
28.	Are you a "leader" or a "follower" in announcing your price reductions? (The follower, even though he matches his competitors, creates a negative impression on his customers.)	____	____
29.	Have you studied your competitors to see whether they follow any sort of pattern when making price changes? (For example, do some of them run clearance sales earlier than others?)	____	____
30.	Is there a pattern to the kinds of items which competitors promote at lower prices at certain times of the month or year?	____	____
31.	Have you decided whether it is better to take early markdowns on seasonal or style goods or to run a clearance sale at the end of the season?	____	____
32.	Have you made regular annual sales, such as Anniversary Sales, Fall Clearance, or Holiday Cleanup, so popular that many customers wait for them rather than buying in season?	____	____
33.	When you change a price, do you make sure that *all* customers know about it through price tags and so on?	____	____
34.	Do you try to time price reductions so they can be promoted in your advertising?	____	____

Competition and Pricing

When you set prices, you have to consider how your competitors might react to your prices. The starting place is learning as much as you can about their price structures. The following questions are designed to help you check out this phase of pricing.

		Yes	No
35.	Do you use all the available channels of information to keep you up to date on your competitors' price policies? (Some useful sources of information are: things your customers tell you; the competitor's price list and catalogs, if he uses them; his advertising; reports from your suppliers; trade paper studies; and shoppers employed by you.)	____	____
36.	Should your policy be to try always to sell above or below competition? Only to meet it?	____	____
37.	Is there a pattern to the way your competitors respond to your price cuts?	____	____
39.	Is the leader pricing of your competitors affecting your sales volume to such an extent that you must alter your pricing policy on individual items (or types of items) of merchandise?	____	____

                                                                                        Yes   No

40. Do you realize that no two competitors have identical
    cost curves? (This difference in costs means that certain
    price levels may be profitable for you but unprofitable for
    your competitor or vice versa.)   _____   _____

Practices Which Can Help Offset Price

Some small retailers take advantage of the fact that price is not always the determining factor in making a sale. They supply customer services and offer other in-
ducements to offset the effect of competitors' lower prices. Delivery service is an
example. Comfortable shopper's meeting place is another. The following questions are designed to help you take a look at some of these practices.

41. Do the items or services which you sell have advantages
    for which customers are willing to pay a little more?   _____   _____

42. From personal observation of customer behavior in your
    store can you tell about how much more customers will
    pay for such advantages?   _____   _____

43. Should you change your services so as to create an ad-
    vantage for which your customers will be willing to
    pay?   _____   _____

44. Does your advertising emphasize customer benefits
    rather than price?   _____   _____

45. Are you using the most common nonprice competitive
    tools? (For example, have you tried to alter your product
    or service to the existing market? Have you tried stamps,
    bonus purchase gifts, or other plans for building repeat
    business?)   _____   _____

46. Should policies on returned goods be changed so as to im-
    press your customers better?   _____   _____

47. If you sell repair services, have you checked out your
    guarantee policy?   _____   _____

48. Should you alter assortments of merchandise to increase
    sales?   _____   _____

Checklist Two: Pricing Checklist for Small Retailers

1. Is the relative price of this item very important to your
   target consumers? The importance of price depends on
   the specific product and on the specific individual. Some
   shoppers are very price-conscious, others want convenience and knowledgeable sales personnel. Because of
   these variations, you need to learn about your customers'
   desires in relation to different products. Having sales
   personnel seek feedback from shoppers is a good starting
   point.   _____   _____

2. Are prices based on estimates of the number of units that
   consumers will demand at various price levels? Demand-
   oriented pricing such as this is superior to cost-oriented
   pricing. In the cost approach, a predetermined amount is
   added to the cost of the merchandise, whereas the de-

	Yes	No

mand approach considers what consumers are willing to pay.

3. Have you established a price range for the product? The cost of merchandise will be at one end of the price range and the level above which consumers will *not* buy the product at the other end.

4. Have you considered what price strategies would be compatible with your store's total retailing mix that includes merchandise, location, promotion, and services?

5. Will trade-ins be accepted as part of the purchase price on items such as appliances and television sets?

Supplier and Competitor Considerations

This set of questions looks outside your firm to two factors that you cannot directly control—suppliers and competitors.

6. Do you have final pricing authority? With the repeal of fair trade laws, "yes" answers will be more common than in previous years. Still, a supplier can control retail prices by refusing to deal with non-conforming stores (a tactic which may be illegal) or by selling to you on consignment.

7. Do you know what direct competitors are doing price-wise?

8. Do you regularly review competitors' ads to obtain information on their prices?

9. Is your store large enough to employ either a full-time or part-time comparison shopper? These three questions emphasize the point that you must watch competitors' prices so that your prices will not be far out of line—too high *or* too low—without good reason. Of course, there may be a good reason for out-of-the-ordinary prices, such as seeking a special price image.

A Price Level Strategy

Selecting a general level of prices in relation to competition is a key strategic decision, perhaps the most important.

10. Should your overall strategy be to sell at prevailing market price levels? The other alternatives are an above-the-market strategy or a below-the-market strategy.

11. Should competitors' temporary price reductions ever be matched?

12. Could private-brand merchandise be obtained in order to avoid direct price competition?

Calculating Planned Initial Markup

In this section you will have to look *inside* your business, taking into account sales, expenses, and profits before setting prices. The point is that your initial markup must be large enough to cover anticipated expenses and reductions *and* still produce a satisfactory profit.

	Yes	No

13. Have you estimated sales, operating expenses, and reductions for the next selling season?

14. Have you established a profit objective for the next selling season?

15. Given estimated sales, expenses, and reductions, have
you planned initial markup?
This figure is calculated with the following formula:

$$\text{Initial markup percentage} = \frac{\text{operating expenses} + \text{reductions} + \text{profit}}{\text{Net sales} + \text{reductions}}$$

Reductions consist of markdowns, stock shortages, and
employee and customer discounts. The following example uses dollar amounts, but the estimates can also be
percentages. If a retailer anticipates $94,000 in sales for a
particular department, $34,000 in expenses, and $6,000 in
reductions, and if the retailer desires a $4,000 profit, ini-
tial markup percentage can be calculated:

$$\text{Initial markup percentage} = \frac{\$34,000 + \$6,000 + \$4,000}{\$94,000 + \$6,000} = 44\%$$

The resulting figure, 44 percent in this example, indicates
what size initial markup is needed *on the average* in
order to make the desired profits.

16. Would it be appropriate to have different initial markup
figures for various lines of merchandise or services? You
would seriously consider this when some lines have
much different characteristics than others. For instance, a
clothing retailer might logically have different initial
markup figures for suits, shirts and pants, and accessories. (Various merchandise characteristics are covered in
an upcoming section.) You may want those items with
the highest turnover rates to carry the lowest initial
markup.

Store Policies

Having calculated an initial markup figure, you could proceed to set prices on
your merchandise. But an important decision such as this should not be rushed.
Instead, you should consider additional factors which suggest what would be the
best price.

17. Is your tentative price compatible with established store
policies? *Policies* are written guidelines indicating appropriate methods or actions in different situations. If established with care, they can save you time in decision making and provide for consistent treatment of shoppers.
Specific policy areas that you should consider are as follows:

18. Will a one-price system, under which the same price is
charged every purchaser of a particular item, be used on
all items?

Yes No

The alternative is to negotiate price with consumers.

19. Will odd-ending prices, such as $1.98 and $44.95, be more appealing to your customers than even-ending prices? _____ _____

20. Will consumers buy more if multiple pricing, such as 2 for $8.50, is used? _____ _____

21. Should any leader offerings (selected products with quite low, less profitable prices) be used? _____ _____

22. Have the characteristics of an effective leader offering been considered? Ordinarily, a leader offering needs the following characteristics to accomplish its purpose of generating much shopper traffic: used by most people, bought frequently, very familiar regular price, and not a large expenditure for consumers.

23. Will price lining, the practice of setting up distinct price points (such as $5.00, $7.50, and $10.00) and then marking all related merchandise at these points, be used? _____ _____

24. Would price lining by means of zones (such as $5.00–$7.50 and $12.50–$15.00) be more appropriate than price points? _____ _____

25. Will cent-off coupons be used in newspaper ads or mailed to selected consumers on any occasion? _____ _____

26. Would periodic special sales, combining reduced prices and heavier advertising, be consistent with the store image you are seeking? _____ _____

27. Do certain items have greater appeal than others when they are part of a special sale? _____ _____

28. Has the impact of various sale items on profits been considered? Sale prices may mean little or no profit on these items. Still, the special sale may contribute to *total* profits by bringing in shoppers who may also buy some regular-price (and profitable) merchandise and by attracting new customers. Also, you should avoid featuring items that require a large amount of labor, which in turn would reduce or erase profits. For instance, according to this criterion, shirts would be a better special sale item than men's suits that often require free alterations. _____ _____

29. Will "rain checks" be issued to consumers who come in for special-sale merchandise that is temporarily out of stock? You should give particular attention to this decision since rain checks are required in some situations. Your lawyer or the regional Federal Trade Commission office should be consulted for specific advice regarding whether rain checks are needed in the special sales you plan. _____ _____

Nature of the Merchandise

In this section you will be considering how selected characteristics of particular merchandise affect a planned initial markup.

	Yes	No

30. Did you get a "good deal" on the wholesale price of this merchandise?

31. Is this item at the peak of its popularity?

32. Are handling and selling costs relatively great due to the product being bulky, having a low turnover rate, and/or requiring much personal selling, installation, or alterations?

33. Are relatively large levels of reductions expected due to markdowns, spoilage, breakage, or theft? With respect to the preceding four questions, "Yes" answers suggest the possibility of or need for larger-than-normal initial markups. For example, very fashionable clothing often will carry a higher markup than basic clothing such as underwear because the particular fashion may suddenly lose its appeal to consumers.

34. Will customer services such as delivery, alterations, gift wrapping, and installation be free of charge to customers? The alternative is to charge for some or all of these services.

Environmental Considerations

The questions in this section focus your attention on three factors outside your business, namely economic conditions, laws, and consumerism.

35. If your state has an unfair sales practices act that requires minimum markups on certain merchandise, do your prices comply with this statute?

36. Are economic conditions in your trading area abnormal? Consumers tend to be more price-conscious when the economy is depressed, suggesting that lower-than-normal markups may be needed to be competitive. On the other hand, shoppers are less price-conscious when the economy is booming, which would permit larger markups *on a selective basis.*

37. Are the ways in which prices are displayed and promoted compatible with consumerism, one part of which has been a call for more straightforward price information?

38. If yours is a grocery store, is it feasible to use unit pricing in which the item's cost per some standard measure is indicated?

Having asked (and hoperfully answered) more than three dozen questions, you are indeed ready to establish retail prices. When you have decided on an appropriate percentage markup, 35 percent on a garden hose for example, the next step is to determine what percentage of the still unknown retail price is represented by the cost figure. The basic markup formula is simply rearranged to do this:

Yes   No

$$Cost = Retail\ price - Markup$$
$$Cost = 100\% - 35\% = 65\%$$

Then the dollar cost, say $3.25 for the garden hose, is plugged into the following formula to arrive at the retail price:

$$Retail\ price = \frac{Dollar\ cost}{Percentage\ cost} = \frac{\$3.25}{65\%\ (or\ .65)} = \$5.00$$

One other consideration is necessary:

39. Is the retail price consistent with your planned initial markups?

Adjustments

It would be ideal if all items sold at their original retail prices. But we know that things are not always ideal. Therefore, a section on price adjustments is necessary.

40. Are additional markups called for, because wholesale prices have increased or because an item's low price causes consumers to question its quality?

41. Should employees be given purchase discounts?

42. Should any groups of customers, such as students or senior citizens, be given purchase discounts?

43. When markdowns appear necessary, have you first considered other alternatives such as retaining price but changing another element of the retailing mix or storing the merchandise until the next selling season?

44. Has an attempt been made to identify causes of markdowns so that steps can be taken to minimize the number of avoidable buying, selling, and pricing errors that cause markdowns?

45. Has the relationship between timing and size of markdowns been taken into account? In general, markdown taken *early* in the selling season or shortly after sales slow down can be smaller than *late* markdowns. Whether an early or late markdown would be more appropriate in a particular situation depends on several things: your assessment of how many consumers might still be interested in the product, the size of the initial markup, and the amount remaining in stock.

46. Would a schedule of automatic markdowns after merchandise has been in stock for specified intervals be appropriate?

47. Is the size of the markdown "just enough" to stimulate purchases? Of course, this question is difficult—perhaps impossible—to answer. Nevertheless, it stresses the point that you have to carefully observe the effects of different size markdowns so that you can eventually acquire some insights into what size markdowns are "just enough" for different kinds of merchandise.

Yes   No

48. Has a procedure been worked out for markdowns on price-lined merchandise?

_____   _____

49. Is the markdown price calculated from the off-retail percentage? This question gets you into the arithmetic of markdowns. Usually, you first tentatively decide on the percentage amount price must be marked down to excite consumers. For example, if you think a 25 percent markdown will be necessary to sell a lavender sofa, the dollar amount of the markdown is calculated as follows:

Dollar   Off-retail
markdown = percentage × Previous retail price
Dollar markdown = 25% (or .25) × $500. = $125.

Then the markdown price is obtained by subtracting the dollar markdown from the previous retail price. Hence, the sofa would be $375.00 after taking the markdown.

50. Has cost of the merchandise been considered before setting the markdown price? This is not to say that a markdown price should never be lower than cost; on the contrary, a price that low may be your only hope of generating some revenue from the item. But cost should be considered to make sure that below-cost markdown prices are the *exception in your store rather than being so common that your total profits are really hurt.*

_____   _____

51. Have procedures for recording the dollar amounts, percentages, and probable causes of markdowns been set up?

_____   _____

Analyzing markdowns is very important since it can provide information that will assist in calculating planned initial markup, in decreasing errors that cause markdowns, and in evaluating suppliers.

You may be weary from thinking your way through the preceding sections, but don't overlook an important final question:

52. Have you marked the calendar for a periodic review of your pricing decisions?

_____   _____

Rather than "laying an egg" due to careless pricing decisions, this checklist should help you lay a solid foundation of effective prices as you try to build retail profits.

SOURCES OF ADDITIONAL INFORMATION

Price and Price Policies, by Walton Hamilton, published by McGraw-Hill Book Co., 1221 Avenue of the Americas, New York, NY 10020.

Pricing Decisions in Small Business, by W. Warren Haynes, published by University of Kentucky Press, Lexington, KY 40506.

Pricing for Marketing Executives, by Alfred R. Oxenfeldt, published by Wadsworth Publishing Co., Inc., 10 Davis Drive, Belmont, CA 94002.

Pricing for Profit and Growth, by Albert U. Bergfeld, James S. Earley, and William R. Knobloch, published by Prentice-Hall, Inc., Englewood Cliffs, NJ 07632.

Pricing Strategies, by Alfred R. Oxenfeldt, published by AMACOM, a division of the American Management Association, 135 West 50 St., New York, NY 10020.

19

How to Find and
Introduce a New Product

THE IMPORTANCE OF NEW PRODUCT INTRODUCTION

It is an unfortunate fact that eight out of ten new products fail in the marketplace. Yet, new product introduction is absolutely essential. Why is this so? Without new products your business cannot survive. You cannot continue to produce the old products that have made your company successful because of the product life cycle. The product life cycle, which is explained more thoroughly in Chapter 4, shows that every product goes through the stages of introduction, growth, maturity, and saturation, and finally goes into decline. In this final phase, while sales may continue to be made, the product becomes more and more unprofitable. Now, naturally, life cycles are of different lengths for different products. Some life cycles are extremely long, such as those for the safety pin or the hairpin. Others, such as those for electronic calculators and electronic watches, are extremely short. However, no product or service can be offered in one form forever.

Of course, a company does not introduce a new product only because it is forced to do so. Below is a listing of some of the possible reasons for a company's decision to offer something new.

1. Your product has become noncompetitive because improvements in competitive products have rendered yours obsolete.
2. The use for which your product was created has either disappeared or has gone into decline.
3. Your product may be related to some phase of the national or local economy. This may be war or peace; it may be heavy industry, the military, energy, agriculture, or any other facet of economic life.
4. A new product may be desirable to take up excess plant capacity.
5. You may have surplus capital which you wish to utilize.
6. You may find the opportunity to utilize by-products and materials in the manufacture of other products.
7. You may want to make maximum use of your sales organization and have additional products which will allow you to amortize these overhead costs over a broader base.
8. You may be in a business that has cycles known as "peaks and valleys," either due to seasonal fluctuations or ordering phases. Sometimes these upswings and downturns can be leveled out by the use of new products which sell during the valleys.
9. You may wish to make use of marginal or partly used manpower or other facilities.

As noted earlier, the mortality of new product ideas is extremely high. Alan A. Smith, of the consulting firm of Arthur D. Little, Inc., of Cambridge, Massachusetts, researched the experience of 20 companies concerned with successful new product development. Here is the experience of these 20 companies.

There were 540 possibilities in the idea stage which were considered for research. 448 of these 540 were eliminated during initial screening of items which should be pursued. This left 92 which were selected for preliminary laboratory investigation. Only 8 of the 92 appeared sufficiently promising to warrant development, and 7 of the 8 were dropped as unsalable or unprofitable as determined during some process of development or introduction into the marketplace. Only 1 of these 7, or 1 out of the original 540 idea possibilities, was placed in regular production.

While many possibilities for new ideas and new products should be considered, you can see that 92 to 1 or even 8 to 1 is not a terrific success ratio, and much money was wasted finding the one product that was successful. In this chapter you will see how to increase your new products' success ratio dramatically.

THE ADVANTAGES OF NEW PRODUCT INTRODUCTION

Earlier we gave several reasons for introducing a new product. Here are some clear-cut advantages for new product development which should encourage you to look at new products and introduce them to the marketplace.

A new product may reduce your overhead by allowing you to amortize administrative sales, advertising and distribution costs over additional products.

Your new product may lead you into new markets which may be even greater than the current market which you are serving.

New products may add substantially to your profit as well as to the stability of your company.

New products may lead you into using distribution channels that will benefit your old product line and working together may synergistically help both.

Tax laws frequently encourage you and in effect share the cost of developing new products.

PRODUCT INTEREST CHECKLIST

I am going to give you a list of sources of new product ideas, but before you look these over, you should have a general idea of the type of product that you're looking for based on factors such as your company's strengths, market preference, the sales volume you desire, product status, the product configuration you may be interested in, and finance. This will give you a profile of product interest. The following checklist was developed by John B. Lang, technology utilization officer of the Small Business Administration in Los Angeles.[1] Use it to develop a profile of product interest.

[1] John B. Long, *Finding a New Product for Your Company*, Small Business Administration (1980).

Your Company's Strengths

		Yes	No
1.	Is manufacturing your company's strength?		
2.	Do you prefer a highly automated production line?		
3.	Do you prefer a product with a high ratio of labor to production costs?		
4.	Are your production personnel highly skilled?		
5.	Are your industrial product designers exceptionally skilled?		
6.	Does your present equipment have a long usable life?		
7.	Is your present equipment largely underutilized?		
8.	Do you have a strong sales force?		
9.	Is your sales force hampered by too-narrow a product?		
10.	Do you have strong capability in a particular technology?		
11.	Does your company have cash or credit resources not used in your present operations?		
12.	Does your company have a reputation for high quality products?		
13.	Does your company have a reputation for low cost production?		

Market Preference

		Yes	No
14.	Do you prefer a particular industry?		
15.	Do you prefer a product sold to retail consumers?		
16.	Do you prefer a product sold to industrial users?		
17.	Do you prefer a product sold to the government?		
18.	Do you prefer a product with long usage?		
19.	Will you accept a product that may be a fad item?		
20.	Do you prefer a consumable item?		
21.	Is there a distribution system (trade practice) you prefer?		
22.	Would you consider a product limited to a given locality? (Or a product in demand largely in overseas markets?)		
23.	Is a product that requires specialty selling desirable?		
24.	Is a product that needs mass merchandising suitable?		
25.	Do you intend overseas distribution?		
26.	Must your present sales department be able to sell a new product?		
27.	Are you willing to create a new or separate marketing department to sell a new product?		

Sales Volume Desired

		Yes	No
28.	Have you determined the optimum annual volume from the product over the next 3 years?		

	Yes	No
29. Do you have any preference for a unit price range in a product?	____	____
30. Do you have 5 and 10 year volume objectives for a new product?	____	____
31. Will this product have to support its own sales organization?	____	____
32. Will the product support its own manufacturing equipment?	____	____
33. At what volume does a product exceed your company's capability?	____	____

Product Status

34. Will you accept an idea for a product?	____	____
35. Will you accept an unpatentable product?	____	____
36. Is a non-exclusive license of a patent acceptable?	____	____
37. Are you willing to develop an idea to a patentable stage?	____	____
38. Will you develop a patent without acceptable prototype?	____	____
39. Will you accept a product that has been on the market but is not yet profitable?	____	____
40. Will you license a patent?	____	____
41. Do you insist on owning the product's patent?	____	____
42. Will you enter a joint venture for a new product with another company?	____	____
43. Would you merge with or buy a company that has good products but needs your company's strengths in manufacturing, sales, finances, or management?	____	____

The Product Configuration

44. Are there any maximum size limitations to a product you can manufacture?	____	____
45. Would weight of a product be a factor?	____	____
46. Do warehousing facilities or yard space impose size limitation?	____	____
47. Does length of production time influence the desirability of a product?	____	____
48. Have you determined your equipment tolerance?	____	____
49. Do you have adequately trained personnel to do the job?	____	____
50. Would you prefer that a product be made of certain materials?	____	____
51. Are there manufacturing processes that should constitute the major portion of a new product?	____	____
52. Are there any manufacturing processes the product should not have?	____	____

		Yes	No
53.	Would a product requiring extensive quality control costs be desirable?	_____	_____

Finance

54.	Has an overall budget been established for a new product?	_____	_____
55.	Have separate budgets been established for finding, acquisition, development, market research, manufacturing, and marketing the new product?	_____	_____
56.	Has a time period been established by which a new product must become self-supporting, profitable, or capable of generating cash?	_____	_____
57.	Does the new product require a certain profit margin to be compatible with your financial resources or company objectives?	_____	_____
58.	Has external long-range financing been explored for your new product?	_____	_____
59.	Is the length of the sales cycle for the new product known?	_____	_____
60.	Do trade practices require you to furnish financial assistance, such as floor planning or dating plans, for distribution of your product?	_____	_____
61.	Have you determined average inventory to sales ratio for the new product?	_____	_____
62.	Have you determined average aging of accounts receivable for your new product?	_____	_____
63.	Does the product have seasonal aspects?	_____	_____

Profile of Product Interest

Your answers to the 63 questions above can lead to a well thought-out guide as to the acceptability of any potential new product. A short condensed profile helps communicate your needs. Such a profile also indicates a high degree of professional management which sources of new products will welcome. For illustrative purposes a fictitious sample profile follows:

The XYZ company, a defense-aerospace oriented precision metal stamping and machine shop, desires to acquire a product or product line to the following specifications:

Market—The product desired is one for use by industrial or commercial firms of a specific industry but not by the government or general public except incidentally.

Product—The product sought is one in which 60 percent of the total direct manufacturing cost consists of metal stamping and/or machining processes.

Price range—Open, but preferably the unit price to the user will be in the $100 to $400 range.

Volume—Open, but preferably a product which aggressively marketed will produce $500,000 in sales the first year with an annual potential sale of 3 to 5 million dollars.

Finance—Initial resources to $150,000 in addition to present plant capacity are available for manufacturing a new product.

Type of acquisition—Prefer royalties to a patent but will consider purchase of a patent, joint venture, merger, or purchase of a company outright.

EIGHTEEN SOURCES FOR NEW PRODUCTS

Any of these sources may give you a new product idea which will make you a fortune.

1. *Currently successful products.* Look at currently successful products, but be careful not to copy them. Copy only the concept. If you copy the idea exactly, you may be in violation of the law if the idea is covered by a patent, copyright, or other type of protection. But even if you don't copy an idea exactly, if your product is very much like another one, the individual who has introduced the product into the market has already captured a fair share, and you will be in the position of trying to take away that share.

2. *Inventor shows.* Many inventors are not good marketers. In fact, most inventions that are patented are never actually produced in quantity. At inventor shows you will have the opportunity to see hundreds of new products that the inventors would like to license for someone else to manufacture and sell for a royalty; perhaps they would like to sell the invention outright. You can find the inventor shows in your area by contacting your local chamber of commerce. Or, you can write to the Office of Inventions and Innovations, National Bureau of Standards, Washington, D.C. 20234, for a listing of the major inventor shows throughout the United States.

3. *Foreign products.* Foreign products are not always available in the United States, and frequently these products which are unfamiliar here may be outstanding and sell quite well. Also, every country would like to see the number of its exports increased. This points to one primary source of foreign products: the commercial attachés of foreign consulates and embassies. You can find the numbers of foreign consulates or embassies in your telephone book if you happen to live in or near a large city. If you do not live close enough to these offices to make calling feasible, get a copy of the *International Commerce Magazine Weekly,* published by the U.S. Department of Commerce. This magazine contains a license opportunity section in which many foreign-made products available for licensing in the United States are listed. To get a copy, contact the Department of Commerce's local field office which you will find in your telephone book. There are other books available that will help you if you are looking for products which you want to import. One is the *American Register of Exporters and Importers,* published by the American Register of Exporters and Importers Corp., 38 Park Row, New York, N.Y. 10038. Another is the *Directory of New York Importers,* published by Commerce Industry Association Institute, Inc., 65 Liberty St., New York, N.Y. 10005. Also, in your local library, you will find at least one directory of importers and exporters published annually for almost every country in the world. Check in the reference or business section of your library. There are also overseas trade publications which will help you. Some that are excellent sources of new product ideas are:

Hong Kong Enterprise, 3rd floor, Connaught Center, Connaught Road Central, Hong Kong.

Made In Europe, P.O. Box 174027, D-6, Frankfurt Am Main, West Germany.

Canada Commerce, Department of Industry, Trade and Commerce, Ottowa, Ontario, Canada K1A0H5.

Commerce in France at the Chamber, 21 Avenue George V, Paris 8E France.

Other foreign trade magazines can be found in your local library and will contain many additional products for you to manufacture or sell. Write to each and ask for a sample of the magazine.

4. *Newspapers.*   Read the business opportunity section of your local paper as well as such publications as the *Wall Street Journal.* Very frequently individuals who have a product to sell will advertise. You can contact them to negotiate the best deal possible for a product that may be very successful. In addition, you may consider advertising in these publications yourself, or in trade magazines, stating that you are interested in acquiring certain types of new products.

5. *Local manufacturers.*   Many manufacturers have created a product at one time or another that was not successful for his or her particular line of work or business, but which you may be able to make very successful. Simply call the president of each company and ask whether any old tooling exists for discontinued products from your line. Sometimes you can buy this tooling very cheaply, for perhaps only a couple hundred dollars, even though it may be worth $40,000 or more. This is one of Joe Cossman's secrets which helped to make him a multimillionaire. He frequently purchased old tooling from manufacturers, turned the product around, and made a fortune with it. Among the products acquired in this way were his famous Potato Spud Gun and Flippy the Frogman, both toy products which sold in the millions.

6. *NASA's Tech Briefs.*   These bulletins are published periodically by the National Aviation and Space Administration. They describe new ideas, concepts, and patents for new products, all by-products of the space program. All of these are available for licensing from NASA. To get a copy of NASA's *Tech Briefs,* write to National Technical Information Service, U.S. Department of Commerce, Springfield, Va. 22151.

7. *Patent Abstracts Bibliography.*   This semiannual publication lists NASA- and government-owned patents and applications for patents as a service to those seeking new licensable products for the commercial market. This may be ordered from the address above.

8. *New products from corporations.*   You can write or contact major U.S. corporations. Most have research and development divisions which develop products the corporation has no interest in producing or selling. As a result, many have established special offices to market the licensing of their patents to individuals outside of their company. The titles of these individuals vary; however, you can usually get in touch with them by contacting any corporation which is large enough to have a research and development division and asking for the director of patent licensing.

9. *Distress merchandise.*   Every retailer has been in a situation where certain merchandise could not be sold. Under these circumstances, he cuts the price tremendously and then attempts to sell it at bargain rates. This material is called distress merchandise. When you see distress merchandise, if you think that you have a market for it, look at the product and see if there is a patent number on it. If there is, you can locate the inventor by purchasing a copy of the patent from the patent office. Or, if you live close to a depository for patents, you can look at the patent and find out the inventor's name and address at no cost at all. As I mentioned earlier, inventors are frequently poor marketers, and the fact that this is distress merchandise indicates that if the inventor still controls the patent, he or she may well be interested in licensing or outright sale. The address to write is U.S. Patent Office, Washington, D.C. 20231.

10. *The Official Gazette of the U.S. Patent Office.* This bulletin is published weekly and lists all the patents granted by the patent office. Annual subscriptions are available from the Superintendent of Documents, Government Printing Office, Washington, D.C. 20402. The gazette contains a section that lists one-time-only patents available for sale or licensing. Many libraries also subscribe to the *Official Gazette* of the U.S. Patent Office. Patent attorneys in your area also may know of new products recently patented and available for licensing.

11. *Expired patents.* In the United States, a patent is good for only 17 years. The only exception is an ornamental design patent which is good for 3½, 7, or 14 years. After that period, the patent is in the public domain and may be produced and sold by anyone. Also, you can look at the entire technology of any general product area by writing the patent office and asking for a list of all the patent numbers falling into a specified product area. The patent office will charge you for this service, but once you have the list of numbers you can go to a federal depository of patents which is usually located in a major library. All you need to do then is look up the patent number and you can get the full information. If the patent on the invention has expired, you are free to do with it as you want. If it has not expired, you may approach the inventor, getting his name and address from the patent, about licensing or purchasing the idea outright.

12. *Trade shows.* Like inventor shows, trade shows will have hundreds of products, some of which will be outstanding for your particular purposes. To find out about trade shows, get a copy of the *Directory of the United States Trade Shows, Expositions and Conventions.* Write to the United States Travel Service, U.S. Department of Commerce, Washington, D.C. 20230. Or, you may ask your local chamber of commerce about upcoming trade shows. Also, see Chapter 17.

13. *Old items from magazines.* If you look through an old Sears or Montgomery Ward catalog, you will notice how many of the products described therein are still of tremendous interest. You can also get good ideas from old magazines. Old mail order products are especially well suited for reissue. An afternoon spent in the library looking at old magazines may give you an idea which you may use as is or one to which you can give a new twist.

14. *Personalizing items.* People like to see items and like to buy items that have their names on them. This idea has been used again and again, every single day, to sell products of all sorts, from brass business card cases sold through the *Wall Street Journal* to briefcases, wallets, address labels, and paperweights. Do some research, because the field is far from exhausted. If you can find a product on which you can imprint someone's name, you probably have a winner.

15. *Commercial banks.* If you acquire all or part of another business, you may also acquire the products which that business controls. Many small companies will find outstanding products that may need the strength that your company can provide to become successful. This strength may have to do with personnel, facilities, equipment, know-how, marketing, or capital. Frequently, commercial banks will know of such a situation and can arrange the meeting between you and someone with a product that you might be interested in. The bank does this for no charge with the expectation of receiving banking business which might ensue from some sort of an arrangement.

16. *Small Business Investment Companies (SBICs) and investment bankers.* These companies are continually examining potential businesses, all of which have products of one sort or another. If you contact SBICs and investment bankers, they might well lead you to new products or an equity position in a business that has products which are desirable for your firm. You can obtain a list of SBICs from your local SBA office as well as from Appendix IV of this book.

17. *Licensing brokers.* A licensing broker is a type of consultant having a wide range of contacts in the licensing field. They represent companies seeking licenses, that is, companies with products that they wish to license, as well as companies searching for products to license. They often have considerable experience in developing fair and reasonable licensing arrangements and can advise you or their client along these lines. You can locate licensing brokers through patent attorneys, in your local telephone book, and sometimes in your local newspapers under the Business Opportunities heading.

18. *The Thomas Register of Manufacturers.* This publication consists of several volumes listing manufacturers of all types of items in the United States. There are several such directories, and you can find them at your local library. You will find not only the names and addresses of the individuals running these companies, but also products that are available and the individuals to write about obtaining them. Every single page is a source of another potential product for your business.

HOW TO DECIDE WHICH NEW PRODUCT TO DEVELOP OR INTRODUCE

As you begin thinking about new product introduction and development, you will discover that there are many products among which to choose. Of course you can't develop them all; the problem then is deciding which products are best for your company. You may think that this will be fairly easy; you simply introduce those products that will bring you the most profit. However, the choice is *not* easy. You may have limited financial resources and a more profitable product will have to be passed over in favor of one that you can afford. Or, it may be important to you to recoup your investment rapidly. Then, too, you must consider the particular background and experience you have, either with the type of product or with marketplaces. Here are 10 different questions which Alan A. Smith recommends that you ask yourself about each product you are considering.

1. Is the product one which fits the company's needs, interests and abilities?
2. Is the chance of success good within the limits of reasonable time and expenditure?
3. Are the people connected with the project capable of carrying it to completion or can suitable people be hired?
4. Will a successfully completed project result in
   (a) New products?
   (b) Improved products?
   (c) Reduced cost

5. Is there a market for the new or improved product?

6. Is the market substantial and profitable?

7. Can the present marketing organization really sell the product?

8. Will the product expand the base of operations of the company?

9. Will the product fill a real need or will it be only a momentary fad?

10. Can the product be made with the present equipment? If not, can the estimated cost of tooling up be covered by increased sales?

These questions will help you screen out many products which will clearly be unsuited to your company or your particular situation.

Other factors which you must consider in comparing potential new products for development and for which you must obtain factual information or forecasts include the following:

Total profit

Profitability

The cost to develop

The market for the product

The life cycle, including estimated length

The cost of research and development

The plant overcapacity or undercapacity

The synergistic effect with other products in your product line

The cost of putting the product on the market

Technical know-how required

Labor skills required

Availability of raw materials

By-products that may be sold from the manufacture of this product

Good will

Marketing know-how available

Physical distribution facilities

Available distribution channels

You can see that deciding which product to introduce is no five-minute task, but the effort is worthwhile. You want the product you select to be a success.

Now, we are getting down to the serious assessment of the wisdom of spending money for one project over another. The end result is which potential products you will introduce and which you will not. First, list what factors you will use for comparison, those which you think are most important: high return on investment, a proprietary position, a large market share, low risk of failure in development, low risk of failure in marketing, huge demand, and so forth. Certain quantitative methods of comparison are also recommended. For example, you can calculate the total profit of a particular project if you can estimate its life cycle by using either the present value or internal rate of return methods shown you for comparison in Chapter 8. You can compare the return for each investment, for each project, by dividing the projected return by the investment and choosing those projects which have the larger return. If time to recoup your investment is important, compare using the pay-back formula, investment divided by the return per year. All of these various quantitative and nonquantitative comparisons are placed on a rating sheet as shown in Figure 19.1.

FIGURE 19-1   RELEVANT FACTORS FOR SELECTING NEW PRODUCTS
                              FOR INTRODUCTION

RELEVANT FACTOR	RELATIVE FACTOR WEIGHTING
DEMAND FOR PRODUCT	
1. Strength	3%
2. Period	3
3. Need	4
MARKET	
1. Size	6
2. Location	5
3. Competition	5
PRODUCT	
1. Compatibility with current line	1
2. Uniqueness of features	8
3. Price	4
4. Protection	3
COMPANY STRENGTHS	
1. Marketing	6
2. Location	2
3. Special facilities	4
4. Production	2
FINANCIAL CONSIDERATIONS	
1. Capital budgeting	8
2. ROI	8
3. Pay-back	8
4. Cash flow	8
PRODUCT DEVELOPMENT	
1. Technical risk	5
2. Producibility	4
3. Scheduling	3
TOTAL	100 %

Figure 19.1. Relevant factors for selecting new products for introduction.

Now, you must determine factor weighting. You do this by taking your list of important factors and deciding which of these factors are more important than others. Let us say that you have four factors which you consider to be of equal importance. These four factors may be technical know-how, profitability, product synergism with other products in your product line, and marketing know-how. If these are your only factors and you consider them to be of equal importance, each would be assigned a weighting of 25%. However, if this is not the case, then the importance of the factors to you will be indicated by the percentages. Let's say that you consider profitability the main item, far and away the most important of the four factors. Perhaps you will assign it 50%. This then leaves 50% to be apportioned among the other three factors. You might assign 10% to technical know-how, 20% to product synergism, and 20% to marketing know-how. In all cases, the total percentages assigned to all the different factors that you have listed should equal exactly 100%.

Now, look at each product you are considering and assign points to the project for each factor that you have listed. The points assigned are from 1 to 10. Those products that seem very good in relation to a particular factor receive 10 points. Those that are very poor receive only 1 point. For example, consider technical know-how. If you have the technical know-how to develop a particular product easily, give it a 10-point rating. On the other hand, if you do not have the technical know-how to develop a certain product, you may give it a very low point score, perhaps only 1 or 2 points.

Factor	Relative Weight	Point Value	Final Value
Demand for product			
Strength	0.03	7	0.21
Period	0.03	3	0.09
Need	0.04	1	0.04
Market			
Size	0.06	4	0.24
Location	0.05	2	0.10
Competition	0.05	7	0.35
Product			
Compatibility with current line	0.01	6	0.06
Uniqueness of features	0.08	2	0.16
Price	0.04	1	0.04
Protection	0.03	1	0.03
Company Strengths			
Marketing	0.06	2	0.12
Location	0.02	8	0.16
Special facilities	0.04	1	0.04
Production	0.02	1	0.02
Financial Considerations			
Capital budgeting	0.08	5	0.40
ROI	0.08	4	0.32
Pay-back	0.08	3	0.24
Cash flow	0.08	2	0.16
Product Development			
Technical risk	0.05	1	0.05
Producibility	0.04	7	0.28
Scheduling	0.03	2	0.06
	1.00	Total point value for this product	3.17

Figure 19.2. New product selection matrix (analysis for a simulated product).

Now that you have completed the point assignments, you must multiply the weighting percentage by the points assigned. The result (shown in Figure 19.2) is a total point rating for each project. Now, you simply pick those projects with the highest ratings. These are the ones you will introduce.

HOW TO BEAT YOUR COMPETITION IN NEW PRODUCT INTRODUCTION AND DEVELOPMENT

You may feel that because you are a small firm you have little or no chance to beat your larger competitors, especially in introducing a new product or a new service. This is wrong, and very frequently a small firm can win out over its competition. Here's how.

Ability to Make Decisions Fast

A small company, where one man or a few men make decisions, has an extremely big advantage in terms of time. Larger companies act slowly, because of a bureaucracy and many levels in the managerial chain of command, when making even simple decisions, while you can operate much more rapidly and efficiently. It is not unusual for a small firm to make a decision in one day that would take a large firm several months or even a year or more to make.

Lower Break-Even Point

Because a smaller firm carries a much lower overhead, the break-even point for your introduction of a new product or a new service will be much lower than that of a larger firm. Also, because as a smaller firm you can be more efficient, your break-even point can be lower than that of a larger competitor. As a result of this, many large firms cannot introduce certain new products or services unless the volume is sufficiently large. On the other hand, you are able to introduce products or services to service a smaller market. A volume that is tremendously profitable for you may be unprofitable for a larger company.

Regional Sales

For the same reason as above, many small firms can serve a specific region in their locality and provide much better customer service and a far more effective and efficient promotional effort than can their larger competitors. This is the reason that many local areas have their own brands of beer and other commodities. Further, in this local area, the small company frequently outsells the larger competitor many times over.

Custom-Made Quality Products

Large firms, because of their volume requirements, frequently cannot do custom work. And for the same reason, quality sometimes suffers. This leaves a nice niche for the smaller company that can do custom work with individuals or other companies that desire this type of product or service. Because of this, some small companies absolutely monopolize the custom-made quality markets in their industries. They charge high prices and make huge profit margins because they have developed this market, a market their bigger competitors cannot reach.

SOURCES OF HELP IN DEVELOPING AND INTRODUCING NEW PRODUCTS

Much of the work necessary in order to introduce a new product or service can be purchased by you, and other help can be obtained at no cost or very little cost. Here are some sources that will help you with your development and introduction of new products.

Management and Marketing Consultants

Management and marketing consultants exist which perform a wide range of services for you in the development and introduction of a new product. These services include evaluating potential sales, creating a marketing plan, setting up pricing, locating executives to run your programs, investigating material costs and sources, checking out competitive problems with which the new product will be faced, budgets, developing financial schedules, and other tasks.

Industrial Designers and Engineers

These individuals will help you to design the new product, help you make it more efficient, or allow you to produce it cheaper. They can improve the physical appearance of the product, making old products look new and visually appealing.

They can redesign products, correct product defects, reduce noise vibration, reduce weight and bulk, eliminate hazards, reduce the number of parts, solve engineering problems, suggest new materials, and do many other similar types of work.

Patent Attorneys and Agents

Patent attorneys and agents can help you make patent searches and applications and help you with related patent, copyright, and trademark work.

Package Designers

Package designers will design the packaging of your product, including developing trademarks or logos, designing containers to hold the product, recommending sizes and shapes of packages, bottles, and enclosures, designing merchandise tags, advising on label requirements levied by city, state, or federal government, conducting drop tests for packaging, and so forth.

Advertising Agencies

Advertising agencies can handle your entire promotional effort, including writing copy, preparing graphics, suggesting other means of promotion, and suggesting which medium and vehicle to choose for your ad.

Marketing Research Firms

Marketing research firms can help you decide what new products to introduce. They offer preliminary consumer research, preliminary industrial research, exploratory research, and other means of determining whether it makes sense to introduce a new product at all.

All of the commercial firms above can be located either through the yellow pages under the appropriate headings or through engineering, marketing, or consultant trade associations. Before engaging any firm, it is wise to check their references; talk to at least three firms who have used their services. And you might also check with their trade association and with your local Better Business Bureau. Remember that this book shows you how to do many of these services yourself, if you desire, at a much reduced cost.

Noncommercial Sources

Some universities have centers funded by the National Science Foundation for helping inventors and innovators with their new product development and introduction into the marketplace. One of the better ones is the University of Oregon's Experimental Center for the Advancement of Invention and Innovation. Much of the information that the University of Oregon has is computerized. This allows the university to evaluate any new product idea on 33 different criteria and help you screen out bad ideas. Each submitted idea is evaluated against the following criteria: legality, safety, environmental impact, societal impact, potential market, product life cycle, usage for learning, product visibility, service, durability, new competition, functional feasibility, production feasibility, development status, investment cost, trend of demand, product line potential, need, promotion, appearance, price, protection, pay-back period, profitability, product interdependence, research and development, stability of demand, consumer, user compatibility, marketing research, distribution, perceived function, existing competition, and potential sales. The address is: Experimental Center for the Advancement of Invention and Innovation, College of Business Administration, 131 Gilbert Hall, University of Oregon, Eugene, Ore. 97403.

The Small Business Institute (SBI) is sponsored by the Small Business Administration and currently is located at 450 colleges and universities around the country. The help provided by the SBI is usually concerned with the business part of new product introduction, including marketing, finances, accounting, management problems, and so forth. Business students of the university supervised by professors provide this service to you free of charge. Contact your local Small Business Administration to learn more. The addresses of the SBA are listed in Appendix II.

The following two organizations may also be of assistance to you with your new product development and introduction problems: (1) the American Association of Small Research Companies, 8794 West Chester Pike, Upper Darby, PA 19082, and (2) the Association for the Advancement of Invention and Innovation, Suite 605, 1735 Jefferson Davis Highway, Arlington, VA 22202.

CHAPTERS TO REREAD BEFORE CONSIDERING NEW PRODUCT DEVELOPMENT AND INTRODUCTION

Several chapters in this book are critical to new product introduction or development. Please reread them before beginning work on your new product or service. They are: Chapter 7, "Protecting Your Idea"; Chapter 4, "Business Planning"; Chapter 15, "Marketing Research"; and Chapter 14, "Advertising and Public Relations."

TWENTY-ONE WARNING SIGNALS

Peter Hilton, founder of the New Product Institute and the president of Kastor, Hilton, Chesley, Clifford and Atherton, Inc., an advertising agency in New York, has documented 21 warning signals from the consumer, the trade, or company management that something is wrong with new product or new service introduction.[2] Action should be taken as soon as possible to correct the problem. If any of these occur as you begin new product introduction or development, stop, heed, and take the required action.

From the consumer:

1. The price is too high.
2. I don't know how to use it—I must be educated.
3. Certainly it's a better product, but it's not quite worth the extra money.

From the trade:

4. The product will have a low rate of turnover.
5. The product will disturb our business on established items, maybe destroy more business than it creates.

[2] Peter Hilton, *New Product Introduction*, Small Business Administration (1961).

6. We are afraid of the servicing problems this new item may create.

7. The product is an unwanted addition to a field already crowded.

8. There is no retail shelf space or floor space available for this product.

9. The nature of the product is such that it must be sold in an odd size or shape ill suited to shipping or display facilities.

10. This product cannot be sold without individual demonstration.

From company management:

11. It is difficult to procure or procure consistently the right raw materials for this product.

12. It is difficult to project costs because the raw material market is subject to considerable price fluctuation.

13. Plant production would be seriously hampered if changes were made to handle the manufacture of this new product.

14. The product is good but impossible to package.

15. The patent situation is confused and we would be vulnerable.

16. The probably channel of distribution of this new product is not clearly defined.

17. To make salesmen's time available for this product would jeopardize our established line.

18. The new product does not hold promise of sufficient volume or frequency of purchase to maintain distribution.

19. The trademark situation is unsatisfactory.

20. Certain government regulations would make marketing of this product difficult.

21. With this product we would be competing in a field dominated by strong, aggressive companies with superior marketing resources.

SOURCES OF ADDITIONAL INFORMATION

Corporate Strategy and New Product Innovation, edited by Robert R. Rothberg, published by The Free Press, a division of MacMillan Publishing Co., Inc., 866 Third Ave., New York, N.Y. 10022.

Handbook of New Product Development, by Peter Hilton, published by Prentice-Hall, Inc., Englewood Cliffs, N.J. 07632.

New Product Introduction for Small Business Owners, by Peter Hilton, published by the Small Business Administration, Washington, D.C. 20402.

New Products, New Profits, edited by Elibeth Marting, published by the American Management Association, 135 West 50th St., New York, N.Y. 10020.

Planning New Products, by Philip Marvin, published by The Penton Publishing Co., Cleveland, Ohio 44101.

Product Planning, edited by A. Edward Spitz, published by Auerbach Publishers, 121 North Broad St., Philadelphia, Pa. 19107.

Technology and Your New Products, by Alan A. Smith, published by the Small Business Administration, Washington, D.C. 20402.

Appendix I

Department of Commerce Addresses

U.S. DEPARTMENT OF COMMERCE DISTRICT OFFICE DIRECTORY

Industry and Trade Administration[1]

ALABAMA

Birmingham—Gayle C. Shelton, Jr., Director, Suite 200-201, 908 South 20th Street, 35205, Area Code 205 Tel 254-1331

ALASKA

Anchorage—Sara L. Haslett, Director, 412 Hill Building, 632 Sixth Avenue 99501, Area Code 907 Tel 265-5307

ARIZONA

Phoenix—Donald W. Fry, Director, Suite 2950 Valley Bank Center, 201 North Central Avenue 85073, Area Code 602 Tel 261-3285

ARKANSAS

Little Rock **(Dallas, Texas District)**—1100 North University, Suite 109 72207, Area Code 501 Tel 378-5157

CALIFORNIA

Los Angeles—Eric C. Silberstein, Director, Room 800, 11777 San Vincente Boulevard 90049, Area Code 213 Tel 824-7591

San Diego[1]—233 A Street, Suite 310 92101, Area Code 714 Tel 293-5395

San Francisco—Philip M. Creighton, Director, Federal Building, Box 36013, 450 Golden Gate Avenue 94102, Area Code 415 Tel 556-5860

COLORADO

Denver—Norman Lawson, Director, Room 165, New Customhouse, 19th & Stout Street 80202, Area Code 303 Tel 837-3246

CONNECTICUT

Hartford—Richard C. Kilbourn, Director, Room 610-B, Federal Office Building, 450 Main Street 06103, Area Code 203 Tel 244-3530

[1] Denotes trade specialist

FLORIDA

Miami—Roger J. LaRoche, Director, Room 821, City National Bank Building, 25 West Flagler Street 33130, Area Code 305 Tel 350-5267

Clearwater[1]—128 North Osceola Avenue 33515, Area Code 813 Tel 446-4081

Jacksonville[1]—815 S. Main Street, Suite 100, 32207, Area Code 904 Tel 791-2796

Tallahassee[1]—Collins Bldg., Rm. G-20 32304, Area Code 904 Tel 488-6469

GEORGIA

Atlanta—David S. Williamson, Director, Suite 600, 1365 Peachtree Street, N.E. 30309, Area Code 404 Tel 881-7000

Savannah—James W. McIntire, Director, 222 U.S. Courthouse & P.O. Box 9746, 125-29 Bull Street 31402, Area Code 912 Tel 232-4321

HAWAII

Honolulu—John S. Davies, Director, 4106 Federal Building, P.O. Box 50026, 300 Ala Moana Boulevard, 96850, Area Code 808 Tel 546-8694

ILLINOIS

Chicago—Gerald M. Marks, Director, 1406 Mid Continental Plaza Building, 55 East Monroe Street 60603, Area Code 312 Tel 353-4450

INDIANA

Indianapolis—Mel R. Sherar, Director, 357 U.S. Courthouse & Federal Office Building, 46 East Ohio Street 46204, Area Code 317 Tel 269-6214

IOWA

Des Moines—Jesse N. Durden, Director, 817 Federal Building, 210 Walnut Street 50309, Area Code 515 Tel 284-4222

KENTUCKY

Frankfort **(Memphis, Tennessee District)**[1]—Capitol Plaza Office Tower, Room 2425, 40601, Area Code 502 Tel 875-4421

LOUISIANA

New Orleans—Edwin A. Leland, Jr., Director, 432 International Trade Mart, No. 2 Canal Street 70130, Area Code 504 Tel 589-6546

MAINE

Portland **(Boston, Massachusetts District)**[1]—Maine State Pier, 40 Commercial Street 04111, Area Code 207 Tel 773-5608

MARYLAND

Baltimore—Carroll F. Hopkins, Director, 415 U.S. Customhouse, Gay and Lombard Streets, 21202, Area Code 301 Tel 962-3560

MASSACHUSETTS

Boston—Francis J. O'Connor, Director, 10th Floor, 441 Stuart Street 02116, Area Code 617 Tel 223-2312

MICHIGAN

Detroit—William L. Welch, Director, 445 Federal Building, 231 West Lafayette 48226, Area Code 313 Tel 226-3650

Grand Rapids[1]—350 Ottawa Street N.W. 49503, Area Code 616 Tel 456-2411/33

MINNESOTA

Minneapolis—Glenn A. Matson, Director, 218 Federal Building, 110 South Fourth Street 55401
Area Code 612 Tel 725-2133

MISSISSIPPI

Jackson (Birmingham, Alabama District)[1]—P.O. Box 849, 1202 Walter Sillers Building 39205,
Area Code 601 Tel 969-4388

MISSOURI

St. Louis—Donald R. Loso, Director, 120 South Central Avenue 63105, Area Code 314 Tel 425-
3302-4

Kansas City[1]—Room 1840, 601 East 12th Street 64106, Area Code 816 Tel 374-3142

MONTANA

Butte (Cheyenne, Wyoming District)[1]—225 S. Idaho Street, Room 101 P.O. Box 3809, 59701, Area
Code 406 Tel 723-6561, Ext. 2317

NEBRASKA

Omaha—George H. Payne, Director, Capitol Plaza, Suite 703A, 1815 Capitol Avenue 68102, Area
Code 402 Tel 221-3665

NEVADA

Reno—Joseph J. Jeremy, Director, 777 W. 2nd Street, Room 120, 89503, Area Code 702 Tel 784-
5203

NEW JERSEY

Newark—Clifford R. Lincoln, Director, 4th Floor, Gateway Building, Market Street & Penn Plaza
07102, Area Code 201 Tel 645-6214

NEW MEXICO

Albuquerque—William E. Dwyer, Director, 505 Marquette Ave., NW, Suite 1015, 87102, Area
Code 505 Tel 766-2386

NEW YORK

Buffalo—Robert F. Magee, Director, 1312 Federal Building, 111 West Huron Street 14202, Area
Code 716 Tel 846-4191

New York—Arthur C. Rutzen, Director, Room 3718, Federal Office Building, 26 Federal Plaza,
Foley Square 10007, Area Code 212 Tel 264-0634

NORTH CAROLINA

Greensboro—Joel B. New, Director, 203 Federal Building, West Market Street, P.O. Box 1950
27402, Area Code 919 Tel 378-5345

OHIO

Cincinnati—Gordon B. Thomas, Director, 10504 Federal Office Building, 550 Main Street, 45202,
Area Code 513 Tel 684-2944

Cleveland—Charles B. Stebbins, Director, Room 600, 666 Euclid Avenue 44114, Area Code 216
Tel 522-4750

OKLAHOMA

Oklahoma City (Dallas, Texas District)[1]—4020 Lincoln Boulevard 73105, Area Code 405 Tel 231-
5302

OREGON

Portland—Lloyd R. Porter, Director, Room 618, 1220 S.W. 3rd Avenue 97204, Area Code 503 Tel 221-3001

PENNSYLVANIA

Philadelphia—Patric P. McCabe, Director, 9448 Federal Building, 600 Arch Street 19106, Area Code 215 Tel 597-2850

Pittsburgh—William M. Bradley, Trade Specialist-in-Charge, 2002 Federal Building, 1000 Liberty Avenue 15222, Area Code 412 Tel 644-2850

PUERTO RICO

San Juan (Hato Rey)—Enrique Vilella, Director, Room 659 Federal Building 00918, Area Code 809 Tel 753-4555, Ext. 555

RHODE ISLAND

Providence (Boston, Massachusetts District)—1 Weybossett Hill 02903, Area Code 401 Tel 277-2605, Ext. 22

SOUTH CAROLINA

Columbia—Philip A. Ouzts, Director, 2611 Forest Drive, Forest Center 29204, Area Code 803 Tel 765-5345

Charleston[1]—Suite 631, Federal Building, 334 Meeting Street 29403, Area Code 803 Tel 577-4361

TENNESSEE

Memphis—Bradford H. Rice, Director, Room 710, 147 Jefferson Avenue 38103, Area Code 901 Tel 521-3213

Nashville[1]—4014 Aberdeen Road, 37216, Area Code 615 Tel 297-5233

TEXAS

Dallas—C. Carmon Stiles, Director, Room 7A5, 1100 Commerce Street 75242 Area Code 214 Tel 749-1515

Houston—Felicito C. Guerrero, Director, 2625 Federal Bldg., Courthouse, 515 Rusk Street 77002, Area Code 713 Tel 226-45231

San Antonio[1]—University of Texas at San Antonio, Div. of Continuing Education 78285, Area Code 512 Tel 229-5875

UTAH

Salt Lake City—George M. Blessing, Jr., Director, 1203 Federal Building 125 South State Street 84138, Area Code 801 Tel 524-5116

VIRGINIA

Richmond—8010 Federal Building, 400 North 8th Street 23240, Area Code 804 Tel 782-2246

Fairfax[1]—8550 Arlington Blvd., 22031, Area Code 703 Tel 560-6460

WASHINGTON

Seattle—Judson S. Wonderly, Director, Room 706, Lake Union Building, 1700 Westlake Avenue North 98109, Area Code 206 Tel 442-5615

WEST VIRGINIA

Charleston—Roger L. Fortner, Director, 3000 New Federal Building, 500 Quarrier Street 25301, Area Code 304 Tel 343-6181, Ext. 375

WISCONSIN

Milwaukee—Russell H. Leitch, Director, Federal Bldg/U.S. Courthouse, 517 East Wisconsin Avenue 53202, Area Code 414 Tel 291-3473

WYOMING

Cheyenne—Lowell O. Burns, Director, 6022 O'Mahoney Federal Center, 2120 Capitol Avenue 82001, Area Code 307 Tel 778-2220, Ext. 2151

Appendix II

OMBE Regional Offices

Charles McMillan
Regional Director
Office of Minority Business Enterprise
U.S. Department of Commerce
1371 Peachtree Street, NE, Suite 505
Atlanta, Georgia 30309
404/881-5091

Henry Zuniga
Regional Director
Office of Minority Business Enterprise
U.S. Department of Commerce
1412 Main Street, Room 1702
Dallas, Texas 75202
214/749-7581

Ramon V. Romero
Regional Director
Office of Minority Business Enterprise
U.S. Department of Commerce
Federal Building, Room 15045
450 Golden Gate Avenue
San Francisco, California 94102
415/556-7234

Daniel V. Lemanski
Regional Director
Office of Minority Business Enterprise
U.S. Department of Commerce
55 East Monroe Street, Suite 1438
Chicago, Illinois 60603
312/353-8375

Newton S. Downing
Regional Director
Office of Minority Business Enterprise
U.S. Department of Commerce
Federal Office Building
26 Federal Plaza, Room 1307
New York, New York 10007
212/264-3262

Luis Encinias
Acting Regional Director
Office of Minority Business Enterprise
U.S. Department of Commerce
1730 K Street, NW Suite 420
Washington, D.C. 20006
202/634-7897

Appendix III

SBA Field Office Addresses

New England (Region 1)

Boston	Massachusetts 02114, 150 Causeway Street, 617/223-2100
Holyoke	Massachusetts 01050, 302 High Street, 413/536-8770
Augusta	Maine 04330, 40 Western Avenue, Room 512, 207/622-6171
Concord	New Hampshire 03301, 55 Pleasant Street, 603/224-4041
Hartford	Connecticut 06103, One Financial Plaza, 203/244-3600
Montpelier	Vermont 05602, 87 State Street, P.O. Box 605, 802/229-0538
Providence	Rhode Island 02903, 40 Fountain Street, 401/528-4586

Eastern (Region 2)

New York	New York 10007, 26 Federal Plaza, Room 3100, 212/264-4355
Albany	New York 12210, 99 Washington Avenue, 518/472-6300
Elmira	New York 14901, 180 State Street, Room 412, 607/734-4686
Hato Rey	Puerto Rico 00919, Chardon and Bolivia Streets, 809/753-4572
Melville	New York 11746, 425 Broad Hollow Road, 516/752-1626
Newark	New Jersey 07102, 970 Broad Street, Room 1635, 201/645-2434
Camden	New Jersey 08104, 1800 East Davis Street, 609/757-5183
Rochester	New York 14014, 100 State Street, 716/263-6700
Syracuse	New York 13260, 100 South Clinton Street, Room 1071, 315/423-5383
Buffalo	New York 14202, 111 West Huron Street, 716/846-4301
St. Thomas	Virgin Islands 00801, Federal Office Building, Veterans' Drive, 809/774-8530

Mid-Atlantic (Region 3)

Philadelphia	Bala Cynwyd, Pennsylvania 19004, One Bala Cynwyd Plaza, 215/596-3311
Harrisburg	Pennsylvania 17101, 100 Chestnut Street, 717/782-3840
Wilkes Barre	Pennsylvania 18702, 20 North Pennsylvania Avenue, 717/826-6497
Baltimore	Towson, Maryland 21204, 8600 La Salle Road, 301/962-4392
Wilmington	Delaware 19801, 844 King Street, 302/573-6294
Clarksburg	West Virginia 26301, 109 N. 3rd Street, 304/623-5631
Charleston	West Virginia 25301, Charleston National Plaza, Suite 628, 304/343-6181
Pittsburgh	Pennsylvania 15222, 1000 Liberty Avenue, 412/644-2780
Richmond	Virginia 23240, 400 N. 8th Street, Room 3015, 804/771-2617
Washington	D.C. 20417, 1030 15th Street, N.W., Suite 250, 202/653-6965

Southeast (Region 4)

Atlanta	Georgia 30309, 1720 Peachtree Road, N.W., 404/881-4325
Biloxi	Mississippi 39530, 111 Fred Haise Boulevard, 601/435-3676
Birmingham	Alabama 35205, 908 South 20th Street, 213/688-2956
Charlotte	North Carolina 28202, 230 South Tryon Street, Suite 700, 704/371-6111
Greenville	North Carolina 27834, 215 South Evans Street, 919/752-3798
Columbia	South Carolina 29201, 1801 Assembly Street, 803/765-5376
Coral Gables	Florida 33134, 2222 Ponce de Leon Boulevard, 305/350-5521
Jackson	Mississippi 39201, 100 West Capitol Street, 601/969-4371
Jacksonville	Florida 32202, 400 W. Bay Street, 904/791-3782
West Palm Beach	Florida 33402, 701 Clematis Street, 305/659-7533
Tampa	Florida 33602, 700 Twiggs Street, 813/228-2594
Louisville	Kentucky 40202, 600 Federal Place, Room 188, 502/582-5971
Nashville	Tennessee 37219, 404 James Robertson Parkway, Suite 1012, 615/251-5881
Knoxville	Tennessee 37902, 502 South Gay Street, Room 307, 615/637-930
Memphis	Tennessee 38103, 167 North Main Street, 901/521-3588

Great Lakes (Region 5)

Chicago	Illinois 60604, 219 South Dearborn Street, 312/353-4528
Springfield	Illinois 62701, 1 North Old State Capitol Plaza, 217/525-4416
Cleveland	Ohio 44199, 1240 East 9th Street, Room 317, 216/522-4180
Columbus	Ohio 43215, 85 Marconi Boulevard, 614/469-6860
Cincinnati	Ohio 45202, 550 Main Street, Room 5028, 513/684-2814
Detroit	Michigan 48226, 477 Michigan Avenue, 313/266-6000
Marquette	Michigan 49885, 540 West Kaye Avenue, 906/225-1108
Indianapolis	Indiana 46204, 575 North Pennsylvania Street, 317/269-7272
Madison	Wisconsin 53703, 122 West Washington Avenue, 608/264-5261
Milwaukee	Wisconsin 53202, 517 East Wisconsin Avenue, 414/291-3941
Eau Claire	Wisconsin 54701, 500 South Barstow Street, Room B9AA, 715/834-9012
Minneapolis	Minnesota 55402, 12 South Sixth Street, 612/725-2362

Southwest (Region 6)

Dallas	Texas 75242, 1100 Commerce Street, 214/767-0605
Albuquerque	New Mexico 87110, 5000 Marble Avenue, NE., 505/766-3430
Houston	Texas 77002, 1 Allen Center, 500 Dallas Street, 713/226-4341
Little Rock	Arkansas 72201, 611 Gaines Street, 507/378-5871
Lubbock	Texas 79401, 1205 Texas Avenue, 806/762-7466
El Paso	Texas 79902, 4100 Rio Bravo, Suite 300, 915/543-7586
Lower Rio Grande Valley	Harlington, Texas 78550, 222 East Van Buren, 512/423-4534
Corpus Christi	Texas 78408, 3105 Leopard Street, 512/888-3331
Marshall	Texas 75670, 100 South Washington Street, Room G12, 214/935-5257
New Orleans	Louisiana 70113, 1001 Howard Avenue, 504/589-6685
Shreveport	Louisiana 71101, 500 Fannin Street, 318/226-5196
Oklahoma City	Oklahoma 73102, 200 N.W. 5th Street, 405/231-4301
San Antonio	Texas 78206, 727 East Durango, Room A-513, 512/229-6250

Mid-Continent (Region 7)

Kansas City	Missouri 64106, 1150 Grand Avenue, 816/374-3416
Des Moines	Iowa 50309, 210 Walnut Street, 515/284-4422
Omaha	Nebraska 68102, Nineteenth and Farnam Streets, 402/221-4691
St. Louis	Missouri 63101, Mercantile Tower, Suite 2500, 314/425-4191
Wichita	Kansas 67202, 110 East Waterman Street, 316/267-6311

Rocky Mountain (Region 8)

Denver	Colorado 80202, 721 19th Street, 303/837-2607
Casper	Wyoming 82601, 100 East B Street, Room 4001, 307/265-5550
Fargo	North Dakota 58102, 657 2d Avenue, North, Room 218, 701/237-5771
Helena	Montana 59601, 301 South Park, 406/449-5381
Salt Lake City	Utah 84138, 125 South State Street, Room 2237, 801/524-5800
Rapid City	South Dakota 57701, 515 9th Street, 605/343-5074
Sioux Falls	South Dakota 57102, 8th and Main Avenue, 605/336-2980

Western (Region 9)

San Francisco	California 94105, 211 Main Street, 415/556-7487
Fresno	California 93712, 1229 N Street, 209/487-5189
Sacramento	California 95825, 2800 Cottage Way, 916/484-4726
Honolulu	Hawaii 96850, 300 Ala Moana, 808/546-8950
Agana	Guam 96910, Pacific Daily News Building, 671/477-8420
Los Angeles	California 90071, 350 South Figueroa Street, 213/688-2956
Las Vegas	Nevada 89101, 301 East Stewart, 702/385-6611
Reno	Nevada 89505, 50 South Virginia Street, 702/784-5268
Phoenix	Arizona 85012, 3030 North Central Avenue, 602/261-3611
San Diego	California 92188, 880 Front Street, 714/293-5440

Northwest (Region 10)

Seattle	Washington 98174, 915 Second Avenue, 206/442-5534
Anchorage	Alaska 99501, 1016 West Sixth Avenue, Suite 200, 907/271-4022
Fairbanks	Alaska 99701, 101 12th Avenue, 907/452-1951
Boise	Idaho 83701, 1005 Main Street, 208/334-1096
Portland	Oregon 97204, 1220 South West Third Avenue, 503/221-2682
Spokane	Washington 99120, Courthouse Bldg., Room 651, 509/456-5310

Appendix IV

Management Assistance Publications

Publications

SBA 115A

U.S. Small Business Administration
Office of Management Assistance

Free Management Assistance Publications

The **Management Aids (MAs)** and **Small Marketers' Aids (SBMs)** series titles are now combined into one series with one title—**Management Aids (MAs).** MAs recommend methods and techniques for handling management problems and business operations. The series is categorized into seven topic areas and numbered within each category. The conversion to new MA numbers is being done as aids are reprinted. Aids already converted are marked with an asterik.

To get copies of the listed publications, check the titles you want, fill in your name and address, and mail this order form to:

U.S. Small Business Administration　　or call toll free 800-433-7212 (Texas only call 800-792-8901).
P.O. Box 15434
Ft. Worth, Texas 76119

Notice: Five (5) copy limit per publication requested. Requests for *more than five (5)* copies of a publication must be sent to the SBA District Office nearest you. Please give the reason you need more than *Five (5)* copies.

Name _____
(Please Print or Type)

Street _____

City/State/Zip _____

Management Aids

Accounting, Financial Management and Analysis

New	Old	Title	New	Old	Title
_*_ MA 1.001	MA 170	The ABC's of Borrowing	_*_ MA 1.014	SMA 144	Getting the Facts for Income Tax Reporting
_*_ MA 1.002	MA 193	What Is the Best Selling Price?			
_*_ MA 1.003	MA 206	Keep Pointed Toward Profit	_*_ MA 1.015	SMA 146	Budgeting in a Small Business Firm
__ MA 1.004	MA 220	Basic Budgets for Profit Planning			
__ MA 1.005	MA 226	Pricing for Small Manufacturers	_*_ MA 1.016	SMA 147	Sound Cash Management and Borrowing
_*_ MA 1.006	MA 229	Cash Flow in a Small Plant			
_*_ MA 1.007	MA 232	Credit and Collections	_*_ MA 1.017	SMA 155	Keeping Records in Small Business
_*_ MA 1.008	MA 234	Attacking Business Decision Problems With Breakeven Analysis	_*_ MA 1.018	SMA 165	Check List for Profit Watching
			__ MA 1.019	SMA 166	Simple Breakeven Analysis for Small Stores
__ MA 1.009	MA 235	A Venture Capital Primer For Small Business			
			__ MA 1.020		Profit Pricing and Costing for Services
_*_ MA 1.010	SMA 126	Accounting Services For Small Service Firms			
__ MA 1.011	SMA 130	Analyze Your Records To Reduce Costs	*Planning*		
_*_ MA 1.012	SMA 140	Profit By Your Wholesalers' Services	_*_ MA 2.001	MA 189	Should You Make or Buy Components
_*_ MA 1.013	SMA 142	Steps in Meeting Your Tax Obligations	_*_ MA 2.002	MA 201	Locating or Relocating Your Business

474

New	Old	Title
* MA 2.003	MA 207	Pointers on Scheduling Production
* MA 2.004	MA 208	Problems in Managing a Family-Owned Business
__ MA 2.005	MA 212	The Equipment Replacement Decision
* MA 2.006	MA 216	Finding a New Product for Your Company
__ MA 2.007	MA 218	Business Plan for Small Manufacturers
* MA 2.008	MA 221	Business Plan for Small Construction Firms
__ MA 2.009	MA 222	Business Life Insurance
* MA 2.010	MA 233	Planning and Goal Setting for Small Business
__ MA 2.011	MA 242	Fixing Production Mistakes
* MA 2.012	MA 243	Setting Up a Quality Control System
__ MA 2.013	MA 248	Can You Make Money With Your Idea or Invention
* MA 2.014	MA 249	Can You Lease or Buy Equipment
* MA 2.015	MA 250	Can You Use a Minicomputer
__ MA 2.016	SMA 71	Check List for Going Into Business
__ MA 2.017	SMA 143	Factors in Considering a Shopping Center Location
* MA 2.018	SMA 148	Insurance Checklist for Small Business
* MA 2.019	SMA 149	Computers for Small Business–Service Bureau or Time Sharing
* MA 2.020	SMA 150	Business Plan for Retailers
* MA 2.021	SMA 152	Using a Traffic Study to Select a Retail Site
* MA 2.022	SMA 153	Business Plan for Small Service Firms
__ MA 2.023	SMA 154	Using Census Data to Select a Store Site
__ MA 2.024	SMA 168	Store Location "Little Things" Mean a Lot
* MA 2.025	SMA 170	Thinking About Going Into Business?

General Management and Administration

New	Old	Title
__ MA 3.001	MA 191	Delegating Work and Responsibility
* MA 3.002	MA 225	Management Checklist for a Family Business
__ MA 3.003	MA 239	Techniques of Time Management
* MA 3.004	SMA 119	Preventing Retail Theft
* MA 3.005	SMA 123	Stock Control for Small Stores
* MA 3.006	SMA 129	Reducing Shoplifting Losses
* MA 3.007	SMA 134	Preventing Burglary and Robbery Loss
* MA 3.008	SMA 137	Outwitting Bad-Check Passers
* MA 3.009	SMA 151	Preventing Embezzlement

Marketing

New	Old	Title
__ MA 4.001	MA 178	Effective Industrial Advertising for Small Plants
__ MA 4.002	MA 187	Using Census Data in Small Plant Marketing
__ MA 4.003	MA 190	Measuring Sales Force Performance
__ MA 4.004	MA 192	Profile Your Customers to Expand Industrial Sales
* MA 4.005	MA 200	Is the Independent Sales Agent for You?
__ MA 4.006	MA 203	Are Your Products and Channels Producing Sales?
* MA 4.007	MA 230	Selling Products on Consignment

New	Old	Title
* MA 4.008	MA 236	Tips on Getting More for Your Marketing Dollar
__ MA 4.009	MA 245	Exhibiting at Trade Shows
* MA 4.010	MA 246	Developing New Accounts
__ MA 4.011		
* MA 4.012	SMA 156	Marketing Checklist for Small Retailers
* MA 4.013	SMA 158	A Pricing Checklist for Small Retailers
* MA 4.014	SMA 159	Improving Personal Selling in Small Retail Stores
* MA 4.015	SMA 160	Advertising Guidelines for Small Retail Firms
__ MA 4.016	SMA 161	Signs in Your Business
__ MA 4.017	SMA 163	Public Relations for Small Business
* MA 4.018	SMA 164	Plan Your Advertising Budget
* MA 4.019	SMA 167	Learning About Your Market
__ MA 4.020	SMA 169	Do You Know the Results of Your Advertising

Organization and Personnel

New	Old	Title
__ MA 5.001	MA 186	Checklist for Developing a Training Program
* MA 5.002	MA 195	Setting Pay for Your Management Jobs
__ MA 5.003	MA 197	Pointers on Preparing an Employee Handbook
* MA 5.004	MA 205	Pointers on Using Temporary-Help Services
__ MA 5.005	MA 209	Preventing Employee Pilferage
__ MA 5.006	MA 241	Setting Up a Pay System
* MA 5.007	SMA 162	Staffing Your Store
* MA 5.008	— —	Managing Employee Benefits

Legal and Governmental Affairs

New	Old	Title
* MA 6.001	MA 217	Reducing Air Pollution in Industry
* MA 6.002	MA 219	Solid Waste Management in Industry
* MA 6.003	MA 223	Incorporating a Small Business
* MA 6.004	MA 231	Selecting the Legal Structure for Your Business
__ MA 6.005	MA 240	Introduction to Patents
__ MA 6.006	MA 244	Product Safety Checklist

Miscellaneous

New	Old	Title
__ MA 7.001	MA 214	The Metric System and Small Business
* MA 7.002	MA 224	Association Services for Small Business
__ MA 7.003	MA 237	Marketing Overseas with U.S. Government Help
__ MA 7.004	MA 247	Negotiating International Sales Contracts
__ MA 7.005	SMA 135	Arbitration: Peace-Maker in Small Business
* MA 7.006	SMA 157	Efficient Lighting for Small Stores

For reference, the following conversion list shows OLD numbers to NEW numbers.

* Aids converted to new number.

MAs				SMAs			
Old	New	Old	New	Old	New	Old	New
170	1.001	223	6.003	71	2.016	161	4.016
178	4.001	224	7.002	119	3.004	162	5.007
186	5.001	225	3.002	123	3.005	163	4.017
187	4.002	226	1.005	126	1.010	164	4.018
189	2.001	229	1.006	129	3.006	165	1.018
190	4.003	230	4.007	130	1.011	166	1.019
191	3.001	231	6.004	134	3.007	167	4.019
192	4.004	232	1.007	135	7.005	168	2.024
193	1.002	233	2.010	137	3.008	169	4.020
195	5.002	234	1.008	140	1.012	170	2.025
197	5.003	235	1.009	142	1.013		
200	4.005	236	4.008	143	2.017		
201	2.002	237	7.003	144	1.014		
203	4.006	239	3.003	146	1.015		
205	5.004	240	6.005	147	1.016		
206	1.003	241	5.006	148	2.018		
207	2.003	242	2.011	149	2.019		
208	2.004	243	2.012	150	2.020		
209	5.005	244	6.006	151	3.009		
212	2.005	245	4.009	152	2.021		
214	7.001	246	4.010	153	2.022		
216	2.006	247	7.004	154	2.023		
217	6.001	248	2.013	155	1.017		
218	2.007	249	2.014	156	4.012		
219	6.002	250	2.015	157	7.006		
220	1.004		5.008	158	4.013		
221	2.008			159	4.014		
222	2.009			160	4.015		

Small Business Bibliographies (SBBs) list key reference sources for many business management topics. (The **SBBs** numbering is the same as before and is unaffected by the **MA** conversion.)

SBBs

- __ 1. Handicrafts
- __ 2. Home Businesses
- __ 3. Selling By Mail Order
- __ 9. Marketing Research Procedures
- __ 10. Retailing
- __ 12. Statistics and Maps for National Market Analysis
- __ 13. National Directory for Use in Marketing
- __ 15. Recordkeeping Systems—Small Store and Service Trade
- __ 18. Basic Library Reference Sources
- __ 20. Advertising—Retail Store
- __ 29. National Mailing-List Houses
- __ 31. Retail Credit and Collection
- __ 37. Buying for Retail Stores
- __ 55. Wholesaling
- __ 72. Personnel Management
- __ 75. Inventory Management
- __ 79. Small Store Planning and Design
- __ 80. Data Processing for Small Businesses
- __ 85. Purchasing for Owners of Small Plants
- __ 86. Training for Small Business
- __ 87. Financial Management
- __ 88. Manufacturing Management
- __ 89. Marketing for Small Business
- __ 90. New Product Development
- __ 91. Ideas Into Dollars

Check to receive another copy of the following:

☐ **115-A List of Free Publications**
☐ **115-B List of For-Sale Publications**

Publications

SBA 115B

U.S. Small Business Administration
Office of Management Assistance

For-Sale Booklets

To Order: Complete the order blank on page 4. Send it with your check or money order to the **Superintendent of Documents**, Government Printing Office, Washington, D.C. 20402. Make check or money order payable to the Superintendent of Documents. Do not send postage stamps or cash. These booklets are not sold by the Small Business Administration. Foreign remittances should be made by international money order payable to the Superintendent of Documents, by draft on an American or Canadian bank located in the U.S. or Canada, or by UNESCO coupons. All orders may be charged to MasterCard, Visa, or Superintendent of Documents deposit accounts. Please include your card number and date of expiration. Prices subject to change without notice.

Small Business Management Series

The booklets in this series provide discussions of special management problems in small companies.

No.		Stock No.	Pages	Price
1.	**An Employee Suggestion System for Small Companies** Explains the basic principles for starting and operating a suggestion system.	045–000–00020–6	18	**$1.10**
9.	**Cost Accounting for Small Manufacturers** Assists managers of small manufacturing firms establish accounting procedures that help control production and business costs.	045–000–00162–8	180	**4.25**
15.	**Handbook of Small Business Finance** Indicates the major areas of financial management and describes a few techniques that can help the small business owner.	045–000–00139–3	63	**3.00**
20.	**Ratio Analysis for Small Business** The purpose of the booklet is to help the owner-manager in detecting favorable or unfavorable trends in the business.	045–000–00150–4	65	**2.20**
22.	**Practical Business Use of Government Statistics** Illustrates some practical uses of Federal Government statistics.	045–000–00131–8	28	**1.40**
25.	**Guides for Profit Planning** Guides for computing and using the breakeven point, the level of gross profit, and the rate of return on investment.	045–000–00137–7	59	**2.50**
27.	**Profitable Community Relations for Small Business** Practical information on how to build and maintain sound community relations by participation in community affairs.	045–000–00033–8	36	**1.50**
28.	**Small Business and Government Research and Development** Includes a discussion of the procedures necessary to locate and interest Government markets.	045–000–00130–0	41	**1.25**
29.	**Management Audit for Small Manufacturers** A series of questions about small manufacturing plant planning, organizing, directing, and coordinating efficiency.	045–000–00151–2	44	**1.60**
30.	**Insurance and Risk Management for Small Business** A discussion of what insurance is, the necessity of obtaining professional advice on buying insurance, and the main types of insurance a small business may need.	045–000–00037–1	72	**3.00**

No.	Stock No.	Pages	Price
31. **Management Audit for Small Retailers** 149 questions guide the owner-manager in a self examination and a review of the business operation.	045-000-00149-1	61	**1.80**
32. **Financial Recordkeeping for Small Stores** Written primarily for the small store owner or prospective owner whose business doesn't justify hiring a full-time bookkeeper.	045-000-00142-3	135	**4.00**
33. **Small Store Planning for Growth** Included is a consideration of merchandising, advertising and display, and checklists for increase in transactions and gross margins.	045-000-00152-1	102	**2.40**
35. **Franchise Index/Profile** Presents an evaluation process that may be used to investigate franchise opportunities.	045-000-00125-3	56	**2.00**
36. **Training Salesmen to Serve Industrial Markets** Discusses role of sales in marketing program of small manufacturer and offers suggestions for sales force to use in serving customers.	045-000-00133-4	85	**2.20**
37. **Financial Control by Time-Absorption Analysis** A profit control technique that can be used by all types of businesses.	045-000-00134-2	138	**2.75**
38. **Management Audit for Small Service Firms** A do-it-yourself guide for owner-managers of small service firms to help them evaluate and improve their operations.	045-000-00203-9	67	**3.75**
39. **Decision Points in Developing New Products** Provides a path from idea to marketing plan for the small manufacturing or R & D firm that wants to expand or develop a business around a new product, process, or invention.	045-000-00146-6	64	**1.50**
40. **Management Audit for Small Construction Firms** Helps top executives of small construction firms to make a self-appraisal of their management practices.	045-000-00161-0	53	**2.50**
41. **Purchasing Management and Inventory Control for Small Business** Explains how to manage purchasing and inventory dollars.	045-000-00167-9	66	**3.25**
42. **Managing the Small Service Firm for Growth and Profit** This booklet aids you in developing a marketing strategy to improve services to assure growth as customer needs change.	045-000-00165-2	58	**3.50**
43. **Credit and Collections for Small Stores** Discusses credit plans to help owner-managers pick and run credit systems. Includes information on legal restrictions recordkeeping, and trade credit.	045-000-00169-5	66	**3.50**

Starting And Managing Series

This series is designed to help the small entrepreneur "to look before leaping" into a business. The first volume in the series—Starting and Managing a Small Business of Your Own—deals with the subject in general terms. Each of the other volumes deals with one type of business in detail. Available titles:

No.	Stock No.	Pages	Price
1. **Starting and Managing a Small Business of Your Own**	045-000-00123-7	95	**3.75**

Nonseries Publications

	Stock No.	Pages	Price
Export Marketing for Smaller Firms A manual for owner-managers of smaller firms who seek sales in foreign markets.	045-000-00158-0	84	**2.20**
U.S. Government Purchasing and Sales Directory A directory for businesses that are interested in selling to the U.S. Government. Lists the purchasing needs of various Agencies.	045-000-00153-9	204	**5.50**
Managing for Profits Ten chapters on various aspects of small business management, for example, marketing, production, and credit.	045-000-00005-2	155	**2.75**

No.	Stock No.	Pages	Price
Buying and Selling a Small Business Deals with the problems that confront buyers and sellers of small businesses.	045–000–00164–4	122	**3.50**
Strengthening Small Business Management Twenty-one chapters on small business management.	045–000–00114–8	155	**4.00**
Small Business Goes to College This booklet traces the development of small business management as a college subject and provides samples of courses offered at 200 colleges and universities.	045–000–00159–8	82	**3.25**
The Best of the SBI Review —1973-1979 Management ideas for the small business owner-manager.	045-000-00172-5	145	**4.50**

Business Basics

Each of the 23 self-study booklets in this series contains text, question, and exercises that teach a specific aspect of small business managment.

Business Basics

No.		Stock No.	Pages	Price
1001	The Profit Plan	045–000–00192–0	33	**$2.25**
1002	Capital Planning	045–000–00193–8	42	**2.50**
1003	Understanding Money Sources	045–000–00194–6	50	**3.50**
1004	Evaluating Money Sources	045–000–00174–1	64	**3.75**
1005	Asset Management	045–000–00175–0	20	**1.50**
1006	Managing Fixed Assets	045–000–00176–8	48	**2.50**
1007	Understanding Costs	045–000–00195–4	48	**2.75**
1008	Cost Control	045–000–00187–3	48	**2.75**
1009	Marketing Strategy	045–000–00188–1	52	**3.50**
1010	Retail Buying Function	045–000–00177–6	40	**2.25**
1011	Inventory Management–Wholesale/Retail	045–000–00190–3	40	**2.50**
1012	Retail Merchandise Management	045–000–00178–4	52	**3.25**
1013	Consumer Credit	045–000–00179–2	40	**2.25**
1014	Credit and Collections: Policy and Procedures	045–000–00180–6	48	**2.50**
1015	Purchasing for Manufacturing Firms	045–000–00181–4	52	**3.25**
1016	Inventory Management—Manufacturing/Service	045–000–00182–2	52	**3.25**
1017	Inventory and Scheduling Techniques	045–000–00183–1	60	**3.50**
1018	Risk Management and Insurance	045–000–00184–9	44	**2.25**
1019	Managing Retail Salespeople	045–000–00189–0	60	**3.75**
1020	Job Analysis, Job Specifications, and Job Descriptions	045–000–00185–7	40	**2.25**
1021	Recruiting and Selecting Employees	045–000–00186–5	40	**2.25**
1022	Training and Developing Employees	045–000–00191–1	40	**2.50**
1023	Employee Relations and Personnel Policies	045–000–00196–2	36	**2.25**

Small Business Management Series

No.	Stock No.	Price	No.	Stock No.	Price
1. ____	045-000-00020-6—	$1.10	32. ____	045-000-00142-3—	4.00
9. ____	045-000-00162-8—	4.25	33. ____	045-000-00152-1—	2.40
15. ____	045-000-00139-3—	3.00	35. ____	045-000-00125-3—	2.00
20. ____	045-000-00150-4—	2.20	36. ____	045-000-00133-4—	2.20
22. ____	045-000-00131-8—	1.40	37. ____	045-000-00134-2—	2.75
25. ____	045-000-00137-7—	2.50	38. ____	045-000-00203-9—	3.75
27. ____	045-000-00033-8—	1.50	39. ____	045-000-00146-6—	1.50
28. ____	045-000-00130-0—	1.25	40. ____	045-000-00161-0—	2.50
29. ____	045-000-00151-2—	1.60	41. ____	045-000-00167-9—	3.25
30. ____	045-000-00037-1—	3.00	42. ____	045-000-00165-2—	3.50
31. ____	045-000-00149-1—	1.80	43. ____	045-000-00169-5—	3.50

Nonseries Publications

Stock No.	Price
____ 045-000-00158-0—	$2.20
____ 045-000-00153-9—	5.50
____ 045-000-00005-2—	2.75
____ 045-000-00159-8—	3.25
____ 045-000-00164-4—	3.50
____ 045-000-00114-8—	4.00
____ 045-000-00172-5—	4.50

Starting and Managing Series

No.	Stock No.	Price
1. ____	045-000-00123-7—	$3.75

Business Basics

No.	Stock No.	Price	No.	Stock No.	Price	No.	Stock No.	Price	No.	Stock No.	Price
1001. ____	045-000-00192-0—	$2.25	1007. ____	045-000-00195-4—	2.75	1013. ____	045-000-00179-2—	2.25	1019. ____	045-000-00189-0—	3.75
1002. ____	045-000-00193-8—	2.50	1008. ____	045-000-00187-3—	2.75	1014. ____	045-000-00180-6—	2.50	1020. ____	045-000-00185-7—	2.25
1003. ____	045-000-00194-6—	3.50	1009. ____	045-000-00188-1—	3.50	1015. ____	045-000-00181-4—	3.25	1021. ____	045-000-00186-5—	2.25
1004. ____	045-000-00174-1—	3.75	1010. ____	045-000-00177-6—	2.25	1016. ____	045-000-00182-2—	3.25	1022. ____	045-000-00191-1—	2.50
1005. ____	045-000-00175-0—	1.50	1011. ____	045-000-00190-3—	2.50	1017. ____	045-000-00183-1—	3.50	1023. ____	045-000-00196-2—	2.25
1006. ____	045-000-00176-8—	2.50	1012. ____	045-000-00178-4—	3.25	1018. ____	045-000-00184-9—	2.25			

ORDER FORM To: Superintendent of Documents, U.S. Government Printing Office, Washington, D.C. 20402

Enclosed is $ _____ ☐ check,
☐ money order, or charge to my
Deposit Account No.

Order No. _____

VISA®

master charge THE INTERBANK CARD

Credit Card Orders Only

Total charges $_____ Fill in the boxes below.

Credit Card No.

Expiration Date
Month/Year

Company or personal name

Additional address/attention line

Street address

City   State   ZIP Code

(or Country)

PLEASE PRINT OR TYPE

For Office Use Only

	Quantity	Charges
Enclosed		
To be mailed		
Subscriptions		
Postage		
Foreign handling		
MMOB		
OPNR		
UPNS		
Discount		
Refund		

Prices shown were in effect in February 1981. Prices of Government publications are subject to change without notice and the prices charged on your order will be those in effect when your order is processed.

A 25-percent discount is given for quantities of 100 or more of the same publication to a single address. For foreign mailings, please add 25 percent to prices shown above.

The publications listed above may also be purchased from U.S. Department of Commerce field offices. If one is located in your city, consult your telephone directory for the address.

A Companion Form, SBA-115A, Lists Current Free Publications and Is Available Without Charge From SBA, P.O. Box 15434, Fort Worth, Texas 76119 or by calling toll free 800-433-7212.

Appendix V

Directory of Operating Small Business Investment Companies

Published by the Small Business Administration, December 1981.

This is a list of all Small Business Investment Companies, including their branch offices, whose licenses, issued by SBA, remain outstanding except those companies that are in process of surrendering their licenses or are subject to legal proceedings, which may have the effect of terminating their activity as Small Business Investment Companies. This list does not purport to characterize the relative merits, as investment companies or otherwise, of these licensees. Inclusion on this list may in no way be construed as approval of a company's operations or as a recommendation by the Small Business Administration.

PART I: SMALL BUSINESS INVESTMENT COMPANIES LISTED ALPHABETICALLY BY STATE

Licensee	Private Capital($)	SBA Lever-age($)	Investment Policy	Owner Code
Alabama				
Benson Investment Company, Inc. William T. Benson, President 406 South Commerce Street Geneva, Alabama 36340 (205) 684-2824	1,000,000	1,000,000	Diversified	5

Licensee	Private Capital($)	SBA Leverage($)	Investment Policy	Owner Code
Coastal Capital Company Arthur C. Tonsmeire Jr., President 3201 Dauphin St., Suite B Mobile, Alabama 36606 (205) 476-0700	950,000	2,400,000	Builders	3
First SBIC of Alabama David Delaney, President 3201 Dauphin St., Suite B Mobile, Alabama 36606 (205) 476-0700	1,278,000	3,100,000	Diversified	5
H & T Capital Corp. John R. Bloom, President 4750 Selma Highway P.O. Drawer Q Montgomery, Alabama 36105 (205) 288-6250	305,000	600,000	Diversified	5

Arizona

Licensee	Private Capital($)	SBA Leverage($)	Investment Policy	Owner Code
American Business Capital Corp. Leonard A. Frankel, President 3550 North Central Ave. Suite 1305 Phoenix, Arizona 85012 (602) 277-6259	500,000	300,000	Diversified	5
Rocky Mountain Equity Corporation Anthony J. Nicoli, President	500,000	0	Diversified	5

Licensee	Private Capital($)	SBA Lever-age($)	Investment Policy	Owner Code
4949 East Lincoln Drive, La Posada Scottsdale, Arizona 85253 (602) 959-4210				
Arkansas				
First SBIC of Arkansas, Inc. Fred Burns, President Worthen Bank Building Suite 706 Little Rock, Arkansas 72201 (501) 378-1876	619,728	0	Diversified	1
Small Business Inv. Cap. Inc. Charles E. Toland, President 10003 New Benton Hwy. Mail: P.O. Box 3627 Little Rock, Arkansas 72203 (501) 455-3590	750,000	2,250,000	Retail grocers	4
California				
Asset Management Capital Co. Franklin Johnson, Jr., President 1417 Edgewood Drive Palo Alto, California 94301 (415) 321-3131	1,320,408	600,000	Diversified	5
Atlanta Investment Capital Corp. (Main Office: New York, NY) 141 El Camino Drive				

Licensee	Private Capital($)	SBA Lever- age($)	Investment Policy	Owner Code
Beverly Hills, California 90212 (213) 273-1730				
Bay Venture Group William R. Chandler, General Partner 1 Embarcadero Center, Suite 3303 San Francisco, California 94111 (415) 989-7680	542,763	0	Diversified	5
Benox, Incorporated John C. Bernett, President 17295 East Railroad Street City of Industry, California 91749 (213) 965-1541	500,000	0	Diversified	5
Brantman Capital Corp. William T. Brantman, President 2476 Mar East Mail: P.O. Box 877 Tiburon, California 94920 (415) 435-4747	350,100	750,000	Diversified	5
Brentwood Associates, Incorporated Timothy Pennington 3rd, President 11661 San Vincente Blvd. Los Angeles, California 90049 (213) 826-6581	2,000,000	5,000,000	Diversified	3
Brentwood Capital Corporation T. M. Pennington, Chairman of Board	6,060,510	8,000,000	Diversified	3

Licensee	Private Capital($)	SBA Lever- age($)	Investment Policy	Owner Code
11661 San Vincente Blvd. Los Angeles, California 90049 (213) 826-6581				
Bryan Capital, Inc. John M. Bryan, President 235 Montgomery St. Suite 2220 San Francisco, California 94104 (415) 421-9990	1,028,720	3,180,000	50% major group 36	5
Builders Capital Corp. Victor H. Indiek, President 2716 Ocean Park Boulevard Santa Monica, California 90404 (213) 450-0779	3,500,000	13,000,000	100% major group 15	5
California Capital Investors Harold A. Haytin, Chairman of the Board 11812 San Vincente Boulevard Los Angeles, California 90049 (213) 820-7222	950,000	0	Diversified	5
California Partners Draper Assoc. CGP Two Palo Alto Square Suite 700 Palo Alto, California 94304 (415) 493-5600	500,000	0	Diversified	5-P

Licensee	Private Capital($)	SBA Lever- age($)	Investment Policy	Owner Code
City Capital Corp. Morton Heller, President 9080 Santa Monica Boulevard Suite 201 Los Angeles, California 90069 (212) 273-4080	400,000	250,000	Diversified	5
Crocker Capital Corp. Charles Crocker, President 111 Sutter St., Suite 600 San Francisco, California 94104 (415) 983-2156	1,204,589	2,205,834	66-⅔% major group 36	2
Crocker Ventures Incorporated John M. Boyle, General Manager One Montgomery Street San Francisco, California 94104 (415) 983-7024	1,000,000	0	Diversified	1
Crosspoint Invest- ment Corporation Max Simpson, Pres. & Chief Fin. Officer 1015 Corporation Way Palo Alto, California 94303 (415) 964-3723	502,000	900,000	Diversified	3
Developers Equity Capital Corp. Larry Sade, Chairman of Board 9201 Wilshire Blvd. Suite 204 Beverly Hills, California 90210 (213) 278-3611	583,000	225,000	100% real estate	5

Licensee	Private Capital($)	SBA Lever- age($)	Investment Policy	Owner Code
Edvestco, Inc. William C. Ed- wards, President 150 Isabella Avenue Atherton, California 94025 (415) 421-9990	1,228,802	3,167,500	50% major group 36	5
Equilease Capital Corp. (Main Office: New York, NY) 315 So. Beverly Drive Beverly Hills, Cali- fornia 90212 (213) 445-7211				
First Interstate Cap- ital, Inc. David B. Jones, President 707 Wilshire Blvd., Suite 1850 Los Angeles, Cali- fornia 90017 (213) 614-5903	5,000,000	1,250,000	Diversified	1
First SBIC of Cali- fornia (Main Office: New- port Beach, CA) 333 South Hope Street Los Angeles, Cali- fornia 90071 (213) 613-5215				
First SBIC of Cali- fornia Tim Hay, President 4000 MacArthur Blvd., Suite 950 Newport Beach, California 92660 (714) 754-4780	12,500,000	0	Diversified	1

Licensee	Private Capital($)	SBA Leverage($)	Investment Policy	Owner Code
Florists Capital Corporation Christopher M. Conroy, Chairman 10524 West Pico Blvd. Los Angeles, California 90064 (213) 836-6169	1,020,286	2,000,000	Diversified	5
Foothill Venture Corp. Pauline Krips Newman, President 2049 Century Park East Los Angeles, California 90067 (213) 556-1222	655,000	1,800,000	Diversified	3
Grocers Capital Co. Elliot Goldstone, Manager 2601 S. Eastern Avenue Los Angeles, California 90040 (213) 728-3322	1,500,000	800,000	Grocery stores	4
H & R Investment Capital Co. Herman Christensen, President 801 American Street San Carlos, California 94070 (415) 365-4691	483,000	185,036	66-⅔% Real estate	5
I.B.S.I. Capital Corp. Melvin Balcharach, President 765 Bridgeway Sausalito, California 94965 (415) 331-2262	545,000	0	Diversified	5

Licensee	Private Capital($)	SBA Lever- age($)	Investment Policy	Owner Code
Imperial Ventures Incorporated	500,000	0	Diversified	1
Donald B. Prell, President				
9920 South Lacien- ega Blvd.				
Mail: P.O. Box 92991; L.A. 90009				
Inglewood, Califor- nia 90301				
(213) 649-3886				
Krasne Fund for Small Business, Inc.	440,000	200,833	90% Real estate	5
Clyde A. Krasne, President				
432 South Arnza Drive, Suite 4				
Los Angeles, Cali- fornia 90048				
(213) 274-7007				
Marwit Capital Corp.	918,314	1,321,800	Diversified	5
Martin W. Witte, President				
180 Newport Center Drive				
Suite 200				
Newport Beach, California 92660				
(714) 640-6234				
Menlo Venture Corp.	5,409,582	4,750,000	Diversified	2
Kirk L. Knight, President				
3000 Sand Hill Road				
Menlo Park, Cali- fornia 94025				
(415) 854-8540				
Merrill Pickard I	11,211,532	0	Diversified	1
Steven L. Merrill, President				

Licensee	Private Capital($)	SBA Leverage($)	Investment Policy	Owner Code
555 California Street, Suite 2170 San Francisco, California 94104 (415) 622-2582				
Metropolitan Venture Company, Inc. Rudolph J. Lowy, Chairman of the Board 8200 Wilshire Boulevard, Suite 314 Beverly Hills, California 90211 (213) 653-1252	1,200,000	0	Diversified	5
Novus Capital Corporation Errol M. Gerson, President 5670 Wilshire Boulevard Los Angeles, California 90036 (213) 932-4051	2,500,000	0	Diversified	3
Oceanic Capital Corp. Robert C. Weeks, President 545 Middlefield Road, Suite 160 Menlo Park, California 94025 (415) 328-4401	1,754,000	4,033,475	Diversified	4
Pan American Investment Co. Spencer Hoopes, Managing Director 545 Middlefield Road, Suite 160 Menlo Park, California 94025 (415) 328-4401	4,824,484	0	Diversified	5

Licensee	Private Capital($)	SBA Lever-age($)	Investment Policy	Owner Code
PBC Venture Capital, Incorporated Philip E. Zachary, President 1408 18th Street Mail: P.O. Box 6008; Bakersfield 93386 Bakersfield, California 93301 (805) 395-3555	540,000	0	Diversified	1
Professional SBIC David M. Zerner, President 954 Schumacher Drive Los Angeles, California 90048 (213) 936-5243	897,115	653,545	66-⅔% Real estate	5
Round Table Capital Corporation Richard Dumke, President 601 Montgomery Street San Francisco, California 94111 (415) 392-7500	500,000	1,500,000	Diversified	5
San Joaquin Capital Corporation Chester Troudy, Executive Vice-President 1675 Chester Ave., Third Floor Mail: P.O. Box 2538 Bakersfield, California 93303 (805) 323-7581	837,330	2,121,311	Diversified	5
San Jose Capital Corp. Daniel Hochman, President	862,433	1,800,000	Diversified	5

Licensee	Private Capital($)	SBA Lever- age($)	Investment Policy	Owner Code
130 Park Center Plaza San Jose, California 95113 (408) 293-7708				
Small Business Enterprises Co. Charles R. Yirchott, Jr., President 555 California Street San Francisco, California 94104 (415) 622-2582	12,500,000	0	45% major groups 26 & 38	1
Union Venture Corp. Brent T. Rider, President 445 S. Figueroa Street Los Angeles, California 90017 (213) 687-5797	6,500,000	3,000,000	Diversified	1
Walden Capital Corp. Arthur S. Berliner, President 303 Sacramento Street San Francisco, California 94109 (415) 391-7225	1,090,184	1,350,000	Diversified	2
Warde Capital Corp. Thomas R. Warde, President 8929 Wilshire Blvd., Suite 500 Beverly Hills, California 90211 (213) 657-0500	600,000	394,497	66-⅔% Real estate	5
Wells Fargo Investment Robert G. Perring, President	3,952,200	7,740,000	Diversified	1

Licensee	Private Capital($)	SBA Lever- age($)	Investment Policy	Owner Code
475 Sansome Street San Francisco, California 94111 (415) 396-3293				
West Coast Venture Capital Gary W. Kalbach, President 10440 South Deanza Blvd., Suite D-2 Cupertino, California 95014 (408) 996-2702	1,096,500	1,000,000	Diversified	5
Westamco Investment Company Leonard G. Muskin, President 8929 Wilshire Blvd., Suite 400 Beverly Hills, California 90211 (213) 652-8288	800,000	808,000	66-⅔% Real estate	4

Colorado

Associated Capital Corporation Rodney J. Love, President 5151 Bannock Street Denver, Colorado 80216 (303) 534-1155	1,435,028	550,000	Grocery stores	4
Central Investment Co. Corp. of Denver (M.O.: Northwest Growth Fund, Inc. Minneapolis, Minnesota) 811 Central Bank Bldg. Denver, Colorado 80202 (303) 825-3351				

Licensee	Private Capital($)	SBA Lever- age($)	Investment Policy	Owner Code
Colorado Growth Capital, Inc. Nicholas H. C. Davis, President 950 Seventeenth Street, Suite 1730 Denver, Colorado 80202 (303) 629-0205	1,049,330	0	Diversified	5
Colorado SBIC Melvin J. Roberts, President 918 Seventeenth Street P.O. Box 5168 Denver, Colorado 80217 (303) 629-1968	699,800	0	Diversified	1
Denver Ventures, Inc. Stanley Perea, Pres- ident 4142 Tejon Street Denver, Colorado 80211 (303) 433-8636	150,000	0	Diversified	3
E S One Capital Corp. Harvey J. Wachtel, President 1905 Sherman Street, Ninth Floor Denver, Colorado 80203 (303) 555-1212	3,625,000	0	Diversified	5
Enervest, Inc. Mark Kimmel, Pres- ident 7000 East Belleview Avenue Suite 310 Englewood, Colo- rado 80110 (303) 771-9650	1,069,258	1,500,000	Diversified	5

Licensee	Private Capital($)	SBA Leverage($)	Investment Policy	Owner Code
Equilease Capital Corp. (Main Office: New York, NY) 120 Bryant Street Denver, Colorado 80219 (303) 573-1374				
Northwest Growth Fund Incorporated (Main Office: Minneapolis, MN) 7625 West 5th Avenue, Suite 202 Lakewood, Colorado 80226 (303) 232-3018				

Connecticut

Licensee	Private Capital($)	SBA Leverage($)	Investment Policy	Owner Code
AB SBIC, Inc. Adam J. Bozzuto, President School House Road Cheshire, Connecticut 06410 (203) 272-0203	500,000	1,000,000	Retail grocery stores	4
Activest Capital Corp. William N. Vitalis, President P.O. Box 76 Cornwall Bridge, Connecticut 06754 (203) 672-6651	500,000	471,300	100% Real estate	4
All State Venture Capital Corporation Thomas H. Brown, Jr., President 830 Post Road East P.O. Box 442 Westport, Connecticut 06880 (203) 226-9376	338,230	225,000	Diversified	6

Licensee	Private Capital($)	SBA Lever- age($)	Investment Policy	Owner Code
Apco Capital Corp. S. David Leibowitt, President 63 Broad Street Milford, Connecti- cut 06460 (203) 877-5101	853,998	1,958,000	Diversified	5
Asset Capital and Management Corp. Ralph Smith, Presi- dent 608 Ferry Blvd. Stratford, Connecti- cut 06497 (203) 375-0299	720,094	1,850,000	Diversified	5
Capital Resource Co. of Connecti- cut I. Martin Fierberg, President 345 North Main Street, Suite 304 West Hartford, Connecticut 06117 (203) 232-4419	617,000	1,676,000	Diversified	5
Dewey Investment Corp. George E. Mrosek, President 101 Middle Turn- pike West Manchester, Con- necticut 06040 (203) 649-0654	484,750	1,370,000	Diversified	6
First Connecticut SBIC David Engelson, President 177 State Street Bridgeport, Con- necticut 06604 (203) 366-4726	7,402,968	20,906,262	50% Real estate	6

Licensee	Private Capital($)	SBA Leverage($)	Investment Policy	Owner Code
First Miami SBIC (Main Office: Miami Beach, FL) 293 Post Road Orange, Connecticut 06477 (203) 227-6824				
J. H. Foster & Co. Ltd. FPI, Inc. John H. Foster, President 999 Summer Street Stamford, Connecticut 06905 (203) 348-4385	2,595,622	3,000,000	Diversified	5-P
Manufacturers SBIC, Incorporation Frank D'Engenio, President 310 Main Street East Haven, Connecticut 06512 (203) 469-7901	408,326	1,314,714	Diversified	6
Marcon Capital Corp. Martin A. Cohen, President 49 Riverside Avenue Westport, Connecticut 06880 (203) 226-7751	500,000	1,500,000	Diversified	4
Nationwide Funding Corporation Neil H. Ellis, President 306 Progress Drive P.O. Box 209 Manchester, Connecticut 06040 (203) 646-6555	156,000	20,000	Diversified	5

Licensee	Private Capital($)	SBA Lever-age($)	Investment Policy	Owner Code
Regional Financial Enterprises, Inc. Robert M. Williams, Chairman 1111 Summer Street Stamford, Connecticut 06905 (203) 356-1730	9,186,000	0	Diversified	1
SBIC of Connecticut Inc. (The) Kenneth F. Zarrilli, President 1115 Main Street Bridgeport, Connecticut 06603 (203) 367-3282	581,940	820,000	Diversified	6

DC

Licensee	Private Capital($)	SBA Lever-age($)	Investment Policy	Owner Code
Allied Investment Corporation George C. Williams, President 1625 Eye Street, N.W. Suite 603 Washington, DC 20006 (202) 331-1112	3,284,708	8,023,956	100% In any one industry	6
Capital Investment Co. of Washington John Katkish, President 1010 Wisconsin Ave., N.W. Washington, DC 20007 (202) 298-3229	502,097	266,744	Diversified	5
Greater Washington Investors, Inc. Don A. Christensen, President 1015 18th St., N.W. Washington, DC 20036 (202) 466-2210	1,731,387	4,177,803	Diversified	6

Licensee	Private Capital($)	SBA Lever- age($)	Investment Policy	Owner Code
Housing Capital Corp. George W. Defran- ceaux, Chairman 1133 Fifteenth St., N.W. Washington, DC 20005 (202) 857-5757	3,500,000	10,500,000	Operative builders	4

Florida

Licensee	Private Capital($)	SBA Lever- age($)	Investment Policy	Owner Code
Allied Capital Corp. (Main Office: Wash- ington, DC) Warren L. Miller, Vice-President One Financial Plaza, Suite 1614 Fort Lauderdale, Florida 33301 (305) 763-8484				
First Miami SBIC Irve L. Libby, Presi- dent 1195 N.E. 125 Street North Miami, Flor- .ida 33161 (305) 891-2534	630,520	432,029	50% Real estate	5
First North Florida SBIC J. B. Higdon, Presi- dent 1400 Gadsden Street P.O. Box 1021 Quincy, Florida 32351 (904) 875-2600	300,000	75,000	Grocery stores	5
Gold Coast Capital Corporation William I. Gold, President 3550 Biscayne Blvd., Room 601 Miami, Florida 33137 (305) 576-2012	521,997	1,034,076	Diversified	5

Licensee	Private Capital($)	SBA Lever- age($)	Investment Policy	Owner Code
Gulf Coast Capital Corporation Oscar M. Tharp, President 70 North Baylen Street Mail: P.O. Box 12790 Pensacola, Florida 32575 (904) 434-1361	500,000	0	Diversified	3
J & D Capital Corp. Jack Carmel, President 12747 Biscayne Blvd. North Miami, Florida 33181 (305) 893-0303	500,000	0	Diversified	5
Market Capital Corp. E. E. Eads, President 1102 North 28th Street P.O. Box 22667 Tampa, Florida 33622 (813) 247-1357	515,400	945,600	Grocery stores	4
Massachusetts Capital Corporation (Main Office: Boston, MA) One Financial Plaza Suite 1614 Fort Lauderdale, Florida 33301 (305) 763-8484				
Quiet SBIC (The) Alton Woody, President 105 East Garden Street Pensacola, Florida 32501 (904) 434-5090	500,000	0	Diversified	5

Licensee	Private Capital($)	SBA Lever- age($)	Investment Policy	Owner Code
Servico Business Inv. Corporation Gary O. Marino, President 2000 Palm Beach Lakes Blvd. West Palm Beach, Florida 33409 (305) 689-9970	500,000	0	Diversified	5
SBAC of Panama City Florida J. R. Arnold, President 2612 West Fifteenth Street Panama City, Florida 32401 (904) 785-9577	3,600,000	12,661,380	80% In lodging places, amusement, and recreation	1
Southeast Venture Capital, Inc. Clement L. Hofmann, President 1 Biscayne Tower, 34th Floor Miami, Florida 33131 (305) 577-4680	2,501,169	4,000,000	Diversified	1
Suwannee Capital Corp. William Lovett, Chairman of Board 1010 East Adams Street (Mail: P.O. Box 2836, Jacksonville 32201 Jacksonville, Florida 32202 (904) 355-8315	1,005,000	1,500,000	Retail grocery stores	5
Western Financial Capital Corp. Dr. F. M. Rosemore, President	991,000	1,000,000	Medical	5

Licensee	Private Capital($)	SBA Leverage($)	Investment Policy	Owner Code
12550 Biscayne Blvd., Suite 406 North Miami, Florida 33181 (305) 891-0823				
Georgia				
Affiliated Investment Fund, Inc. Samuel Weissman, President 2225 Shurfine Drive College Park, Georgia 30337 (404) 766-0221	512,000	500,000	Retail grocer	4
Equilease Capital Corp. (Main Office: New York, NY) 22-61 Penimeter Pk., Suite 12 Atlanta, Georgia 30309 (404) 457-8278				
First American Investment Corporation Cecil D. Conlee, President 300 Interstate North Suite 400 Atlanta, Georgia 30339 (404) 955-0000	3,710,132	9,472,929	100% Real estate	4
Investor's Equity, Inc. I. Walter Fisher, President 2940 First National Bank Tower Atlanta, Georgia 30383 (404) 523-3999	315,500	162,500	Diversified	5

Licensee	Private Capital($)	SBA Lever-age($)	Investment Policy	Owner Code
Mome Capital Corp. James A. Hutchin-son, President 518 Jackson Street Thomson, Georgia 30824 (404) 595-1507	700,000	1,600,000	Mobile homes	5
Peachtree Capital Corporation David Howe, Presi-dent 1611 Gas Light Tower 235 Peachtree Street Atlanta, Georgia 30303 (404) 522-9000	700,000	0	Diversified	5
Southeastern Capi-tal SBI Corp. J. Ray Efird, Presi-dent Suite 60, Northcreek 3715 Northside Parkway, N.W. Atlanta, Georgia 30327 (404) 237-1567	1,500,000	1,000,000	Diversified	6

Hawaii

SBIC of Hawaii James Wong, Chair-man of Board 1575 South Bere-tania St. Honolulu, Hawaii 96814 (808) 949-3677	332,291	240,000	66-⅔% Real estate	3

Idaho

First Idaho Venture Capital Corp. Jack J. Winderal, President	1,000,000	1,500,000	Diversified	3

Licensee	Private Capital($)	SBA Lever- age($)	Investment Policy	Owner Code
205 N. 10th St. P.O. Box 1739 Boise, Idaho 83701 (208) 345-3460				

Illinois

Abbott Capital Corp. Richard E. Lassar, President 120 South LaSalle St. Chicago, Illinois 60603 (312) 726-3803	727,840	1,975,000	Diversified	5
Advance Growth Capital Corpora- tion Charles F. Sebas- tion, President Radio Center 9355 West Joliet Road Lagrange, Illinois 60526 (312) 352-2650	3,901,186	233,333	Diversified	6
Certified Grocers Inv. Corporation Charles D. Nipp, President 4800 South Central Avenue Chicago, Illinois 60638 (312) 585-7000	500,000	0	Retail grocery stores	4
Claremont/LaSalle Corp. Steven B. Randall, President 29 South LaSalle St. Suite 430 Chicago, Illinois 60603 (312) 236-5888	505,000	0	Diversified	5

Licensee	Private Capital($)	SBA Leverage($)	Investment Policy	Owner Code
Continental Illinois Venture Corp. John L. Hines, President 231 South LaSalle St. Suite 1617 Chicago, Illinois 60693 (312) 828-8023	25,011,800	2,500,000	Diversified	1
Equilease Capital Corp. (Main Office: New York, NY) 2400 East Devon Des Plaines, Illinois 60018 (312) 981-1710				
First Capital Corp. of Chicago John A. Canning, Jr., President One First National Plaza Chicago, Illinois 60670 (312) 732-8068	20,000,000	2,500,000	Diversified	1
Frontenac Capital Corporation Martin J. Koldyke, President 208 South LaSalle Street, Room 1900 Chicago, Illinois 60604 (312) 368-0047	3,000,000	600,000	Diversified	2
Golder, Thoma Capital Company Carl Thoma, General Partner 120 South LaSalle Street, Suite 630 Chicago, Illinois 60604 (312) 853-3322	5,000,000	0	Communications	5

Licensee	Private Capital($)	SBA Lever- age($)	Investment Policy	Owner Code
SB Management In- vestors, Inc. Kenneth Eaton, President 17 East Chestnut Chicago, Illinois 60611 (312) 943-0750	150,650	150,000	Diversified	5
United Capital Corp. of Illinois John R. Henriksen, President United Center, State & Wyman Sts. P.O. Box 998 Rockford, Illinois 61105 (815) 987-2179	3,100,000	1,400,000	Diversified	4

Indiana

Licensee	Private Capital($)	SBA Lever- age($)	Investment Policy	Owner Code
Heritage Venture Group Incor- porated Arthur A. Angotti, President 3375 One Indiana Square Indianapolis, Indi- ana 46204 (317) 635-5696	960,000	0	Diversified	5
Tyler Refrigeration Capital Corp. Gary Slock, Presi- dent 2222 East Michigan Blvd. Michigan City, Indi- ana 46360 (219) 874-3181	303,000	0	Diversified	4

Iowa

Licensee	Private Capital($)	SBA Lever- age($)	Investment Policy	Owner Code
Moramerica Capital Corporation Jerome Burrows, President	3,700,000	14,099,889	Diversified	1

Licensee	Private Capital($)	SBA Lever-age($)	Investment Policy	Owner Code
Suite 200, American Bldg. Cedar Rapids, Iowa 52401 (319) 363-0263				
R. W. Allsop Capital Corporation Robert W. Allsop, President Corporate Center East 2750 First Avenue N.E., Suite 210 Cedar Rapids, Iowa 52402 (319) 363-8971	2,500,000	0	Diversified	3

Kansas

Licensee	Private Capital($)	SBA Lever-age($)	Investment Policy	Owner Code
Kansas Venture Capital Inc. George L. Doak, President 1030 First National Bank Tower One Townsite Plaza Topeka, Kansas 66603 (913) 235-3437	1,075,240	0	Diversified	3

Kentucky

Licensee	Private Capital($)	SBA Lever-age($)	Investment Policy	Owner Code
Financial Opportunities, Inc. Joe P. Peden, President 981 South Third Street Louisville, Kentucky 40203 (502) 584-1281	800,000	2,000,000	Diversified	4
Mountain Ventures, Incorporated Frederick J. Beste II, President 911 North Main Street	1,300,000	0	Diversified	5

Licensee	Private Capital($)	SBA Lever-age($)	Investment Policy	Owner Code
Mail: P.O. Box 628; London, KY 40741 London, Kentucky 40741 (606) 864-5175				
Louisiana				
Caddo Capital Corp. Thomas L. Young, Jr., President 3010 Knight Street, Suite 240 Shreveport, Louisiana 71105 (318) 869-1689	520,000	1,000,000	Diversified	5
Capital for Terrebonne, Inc. Hartwell A. Lewis, President 1613 Barrow Street Houma, Louisiana 70360 (504) 868-3930	750,000	1,680,000	Diversified	5
Commercial Capital, Incorporated Frederick W. Pierce, President P.O. Box 939 Covington, Louisiana 70433 (504) 892-4921	860,000	2,425,900	Diversified	3
Commercial Capital, Inc. (Main Office: Covington, LA) 1809 West Thomas Street Hammond, Louisiana 70404 (504) 892-4921				

Licensee	Private Capital($)	SBA Lever- age($)	Investment Policy	Owner Code
Commercial Ven- ture Capital Corp. William H. Jackson, President 329 Texas Street Shreveport, Louisi- ana 71101 (318) 226-4602	1,000,000	0	Diversified	1
Dixie Business In- vestment Co. Steve K. Cheek, President 401-½ Lake Street P.O. Box 588 Lake Providence, Louisiana 71254 (318) 559-1558	543,193	1,200,000	Diversified	2
First SBIC of Loui- siana, Inc. Mrs. N. Hooper, Exec. V.P. 2852 Carey Street, P.O. Box 1336 Slidell, Louisiana 70459 (504) 641-2404	161,801	225,000	Water transporta- tion	5
First Southern Cap- ital Corporation John H. Crabtree, President 6161 Perkins Rd., Suite 2C Mail: P.O. Box 14205 Baton Rouge, Loui- siana 70808 (504) 769-3004	1,500,000	3,400,000	Diversified	6
Louisiana Equity Capital Corp. G. Lee Griffin, Pres- ident 451 Florida Street Baton Rouge, Loui- siana 70801 (504) 389-4421	1,700,000	1,000,000	Diversified	1

Licensee	Private Capital($)	SBA Leverage($)	Investment Policy	Owner Code
Royal Street Investment Corp. William D. Humphries, President 618 Baronne Street Mail: P.O. Box 2349; New Orleans, 70176 New Orleans, Louisiana 70113 (504) 588-9271	1,773,500	1,383,332	Diversified	4
Savings Venture Capital Corp. Dale Anderson, President 6001 Financial Plaza P.O. Box 33888 Shreveport, Louisiana 71130 (318) 687-8996	1,000,000	2,650,000	Diversified	4
Venturtech Capital, Incorporated W. A. Bruce, Exec. V.P. Suite 220, Republic Tower 5700 Florida Blvd. Baton Rouge, Louisiana 70806 (504) 926-5482	1,115,200	4,230,000	Technology field	4

Maine

Licensee	Private Capital($)	SBA Leverage($)	Investment Policy	Owner Code
Great Northern Capital Corporation Barry Goldman, President 1 Monument Square Portland, Maine 04101 (207) 774-5557	504,000	0	Diversified	5

Licensee	Private Capital($)	SBA Lever-age($)	Investment Policy	Owner Code
Hampshire Capital Corporation William Darling, Chairman P.O. Box 659 Portland, Maine 04104 (207) 775-2371	525,000	0	Diversified	5
Maine Capital Corp. Philip W. Hussey, Jr., President One Memorial Circle Augusta, Maine 04330 (207) 623-1686	1,000,000	0	Diversified	1

Massachusetts

Licensee	Private Capital($)	SBA Lever-age($)	Investment Policy	Owner Code
Advent Capital Corp. David D. Croll, Chairman 111 Devonshire Street Boston, Massachusetts 02109 (617) 725-2301	3,000,000	8,000,000	Diversified	5
Alta Capital Corp. William P. Egan, President 175 Federal Street Boston, Massachusetts 02110 (617) 482-8020	2,000,000	1,000,000	Diversified	5
Atlas Capital Corp. Herbert Carver, President 55 Court Street Boston, Massachusetts 02108 (617) 482-1218	1,254,156	2,511,417	50% Real estate	3

Licensee	Private Capital($)	SBA Lever- age($)	Investment Policy	Owner Code
Boston Hambro Capital Company Edwin Goodman, President of Corp. G.P. One Boston Place Boston, Massachu- setts 02106 (617) 722-7055	5,400,000	1,000,000	Diversified	5
Business Achieve- ment Corporation Julian H. Katzeff, President 1280 Centre Street Newton Centre, Massachusetts 02159 (617) 965-0550	361,870	430,000	Diversified	5
Chestnut Capital Corp. David D. Croll, Chairman and CEO 111 Devonshire Street Boston, Massachu- setts 02109 (617) 725-2302	1,500,000	2,000,000	Diversified	5
Devonshire Capital Corporation David D. Croll, Chairman 111 Devonshire Street Boston, Massachu- setts 02109 (617) 725-2306	2,532,750	7,000,000	Diversified	5
Equilease Capital Corp. (Main Office: New York, NY) 393 Totten Pond Rd., Suite 651 Waltham, Massa- chusetts 02154 (617) 826-9056				

Licensee	Private Capital($)	SBA Lever- age($)	Investment Policy	Owner Code
First Capital Corp. of Boston Charles Klotz, President 100 Federal Street Boston, Massachusetts 02110 (617) 434-2441	5,000,000	7,500,000	Diversified	1
First United SBIC, Incorporated Alfred W. Ferrara, Vice President 135 Will Drive Canton, Massachusetts 02021 (617) 828-6150	300,000	300,000	Diversified	4
International Film Investors (LP) (Main Office: New York, NY) Suite 1400, One Federal Street Boston, Massachusetts 02110				
Massachusetts Capital Corporation David Harkins, President 75 Federal Street Boston, Massachusetts 02110 (617) 426-2488	1,695,445	3,345,000	Diversified	5
New England Enterprise Capital Corp. Z. David Patterson, Vice President 28 State Street Boston, Massachusetts 02106 (617) 742-0285	2,500,000	990,002	Diversified	1

Licensee	Private Capital($)	SBA Lever- age($)	Investment Policy	Owner Code
Northeast SBI Corp. Joseph Mindick, Treasurer 16 Cumberland Street Boston, Massachusetts 02115 (617) 267-3983	378,802	1,130,000	Diversified	5
Orange Nassau Capital Corporation G. Kenneth Macrae, President One Post Office Square, Suite 1760 Boston, Massachusetts 02109 (617) 451-6220	2,000,000	0	Diversified	5
Prime Capital Corp. Jason Rosenberg, President 381 Congress Street Boston, Massachusetts 02210 (617) 542-1854	353,000	200,000	Diversified	5
Schooner Capital Corp. Vincent Ryan, Jr., President 77 Franklin Street, 9th Floor Boston, Massachusetts 02110 (617) 357-9031	1,885, 979	2,952,797	Diversified	5
Transatlantic Capital Corporation Bayard Henry, President 60 Batterymarch Street, Room 728 Boston, Massachusetts 02110 (617) 482-0015	3,009,000	0	Diversified	2

Licensee	Private Capital($)	SBA Lever-age($)	Investment Policy	Owner Code
UST Capital Corp. Stephen R. Lewin-stein, President 40 Court Street Boston, Massachu-setts 02108 (617) 726-7129	682,800	716,767	Diversified	1
Vadus Capital Corp. Peter A. Brook, Chairman of the Board One Post Office Square, Suite 1760 Boston, Massachu-setts 02109 (617) 451-6220	1,000,000	0	Diversified	5
Worcester Capital Corp. Kenneth Kidd, Man-ager 446 Main Street Worcester, Massa-chusetts 01608 (617) 853-7298	650,000	200,000	Diversified	1

Michigan

Licensee	Private Capital($)	SBA Lever-age($)	Investment Policy	Owner Code
DBT Capital Corp. John D. Berkaw, President 211 West Fort Street Detroit, Michigan 48226 (313) 222-3907	1,250,000	0	Diversified	1
Doan Resources Corp. Herbert D. Doan, President 110 East Grove Street Midland, Michigan 48640 (517) 631-2623	3,300,000	5,025,000	Diversified	3

Licensee	Private Capital($)	SBA Lever- age($)	Investment Policy	Owner Code
Federated Capital Corporation Louis P. Ferris, Jr., President 20000 West Twelve Mile Road Southfield, Michigan 48076 (313) 557-9100	400,000	600,000	Diversified	3
Michigan Capital & Service, Inc. Joseph Conway, President 740 City Center Building Ann Arbor, Michigan 48104 (313) 663-0702	2,552,265	1,600,000	Diversified	2
Tyler Refrigeration Capital Corp. (Main Office: Michigan City, IN) 1329 Lake Street Niles, Michigan 49120 (616) 683-2000				

Minnesota

Consumer Growth Capital, Inc. John T. Gerlach, President 430 Oak Grove, Suite 404 Minneapolis, Minnesota 55403 (612) 874-0694	1,524,976	1,000,000	Diversified	5
Control Data Capital Corporation W. D. Anderson, Secretary/Treasurer	2,500,000	5,000,000	Diversified	4

Licensee	Private Capital($)	SBA Lever- age($)	Investment Policy	Owner Code
8100 34th Avenue South Bloomington, Minnesota 55420 (612) 853-8100				
Eagle Ventures, Inc. Lawrence L. Horsch, President Suite 700, Soo Line Building Minneapolis, Minnesota 55402 (612) 339-9694	1,323,871	470,000	Diversified	4
First Midwest Capital Corporation Alan K. Ruvelson, President 15 South Fifth St., Suite 700 Minneapolis, Minnesota 55402 (612) 339-9391	1,325,000	2,825,000	Diversified	3
North Star Ventures, Incorporation Terrence W. Glarner, General Manager Suite 1258 7900 Xerxes Avenue South Minneapolis, Minnesota 55431 (612) 830-4550	3,000,000	3,250,000	Diversified	5
Northland Capital Corporation George G. Barnum, Jr. 613 Missabe Building Duluth, Minnesota 55802 (218) 722-0545	762,850	500,000	Diversified	5

Licensee	Private Capital($)	SBA Lever- age($)	Investment Policy	Owner Code
Northwest Growth Fund, Incor- porated Daniel J. Haggerty, President 1730 Midwest Plaza Bldg. 801 Nigollet Mall Minneapolis, Min- nesota 55402 (612) 372-8770	10,000,000	19,773,980	Diversified	1
P. R. Peterson Ven- ture Capital Corp. P. R. Peterson, Pres- ident 7301 Washington, Ave., South Minneapolis, Min- nesota 55435 (612) 941-8285	428,500	0	Diversified	5
Pathfinder Venture Capital Corp. Andrew J. Green- shields, President 7300 Metro Blvd., Suite 585 Minneapolis, Min- nesota 55435 (612) 835-1121	2,000,000	0	Medical, computer, and data communi- cations	5
Retailers Growth Fund, Incor- porated Cornell L. Moore, President 5100 Gamble Drive Minneapolis, Min- nesota 55416 (612) 546-8989	630,000	1,890,000	Franchised retailers	4
Shared Ventures, Inc. Howard W. Weiner, President	500,000	0	Diversified	5

Licensee	Private Capital($)	SBA Leverage($)	Investment Policy	Owner Code
4601 Excelsior Boulevard St. Louis Park, Minnesota 55416 (612) 925-3411				

Mississippi

Licensee	Private Capital($)	SBA Leverage($)	Investment Policy	Owner Code
Invesat Corporation J. Thomas Noojin, President 162 E. Amite Street, Suite 204 Jackson, Mississippi 39207 (601) 969-3242	3,300,000	2,100,000	Diversified	6
Vicksburg SBIC David L. May, President 302 First National Bank Bldg. Vicksburg, Mississippi 39180 (601) 636-4762	550,000	1,037,468	Diversified	5

Missouri

Licensee	Private Capital($)	SBA Leverage($)	Investment Policy	Owner Code
Atlas SBI Corp. Ronald Jarvis, Jr., President 1617 Baltimore Mail: P.O. Box 19657; K.C., MO 64141 Kansas City, Missouri 64108 (816) 471-1750	187,750	0	Diversified	4
Bankers Capital Corp. Raymond E. Glasnapp, President 4049 Pennsylvania, Suite 304 Kansas City, Missouri 64111 (816) 531-1600	302,000	900,000	Diversified	5

Licensee	Private Capital($)	SBA Lever- age($)	Investment Policy	Owner Code
Capital for Busi- ness, Incor- porated James Lynn, Presi- dent P.O. Box 13686 Kansas City, Mis- souri 64199 (816) 234-2344	2,500,000	0	Diversified	1
Equilease Capital Corp. (Main Office: New York, NY) 7700 Clayton Road St. Louis, Missouri 63117				
Intercapco West, Inc. Thomas E. Phelps, President 7800 Bonhomme Avenue St. Louis, Missouri 63105 (314) 863-0600	525,000	500,000	Diversified	4
Moramerica Capital Corp. (Main Office: Cedar Rapids, Iowa) 911 Main Street, Suite 2724A Commerce Tower Building Kansas City, Mis- souri 64105 (816) 842-0114				
R. W. Allsop Capi- tal Corporation (Main Office: Cedar Rapids, Iowa) 111 West Park Plaza, Suite 600 Saint Louis, Mis- souri 63141 (314) 434-1688				

Licensee	Private Capital($)	SBA Lever- age($)	Investment Policy	Owner Code
Nevada				
Universal Invest- ment Corporation Bernard N. Ne- merov, President 300 South Curry Street Carson City, Ne- vada 89701 (702) 883-7585	400,000	400,000	Diversified	5
Westland Capital Corporation Robert S. Dunbar, President 100 West Grove Street Reno, Nevada 89509 (702) 826-8221	1,000,000	1,240,000	Diversified	6
New Jersey				
Capital SBIC, Inc. Isadore Cohen, President 143 East State Street Trenton, New Jer- sey 08608 (609) 394-5221	593,000	202,600	85% Real estate	5
Engle Investment Co. Murray Hendel, President 35 Essex Street Hackensack, New Jersey 07601 (201) 489-3583	500,657	587,500	Diversified	5
Equities Capital Co., Inc. Leon Scharf, Presi- dent 2175 Lemoine Ave- nue Fort Lee, New Jer- sey 07024 (201) 947-0070	502,500	0	Diversified	5

Licensee	Private Capital($)	SBA Lever-age($)	Investment Policy	Owner Code
Eslo Capital Leo Katz, President 485 Morris Avenue Springfield, New Jersey 07080 (201) 267-3152	500,000	500,000	Diversified	5

Interstate Capital
  Co., Inc.
David Scharf, Presi-
  dent
77 Highway 5
Edgewater, New
  Jersey 07020
(201) 224-2403
	502,500	500,000	Diversified	5

Lloyd Capital Corp.
Solomon Scharf,
  President
77 State Highway 5
P.O. Box 180
Edgewater, New
  Jersey 07020
(201) 947-6000
	2,500,000	7,500,000	Diversified	6

Monmouth Capital
  Corp.
Eugene W. Landy,
  President
125 Wickoff Road
1st Merchants Bank
  Bldg.-P.O. Box
  335
Eatontown, New
  Jersey 07724
(201) 542-4927
	2,453,931	6,164,533	Diversified	6

Quidnet Capital
  Corp.
Reid White, Presi-
  dent
909 State Road
Princeton, New Jer-
  sey 08540
(609) 924-7665
	1,500,000	1,700,000	Diversified	3

Licensee	Private Capital($)	SBA Leverage($)	Investment Policy	Owner Code
Unicorn Ventures, Ltd. Frank P. Diassi, President 14 Commerce Drive Cranford, New Jersey 07016 (201) 276-7880	717,917	0	Diversified	5

New Mexico

Licensee	Private Capital($)	SBA Leverage($)	Investment Policy	Owner Code
Albuquerque SBIC Albert T. Ussery, President 501 Tijeras Avenue, N.W. P.O. Box 487 Albuquerque, New Mexico 87103 (505) 247-0145	302,000	0	Diversified	5
First Capital Corp. of New Mexico Shirley Ann Williams, President 3815 Eubank Boulevard Albuquerque, New Mexico 87110 (505) 296-7135	504,000	1,500,000	Diversified	5
Fluid Capital Corp. George T. Slaughter, President 200 Lomas Blvd., N.W., Suite 527 Albuquerque, New Mexico 87110 (505) 243-2279	1,255,000	1,900,000	Diversified	4
Franklin Corp. (The) (Main Office: New York, NY) 4209 San Mateo, N.E. Albuquerque, New Mexico 87110 (505) 243-9680				

Licensee	Private Capital($)	SBA Leverage($)	Investment Policy	Owner Code
New Mexico Capital Corporation S. P. Hidalgo, Exec. Vice-President 2900 Louisiana Blvd., N.E. Suite 201 Albuquerque, New Mexico 87110 (505) 884-3600	2,985,001	11,897,500	Diversified	5
Southwest Capital Investments, Inc. Martin J. Roe, President 8000 Pennsylvania Circle, N.E. Albuquerque, New Mexico 87110 (505) 265-9564	830,552	2,450,000	Diversified	3
Venture Capital Corp. of New Mexico Benirwin Bronstein, President 5301 Central Avenue, N.E. Suite 1600 Albuquerque, New Mexico 87108 (505) 266-0066	944,938	3,760,000	Diversified	5

New York

Licensee	Private Capital($)	SBA Leverage($)	Investment Policy	Owner Code
Amev Capital Corp. Martin Orland, President Two World Trade Center Suite 9766 New York, New York 10048 (212) 775-1912	3,000,000	1,000,000	Diversified	5

Licensee	Private Capital($)	SBA Lever- age($)	Investment Policy	Owner Code
Atalanta Invest- ment Company, Inc. L. Mark Newman, Chairman of Board 450 Park Avenue New York, New York 10022 (212) 832-1104	6,700,500	15,000,000	Diversified	4
Basic Capital Corp. Paul Kates, Presi- dent 32 West 39th St., 3rd Fl. New York, New York 10018 (212) 944-9874	450,000	116,333	Diversified	4
Beneficial Capital Corporation John Hoey, Presi- dent 645 Fifth Avenue New York, New York 10022 (212) 752-1291	500,000	1,450,000	Diversified	5
Bohlen Capital Corp. Harvey J. Werth- eim, President Suite 1260 - 230 Park Avenue New York, New York 10017 (212) 867-9706	1,500,000	3,500,000	Diversified	5
Boston Hambro Capital Company (Main Office: Bos- ton, MA) 17 East 71st Street New York, New York 10021 (212) 288-9106				

Licensee	Private Capital($)	SBA Lever- age($)	Investment Policy	Owner Code
BT Capital Corp. James G. Hellmuth, President 280 Park Avenue New York, New York 10017 (212) 850-1916	5,007,024	2,400,000	Diversified	1
Central New York SBIC (The) Robert E. Romig, President 351 So. Warren Street Syracuse, New York 13202 (315) 478-5026	150,000	180,000	Vending machine	4
Chase Manhattan Capital Corp. Robert Hubbard, President 1 Chase Manhattan Plaza - 30th Floor New York, New York 10081 (212) 552-6275	24,785,000	13,000,000	Diversified	1
Cineffects Capital Corporation Joseph J. Macaluso, President 115 West 45th Street New York, New York 10036 (212) 575-5161	510,000	0	Diversified	5
Citicorp Venture Capital Ltd. John Murphy, Asst. V.P. 399 Park Avenue New York, New York 10022 (212) 559-1127	37,000,000	12,500,000	Diversified	1

Licensee	Private Capital($)	SBA Lever-age($)	Investment Policy	Owner Code
Clinton Capital Corp. Mark Scharfman, President 35 Middagh Street Brooklyn, New York 11201 (212) 260-5329	600,000	0	Diversified	5
CMNY Capital Company, Incorporation Robert Davidoff, Vice President 77 Water Street New York, New York 10005 (212) 437-7078	1,776,480	5,060,000	Diversified	3
College Venture Equity Corporation Francis M. Williams, President 1222 Main Street P.O. Box 791 Niagara Falls, New York 14301 (716) 285-8455	620,000	0	Diversified	5
Columbia Pictures Capital Corp. Francis T. Vincent, Jr., President 711 Fifth Avenue New York, New York 10022 (212) 751-4400	501,000	0	Diversified	5
Cornell Capital Corp. Barry M. Bloom, President 8-B Main Street East Hampton, New York 11937 (516) 324-0408	558,000	0	Diversified	5

Licensee	Private Capital($)	SBA Lever- age($)	Investment Policy	Owner Code
EAB Venture Corp. Richard C. Burcaw, President 90 Park Avenue New York, New York 10016 (212) 437-2283	3,000,000	0	Diversified	5
Edwards Capital Company Edward H. Teitle- baum, President 215 Lexington Ave- nue, Suite 805 New York, New York 10016 (212) 686-2568	1,817,490	4,650,000	Diversified	5
Engle Investment Co. (Main Office: Hack- ensack, NJ) 135 West 50 Street New York, New York 10020 (212) 757-9580				
Equilease Capital Corp. Norbert Weissberg, President 750 Third Avenue New York, New York 10017 (212) 557-6800	2,500,000	1,250,000	Diversified	3
Equitable SBI Corp. David Goldberg, President 350 Fifth Ave., Suite 5805 New York, New York 10001 (212) 564-5420	250,200	150,000	66-⅔% Health and related	5
ESIC Capital, Inc. George Bookbinder, President	2,030,333	7,139,300	Diversified	5

Licensee	Private Capital($)	SBA Lever- age($)	Investment Policy	Owner Code
516 Fifth Avenue Suite 706 New York, New York 10036 (212) 944-5860				
European Develop- ment Capital Corp. Harvey J. Werth- eim, President 230 Park Ave., Suite 1260 New York, New York 10017 (212) 867-9709	2,008,620	1,250,000	Diversified	5
Fairfield Equity Corp. Matthew A. Berdon, President 200 East 42 Street New York, New York 10017 (212) 867-0150	997,109	2,400,003	Diversified	5
Faulkner Invest- ment Company Theodore Cross, General Partner 870 Seventh Ave- nue New York, New York 10019 (212) 977-7412	510,000	0	Diversified	5
Fifty-Third Street Ventures Alan J. Patricof, Chairman 545 Madison Ave- nue New York, New York 10022 (212) 753-6300	2,600,000	5,460,000	Diversified	5
Finevalor Capital Corporation Juan Zavala, Presi- dent	1,020,000	O	Diversified	5

Licensee	Private Capital($)	SBA Lever- age($)	Investment Policy	Owner Code
745 Fifth Avenue New York, New York 10022 (212) 223-0569				
First Connecticut SBIC (Main Office: Bridgeport, CT) 68 Fifth Avenue New York, New York 10003 (212) 541-6222				
First Wall Street SBIC, Inc. John W. Chappell, President 767 Fifth Ave., Suite 4403 New York, New York 10022 (212) 355-6540	504,380	0	Diversified	5
Franklin Corp. (The) Herman E. Good- man, President One Rockefeller Plaza Suite 2614 New York, New York 10022 (212) 581-4900	9,183,027	15,860,000	Diversified	6
Fundex Capital Corp. Howard Sommer, President 525 Northern Blvd. Great Neck, New York 11021 (516) 466-8551	596,398	1,800,000	Diversified	5
Hanover Capital Corp. Daniel J. Sullivan, President	847,944	1,467,500	Diversified	5

Licensee	Private Capital($)	SBA Lever-age($)	Investment Policy	Owner Code
150 East 58th Street, Suite 3520 New York, New York 10022 (212) 532-5173				
Heller Capital Services, Inc. J. Allen Kerr, President 200 Park Avenue New York, New York 10017 (212) 880-7047	2,015,000	0	Diversified	5
Holding Capital Management Co., L.P. Sash A. Spencer, President, Corp. G/P 711 Fifth Avenue New York, New York 10022 (212) 888-8478	665,000	0	Diversified	5-P
Intercoastal Capital Corp. Herbert Krasnow, President 380 Madison Avenue New York, New York 10017 (212) 986-0482	608,800	924,235	66% Real estate	6
Intergroup Venture Capital Corp. Ben Hauben, President 230 Park Avenue New York, New York 10017 (212) 661-5428	502,500	1,000,000	Diversified	5
International Film Investors, L.P. Josiah H. Child., Jr. Pres.-Corp. G.P.	10,232,500	10,000,000	100% Movie specialist	4-P

Licensee	Private Capital($)	SBA Lever-age($)	Investment Policy	Owner Code
595 Madison Ave., 11th Fl. New York, New York 10022 (212) 310-1500				
Irving Capital Corp. Andrew McWethy, V.P. and Gen. Mgr. 1290 Avenue of the Americas New York, New York 10019 (212) 487-3474	6,900,000	0	Diversified	1
Kwiat Capital Corp. David Kwiat, President 576 Fifth Avenue New York, New York 10036 (212) 391-2416	510,000	0	Diversified	5
Lincoln Capital Corp. Martin Lifton, President 41 East 42nd Street New York, New York 10017 (212) 697-0610	1,212,950	169,492	50% Real estate	5
M & T Capital Corp. Harold M. Small, President One M & T Plaza Buffalo, New York 14240 (716) 842-4200	2,200,000	4,500,000	Diversified	1
Marwit Capital Corp. (Main Office: Newport Beach, CA) 6 East 43rd Street New York, New York 10017 (212) 867-3906				

Licensee	Private Capital($)	SBA Lever- age($)	Investment Policy	Owner Code
Menlo Venture Corp. (Main Office: Menlo Park, CA) 230 Park Avenue New York, New York 10169 (212) 697-7667				
Midland Venture Capital Ltd. R. Machinist & M. Stanfield, Managers 110 William Street New York, New York 10038 (212) 577-0750	15,000,000	9,495,000	Diversified	6
Multi-Purpose Capital Corporation Eli B. Fine, President 31 South Broadway Yonkers, New York 10701 (914) 963-2733	190,300	278,400	Diversified	5
Nelson Capital Corp. Irwin Nelson, President 591 Stewart Avenue Garden City L.I., New York 11530 (516) 222-2555	449,000	1,170,000	Diversified	5
NIS Capital Corp. Howard Blank, President 34 S. Broadway White Plains, New York 10601 (914) 428-8600	500,000	1,500,000	Diversified	4
Noro Capital Corp. Harvey J. Wertheim, President	1,000,000	2,000,000	Diversified	5

Licensee	Private Capital($)	SBA Lever- age($)	Investment Policy	Owner Code
230 Park Avenue New York, New York 10017 (212) 661-5281				
NYBDC Capital Corp. Marshall R. Lustig, President 41 State Street Albany, New York 12207 (518) 463-2268	300,000	0	Diversified	4
Percival Capital Corp. George A. Simpson, President 29 Broadway - Suite 1801 New York, New York 10004 (212) 785-7008	505,000	500,000	Diversified	5
Peter J. Schmitt SBIC, Incor- porated William Wanstedt, President 678 Bailey Avenue Buffalo, New York 14206 (716) 825-1111	500,000	100,000	Retail grocers	4
Pioneer Investors Corporation James G. Niven, President 113 East 55th Street New York, New York 10022 (212) 980-9090	2,510,000	6,500,000	Diversified	5
Preferential Capital Corporation Bruce Bayroff, Sec.- Treas.	419,381	617,926	Diversified	5

Licensee	Private Capital($)	SBA Lever- age($)	Investment Policy	Owner Code
16 Court Street Brooklyn, New York 11241 (212) 855-2728				
Printers Capital Corp. Herbert Brandon, President 1 World Trade Center Suite 3169 New York, New York 10048 (212) 432-0750	154,720	142,500	Printing and duplicating	5
Questech Capital Corp. Earl W. Brian, M.D., President 11 Hanover Square New York, New York 10065 (212) 483-1335	3,500,000	0	Diversified	5
R & R Financial Corp. Imre Rosenthal, President 1451 Broadway New York, New York 10066 (212) 564-4500	305,000	474,494	Diversified	3
Rand SBIC, Inc. Donald Ross, President 2600 Rand Building Buffalo, New York 14203 (716) 853-0802	605,000	600,000	Diversified	6
Realty Growth Capital Corporation Lawrence Benenson, President	500,000	1,505,000	100% Real estate specialist	5

Licensee	Private Capital($)	SBA Lever-age($)	Investment Policy	Owner Code
575 Lexington Avenue New York, New York 10022 (212) 755-9043				
Roundhill Capital Corporation Joseph M. Javis, President 44 Wall Street New York, New York 10005 (212) 747-0144	505,000	0	Diversified	5
Royal Business Funds Corporation S. P. Bonan, President 60 East 42nd Street New York, New York 10017 (212) 986-8463	6,370,481	18,646,565	100% Real estate	6
S & S Venture Associates Ltd. Donald Smith, President 352 Seventh Avenue New York, New York 10001 (212) 736-2423	510,000	500,000	Diversified	5
SB Electronics Investment Co. Stanley Meisels, President 60 Broad Street New York, New York 10004 (212) 952-7531	497,125	855,336	Diversified	5
Sherwood Business Capital Corp. Lewis R. Eisner, President	504,000	0	Diversified	5

Licensee	Private Capital($)	SBA Lever-age($)	Investment Policy	Owner Code
770 King Street Port Chester, New York 10573 (914) 937-6000				
Southern Tier Capital Corporation Harold Gold, Secretary-Treasurer 55 South Main Street Liberty, New York 12754 (914) 282-3030	350,111	847,500	Major group 70 (hotels and rooming houses)	5
Sprout Capital Corp. Lawrence R. Johnson, President 140 Broadway New York, New York 10005 (212) 943-0300	5,000,000	2,000,000	Diversified	3
Tappan Zee Capital Corporation Karl Kirchner, President 120 North Main Street New City, New York 10956 (914) 634-8890	659,280	1,344,000	66% Real estate	5
Telesciences Capital Corporation George E. Carmody, President 135 East 54th Street New York, New York 10022 (212) 935-2550	1,250,000	0	Diversified	4
TLC Funding Corp. Philip G. Kass, President 200 East 42nd Street New York, New York 10017 (212) 682-0790	700,000	696,000	Diversified	5

Licensee	Private Capital($)	SBA Lever-age($)	Investment Policy	Owner Code
Van Rietschoten Capital Corp. Harvey J. Werth-eim, President Suite 1260 - 230 Park Avenue New York, New York 10017 (212) 867-9705	2,000,000	4,000,000	Diversified	5
Vega Capital Corp. Victor Harz, President 10 East 40th Street New York, New York 10016 (212) 685-2222	2,425,625	7,183,336	Diversified	6
Venture SBIC, Inc. Arnold Feldman, President 249-12 Jericho Turn-pike Bellerose, New York 11426 (212) 343-8188	612,000	1,800,000	Diversified	5
Winfield Capital Corp. Stanley M. Pech-man, President 237 Mamaroneck Avenue White Plains, New York 10605 (914) 949-2600	700,000	2,100,000	Diversified	5
Wood River Capital Corporation Richard M. Drys-dale, President 645 Madison Ave-nue New York, New York 10022 (212) 750-9420	6,012,000	6,000,000	Diversified	5

Licensee	Private Capital($)	SBA Lever- age($)	Investment Policy	Owner Code

North Carolina

Licensee	Private Capital($)	SBA Leverage($)	Investment Policy	Owner Code
Delta Capital, Inc. Alex B. Wilkins, Jr., President 202 Latta Arcade 320 South Tryon Street Charlotte, North Carolina 28202 (704) 372-1410	1,250,000	4,103,070	50% Real estate	3
Heritage Capital Corp. J. Randolph Gregory, President 2290 Jefferston First Union Plaza Charlotte, North Carolina 28282 (704) 334-2867	1,250,265	1,923,135	50% Real estate	3
Kitty Hawk Capital, Incorporated Walter H. Wilkinson, President 2195 First Union Plaza Charlotte, North Carolina 28282 (704) 333-3777	1,305,000	0	Diversified	5-P
Lowcountry Investment Corporation (Main Office: Charleston Heights, SC) Vernon Avenue Kinston, North Carolina 28659				
Northwestern Capital Corporation Clyde R. Brown, President	1,363,000	2,639,995	Diversified	6

Licensee	Private Capital($)	SBA Lever-age($)	Investment Policy	Owner Code

924 B Street
Mail: P.O. Box 310
North Wilkesbor,
  North Carolina
  28659
(919) 667-2111				

North Dakota

First Dakota Capital
  Corporation
James S. Lindsay,
  President
2800 7th Avenue,
  North
Fargo, North Da-
  kota 58102
(701) 237-0450
	365,000	600,000	Diversified	5

Ohio

Banc One Capital
  Corporation
James E. Kolls, Vice
  President
100 East Broad
  Street
Columbus, Ohio
  43215
(614) 461-5832
	340,000	0	Diversified	1

Capital Funds Corp.
Richard Berndt,
  Chief Inv. Officer
127 Public Square
Cleveland, Ohio
  44114
(216) 861-4000
	1,750,000	0	Communications	1

Clarion Capital
  Corp.
Peter Van Ooster-
  hout, President
The Chesterfield,
  Suite 201
1801 East 12th
  Street
Cleveland, Ohio
  44114
(216) 687-1096
	7,903,628	15,500,000	Diversified	6

Licensee	Private Capital($)	SBA Lever-age($)	Investment Policy	Owner Code
DYCAP, Inc. A. G. Imhoff, President 88 East Broad Street Suite 1980 Columbus, Ohio 43215 (614) 228-6641	450,000	650,025	Diversified	5
Greater Miami Inv. Services, Inc. Emmett B. Lewis, President 3131 South Dixie Drive, Suite 505 Dayton, Ohio 45439 (513) 294-6124	650,000	0	Diversified	2
Gries Investment Corp. Robert D. Gries, President 2310 Terminal Tower Bldg. Cleveland, Ohio 44113 (216) 861-1146	682,957	921,200	Diversified	5
Intercapco, Inc. Robert B. Haas, President One Erieview Plaza, 10th Floor Cleveland, Ohio 44114 (216) 241-7170	1,510,000	4,000,000	Diversified	5
National City Capital Corporation Michael Sherwin, President 1900 East Ninth Street Cleveland, Ohio 44114 (216) 575-2491	2,500,000	0	Diversified	1

Licensee	Private Capital($)	SBA Lever-age($)	Investment Policy	Owner Code
Tamco Investors (SBIC) Incor-porated Nathan H. Monus, President 375 Victoria Road Youngstown, Ohio 44515 (216) 792-3811	300,000	600,000	Retail grocers	4
Tomlinson Capital Corporation John A. Chernak, Vice President 3055 East 63rd Street Cleveland, Ohio 44127 (216) 271-2103	550,000	1,500,000	Miniature super-market	4

Oklahoma

Licensee	Private Capital($)	SBA Lever-age($)	Investment Policy	Owner Code
Alliance Business Investment Co. Barry Davis, Presi-dent 500 McFarlin Bldg. Tulsa, Oklahoma 74103 (918) 584-3581	2,503,018	3,521,083	Diversified	5
Bartlesville Invest-ment Corp. James L. Diamond, President P.O. Box 548 Bartlesville, Okla-homa 74003 (918) 333-3022	645,000	1,822,500	Diversified	5
First Oklahoma Inv. Capital Corpora-tion Eldon Beller, Presi-dent	505,100	0	Diversified	1

Licensee	Private Capital($)	SBA Lever-age($)	Investment Policy	Owner Code
120 North Robinson Mail: P.O. Box 25189; OK City, OK 73225 Oklahoma City, Oklahoma 73102 (405) 272-4660				
First Venture Corp. Jon R. K. Tinkle, President Venture Building, The Quarters Bartlesville, Oklahoma 74003 (918) 333-8820	1,459,033	5,000,000	Diversified	1
Investment Capital, Incorporated James J. Wasson, President 300 North Harrison Mail: P.O. Box 1071 Cushing, Oklahoma 74023 (918) 225-5850	1,049,981	2,880,000	Diversified	5
Oklahoma Capital Corp. Bill Daniel, Sr., Chairman of Board Suite 550 2200 Classen Blvd. Oklahoma City, Oklahoma 73106 (405) 525-5544	411,300	1,200,000	Diversified	5
Southwest Venture Capital, Inc. Donald J. Rubottom, President 1920 First Place Tulsa, Oklahoma 74103 (918) 584-4201	500,000	500,000	Diversified	5

Licensee	Private Capital($)	SBA Lever- age($)	Investment Policy	Owner Code
Utica Investment Corp. David D. Nunneley, President 1924 South Utica Avenue Suite 418 Tulsa, Oklahoma 74104 (918) 747-7581	505,000	0	Diversified	1
Western Venture Capital Corp. Gary L. Smith, President 4900 South Lewis Tulsa, Oklahoma 74105 (918) 749-7981	1,048,214	0	Diversified	2

Oregon

Cascade Capital Corp. (M.O: Northwest Growth Fund, Inc. Minneapolis, MN) 1300 S.W. 5th St., Suite 3018 Portland, Oregon 97201 (503) 223-6622				
Northern Pacific Capital Corp. John J. Tennant, Jr., President 1201 S.W. 12th Ave., Suite 608 Mail: P.O. Box 1658; Portland, OR 97207 Portland, Oregon 97205 (503) 245-3147	750,000	800,000	Diversified	5

Licensee	Private Capital($)	SBA Lever-age($)	Investment Policy	Owner Code
Pennsylvania				
American Venture Capital Co. Knute C. Albrect, President Suite 122, Blue Bell West 650 Skippack Pike Blue Bell, Pennsylvania 19422 (215) 278-8907	1,200,000	0	Diversified	1
Capital Corporation of America Martin M. Newman, President 1521 Walnut Street Philadelphia, Pennsylvania 19102 (215) 563-7423	1,302,135	1,065,000	Diversified	6
Central Capital Corp. W. D. McElhinny, Chairman of Board 1097 Commercial Avenue Lancaster, Pennsylvania 17604 (717) 569-9650	1,000,000	0	Diversified	1
Equilease Capital Corporation (Main Office: New York, NY) One Parkway Center, RM, 213 Pittsburgh, Pennsylvania 19102 (215) 265-8590				
Fidelity America SBIC Howard I. Green, President	560,359	1,363,031	Diversified	6

Licensee	Private Capital($)	SBA Lever- age($)	Investment Policy	Owner Code
3 Penn Center Plaza, Suite 1420 Philadelphia, Pennsylvania 19102 (215) 568-3550				
Osher Capital Corp. Leonard Cantor, President Wyncote House Township Line Rd. & Washington Lane Wyncote, Pennsylvania 19095 (215) 624-4800	300,000	300,000	Diversified	5
Pennsylvania Growth Investment Corp. William L. Mosenson, President 1000 RIDC Plaza Pittsburgh, Pennsylvania 15238 (412) 963-9339	627,375	379,413	Diversified	3
Real Estate Capital Corporation William J. Levitt, Jr., President 111 Presidential Blvd. Bala Cynwyd, Pennsylvania 19004 (215) 569-4400	1,260,444	947,518	100% Real estate specialists	5
Sharon SBIC Nels Scheel, President 385 Shenango Avenue Sharon, Pennsylvania 16146 (412) 981-1500	255,000	487,500	Grocery store	4

Licensee	Private Capital($)	SBA Lever- age($)	Investment Policy	Owner Code
TDH Capital Corp. J. Mahlon Buck, Jr., President 2 Radnor Corporate Center Radnor, Pennsylvania 19087 (215) 293-9787	4,000,000	0	Diversified	5

Rhode Island

| Industrial Capital Corporation Albert A. T. Wickersham, President 111 Westminster Street Providence, Rhode Island 02903 (401) 278-6770 | 3,000,000 | 500,000 | Diversified | 1 |
| Narragansett Capital Corporation Robert D. Manchester, President 40 Westminster Street Providence, Rhode Island 02903 (401) 751-1000 | 20,000,203 | 34,930,000 | Diversified | 6 |

South Carolina

| Carolina Venture Cap. Corporation Thomas H. Harvey III, President Suite 109, Sea Pines Exec. Office Bldg. Mail: P.O. Box 3110 Hilton Head Isl, South Carolina 29928 (803) 842-3101 | 500,000 | 0 | Diversified | 5 |
| Charleston Capital Corporation Henry Yaschik, President | 637,000 | 1,032,625 | Diversified | 5 |

Licensee	Private Capital($)	SBA Lever- age($)	Investment Policy	Owner Code
111 Church Street P.O. Box 328 Charleston, South Carolina 29402 (803) 723-6464				
Falcon Capital Corp. Mona G. Sokol, President 100 Broad Street Charleston, South Carolina 29401 (803) 723-8624	152,237	150,000	Diversified	5
Floco Investment Company, Inc. (The) William H. Johnson, Sr., President P.O. Box 216 Scranton, South Carolina 29561 (803) 389-2731	502,464	87,500	Food retailers	5
Lowcountry Invest- ment Corporation Joseph T. Newton, Jr., President 4444 Daley Street P.O. Box 10447 Charleston, South Carolina 29411 (803) 554-9880	1,908,950	5,395,000	Grocery store	4
Reedy River Ven- tures, Incor- porated John M. Sterling, President 60 Camperdown Way P.O. Box 8931 Greenville, South Carolina 29601 (803) 233-2374	1,254,500	0	Diversified	5

Licensee	Private Capital($)	SBA Lever- age($)	Investment Policy	Owner Code

Tennessee

Licensee	Private Capital($)	SBA Lever- age($)	Investment Policy	Owner Code
C & C Capital Corp. T. Wendell Holli- day, President 531 S. Gay Street P.O. Box 90 Knoxville, Tennes- see 37901 (615) 637-0521	1,000,000	1,100,000	Diversified	1
De Soto Capital Corp. William B. Rudner, President 5050 Poplar Ave., Suite 2429 Memphis, Tennes- see 38157 (901) 682-9072	500,000	400,000	Diversified	5
Financial Re- sources, Incor- porated Milton Picard, Chairman of Board 2800 Sterick Blvd. Memphis, Tennes- see 38103 (901) 527-9411	405,320	416,500	Diversified	5

Texas

Licensee	Private Capital($)	SBA Lever- age($)	Investment Policy	Owner Code
Alliance Business Investment Co. (Main Office: Tulsa, OK) 2660 South Tower Houston, Texas 77002 (713) 224-8224				
Allied Bancshares Capital Corp. D. Kent Anderson, President	6,250,000	0	Diversified	1

Licensee	Private Capital($)	SBA Leverage($)	Investment Policy	Owner Code
P.O. Box 3326 Houston, Texas 77001 (713) 224-6611				
American Energy Investment Corp. Robert J. Moses, Executive V.P. 1010 Lamar, Suite 1680 Houston, Texas 77002 (713) 651-0220	2,500,000	0	Energy industries	5
Aspen Financial Corp. William E. Dueease, President 333 North Belt, Suite 660 Houston, Texas 77060 (713) 999-0011	505,000	0	Diversified	5
Bow Lane Capital Corporation Stuart Schube, President Suite 950, 2401 Fountainview Houston, Texas 77057 (713) 977-7421	2,500,000	1,000,000	Diversified	5
Brittany Capital Corp. Robert E. Clements, President 1525 Elm Street 2424 LTV Tower Dallas, Texas 75201 (214) 742-5810	500,000	1,380,000	Diversified	2
Cameron Financial Corporation A. Baker Duncan, President	512,000	300,000	Diversified	5

Licensee	Private Capital($)	SBA Lever- age($)	Investment Policy	Owner Code
Dullnig Building 262 Losoya San Antonio, Texas 78205 (512) 223-9768				
Capital Marketing Corporation Nathaniel Gibbs, Chairman of Board 9004 Ambassador Row P.O. Box 225293 Dallas, Texas 75222 (214) 638-1913	7,796,838	23,390,000	Retail grocers	4
Central Texas SBI Corporation Walter G. Lacy, Jr., President P.O. Box 829 Waco, Texas 76703 (817) 753-6461	300,000	212,500	Diversified	1
Commerce South- west Capital, Inc. Harold W. McNabb, President 1525 Elm Street - Room 202 Dallas, Texas 75201 (214) 658-6231	1,003,500	0	Diversified	5
CSC Capital Corp. William R. Thomas, President Suite 700, 12900 Preston Road Dallas, Texas 75230 (214) 233-8242	3,065,585	6,000,000	Diversified	6
Dallas Business Capital Corp. Edgar S. Meredith, Sr. V.P.	6,330,830	1,900,000	Diversified	6

Licensee	Private Capital($)	SBA Leverage($)	Investment Policy	Owner Code
Suite 333, Meadows Bldg. 5646 Milton Street Dallas, Texas 75206 (214) 691-0711				
Diman Financial Corp. Don Mann, President 13601 Preston Rd., Suite 717E Dallas, Texas 75240 (214) 233-7610	444,000	1,330,000	Diversified	4
Energy Assets, Inc. Laurence E. Simmons, Exec. V.P. 1800 South Tower Pennzoil Place Houston, Texas 77002 (713) 236-9999	546,351	500,000	Various firms in energy industry	4
Energy Capital Corporation Herbert F. Poyner, President 953 Esperson Building Houston, Texas 77002 (713) 236-0006	11,285,613	0	Diversified	5
Enterprise Capital Corporation Ms. Deborah A. Frost, Sec./Treasurer Suite 465 W. Executive Plaza 4635 Southwest Freeway Houston, Texas 77027 (713) 626-7171	750,000	2,924,583	Diversified	5

Licensee	Private Capital($)	SBA Lever-age($)	Investment Policy	Owner Code
First Bancorp Capital, Inc. George F. Baum, Jr., President 100 North Main Street P.O. Box 613 Corsicana, Texas 75110 (214) 874-4711	505,000	0	Diversified	1
First Business Investment Corp. Albert J. Prevot, President One West Loop South, Suite 807 Houston, Texas 77027 (713) 840-7337	542,000	789,166	Diversified	5
First Capital Corp. John R. Payne, President 7100 Grapevine Hwy., Suite 105 Fort Worth, Texas 76118 (817) 284-0166	1,000,310	0	Diversified	5
First City Capital Corporation William E. Ladin, President One West Loop South, Suite 809 Houston, Texas 77027 (713) 623-6151	520,005	1,560,000	Diversified	5
Great American Capital Investors, Inc. Albert S. Dillard, President 1006 Holliday Street Wichita Falls, Texas 76307 (817) 322-4448	510,000	500,000	Diversified	1

Licensee	Private Capital($)	SBA Leverage($)	Investment Policy	Owner Code
Grocers SBI Corp. Milton E. Levit, President 3131 East Holcombe Blvd. Suite 101 Houston, Texas 77021 (713) 747-7913	1,000,000	2,000,000	Retail grocers	4
Interfirst Venture Corporation Eric C. Neuman, President 245 First International Bldg. Dallas, Texas 75270 (214) 744-8050	12,500,044	7,430,000	Diversified	1
Livingston Capital, Ltd. J. Livingston Kosberg, Ltd. Partner 5701 Woodway, Suite 332 Houston, Texas 77057 (713) 977-4040	1,000,000	950,000	Diversified	5-P
Mapleleaf Capital Corporation Edward Barton Scott, President 7500 San Felipe Houston, Texas 77063 (713) 975-8060	3,331,625	2,000,000	Diversified	2
Mercantile Dallas Corporation John G. Farmer, President 1704 Main Street P.O. Box 222090 Dallas, Texas 75222 (214) 741-1469	11,500,000	28,000,000	Diversified	1

Licensee	Private Capital($)	SBA Lever-age($)	Investment Policy	Owner Code
Permian Basin Capital Corporation Douglas B. Henson, President P.O. Box 1599 Midland, Texas 79701 (915) 683-4231	500,000	0	Diversified	1
Rainbow Capital Corp. William A. Anderson, Jr., President 1100 One Allen Center Houston, Texas 77002 (713) 757-0461	500,000	0	Diversified	5
Red River Ventures, Incorporated Thomas H. Schnitzius, President 535 Houston Natural Gas Bldg. Houston, Texas 77002 (713) 658-9806	751,000	1,800,000	Diversified	3
Republic Venture Group Incorporated Robert H. Wellborn, V.P. & General Mgr. P.O. Box 225961 (214) 653-5078	5,000,000	0	Diversified	1
Retail Capital Corp. William J. Boschma, President 13403 Northwest Freeway Suite 160 Houston, Texas 77040 (713) 462-8517	510,000	1,000,000	Diversified	5

Licensee	Private Capital($)	SBA Lever-age($)	Investment Policy	Owner Code
Rice Country Capital, Incorporated William H. Harrison, Jr., President P.O. Box 215 Eagle Lake, Texas 77434 (713) 234-2506	405,000	0	Diversified	1
Rice Investment Company Alvin Diamond, Secretary 3200 Produce Row Houston, Texas 77023 (713) 797-1990	1,320,001	3,815,500	Retail grocers	5
Rust Capital Limited Jeffery Garvey, Partner 605 Brazos, Suite 300 Austin, Texas 78701 (512) 479-0055	2,000,000	1,500,000	Diversified	3
San Antonio Venture Group, Inc. William A. Fagan, President 2300 West Commerce Street San Antonio, Texas 78207 (512) 223-3633	1,050,000	0	Diversified	4
SBI Capital Corp. William E. Wright, President 6305 Beverly Hill Lane Mail: P.O. Box 1597; Bellaire, TX 77401 Houston, Texas 77057 (713) 975-1188	1,000,000	0	Diversified	5

Licensee	Private Capital($)	SBA Leverage($)	Investment Policy	Owner Code
South Texas SBIC Arthur E. Buckert, Treasurer 120 South Main Street P.O. Box 1698 Victoria, Texas 77901 (512) 573-5151	400,000	0	Diversified	1
Southwestern Venture Cap. of Texas, Inc. James A. Bettersworth, President 113 South River Street, Suite 205 P.O. Box 1169 Seguin, Texas 78155 (512) 379-2258	1,001,000	0	Diversified	2
Texas Capital Corp. W. Grogan Lord, President 2424 Houston Natural Gas Bldg. 1200 Travis Street Houston, Texas 77002 (713) 658-9961	3,050,000	6,961,667	Diversified	4
Trammell Crow Investment Co. Henry W. Billingsley, President 2001 Bryan Tower Suite 3200 Dallas, Texas 75201 (214) 747-0643	529,000	150,000	100% Real estate	5
TSM Corporation Joe Justice, General Manager 444 Executive Center Blvd., Suite 237	499,847	1,150,000	Diversified	5

Licensee	Private Capital($)	SBA Lever- age($)	Investment Policy	Owner Code
Mail: Box 9938; El Paso, TX 79990 El Paso, Texas 79902 (915) 533-6375				
West Central Capi- tal Corporation Howard W. Jacob, President Suite 206 440 Northlake Cen- ter Dallas, Texas 75238 (214) 348-3969	152,853	75,000	Diversified	5
Zenith Capital Corp. Jerry E. Finger, President Suite 218 5150 North Shep- herd Houston, Texas 77018 (713) 692-6121	505,000	0	Diversified	1

Vermont

Mansfield Capital Corporation Stephen H. Farring- ton, President Mountain Road Stowe, Vermont 05672 (802) 253-9400	350,010	0	Diversified	5
SBIC of Vermont, Inc. Robert B. Manning, President 121 West Street Rutland, Vermont 05701 (802) 775-3393	1,316,000	1,100,000	Diversified	1

Licensee	Private Capital($)	SBA Lever- age($)	Investment Policy	Owner Code
Vermont Invest- ment Capital, Inc. Harold Jacobs, Pres- ident South Windsor Street, Box 590 South Royalton, Vermont 05068 (802) 763-7716	228,344	550,000	Diversified	5

Virginia

Licensee	Private Capital($)	SBA Lever- age($)	Investment Policy	Owner Code
Inverness Capital Corporation Harry S. Flemming, President 424 N. Washington Street Alexandria, Vir- ginia 22314 (703) 549-5730	2,423,963	7,453,543	Diversified	5
James River Capital Associates A. Hugh Ewing, President 9 South 12th Street Mail: P.O. Box 1776 Richmond, Virginia 23214 (804) 643-7323	1,075,000	0	Diversified	5-P
Metropolitan Capi- tal Corporation F. W. Scoville, Pres- ident 2550 Huntington Avenue Alexandria, Vir- ginia 22303 (703) 960-4698	548,418	1,560,000	Diversified	4
SBI Corporation of Norfolk D. H. Burlage, Pres- ident	300,606	356,151	Diversified	4

Licensee	Private Capital($)	SBA Lever- age($)	Investment Policy	Owner Code
1216 Granby St., Suite 3 Norfolk, Virginia 23510 (804) 625-0534				
Tidewater Indus- trial Capital Corp. Armand Caplan, President Suite 1424 United Virginia Bank Bldg. Norfolk, Virginia 23510 (804) 622-1501	758,200	1,200,000	Diversified	4
Tidewater SBI Corp. Robert H. Schmidt, President 234 Monticello Ave- nue 1106 Maritime Tower Norfolk, Virginia 23510 (804) 627-2315	1,000,000	1,240,032	Diversified	4
Virginia Capital Corp. Robert H. Pratt, President 801 East Main Street Mail: P.O. Box 1493; Richmond, Virginia 23121 Richmond, Virginia 23219 (804) 644-5496	1,400,197	4,041,668	Diversified	6
Washington				
Capital Resource Corporation T. Evans Wyckoff, President	500,000	0	Diversified	5

Licensee	Private Capital($)	SBA Lever-age($)	Investment Policy	Owner Code
1001 Logan Building Seattle, Washington 98101 (206) 623-6550				
CH Capital Corp. Elwood D. Howse, President 11201 Southeast 8th, Suite 163 Bellevue, Washington 98004 (206) 455-5522	2,501,922	0	Diversified	5
Northwest Business Investment Corp. C. Paul Sandifur, President 929 West Sprague Avenue Spokane, Washington 99204 (509) 838-3111	250,200	484,875	Diversified	5
Peoples Small Business Investment Corp. James G. Cairns, Jr., President 1414 Fourth Avenue Seattle, Washington 98171 (206) 344-8105	500,000	0	Diversified	1
Seafirst Capital Corp. Steven G. Blanchard, Manager Fourth & Blanchard Building Seattle, Washington 98121 (206) 583-3278	2,500,000	0	Diversified	1
Washington Capital Corporation James F. Aylward, President	5,591,500	13,985,825	50% Real estate	3

Licensee	Private Capital($)	SBA Leverage($)	Investment Policy	Owner Code
1417 Fourth Avenue P.O. Box 1770 Seattle, Washington 98111 (206) 682-5400				
Washington Trust Equity Corp. Dan T. Lacy, Manager Washington Trust Financial Ctr. P.O. Box 2127 Spokane, Washington 99210 (509) 455-4106	700,000	500,000	Diversified	1

Wisconsin

Licensee	Private Capital($)	SBA Leverage($)	Investment Policy	Owner Code
Bando-McGlocklin Investment Co., Inc. George Schonath, Investment Advisor 13555 Bishops Court Brookfield, Wisconsin 53005 (414) 784-9010	1,150,000	0	Diversified	5
Bankit Financial Corp. Roy D. Terracina, Exec. V.P. 733 North Vanburen Street Milwaukee, Wisconsin 53202 (414) 271-5050	350,000	300,000	Grocery stores	4
Capital Investments, Incorporated Robert L. Banner, Vice President 515 West Wells Street Milwaukee, Wisconsin 53203 (414) 273-6560	3,159,044	9,439,000	Diversified	6

Licensee	Private Capital($)	SBA Lever-age($)	Investment Policy	Owner Code
Certco Capital Corp. Howard E. Hill, President 6150 McKee Road Madison, Wisconsin 53507 (608) 271-4500	405,000	0	Retail grocers	4
Moramerica Capital Corporation (Main Office: Cedar Rapids, Iowa) 710 N. Plankinton Ave. Suite 333 Milwaukee, Wisconsin 53203 (414) 276-3839				
Super Market Investors Incorporated John W. Andorfer, President 11300 West Burleigh Street Mail: P.O. Box 473; Milwaukee, Wisconsin 53202 Wauwautosa, Wisconsin 53201 (414) 453-6211	500,000	1,000,000	Retail grocers	4

Wyoming

Licensee	Private Capital($)	SBA Lever-age($)	Investment Policy	Owner Code
Capital Corporation of Wyoming, Inc. Larry J. McDonald, Exec. V.P. P.O. Box 612 145 South Durbin Street Casper, Wyoming 82602 (307) 234-5351	450,000	300,000	Diversified	3

SBIC Totals by States

State	Number of SBICS					Total Private Capital ($)	Total Obligations to SBA ($)
	Size 1	Size 2	Size 3	Size 4	Total		
Alabama	0	3	1	0	4	3,533,000	7,100,000
Alaska	0	0	0	0	0	0	0
Arizona	0	2	0	0	2	1,000,000	300,000
Arkansas	0	2	0	0	2	1,369,728	2,250,000
California	0	22	16	6	44	102,307,852	73,986,831
Colorado	1	1	4	0	6	8,028,416	2,050,000
Connecticut	1	10	1	2	14	24,844,928	36,111,276
Delaware	0	0	0	0	0	0	0
D.C.	0	1	3	0	4	9,018,192	22,968,503
Florida	1	8	3	0	12	12,065,086	21,648,085
Georgia	0	4	2	0	6	7,437,632	12,735,429
Hawaii	0	1	0	0	1	332,291	240,000
Idaho	0	1	0	0	1	1,000,000	1,500,000
Illinois	1	3	4	2	10	61,896,476	9,358,333
Indiana	0	2	0	0	2	1,263,000	0
Iowa	0	0	2	0	2	6,200,000	14,099,889
Kansas	0	0	1	0	1	1,075,240	0
Kentucky	0	1	1	0	2	2,100,000	2,000,000
Louisiana	1	6	4	0	11	10,923,694	19,194,232
Maine	0	3	0	0	3	2,029,000	0
Maryland	0	0	0	0	0	0	0
Massachusetts	1	6	11	1	19	35,503,802	39,275,983
Michigan	0	1	3	0	4	7,502,265	7,225,000
Minnesota	0	4	6	1	11	23,995,197	34,708,980
Mississippi	0	1	1	0	2	3,850,000	3,137,468
Missouri	1	2	1	0	4	3,514,750	1,400,000
Montana	0	0	0	0	0	0	0
Nebraska	0	0	0	0	0	0	0
Nevada	0	2	0	0	2	1,400,000	1,640,000
New Hampshire	0	0	0	0	0	0	0
New Jersey	0	6	3	0	9	9,770,505	17,154,633
New Mexico	0	4	2	0	6	6,821,491	21,507,500
New York	5	34	19	10	68	190,904,278	183,082,920
North Carolina	0	0	4	0	4	5,168,265	8,666,200
North Dakota	0	1	0	0	1	365,000	600,000
Ohio	1	5	3	1	10	16,636,585	23,171,225
Oklahoma	0	5	4	0	9	8,626,646	14,923,583
Oregon	0	1	0	0	1	750,000	800,000
Pennsylvania	2	3	4	0	9	10,505,313	4,542,462
Puerto Rico	0	0	0	0	0	0	0
Rhode Island	0	0	1	1	2	23,000,203	35,430,000
South Carolina	1	3	2	0	6	4,955,151	6,665,125
South Dakota	0	0	0	0	0	0	0
Tennessee	0	3	0	0	3	1,905,320	1,916,500
Texas	2	22	12	6	42	95,872,402	98,618,416
Utah	0	0	0	0	0	0	0
Vermont	1	1	1	0	3	1,894,354	1,650,000
Virginia	0	4	3	0	7	7,506,384	15,851,394
Washington	1	3	2	1	7	12,543,622	14,970,700
West Virginia	0	0	0	0	0	0	0
Wisconsin	0	3	2	0	5	5,564,044	10,739,000
Wyoming	0	1	0	0	1	450,000	300,000
Total	20	185	126	31	362	735,430,112	773,519,667

SBIC Totals by Private Capital Size Class

Total Private Capital Size Class	Total Number of SBICs	Total Private Capital ($)	Total Obligations to SBA ($)
Size 1: Below $300,000	20	4,390,055	4,380,775
Size 2: $300,001 to $1 million	185	109,461,985	132,832,273
Size 3: $1 million to $5 million	126	274,046,492	345,838,987
Size 4: Over $5 million	31	347,531,580	290,467,632
Total	362	735,430,112	773,519,667

SBIC Totals by Type of Ownership

Size Class	Total Number of SBICs	Total Private Capital ($)	Total Obligations to SBA ($)
Bank dominated	57	277,847,230	154,674,518
Bank associated	12	23,339,652	15,085,834
Financial organization	30	49,196,369	70,153,254
Non-financial organization	51	72,136,244	129,271,319
Individually owned	183	203,245,277	216,271,311
40 act company	29	109,665,340	188,063,431
Total	362	735,430,112	773,519,667

SBIC Private Capital by Type of Ownership

	Private Capital Size Class							
	Size 1		Size 2		Size 3		Size 4	
Type of ownership	Number	Dollars	Number	Dollars	Number	Dollars	Number	Dollars
Bank dominated	1	300,000	22	14,067,428	19	52,628,402	15	210,851,400
Bank associated	0	0	3	1,693,193	8	16,236,877	1	5,409,582
Financial organization	1	150,000	13	8,163,218	14	29,231,141	2	11,652,010
Non-financial organization	6	1,492,750	27	15,687,975	15	30,225,681	3	24,729,838
Individually owned	12	2,447,305	112	65,262,766	56	112,837,593	3	22,697,613
40 ACT company	0	0	8	4,587,405	14	32,886,798	7	72,191,137

PART II: 301(D) LICENSEES LISTED ALPHABETICALLY BY STATE

This listing is limited to licensees assisting small business concerns owned by socially or economically disadvantaged persons.

Licensee	Private Capital($)	SBA Leverage($)	Investment Policy	Owner Code
Alabama				
First Alabama Capital Corporation David C. Delaney, President 3201 Dauphin Street, Suite B Mobile, Alabama 36606 (205) 476-0700	500,000	0	Diversified	5
Arkansas				
Capital Management Services, Inc. David L. Hale, President 1910 North Grant Street, Suite 200 Little Rock, Arkansas 72207 (501) 664-8613	500,500	500,000	Diversified	5
Kar-Mal Venture Capital, Inc. Thomas Karam, President Suite 610 Plaza West Office Bldg. Little Rock, Arkansas 72205 (501) 661-0010	500,000	1,000,000	Diversified	4
Power Ventures Inc. Dorsey D. Glover, President 829 Highway 270 North Malvern, Arkansas 72104 (501) 332-3695	500,000	500,000	Diversified	5

Licensee	Private Capital($)	SBA Leverage($)	Investment Policy	Owner Code
California				
Asian American Capital Corporation John F. Louie, General Manager 1911 West Tennyson Road Suite #3 Hayward, California 94546 (916) 444-6778	500,000	0	Diversified	5
Associates Venture Capital Corp. Walter P. Strycker, President 611 Front Street San Francisco, California 94111 (415) 397-0351	540,000	525,000	Diversified	5
Bay Area Western Venture Group Samuel Burford, President 383 Diablo Road, Suite 100 Danville, California 94526 (408) 688-5080	742,900	1,450,000	Diversified	5
Continental Investors, Incorporated (Main Office: District of Columbia) d/b/a/ California Continental Investors 8781 Seaspray Drive Huntington, California 92646 (714) 964-5207				
Equitable Capital Corporation John C. Lee, President	500,000	1,000,000	Diversified	5

Licensee	Private Capital($)	SBA Leverage($)	Investment Policy	Owner Code
855 Sansome Street San Francisco, California 94111 (415) 434-4114				
Hub Enterprises, Ltd. John B. Lacoste, President 5874 Doyle Street Emeryville, California 94608 (415) 653-5707	318,500	600,000	Diversified	5
Lasung Investment & Finance Co. Mr. Jung Su Lee, President 3600 Wilshire Boulevard, Suite 1410 Los Angeles, California 90010 (213) 382-6297	500,000	1,500,000	Diversified	5
MCA New Ventures, Inc. Norbert A. Simmons, President 100 Universal City Plaza Universal City, California 91608 (213) 985-4321	3,140,000	3,000,000	Entertainment field	4
Milestone Capital Corporation Zoilo R. Inacay, President 5401 Mission Street San Francisco, California 94112 (415) 586-5702	500,000	0	Diversified	5
Minority Enterprise Funding, Inc. Howard D. Balshan, President	500,000	0	Diversified	5

Licensee	Private Capital($)	SBA Lever- age($)	Investment Policy	Owner Code
7171 Patterson Dr. Garden Grove, California 92641 (714) 892-7706				
Myriad Capital, Inc. Mr. Chuang-I Lin, President 8820 Sepulveda Blvd., Suite 109 Los Angeles, California 90045 (213) 641-7936	520,000	0	Diversified	5
Opportunity Capital Corporation J. Peter Thompson, President 100 California St., Suite 714 San Francisco, California 94111 (415) 421-5935	2,580,849	3,135,849	Diversified	2
Pacific Capital Fund, Incorporated Victor H. Gallego, President 500 Airport Boulevard, Suite 400 Burlingame, California 94010 (405) 342-0748	1,000,000	0	Diversified	5
Positive Enterprises, Incorporated Mr. Kwok Szeto, President 399 Arguello Street San Francisco, California 94118 (415) 386-6600	505,000	505,000	Diversified	5
Sam Woong Investment Company Masoa Aoki, President	500,000	0	Diversified	5

Licensee	Private Capital($)	SBA Leverage($)	Investment Policy	Owner Code
1625 West Olympic Blvd., Suite 1007 Los Angeles, California 90037 (213) 232-5194				
Space Ventures, Inc. William J. Smollen, President 3901 MacArthur Blvd. Newport Beach, California 92660 (714) 851-0855	1,010,000	1,000,000	Diversified	4
Unity Capital Corp. Frank W. Owen, President 4343 Morena Boulevard, Suite 3A San Diego, California 92117 (714) 275-6030	310,000	300,000	Diversified	5
YFY Capital Corp. Richard Lim, President 533 Jackson Street San Francisco, California 94133 (415) 433-5346	500,000	0	Diversified	5
Yosemite Capital Inv. Company J. Horace Hampton, President 448 Fresno Street Fresno, California 93706 (209) 485-2431	305,300	300,000	Diversified	5

Connecticut

Licensee	Private Capital($)	SBA Leverage($)	Investment Policy	Owner Code
Cominvest of Hartford Incorporated Bessye W. Bennett, President	550,119	1,500,000	Diversified	1

Licensee	Private Capital($)	SBA Lever- age($)	Investment Policy	Owner Code
18 Asylum Street Hartford, Connecti- cut 06105 (203) 246-7259				

DC

Licensee	Private Capital($)	SBA Lever- age($)	Investment Policy	Owner Code
Broadcast Capital Inc. Samuel D. Ewing, Jr., President 1771 N Street, NW Washington, DC 20036 (202) 293-3575	1,000,000	1,000,000	Communications media	5
Continental Inves- tors Lac Thantrong, President 2020 K Street, N.W. Washington, DC 20006 (202) 466-3709	2,000,000	1,750,000	Diversified	5
District of Colum- bia Investment Company Joseph D. Jackson, President 1133 North Capitol Street, N.E. Washington, DC 20002 (202) 842-4680	1,750,000	2,350,000	Diversified	4
Fulcrum Venture Capital Corp. Stephen L. Lilly, President 2021 K Street, N.W. Suite 701 Washington, DC 20006 (202) 833-9580	2,000,000	2,000,000	Diversified	3

Licensee	Private Capital($)	SBA Lever- age($)	Investment Policy	Owner Code
Minority Broadcast Investment Corp. Walter Threadgill, President 1220 - 19th Street, N.W. Suite 501 Washington, DC 20036 (202) 293-2977	1,000,100	2,000,100	Communications	5
NBL Capital Corp. Theodore H. Hagans, Jr. 4324 Georgia Ave., N.W. Washington, DC 20011 (202) 829-5900	200,000	450,000	Diversified	5
Syncom Capital Corporation Herbert P. Wilkins, President 1625 I Street, N.W., Suite 414 Washington, DC 20006 (202) 293-9428	2,250,000	2,250,000	Communications media	4

Florida

Broward Venture Capital Corp. William H. Lackey, President 660 S. Federal High- way, Suite 300 Pompano Beach, Florida 33062 (305) 463-3399	500,000	0	Diversified	5
Cubico Ltd., Inc. Anthony G. Marina, President 7425 N.W. 79th Street Miami, Florida 33166 (305) 885-8881	500,000	500,000	Diversified	5

Licensee	Private Capital($)	SBA Lever-age($)	Investment Policy	Owner Code
Feyca Investment Co. Felipe de Diego, President 161 Almeria Avenue, Suite 103W Coral Gables, Florida 33134 (305) 643-1822	511,500	1,000,000	Diversified	5
First American Lending Corp. (The) Roy W. Talmo, Chairman 1200 N. Dixie Highway Lake Worth, Florida 33460 (305) 947-6678	500,000	500,000	Diversified	1
First B.D.J. Financial Service, Inc. John Rhodes, President 4747 North Ocean Blvd. Suite 215 Fort Lauderdale, Florida 33308 (305) 782-9494	500,000	0	Diversified	5
Jets Venture Capital Corporation Larry D. Barnette, President 2721 Park Street Jacksonville, Florida 32205 (904) 384-3477	1,000,000	1,020,000	Diversified	5
Safeco Capital, Inc. Rene J. Leonard, President 8770 S.W. 8th Street Miami, Florida 33174 (305) 551-0809	500,000	1,000,000	Diversified	5

Licensee	Private Capital($)	SBA Lever- age($)	Investment Policy	Owner Code
Trans Florida Capital Corporation Pedro L. Logez, President 747 Ponce de Leon Blvd. Coral Gables, Florida 33134 (305) 442-0444	500,000	0	Diversified	5
Universal Financial Services, Inc. Norman Zipkin, President 225 N.E. 35th Street Miami, Florida 33137 (305) 573-7496	500,000	500,000	Diversified	5
Venture Opportunities Corporation A. Fred March, President 444 Brickell Ave., Suite 750 Miami, Florida 33131 (305) 358-0359	575,000	1,725,000	Diversified	5
Verde Capital Corp. Steven J. Green, Chairman of Board 6701 Sunset Drive South Miami, Florida 33143 (305) 666-8789	1,005,000	4,000,000	Diversified	5

Georgia

Sunbelt Funding Corp. Charles H. Jones, President 2720 Riverside Drive Mail: P.O. Box 7006 Macon, Georgia 31298 (912) 742-0177	500,000	500,000	Diversified	5

Licensee	Private Capital($)	SBA Lever-age($)	Investment Policy	Owner Code
Hawaii				
Pacific Venture Capital, Ltd. Dexter J. Taniguchi, President 1505 Dillingham Blvd. Honolulu, Hawaii 96817 (808) 847-6502	721,000	700,000	Diversified	4
Illinois				
Amoco Venture Capital Company Lyle E. Schaffer, President 200 E. Randolph Dr. Chicago, Illinois 60601 (312) 856-6523	776,750	2,525,000	Diversified	4
Cedco Capital Corp. Frank B. Brooks, President 180 North Michigan Avenue Chicago, Illinois 60601 (312) 984-5950	668,800	500,000	Diversified	4
Chicago Community Ventures, Inc. Phyllis George, President 108 North State Street Chicago, Illinois 60603 (312) 726-6084	1,005,000	1,505,000	Diversified	4
Combined Opportunities Incorporated Wallace Buya, President 300 North State Street Chicago, Illinois 60610 (312) 266-3050	500,000	500,000	Diversified	4
Neighborhood Fund, Inc. (The) James Fletcher, President 1950 East 71st Street Chicago, Illinois 60649 (312) 684-8074	170,000	320,000	Diversified	1

Licensee	Private Capital($)	SBA Leverage($)	Investment Policy	Owner Code
Tower Ventures, Inc. Robert A. Comey, President Sears Tower, BSC 9-29 Chicago, Illinois 60684 (312) 875-9628	1,500,000	3,000,000	Diversified	4
Urban Fund of Illinois Inc. (The) Peter H. Ross, President 300 N. State Street Chicago, Illinois 60610 (312) 266-3050	650,000	1,293,000	Diversified	1

Kansas

Central Systems Equity Corporation Clarence E. Wesley, President 350 West Douglas Wichita, Kansas 67202 (316) 265-7771	1,076,066	0	Diversified	5

Kentucky

Equal Opportunity Finance, Inc. Franklin Justice, Jr., V.P. and Mgr. 9502 Williamsburg Plaza Mail: P.O. Box 1915 Louisville, Kentucky 40201 (502) 423-1943	742,395	1,000,000	Diversified	4

Louisiana

Business Capital Corp. David R. Burrus, President 1732 Canal Street New Orleans, Louisiana 70112 (504) 581-4002	4,700,000	8,200,000	Diversified	5

Licensee	Private Capital($)	SBA Lever- age($)	Investment Policy	Owner Code
Central Venture Capital Corporation Louis A. Gerdes, Jr., President 1739 St. Bernard Ave. New Orleans, Louisiana 70116 (504) 822-4110	196,709	0	Insurance com- panies	4
Edict Investment Corp. Rev. Robert P. Morin, President 2908 S. Carrollton Ave. New Orleans, Louisiana 70118 (504) 861-2364	218,500	150,000	Diversified	4
Louisiana Venture Capi- tal Corp. Ben D. Johnson, Presi- dent 315 North Street Natchitoches, Louisiana 71457 (318) 352-9138	510,000	500,000	Diversified	4
SCDF Investment Corp. Rev. Albert J. McKnight, President 1006 Surrey Street Lafayette, Louisiana 70501 (318) 232-3769	1,000,010	2,419,549	Diversified	4

Maryland

Licensee	Private Capital($)	SBA Lever- age($)	Investment Policy	Owner Code
Albright Venture Capital Incorporated William A. Albright, President 8005 Rappahannock Av- enue Jessup, Maryland 20794 (301) 490-4441	500,000	1,000,000	Diversified	5

Licensee	Private Capital($)	SBA Lever- age($)	Investment Policy	Owner Code
Massachusetts				
Massachusetts Venture Capital Corp. Charles T. Grigsby, President 59 Temple Place Boston, Massachusetts 02111 (617) 426-0208	700,000	1,400,000	Diversified	2
W.C.C.I. Capital Corp. Charles R. Valade, President 791 Main Street Worcester, Massachusetts 01610 (617) 791-3259	350,049	0	Diversified	4
Michigan				
Dearborn Capital Corp. Robert C. Chambers, President P.O. Box 1729 Dearborn, Michigan 48121 (313) 337-8577	1,219,607	1,000,000	Diversified	4
Independence Capital Formation, Inc. Walter M. McMurtry, Jr., President 1505 Woodward, Suite 700 Detroit, Michigan 48226 (313) 961-2470	1,033,293	4,132,986	Diversified	4
Innercity Cap. Access Center, Inc. Walter M. McMurtry, Jr., President 1505 Woodward, Suite 700 Detroit, Michigan 48226 (313) 961-2470	250,000	0	Diversified	5

Licensee	Private Capital($)	SBA Lever-age($)	Investment Policy	Owner Code
Metro-Detroit Inv. Co. William J. Fowler, President 18481 West Ten Mile Road Suite 202 Southfield, Michigan 48075 (313) 557-3818	1,000,000	3,000,000	Food stores	4
Motor Enterprises, Incorporated James Kobus, Manager 3044 West Grand Blvd. Detroit, Michigan 48202 (313) 556-4273	1,250,000	2,000,000	Diversified	4
Mutual Investment Co. Incorporated Jack Najor, President 29100 Wixom Road Wixom, Michigan 48096 (313) 552-8515	600,000	1,200,000	Diversified	5
Prime, Inc. Jimmy N. Hill, President 1845 David Whitney Bldg. Detroit, Michigan 48226 (313) 964-3380	1,097,500	2,380,000	Diversified	4

Minnesota

Licensee	Private Capital($)	SBA Lever-age($)	Investment Policy	Owner Code
Control Data Community Ventures Fund W. D. Anderson, Secretary/Treasurer 8100 34th Avenue South Bloomington, Minnesota 55420 (612) 853-8100	2,002,500	2,000,000	Diversified	4

Mississippi

Licensee	Private Capital($)	SBA Lever-age($)	Investment Policy	Owner Code
Sun-Delta Cap. Access Center, Inc. Charles Bannerman, President	1,250,100	0	Diversified	5

Licensee	Private Capital($)	SBA Lever- age($)	Investment Policy	Owner Code
819 Main Street Greenville, Mississippi 38701 (601) 335-5291				
Nebraska				
Community Equity Corp. of Nebraska William C. Moore, President 5620 Ames Ave., Room 109 Omaha, Nebraska 68104 (402) 455-7722	500,000	1,100,000	Diversified	4
New Jersey				
Broad Arrow Investment Corporation Charles N. Bellm, President 33 South Street P.O. Box 2231R Morristown, New Jersey 07960 (609) 924-8640	157,200	150,000	Diversified	5
Rutgers Minority Inv. Co. Louis T. German, President 180 University Avenue Newark, New Jersey 07102 (201) 648-5287	1,320,000	1,155,000	Diversified	4
New Mexico				
Associated Southwest Investors, Inc. John R. Rice, General Manager 2425 Alamo S.E. Albuquerque, New Mexico 87106 (505) 842-5955	707,000	1,700,000	Diversified	4

Licensee	Private Capital($)	SBA Lever-age($)	Investment Policy	Owner Code
New York				
American Asian Capital Corporation Howard H. Lin, President 79 Wall St., Room 907 New York, New York 10005 (212) 422-6880	503,000	500,000	Diversified	5
Amistad Dot Venture Capital, Inc. Percy E. Sutton, President 805 Second Avenue, Suite 303 New York, New York 10017 (212) 537-6600	3,500,000	2,000,000	Communications and trans-portation	5
Bancap Corporation William L. Whitely, President 155 East 42nd Street, Suite 305 New York, New York 10017 (212) 687-6470	1,000,000	2,000,000	Diversified	1
Capital Investors & Man-agement Corp. Rose Chao, Manager 3 Pell Street, Suite 3 New York, New York 10013 (212) 964-2480	500,000	500,000	Diversified	5
CEDC MESBIC, Inc. John L. Kearse, President 106 Main Street Hempstead, New York 11550 (516) 292-9710	500,000	500,000	Diversified	4
Cohen Capital Corp. Edward H. Cohen, President	500,000	1,500,000	Diversified	5

Licensee	Private Capital($)	SBA Lever- age($)	Investment Policy	Owner Code
163 East 36th Street, Suite 2A New York, New York 10016 (212) 689-9030				
Croesus Securities Limited George L. Wallace, President 1290 Avenue of the Americas New York, New York 10104 (212) 245-2794	1,500,000	0	Diversified	5
CVC Capital Corp. Joerg G. Klebe, President 666 Fifth Avenue New York, New York 10019 (212) 246-1980	2,005,000	4,000,000	Television industry	5
ELK Associates Funding Corp. Gary C. Granoff, President 31 East Mall Plainview, New York 11803 (516) 249-3387	507,500	1,000,000	Diversified	5
Equico Capital Corp. Joseph Di Blasi, Dir. of Fin. Affairs 1290 Avenue of the Americas Suite 3400 New York, New York 10019 (212) 554-8413	6,950,000	7,970,000	Diversified	4
EXIM Capital Corp. Victor K. Chun, President 290 Madison Avenue New York, New York 10017 (212) 683-3200	510,000	500,000	Diversified	5

Licensee	Private Capital($)	SBA Lever-age($)	Investment Policy	Owner Code
H.B.R. Capital Corp. Eric Boswell, Manager 1775 Broadway, Suite 417 New York, New York 10019 (212) 247-8040	505,000	0	Diversified	5
Hop Chung Capital Cor-poration Yon Hon Lee, President 74-A Mott Street New York, New York 10013 (212) 267-2727	500,000	500,000	Diversified	5
Ibero American Inves-tors Corp. Domingo Garcia, Presi-dent Chamber of Commerce Building 55 Saint Paul Street Rochester, New York 14604 (716) 544-0450	324,787	317,500	Diversified	5
Intercontinental Capital Funding Corp. James S. Yu, President 80 Mott Street New York, New York 10013 (212) 226-6260	500,000	0	Diversified	5
Intergroup Funding Cor-poration Ben Hauben, President 230 Park Avenue New York, New York 10017 (212) 661-5428	510,000	1,000,000	Diversified	5
International Paper Cap. Formation, Inc. Bernard L. Riley, Presi-dent	1,000,000	0	Diversified	5

Licensee	Private Capital($)	SBA Leverage($)	Investment Policy	Owner Code
77 West 45th Street New York, New York 10036 (212) 536-6000				
Japanese American Cap. Corporation Stephen C. Huang, President 120 Broadway New York, New York 10005 (212) 964-4077	525,000	1,050,001	Diversified	5
King SBI Corp. Neil Ritz, President 4444 River Road Tonawanda, New York 14150 (716) 856-4413	500,183	1,500,000	Diversified	4
Korean Capital Corp. Jae Hoon Hwang, President 222-48 Birmington Parkway Mail: P.O. Box 12; Bayside, N.Y. 11361 Bayside, New York 11364 (212) 224-5891	516,000	0	Diversified	5
Medallion Funding Corporation Alvin Murstein, President 205 E. 42nd St., Suite 2020 New York, New York 10017 (212) 682-3300	1,239,000	2,189,000	Transportation	5
Medallion Funding Corporation (Main Office: New York, NY) 86 Glen Cove Road East Hills, New York 11577 (212) 682-3300				

Licensee	Private Capital($)	SBA Lever- age($)	Investment Policy	Owner Code
Merit Funding, Inc. Roger L. Cohen, President One Battery Park Plaza New York, New York 10004 (212) 344-6254	500,000	500,000	Diversified	5
Minority Equity Cap. Co., Inc. Patrick O. Burns, Gen'l Mgr. 275 Madison Avenue New York, New York 10016 (212) 686-9710	2,204,047	1,707,000	Diversified	4
New Oasis Capital Corporation James Haung, President 114 Liberty Street, Suite 404 New York, New York 10006 (212) 349-2804	500,000	500,000	Diversified	5
North American Funding Corporation Franklin F. Y. Wong, V.P. and Gen. Mgr. 177 Canal Street New York, New York 10013 (212) 226-0080	500,000	0	Diversified	5
North Street Capital Corporation Ralph McNeal, President 250 North Street White Plains, New York 10625 (914) 683-2500	500,000	1,500,000	Diversified	4
ODA Capital Corp. Philip Klein, Executive Director 82 Lee Avenue Brooklyn, New York 11211 (212) 963-9270	401,500	1,200,000	Diversified	5

Licensee	Private Capital($)	SBA Lever-age($)	Investment Policy	Owner Code
Pan Pac Capital Corp. Dr. In Ping Jack Lee, President 120 Broadway New York, New York 10271 (212) 619-2445	503,000	503,000	Diversified	5
Pierre Funding Corp. Elias Debbas, President 270 Madison Avenue, Suite 1608 New York, New York 10017 (212) 689-9361	604,500	0	Diversified	5
Pioneer Capital Corp. James G. Niven, President 113 East 55th Street New York, New York 10022 (212) 344-4490	701,261	1,400,000	Diversified	5
Rainbow Bridge Capital Corporation Baldwin T. Ching, President 52-25 Barnett Avenue Long Island City, New York 11104 (212) 896-9300	500,000	500,000	Diversified	5
Situation Ventures Corporation Sam Hollander, President 502 Flushing Avenue New York, New York 11205 (212) 855-1835	1,000,200	1,500,000	Diversified	5
Square Deal Venture Capital Corp. Mordechai Z. Fledman, President	546,000	200,000	Diversified	5

Licensee	Private Capital($)	SBA Lever- age($)	Investment Policy	Owner Code
Lincoln & Jefferson Ave- nues VG of New Square, New York 10977 (914) 354-7774				
Taroco Capital Corp. David R. C. Chang, Pres- ident 120 Broadway New York, New York 10005 (212) 964-6877	505,000	2,020,000	Chinese Ameri- cans	5
Transportation SBIC, In- corporated Melvin L. Hirsch, Presi- dent 122 East 42nd Street, 46th Fl. c/o Melvin L. Hirsch New York, New York 10168 (212) 986-6050	505,000	0	Diversified	5
Watchung Capital Corp. S. T. Jeng, President 111 Broadway, Room 2002 New York, New York 10006 (212) 227-4597	500,000	1,000,000	Diversified	5

North Carolina

Licensee	Private Capital($)	SBA Lever- age($)	Investment Policy	Owner Code
Vanguard Investment Company, Inc. James F. Hansley, Presi- dent Suite 309, Pepper Bldg. Fourth and Liberty St. Winston-Salem, North Carolina 27101 (919) 724-3676	900,053	1,770,000	Diversified	4

Licensee	Private Capital($)	SBA Leverage($)	Investment Policy	Owner Code
Ohio				
Center City Minority Enterprise Inv. Co. Thomas V. Wright, President Centre City Office Building, Suite 762 40 South Main Street Dayton, Ohio 45402 (513) 461-6164	500,000	0	Diversified	5
Glenco Enterprises, Incorporated Dr. Lewis F. Wright, V.P. 1464 E. 105 St., Suite 101 Cleveland, Ohio 44106 (216) 721-1200	500,000	1,000,000	Diversified	5
Pennsylvania				
Alliance Enterprise Corporation Shallie M. Bey, Jr., President 1616 Walnut St., Suite 802 Philadelphia, Pennsylvania 19103 (215) 972-4230	2,715,200	2,700,000	Diversified	4
Greater Phila. Venture Cap. Corp. Inc. J. Walton St. Clair, Jr., President 920 Lewis Tower Bldg. 225 South Fifteenth St. Philadelphia, Pennsylvania 19102 (215) 732-3415	756,583	1,255,000	Diversified	2
Puerto Rico				
Credi-I-F.A.C., Inc. Manuel L. Prats, Manager	500,000	0	Diversified	1

Licensee	Private Capital($)	SBA Leverage($)	Investment Policy	Owner Code
Banco Cooperative Plaza, Suite 1001 623 Ponce de Leon Avenue Hato Rey, Puerto Rico 00918 (809) 765-0070				
First Puerto Rico Capital, Inc. Eliseo E. Font, President 54 W. McKinley Street Mayaguez, Puerto Rico 00708 (809) 833-2929	500,000	0	Diversified	1
North America Inv. Corp. Santigo Ruz Betacourt, President Banco CTR #1710, M Rivera Av Stop 34 Mail: P.O. Box 1831 Hato Rey Sta., PR 00919 Hato Rey, Puerto Rico 00936 (809) 751-6178	750,000	2,250,000	Diversified	5
Venture Capital P.R., Incorporated Manuel L. Prats, President Executive Building, Suite 1204 Ponce de Leon Avenue, #623 Hato Rey, Puerto Rico 00918 (809) 763-0581	505,000	500,000	Diversified	5

Tennessee

Licensee	Private Capital($)	SBA Leverage($)	Investment Policy	Owner Code
Chickasaw Capital Corporation Wayne J. Haskins, President	500,000	500,000	Diversified	1

Licensee	Private Capital($)	SBA Lever-age($)	Investment Policy	Owner Code
67 Madison Ave., Suite 813 P.O. Box 387 Memphis, Tennessee 38103 (901) 523-6404				
R.P.B. Investment Enter-prises, Inc. M. Hall Oakley, Presi-dent Falls Building 22 North Front Street Memphis, Tennessee 38103 (901) 526-0063	500,000	500,000	Diversified	5
Tennessee Equity Cap. Corp. Richard Kantor, Presi-dent 4515 Poplar Avenue Memphis, Tennessee 38117 (901) 761-3410	502,000	500,000	Diversified	5
Tennessee Equity Cap. Corp. (Main Office: Memphis, TN) 1102 Stonewall Jackson Court Nashville, Tennessee 37220 (615) 373-4502				
Tennessee Venture Cap-ital Corp. Wendell P. Knox, Presi-dent 170 Fourth Avenue North Room 622 Nashville, Tennessee 37219 (615) 244-6935	500,000	500,000	Diversified	5

Licensee	Private Capital($)	SBA Leverage($)	Investment Policy	Owner Code
Texas				
MESBIC Financial Corp. of Dallas Walter W. Durham, President 7701 N. Stemmons Freeway Suite 836 Dallas, Texas 75247 (214) 637-0445	1,946,667	1,850,000	Diversified	2
MESBIC Financial Corp. of Houston Richard Rothfeld, President 717 Travis, Suite 600 Houston, Texas 77002 (713) 228-8321	854,900	854,000	Diversified	2
MESBIC of San Antonio Incorporated Juan J. Patlan, President 2300 West Commerce San Antonio, Texas 78207 (512) 224-0909	751,000	0	Diversified	5
Southern Orient Cap. Corporation Min H. Liang, President 2419 Fannin, Suite 200 Houston, Texas 77002 (713) 225-3369	550,000	550,000	Diversified	5
Virginia				
East West United Inv. Co. Bui Trac, Chairman 6723 Whittier Ave., Suite 205B McLean, Virginia 22101 (703) 821-6616	500,000	1,500,000	Diversified	5
Norfolk Investment Company, Inc. Kirk W. Saunders, Gen'l Mgr.	700,000	1,400,000	Diversified	4

Licensee	Private Capital($)	SBA Lever- age($)	Investment Policy	Owner Code
Suite 515, Granby Mall Bldg. 201 Granby Street Norfolk, Virginia 23510 (804) 623-1042				
Washington				
Model Capital Corp. Thomas Bangasser, Manager c/o Seattle Urban League 105 14th Avenue Seattle, Washington 98122 (206) 447-3799	150,000	0	Diversified	4
Wisconsin				
SC Opportunities, Inc. Robert L. Ableman, Sec- retary 1112 Seventh Avenue Monroe, Wisconsin 53566 (608) 328-8400	300,000	600,000	Swiss Colony franchises	5

301(D) SBIC Totals by States

State	Number of SBICS					Total Private Capital ($)	Total Obligations to SBA ($)
	Size 1	Size 2	Size 3	Size 4	Total		
Alabama	0	1	0	0	1	500,000	0
Alaska	0	0	0	0	1	0	0
Arizona	0	0	0	0	0	0	0
Arkansas	0	3	0	0	3	1,500,500	2,000,000
California	0	15	3	0	18	14,472,549	13,315,849
Colorado	0	0	0	0	0	0	0
Connecticut	0	1	0	0	1	550,119	1,500,000
Delaware	0	0	0	0	0	0	0
D.C.	1	1	5	0	7	10,200,100	11,800,100
Florida	0	10	1	0	11	6,591,500	10,245,000
Georgia	0	1	0	0	1	500,000	500,000
Hawaii	0	1	0	0	1	721,000	700,000
Idaho	0	0	0	0	0		0
Illinois	1	4	2	0	7	5,270,550	9,643,000
Indiana	0	0	0	0	0	0	0
Iowa	0	0	0	0	0	0	0
Kansas	0	0	1	0	1	1,076,066	0
Kentucky	0	1	0	0	1	742,395	1,000,000
Louisiana	2	1	2	0	5	6,625,219	11,269,549
Maine	0	0	0	0	0	0	0
Maryland	0	1	0	0	1	500,000	1,000,000
Massachusetts	0	2	0	0	2	1,050,049	1,400,000
Michigan	10	2	4	0	7	6,450,400	13,712,986
Minnesota	0	0	1	0	1	2,002,500	2,000,000
Mississippi	0	0	1	0	1	1,250,100	0
Missouri	0	0	0	0	0	0	0
Montana	0	0	0	0	0	0	0
Nebraska	0	1	0	0	1	500,000	1,100,000
Nevada	0	0	0	0	0	0	0
New Hampshire	0	0	0	0	0	0	0
New Jersey	1	0	1	0	2	1,477,200	1,305,000
New Mexico	0	1	0	0	1	707,000	1,700,000
New York	0	29	6	1	36	34,065,978	39,556,501
North Carolina	0	1	0	0	1	900,053	1,770,000
North Dakota	0	0	0	0	0	0	0
Ohio	0	2	0	0	2	1,000,000	1,000,000
Oklahoma	0	0	0	0	0	0	0
Oregon	0	0	0	0	0	0	0
Pennsylvania	0	1	1	0	2	3,471,783	3,955,000.
Puerto Rico	0	4	0	0	4	2,255,000	2,759,000
Rhode Island	0	0	0	0	0	0	0
South Carolina	0	0	0	0	0	0	0
South Dakota	0	0	0	0	0	0	0
Tennessee	0	4	0	0	4	2,002,000	2,000,000
Texas	0	3	1	0	4	4,102,567	3,254,000
Utah	0	0	0	0	0	0	0
Vermont	0	0	0	0	0	0	0
Virginia	0	2	0	0	2	1,200,000	2,900,000
Washington	1	0	0	0	1	150,000	0
West Virginia	0	0	0	0	0	0	0
Wisconsin	1	0	0	0	1	300,000	600,000
Wyoming	0	0	0	0	0	0	0
Total	8	92	29	1	130	112,134,628	141,976,985

SBIC Totals by Private Capital Size Class

Total Private Capital Size Class	Total Number of SBICs	Total Private Capital ($)	Total Obligations to SBA ($)
Size 1: Below $300,000	8	1,642,409	1,670,000
Size 2: $300,001 to $1 million	92	52,242,080	67,112,501
Size 3: $1 million to $5 million	29	51,300,139	65,224,484
Size 4: Over $5 million	1	6,950,000	7,970,000
Total	130	112,134,628	141,976,985

301(D) SBIC Totals by Type of Ownership

Size Class	Total Number of SBICs	Total Private Capital ($)	Total Obligations to SBA ($)
Bank dominated	8	4,370,119	6,113,000
Bank associated	5	6,838,999	8,494,849
Financial organization	1	2,000,000	2,000,000
Non-financial organization	35	42,088,596	59,914,535
Individually owned	81	56,836,914	65,454,601
40 act company	0	0	0
Total	130	112,134,628	141,976,985

301(D) SBIC Private Capital by Type of Ownership

Type of ownership	Size 1 Number	Size 1 Dollars	Size 2 Number	Size 2 Dollars	Size 3 Number	Size 3 Dollars	Size 4 Number	Size 4 Dollars
Bank dominated	1	170,000	7	4,200,119	0	0	0	0
Bank associated	0	0	3	2,311,483	2	4,527,516	0	0
Financial organiza-tion	0	0	0	0	1	2,000,000	0	0
Non-financial organi-zation	3	565,209	16	10,076,230	15	24,497,157	1	6,950,000
Individually owned	4	907,200	66	35,654,248	11	20,275,466	0	0
40 ACT company	0	0	0	0	0	0	0	

Key for Code Number of Each Type of Ownership

Code Number	Type of Ownership
1	Bank dominated (50% or more owned by bank or bank holding company)
2	Bank associated (10% to 49% owned by bank or bank holding company)
3	Financial organization other than bank or bank holding company (public or nonpublic)
4	Nonfinancial organization (public or nonpublic)
5	Individually owned (privatedly held)
6	40' ACT company

Appendix VI

Small Business Administration Business Plan and Qualifications Résumé

(Each item should be completed, if none or not applicable so state).

I. Firm Identification:

Name _____

Trade Name _____

Address _____

        Street   P.O. Box

_____

      City   County   State   Zip

Business Phone _____ _____ Home Phone _____ _____

     Area code   Number   Area Code   Number

Type of Business _____ SIC Code _____

Employees Identification Number _____ Tax Exemption No. _____

Number of Employees: _____ as of _____

Indicate if supply, service, construction or concession _____

Month and Year Business Established _____

Fiscal Year Ends _____

Is concern organized for profit? Yes ☐ No ☐

Is concern associated in any way with a non-profit organization?

                     Yes ☐ No ☐

If yes, specify name of non-profit organization and the nature of the association ____

_____

_____

Does concern and affiliates meet small business size standard as defined in Part 121 SBA Rules and Regulations? Yes ☐ No ☐

If answer is *no*, Divestitute Agreement must be submitted.

II. List other types and locations of business in which firm is or has recently been engaged.

Types of Business: _____

Address of Facility: _____

_____

Presently Operating: Yes ☐ No ☐   If operating, how long? _____

III. Ownership:

A. Type of Ownership

    Sole Proprietorship ☐

    Partnership ☐ (Attach copy of partnership agreement.)

    Corporation ☐ (Attach copy of certificate from Secretary of State, Articles of State, Articles of Incorporation, and By-Laws.)

If corporation: Total no. of shares authorized: _____

Total no. of shares issued: _____

B. Is concern owned and controlled by one or more persons who have been deprived of the opportunity to develop and maintain a competitive position in the economy because of social or economic disadvantages?   Yes ☐   No ☐

C. Name and address of all stockholders and/or partners and their ethnic identification; i.e., Aleuts, Black American, Eskimo, Indian, Oriental, Spanish-American, White American, etc.

Name	Address	*Number and Class of Shares	Office Held	Ethnic Ident.
_____	_____	____	____	____
_____	_____	____	____	____
_____	_____	____	____	____
_____	_____	____	____	____
_____	_____	____	____	____
_____	_____	____	____	____

[1] Attach copy of Stock Certificate(s) issued.

D. Attach copy of all Divestiture and/or Ownership Agreements.

E. Attach personal financial statement on above principals (SBA Form 413 may be used to submit this statement).

F. SBA Form 912, "Statement of Personal History" must be completed according to the instructions contained therein and submitted with this Business Plan and Qualifications Resume.

G. Show names of social and/or economic disadvantaged persons listed in III C above. Give a narrative summary of cultural, social, chronic economic circumstances and background on each to support disadvantaged status. (Continue on separate sheet as necessary.)

Name: _____

Narrative Summary:

Name: _____

Narrative Summary:

Name: _____
Narrative Summary:

Name: _____
Narrative Summary:

H. List all entities that owners, directors, officers, partners and managers of applicant have a financial interest in or hold a management or board position. If none, so state.

Name of Entity	Name of Person	Position Held	% or Ownership
_____	_____	_____	_____
_____	_____	_____	_____
_____	_____	_____	_____
_____	_____	_____	_____

I. Have any of the above firms received or applied for 8(a) approval:

Yes ☐ No ☐ If yes, identify _____

VI. Company History: (Narrative of purpose chronological development, problems and successes).

V. Product or Service: (Narrative of characteristics, uses and applicability to commercial market. Nature of work performed with own forces, area of operations).

VI. A. Management: (A copy of this form must be completed by all directors, officers and senior management personnel.)

1. Name: _____ 2. Age ____ 3. Sex ____

4. Marital Status _____ 5. Social Security Number _____

6. Military Serial Number _____
7. Present Position: (Include description of duties)

8. Other jobs and positions held and salaries.

9. Formal schooling

10. Technical training and qualifications

11. Management training

12. Military Experience

(a)

Branch of Service	Place of Service	Period of Service	MOS	Rank
————	————	————	———	—————
————	————	————	———	—————

(b) Service Schools attended and date of attendance

————————————————————

————————————————————

————————————————————

B. List professional, management and technical resource support to be received by your company. (Attach copies of all Management and Technical Support Agreements.)

Name	Address	Phone	Service Performed	Compensation to Be Paid
————	————	————	————	————
————	————	————	————	————
————	————	————	————	————
————	————	————	————	————

C. Diagram Organizational Chart of Firm.

VII. Marketing:
    A. Market Area:

    B. Market Potential:

    C. Commercial Customers:

    D. Government Customers: (Include name and phone number of contracting officers and small business specialist contacted).

    E. Competitors

    F. Advantage over Competitors

    G. Pricing and Bidding Procedures (attach sample of pricing and bidding documents)

    H. Sales Forecast by Product or Service Category

    I. Sales and Distribution Plan (Including advertising pricing, credit terms, etc.):

    J. Business Plan Graph (Reflect commercial and non 8(a) government sales, 8(a) projected support, and break-even point).

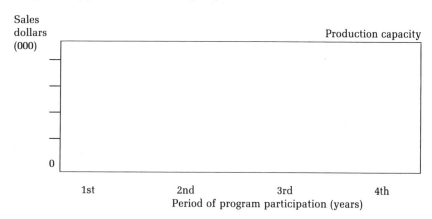

K. Break-Even chart (Reflect income from sales, fixed cost, variable cost and break-even point).

Cost in
dollars

```
        ┌──────────────────────────────────────────┐
        │                                          │
        │                                          │
        │                                          │
        │                                          │
        │                                          │
        │                                          │
        │                                          │
      0 └──────────────────────────────────────────┘ 100
                            50
```

Percentage of plant capacity in operation

VIII. Production:
   A. Plant: (Include location, total square footage, and layout and sketch of office and storage areas. Also include copy of lease deed or proposed lease).

   B. Equipment:

Quantity	Description	Age	Buying or Leasing	Cost

   C. Equipment Layout and Production Flow Plan:

   D. Supervisory Personnel (names and responsibilities):

   E. Labor Skill and Source (detailed list by classification, number and pay rate):

Skill Classification	Number	Pay Rate	Source

   F. Materials Used, Source of Supply, and Average Delivery Time:

G. Shipping Facilities and Accessibility to Transportation:

H. Quality Control System:

I. Workforce Classified as Disadvantaged and Training Programs:

J. Expansion Capability:

IX. Operational Plan:

X. Financial:
Attach year-end and current business balance sheet on applicant and affiliates, year-end and current profit and loss statements on applicant and affiliates, aging of accounts receivable and payables on applicant, monthly cash flow for twelve months on applicant and annual detail projection for two years on applicant.

A. Sales History: (Applicant)

	FY_____	FY_____	FY_____	Year-end to date as of _____
Commercial	_____	_____	_____	_____
Government 8(a)	_____	_____	_____	_____
Government Other	_____	_____	_____	_____
Total _____	_____	_____	_____	_____

B.   Profits of Losses (Applicant)

	FY____	FY____	FY____	Year-end to date as of____
	____	____	____	____

C.   Projection (Applicant)

	1st Year	2nd Year	3rd Year	4th Year
8(a) Projected support	____	____	____	____
Commercial sales	____	____	____	____
Other government	____	____	____	____
Total	____	____	____	____

Note: Projected 8(a) support should decline with each progressive year. Commercial and other Government sales should increase.

D.   Condensed Balance Sheets History (Applicant):

Current as of____		FY ending 19___	
C/A_____	C/L_____	C/A_____	C/L_____
F/A_____	LT/L_____	F/A_____	LT/L_____
O/A_____	N/W_____	O/A_____	N/W_____
Total_____	_____	_____	_____

FY Ending 19___		FY Ending 19___	
C/A_____	C/L_____	C/A_____	C/L_____
F/A_____	LT/L_____	F/A_____	LT/L_____
O/A_____	N/W_____	O/A_____	N/W_____
Total_____	_____	_____	_____

Key: C/A—current assets   O/A—other assets   LT/L—Long term liabilities
       F/A—Fixed assets   C/L—current liabilities   N/W—Networth

E.   Sales History (Affiliates—Sponsors)

Name of Affiliate_____

	FY____	FY____	FY____	Year end to date as of____
Commercial	_____	_____	_____	_____
Government	_____	_____	_____	_____
Total	_____	_____	_____	_____

F.   Condensed Balance Sheets (Affiliates—Sponsors)

Name of Affiliate_____

Current as of____		FY Ending 19___	
C/A_____	C/L_____	C/A_____	C/L_____
F/A_____	LT/L_____	F/A_____	LT/L_____
O/A_____	N/W_____	O/A_____	N/W_____
Total_____	_____	_____	_____

FY Ending 19___		FY Ending 19___	
C/A_____	C/L_____	C/A_____	C/L_____
F/A_____	LT/L_____	F/A_____	LT/L_____
O/A_____	N/W_____	O/A_____	N/W_____
Total_____	_____	_____	_____

XI. Other Pertinent Information:
   A. Contracts or Jobs In-House:

Customer & Representative	Description	Amount ($)	%Completed	Scheduled Completion
_____	_____	_____	_____	_____
_____	_____	_____	_____	_____
_____	_____	_____	_____	_____
_____	_____	_____	_____	_____
_____	_____	_____	_____	_____
_____	_____	_____	_____	_____

   B. Average Monthly Billings—$:
   C. Record of Surety and Fidelity Bonds:

Date	Job or Person	Type of Bond	Amount	Surety Company	Agent or Agency
____	_____	_____	_____	_____	_____
____	_____	_____	_____	_____	_____
____	_____	_____	_____	_____	_____
____	_____	_____	_____	_____	_____
____	_____	_____	_____	_____	_____
____	_____	_____	_____	_____	_____

   D. Contracts or Jobs Completed within the Last Two Years

Customer	Description	Amount ($)
_____	_____	_____
_____	_____	_____
_____	_____	_____
_____	_____	_____
_____	_____	_____
_____	_____	_____
_____	_____	_____

_____ _____ _____

_____ _____ _____

_____ _____ _____

_____ _____ _____

_____ _____ _____

_____ _____ _____

_____ _____ _____

E. Schedule of Insurance:

Company	Coverage	Amount	Expiration Date	Agents or Agency
____	____	____	____	____
____	____	____	____	____
____	____	____	____	____
____	____	____	____	____

F. Bank and Trade Reference:

Name and Address	Contact Person and Position
_____	_____
_____	_____
_____	_____
_____	_____

G. Availability of credit and Financial Assistance:

Source	Amount	Terms	Degree of Commitment (Attach any documentation of commitment
____	____	____	_____
____	____	____	_____
____	____	____	_____

H. List of Loans or Loan Guarantees Provided by the Small Business Administration:

Names and Address of Lender	Loan Number	Original Amount of Loan	Amount Outstanding
_____	_____	_____	_____
_____	_____	_____	_____
_____	_____	_____	_____

I. Outline of Business Goals: (Necessary to become competitive)

Annual Sales	$_____	Current Ratio_____	to_____
Annual Profits	$_____	Debt to Net_____ Worth Ratio	to_____
Bondability	$_____	Estimated number of_____ years to become competitive	to_____

J. Additional Equipment Necessary to Conduct Competitive Business:

Description	Purchase Cost	Lease Cost
_____	$_____	$_____
_____	$_____	$_____
_____	$_____	$_____
_____	$_____	$_____
_____	$_____	$_____
_____	$_____	$_____
_____	$_____	$_____
_____	$_____	$_____
Total	$_____	$_____Per Month

K. Other Resources Needed to Become Competitive:

Type	Amount	Anticipated Source
_____	_____	_____
_____	_____	_____
_____	_____	_____

L. Licenses and Certificates in Effect:

Type	Amount	Place of Issue
_____	_____	_____
_____	_____	_____
_____	_____	_____

M. List trade association and other organizations of which company is a member.

N. Labor Agreements in effect.

O. Contracts with suppliers

P. List law suits in force or pending

Q. Patents, royalties, etc.

R. Product research and development

S. Annual sales volume in dollars required for company to breakeven. $___

VII. Statement of Cooperation:
I understand that if approved for participation in the 8(a) Program I will assume certain obligations as listed below. I understand and agree that if I do not meet these obligations, Small Business Administration may, in its sole discretion, remove me from further participation. I further understand that SBA cannot assure the availability of 8(a) contracts to my company, either now or in the future.

I pledge to use my best efforts to develop my business by actively soliciting business (either commercial or competitive Federal) in accordance with the projections made in my business plan.

I pledge to provide SBA with timely and accurate financial information which will consist of at least quarterly profit or loss statements and quarterly balance sheet. The income from 8(a) contracts is to be shown separately from other income. If requested, I will provide such other information as may be required.

I further agree that any duly authorized representative of the Small Business Administration shall have access to and the right to examine any pertinent books, documents, papers, and records involving transactions related to any contract awarded under the 8(a) Program.

To the best of my ability, I will put into practice the business methods and advice provided to me by Small Business Administration. I will discuss with appropriate SBA personnel any major changes or long-term commitments prior to entering into such commitments.

I will conduct my business affairs in an ethical manner.

I hereby certify that I have not paid fees to third parties, whether directly or indirectly, in the process of obtaining 8(a) subcontracts. If such fees have been paid, or contracted to be paid, I attach full details of such agreement.

I further certify that the statements contained in this application and attachments are true and correct to the best of my knowledge and belief.

Signature of Authorized Officer of Firm	Title of Officer	Date

Technical and Management Assistance Agreement:

The undersigned requests the SBA to provide technical and management assistance in connection with this Business Plan and Qualifications Resume. It is understood that said assistance shall be performed free of charge. I hereby authorize SBA to furnish information and data contained in the Business Plan and Qualifications Resume to those persons providing this company with technical and management assistance. All information will be treated in strict confidence.

In consideration of this assistance, I hereby waive all claims arising therefrom against SBA and aforeferenced persons.

Signature of Authorized Officer of Firm	Title of Officer	Date

Appendix VII

Small Business Organizations

There are many organizations throughout the Nation which represent small business interests. The following list of general small business organizations is by no means exhaustive but does represent several of the major organizations which deal with the Federal government on a regular and on-going basis.

COALITION OF SMALL AND INDEPENDENT BUSINESS ASSOCIATIONS (COSIBA)

Council of Smaller Enterprises (COSE)
690 Union Commerce Building
Cleveland, Ohio 44115

Director	Michael Benz	(216) 621-3300

Independent Business Association of Wisconsin
7635 Bluemound Road, Milwaukee, Wisconsin 53214

President	Dean Treptow	(414) 258-7055

National Association of Small Business Investment Companies (NASBIC)
618 Washington Building, Washington, DC 20005

President	Arthur D. Little	(202) 638-3411
Exec. V.P.	Walter Stults	

National Business League (NBL)
4324 Georgia Ave., NW, Washington, DC 20011

President	Theodore R. Hagans, Jr.	(202) 829-5900

National Federation of Independent Business
Suite 3206, 490 L'Enfant Plaza East, S.W.,
Washington, DC 20024

President	Wilson Johnson*	(415) 341-7441
Washington Counsel	James D. "Mike" McKevitt	(202) 554-9000

* at National Headquarters, San Mateo, Calif.

National Small Business Association (NSBA)
1604 K St., NW, Washington, DC 20006

President	John E. Lewis	(202) 296-7400

Smaller Business Association of New England (SBANE)
69 Hickory Drive, Waltham, MA 02154

President	Daniel A. Cronin, Jr.	(617) 890-9070
Exec. V.P.	Lewis A. Shattuck	

New York Association of Small Business Councils
1500 One MONY Plaza, Syracuse, NY 13202

President	Erwin G. Shultz	(315) 422-1343

Smaller Manufacturers Council (SMC)
339 Boulevard of the Allies, Pittsburgh, PA 15222

President	Barrie D. Gibbs	(412) 391-1622
Exec. V.P.	Leo McDonough	

Appendix VIII

Other Small Business Contacts

	Center for Small Business **Chamber of Commerce of the United States** 1615 H Street, NW, Washington, DC 20062	
Director	Ivan Elmer	(202) 659-6180
	Latin American Manufacturing Association (LAMA) 1325 18th St., NW Washington, DC 20036	
President	Steven Denlinger	(202) 467-5803
	National Association of Black Manufacturers 1625 Eye Street, NW, Washington, DC	
President	Eugene Baker	(202) 785-5133
	National Association of Women Business Owners 2000 P Street, NW, Washington, DC 20036	
President	Susan Cavanaugh	(202) 338-8966
	National Economic Development Association 1636 R St., NW, Washington, DC 20009	
President	Jose C. Gomez	(202) 232-1666

Appendix IX

NTIS: Thousands of Additional Sources of Information for Small Business

At least 26 million referrals annually are made to specific titles in the NTIS system, three each second of the NTIS workday. And every second of the NTIS workday, a buyer receives a specially requested information time. About 3,600 new buyers are added to the NTIS customer list monthly and 10,000 customers make repeat purchases, resulting in 23,500 items of information being shipped daily. Every three minutes during the NTIS workday two new technical reports enter the NTIS system.

A STATEMENT OF PURPOSE

NTIS is an information service organization stemming from a congressionally created predecessor. It channels information about technological innovations and other specialized information to business, educators, government, and the public. Its products and services are intended to increase the efficiency and effectiveness of U.S. research and development, to support U.S. foreign policy goals by assisting the social and economic development of other nations, and to increase the availability of foreign technical information in the United States. NTIS undertakes and develops innovative information products and programs appropriate for Government, but which have the potential to become self-supporting.

37TH ANNIVERSARY FOR NTIS, PREDECESSOR ORGANIZATIONS

NTIS became twelve years old in 1982, but its predecessor organizations go back 37 years to 1945 when President Truman signed Executive Order 9568 establishing the Publication Board to make available Government research that had been withheld during the war because of security classifications. Soon thereafter, an amendment extended the Publication Board's mission to include the handling of enemy scientific and industrial information.

By early 1946 declassified documents were arriving at the rate of 5,000 a month, an interesting comparison to the current acquisition rate of some 5,800 reports monthly.

From the Publication Board there evolved the Office of Technical Services, under the Assistant Secretary for Foreign and Domestic Commerce, and after that the Clearinghouse for Federal Scientific and Technical Information, under the Assistant Secretary for Science and Technology.

The designation of the agency as the National Technical Information Service was made by the Secretary of Commerce in 1970, along with an expanded mission to acquire and promote domestic and foreign technological information.

GETTING STARTED; LOCATING AND HANDLING TECHNICAL INFORMATION

Anyone can be a beginner in approaching new technical information regardless of accomplishments or experience in other areas.

The following publications have been selected as basic guides to the NTIS collection, the specialized collections of NTIS's information sources and technical information in general.

1. How to Get It—A Guide to Defense-Related Documents (AD-769 220), A15.
2. Source Header List DTIC (AD-A041 700), $36.00.
3. Government Acronyms and Alphabetic Organizational Designators Used in DDC (AD-A044 000), A12.
4. Especially DTIC (AD-A005 400), A05.
5. DTIC Referral Data Bank Directory (AD-A055 700), A18.
6. How to Obtain Information in Different Fields of Science & Technology (AD-780 061), A06.
7. Energy Information in the Federal Government (PB-246 703), $45.00.
8. Directory of Cancer Research Information Resources (PB-293 187), A12.
9. Integrated Energy Vocabulary (PB-259 000), E11.
10. Medical Subject Headings (Annotated List) (PB-300 500) $15.00. Medical Subject Headings (Tree Structures) (PB-300 498) $10.50. Medical Subject Headings (Tree Annotations) (PB80-104706) $7.25. MESH Permuted Medical Subject Headings (PB-300 499), E05.
11. Online Services Reference Manual (MEDLARS) (PB80-114531) $10.50.
12. List of Serials and Monographs for Online Users (PB80-131204) $6.50.
13. U.S. Directory of Environmental Sources (PB-274 110), $34.00.
14. Market Share Reports Catalog (PB-294 300), free.
15. User's Guide to the Environmental Protection Agency Library System (PB-238 932), A03.
16. Information Services on Research in Progress (PB-282 025), A20.

NTIS IN THE 1980'S: TECHNOLOGY FOR PRODUCTIVITY AND INNOVATION

The Basic NTIS Product Is Federal Research and Technical Information in Paper, Film, and Machine-Readable Formats

As a cornerstone of the technological publishing structure in the United States, the National Technical Information Service (NTIS) is a key participant in the development of advanced information products and services for the achievement of U.S. productivity and innovational goals in the 1980's.

Three of the developmental areas in which progress is well under way are:

1. The greatly increased public availability of Federal computer software, programs, and data files.
2. The planned systematic acquisition of generally unpublished foreign technology, worldwide, of particular interest to U.S. industrialists.
3. The promotion of U.S. Government-owned patents for licensing by U.S. manufacturers, and the public availability of U.S. Patent and Trademark Office data files on magnetic tape.

NTIS, an agency of the U.S. Department of Commerce, is the central source for the public sale of U.S. Government-sponsored research, development, and engineering reports, as well as for foreign technical reports and other analyses prepared by national and local government agencies, their contractors, or grantees. It is the central source for federally generated machine processable data files and manages the Federal Software Center for intragovernment distribution. NTIS is one of the world's leading processors of specialty information.

The NTIS information collection exceeds 1.2 million titles, about 300,000 of which contain foreign technology or marketing information. All are permanently available for sale, either directly from the 80,000 titles in shelf stock or from the microfiche masters of titles less in demand. Seventy thousand new reports of completed research are added to the data base annually. In the same period NTIS supplies its customers with more than 6 million documents and microforms. It ships about 23,500 information products daily.

Full summaries of current U.S. and foreign research reports and other specialized information, in hundreds of subject categories, are published regularly by NTIS in a wide variety of weekly newsletters, a biweekly journal, an annual index, and in various subscription formats for other Federal agencies. The complete texts of the reports cited are sold in paper and microform.

Anyone seeking the latest technical reports or wanting to compile unique subject groups of abstracts may search the *NTIS Bibliographic Data Base* online, using the services of organizations that maintain the data base for public use through contractual relationships with NTIS. Or, the whole data base may be leased in machine-readable form directly from NTIS. The more timely abstracts are continually grouped by NTIS into paperbound *Published Searches*, covering some 2,200 topical subject areas.

Customers with well defined continuing interests subscribe to a standing order microfiche service (SRIM) which enables them automatically to receive the full texts of only those documents relating to their individual requirements. A similar service provides the automatic distribution of paperbound reports.

NTIS sells its technical information products and services under the provisions of Title 15 of the U.S. Code (1151-7). The law establishes a clearinghouse for scientific, technical, and engineering information and directs NTIS to be self supporting.

NTIS, therefore, is a unique Government agency sustained only by its customers. It operates very much as a business, but in the public service. All the costs of NTIS products and services, including rent, telephone, salaries, marketing, postage, and all other usual costs of doing business are paid from sales income; not from tax-supported congressional appropriations.

SCIENCE INFORMATION EXCHANGE DATA BASE; 200,000 ONGOING PROJECTS

The SIE Data Base consists of summaries of federally funded research in progress. The Data Base is very dynamic in that old records are retired and new records are added as projects are completed and new projects begun. There are approximately 100,000 new projects announced annually, with over 200,000 projects existing in the Data Base at any one time.

The SIE Data Base of information about ongoing Federal research projects is available on lease from NTIS. But, the SIE will continue to provide its other information products to the public.

INFORMATION FOR INNOVATORS IS UNIQUE NEW SERVICE

A powerful new interdisciplinary information service for innovators is now available from NTIS. *Information for Innovators* uncovers technical and market opportunities for industry by interpreting the innovation potential in existing federally sponsored R&D and foreign technology.

The plain language briefs, written for professionals responsible for keeping informed beyond their own fields of expertise, enable you to scan the innovation-relevant cream of 2,500 new reports in 20 minutes every two weeks. Each item is linked to available original sources, people and organizations, and other useful data bases.

Information for Innovators every other week service is $85 annually. An additional option, *Innovators Source Library,* simultaneously provides in microfiche all original reports on which each issue is based, for $365 additional, annually. Use the order form on page 31.

WHO PREPARES GOVERNMENT RESEARCH?

Most Government research is conducted by U.S. corporations, Federal Laboratories, and universities under contract to Government agencies. The NTIS collection is the largest and best publicly available pool of widely varied research results in the world. Corporate authors of reports in the NTIS system include:

Massachusetts Institute of Technology, Allied Chemical, Harvard University, Standard Oil of Indiana, Yale University, Owens Illinois, New York University, Aluminum Co. of America, University of Pennsylvania, Combustion Engineering, Stanford University, Deere & Co., Cornell University, IBM, Texas A&M University, General Electric, University of Rochester, General Motors, Johns Hopkins University, Rockwell International, University of California, Eastman Kodak, University of Illinois, Rand Corp., University of Wisconsin, Tennessee Valley Authority, University of Michigan, International Telephone & Telegraph, Columbia University, Honeywell, University of Minnesota, Fairchild, University of Washington, Ford Motor Co., University of Chicago, Hewlett-Packard, Sperry Rand, Babcock & Wilcox, Reynolds Metals, Norton Co., Shell Oil, Union Carbide, Crown Zellerbach, Swift & Co., Monsanto, Gulf Oil, Carborundum, Kaiser Aluminum & Chemical, Control Data, RCA, and Westinghouse Electric Corporation.

UNIQUE DATA BASE SERVICES AND MACHINE-READABLE INFORMATION TO AID U.S. INNOVATION, RAISE PRODUCTIVITY

In its continuing effort to provide the widest possible access to specialized scientific, technical, and business information, NTIS has become increasingly responsible for expanding the public access to the machine-readable information products of Federal agencies.

In the initial stages of the current expansion program, special attention is being given to the following areas of concern:

Providing access to bibliographic data files produced by agencies other than NTIS.

Cataloging and indexing machine-readable statistical data files.

Providing online access to various data bases processed by Federal agencies.

Expanding the NTIS collection of available machine-readable data files and software.

Providing access to the full range of Federal statistical data files through reference and tabulation services.

A wide range of machine-readable products and services already is available from NTIS in these areas:

Bibliographic Data Bases

NTIS Bibliographic Data Base—All items announced by NTIS are included in the NTIS Bibliographic Data Base (on magnetic tape). It is available for lease.

Energy Data Base (EDB)—The world's largest and most comprehensive data base on energy, created and maintained by the Technical Information Center, U.S. Department of Energy, is available for lease through NTIS.

Patent Tapes—From the U.S. Patent and Trademark Office, U.S. Department of Commerce, the Patent Tapes are being made publicly available for the first time through NTIS.

Selected Water Resources Abstracts (SWRA) Data Base—From the Office of Water Research and Technology, U.S. Department of the Interior, the *SWRA* is available for lease through NTIS. The *SWRA* contains abstracts covering aspects of the characteristics, conservation, control, use, and management of water.

Online Access Services

NTIS plans to provide online access to data bases processed by Federal agencies when a comparable service is not offered by a commercial vendor. Services being considered will stem from data bases containing information in the areas of economics, the labor force, environment, chemical substances, and others.

Batch Services

NTIS provides custom reports from an enormous data base of 1970 Census data developed and maintained by the Lawrence Berkeley Laboratory of the U.S. Department of Energy. The data base contains all of the employment-related information of the 1970 Census. A comparable service based on 1980 Census data is planned.

Magnetic Tapes

The present collection of magnetic tapes contains more than 1,200 data files and computer programs from more than 100 Federal agencies, covering an array of subject fields.

The 1980 Directory of Computer Software and Related Technical Reports is a unique guide to machine-readable software and related technical reports available to the public from Federal agencies. More than 350 programs are listed and described in the Directory, along with applicable technical reports.

References and Tabulation Services

The *Statistical Data Reference Service* makes information available on the full range of Federal statistical resources, covering major subject areas based on social, economic, and environmental statistical programs of the U.S. Government.

The *Statistical Data Tabulation Service* provides low-cost easy access to data from Federal data files, through standardization of the programs used to prepare tabulations.

Foreign Technology

NTIS is negotiating with foreign data base operators to make their data directly accessible in the United States. Several data bases, bibliographic and nonbibliographic, that heretofore have been accessible only in Europe and Japan are expected to be made available in the U.S. through NTIS.

NTIS Bibliographic Data Base

All of the research summaries announced by NTIS are included in the *NTIS Bibliographic Data Base* (on magnetic tape). Most are complete bibliographic citations and may be used to create a wide variety of information products.

Users of the *NTIS Bibliographic Data Base* are uniquely able to search a multiplicity of technical information input styles within the uniform NTIS format. There is no need for the user to acquire familiarity with different search strategies in order to search the several source tapes contributing to the NTIS file. Such "single" searching saves both computer and communication costs.

Subscribers may search any or all of the file elements: research report title; personal or corporate author; NTIS order/report number or contract/grant number; by subject, using keywords, descriptors, or subject codes.

The files are arranged in the NTIS modification of the COSATI implementation of the ANSI standard (Z39.2, 1971) specifying a format for bibliographic information interchange on magnetic tapes. The character code is convertible to the standard ASCII code.

Tapes are available as 7-track, 800 BPI and as 9-track, 800, 1,600 or 6,250 BPI, odd parity only.

The magnetic tape containing the data file may be leased annually and files back to 1964 may be acquired. Current tapes are shipped to subscribers biweekly.

Basic Guides to NTIS Files

The following publications are basic guides to the NTIS collection.

NTIS Subject Classification (Past & Present) (PB-270 575) Price code A05

A Reference Guide to the NTIS Bibliographic Data Base (NTIS-PR-253) No charge

Environmental Microthesaurus (PB-265 261) Price code E06

Energy Microthesaurus (PB-254 800) Price code E06

Health Care Microthesaurus (PB-290 776) Price code E06

Computer Sciences Microthesaurus (PB80-207814) Price code E04

Standard for Cataloging of Government Scientific and Technical Reports (PB-277 951) Price code A04

COSATI Corporate Author Headings (PB-198 275) Price code A99

COSATI Subject Categories (AD-612200) Price code A04

The *NTIS Bibliographic Data Base* is available online from the following U.S. commercial vendors:

Lockheed Information Service
3460 Hillview Avenue
Palo Alto, California 94304

System Development Corporation
2500 Colorado Avenue
Santa Monica, California 90406

Bibliographic Retrieval Services Inc.
Corporation Park, Bldg. 702
Scotia, New York 12302

SEARCHES, ABSTRACT NEWSLETTERS, TECH NOTES, FULL-TEXT FICHE SERVICE

The basic *NTIS Bibliographic Data Base* on magnetic tape is the resource from which NTIS designs and produces an array of information, products, and services. But the principal NTIS product for thousands of its users remains its inventory and current acquisition of federally sponsored research and technical reports. Only abstracts of the full-text reports are on the magnetic tape.

The primary NTIS products and services, aside from the technical reports, are briefly described on the following pages 5 thru 8. More detailed information may be obtained on request to the appropriate product manager.

3,000-Plus Published Searches

Most of these 3,000 or so specially priced *Published Searches* consist of between 100 and 200 different thorough research summaries (abstracts) of advanced technology for business people, scientists, and specialists in urban, economic, and social affairs. Most of the reports summarized also are sold by NTIS.

Users of NTIS *Published Searches* may multiply their search benefits and applications in many instances where the NTISearch subjects are offered with identical subject searches from the data bases of the **Department of Energy, Engineering Index, American Petroleum Institute, Institute of Paper Chemistry, Food Science and Technology Abstracts; and International Aerospace Abstracts.** And, other data bases are being added. Such opportunities are indicated in current lists of available NTIS *Published Search* subjects. Ask for PR-186.

Abstract Newsletters

Abstract Newsletters provide thousands of readers with timely research summaries within three weeks of their receipt by NTIS from the originating agencies. Abstract Newsletters ensure maximum coverage of broad areas of Government research in brief and convenient form and at minimal cost. Summaries of special interest are noted by the terms, *Highlight, Published Search, Foreign Technology, or Foreign Marketing Information.*

    The final issue of the year is a special subject and order number index containing up to 10 cross references for each research summary indexed. The Abstract Newsletter titles and annual subscription rates are:

Administration & Management	$70
Agriculture & Food	$60
Behavior & Society	$60
Biomedical Technology & Human Factors Engineering	$50
Building Industry Technology	$65
Business & Economics	$65
Chemistry	$70
Civil Engineering	$70
Communication	$55
Computers, Control & Information Theory	$80
Electrotechnology	$55
Energy	$80
Environmental Pollution & Control	$80
Government Inventions for Licensing	$180
Health Planning & Health Services Research	$60
Industrial & Mechanical Engineering	$65
Library & Information Sciences	$50
Materials Sciences	$70
Medicine & Biology	$60
NASA Earth Resources Survey Program (Bimonthly)	$50
Natural Resources & Earth Sciences	$60
Ocean Technology & Engineering	$55
Physics	$60
Problem Solving Information for State & Local Governments	$50
Transportation	$70
Urban & Regional Technology & Development	$50

All NTIS Abstracts in One Volume

Summaries of U.S. Government research are published in one biweekly volume that includes five indexes. Coverage is comprehensive—about 70,000 new summaries annually, more than 10,000 pages—and is indexed by subject, personal and corporate author, and Government contract and NTIS order/report numbers.

The Government Reports Announcements & Index was designed for librarians and technical information specialists and for those used to working with technical information terms and sources.

GRA&I Annual subscription: $275. Multiple subscriptions ordered at the same time for the same address are sold at a 15 percent discount.

Special Six-Volume Annual Index

A cumulation of the 26 issues of the biweekly GRA&I Index is included in the Annual Index. It consists of six volumes: Subject, Personal Author, Corporate Author, and Contract Numbers & NTIS order/report Numbers.

Indexes prior to 1974 are softbound.

Write for special quotation for combinations of earlier year indexes.

Full-Text Profiles in Fiche

You can vastly expand your coverage of U.S. Government research and development with only a modest information budget. *Selected Research in Microfiche* (SRIM) limits your expense by sending you complete research reports (not just abstracts) in microfiche in *only* the subject areas you select.

Our analysts will help choose from 390 categories and subcategories and 200,-000 descriptive terms. Full-text microfiche copies of the reports are sent to you biweekly, and instead of the regular single fiche report price of $3.50 you pay only 85 cents for each SRIM microfiche title *automatically selected from your category.*

Each microfiche can contain the equivalent of 98 pages of text arranged in 4x6 inches (105mm x 148mm) and may be easily read with any microfiche viewer. You can easily carry the equivalent of fifty 300-page books in one pocket.

You don't have to wait to track down a specific report, order it, and wait for reprinting if it's out of stock. You get the full report, complete with every illustration and notation. By the time you read of a report's availability, the report will have been selected by SRIM and be on its way to you. You can arrange for SRIM in a variety of information patterns.

The usefulness of a SRIM subscription can be extended and increased through the use of the quarterly SRIM Index in paper or microfiche, or both.

Each Index is individual and designed to list only the microfiche covered by a particular subscription.

Here are two typical examples of *Selected Research in Microfiche:*

Energy/Energy Use, Supply and Demand: 480 complete report texts were sent out over a 12-month period, costing the customer $408. The same titles ordered individually in microfiche form would cost $1,680; and in paper copy, about $3,800.

Administration/Public Administration and Government: 559 complete report texts were sent out over a 12-month period, costing the customer $475. The same titles ordered individually in microfiche form would have cost $1,956; in paper copy, total cost would have been more than $4,440.

Tech Notes from Nine U.S. Agencies

Tech Notes pulls together into a single convenient monthly package summaries of new applications for technology developed by different Federal agencies and their contractors.

The individual *Tech Notes* entries are prepared by the various agencies and are generally patterned after the Tech Briefs pioneered by NASA, which are now part of the new package. *Tech Notes* includes the following:

NASA Tech Briefs:

> Army—Office of Manufacturing Technology (Manufacturing Technology Note)
> Air Force—Abstracts of New Technology
> Air Force—Manufacturing Technology
> Navy—Manufacturing Technology
> Navy—Technology Transfer Fact Sheets
> Interior—Bureau of Mines Technology News
> Agriculture—Forest Service Equip Tips
> Commerce—NBS Staff Report
> DOE—Union Carbide TU Bulletin,
>   Department of Energy Notes
> NSF/RANN—UTS Briefs

To avoid overwhelming users with massive outpourings of new applications for Federal technology in all fields, *Tech Notes* is available in various subject categories. Currently these are:

Computers, Electrotechnology, Energy, Engineering, Life Sciences, Physical Sciences, Machinery, Materials, Manufacturing, Ordnance, and Testing and Instrumentation.

Selected Technology for Licensing, one-page summaries of the better Government inventions from all agencies, is another feature of the package.

Users may subscribe to any one category or any combination of categories. Substantial discounts are offered to those who order more than one category. To qualify for the discount all categories must be mailed to the same person, to a single address. A typical monthly issue for a single category includes about 12 individual *Tech Notes*.

Most Tech Notes in the package are supported by backup material that may be obtained from NTIS when additional information is required.

Prices: One category, $50; two categories, $95; three categories, $135; four categories, $170; five categories, $205; six categories, $240; seven categories, $275; eight categories, $310; nine categories, $345; ten categories, $380; *All Categories $250.*

Today's personal professional library can be portable, thanks to microforms on which the printed page has been photographically reduced to thumbnail size, or smaller. You may comfortably carry fifty 300-page volumes on microfiche in your pocket. There is space for the equivalent of 98 pages, each a twenty-fourth the size of the original, on each 4x6 inch (105mm x 148mm) film sheet. One hundred and fifty sheets of film are 1 inch thick. Microfilm is on reels, about the size and shape of 16mm movie film. Each 100-foot reel contains about 2,200 printed pages, or 22 pages a foot. Aperture cards are standard tabulating cards into which microfilm images have been inserted. They are often key-punched for mechanical retrieval.

Microforms (film, fiche, or aperture cards) have other very practical qualities besides their uses for daily reference. One is "previewing" large and expensive volumes where there is uncertainty about the immediate usefulness or relevance of a particular work to a task at hand. Another is when only a chapter, one or two pages, or even a paragraph, of a volume is required. In both cases microforms are most satisfactory.

Portable fiche and film readers, some less than book size and very lightweight, are available for about $100. Some may be operated from self-contained rechargeable cells or from an automobile cigarette lighter. Readers which also print selected pages on paper are higher priced.

Practically all periodicals and vast varieties of historic and contemporary information are available on microforms.

Information Source for Equipment
and Supplies
NATIONAL MICROGRAPHICS
ASSOCIATION
8728 Colesville Road
Silver Spring, Maryland 20910

NEW GOVERNMENT INVENTIONS OFFER OPPORTUNITIES TO ACQUIRE TECHNOLOGY

NTIS is the central source for information on all new U.S. Government-owned patents and patent-pending applications. These inventions primarily come out of Government laboratories but also include contractor inventions to which the Government has title.

Information is available on nearly 1,500 new Government inventions annually. (More than 25,000 U.S. Government inventions are now in the NTIS data base.) Cooperating agencies submit their new inventions to NTIS when patent applications are filed with the U.S. Patent and Trademark Office and again when the patents are issued. These inventions are summarized in the NTIS illustrated abstract newsletter, *Government Inventions for Licensing,* (see page 5).

New inventions are evaluated by specialists under contract to NTIS to determine their potential for commercial application. The most commercially promising inventions are summarized in *Selected Technology for Licensing,* the publication series available to *NTIS Tech Notes* subscribers (see page 6).

Copies of pending patent applications announced by NTIS are available in paper and microfiche. Claims are deleted before sale to the public to avoid premature disclosure. Claims and related technical data usually will be made available to serious prospective licensees.

NTIS obtains foreign patent protection on selected inventions which are in the custody of the Department of Commerce or are assigned to the Department by other Federal agencies. Foreign patent protection provides U.S. firms with more attractive licensing packages.

Inventions in the NTIS portfolio are normally licensed on a non-exclusive basis. Exclusive licenses may be granted when there is no interest in non exclusive licenses because of the significant capital investment required. Nominal fees are charged to permit NTIS to operate its invention promotion program on a self-supporting basis.

GOVERNMENT PATENTS CATALOG IS UNIQUE; AVAILABLE IN 1981

NTIS is pleased to announce its *Catalog of Government Patents*, known during its developmental stages as the *U.S. Government Patent Portfolio Listing*. This unique catalog presents information on thousands of Government-owned inventions, most of which are available for licensing. These inventions have resulted from billions of Federal dollars invested in a variety of research and development projects. The catalog comprises three basic portions:

Part A contains about 16,000 patents and patent applications contained in three hardbound volumes. This basic section, which contains all patents issued to Federal agencies from 1966 through 1974, includes an abstract of each invention and, in some 40 percent, also includes an illustration. The three volumes of Part A are arranged generally along the lines of the Patent and Trademark Office classification system, as is the Table of Contents. Price: $120.

Part B of the *Catalog of Government Patents* covers the years 1975 through 1980. It is planned as a hard bound, two- or three-volume edition with index. The entries are sorted in a unique subject arrangement that includes the Patent and Trademark Office's classification system, plus some specially developed NTIS subcategories. These entries are sorted by Federal agency, by patent application or issued patent, and then listed sequentially by number. Patent applications in this section include only those for which patents have not been subsequently issued. Inventions are indexed both by subject and by agency. Buyers of Part A will be notified when Part B is ready for distribution.

Part C is already available as the weekly Newsletter, *Government Inventions for Licensing*. Sample copies are available on request.

The patents and patent applications cover all fields of science and technology and should find application in the solution of commercial, manufacturing, and production problems.

TIMELY & TOPICAL: *ENERGY*

New research reports relating to energy are 34 percent of all the information added to the NTIS collection each year. Of the 24,000 documents, 4,000 are from foreign sources. The following descriptions are condensed because the whole energy product line is described in detail in a separate free catalog, PR-593, obtainable by checking the order form on page 31.

World's Largest Energy Data Base

The world's largest and most comprehensive bibliographic data base on energy is created and maintained by the Department of Energy's Technical Information Center, Oak Ridge, Tennessee, and is available for lease through NTIS. The *Energy Data Base* (EDB) includes more than 600,000 items.

For more information on leasing the *EDB*, please telephone (703) 487-4808.

Energy Abstract Newsletter

The *Energy Abstract Newsletter* provides thousands of readers with timely research summaries within three weeks of their receipt by NTIS from the originating agencies. Summaries of special interest are highlighted and foreign technology is identified. Annual subscription: $80.

Tech Notes Includes Energy

Tech Notes pulls together into a single convenient monthly package summaries of new applications for technology developed by different Federal agencies and their contractors. The individual *Tech Notes* entries are prepared by the various agencies, including the Department of Energy *Tech Notes* which may be subscribed to separately at $50 annually.

DOE Periodicals

The monthly *Fusion Energy Update* abstracts and indexes current scientific and technical reports, journal articles, conference papers and proceedings, books, patents, theses, and monographs for all sources of fusion energy.

Subjects covered include plasma physics, physics and engineering of blankets, magnetic fields and coils, power supplies and circuitry, cooling systems, fuel systems, radiation hazards, power conversion systems, inertial confinement systems, and component development and testing.

The monthly *Solar Energy Update* announces research, development, and demonstration information from all sources. It abstracts and indexes reports, journal articles, conference proceedings, patents, theses, and monographs. Corporate and personal author, subject, and report number indexes are included and are cumulated annually.

The monthly *Fossil Energy Update* abstracts and indexes current scientific and technical reports, journal articles, conference papers and proceedings, books, patents, theses, and monographs from all sources on fossil energy. Subjects include coal, petroleum, natural gas, oil shale, hydrogen production, hydrocarbon and alcohol fuels, electric power engineering, and magnetohydrodynamic generators.

The monthly *Geothermal Energy Update* contains references to reports, journal articles, conference proceedings, patents, theses, and monographs. Citations and abstracts are grouped under subject categories.

The monthly *Energy Conservation Update* provides abstracts and an index to the latest studies of energy conservation worldwide. It covers a broad spectrum from transportation and industrial energy savings to the latest research dealing with techniques for residential and commercial heating, lighting, and hot water conservation.

NASA Energy Bibliography Quarterly

Coverage includes regional, national, and international energy systems; research and development on fuels and other sources of energy; energy conversion, transport, transmission, distribution, and storage, with special emphasis on the use of hydrogen and of solar energy.

The *NASA energy quarterly* has five indexes which are cumulative through the year. They include subject, personal author, corporate source, contract number, and report number.

Nuclear Regulatory Commission Reports

The *Standard Review Plan* published by the Nuclear Regulatory Commission's (NRC) Office of Nuclear Reactor Regulation is a safety review of applications to build and operate light-water-cooled nuclear power reactors.

Standard Review Plan (*Environmental*): These Environmental Standard Review Plans (ESRPs) constitute a series of instructions developed for the Nuclear Regulatory Commission (NRC) staff's environmental review of applications for nuclear power plant construction permits.

The *Water Reactor Safety Research Status Summary Report* reviews the status and overall progress of the Nuclear Regulatory Commission's safety research program from a managerial point of view.

Energy Research on Standing Order

Energy SOS (Standing Order Service) automatically brings you the full text of every printed energy report published by NTIS—as many as 11,000 reports annually.

If your needs are specific you can limit the reports you receive to any one or combination of subjects.

You will receive your energy reports weeks before you would if ordering them separately. No ordering is required after your first request. Each time a report is issued in your area of interest it will be directed to you automatically.

Energy SOS subscribers pay 20 percent less for reports than buyers of single titles—a savings of about $1.30 on each report—so that a subscriber to the entire output could save $14,000 or more in one year.

DOE Nuclear Operations, Research

These are the Department of Energy's unclassified technical reports, critical reviews, conference papers, and symposia results. These reports are described in *NTIS Abstract Newsletters* and journals (GRA&I). Complete texts are sold in paper copy and microfiche in 56 categories.

FIRST FEDERAL RESEARCH REFLECTED BY THREE PIONEER UNDERTAKINGS

The first federally funded research was in 1768, or in 1803, or in 1830. You may choose the date according to your interpretation of three pioneer undertakings.

In 1768 the colonial Philadelphia Assembly authorized 100 pounds in public funds to be spent for a telescope that would enable local academicians to observe the transit of Venus.

In 1803 Congress authorized $2,500 for the exploration of the upper Missouri River, "so as to extend the external commerce of the United States."

In 1830, after a series of catastrophic steamboat boiler explosions, Congress appropriated $1,500 for experiments to determine how such explosions could be prevented. The project is generally considered the first Federal research contract and it was undertaken by the Franklin Institute of Philadelphia.

Possibly never since has $1,500 worth of research bought such success. The investigating committees' six detailed recommendations revolutionized steam boiler manufacture and use in the U.S. and contributed to legislation that set the standards for steam boilers for years to come.

TIMELY & TOPICAL: *ENVIRONMENT & HEALTH*

Environment and health research reports are among those most sought by NTIS customers. Some 15,000 documents on these subjects are acquired by NTIS annually and announced in its *Abstract Newsletters* and *Government Reports Announcements and Index* (GRA&I).

FDA Field Operations Manual

The *Compliance Program Guidance Manual* was developed to instruct those involved in Food and Drug Administration Field operations. The plans and instructions are surveillance or compliance oriented in accomplishing FDA's regulatory obligations. The manual's six major categories are: 1) Food and Cosmetics; 2) Drugs; 3) Biologics; 4) Veterinary Medicine; 5) Medical Devices; 6) Radiological Health. Almost every page in the manual is reissued or superseded during a fiscal year. Updates will be on a monthly basis, issued by NTIS on Standing Order.

Other FDA Subscription Items

The FDA *Compliance Policy Guides* include all official statements of FDA compliance policy and describe the Food and Drug Administration's official policies on compliance matters. This series is issued as a basic report with approximately 12 updates a year.
Price: $100 annually. Order: PB81-915400.

The *Monthly Import Detention List* tabulates currently detained imported items such as foodstuffs and pharmaceuticals. The detentions are arranged by product code; sample number; the product, district, and port of entry; manufacturer's and shipper's name; city and country of origin; the primary and secondary reason for detention; unit type, quantity, and value. Each issue is about 90 pages.
Price: $50 annually. Order: PB81-923600

FDA Drug and Device Product Approvals is published monthly and lists the most recent New Drug Approvals (NDA's); Abbreviated New Drug Applications (ANDA's); New Animal (veterinary) Drug Applications (NADA's); medical devices and licenses issued for biological products.
Price: $50 annually. Order: PB81-923700.

The *Drug Summary Basis for Approval* (SBA) contains the SBA for each original New Drug Application (NDA) approved by the FDA during the preceding month. This monthly publication complements the *FDA Drug and Device Product Approvals* by providing the summaries of the scientific studies evaluated by FDA during the drug approval process. Approximately 7 reports of 25 pages each per issue.
Price: $140. Order: PB81-915900.

FDA Pesticide Manual

This two-volume laboratory manual describes methods for the analysis of pesticide residues in foods and feeds. Details are presented for the methods used by the Food and Drug Administration to enforce the pesticide tolerances set by the Environmental Protection Agency.

Volume I: Gives complete details of FDA multi-pesticide residue methods. Sample preparation, gas chromatographic operating conditions, confirming techniques, and tabulations of analytical behavior of various chemicals through each procedure are included.

Volume II: Presents methods for determining single pesticide residues. Appropriate cross-references to Volume I are included.

Prices include revised pages as published.

Volume I $35	Order PB81-911800.
Volume II $50	Order PB81-911900.
Volumes I & II $75	Order PB81-911700.

EPA Pesticide Data

The Environmental Protection Agency, Office of Pesticide Programs, has amassed a comprehensive computerized collection of information on specific pesticide products, which includes product names, manufacturers, active ingredients, tolerance for residues, and site and pest information for particular products and active chemical ingredients.

These data are on microfiche in two sets. Set "A" is updated biannually and consists of the subsets:

Product Name List (alpha and numeric)
Company List (alpha and numeric)
Chemicals (alpha and numeric)
Residue Tolerances (chemical and commodity)
Registration Numbers by Chemical
Label Profiles

Set "B" is redone biannually and consists of the following subsets and numbers of fiche:

Chemical/Site/Pest
Site/Pest/Chemical/Registration Numbers
Pest/Chemical

Price annually:
Sets A & B $150 Order PB81-921900
Set A $120 Order PB81-922000
Set B $120 Order PB81-922100

NCI's Oncology Overviews

The information in these overviews is assembled to promote the exchange of information among cancer scientists. Abstracts of articles dealing with each of the three specific topics—carcinogenesis, virology, and therapy—are drawn from the International Cancer Research Data Bank of the National Cancer Institute.

Carcinogenesis: Subscribers will receive about 10 titles a year which will be renewed in 12- to 24-month cycles. Price: $2 a title on a standing-order basis. Order PB81-922900.

Virology, Immunology and Biology: Subscribers will receive about 10 titles a year which will be renewed in 12- to 24-month cycles. Price: $2 a title on a standing-order basis. Order PB81-923000.

Therapy: Subscribers will receive about 10 titles a year which will be renewed in 12- to 24-month cycles. Price: $2 a title on a standing-order basis. Order PB81-922800.

Special listings of current cancer research contain descriptions of ongoing projects in specific cancer research areas. These listings are derived from research project descriptions provided to the International Cancer Research Data Bank (ICRDB) by investigators worldwide.

Cancergrams

Cancergrams is a service of the International Cancer Research Data Bank (ICRDB) program of the National Cancer Institute. It is distributed approximately monthly and contains abstracts of recently published articles. More than 60 topics available. Annual subscription $24 per topic. For more detailed information, request PR-412.

EPA Quarterly Reports

All EPA items in the NTIS collection are indexed quarterly in a continuing series. The new quarterly evolved from the original master bibliography and its supplements, from 1970.

An annual subscription to *EPA Publications Bibliography Quarterly Abstract Bulletin* is $60. Order PB81-904200.

SWRA Data Base

Selected Water Resources Abstracts (journal and index) covers water pollution, water law, ground water, lakes and estuaries, water yield, watershed protection, waste treatment, water demand, hydraulics, and soil mechanics. It reviews current reports and articles on water-related aspects of the life, physical, and social sciences, and the conservation, control, use, management, other engineering, and legal aspects of water. Entries contain abstracts and full bibliographic citations.

Each issue indexed by subject, personal and corporate author, and accession number. Compiled by the U.S. Department of the Interior.

Issued semimonthly. Annual subscription, $100; $125 with index. Annual index alone, $50. Order PB81-910200.

Aerospace Medicine and Biology

A subscription series emphasizing applied research, refers to basic studies and theoretical principles related to experimental developments.

Zeroes in on biological, physiological, and environmental effects to which humans are subjected during and following space flights.

Issued monthly. Annual subscription for *Aerospace Medicine and Biology*, $65. Order PB81-912300. Complete set of 1964–1970 issues, $400.

TIMELY & TOPICAL: *ECONOMIC DATA*

Current information bearing on the U.S. economy and national demographics is available from NTIS in a variety of data bases and some paper products. This NTIS product line is rapidly expanding, so there may be more economic data services available than are listed here. Request an up-to-date list of data base products and services, using the order form on page 31.

Consumer Price Index Mailgram

This three-page monthly report by the Bureau of Labor Statistics contains the Consumer Price Index (CPI) for all urban consumers and urban wage earners and clerical workers.

The CPI is a measure of the average change in prices over time, in a fixed basket of goods and services. The report is delivered by Western Union Mailgram. Price: $95 annually in the contiguous United States and Hawaii; $110 in Alaska and Canada. PB81-915800.

Bibliographic and Nonbibliographic

Engineering Index (Ei) recently characterized **bibliographic** data bases as *pointers which refer users somewhere else for detailed information*. Ei then listed the contrasting elements of a **nonbibliographic** data base, as follows:

the base itself holds the written or numeric information;

access is frequently restricted to a particular user community or to a particular communications carrier;

it is likely to be coupled with a particular kind of software or computer;

about 79 percent of its use is performed by the end user, while information **intermediaries** are the prime users of **bibliographic** data bases;

initially, users tend to be commercial enterprises; and the cost of producing a **nonbibliographic** data base is greater than for a **bibliographic** one.

Statistical Data Reference Service

The *Statistical Data Reference Service* (SDRS) makes information available on the full range of Federal statistical resources.

The major subject areas covered are based on social, economic, and environmental statistical programs of the U.S. Government.

The *SDRS* is sponsored by NTIS through a commercial contractor. For more information, please telephone (703) 487-4808.

Statistical Data Tabulation Service

The *Statistical Data Tabulation Service* (SDTS) provides low-cost easy access to data from Federal data files.

Through standardization of the program used to prepare tabulations, *SDTS* transforms the data into needed information at low cost.

SDTS can rapidly make available tabulations from the following data files:

1976 Survey of Income and Education
1970 Census Public Use Samples
Current Population Surveys (all recent years)
National Crime Surveys

The service is provided by NTIS through a commercial contractor. For more information on *SDTS*, please telephone (703) 487-4808.

LBL Employment Information

The Lawrence Berkeley Laboratory (LBL) data base contains all of the employment-related information produced by the 1970 Census and will be updated with the 1980 Census data in mid 1981. The data can be used in planning for school vocational training, market projection when population or salary levels are a consideration, transportation planning, and so forth. Reports can also be produced that reflect the labor force by various breakouts such as industry, salary levels, age, education, and so forth. Custom reports by any Census area are available.

GPO, SupDocs, NTIS: HOW THEY DIFFER

The **Government Printing Office** (GPO) is the principal printing agency of the Federal Government. GPO is part of the Legislative Branch and derives its authority and direction from Congress. Its primary products and services are the printing and distribution of the Congressional Record, the Federal Register, and the Weekly Compilation of Presidential Documents. In addition, important and quick turn-around printing jobs are done within GPO and others are contracted out commercially. GPO printing and binding operations are paid for by direct appropriations or by reimbursements from the Federal agencies requisitioning printing services.

The Superintendent of Documents (SupDocs) is responsible for:

The compilation of catalogs and indexes of Government publications.

The administration of the Federal Depository Library System. Some 1,200 such libraries receive free Federal publications of their choice for the public. These are funded by a direct appropriation from Congress.

Distribution of publications specifically authorized by law or Congressional Resolution.

The sales program offers 25,000 popular titles and over 400 Federal subscriptions to domestic and foreign customers on a current basis. The price of each publication and subscription includes domestic postage. Overseas customers are charged an additional 25 percent to cover handling charges. Twenty-six Government bookstores, located in 20 cities within the United States, sell many popular publications directly to customers. A list of locations is available from SupDocs.

The **National Technical Information Service** (NTIS) is a central *permanent* source of specialized business, economic, scientific, and social information of varied origins. NTIS's information is always available; single copies of any of its million titles are printed to order when not in stock. Its customers are mostly business people and professionals accustomed to locating and applying specialized information to problem solving. NTIS titles are promoted through a wide variety of media.

A FEW WORDS ABOUT APPEARANCE

The legibility of the research reports provided to NTIS by the originating organizations varies. The documents received by NTIS may be the originals, or they may be copies of the originals, or copies of copies. Often, NTIS receives only a microfiche copy of an original document (or microfiche of copies) from which it must reproduce paper copies or other microfiche.

NTIS customers have about a one in five chance of receiving their full-text technical reports in the attractive hardbound covers and colorful soft bindings sometimes provided to NTIS by the originating organizations.

These original covers and bindings are not usually duplicated after the limited initial stocks are depleted. Paper covers replace hardbound covers and bright designs give way to the photographic grays and blacks of simple covers. It is the only practical way to ensure the permanent convenient accessibility of information for which the demand may be only a few copies a month.

The text pages are reproduced according to customer demand, and therefore are permanently available. Their appearance is similar to photocopied or photo-offset copies. Illustrations may not show fine details. The nature of the NTIS high-speed production equipment is such that the most efficient and inexpensive method of binding this very low volume production is stapling the pages together.

NTIS conveys technical information at the lowest possible cost while maintaining its permanent availability. That would be impossible if NTIS were to strive for the fine appearance of commercial technical books.

This restraint on impressive appearance allows NTIS to intensify its identification, acquisition, and computer processing of timely technical information, more directly benefiting its customers.

TIMELY & TOPICAL: *LOCAL GOVERNMENT*

The NTIS system of local government information was designed to meet the practical problem-solving needs of local governments as information users as well as information sources.

NTIS' approach has been to differentiate between hard core problem-solving technology and general research and to work toward establishing an information exchange center that would acquire pertinent information generated outside State and local governments.

The abstract newsletters *Problem-Solving Information for State & Local Governments* and *Urban & Regional Technology & Development* report on the various aspects of urban area management.

Only the NTIS system includes Federal, international, and other nonproprietary information carefully selected for direct applicability in local government problem-solving situations where timeliness and practicality are vital.

Software for Local Governments

Problem-solving computer software for State, county, and city governments is available for sale from NTIS at prices within most local budgets.

Federally tested programs, based on thorough research by many Government agencies, are available. Write for further information. Most are of specific interest to experts and educators in urban and suburban affairs.

Highway Planning

This software package was developed by the Department of Transportation's Rural Highway Transportation Planning System. It consists of six magnetic tape reels of software and test data, a user manual, and a guidebook to highway planning.

The elements of the program, aside from the test data are indicated by the coverage of the guidebook. Its six sections cover: *The Highway Planning Process; Instructions for Road Inventory; Instructions for Traffic Surveys; Functional Classification of Highways; Highway Adequacy Rating;* and *Measuring Highway Improvement Needs and Priority Analysis.* The guidebook is also available in Spanish.

Project Share Documents

The *Journal of Human Services Abstracts* announces documents received by HHS's Project Share, a national clearinghouse for human services information.

The quarterly *Journal* contains some 150 abstracts of documents included in the Project Share data base. It is indexed.

Price: $10.50 a copy on standing order. Order PB81-903400.

Local Government Credit Plan

No advance funds are necessary for local governments and State universities to obtain credit and immediate shipments of NTIS products and services.

Upon receipt of the special credit account application NTIS PR 220 (free on request), NTIS will mail a supply of preaddressed order forms bearing a special account number. These forms also will show a "ship to" address if one is required.

Subsequently, orders will be processed directly into the NTIS automated system, eliminating several steps in normal order handling and minimizing errors.

The outstanding feature of the NTIS billing system is that it lists, item by item, the purchases made by an institution, along with the corresponding costs. Such billing saves acquisition librarians considerable record keeping.

Monthly statements will show all charges, credits, deposits, and the balance. The charges may easily be verified from the Record of Shipment Cards included with every shipment. The local government's or the library's signed payment voucher (which we will keep on hand) will be mailed with each statement. Payment is due upon its receipt. Officials need not be concerned with special funding, delays, or price changes.

The charge for this service is 10 cents a line item.

REVIEWS OF NTIS PRODUCTS AND SERVICES

Reviews of NTIS products and services were published in the following periodicals in 1979–80. American Reference Books Annual, Arctic and Alpine Research, Book News-Citizen Housing & Planning Council of NY, Building Design COMPUTING, Concrete Abstracts-American Concrete Institute, Crime Control Digest, Computers and Medicine, Civil Engineering, Chemical Engineering Progress, Solar Heating and Cooling, Combined Book Exhibit, The Construction Specifier, Chemical Times Trends, Environmental Science & Technology, DM-Data Processing Management Association, INFORMATION HOTLINE, ISI Institute for Scientific Information, INFODOC REVIEWS - Nelinet Government Document Task Group, Information Manager, Future Life, Platt's Oilgram News, New Roots for the Northeast, Marine Policy, Energy Research Reports, Korean American Times, Mechanical Engineering, The Grapevine, Sage Public Administration Abstracts, Sage Human Resources Abstracts, The White House Conference on Library and Information Services, Information Manager, RR Bowker Book News, Security Management, Rural America, SIE-Select Information Exchange, NAHRO-National Association of Housing & Redevelopment Officials, The Police Chief, Industrial Engineering, FORBES, Health & Safety in Industry, Concrete Abstracts-American Concrete Institute, Journal of the American Dietetic Association, Federal Construction Council Newsletter - BRAB, The Work Book - SW Research & Information Center, STS Newsletter, The Acquisitive Librarian, On Campus with Women, Space Age Times; Science Trends, Scientific Information Notes, Pit & Quarry, Energy Today, Environmental Report, Radiation Reports, EARS, GEOTIMES, Information Retrieval and Library Automation, R & D Management Digest, Pension & Profit Sharing Report, Civil Engineering, IEEE Spectrum, Journal of Industrial Engineering, SHOPPING CENTER TODAY, Information Please Almanac, SIGHTLINES, and Vertical File Index.

NTIS TITLE INDEX ALLOWS KEYWORD SEARCH OF SYSTEM

The *RETROSPECTIVE INDEX* covers July 1964 through December 1978 and references more than 750,000 publications on 1,332 sheets of microfiche. This product is in three sections:

KEYWORD OUT OF CONTEXT (KWOC) TITLE INDEX. Any keyword in the title can lead to the relevant reports. Along with the titles, order numbers, dates, price codes, and number of pages are given.

AUTHOR INDEX. Here you can find multiple titles by the same author, most of the title, and order numbers and price codes.

REPORT/ACCESSION NUMBER INDEX. This index is used to verify a publication's title, order number, and price code when you have only the report/accession number at hand. The price is $600. Order PB80-139900.

The *CURRENT INDEX* is a quarterly cumulation of new publications. Approximately 17,500 new titles are added each quarter. The cumulations are merged quarterly on a two-year cycle. The index is published within two weeks after the closing of the final GRA&I for the quarter.

Price when subscription is in force during both years of any two-year cycle is $400. Price when subscription is entered during the second year of any two-year cumulating cycle is $300. Order PB80-916000.

Save $100 by ordering both the Retrospective and Current Index. PB80-916100.

SPECIAL TECHNOLOGY GROUPS OFFER UNIQUE HIGHLY REFINED RESEARCH DATA

Special Technology Groups are an important information resource for the NTIS Bibliographic Data Base.

Some Special Technology Groups are called Information Analysis Centers (IACs). These are mainly concerned with the analysis and communication of information relating to the very latest in the state of an art. Some IACs concentrate on the evaluation of cultural, educational, and socio-economic data. The 100 or more federally sponsored IACs in the United States are considered national resources of particular knowledge.

NTIS is the national marketing coordinator for many Special Technology

Groups, many of which have been required to recover their costs by making their products and services publicly available.

Usually Special Technology Groups, including IACs, define their operations within three principal areas:

Inquiry Services: The custom searching of an information collection relevant to specific queries; combined, by some, with analytical research and evaluation.

Data Books & Research Reports: Often these are state-of-the-art reports; that is, the best information available on a subject. Also published in this category are annotated bibliographies, technical guides, and directories of terms and processes.

Newsletters: These reflect the latest technical achievements, in brief, as they are observed and recorded for subsequent detailed evaluation; usually available on a subscription basis.

NTIS is the national marketing coordinator for the following Information Analysis Centers.

Chemical Propulsion Information Agency

Covers performance calculations, chemical synthesis programs, combustion studies, propellant formulation efforts, physical and ballistic characteristics, rocket design, ground testing of rockets, integration of rockets and flight vehicles, and correlation of flight data with static test data.

Publishes extensively and maintains mailing list for exchange of chemical propulsion technical information.

Electromagnetic Compatibility Analysis Center

Maintains a comprehensive data base, a large-scale computer with appropriate software systems for analysis and data manipulation in spectrum planning, emission and susceptibility characteristics evaluation, and deployment and siting analysis.

Energetic Materials Division, Army Armament Research and Development Command

Covers basic and applied research on explosives and related substances.

Basic and applied research is done on the mechanical, thermal, and electrostatic response of explosives for the purpose of developing better tests and elucidating the initiation process under these stimuli.

Answers inquiries, publishes state-of-the-art reports, bibliographies, indexes, and directories.

Infrared Information and Analysis Center

Covers infrared sources, characteristic radiation from natural and manmade objects; optical properties of materials, infrared detection materials and elements, laboratory components and techniques; infrared spectra; lasers and masers; military infrared systems and components.

Provides references to scientific and technical documents, answers queries on current research and development, answers specific technical questions; publishes bibliographies, state-of-the-art reports; conducts annual Infrared Information Symposia and DOD conference on laser technology.

Machinability Data Center

Covers the evaluation, storage, and dissemination of material removal information; strongly emphasizes engineering evaluation to develop optimized material removal parameters.

Answers technical inquiries concerning material removal, maintains a user file for distribution of information products, including machine data pamphlets and tables on materials of current interest, state-of-the-art reports, technical announcements.

Mechanical Properties Data Center

Covers mechanical properties of structural materials and interacting variables, with major emphasis on metal alloys; maintains data on more than 4,000 specific alloys.

Answers questions, provides special bibliographies and technical evaluations, prepares Aerospace Structural Metals Handbook, issues special publications and inventory reports on the MPDC system.

Metals and Ceramics Information Center

Covers the characteristics and utilization of advanced metals, ceramics, and selected composites.

Answers technical inquiries and requests for literature searches, publishes state-of-the-art reports, handbooks, and two reviews available on subscription; *Review of Metals Technology* and *Review of Ceramic Technology*.

Non-Destructive Testing Information Analysis Center

Coverage includes radiography, acoustics, ultrasonics, magnetics, eddy currents, optical and ultrasonic holography, penetrant testing, and optical, thermal, and infrared sensing.

Its 16,000 documents and abstracts range from basic studies in physical sciences for non-destructive testing to applied techniques for examining structures and finished components.

Nuclear Safety Information Center

Covers nuclear safety—general criteria, analysis, operating systems, accident analysis, environmental surveys, monitoring and radiation exposure of humans, siting and containment of facilities, transporting and handling of radioactive materials, reactor transients, kinetics and stability, and nuclear instrumentation.

Answers technical inquiries, publishes state-of-the-art reports and bibliographies, and provides current-awareness services.

Plastics Technical Evaluation Center

Covers structural composites, electrical and electronic applications, packaging, mechanical goods applications, microbiological deterioration, test methods and specifications, compatibility, and reactivity.

Answers inquiries, and publishes state-of-the-art reports, bibliographies, indexes, and directories.

Reliability Analysis Center

Covers microelectronic circuit devices including monolithic integrated circuits, metal oxide semiconductor integrated circuits, hybrid circuits, thin film circuits, integrated arrays, and device fabrication, testing, equipment assembly, and operation.

Answers direct user inquiries and publishes technical monographs.

Technology Application Center

Covers heat pipe technology, secondary uses of waste glass, noise pollution, and hydrogen and solar energy.

Answers inquiries. Publishes handbooks, data books, current awareness bulletins, and state-of-the-art reviews.

Thermophysical & Electronic Properties Information Analysis Center

Covers 16 thermophysical properties of matter keyed to representative groups: High temperature solid materials, thermal conductivity, thermal diffusivity, absorptance, reflectance, viscosity, specific heats, and constant pressures.

Answers technical inquiries; makes referrals and literature and data searches; provides technical advisory and consulting services; and reproduces research documents on microfiche.

Toxicology Information Response Center

Covers general scope of toxicology. Concentrates on pesticides, bioenvironmental toxicants, toxis chemicals, food additives, and drugs. Provides literature searches, critical reviews, state-of-the-art reviews, current awareness service, and specialized bibliographies.

TIMELY FOREIGN TECHNOLOGY, MARKET DATA FOR U.S. INNOVATORS AND EXPORTERS

Acquisition of Foreign Technology Is the Prime Target of NTIS Office of International Affairs

The National Technical Information Service (NTIS), as the central source for scientific and technical information sponsored by the United States Government, plays a key role in the international exchange of information. NTIS increasingly has become the lead agency within the Federal establishment responsible for participation in bilateral, regional, and worldwide activities involving technology transfer and information. This has come about because of the growing recognition of the importance of technical information in the conduct of U.S. business overseas and in the conduct of U.S. international relations.

In order to respond to this growing responsibility, an Office of International Affairs has been created within NTIS. NTIS' objective in forming this new office is to help create a positive climate and provide a mechanism for an equitable exchange of information among all nations. This is based on the United States' historical commitment to the open access to public information in our free society.

This international flow of information through NTIS is shown in these figures—

There are 300,000 reports based on foreign technology in the NTIS collection.

20% of the products and services provided by NTIS go to non-U.S. destinations.

Some 90 countries regularly receive information from NTIS.

20% of the authors represented in the NTIS collection of one million titles are attached to non-U.S. organizations.

Some 10% of current annual acquisitions are from non-U.S. sources.

More than 25 nations regularly contribute information items to the NTIS Bibliographic Data Base.

NTIS has bilateral agreements with non-U.S. governmental, regional, or private information organizations in 37 countries which stimulate the international exchange of information through local sales services and the acquisition of new information.

Such organizations as Netherlands Organization for Applied Scientific Research, and the Delft Hydraulic Laboratory; the United Kingdom's National Coal Board, National Physical Laboratory, and the Japan Information Center of Science & Technology have already made many valuable contributions.

Foreign acquisitions are concentrated in the fields of solar energy, health care, metallurgy, mass transportation, building, research, and scientific instruments. Abstracts of all foreign technical reports are published in NTIS' abstract newsletters and journals. In most cases, the complete texts in the original language also are available from NTIS.

Several other new programs are expected to spur industrial innovations in the United States. Specific actions to aid the development and commercialization of new U.S. products and processes will emphasize an increased flow of foreign technical information to the United States.

In addition to augmenting its long-standing translations program, NTIS will develop a pilot international technology information exchange system to provide for the identification, collection, evaluation, and dissemination of foreign technology.

Translation into English of significant research literature from languages such as Russian, Chinese, and Japanese, is important both for the promotion of international scientific cooperation and the expansion of technical innovation in the United States. Although study of foreign languages has been traditionally encouraged among scientists, the language barrier still is a formidable obstacle at technical operating levels in business and industry.

To alleviate this, NTIS will expand the long-established Special Foreign Currency Science Information Program that it conducts for the National Science Foundation.

Research scientists and technical experts from all Federal agencies select foreign material to be translated into English.

CIA Reports Cover World Affairs

Central Intelligence Agency (CIA) publications cover a variety of unclassified foreign information. The subject areas are political, statistical, and economic, with reports on agriculture, metals, minerals, natural gas, oil, and military and official structures.

CIA reports and analyses are sold singly and by subscription; irregularly issued recurring reports are sold on a standing order basis.

International Telecommunications Union

NTIS now offers the CCITT *Orange Book* from the International Telecommunications Union in Geneva, Switzerland. It contains the most current International Recommendations adopted by the Sixth Plenary Assembly of the International Telegraph and Telephone Consultative Committee (CCITT).

The nine-volume *Orange Book* is published in 16 separately available publications. It is available in paper copy in English, Spanish, and French.

International Radio Proceedings

Also from the International Telecommunications Union in Geneva, NTIS offers the proceedings of the XIVth Plenary Assembly of the CCIR, held in Kyoto, 1978. The *Recommendations and Reports of the CCIR* (Green Book) contains questions, study programs, decisions, resolutions, and opinions of the Assembly.

Foreign Translations

More than a million pages of scientific material has been translated since the Special Foreign Currency Science Information Program (SFCSIP) was started.

Four bibliographies listing more than 5,000 titles are available from NTIS.

Daily Foreign Press, Radio Translations

Hundreds of *Foreign Broadcast Information Service* (FBIS) radio news transmissions, newspaper editorials, articles, and magazine features are monitored daily by expert U.S. analysts. The best of these translations are grouped in eight areas (volumes) of interest and are sold through NTIS.

Substantial discounts are offered to those who order more than one volume. All volumes are mailed daily.

Translations of Communist Media

The Joint Publications Research Service (JPRS), 1000 N. Glebe Rd., Arlington, VA 22201, translates and abstracts foreign language political and technical media for Federal agencies. More than 80,000 reports published since 1957 are available to the public through the NTIS Bibliographic Data Base.

Most JPRS reports are concerned with publications in communist countries, though materials from all nations may be translated. About half of the reports are in the scientific and technical fields.

Trends in Communist Media

The Foreign Broadcast Information Service's weekly analytical report titled *Trends in Communist Media* analyzes Chinese, Soviet, and other communist media discussions of key issues under a confidential classification limited to six months. The declassified *Trends* averages between 20 and 30 pages and is sent to subscribers weekly either in paper or microfiche.

Worldwide Exported Products Standards

U.S. exporters now have access to current multinational government regulations and codes of practice involving the sale of manufactured products worldwide.

The *Technical Help to Exporters* (THE) service of the British Standards Institution provides this vital information through NTIS.

U.S. Market Share Reports

U.S. Market Share Reports give a statistical picture of international trade in manufactured products, covering more than three-quarters of the total exported output of all the free world's factories.

These are unique references that trace shifting trends in the movement of goods between countries. The five-year spread of data on the imports of some 1,100 commodities by 90 countries reflects both the changing levels of those countries' import demands and shifts in the relative competitive positions of exporting countries.

A TOPICAL SAMPLING OF THE 1.2 MILLION RESEARCH AND TECHNICAL REPORTS IN THE NTIS COLLECTION

The core of the NTIS information system is its collection of 1.2 million different technical reports on completed Government research—any one of which is *permanently* available in film or paper copy.

All the report titles, with complete abstracts, may be searched by computer, using the NTIS Bibliographic Data Base directly or through a commercial vendor.

The titles acquired in a year—about 70,000 currently—are compiled in the NTIS Annual Index, available by subscription (see page 6) or in many libraries.

Current titles are announced weekly by subject in 26 various Abstract Newsletters, *all* of which are accumulated and published biweekly in *Government Reports Announcements & Index.*

Specially newsworthy titles are advertised or directed to the trade press in announcements to publishers.

It is virtually impossible to present a representative listing of NTIS technical report titles in a catalog the size of this one (the Annual Index is 7,000 pages). You can find a more representative listing in any issue of *Government Reports Announcements & Index* but you will see that it requires hundreds of pages.

The following list, then, is an attempt only to depict the scope of a very few of the titles in which customers were particularly interested when this catalog was printed.

General Technical Reports (*PC* = paper copy; *MF* = microfiche)

Guide to Technical Services and Information Sources for ADP Managers and Users
PB-294 845   PC A03/MF A01

Design and Installation Manual For Thermal Energy Storage
ANL-79-15   PC A07/MF A01

The Report of the Alcohol Fuels Policy Review
DOE/PE-0012   PC A06/MF A01

Energy Efficiency and Electric Motors
PB-259 129   PC A08/MF A01

Oven Curing: Energy Conservation and Emission Control in Coil Coating
TID-28705   PC A03/MF A01

The Coating Industry
TID-28706   PC A06/MF A01

Maintenance and Adjustment Manual for Natural Gas and No. 2 Fuel Oil Burners
TID-27600   PC A03/MF A01

Upgrading Existing Evaporators to Reduce Energy Consumption
COO/2870-2   PC A05/MF A01

Costs of Owning, Borrowing, and Disposing of Periodical Publications
PB-274 821   PC A04/MF A01

Coal Conversion Systems Technical Data Book
HCP/T2286-01   PC A25/MF A01

Scientific Problems of Coal Utilization
CONF-770509   PC A18/MF A01

Fundamentals of Solar Heating
HCP/M 4038-01   PC A06/MF A01

Fuel Efficient Vehicles & Consumer Behavior
PB-298 569   PC A10/MF A01

Aircraft Noise & Property Values
PB-297 681   PC A08/MF A01

Chinese-English Dictionary of Modern Communist Usage, 2nd Edition
JPRS-20904   PC A99/MF A01

Energy Audit Workbook For Schools
DOE/CS-0041/2   PC A05/MF A01

Energy Audit Workbook for Hotels and Motels
DOE/CS-0041/4   PC A05/MF A01

Energy Audit Workbook for Apartment Buildings
DOE/CS-0041/1   PC A05/MF A01

Energy Audit Workbook for Office Buildings
DOE/CS-0041/6   PC A05/MF A01

Energy Audit Workbook for Hospitals
DOE/CS-0041/3   PC A05/MF A01

Energy Audit Workbook for Retail Stores
DOE/CS-0041/11   PC A05/MF A01

Energy Audit Workbook for Bakeries
DOE/CS-0041/10   PC A05/MF A01

Energy Audit Workbook for Bus Stations
DOE/CS-0041/8   PC A05/MF A01

Energy Audit Workbook for Restaurants
DOE/CS-0041/7   PC A05/MF A01

Energy Audit Workbook for Die Casting Plants
DOE/CS-0041/5   PC A05/MF A01

Guidelines For Saving Energy In Existing Buildings. Engineers, Architects, and Operators Manual: ECM 2
PB-249 929   PC A19/MF A01

Preliminary Forecast of Likely U.S. Energy Consumption/Production Balances for 1985 and 2000 by States
PB-287 486   PC A08/MF A01

Campaign Finance Law '78
PB-299 628 Set   PC E08/MF A01

U.S. Transportation Trends and Choices to 2000 A.D.
PB-282 230   PC A18/MF A01

Financing Problems in Coal and Shale Boom Towns
PB-259 438   PC A11/MF A01

Energy Accounting and Management
TID-3375   PC A06/MF A01

Solar Legislation: A Review of The State Statutes
PB-295 642   PC A17/MF A01

Solar Energy Engineer's Guide
PB-297 043   PC E13/MF E13

Fuels From Sugar Crops
TID-22781   PC A00($4.75) MF A01

Soviet Officials
PB-299 682 Set (3v.)   PC A99/MF A01

Low Cost Solar Heating For Homes
N76-27671   PC A04/MF A01

"Legionnaires' ": The Disease, the Bacterium and Methodology
PB-297 957   PC A09/MF A01

Received Signal Level (RSL) Measurement and Analysis With A Desk-Top Computer
PB-294 820   PC A08/MF A01

Weatherization Materials Handbook
PB-297 212   PC A06/MF A01

Evaluation of Signal/Control System Equipment and Technology. Task 2: Status of Present Signal/Control Equipment
PB-299 891   PC A06/MF A01

Evaluation of Signal/Control System Equipment and Technology. Task 1: Assessment of Signal/Control Technology and Literature Review
PB-296 494   PC A09/MF A01

Characteristics of Urban Transportation Systems: A Handbook For Transportation Planners
PB-301 319   PC A09/MF A01

Health Effects Associated With Diesel Exhaust Emissions, Literature Review and Evaluation
PB-289 817   PC A08/MF A01

A Safe Practices Manual For The Manufacturing, Transportation, Storage, and Use of Explosives
PB-297 827   PC A09/MF A01

Urban Family Building Patterns: The Social Mobility-Fertility Hypothesis Re-Examined
PB-299 425   PC A10/MF A01

Mid-America Ports Study, Vol. 1
PB-299 562   PC A16/MF A01

Fluorescent Antibody Techniques and Bacterial Applications
PB-297 961   PC A06/MF A01

Channel Level Power Control Interface. Category: Hardware Standard, Sub-category: Interface
FIPSPUB61   PC A02/MF A01

Symbol Signs. The Development of Passenger/Pedestrian Oriented Symbols For Use In Transportation-Related Facilities
PB-239 352   PC A08/MF A01

Telecommunications for Metropolitan Areas: Opportunities for the 1980s
PB-286 609   PC A06/MF A01

Alcohol Abuse and Alcoholism Programs: A Technical Assistance Manual for Health Systems Agencies
HRP0900411   PC A06/MF A01

A Ship Repair Market Assessment: Final Report
PB-288 845   PC A07/MF A01

New Plastics: Properties, Processing and Potential Uses
ADA-056 990   PC E07/MF A01

A System for Fire Safety Evaluation of Health Care Facilities
PB-292 273   PC A07/MF A01

Common Blood and Tissue Parasites of Man; Life Cycle Charts
PB-297 959   PC A03/MF A01

Client Assessment: A Manual for Employment and Training Agencies
PB-300 452   PC A09/MF A01

Leadership and Exchange in Formal Organizations
AD-725 584   PC A16/MF A01

Gasohol: A Technical Memorandum
PB80-105885   PC A05/MF A01

Wind Power for Farms, Homes, and Small Industry
RFP-28411270784   PC A11/MF A01

New Drug Evaluation Project Briefing Book
PB80-116346   PC A07/MF A01

The Cost of Clean Air and Water Report to Congress
PB-300 446   PC A15/MF A01

Index of Federal Labor Relations Cases
PB-300 963   PC A13/MF A01

Radiation Safety Technician Training Course
ANL7291 Rev 1   PC A22/MF A01

What Everyone Solving Differential Equations Numerically Should Know
SAND78 0315   PC A02/MF A01

The Initial Growth and Expanding Opportunities of U.S. Domestic Satellite Service
PB-300 438   PC A08/MF A01

The State of School Science: A Review of the Teaching of Mathematics, Science and Social Studies in American Schools, and Recommendations for Improvements
PB-300 490   PC A05/MF A01

Manual of Septic-Tank Practice Developed in Cooperation With The Joint Committee On Rural Sanitation
PB-218 226   PC A05/MF A01

Manual of Respiratory Protection Against Airborne Radioactive Materials
PB-258 052   PC A07/MF A01

Handbook on Aerosols
TID-26608   PC $6/MF A01

Interagency Task Force on Product Liability
PB-273 220   PC $20/MF A01

Market Share Reports Catalog
PB-294 300   PC Free

Codes For Named Populated Places and Related Entities of the States of the United States
FIPSPUB55   PC E05/MF E05

Forecast of Likely U.S. Energy Supply/Demand Balances for 1985 and 2000, and Implications for U.S. Energy Policy
PB-266 240   PC A08/MF A01

Interagency Task Force on Product Liability Legal Study
PB-263 601   PC A99/MF A01

Reducing Excess Hospital Capacity
HRP0015199   PC A11/MF A01

Impacts of Construction Activities in Wetlands of the United States
PB-256 674   PC A19/MF A01

Evaluation of the Health Aspects of Sucrose as a Food Ingredient
PB-262 668   PC A03/MF A01

Women and Their Health: Research Implications for a New Era. Proceedings of a Conference Held at San Francisco, California on August 1–2, 1975
PB-264 359   PC A06/MF A01

KEY WORD TITLE INDEX

The current *NTIS Title Index* is a quarterly cumulation of new publications. Approximately 17,500 new titles are added each quarter. The cumulations are merged quarterly on a two-year cycle. The *Index* is published within two weeks after the closing of the final Government Reports Announcement Index for the quarter.

Price when subscription is in force during both years of any 2-year cumulating cycle is $400. Price when subscription is entered during second year of any 2-year cumulating cycle is $300. Order: PB81-916000.

Save $100 by ordering both the Retrospective and Current Index. Order PB81-916100.

HOW TO ORDER

The prices listed cover sales in the United States, Canada and Mexico only.
Three categories of order fulfillment are offered.

1. **Rush handling** (replaces "Rush Order") is for customers who must have immediate delivery.

Rush Handling guarantees that a particular order will be filled within 24 hours of receipt. *Rush Handling* orders receive immediate validation, verification of availability, and individual hand processing through inventory control and the warehouse; priority printing if reproduction from film is required, and priority mailing.

Rush Handling orders for mailing rather than pickup are accepted only from customers having NTIS Deposit Accounts or American Express, Visa, or Master-Card Accounts.

Rush Handling orders may be placed only by telephone, telegram, Telex, Tele-copier (numbers inside back cover) or customers in person; not by mail. Customers must use order numbers.

Rush Handling for delivery to customers by First Class Mail adds $10 to the cost of each item or copy ordered.

Rush Handling for pickup in Springfield or D.C. adds $6 to the cost of each item or copy ordered.

2. Premium service is a day and night toll-free telephone ordering procedure ensuring order processing and mailing within four to nine days to NTIS Deposit Account or American Express, Visa, or MasterCard customers. The $3.50 fee for each item is waived if the order is not mailed within the specified period. Customers must use order numbers. Titles alone cannot be accepted in this procedure.

All Deposit Account, American Express, Visa, and MasterCard customers receive *Premium Service* identification numbers with which they may place telephone orders at any time. *Premium Service* benefits are toll-free calls within 24-hour availability, no busy signals, simplified ordering techniques (details with the identification number), postage savings, and priority delivery.

Premium Service adds $3.50 to the cost of each item ordered.

3. Regular service will continue to operate with improved processing and stocking methods, optional priority mail delivery ($3 North America; $4 outside) and optional pickup in Springfield or D.C. Current parcel post deliveries using the U.S. Postal Service are completed within 9 to 30 days.

4. Online ordering: The commercial vendors of the NTIS Bibliographic Data Base are experimenting with the convenience of online ordering of NTIS documents for their customers. Currently, online ordering is offered by the Systems Development Corporation (SDC). It permits SDC customers to charge their NTIS Deposit Accounts for orders that are transmitted daily to NTIS. Inquiries should be addressed to SDC, 2500 Colorado Avenue, Santa Monica, California 90406.

5. Telex: Ordering from NTIS may be speeded by the use of Telex. Customers may charge their Deposit Accounts, credit cards or ask for Ship & Bill Service. Ship & Bill Service costs $5 extra for each order.

For information not covered, direct your inquiry to Customer Services, NTIS, 5285 Port Royal Road, Springfield, VA 22161; or telephone (703) 487-4600 or (202) 724-3509.

Discount on Multiple Copies

When 20 or more paper copies of one title are ordered, NTIS automatically reduces the total price by 15 percent.

HOW TO PAY

The fastest service is provided to customers who charge against their NTIS Deposit Accounts or their American Express, Visa, or MasterCard accounts, because the processing of such orders is simplest for NTIS. Holders of NTIS Deposit

Accounts may replenish their accounts using the above credit cards. And new Deposit Accounts may be opened in the same manner.

Otherwise, payment by check or money order must accompany each order.

As an added convenience to customers who have established credit, a Ship and Bill Service is provided generally at a $5 surcharge on each total order for documents, regardless of the number of documents ordered.

Retail Sales at Two Locations

NTIS has two retail sales locations in the Washington area.

In the District of Columbia, the *NTIS Information Center and Bookstore* is in the Pennsylvania Building, Suite 620, 425 13th Street N.W. Telephone (202) 724-3382. Several hundred best selling titles are displayed for sale and for immediate delivery without Rush Handling surcharge.

The *Springfield Operations Center* has a much more limited display of research reports, but any titles may be ordered for future delivery.

How to Open a Deposit Account

Use the order form on page 32 and send at least $25, or enough to cover your first order, to NTIS Deposit Account, 5285 Part Royal Road, Springfield, VA 22161. Thereafter, keep at least $25 on deposit or enough to cover two months' charges. *Orders will not be processed for overdrawn accounts.* You may deposit any amount prior to ordering. Some active customers keep several thousand dollars in their accounts to ensure the fastest possible service for large orders.

When your account is opened, you will receive preaddressed order forms to speed your shipments and simplify accounting and the recording of tax-deductible expenses.

NTIS Domestic Price Codes

The prices below are for customers in the United States, Canada, and Mexico.

A01	$ 3.50	A14	$ 23.00
A02	5.00	A15	24.50
A03	6.50	A16	26.00
A04	8.00	A17	27.50
A05	9.50	A18	29.00
A06	11.00	A19	30.50
A07	12.50	A20	32.00
A08	14.00	A21	33.50
A09	15.50	A22	35.00
A10	17.00	A23	36.50
A11	18.50	A24	38.00
A12	20.00	A25	39.50
A13	21.50		

A99—For documents over 600 pages, add $1.50 for each additional 25-page increment.

E01	$ 5.50	E14	$ 33.50
E02	6.50	E15	36.50

E03	8.50	E16	39.50
E04	10.50	E17	42.50
E05	12.50	E18	45.50
E06	14.50	E19	50.50
E07	16.50	E20	60.50
E08	18.50	E99—Ask for quote.	
E09	20.50	N01	30.00
E10	22.50	N02	50.00
E11	24.50		
E12	27.50		
E13	30.50		
T01	$110.00	T12	$ 780.00
T02	125.00	T13	840.00
T03	210.00	T14	900.00
T04	300.00	T15	960.00
T05	360.00	T16	1,020.00
T06	420.00	T17	1,080.00
T07	480.00	T18	1,140.00
T08	540.00	T19	1,200.00
T09	600.00	T99—Ask for quote.	
T10	660.00		
T11	720.00		

Index